# *Era of*

# *Emancipation*

## British Government of Ireland, 1812–1830

BRIAN JENKINS

McGill-Queen's University Press
Kingston and Montreal

© McGill-Queen's University Press
ISBN 0-7735-0659-4

Legal deposit third quarter 1988
Bibliothèque nationale du Québec

Printed in Canada on acid-free paper.

This book has been published with the help of a grant from
the Social Science Federation of Canada, using funds
provided by the Social Sciences and Humanities Research
Council of Canada. Funds have also been provided by
Bishop's University.

**Canadian Cataloguing in Publication Data**

Jenkins, Brian, 1939–
    Era of emancipation: British government of Ireland,
    1812–1830
    Includes index.
    Bibliography: p.
    ISBN 0-7735-0659-4
    1. Ireland – Politics and government – 1800–1837. I. Title.
    DA950.2.J36 1988    941.5081    C88-090091-1

*For Lillian, Maldwyn, and Owen Jenkins*

# Contents

# *Acknowledgments*

For its support of this study I wish to thank the Social Sciences and Humanities Research Council of Canada. My University has been generous in granting me time in which to research and write. I owe debts of gratitude to my friend Jeff Jefferis and to my wife Jean who read the entire manuscript and sought to make it more readable. I benefited greatly from the advice of Donald Akenson, the editor of McGill-Queen's University Press and a distinguished historian of Ireland. I wish to thank Lord Sackville for permission to quote from the Whitworth Papers. Quotations from the manuscripts in the British Library and the National Library of Ireland are with the permission of the Trustees. Finally, I wish to express my appreciation of the unfailing helpfulness of the staffs of the British Library, the National Library of Ireland, the State Paper Office, Dublin, the Public Record Office of Ireland, the Public Record Office of Northern Ireland, the Public Record Office, the Devon Record Office, the Kent Archives, the John Rylands University Library of Manchester, the Sheffield Central Library, the Staffordshire Record Office, and the Surrey Record Office.

*Era of Emancipation*

# Introduction

The arrival of the Normans in Ireland in the twelfth century began the long search for an acceptable constitutional and political relationship between the rulers of England and the inhabitants of the neighbouring land. If Gaelic kings swore fealty, the writ of English kings rarely ran large. But the Tudors, having triumphed in England's dynastic wars of the fifteenth century, systematically set about the task of guarding and governing their realms more effectively. In Ireland, the powers of the Parliament were severely curtailed. Then, in June of 1541, it was summoned by Henry VIII to confirm his new title of "King of this land of Ireland as united, annexed, and knit for ever to the Imperial crown of the realm of England." A policy of colonization was slowly implemented. Seeking to create the submissive population so "essential to successful rule," the Tudors decided to plant Englishmen among the fractious Irish. Limited settlements in Leix and Offaly were followed by a more significant experiment in Munster which involved the "Removal of native Irish and their replacement by English-born Protestants."[1]

By 1603 the Tudors had succeeded in imposing English government on Gaelic Ireland but not in winning popular acceptance of English rule. Not surprisingly, therefore, the Stuarts continued the plantation policy. The flight of the earls of Tyrone and Tyrconnell in 1607, and the confiscation of their estates in Ulster, created the opportunity for an ambitious scheme of settlement. Only in the counties of Down and Antrim, however, where the lands attracted substantial numbers of Scots, was the colonization truly successful. Elsewhere, isolated groups of British settlers were surrounded by sullen, alienated native Irish, who believed that the lands had been stolen from them. Their smouldering resentment was fuelled by religious hostility. The Tudors had imposed Protestantism upon the English state, and the settlers were members of the separate branches, Anglicanism and Presbyterianism, of the reformed faith, whereas the Irish had remained loyal to the Church of Rome. In 1641, profiting from Britain's preoccupation with a deepening constitutional crisis which pitted king against Parliament, the native Irish rose in rebellion and put thousands of the British settlers to the sword. The Munster plantation had met a similar fate less than a half-century earlier.[2]

Atrocities committed in 1641, and Ireland's plumping for the royal cause in the English civil war, provided Oliver Cromwell with an excuse to exact a terrible revenge. The brutal Cromwellian conquest prepared the ground for another experiment in colonization, for Catholic landholders were dispossessed and ordered to resettle in the remote region west of the Shannon. Although Irish Catholics made a limited recovery under the restored monarchy, their ownership of the soil increasing marginally during the reign of Charles II, they had reason to expect better things from his brother and successor. James II ascended the throne in 1685 with a "Catholic design" for Ireland. Indeed, it was there that he fled when his English subjects invited his Protestant daughter, Mary, and her husband, William of Orange, to oust him. But Ireland's Protestants, alarmed by the actions of the Catholic Parliament James had summoned in Dublin, rallied to the Williamite cause. The king's men were defeated, first at the Boyne in July 1690, and then at Aughrim one year later. The commemoration of those victories became an annual rite of Irish Protestant triumphalism, as did the celebration of the victor's birthday.

The enthronement of William and Mary had conclusively established the Protestant character of the state. That fact, and the insecurity of Ireland's minority of Protestants, helped both to justify and produce a flood of penal laws in that country which reduced the Roman Catholic majority to a position of political, social, and economic inferiority. Dissenters were also victimized. Subsequently, the ruling Anglican minority exploited Britain's embarrassment during the American revolutionary war to secure, in 1782, the restoration of a measure of legislative independence. Not that the creation of the "Protestant nation" met the expectations of many of the supporters of constitutional reform. Middle-class Protestants had been seeking parliamentary reform, while Catholics had been hopeful of the removal of the penal laws under which they lived and laboured. Concessions were made, especially after the outbreak of the French Revolution and then of war between Britain and revolutionary France. Concerned for the security of their exposed western flank, the British government prodded an often reluctant Irish Parliament into action. Under the terms of the relief bills of 1792 and 1793, restrictions on the education of Catholics and their entry into the legal profession were removed, they were admitted to the franchise, were made eligible for a broad range of civil and military positions, and were permitted to bear arms. Grudging and incomplete, this relaxation of the penal code neither satisfied Catholics nor appeased the Protestant radicals who had been inspired by the doctrines of the French Revolution. They had organized the United Irishmen, which as the name implies repudiated sectarianism and affirmed a national unity. This noble purpose had long since been fatally compromised, however, when Ireland rose in rebellion in 1798, a rebellion which prompted the constitutional reform of union.

William Pitt, as the author of the union of Great Britain and Ireland, had declared himself to be firmly persuaded that if "complete and entire," if "founded on equal and liberal principles, on the similarity of laws, constitutions, and government, and on a sense of mutual interests and affections," it would defeat all enemies and "augment the stability, power and resources of the empire." For such a union would promote the "security, wealth, and commerce, of the respective kingdoms," and allay the "distractions" which had "unhappily prevailed" in Ireland. Unable to defend herself from foreign foes, or to provide for the needs of her inhabitants, or even to establish "internal content and tranquillity," what was more natural, Pitt asked, than that Ireland should seek those blessings through unity with a nation to which she was already bound by so many ties of affinity? "Does an union, under such circumstances, by free consent, and on just and equal terms, deserve to be branded as a proposal for subjecting Ireland to a foreign yoke?"[3]

Inherent in the union, therefore, were promises of far-reaching change in Ireland. That country was "subject to great and deplorable evils, which have a deep root," Pitt observed. They were located "in the situation of the country itself – in the present character, manners and habits of its inhabitants – in their want of intelligence, or, in other words, their ignorance – in the unavoidable separation between certain classes – in the Sate of property – in its religious distinctions – in the rancour which bigotry engenders and superstitution rears and cherishes," and "in the animosities existing between ancient settlers and original inhabitants." Men existing miserably "in a state of poverty" in which it was impossible that they could have any comfort would only be uplifted, and their manners and customs improved, by a "distribution of wealth" itself dependent upon a "distribution of capital." Just such an infusion of capital would result from union, he predicted. English investment would set Irish commerce in motion, open fresh sources of wealth and industry, and finance much-needed improvements in Irish agriculture. Yet Pitt recognized that even prosperity could not ensure tranquillity. Ireland must be liberated not only from poverty but also from "the blind zeal and phrenzy of religious prejudices." So long as she remained a separate kingdom, full concessions could not be made to the Catholic majority "without endangering the state, and shaking the [Protestant] constitution of Ireland to its centre." Once the ruling but insecure Protestant minority had been transformed into part of the larger British majority, and responsibility for Ireland transferred from a partisan local parliament in Dublin to an "impartial legislature" in London, then the emancipation of Catholics from their remaining disabilities, the relief of the overwhelmingly Catholic lower orders from some of the burdens of an Established Church to which they did not belong, even the making of adequate provision for their clergy, would become possible.[4]

The union failed, although 120 years were to elapse before the weary British reluctantly and painfully conceded the point. The seeds of its dissolution were sown at the United Kingdom's birth, as promises of social reform, sectarian reconciliation, and economic development went largely unfulfilled, and they quickly germinated in a soil so rich in nutrients. The union had "only affected the surface of the Irish community," George Cornewall Lewis later wrote, for "the under-currents of society still flowed in their former directions." Pitt had evidently assumed that the rapidly modernizing English core of the union would eventually diffuse prosperity and social well-being to its Irish periphery. That self-same assumption has characterized some of the modern core-periphery models of economic development. Regional inequalities will be counterbalanced, and a core-periphery equilibrium established, the model constructors predict, by countervailing forces. Of these forces government intervention has promised to be the most significant, as politicians respond to the political and social tensions that develop between the deprived periphery and the advantaged core. But Ireland remained an exception to such rules, and the eventual triumph of separatism there has been explained as a natural consequence of her inherently "colonial" relationship with Britain. As applied to Ireland, indeed to the entire Celtic fringe of the United Kingdom, the concept of "internal colonialism" has emphasized not only her position of political and economic dependency but also her ethnic distinctiveness.[5]

In his influential elaboration of the concept, Michael Hechter described Ireland as "an almost ideal-typical example of a colonial situation." High prestige roles and positions, together with commerce, trade, and credit were all monopolized by members of the core, he argued. Further, the periphery's economy was "forced into complementary development to the core," and this economic dependence "reinforced through juridical, political, and military measures." As a result, a relative lack of services and a lower standard of living excited "a higher level of frustration among members of the peripheral group." That frustration was merely heightened by "national discrimination on the basis of language, religion or other cultural forms." Against this background, Irish resistance to political integration appeared readily explicable. Other students of Celtic separatism have suggested that it was the progress of assimilation that reactivated a long latent nationalism. Both cultural decline and economic peripheralism were interpreted as "positive evidence" of the "detrimental effects" of "integration into the British State." In short, "ethnic distinctiveness" rather than uneven economic development lay at the core of separatism on the periphery. Only subsequently was "an economic rationale for self-government" advanced. Of course, in the case of Ireland "malintegration" had been institutionalized at the creation of the United Kingdom. The assurance that she would be elevated "'from the degraded post of a mercenary province to the proud station of an integral and governing member of the greatest empire in the world'" quickly acquired an ironic colouring. The union was never complete and entire. Instead, Ireland was always regarded as something of an oddity. The United Kingdom was founded upon the paradoxical notion of her exceptional status and character, and the maintenance of a semicolonial form of government headed by a lord lieutenant was merely the most obvious manifestation of her peculiarity. In this sense Ireland's relationship with England always appeared to be somewhat less intimate than that between the core and the two other Celtic peripheries. In fact, Scotland retained a broad range of distinctive institutions. Recognizing this, Hechter has recently conceded that she did not experience "internal colonialism to any great degree, but instead had a high level of institutional autonomy."[6]

This imperfect union's prospects of winning and maintaining popular acceptance in Ireland were not enhanced by its identification with the interests of the island's Protestant minority. And critics of internal colonial theories have emphasized their tendency to "overlook interregional anomalies in their emphasis upon interregional differentiation." Many Irish Protestants had waged a vigorous opposition to the loss of their Parliament, and thus to the surrender of nationhood. Some had declined to put "an external extinguisher on the rising genius" of their country, and had denied that union would effect a reconciliation of sectarian differences. Others had disputed the claims that it would spur economic growth, pointing out that there were too many attractive alternative investment opportunities for surplus English capital for much of that precious commodity to find its way to Ireland. Furthermore, whenever the interests of the two countries clashed those of the weaker would inevitably be sacrificed in a legislature in which Irishmen occupied only one-sixth of the seats. Finally, they had warned that union would foster absenteeism. Irishmen of wealth and influence would desert their native land for the capital of the United Kingdom, relegating Dublin to the rank of a provincial centre. It was this last prospect which weighed heavily on the minds of Dublin's army of more than 1,500 barristers and lawyers. They had good reason to fear the consequences of the emigration of their land's wealthiest potential litigants. Moreover, the sixty-seven barristers who were members of the Irish Parliament knew that there would be room for far fewer of them at Westminster, where Irish seats would number only one-third of those in Dublin. Equally self-interested had been the resistance of other borough and county members, or their patrons, who faced the same loss of prestige and of a valuable asset.[7]

To oppose the union did not imply any want of loyalty to the British connection, and conservative Irishmen who resisted it fully expected to preserve an exclusively Protestant Irish Parliament. Yet others already saw the union as essential for the maintenance of the Ascendancy – Protestant state, Protestant church, Protestant land – and this was a position to which it was easier to hold as a result of Pitt's decision not to risk alienating them by fastening Catholic Emancipation to the project of union itself. Defeated, the opponents quickly reconciled themselves to the new situation. As Pitt had foreseen, they felt more secure as an integral part of the United Kingdom's large Protestant majority, and became more British in outlook. But, contrary to his hopes, these developments failed to induce among the generality a greater liberalism in their attitudes towards the four-fifths of their countrymen who were Catholics. Divided among themselves on matters of doctrine, with Dissenters opposing Anglicans, and the latter harbouring evangelicals as well as latitudinarians, they were broadly united by distrust and dislike, even fear, of the Catholic population. Conversely, those Catholics who had supported union in the belief that it would bring their liberation from disabilities, and thus the establishment of true civil equality, were progressively alienated from it by the failure of successive governments to effect emancipation. Moreover, continued discrimination fostered the politicization of the Catholic clergy, and, subsequently, that of the Catholic masses. Neither development contributed to Protestant peace of mind.[8]

A pattern of failure was clearly marked out during the first three decades of the union's existence, and a large measure of responsibility for the sorry course of events can fairly be laid at the door of British politicians. After all, one argument for a union had been "the proved impossibility of so much as commencing the reformation of Ireland so long as a separate Legislature existed there." The subsequent disappointment of expectations has been attributed to British "indifference, neglect and extraordinary ignorance of Ireland and Irish conditions." Englishmen have been convicted of bigotry. According to one indictment, they responded to demands for change with "religious and racial denigration of the Irish as a people rather than serious investigation of their complaints." Yet, even though ignorance of Ireland did abound in Britain, and despite the presence of 100 members from that island was all too often on parade in Parliament, there were frequent investigations of her peculiar problems. Reports recommending the reclamation of bogs, in order to enlarge the area of productive land, were presented to Parliament frequently after 1810. There were several inquiries into the condition of the labouring poor. In all, the first three decades of the union saw more than 100 commissions and 61 committees investigate or report on Irish affairs. The "sufferings of Ireland were made known, and remedies were devised," critics charged, "but never adopted." In the words of one Irishman, it "is not alone of cold indifference to the promotion of her interests, and readiness to assail them, that Ireland has to complain. She complains of the efforts, which have been made, under oligarchical influence, to misrepresent her condition to the world, and persuade her in opposition to her own testimony, that she is improving, while her people are daily sinking deeper in misery." Yet the men charged with her government were devoid neither of intelligence, knowledge, experience, nor good intentions. Further, national self-interest suggested the wisdom of conciliating the Irish. Fighting a war of survival with the French, and then, once that expensive conflict had been won, preoccupied with the recovery of fiscal health, the British had need of a satisfied and tranquil Ireland. Nevertheless, among her countrymen, the belief that "improvement of every kind has been thwarted" became ever more deeply rooted. In truth, British ministers made a series of fateful choices, often preferring inaction to action, or limited reform to far-reaching change, or opting for coercion rather than for conciliation. This study seeks to explain how they approached the task of governing Ireland and why they made those choices at that particular time. Why did they allow the union to become so closely identified with the Protestant minority that not even the belated concession of emancipation could halt the process of Catholic alienation? In short, this is not an history of Anglo-Irish relations in their fullest sense, but rather an examination of the formulation and execution of Irish policy.[9].

Dominated as it was by the issue of Catholic Emancipation, the period which opened with the formation of the Liverpool administration in 1812 and closed eighteen years later with the fall of the Wellington ministry, proved to be an especially crucial one for the union. The implied promise of emancipation, extended to Catholics by William Pitt at the turn of the century, had still not been honoured after more than a decade. Increasingly, the question disrupted British politics. In 1812 the ruling but divided Tories sought refuge in the expedient of cabinet neutrality. Individual members of the government were free to speak and vote on Catholic claims as their consciences dictated, but as a body they refused to take a stand. Not that this strategy always prevented their collective embarrassment, for the disturbed state of Ireland, if nothing else, ensured that emancipation was a recurrent topic of parliamentary debate. Throughout these years, the upholders of the Protestant Ascendancy waged a rearguard action against the advocates of concession. They found within their ranks a precocious general.

Robert Peel went to Ireland in 1812 at the age of twenty-four. As chief secretary, he was the principal instrument of a policy founded upon the notion of the island's exceptionalism. An overwhelmingly Catholic population, now fully incorporated into a Protestant state, was not her least exceptional feature. The extent and depth of Ireland's poverty, and the extraordinary level of violence there, served also to distinguish that country from the rest of the United Kingdom. These were the circumstances which appeared to call for exceptional measures. When Peel left Ireland and office in 1818 his successor as chief secretary attempted to undo this policy. By the time of his dismissal at the end of 1821, Charles Grant's attempt to administer Ireland with the aid of the ordinary law only had been adjudged a failure. And soon after his departure Peel returned to office. As home secretary he assumed a broad responsibility for Irish affairs. However, the task of holding back the swelling tide of support for emancipation had become even more difficult. Sympathizers with that cause were now numerically stronger within the British government, while the Irish executive was ever more sharply divided. "Catholics" and "Protestants" administered the country in uneasy and uncomfortable partnership. Over the course of the next half-decade a series of reforms were enacted in an effort to pacify Ireland. Men such as Peel still hoped to avoid the ultimate concession of emancipation, but by the end of 1828 he had privately accepted its necessity. Together with the then prime minister, the duke of Wellington, he piloted the measure through Parliament. Thus did the champions of the Protestant state reluctantly serve as standard-bearers of Catholic Emancipation. The following year they fell from power and the Whigs, many of whom had long espoused emancipation from the Opposition benches, arguing that it was the vital instrument of tranquillity and improvement, made the discovery that Irish Catholics had developed an entirely new agenda of essential legislation.

Peel's contribution to the government of Ireland was of an order which only one of his contemporaries came near to rivalling. William Gregory was appointed civil under-secretary in 1812, shortly after Peel took office as chief secretary, and he did not long survive the latter's departure from the Home Office in 1830. This symmetry in their careers was entirely appropriate, for they became fast friends and close collaborators. Yet Gregory's influence within the Irish government extended beyond his intimacy with Peel and his faithful execution of the younger man's policies. He serves to illustrate a new breed of able men increasingly if haphazardly appointed to senior administrative positions, and who helped "to advise their political chiefs and shape policy." He acquired unmatched knowledge of the detail of Irish administration, adding the duties of military under-secretary to those of the civil in 1819, and became something of an indispensable man. Nor was he merely a glorified clerk, for during the prolonged absences of the chief secretary in London, attending the sessions of Parliament, viceroys turned to Gregory for advice and relied upon him to supervise day to day affairs and to implement policy. The liberal Charles Grant, ruminating on his failure, remarked that Gregory was for half of the year the master of the whole machine of government. His position was further strengthened by the warmth of the personal relationships he established with several of his superiors. Three of the five lords lieutenant under whom he served (Richmond, Whitworth, and Talbot) and four of the five chief secretaries (Peel, Goulburn, Lamb, and Hardinge), not only invited him into their confidence but also gave him their friendship. One consequence was a general perception of Gregory as the dominating influence at the Castle. Thomas Wyse, the historian of the Catholic Association, complained that "The petitioner at the Castle did not ask what the Lord Lieutenant thought but what the Lord Lieutenant's secretary thought, or rather what his secretary's secretary thought." It was Gregory, he claimed, "who held in his hands the destinies of Ireland." Daniel O'Connell expressed much the same opinion. If critics of the government tended to inflate Gregory's importance, he wielded influence enough. Moreover, he emerged as the most enduring symbol of conservative Protestant control of the administration. He came to epitomize the Ascendancy, and for O'Connell his removal from office became an *idée fixe*, an *"indispensable"* concession to Catholic opinion. Thus his attitudes and opinions are examined at some length, and he is accorded a prominent place, in this account of the era of emancipation.[10]

The structure of this study is straightforward. It opens with an analysis of the principal problems confronting the British governors of Ireland and an explanation of their conviction that the sister island could only be regarded as an exception within the United Kingdom. The second chapter is devoted largely to a discussion of the instruments of government – the means by which policy conceived in London, with advice from Dublin, was implemented. The succeeding chapters are broadly chronological, but this has resulted less from an attachment to narrative history than to the fact that this period witnessed a succession of experiments in Irish government. British ministries, not always with the troubles of Ireland in the forefront of their mind, mixed liberal and conservative agents, and administered liberal doses of repression and more conservative measures of reform, in a forlorn quest for tranquillity.

## CHAPTER ONE

# Britain and Ireland: Kindred Problems, Alien Sentiments

By 1812 Britain had been at war with France for almost a generation. Seemingly endless, the struggle had so exacerbated Britain's already complicated relationship with the United States that in June of that year her former colonies entered the lists agains her. The American conflict not only aggravated Britain's strategic difficulties but further dislocated an economy still struggling to overcome the effects of Napoleon's continental system. The will of a war-weary people appeared to be in grave danger of exhaustion. Ironically, the severe strains to which the British were now subjected ultimately proved to be less debilitating than those Napoleon imposed upon his own subjects as a result of the invasion of Russia. He launched that disastrous enterprise only a few days after the American declaration of war on Britain, but long before word of this development reached Europe. The immensity of the French emperor's miscalculation was not immediately apparent, however. So, beset by commotion at home as well as a widening conflict abroad, the British governing elite again fell prey to anxieties which the French Revolution had first awakened.

The dynamic role played by the *sans-culottes* in the dismantling of the *ancien régime* had excited nervousness, if not apprehension, within the upper ranks of British society. After all, Britain's lower orders enjoyed an unequalled reputation for turbulence. Ignited by an astonishing diversity of factors, popular disturbances had been commonplace in England throughout the eighteenth century. Annual wakes, fairs, and festivals had regularly been scarred by the faction fights that formed part of a popular culture. Even the Gordon Riots, which swept across the capital in June of 1780, leaving an unprecedented trail of destruction, at first reflected the ritualized character of much of this violence. Only when the initial paroxysm of popular anti-catholicism developed into an assault upon the personal and institutional symbols of authority did the government take fright.[1]

The most common form of disturbance was the food riot. Here again a traditional if not reassuring pattern could often be detected within the tumult. Rioters usually had limited ends. They sought to halt the movement of grains out of their own localities and to coerce dealers and the authorities into a reduction of prices. Moreover, they tended to exhibit remarkable "discipline and restraint." Attacks on property were rarely accompanied by assaults on persons, and this discrimination was especially evident in those few rural areas visited by disorders. Whether seeking to enforce a "moral economy," responding to the heightening class tensions in urban communities, or simply demonstrating outrage during exceptional crises in food supply and employment, the rioters rarely posed a serious threat to the established social and political order. Nevertheless, the events of the 1790s gave government and gentry reasonable cause for disquiet. The outbreak of the French Revolution had coincided with the centenary of Britain's, and concern that French principles might prove attractive to discontented Britons was not allayed by the astonishing popularity of Tom Paine's *Rights of Man* and evidence of organized lower-class urban radicalism.[2] Their nervousness increased with the outbreak of war with France in 1793, and the resort by that nation to terror as an instrument of government. Equally worrying at this critical juncture were the coincidental shortages of provisions in Britain. The British government successfully weathered this crisis, as it did the recurrent storms of food rioting, by implementing a policy which tempered coercion with conciliation. Not only did it intervene directly in the cereals market but it also became more involved in the organization of relief. The use of grains in distilling and the manufacture of starch was forbidden. Wheat was imported on the government's account and its release onto the market closely supervised. For their part, the well-to-do volunteered to reduce their consumption of bread and opened subscriptions to assist the poor to purchase the available supplies.

Simultaneously, the heavy hand of repression was laid upon suspected political dissidents. The suspension of habeas corpus, the passage of laws to prevent treasonable practices and seditious meetings, and the outlawing of unofficial oaths, all facilitated the silencing of radical critics. They were also intimidated by "loyal" mobs. "In many areas popular Toryism provided at least as spontaneous an appeal as popular radicalism." Finally, the government resorted to its traditional weapon – the military. Britain lacked an effective police system. The limited ends of the food rioters, the belief that urban growth had not produced a dramatic surge in criminality, and the essentially nonviolent character of the vast majority of offences permitted the English to continue to indulge their traditional and ideological aversion to a highly organized, well-disciplined, and permanent civilian force to maintain the peace. The exception was the capital. There, contemporaries were convinced serious crime was increasing and proposals were advanced from the mid-eighteenth century for the creation of a centralized police force. Instead, a series of limited measures were adopted. The Bow Street magistrates established a company of thief-takers, stipendiary magistrates were appointed, and a force formed to police the Thames while another patrolled the highways around the metropolis. Elsewhere the authorities were obliged to rely on troops for the performance of police functions and within a year of the French declaration of war the Volunteer Act had created a new force intended not merely as a guard against invasion but as an instrument of domestic law and order. Successful as these immediate counter-revolutionary measures proved to be – and their effectiveness was enhanced by the reluctance of radicals to seek violent change – a number of economic and social developments were working towards the same conservative end.[3]

The industrialization of the British economy gathered momentum during the late eighteenth century, though the growth in real output and national income may have been more gradual than economic historians once surmised. Similarly, the conflict with France probably retarded rather than accelerated real growth. Nevertheless, between 1793 and 1815, Britain was in the extraordinary position of "fighting a major war and getting richer at the same time." Her single most important industry remained agriculture, "and it was the state of the harvest which was still the most significant factor in determining change in the national income between one year and the next." Although her rapidly multiplying population remained overwhelmingly rural, town-dwellers were increasing sharply in numbers and proportion. By 1800 "about 30 per cent of the country's population lived in towns of 2,500 inhabitants or more." In response to the demands of an ever-swelling and more urban population, farmers had undertaken improvements to increase the supply of foodstuffs even before the war gave them the additional incentives of rising prices and an assured market. Prosperity bred optimism, and both were the guardians of living standards which impressed many visitors to England. If the man who believed himself to be steadily rising in the world made a poor recruit for a revolution, what of the poor who were left behind by or fell before the economic advance?[4]

Every town had its slums, but they were most obvious in such booming manufacturing centres as Manchester. Overcrowding, a lack of sanitation, poverty, and disease were the ingredients of a potentially volatile brew, especially when the residents of the pestilential "rookeries" found themselves ensnared by the price inflation of the war years. On the land, meanwhile, the poverty was equally harsh. Reduced to the ranks of labourers by the enclosure movement and the development of more highly capitalized farming, agricultural workers had struggled painfully to cope with the moderate price increases which were a feature of the two decades before the French war. In southern and eastern counties, where the supply of agricultural labourers greatly exceeded the demand and opportunities for alternative employment were few, their abject poverty was all too evident in bodies that were undernourished, poorly clad, and ill-housed. Their "Miserable, overcrowded, single-room cottages with turfed roofs, earthen floors and unglazed windows shocked countless travellers" to a country ranked second only to Holland in terms of national prosperity. Observers likened such "wretched hovels" to "wigwams" and "pigsties." Squalor and misery were not universal, for competition for labour in the industrializing northern and midlands counties pushed up agricultural wages too, but they were pervasive.[5]

The depressed condition of labourers attempting to eke out an existence on wages insufficient for subsistence, and evidence of their restiveness, spurred an administrative modification of the Poor Law. The responsibility of each community to make provision for the "deserving poor" had been established by law during the reign of Elizabeth, though disputes over which parish was to be charged for the support of a particular indigent improved neither the law's efficiency nor the system's humanity. Then, early in the eighteenth century, parishes had been empowered to establish workhouses and deny relief to persons who refused to enter them. In little more than a half-century English parishes erected almost 2,000 of them. Later, as the innocent victims of the revolutionary changes in the economy multiplied, there had been a relaxation of the law's harsher provisions. Under the terms of the Poor Act of 1782 the use of the workhouse test as a deterrent to the able-bodied among the paupers was curtailed. After all, the dramatic increase in the number of the poor during cyclical recessions discouraged plans to require residence in workhouses which would have been expensive to construct or purchase. The same considerations – humanitarianism and cost-effectiveness – shaped the Poor Acts of 1793 and 1795, which offered paupers greater protection from the danger of neglect. By this time a public opinion sympathetic to "more widespread *outdoor* relief" provided the background against which magistrates, first in Oxford and then in Speenhamland, devised schemes which guaranteed labourers a subsistence income. Although diversity continued to be an essential characteristic of such a parish-based system, "During the war and its immediate aftermath Speenhamland and its variants were to be applied in most of the counties of England and Wales. Only in the north, where alternative industrial employment helped to raise cash wages in agriculture and where payments in kind were more common, was its influence limited." To use the rates to subsidize the poorly paid risked the pauperization of labour, and these provisions were administered heartlessly in some areas, but the modified law did provide "a safety-net for the unfortunate" and in some instances perhaps even "a welfare state in miniature." The wage allowance "helped keep alive a swelling rural proletariat at the expense of farmers' profits and landlords' rents." Moreover, the fact that the poor rate was a charge on the occupants not the owners of the land allowed the latter in their capacity as magistrates to check the natural parsimony of the ratepayers at comparatively little direct cost to themselves, thereby helping to restore to rural relationships that veneer of paternalism damaged by the rise of commercial farming yet so important to a society founded on deference and subordination. To this extent the Poor Law served to contain disaffection. Of course, few paternalists doubted the inevitability of poverty, citing the Bible as their authority that it would never cease. Consequently, as the numbers in receipt of relief rose steeply, and the costs ballooned, so criticism of the revised system grew louder.[6]

Individual efforts by its clergymen to lessen the suffering of the poor by cooperating with "enlightened justices" did not constitute the largest contribution of the Established Church to the antirevolutionary cause in Britain. In the words of one divine, contemplating the events across the Channel, "'When religion shall have lost its hold on men's consciences, government will lose its authority over their persons, and a state of barbarous anarchy will ensue'." The Church of England "stood for the maintenance of the existing social order" and was regarded as a buttress of the constitution. Thus it demanded the suppression of radical literature and defended social inequality as both natural and providential. More appealing, at least to the poor, were the calls by some clergy for the wealthy to accept their fundamental obligation to aid the needy. Yet the essentials of the Christian ethic, however well taught by the divines and writers of "orthodox eighteenth-century Anglicanism," offer a less than convincing explanation of Britain's avoidance of revolutionary violence. Uncounted numbers of the lower orders did not hold in high esteem an Established Church whose clergy all too often placed secular interests ahead of spiritual duties. In this sense, the crusade for agricultural improvements had had an unforeseen and unfortunate consequence. Progressive landowners and farmers had required the consent of the tithe holders before they could effect enclosures, and they had frequently secured a commutation in exchange for a generous allotment of land. As a result, some parsons were transformed into squires and magistrates. Not a few did show themselves to be paternalists in their administration of the Poor Law, but in all too many cases their removal from village rectories to country houses merely widened the physical distance and deepened the social gulf which separated them from their impoverished parishioners. Conversely, the large number of "meagre" livings encouraged pluralism. Whatever its cause, nonresidence was a discouragement to church attendance. Similarly, the Established Church had failed to adjust successfully to urbanization. In Manchester, for example, there were eight times as many potential parishioners as there were pews while few clergy were attracted to the many poor livings. To the extent that it responded to urban growth, the church located itself in fashionable areas and soon "acquired a distinctly middle-class gloss." The poor were largely ignored.[7]

For all of its failings, by the final quarter of the eighteenth century the church was harbouring a small but vibrant band of activist clergy dedicated to ecclesiastical and social reform. These evangelicals excited the suspicions of their High Church brethren. They tended to associate them with the Methodists whom they were increasingly determined to purge from Anglican ranks. Hence their denunciations of this "'general conspiracy against common sense and rational orthodox Christianity'." Such tensions grew during the 1790s. High Churchmen blamed subversive French ideas for the prevalence of immorality and depravity in British society. The evangelicals, on the other hand, laid vice and sin at the door of "true religion," arguing that it had neglected to reform "the evil heart of man." This implied criticism of their own church was made explicit in attacks upon the lax morality and secular pastimes of a priesthood recruited from otherwise unprovided-for sons of the gentry and aristocracy. Moreover, while they affirmed the necessity of an Established Church to ensure a "basic continuity of religious teaching," the evangelicals attacked the "mere formality of church-attendance" and introduced a notion of the "Invisible Church" which threatened to undermine the Establishment. Nor were the orthodox unmindful of the turmoil in those parishes where congregation and clergy found themselves in opposite camps.[8]

The irony of this internal conflict lay in the combatants' unity of purpose. Reactionaries and evangelicals upheld the same values – stable government and secure property. The essential difference between them was that the latter supported the established order with somewhat greater subtlety. This is not to deny the strength of their humanitarian impulse to aid the unfortunate. Sensible and sensitive men perceived with dismay the embittering contrast between wealth and poverty and the menacing increase in disorders. That evangelical vanguard, the Clapham Sect, was "genuinely concerned" for the poor, but "saw only infinite peril if the poor themselves began in desperation to combine for their own deliverance." Instead, the poor ought to be furnished with somewhat more comfort and made a great deal more pious. This course seemed all the more compelling once the revolution had erupted in France. Both symmetry and symbolism are to be found, therefore, in the report that on his deathbed Edmund Burke, whose *Reflections on the Revolution in France* had acquired the aura of prophecy, read the latest work of the acknowledged evangelical leader, William Wilberforce. In his *Practical View of the Religious System of Professed Christians Contrasted with Real Christians*, he extolled Christianity as the indispensable agent of social cohesion. The assurance of eternal justice in the next world made bearable the transitory injustices of life in this.[9]

Evangelicals of all persuasions sought nothing less than a reformation of British society. They expected the rich to set an example of piety, charity, and responsiblity and the poor to learn patience as well as piety. The work of assistance and instruction was undertaken by a host of philanthropic societies. The London Missionary Society, the Religious Tract Society, and the British and Foreign Bible Society were but three of the most important. Originally founded in 1804 to distribute Bibles, and soon aided by a legion of Auxiliary Societies established in those urban areas most in need of missionaries, the last attracted the vehement criticism of orthodox church-men. They resented the challenge it and its auxiliaries offered to the exclu-sively Anglican Society for the Propagation of Christian Knowledge, founded in 1699, and they suspected it of introducing a fifth column of dissenters into the bosom of the Establishment. Nevertheless, the Bible Society pressed on with its mission of carrying the evangelical message to the artisans left untended by the orthodox pastors of the Established Church, and gave powerful support to the Sunday Schools organized for much the same purpose.[10]

The eighteenth century witnessed a resurgence of interest in education, especially among the swelling ranks of the middle classes. Heavily influ-enced by the works of the materialist philosophers, such as John Locke, they saw it as an instrument for modifying man's nature, forming his char-acter, and developing his moral qualities. Subsequently, the cause was taken up by "philosophic radicals," such as James Mill, who stressed the peculiar importance of education for the working classes. It would bring them "within the orbit of civilization" and was an "essential concomitant of an enlarged suffrage." Needless to say, conservative evangelicals were primarily inter-ested in moral reform of the lower orders. Convinced of the merits of a little Christian education, or at least schooling, they and a number of High Churchmen rallied to Robert Raikes, who had opened his first Sunday School in 1780 and formed with a group of friends the society of that name five years later. By 1787 some 250,000 children were attending these schools, where they were taught to read through the exclusive study of the Bible, the catechism, and other suitable tracts, such as those which flowed from the inspired pen of Hannah More. The schools promoted social contentment as well as piety, and have been interpreted as "clever inventions because they ensured that children who worked from Monday to Saturday were instructed [or indoctrinated] on their day off." Docility was also taught at the charity schools established earlier in the century. They sought to reconcile the children of the poor to their position in society, and therefore "lacked any concept of relating education to social advancement and saw moral reformation as the desperately needed remedy for the social problem of the poor." Of course, once the poor had acquired a rudimentary education it was difficult to restrict them to the Bible or Hannah More's *Cheap Repo-sitory*, and this uneasiness was reflected in the debate over the wisdom of instructing them in writing. In short, the Sunday and other charity schools, together with those subsequently founded by the National Society for Pro-moting the Education of the Poor in the Principles of the Established Church

(1811) and by the nonconformists' British and Foreign School Society (1812), may in the long run have been of questionable value in the struggle against radical or subversive ideas.[11]

Whatever the ultimate shortcomings of some of the evangelicals' endeavours, they were a force for social cohesion during the prolonged crisis of the Revolutionary and Napoleonic wars. They had introduced the rudiments of a religious education to those whose spiritual needs had been ignored by orthodox churchmen. It was during the war that Methodism blossomed in the towns, though it was by no means an exclusively urban phenomenon, and in alliance with other evangelicals Methodists waged war on a popular culture which was characterized by hedonism and violence. The evangelicals genuine concern for the material welfare of the poor did not always result in a truly significant lessening of misery, but it did tend to blunt the bitterness of the lower orders. Then again, they placed heavy emphasis on obedience to established authority. Further, to the extent that evangelicalism diverted the energies of men from political into spiritual channels, it may have denied the radical movements the leadership they required. Certainly, the converted turned away in revulsion from the anticlericalism and irreligion put on display in France. Moreover, evangelicalism "brought together the developing sections of the middle classes, gave them an independent outlook, relieved their fears of the more elemental forms of mass unrest, [and] showed how a respectable working-class could be led by a respectable middle-class." This leadership did not go unchallenged by radical elements within the working class, nor did the social fabric of Britain escape serious rents.[12]

A downturn in the economy in 1810, as Napoleon tightened his continental system, was worsened by a rash of bank failures, a poor harvest, and the Americans' severing of trade in a final effort to avoid a resort to war. Thousands of workers were thrown out of employment in the Manchester textile trades, in the wool trade of the West Riding of Yorkshire, and in the hosiery industry of Nottinghamshire and Leicestershire. Unemployment and low wages combined with expensive food brought in 1811 and 1812 another bout of rioting in the hardest hit areas. The activities of machine-breaking rioters, conducted as they were over an extensive area, which in turn suggested a frightening measure of cooperation, inevitably excited fresh fears of Jacobinism. How genuinely revolutionary this outburst of Luddism was remains a matter of dispute among historians, but at the time the government kept its nerve. Relying in the first instance on local magistrates for the enforcement of the law, it responded to their demands for legislation – frame-breaking bill to make the crime a capital offence and a peace bill to permit the conscription of adults as special constables – and requests for military aid. The 12,000 troops despatched to the disturbed areas overawed the rioters while the subsequent trials served to remind the disaffected of the perils of conduct which had resulted in much destruction of property and several murders. Sixteen men were executed in York early in 1813 for machine-breaking, the theft of arms, or simple robbery, and seven others were transported for taking illegal oaths.[13]

Britain's economic difficulties and related social tensions paled before her sister kingdom's chronic maladies, for which union had been legislated as the cure following the rebellion of 1798 and the landing of a French expeditionary force. The mutual benefits as seen from England were summarized in the British Commons by George Canning, himself of Irish extraction. Britain would be assured of greater military security on her western flank, while the people of Ireland would receive "the real, inspiriting, and enlivening sunshine of English liberty." Nor would the sun know any distinction of sect. Both Protestant minority and Catholic majority would prosper. At last secure, as part of the larger British majority, Protestant Irishmen would surely endorse the repeal of the remaining Catholic disabilities. "It is to put an end to those hopes of our enemies – it is to put Ireland out of danger, both from foreign attack and domestic disturbance and distraction – it is, in every point of view, to ameliorate her condition," Canning declaimed, "that this measure is proposed." The apparent success of the earlier union with Scotland lent credibility to such assertions.[14]

Contemporaries saw the union of 1707 as the means by which Scotland had been rescued from poverty. Free access to Britain's domestic and colonial markets had always promised to spur the growth of the external trade which mercantilists believed to be essential to Scotland's development. Of course, it had taken the Scots time to capitalize fully upon their new opportunities. They had first to improve the quality of their goods, in order to compete within the large protected market. They prudently avoided industrial competition with the more advanced economy of Britain by developing their production along complementary lines. By the end of the century, however, the union seemed to have achieved its purpose. The formerly chaotic finances had been brought under control, capital had moved north from the far richer South, the state had invested heavily in improved communications, bounties had been provided to the fisheries, the producers of whisky had received concessions which gave them an advantage over English competitors, the textile and coal industries had developed, as had trade, while the successful entrepreneurs who invested a portion of their profits in land had led the way in agricultural improvements. Ironically, the union may have succeeded not only because of what amounted to a program of regional development but also because it was an incomplete one. Economic gains had been purchased at a comparatively low price in terms of "real political power." Thus Scotland's great institutions of "law, education, and the Scottish kirk, the primary sources of nationality rather than a Parliament which had only lost its ancient impotence two decades before Union," had been "preserved intact." Moreover, her landowners and merchants had maintained their existing privileges. In short, Scotland had secured vital commercial advantages "while retaining an indigenous élite with an enhanced apparatus of power and also the survival of a series of institutions which both defined her nationality and provided the social base for modernisation." Yet these finer points of the Anglo-Scottish relationships probably escaped most observers.[15]

Whereas Scotland could scarcely be described as a colony of England, the Anglo-Irish relationship had acquired something of a colonial character by the eighteenth century. The Irish had "lost their lands," been obliged "to work for 'strangers'," and had fallen under "new forms of political domination." Conquest and confiscation had produced an élite that was socially, racially, and religiously distinct from the great mass of the population. Similarly, colonization had introduced a substantial minority of English and Scottish Protestants whose presence created ethnic and sectarian divisions within the ranks of the lower orders. That gulf was widened and deepened by the discriminatory penal laws which fell so heavily upon Catholics. Lastly, there was an element of colonialism in Ireland's growing economic dependence on Britain, but it did not inhibit the development of a surprisingly expansive mood of economic optimism.[16]

Confidence had grown with the progressive diversification of the Irish economy. Encouraged by cheap money and substantial public investment, entrepreneurs had enthusiastically embarked upon industrialization. Imitating technological developments in England, Irishmen transformed such traditional industries as milling into "large-scale" enterprises which utilized water power and were housed in substantial buildings. Belfast, in particular, adopted "wholeheartedly the techniques of the Industrial Revolution." By 1800 the cotton industry alone reputedly gave direct employment in that town to 13,500 people. In this and other successful industries, such as linen, the Irish were able to exploit their low labour costs and English manufacturers were by no means scornful of their competitive potential. In 1783 a depression in Ireland's textile industries excited calls for protection from foreign goods, including British, a demand which appeared all the more reasonable given the existing differential in duties charged by the two countries on importations of the other's manufactures. Britain's rates were higher. William Pitt's response to this outburst of "colonial nationalism" was to propose free trade. But the scheme came to naught largely because of the fears of British merchants and manufacturers that industries would emigrate to Ireland and Pitt's misjudgment of the strength of the Irish Parliament's nationalism. Happily, the Irish economy quickly regained its momentum and one measure of its continuing expansion was the proliferation of market centres in the second half of the century. Two hundred patents were granted between 1750 and 1799, and the "significant reductions in size of market areas" was further evidence of thriving provisions and cattle trades and a booming linen industry.[17]

Important as the economic changes were, the prospects of continued diversification and industrialization were less rosy than Irish optimists imagined. Thus the prolonged effort to develop a large-scale commercialized fishing industry, which the Irish government sought to assist with tonnage bounties, foundered with the disappearance of the herring shoals. By the century's end, Scottish herring was being imported for domestic consumption. Significantly, Scottish merchants controlled and Scottish ships carried by far the larger proportion of the small but valuable trade between the two countries. This was only one illustration of the weakness of the Irish commercial sector, which probably owed much to a genteel distate for trade among middle and upper-class Protestants. No less significant was the equally weak domestic demand for Irish manufactures. Ireland's small and remote deposits of coal may not at this stage have been a serious obstacle to industrial expansion, but the growing dependence upon this fuel for domestic heating – her woods had long since been cut and peat was too bulky to ship any distance economically – was costly. Consumers who bought high-priced imported coal necessarily had less disposable income for the purchase of manufactures. The same was true of the many Irishmen who were victims of low agricultural incomes. By 1800 few Irish industries were able to compete with those of Britain where strong domestic and growing foreign demand were already facilitating the introduction of economies of scale. Even Ireland's substantial capital investment in communications perversely served to ease the distribution of British products. Yet the progressive introduction of free trade, following union, was not a sinister device of the English "metropole" to destroy the "manufacturing and much of the remainder of the economic base" of the Irish "satellite." Instead, there was reason to hope that the arrangement which had apparently worked so well for Scotland would work again. Adam Smith certainly thought so. The extent to which Ireland's economic future was already predetermined was not apparent to contemporaries.[18]

Many of the more successful Irish industries were extensions of agriculture. Even the textile trades had an intimate link to rural Ireland. They provided supplementary employment and vital income for a host of small farmers and their families. Her economic growth notwithstanding, Ireland remained a rural country dependent upon agriculture for her well-being. After linens, provisions were her principal exports and by 1800 she was almost entirely dependent on England as a market for these goods. The success of this trade, the growth in British demand for grains, and the desire to provide for the voracious appetite of the inhabitants of Dublin, saw bounties offered to producers and exporters of cereals. This policy, together with high prices, drew grain supplies "out of the countryside and out of rural diets to be replaced by cheaper food stuffs, notably potatoes." No less important, "by the end of the century the trade in foodstuffs from Ireland to Britain reflected, on the one hand, the increasing industrialization of Britain and, on the other, the retardation of Irish economic growth." And this at a time of dramatic population growth. Whatever the explanation for what was a general demographic phenomenon after 1750 – an autonomous decline in the death rate as infectious diseases became less virulent or people developed immunities; improvements in medicine; better nutrition; a lowering of the age of marriage and a consequent rise in fertility – the Irish numbered more than 5 million by the opening of the nineteenth century. It was the soil which had to support a population growing at a peculiarly rapid rate. Agriculture was not only the largest single economic activity, as in Britain, but it continued to dominate the economy in a way that was no longer true on the other side of the Irish Sea. Contemporaries estimated that it gave employment to fully three-quarters of the work force, as opposed to one-third in England. Even more disturbing was its inefficiency.[19]

The stimuli of strong demand and high prices did inspire improvements in the methods of supply, as they had in Britain, but Ireland's agriculture failed to achieve the productivity of that of her principal customer. Perhaps Arthur Young overstated the case when, following his tour of the island, he suggested that in farming Ireland lagged two centuries behind her neighbour, yet the evidence of backwardness was all too visible. Farms were untidy, fencing inadequate, crop rotation unscientific, harvesting practices and implements rudimentary, the use of draft animals and the treatment of livestock savage, while the sharp increase in the size of the population was but one of the factors behind the fragmentation of landholdings. Farms were subdivided by fathers anxious to provide for their children, cottiers paid their rent in labour, and labourers rented small plots in conacre on which to raise the potatoes that were becoming the principal source of nourishment for the very poor. Increasingly, small farmers were also to become dependent on the root.[20]

The profound weaknesses of the economy were obscured after 1793 by a wartime prosperity, as the British demand for wheat, flour, and oats continued to grow. A boom in agricultural exports was accompanied by another leap in prices. A portion of the capital now accumulated was reinvested in agriculture or invested in industry, communications, and urban development, but the combination of large profits from tillage and continuing population pressure had a less fortunate impact upon the economy. Further incentives to subletting and subdivision were being offered at a time when a decline in the domestic woollen industry exposed to disaster those small farmers and cottiers who were dependent upon this source of supplementary income in order to make ends meet. Equally alarming, poor grain and potato harvests in 1799 and 1800 created near-famine conditions for a large class of labourers. Few if any of these ominous problems were solved by the union with Britain. Indeed, in the minds of some observers it became a large part of the problem instead of the solution.[21]

"'The Union has not given us new capital or new trade; the export trade is the old trade of Ireland, increasing from its nature, not from the Union'," Henry Grattan complained privately in 1809. Certainly, the economic hopes of its advocates had not been quickly fulfilled, and before long critics were pointing to Dublin as a doleful example of the union's impact. They recalled a national capital which had been perhaps "one of the most agreeable places of residence in Europe," and had boasted a society "as brilliant and polished as that of Paris in its best days, while social intercourse was conducted with a conviviality that could not be equalled in France, and which, though not always strictly in accordance with modern notions of temperance, seldom degenerated into coarseness." No doubt Dublin had lost some of its social sheen as a result of the migration to Britain of many of Ireland's grandees, while the urban improvements of the late eighteenth century initiated by the Paving Commission and the Wide Steets Commissioners may well have begun to lose their freshness. One Irishman who returned to his native land a decade after the union complained of the capital's shabbiness, of dirty and dark streets, and of the indifference and neglect of those well-paid officials responsible for its administration. However, as one reviewer of this indictment was quick to note, if cleanliness and adequate street-lighting were the standards of national progress, the condition of London gave cause for apprehension for the future of Britain.[22]

Other visitors were more impressed with Dublin. As a city it held "in miniature everything to be met with in the great capital of the British empire," and its environs and natural amenities, particularly the vast expanse of Phoenix Park and the splendid Botanical Garden, were more pleasing than those of London. Admittedly, there remained a "curious contrast between the grandeur of the national buildings and monuments, and the poverty of the great body of the people," but even this contradiction could not entirely erase an impression that Ireland was on "the road to improvement." Dublin remained a manufacturing as well as an administrative centre, with a commercial life that sustained a substantial middle class. Yet the core of the indictment of the union was the accusation that it had stunted the island's economic growth. Critics charged that Ireland's assessment for the support of the united kingdoms, some two-seventeenths of the total, was unfair and resulted in gross overtaxation. Drained of funds through overtaxation and remittances to absentee landowners, she had been robbed of capital so essential for economic diversification and agricultural improvements.[23]

Even before the union Ireland had been obliged to contribute to the cost of the war with France, and a reluctance to meet the increased charges through direct taxation had seen her resort to a number of indirect taxes and heavy borrowings. After 1801 Ireland retained her separate financial structure and currency and successive chancellors of the Irish exchequer pursued the pre-union financial policies. They imposed additional levies on such traditional items as stamps, sugar, and tea, but a growing resistance to an ever heavier burden of indirect taxation had obliged them to persist with the expedient of borrowing. Before the war's end some 85 per cent of current revenues were being applied to the service of a debt which had qradrupled since 1800. If, despite this strategy, the level of taxation was burdensome, much of what was taken from Ireland was returned in the form of the expenditures on the substantial military force stationed there.[24]

To the charge of overtaxation, foes of the terms of union and its disillusioned former friends added the bitter accusation that Ireland's infant industries had deliberately been left virtually defenceless. The lowering of their protective walls had exposed them to the aggressive competition of British concerns which entered the fray armed with superior capital and influence. What was worse, in certain cases, such as the fisheries, Ireland had been the victim of a calculated discrimination. Evidently these critics resented their country's apparent powerlessness and increasing "dependency" upon Britain. She, with her more advanced economy, appeared to have sentenced Ireland to "underdevelopment." Yet some industries did survive and several were able to thrive. Linens remained an important export. Encouraged by parliamentarians anxious to wean Irishmen away from spirits, brewing expanded and the firm of Guinness illustrated its success. Distilling weathered not only the union but also legislative efforts to discourage it, though an important segment of this industry was in the hands of illegal distillers. Nor is it at all certain that high protective walls would have rescued other Irish industries. Moreover, one propagandist for the union, R.M. Martin, later chronicled the development of steam power in Ireland, tracing its growth from Belfast in 1806 to Dublin, Cork, Londonderry, Kilkenny, Limerick, and Waterford in little more than a decade, as proof that despite the cheapness of water power this more advanced method of industrial production had been brought gradually into operation. Further, he totalled up the public investment. He calculated that during the first sixteen years of the union Parliament had made grants to encourage industry, to finance public works and employment, and to support charitable and literary institutions which totalled £4,398,638. In short, what some Irishmen interpreted as exploitation some Britons may well have believed to be development. Union did not create Ireland's dependence upon her trade with Britain, but did facilitate further exploitation of the market so vital to the prosperity of the industry which dominated her economy. Nor did her continued dependence upon agriculture necessarily doom her to impoverishment. "It was not the specialization in agriculture which was the root of Ireland's poverty, but low agricultural productivity itself that was to blame."[25]

The backwardness of Irish agriculture, which Arthur Young and others had noted long before the union, persisted into the nineteenth century despite the pull of an ever enlarging British market and the best efforts of the Farming Society and other progressive agencies. However, the trend towards tillage had accelerated following the complete removal in 1806 of restrictions on the importation of Irish corn into Britain. Within two years Ireland was meeting "four-fifths of Great Britain's imported cereal requirements." Irish farmers also exported large quantities of corn to the British and allied armies fighting in the Iberian peninsula. The happy combination of assured markets and high prices induced those holding substantial areas of land on long leases to grasp for the still easier profits to be made from subdivision and subletting. Since the margin of profit for the proliferating small tillage farmers was rarely adequate, the effect of this parcelling out of land was to deepen the "subsistence stratum" as the "rate of increase in the numbers of cottiers and labourers" outstripped "the rate of expansion of the monetary economy." In short, and for reasons that had little to do with the union, this wartime prosperity excluded vast numbers of Irishmen. Like many Englishmen, they fell victim to the collapse of the trade with America after 1811. Artisans had found wage increases lagging behind price rises even before that hardship was compounded by the dislocation of a linen industry dependent upon American flaxseed. Firms quickly laid off their workers, until by 1814 more than 18,000 had been thrown out of work in Belfast alone. Meanwhile the labourers on the land found themselves imprisoned in an equally painful economic vice – low wages and high rents – as the supply of population exceeded the demand for labour.[26]

Ireland was the poorest of the united kingdoms. A general increase in Irish prosperity during the eighteenth century had failed to lift a rural society out of its exceptional destitution. A local writer described conditions in one district of County Cork in 1775 that were "shocking to humanity," and then observed that they were common to at least one-quarter of the entire population of southwestern Ireland and that an additional quarter were only marginally better off. And while there were suggestions that the "'general appearance of the mass of the people'" had "'greatly improved'" during the profitable years of the Napoleonic Wars, Irish society remained remarkable less for the existence of widespread poverty than for the proportion of the population that was in constant danger of impoverishment. Tax returns compiled during the 1790s suggested the irregular shape of the Irish social pyramid. It had an immensely broad and deep base, surmounted by a narrow and shallow centre which tapered sharply to the characteristic apex. The large landholders, aristocrats and gentry, provided the upper classes who numbered about 10,000 and were predominantly Protestant. The middle was composed of the more substantial farmers, merchants, the professions, and the clergy, and embraced a very considerable number of Catholics. For however small the area of Ireland owned by Catholics – Arthur Young put it at 5 per cent – a substantial amount of land was leased by them. One intelligent and careful observer estimated early in the new century that Catholics were in occupation of more than half of the personal property of the kingdom. Other Catholics had grown affluent as members of the commercial and professional middle classes. Filling the vacuum created by an Ascendancy distaste for a career in business, and exploiting a relaxation of the penal laws which granted them a measure of equality in the enjoyment of property rights, Catholics had acquired prominence in their country's mercantile life. Beneath this small, vibrant middle class lay the great mass of lower orders, a term which the hearth tax returns suggest covered more than 80 per cent of the entire population. Indeed, one-seventh of the houses of Ireland had been exempted from the tax on grounds of poverty. This estimate of the proportion of Irishmen who belonged to the lower orders is not inconsistent with the modern calculation that on the eve of the Famine more than half of the adult male workforce on the land was composed of "landless labourers and landholding labourers." If small farmers were added to this number, and after the middle of the eighteenth century the distinction between them and cottiers began to disappear, the rural poor of Ireland exceeded three-quarters of the total.[27]

The depth of this lower class, which included at one end of the scale men working as many as a score of acres and at the other those tending a plot in conacre or employed in manufacturing, goes far to explain an apparent paradox. The Irish had an enviable reputation for strength, stamina, and vigour, yet recruiting officers during the French wars had reported that the children of the very poor were of stunted growth, a deformity they attributed to the want of proper nourishment in infancy. In fact, for all but the very poorest of the rural poor the mainstay of their diet, the potato, was supplemented by cereals, buttermilk, other dairy products, vegetables and even fish. Reasonably well supplied with nutritious food, they also enjoyed ample supplies of fuel, peat being abundant. However, its time-consuming preparation contributed to the slow pace of agricultural modernization. Common to the poor and very poor alike were housing conditions which amazed many visitors. Even small farmers at the upper end of the poverty scale refrained from investing heavily in their shelter, since landlords were under no obligation to compensate them for any improvements whenever they turned them off the land. These "mansions of miserable existence" moved John Curwen, an English MP, to conclude: "The only wonder is, that the demoralizing influence of such wretchedness on the Irish character, has not long ago been found to be more general and pernicious." The "hilarity and vivacity" of the peasantry "in defiance of their apparent distress" could not mask, however, a dangerous spirit of "insubordination" in the face of the many demands made upon the value of the produce of their holdings – rents, county cess, tithes, vestry cess, and priests' dues. Moreover, their resistance appeared all the more threatening given the absence of those informal and institutional restraints upon the lower orders which were a feature of British society.[28]

There was little likelihood of Irish tenants establishing a bond with their landlords which would lend itself to romanticization. In Ireland, the veneer of paternalism covering an inherently exploitative relationship had always been painfully thin and belief in the justice of gentry rule conspicuously absent. Many of the largest landowners were British and absentees, whereas others, who were Irish by birth, had been educated in England and had acquired English manners and tastes. Absentees naturally tended to be unaware of the miserable plight of their tenantry and were incapable of providing personally "the necessary example of efficient land management and improving cultivation from which their tenants could have substantially profited." But the charge that landlords who failed to improve their estates and to invest their surplus capital in Ireland were largely responsible for the backwardness of agriculture, and thus for poverty, obscures the extent to which Irish tenants, no less than those in Britain, were the victims of agrarian improvements. Some "were forced to replace their consumption-ordered family economy with a more modern production-oriented system," which threatened "their always precarious economic system and the social and moral values which supported it." For others, the projects of improving landlords or larger farmers often involved the invasion of customary rights or even the loss of the plot of land that they believed alone stood between them and absolute destitution. As a result, those efforts that were made to modernize Irish farming were frequently double-edged. They served to increase the strain on those social relations and ties which elsewhere helped to check peasant violence, but in Ireland were already too weak to be effective.[29]

Abuses of landlord power did nothing to lessen peasant alienation. Edward Wakefield, whose encyclopedic account of his visit to Ireland early in the nineteenth century provided Englishmen with a mine of information, recalled seeing a gentleman of some standing lay open a poor man's cheek with a whip for no other reason than that he stood in his way. "'Even more astonishing'," he remarked, was the behaviour of the spectators, who "'dispersed running different ways, like slaves terrified at the rod of their despot'." The same point was made by a prize-winning essayist, who deplored "'a degree of domestic tyranny difficult to imagine'." It was a tyranny landlords exercised for electoral purposes following the enfranchisement of Catholic forty-shilling freeholders in 1793 – a measure which offered them yet another inducement to subdivide landholdings. Of course, the most abrasive issue in landlord/tenant relations was the rent charge. The boom years had seen rents rise steeply. Some tenants were adequately compensated by an accompanying rise in prices, many others were less fortunate. Not that their rents always went to the head landlord. Many of the large and middle-sized farmers holding lengthy leases had been in the best position to capitalize upon the feverish demand for land as profits escalated and population ballooned. They were the beneficiaries of the doubling and even tripling of the rents paid by small farmers and cottiers between 1800 and 1815. Not surprisingly, the disturbances that swept across east Munster during much of this period were not a conflict of the polar extremes of Irish society, of rural poor and great landowners, but a struggle that pitted labourers and their small farmer allies against the large farmers with whom they came into direct contact and upon whom they were dependent for land and employment.[30]

Another point of rural friction was the system of local taxation and justice. Irish grand juries apportioned the county rate or cess which provided the funds for a wide range of local services. The control of these juries by the large landowners and the self-serving ways in which much of the money they voted was expended – such as the construction of roads which led to their own estates – excited complaints that the poor were being taxed for the benefit of the rich. The fact that the juries also had a judicial function and were dominated by Protestants – of the estimated 900 grand jurors in any one year only some eighty, Wakefield calculated, were Catholics, and the magistracy was of the same religious hue – nourished the widespread belief among the Catholic poor that local justice was both partisan and sectarian. "Want of respect for the law, and submission to its administration, are among the many culpable errors to which the Irish are addicted," wrote John Curwen, following his visit to the island in 1813. This was a failing which he attributed to the widespread impression that the laws were less of a shield of the weak against the strong than chains forged by the few to shackle the many. The stream of justice would first have to be purified, he recognized, if the popular mind was ever to be cleansed of such a "fatal delusion."[31]

Among the other serious irritants which inflamed the poor was the tithe. There had been no shortage of criticism of this levy in Britain, where as a result of its survival as a tax in kind in some areas it was regarded as an obstacle to agricultural modernization. Further, those farmers who failed to give adequate notice of their intention to harvest, or who interfered with the tithe-owner or his proctor, were hauled before ecclesiastical courts which were notoriously expensive and dilatory. The commutation effected during the enclosure movement had lessened friction with progressive farmers, but only at the cost of further alienating the clergy from poor labourers. Even the resort to money compositions in most regions of Britain by the end of the eighteenth century had not ended the controversy. Instead, wide variations in assessments provided another rich source of dispute, as did the fact that the tax fell exclusively upon the produce of the land and was levied on the total cropped not the clear profit. The merchant and industrialist escaped. The tithe, therefore, had come to be regarded as a serious injustice and one which fostered anticlericalism and on occasion incited the poor to riot. The grievance cut more deeply in Ireland. As Sir Henry Parnell patiently explained to Parliament in 1810, the tax was justifiably resented by the vast majority of Irishmen. Not only did it support a church they regarded as alien and heretical, but it was often assessed arbitrarity and fell most heavily upon those least able to carry the burden. Whereas in England many among the rural poor could survive on their wages and thereby escape the tithe, although labourers raising potatoes on allotments were liable to encounter the titheman, in Ireland survival depended upon the possession of a plot of land on which to raise a subsistence diet. This food then became titheable, at least in Munster and those parts of Leinster where the tax was levied on potatoes. But opposition to the tithe was not confined to the poor. As land was converted from pasturage (earlier freed of the tax) to tillage, large farmers had reason to acquire a sense of the tax's injustice. Indeed, agitation by landlords "indicates that a portion of tithe expenses was being passed on" to them. As in England, money compositions for the tithe in kind did little to soothe the irritation, especially as some owners resorted to tithe proctors who had a well-earned and unenviable reputation for extortion.[32]

For the clergy of the Established Church the tithe was an essential source of income. Furthermore, they rarely if ever attempted to collect one-tenth of the value of the produce of the land. Rather, they claimed a sum which amounted on average to no more than one-third of their legal due. In their own minds, therefore, they were behaving compassionately. Yet their determination to assert their rights as clergy of the state church and to protect their incomes was only one of several sources of the popular hostility towards them. Their identification with the earlier persecution of Roman Catholics under the penal laws, with the Protestant aristocracy and gentry who expected them to support the landlord class, and with the English state, was not calculated to burnish their image. There were Anglican clergy who earned a measure of popular respect by the faithful performance of their spiritual and charitable duties, but many constituted another class of absentees. Some bishops did not reside in their dioceses while a substantial number of the absent priests were unable to reside in their parishes for want of a glebe-house. Evidently this was not a church likely to justify its existence by launching a crusade to convert the Irish to the reformed faith. Catholics did defect to the Established Church during the eighteenth century, though not in great numbers. The vast mass of the Catholic population was left undisturbed by an indolent and acquiescent Protestant clergy. Then, at the turn of the century, the Established Church rediscovered its missionary purpose. The union of the Church of Ireland with the Church of England under the terms of the larger union was accompanied by a strengthening of the influence of evangelicals within the former. In Britain evangelicalism had acted as another informal restraint upon the potentially dangerous lower orders. In Ireland it always threatened to revitalize sectarian animosities.[33]

The growth of evangelical influence within the Church of Ireland led to the founding in 1792 of the Association for Discountenancing Vice and Promoting the Knowledge and Practice of the Christian Religion. Incorporated in 1800, and securing a parliamentary grant that same year, the society was committed to the education of children of all denominations in schools controlled by the Established Church. This work of religious education was supplemented, as in Britain, by voluntary organizations. The Hibernian Bible Society was founded in 1806 to distribute Bibles and religious tracts, and was soon joined by the Sunday School Society for Ireland (1809 ) and the Religious Tract Society (1810). Inevitably, a rediscovered commitment to carry the reformed word to the mass of the Catholic population, and the strong accompanying undercurrent of proselytism, "provoked intense hostility among Irish catholics and contributed largely to the communal bitterness which was one of the most prominent and ugly features in Irish life."[34]

The renewed missionary purpose exhibited by some Anglican clergy gave a fresh fillip to a reform of the Roman Church which was already under way. The relaxation of the penal laws during the late eighteenth century, and the founding of a seminary at Maynooth, had given encouragement to reformers. They were determined to improve the discipline and reputation of a priesthood which, no less than the Anglican, had succumbed to self-indulgence and laxity. The reclamation of immoral and drunken priests went hand in hand with restrictions on their attendance at public amusements and renewed efforts to recruit a clergy adequate to the needs of 80 per cent of the population. The campaign then advanced into the lay community, as efforts were made to discourage the pattern-day gatherings and festive wakes that ended all too often in disorderly behaviour. A rejuvenated Roman Catholic clergy promised to be a valuable ally in the struggle to restrain a peasantry which had exhibited a worrying propensity for violence. The priests' attitude, however, was ambivalent. While remembrances of past injustices were slowly fading, they were drawn by sympathy for their poor parishioners into confrontations with Protestant landlords, or were angered by the proselytizing evangelicals of the Established Church. At other times they found themselves the victims of agrarian violence for seeking to discourage it or for adding their own exactions to those the rural poor were already required to pay.[35]

The principal sources of income of the Catholic priesthood were "voluntary oblations," which the faithful paid to officiating clergy at christenings, marriages, and funerals, and money dues collected twice yearly from the heads of families. These levies led to friction. Conflict resulted less from

exorbitant demands of socially ambitious priests than from the poverty
of their flocks, whose members "handled very little money, who had other
commitments, such as rents and tithes, to meet out of their slender resources
and who found employment only irregularly and at very low rates."[36]

Could Ireland's rural disturbances be traced, therefore, to a common point
of origin – chronic poverty? Not quite, the intelligent and observant John
Curwen judged. "The just and impartial investigator" would discover that
the seditious or illegal associations which so frequently disturbed Ireland
originated in "causes of substantial complaint," such as "the want of legal
protection or redress" from "tyranny and oppression," as well as in "poverty
and despair in themselves." Not a few observers attributed the destitution
to overpopulation, some hinting darkly that the priests' desire to inflate their
income had resulted in earlier marriages. More recently, it has been argued
that poverty encouraged earlier marriages and thus a rise in the birth rate.
Curwen reported an estimated population of 6 millions and admitted: "In
some places the numbers of people are astonishing; and in many districts,
I am persuaded, an inhabitant would be found for every acre." Yet the
overopulation theory was vigorously disputed by a number of contemporaries. James Hall, following his *Tour through Ireland* in 1812, challenged
the "mistaken notion" that Ireland was too populous. She produced more
than enough provisions for her people, he noted, and "with tolerable culture
and attention to bogs and places" which could be improved might "support
three times her present number of inhabitants." The commissioners on bogs
reached much the same conclusion in their four weighty reports, delivered
between 1810 and 1814. But disagreements over the causes of poverty
implied consensus on its gravity as a problem in a country which had failed
to manufacture as tightly woven an institutional safety-net for the poor as
that erected in Britain.[37]

The Irish Parliament's refusal to imitate the English Poor Law had been
a matter of self-congratulation at the moment of union. The satisfaction the
few derived from the knowledge that they had escaped financially burdensome provisions, which were also denounced as morally harmful to the poor,
was purchased at a high price for the impoverished many. Although a
responsibility for the "deserving poor" had been acknowledged, that description had been reserved in Ireland for the truly helpless – the infirm,
the aged, and the very young. Just as Britain had made provision at the
beginning of the eighteenth century for housing the poor in workhouses, so
did Ireland. One was erected in Dublin and a second in Cork. Then, in 1715,
an act was passed which foresaw a national system for apprenticing "helpless" children. But as in England, the system of pauper relief was overhauled
later in the century. A national plan of workhouses or houses of industry
was drafted which envisaged assistance of the helpless and correction of the
idle. The helpless poor were to be licensed to beg, and greater if unsystematic

support was to be provided for those institutions which cared for sick indigents. Worthy as these measures were, the fundamental weakness of the Irish Poor Law was its permissiveness. Few counties chose to establish houses of industry, and, while most did eventually erect infirmaries, the want of adequate supervision ensured that these were virtually useless. Even more important, such institutions as did exist to provide relief were heavily dependent upon voluntary contributions. The small sums voted by grand juries, and a parliamentary grant to the Dublin House of Industry, did not answer the problems of inadequate funding. Effective legislation to oblige counties to care for the poor was what Ireland required but did not receive. Consequently, few "among the many poor in Ireland could feel that those in charge of public affairs had any concern for their wretchedness or that any significant bond existed between them and the rest of the community." Thus by the time of union Ireland had failed to develop either the institutional support for the poor or those informal constraints which while they had not prevented the oubreak of disturbances in Britain had helped to ensure that they did not endanger the state.[38]

The disorders that had periodically afflicted the Irish countryside acquired a more alarming dimension during the 1760s with the first of the Whiteboy disturbances. The binding of the participants by secret oaths savagely enforced was a disquieting innovation, but the cruelty with which they behaved and the extent of the lawlessness also unnerved local gentry. These associations were subsequently likened to a "sort of trades union," formed for the essential purpose of keeping "the actual occupant in possession of his land, and in general to regulate the relation of landlord and tenant for the benefit of the latter." Their activites were greatly assisted, it was freely conceded, by the "*general and settled hatred of the law* among the great body of the peasantry." And no matter how simple or sophisticated the definition of peasant – "a subsistence, or neo-subsistence farmer"; "the primacy of the household and community interlocked by kinship; production by the family unit with little hired labour; the greater proportion of produce being consumed by the family unit; a strong sense of attachment to locality; and the conception of land as not a saleable produce" – it embraced the vast majority of the population of Ireland. Nor was there any dispute over the causes of outrages. "Where destitution is, there crime will be found as a matter of course," one witness later observed to a parliamentary select committee. Their miserable condition, their liability to charges which they were unable to meet, their inability to find employment, their determination to retain possession of the land, all were factors in the violent behaviour of peasants. So also was the religious and ethnic alienation of tenant from landlord. Yet there was an apparent paradox in all of these explanations of rural disturbances, and it was one which contemporaries did not overlook. The deeper the peasants' misery the less likely their resort to violence. In short, there appeared to be "a certain pitch of wretchedness which breaks the spirit, and produces a dull lethargic languor." Or, as modern sociologists have recast this observation, those "who are at the bottom of the social ladder ... do not enjoy the degree of cultural and structural independence necessary to formulate and strive for a new system of social relations." Disturbances were most likely to prevail where the peasantry were "bold and robust, and one degree removed above the lowest poverty; and where the land [was] productive, and consequently thickly peopled."[39]

However amenable to economic and sociological explanation, the chronic unrest in rural Ireland gave the government ample cause for concern and eventually lent itself to misinterpretation as a fundamental challenge to the authority of the state. Was not Whiteboyism "arbitrary, capricious, violent, unprincipled, and sanguinary, oppressive of the upper, and corruptive of the lower classes, and in the long run most pernicious to the entire society"? In brief, did it not amount to the abrogation of existing law, even the abolition of existing government, intelligent observers asked? Moreover, although assaults upon Catholic priests suggested that economic grievances were preeminent, as did the fact that the vast majority of the mobs' victims were Catholics accused of being parties to injustice, perhaps by taking land from which another had been ejected, sectarianism inevitably surfaced. Most landlords from whose houses arms were stolen and whose property rights were invaded were Protestants. The violence which scarred areas of Ulster during the last two decades of the century reflected sectarian enmities as well as economic jealousies. Protestant peasants resented and resisted the competition of Catholics for land and their efforts to enter the linen industry. It was from these tensions and the resulting conflict that the Defenders and the Orange Order emerged.[40]

Originally a nonsectarian body organized to protect Catholics from Protestant violence, the Defenders mutated into an exclusively Catholic oath-bound secret society. However inchoate their revolutionary ideas, they were a subversive organization whose members "swore to 'sweep clean the Protestants, kill the Lord Lieutenant, and leave none alive'" The tendency of the more traditional apolitical agrarian secret societies to adopt Defender-like oaths inevitably aroused suspicion of their ultimate goals. That distrust grew as radical nationalists exploited the undoubted but poorly focused hatred of English rule which folk culture helped to sustain among the Catholic peasantry, and it was confirmed by the Defenderite character of the rebellion in 1798. So, just as the United Irishmen's leadership of the insurrection ensured that their earlier calls for parliamentary reform and Catholic Emancipation were retroactively interpreted as screens for larger and more subversive aims, the demands of the traditional agrarian secret societies for the lowering of rents, the abolition of tithes, and the regulation of prices and wages acquired the same sinister hue. The fact that Catholic rebels in Wexford were led in 1798 by a priest, and that they slaughtered a substantial number of Protestants who fell into their hands, left a deep and indelible impression on the mind of the religious minority. In the catalogue of atrocities, to the bridge at Portadown had now been added the barn at Scullabogue. If a "Jacobinical conspiracy" had pursued "its object chiefly with Popish instruments," those instruments had proven fatal to Protestants. Here was conclusive proof that a "semi-barbarous Catholic democracy" was animated by a savage hatred of Protestantism, and would never be satisfied until the Protestant Establishment had been toppled and the Protestant control of most of the land of Ireland destroyed.[41]

The defeat of the rebellion in 1798 had not eradicated Defenderism. Within a few years it was slowly reemerging as Ribbonism, a name which the authorities tended not entirely without cause to apply to the revived agrarian secret socities. After all, many of them were believed to have adopted Ribbon oaths. The Whiteboyism which erupted in Tipperary in 1802 had, by 1806, spread to the surrounding counties in the form of a class war between the rural poor and the Catholic middle classes who had been the victims of the initial violence. The middle-class Shanavests were bound by nationalism as well as class interest. Indeed, political and religious alienation may well explain their decision to take matters into their own hands rather than turn to the authorities for protection. In the words of one government informer, the Shanavests were "sworn Republicans." The Threshers terrorizing five counties in the three other provinces may have been more traditionally apolitical, but "most of the resident gentry could not believe that the military parading, the arming and oath-taking of these secret bodies was not based ultimately on ideas of political subversion, and most genuinely believed that tithes were a pretext for 'swearing of United men'." Popular disturbances could not do other than grind and hone religious antagonism and political suspicions at a time when Irish nationalism was becoming exclusively identified with Roman Catholics.[42]

This association of political ambitions with economic grievances, and the sadly deficient instruments for maintaining order which were at their disposal, go far to explain the ambivalent attitude of the authorities in Dublin to the Orange Order organized by militant Protestants. Orange provocations did foment Catholic unrest but the Orangemen professed loyalty to the British connection and their yeomanry was a valued ally in the battle to restore rural peace. In short, "the crown could not disentangle itself from Orange support without depriving itself of an essential part of its police power."[43]

The principal guardians of law and order in Ireland as in England were the local gentry serving as unpaid magistrates, men able to command local respect and to pursue a life of "gentlemanly leisure." But the civil forces at their disposal lacked number, training, and commitment. Measures taken before the union to improve the system of baronial constables had nevertheless left such policemen ill-paid and merely part-time law enforcement officers. Irishmen, no less than Englishmen, were wary of any proposal which might arm the government with the weapons of a despotism; however, such fears did not prevent the creation of a more effective police force for Dublin or the strengthening of the magistracy. Surrounded by unruly peasantry and bereft of adequate police protection, many magistrates had chosen discretion as the better part of valour. They exhibited a sensible concern for their own safety. This brought them chastisement from lord chancellors. Whiteboy rule in Tipperary early in the nineteenth century was attributed to "the apathy and indolence, or connivance" of the local gentry. Although efforts had been made to bolster the magistracy through the employment of paid professionals, such as the provision in 1796 for the appointment of assistant barristers, at the union Ireland found herself with "a weak and inefficient system for law enforcement." Also like Britain, she was heavily dependent upon the military for the maintenance of order. Where the kingdoms appeared to differ markedly was in the extent of the challenge they faced. If, for prolonged periods, certain regions of Ireland were neither endemically nor abnormally violent, some part of that land did seem always to be in a state of near anarchy. Many Britons naturally accepted this as proof of her exceptional condition.[44]

The chronically disturbed Irish countryside fed suspicions of a national disloyalty and hardened the already well-formed British opinion that Ireland posed unique problems which demanded particular solutions. Only in Ireland had a revolutionary leadership succeeded in evoking a widespread popular response. Five years after the great rebellion came Robert Emmet's lesser one. However faint a reprise of 1798, his insurrection had held greater menace than the startled authorities cared publicly to admit. Nor had the treasonable activities of the Irish been confined to their native land. The frustration of Colonel Despard's English conspiracy in November 1802 had provided a timely reminder of the earlier subversive labours of the United Irishmen – their inspiration of the United Scotsmen and the United Englishmen, their association with the more radical elements of the London Corresponding Society (an organization in which Irishmen had taken a leading role), and their involvement in the naval mutinies of 1797 and 1798. Was not Edward Despard himself the son of an Irish landowner? Even the outbreak of machine-breaking and violence in 1811 and 1812 was connected by some observers to Irish immigrants living in English industrial towns and to the arrival of revolutionary delegates from Ireland.[45]

Britain's own political turbulence and criminality seemed of a different and lesser order when compared to the violence in the neighbouring kingdom. "The hegemony of the law was never complete and unbroken" in England, but the torn fabric was constantly and readily reknit. English disturbances had proven more localized than those in Ireland, and, with the exception of the Gordon Riots, less savage and less politically threatening. Rarely had they been a feature of rural life. Whatever the explanation of this passivity – the disappearance of an English peasantry and the "evolutionary nature" of the commercialization of English agriculture have been advanced, together with the deadening influence of the Poor Law – it was reassuringly manifest. Even on the Celtic fringe of British society, where the hardships of the lower orders seemed little different from those of the Irish, and "social and religious barriers between landlord and tenant" were to be found, the up-heavals always seemed less ominous. In Scotland, industrialization and agricultural commercialization had left their scars. Scotsmen did riot fre-quently over food, over patronage appointments of local clergy, over the clearances of tenants from large estates, and against the Militia Act. As in England, however, such eruptions tended to be spontaneous, local, and shortlived, quickly discouraged and controlled by a moderate show of mil-itary strength. Even the Highlanders offered noteworthy resistance to ex-pulsion from their holdings on rare occasions only. Of course, the Scottish Poor Law, for all of its stern exclusion of the able-bodied, was enforced with considerable flexibility and ways were found to afford minimal relief even to the able-bodied poor.[46]

In Wales there appeared to be more than a passing similarity with the situation in Ireland. The so-called "Acts of Union" of the sixteenth century had effectively reduced the principality, it has been argued, to "the earliest of the English colonies, exploited from the homeland, and governed in the interests of the exploiters by a renegade native gentry." By the eighteenth century Wales "was a land of poverty-striken peasants. Their labours sup-ported a class of absentee landlords as well as alien, largely absentee pluralist clergy." They were housed in huts little different from those to be seen in Ireland. This overwhelmingly agrarian economy, for Wales boasted only seven towns of any size and not one of them possessed more than 10,000 residents, was now required to absorb a rapidly swelling population. The pressure led to a proliferation of smallholdings, higher rents, sharp increases in local rates and taxes, an increase in the proportion of men with little or no land, and even a growing dependence upon the potato. The inevitable tensions were heightened by the movement to make farming more efficient and more profitable. The rural poor feared that enclosures would see them driven from their cottages or forced to pay for the commons land on which they had been squatting, and would make more difficult the cutting of the peat which they sold to supplement their meagre incomes. As a result, Wales also was visited with disturbances. Indeed, some of the characteristics of agrarian disorders in nearby Ireland, such as threatening letters to magistrates and oath-taking, were to be found in Wales. That was the extent of the resemblance, however. The authorities were not unduly alarmed, for much of "the rioting was notable for its discipline and good order. It did not bear the character of savage and purposeless violence." Property was destroyed on occasion and occasionally officials were assaulted, but the activities of the mob rarely "were serious enough or sufficiently widespread to cause the government much concern." Perhaps it was significant that evangelicals had long been at work in Wales teaching piety, prudence, humility, and industry in their circulating schools. The relative passivity of the principality also owed much, undoubtedly, to the survival of the paternalist ethic among the resident gentry. In their capacity as magistrates, they took action to ease acute distress. The export of grains was banned, prices were fixed, and relief was provided even to the able-bodied poor.[47]

In contrast to those in Great Britain, the rural disturbances in Ireland were persistent, extensive, destructive, and savage. The smaller island appeared to be forever teetering on the brink of anarchy. Was this evidence that the Irish stood lower on the scale of civilization, a number of observers asked? "Some people in England, terrified by newspaper stories, consider the state of society to be so uncivilized, that it is almost dangerous to visit Ireland," Edward Wakefield noted. Another sympathetic visitor, John Curwen, admitted that his mind was not "wholly free from all unfortunate impressions." Not that the notion of a society overwhelmingly populated by half-savage lower orders, and thus the preserve of "core group members" who defined themselves as civilizers, was exclusively British. Some Irishmen acknowledged "'that the Irish peasant does not much excel the savage in just notions of liberty, or in due respect for the laws and civil institutions of man'." A generation later, Alexis de Tocqueville was surprised when a Catholic bishop endorsed this unflattering assessment of his fellow-countrymen. They possessed "'virtues dear to God'," the bishop remarked, "'but they are ignorant, violent, intemperate, and as incapable of resisting the first impulses as savages'."[48]

This analysis did determine the attitudes of many Britons whose opinion of the "swinish multitudes" had been formed during the horrors of the French Revolution and who regarded the maintenance of order and the protection of property as the essential purposes of government. But it clearly did not satisfy all of those who sought an explanation of the Irish peasant's desperate nature. The essential question was what had produced this frightening figure. By way of an answer, the well-meaning band struggling to overcome British ignorance of Ireland emphasized the wretched condition of the poor and the political and religious injustice superimposed upon this misery.[49]

Ireland's economic backwardness and her greater depth of poverty had not escaped the notice of the British government. A select Committee on the Poor of Ireland reported in 1804 that the law, such as it was, had not been enforced effectively. Acts directing the establishment of houses of industry in every county had not been complied with. Dublin's policy of opening the doors of its house to the poor from across the island had been welcomed elsewhere as an excuse not to make further provision for them. Indeed, the grand juries had even failed to vote the monies necessary for the maintenance of those institutions that had been erected. Yet the response of the united parliament in 1805, and the following year, was merely to extend additional discretionary powers to grand juries. It sanctioned the establishment of dispensaries partially financed out of public funds, where the poor might obtain both medicine and medical attention free of charge. Whatever its importance in theory as an innovation in the field of public health, this measure's dependence on local initiative militated against its success as an instrument for ameliorating the condition of even the sick poor. Significantly, there was no move to require of Ireland assistance similar to that being provided to the healthy poor in much of Britain, where relief was regarded as a valuable safeguard against a revolt by the lower orders. Why?[50]

The answer to this question lay in the combined powers of observation, prejudice, and ideology. Poor as most Irishmen were, it was no less obvious, at least to many contemporaries, that in terms of food and fuel they were often better supplied than many Britons. Another English conviction was that the Irish had greater tolerance than themselves of penury, a belief which blended well with growing anti-Irish prejudice in Britain. There, instead of marvelling at his enterprise in travelling to England in search of employment, there was an increasing tendency to attribute the Irishman's misery to laziness. The protests of the more charitable visitors to Ireland, that the natives' failure to acquire "the laborious habits of the English" ought rather "to be considered a misfortune, than to be imputed to them as blame," fell upon deaf ears. "In a country where there is little demand and no encouragement for industrious exertions," John Curwen reported, "it cannot be surprising that this habit is not acquired." Important as prejudice proved to be, British attitudes toward Irish poverty owed even more to the growing criticism of the English system of poor relief which acquired intellectual respectability as a result of an ideological assault upon the Poor Law.[51]

Britain's first census in 1801 had reported a population approaching eleven millions. The number dependent upon public aid and the cost of aiding them excited both concern and criticism. The poor rate had averaged £2 million a year before the Napoleonic Wars but was rising sharply, until by 1818 it was to approach £8 million. Although much of the additional expense was a result of wartime inflation, inevitably it was Speenhamland and its variants that caught the eye of ratepayers. They were one in the opinion that idleness was a "vice if voluntary and a national burden if involuntary; in either case it was also a social danger." Similarly, Arthur Young gave voice to a common belief when he remarked "that everyone but an idiot knew that the poor must be kept poor, or they would not work." Even during the "Age of Benevolence," when humanity and philanthropy had fostered greater public sympathy for the poor, and more liberal attitudes towards their relief, there had been a persistent ambivalence. Would not "indiscriminate charity" prove a curse to the poor in particular and society in general by undermining habits of industry and frugality? Moreover, those anxious to lighten the misery of the poor for humanitarian reasons had not always been easily distinguished from pragmatists interested only in keeping the poor subdued. But it was Adam Smith and his odd assortment of disciples who exposed and subjected the Poor Law to a thoroughgoing intellectual scrutiny.[52]

In the *Wealth of Nations* Smith foresaw "an active, intelligent, industrious worker, receiving good wages, constantly bettering himself, and sharing in the 'universal opulence' created by the division of labour and the expansion of industry." Such optimism was qualified only by the requirement that the society be "well-governed." Moreover, he challenged the assumption that men would work better when they were ill-fed rather than well-fed, or when they we disheartened instead of in good health. Nevertheless, his "innate conservatism" with respect to the problem of the poor had prompted him to insist that social tranquillity and order took precedence over the relief of the miserable. It was a proposition with which one of his disciples, in particular, was to become identified. Edmund Burke's "Thoughts and Details on Scarcity," which appeared in November 1795, was written to discredit the Speenhamland system. Burke cited "the laws of trade" and "the rules of commerce" in support of his argument that the state ought not to meddle with relief. "The poor might be miserable, but that misery was inevitable and should not be disguised by misguided pity." Certainly, a distinction ought to be made between deserving poor – "the sick and the infirm, orphan infants and the decrepit aged" – and the undeserving. Burke recommended private charity for the former and "Patience, labour, sobriety, frugality and Religion" for the latter. Indeed, his unrelenting assault upon the identification of the labouring people with the poor, and the associated notion that the state had an obligation to assist the impoverished, anticipated Malthus. "'The labouring people are only poor because they are numerous,'" he declared. "'Numbers in their nature imply poverty'."[53]

The first edition of Malthus's *Essay on Population*, which was ultimately to have such a far-reaching effect upon social policy, appeared in 1798. He wrote, as had Burke, against a worrying background of shortages which indicated that food was "not unlimited in supply, and therefore an unlimited right to it could not be recognized." Yet scarcity was not his inspiration. Malthus challenged Smith's fundamental proposition "that an increase in the wealth of the nation would result in an increase in 'the happiness and comfort of the lower orders of society'." It was his contention that by creating wealth and pushing up the wages of a swelling labour force without also increasing the supply of food, industrialization and productivity held out the promise of misery, not plenty, to the lower orders. The "obvious truth," he declared, was that "'population must always be kept down to the level of the means of subsistence'." And the natural instrument for maintaining this equilibrium was misery in its various guises – epidemic, famine, war. It was in the second and much lengthier edition of his *Essay*, published early in the new century, that Malthus added "moral restraint" as an alternative device for controlling population and thus avoiding much human suffering.[54]

Basic to Malthus's argument was the conviction that the poor invited misery and vice. The iniquity of the Poor Laws, he added, was that they abetted improvidence by ensuring that a man's family did not suffer no matter how great his moral failings. Thus the laws were indicted and convicted on charges of promoting "'carelessness and want of frugality'," of encouraging "'drunkenness and dissipation'," and of discouraging "'sobriety and industry'." Their marginal alleviation of individual misery served merely to broaden the "general evil". As for the Speenhamland system, for him it "epitomized the evils of mercantilist paternalism." The solution which Malthus advanced called for the instruction of the poor concerning their complicity in their misery, an increase in agricultural production, and a gradual abolition of the Poor Laws in order to infuse the poor with the spirit of self-help. Nor would anyone starve. Like Burke, he expected private charity to rebuild that protective wall which the state had earlier erected around the poor and he was now seeking to dismantle. Of course, since it enclosed only the truly helpless it would be a much humbler structure.[55]

The apparent inhumanity of Malthusianism attracted a broad spectrum of critics. To Robert Southey and William Cobbett, among others, it seemed that its author was proposing to abolish the poor rates and starve the poor into celibacy. It was illegal to withhold relief from the poor, Cobbett claimed, and unjust to force them to carry society's burdens. Yet Malthus was no "misanthropic philosopher," and those who met the "Ogre" discovered to their surprise that he was "a most amiable man – of strict truth, perfect integrity and rational benevolence," though the unfortunate disfigurement and speech impediment of a hare-lip caused him to talk "snuffily through his nose." Of greater importance was the intellectual attraction his theories held for the powerful and the influential. To them must be added "the untold number of people who accepted his thesis without making a public profession of it, sometimes without being consciously aware of it." Indeed, his works, together with those of Smith, Burke, and David Ricardo, nurtured a belief that efforts by the state to lessen poverty violated scientific laws and were therefore futile.[56]

Ireland's plight had been of peripheral concern at best to the participants in the debate on the Poor Law, but the growing popularity of Malthusianism among Britain's political élite promised to place it at the centre of her social policy. Unwilling to court upheaval by dismantling the Poor Law in England as Malthus proposed, the governing class encouraged workers there to form mutual benefit associations in the hope that these would at least help to solve the problem of rising poor rates by encouraging "independence based upon thrift." By 1815 they were to boast a membership of almost one million. In Ireland, it set its face against the introduction of false philanthropy which would also have conflicted with the country gentleman's faith in permissive as opposed to positive legislation. After all, her greater density of beggars, as compared to England's, had been shown "scientifically" to be the result not of the absence of a poor law but of the "'languid state of industry'." Even more to the point, the introduction of the English system would merely encourage the natural indolence and thirst for dissipation which were in British eyes such prominent features of the Irish character. Malthus had cited Ireland as an example of the misery which inevitably followed from overpopulation. There, the ready availability of potato plots had brought into existence a population which neither the quantity of capital nor the opportunity for employment demanded, he reasoned. As a result, the price of labour had been so depressed that "'complete indigence'" awaited all who could not find employment and "'an incomplete subsistence'" beckoned as the fate even of those who did. The counter-argument that England, and presumably Ireland, possessed the means to sustain larger populations had not impressed him. This was for him "a goal which should only be approached gradually, letting subsistence wait upon the existing social order, and population on both." In short, although the overpopulation theory as an explanation of poverty was criticized and challenged, it nevertheless became an article of faith among those politicians obliged to confront the social problems of Ireland.[57]

The doctrine of self-help implied the futility of state intervention. Speaking in Parliament in 1812, the prime minister, Lord Liverpool, attached to this repudiation of mercantilism and the positive state a classic French term – *laissez-faire*. Smith, Burke, and Malthus had all contributed to the new political economy, each arguing, though in Smith's case with greater subtlety, that government should not meddle with the economic process. The free market was the only natural and efficient regulator of economic life and the duty of government was to enact those laws which "would make institutions of society congruent with natural laws." Put in the simplest terms, the state ought to do no more than preserve the nation, keep the peace, and protect its citizenry from antisocial and corrupt elements. Evidently the restrictive principles of *laissez-faire* promised to limit the response of the British government to Ireland's manifold problems. Fortunately, those principles proved to be less negative in practice than they were in theory. Pragmatists and ideologues alike discovered that a government in pursuit of its fundamental obligation to maintain peace and order was frequently unable to avoid a species of state intervention which exceeded the theoretically desirable. Even Malthus envisaged programs of public works for the un-employed, and together with Smith endorsed public education for the poor. In a little learning they saw a means to control the growth of population, to guarantee social order, and to facilitate national economic development.[58]

Britain also harboured optimists who were convinced that a single remedial measure would satisfy and pacify Ireland. Catholic Emancipation would "strengthen the influence of the gentry over the populace" and "multiply the ties" which bound the gentry "to the Government and to the English connexion," thereby launching "the career of Irish prosperity." Malthus conceded the justice of the Irish Catholics' demand and attributed to their demoralized state their devotion to proliferation. But much depended upon the way in which this concession was extended. To inspire confidence and deserve gratitude it had to be undertaken "with the alacrity of men eager to begin the reparation of long injustice." Further delay would merely afford proof of a "reluctant and sullen submission" to necessity. The call for emancipation therefore mixed expediency with principle. It appealed in the name of a more enlightened age for an end to religious intolerance. This was a plea which Sydney Smith, a great polemicist and wit as well as a member of the Established Church, elegantly made in his *Peter Plymley Letters* and his contributions to the *Edinburgh Review*. Unfortunately, re-ligious toleration had suffered a number of setbacks at the end of the eight-eenth century. Its association with such radical dissenters as Joseph Priestley, who had been unrelenting in his swingeing attacks on the Establishment, did not enhance the doctrine's attractions for the orthodox. Similarly, its expansion to embrace Roman Catholics, especially Irish Catholics, held little appeal for evangelicals.[59]

Evangelicals despised the Roman Church for denying to the laity the Bible and thus the true Word of God. Nevertheless, there were divisions within their ranks on the issue of Catholic Emancipation. Indeed, the confusion was personified by William Wilberforce. He first supported emancipation, then opposed it, and finally returned to his original position. Significantly, the strength of the evangelical opposition lay in the popular wing of the movement, among the Methodists. Their hostility was fashioned out of an inherent distrust of Catholicism and the experiences of their handful of missionaries in Ireland. The mob violence John Wesley himself encountered, his conviction that Roman Catholicism not only caused the island's religious and political problems but also accounted for its poverty, his distrust of the loyalty of Catholics to the crown, and his belief that as a result of its own "intolerance" the Roman Church had forfeited any claim to toleration, all combined to produce an anti-Catholic legacy. Later accounts of missionaries' persecution at the hands or instigation of "Romish priests," of their being forced to seek the protection of magistrates and military, of the "anti-gospel activities" of the Catholic clergy, were widely circulated in Britain and sharpened Methodist opposition to concession. These reports from Ireland were accepted as confirmation of the suspicion, which the rebellion of 1798 had done much to strengthen, that once Roman Catholics "'had the power they wou'd not leave [one] Protestant alive in the Kingdom'." Methodists believed that peace in Ireland depended upon the conversion of her people to Protestantism. Emancipation must therefore be opposed, for if granted it would extinguish their hopes of winning Irish converts in large numbers.[60]

It was among High Churchmen, however, that the measure's most influential opponents were to be found. Not that they conceded the high ground of principle to those who supported the cause in the name of religious toleration. They drew a sharp distinction between freedom of worship and civil equality, the former having been effectively guaranteed to English Catholics in 1791. The Protestantism of the British constitution had been settled by the Glorious Revolution of 1688, when king and people had entered into a solemn compact to maintain the Protestant Ascendancy. Thus if those who dissented from the Establishment wished admission to the full rights of citizenship they must change their religious opinions rather than expect the amendment of the constitution. The state was under an obligation to exclude from Parliament – and the exclusion of Catholics from the legislature was the principal issue – those enemies of an Establishment which was its own moral arm. To admit them would surely result ultimately in disestablishment and thus the demise of the "chief guarantee of civil morality and obedience to government." The alarm was sounded that before long the members of the Established Church would find themselves in a minority, for the number of dissenting chapels and churches was increasing dramatically. Moreover, the Catholic community of England had been showing signs of renewed vigour even before its priesthood was reinforced by refugees from revolutionary France and its ranks bolstered by Irish immigrants. Indeed, the Catholic clergy had recognized the missionary opportunities in the industrial towns. Here was an inkling of the English Catholics' continuing interest in the conversion of their fellow countrymen.[61]

Behind such concerns there lurked a virulent anti-Catholic tradition as well as suspicion of radical dissenters. Protestantism "had originated in a revolt against Popery and was in consequence as good as Popery was bad." The claim of exclusive salvation was paraded as proof of Popery's intolerance, while Papists were accused of an allegiance divided between the pope and their sovereign. The fact that for much of the first decade of the nineteenth century the pontiff was either ally or puppet of Napoleon lent contemporary force to this ancient charge. Of course, the revolution which made possible Napoleon's rise had also reinvigorated the High Church concept of the fundamental partnership of church and state. Ironically, the most influential philosopher of the new conservatism had been a passionate supporter of Catholic Emancipation and bitter opponent of the repeal of the remaining restrictions on dissenters. Although Edmund Burke's "practical arguments" were later adopted by a group of liberal and pragmatic Tories who accepted the necessity of emancipation, his "denunciations of innovation," support of the status quo, and repudiation of natural rights, were employed to good effect by those resisting this measure. And they opposed it in the full confidence that they enjoyed the backing of the overwhelming majority of Britons.[62]

In Britain popular hostility to emancipation was intensified by the ever closer identification of the cause with the Irish. English attitudes towards the Irish were more complex than has sometimes been represented. The stereotype of "Paddy" may have been as much an Irish as an English creation, and he was a character who possessed great virtues as well as conspicuous vices. Restlessness, indolence, improvidence, and impetuosity were balanced by generosity, good-heartedness, and bravery. Also, there is some evidence that by the middle of the eighteenth century "'the Irish had come to be generally well-liked in England'." But Irish involvement in the naval mutinies of the French wars, the activities of the United Irishmen, and then the rebellion of 1798, had convicted them of treason in the minds of many loyalists. They were different from the British, distinguished by their Romanism, revolutionary temper, and rejection of English values. More than once after the rebellion of 1798 loyal Irish regiments serving in England had been provoked to violence by the popular taunts of "Croppies," "Irish Rebels," and "Irish Rascals."[63]

The upper classes of Britain accepted the image of the Irishman as fashioned by historians and other writers. The influence of Giraldus Cambrensis reached across the centuries, for his twelfth-century depiction of a wild and savage people had become part of the British literary tradition. Thus David Hume, "the most influential historian" of the eighteenth century, portrayed the Irish as half-civilized and semibarbarous. A debased character served to explain their refusal to accept the Reformation, he observed, though it was reinforced in this instance by a national enmity towards the English. Little wonder the prospect of one hundred "Paddys" arriving at Westminster evoked expressions of lordly disdain.[64]

Earthier concerns dictated the attitude of the English lower orders. The tension which had long existed between Britons and immigrant Irish in the nation's capital and its industrializing towns, and had occasionally burst into violence, heightened at the beginning of the nineteenth century as the pace of immigration quickened. The Irish formed a considerable part of London's residents and many others had been drawn to Manchester's textile industry. The impact of the arriving Irish on the already squalid living conditions, their congregation together "for protection and communal assistance," their competition for semiskilled or unskilled work, their association with vagrancy (a survey of 2,000 adult beggars in London in the 1790s identified a third of them as Irish), pauperism, disorders and disease, their cultural distinctiveness, and their religion, were all ingredients of the simmering popular hostility towards them. British labourers vented this antipathy in a number of ways, including physical assaults and the founding of Orange lodges. Revealingly, the popular search in London in 1811 for a brutal multiple murderer quickly focused on an Irishman. In the countryside, mean- while, the knowledge that a vegetable the English still raised largely as fodder was becoming the mainstay of many an Irish diet probably nourished greater ethnic scorn than class sympathy. Indeed, resistance to the potato drew strength from the notion that as a food it was "only fit for the despised Irish peasants." Even stronger emotions were aroused by the brutality of soldiers who came from Ireland. During the ill-named Kildonan Rebellion against the Highland Clearances, it had been the Irish serving in a Scots regiment who had behaved most savagely, claiming that they were exacting revenge for the behaviour of Scottish troops during the Rebellion of 1798.[65]

If popular opinion was plainly unsympathetic to the problems of Ireland and the plight of her people, the British government was unlikely to be spurred into remedial action by the great body of Irish members who took their seats in Parliament in 1801. Despite fears of an invasion by an alien horde of barbarians, the Irishmen who arrived at Westminster differed little in origins, education, or temperament from those Britons they were joining there. Lacking cohesion and anxious for preferment, the majority of them tended to give "slavish support" to the ministry of the day. Only on the Catholic question were any number of them inclined to toe a national line, conscious as they were of the Catholic electorate created by the relief bill of 1793 and of the growing Catholic "interest" in many constituencies. Under these circumstances, and absorbed by the life and death struggle with Napoleonic France, successive governments during the decade following the union appeared to have both opportunity and cause to treat Ireland as no more than a peripheral concern. Yet she did bedevil British politics during these years.[66]

The proven vulnerability of her exposed western flank to French subver- sion ensured that Britain stationed a substantial military force in Ireland and did not ignore Irish grievances. Pitt and Castlereagh had given thought in 1800 to ways of lessening the irritation of the tithe. Lord Grenville had planned to take aim at the same target when he formed the coalition Ministry of All the Talents in 1806, only to fail in this good intention as in so many others. The opposition of the Established Church and strengthening of the alliance of church and state in the face of the revolutionary challenge from France ensured that there had been little progress by the time of the sudden fall of the Talents ministry in 1807. During the subsequent decline of anti- tithe agitation the issue quietly expired despite the valiant efforts in the Commons of Sir Henry Parnell, an Irish Whig, to keep it alive. Another conciliatory proposal envisaged state payment of the Catholic clergy. The knowledge that the priests' dues had a prominent place on the peasants' list of complaints sparked periodic reconsideration of this suggestion. Elements within the Catholic hierarchy did show some interest in this scheme, even though it involved granting the state the right to influence senior ecclesiastical appointments. Other Catholics suspected the intent of the exchange. Was it designed to weaken the people's confidence in their clergy? The hostility of the laity eventually prompted the hierarchy to discountenance an agreement.[67]

The Catholic clergy had less difficulty accepting an increased public grant for the seminary at Maynooth. The government had been providing an annual subsidy of £8,000, but this was inadequate, and in 1806 the president of the college appealed to the Talents ministry for additional funding. The cost of putting a son through Maynooth he estimated at no less than £160, which meant that relatively few Irish families could afford this choice of vocation. He stressed that "the prospects in the life of a Roman Catholic clergyman in this country bear no proportion to the expenses and labour necessary to become one; and it is only from the respectability attached among us to the profession, and the piety of the parents that we are to expect any candidates for it." Sensing that the political governors of a Protestant state might require some more expedient spur to generosity, he dwelt upon the advantage to the government of having Roman Catholic priests educated under closer public scrutiny. Then again, it might reasonably expect that greater generosity to their church would inspire greater loyalty to the state among the great majority of the Irish people. Although the sharply increased annual grant of more than £13,000 did not long survive the fall of the Talents, its reduction by £4,000 left it above the original level of support.[68]

The Catholic question also attracted the attention of British governments and politicians as a national campaign for emancipation gathered momentum in Ireland, paralleled as it was by renewed agitation among the English Catholic community. A committee composed of moderate aristocrats and more radical middle-class elements was formed in Dublin in 1804 to agitate the issue in a gentlemanly fashion. By 1807 impatience with the constitutional process brought the more radical agitators to the fore, while economic difficulties fed a popular militancy. The following year saw the formation of the Board of British Catholics, which was the organ of a Catholic Association which offered membership to all who could afford a "moderate" subscription. Yet the need for British politicans to square the circle of Protestant resistance led those of them who were supporters of emancipation to insist upon statutory "securities" for the Protestant State. In Ireland, Daniel O'Connell, a young barrister, who had first come to public notice as a result of his opposition to union, now rallied the Catholic laity in opposition to the proposal that the government have a veto over Catholic episcopal appointments. The Catholic bishops hurriedly followed suit, but the identification of the larger question with "anti-Union sentiments" was an ominous development. More immediately, the opponents of emancipation exploited the "unreasonable refusal" on the part of Catholics "to lodge with the Sovereign a power with respect to the nomination of their bishops." For this power was "not denied to other sovereigns in Europe" and was essential to "that due subordination of ecclesiastical to political authority" which was a "fundamental principle" of the British constitution. [69]

While Ireland continued to simmer and occasionally threatened to boil over, British governments made the discovery that the Irish problem had created a fresh source of ministerial instability. Pitt left office in 1801 ostensibly over his inability to convince the king of the need for Catholic Emancipation. He was the first prime minister of the United Kingdom and the first to resign over Ireland. The Talents ministry was also undone by the Irish question. Grenville had dreamed of introducing a far-reaching program of reform in Ireland, which would include emancipation and tithe reform, only to waken to the reality of his situation. He led a coalition which included stern opponents of those measures as well as Foxite Whig supporters of them, while even his own family and faction were divided on the Catholic question. So he first procrastinated and then, frightened by the mounting unrest in Ireland, agreed to the introduction of an inconsequential proposal. When, under continuing Irish pressure, he attempted by sleight of hand to broaden the effect of this measure, he set in train the events which led to his dismissal in March 1807. By their dogged adherence to emancipation, despite the opposition of the king and its unpopularity in the country, the Grenvillites and the Whigs guaranteed their prolonged exclusion from office. Of course, Grenville continued to believe that "securities" were the means of escaping this cleft stick, but this attachment to them long after their rejection by the Irish Catholic laity and hierarchy simply added to his own and his supporters' political embarrassment. [70]

The dismissal of the Talents restored the Tories to office. Although they had not as yet evolved into a party they were to hold on to power for more than two decades. Significantly, the Irish question produced tension and even divisions within their ranks. Thus the new ministry over which the duke of Portland nominally presided embraced "'red-hot Protestants'," led by Spencer Perceval, and moderates, such as Canning and Castlereagh, who accepted the expediency of concession. The acrimony moved Arthur Wellesley, then the chief secretary for Ireland, to warn that unless the ministers drew together they would "'not only be unable to hold their offices'" but would "'entirely ruin the King's affairs'." Castlereagh and Canning, the two leading moderates, did not improve ministerial harmony when they carried a dispute to the duelling ground on Putney Heath. The exchange, which left Canning wounded and both men in disgrace, was dramatic evidence of the disintegration of the administration, though the handling of the French war rather than of Ireland was the immediate cause of its collapse. After some political skirmishing, Perceval succeeded to the office of prime minister. Nevertheless, at the time of his assassination by a lunatic bankrupt in 1812 the government again included men who differed profoundly on Irish policy. It was left to his successor, Lord Liverpool, to formalize the expedient proposed by the prince regent, that the individual members of the government be left free to speak and vote as they wished on Catholic Emancipation.[71]

Divided counsel did not a coherent policy make, but the Tories had initially been favoured by fortune. In 1807 Ireland was in a state of relative tranquillity. Just how relative the Irish definition of tranquillity was, a Whig matron, Countess Granville, discovered for herself the following year. To describe as tranquil the state of affairs she encountered was "only a proof of the dreadful state it must be in when they think it unquiet." Under Portland, the Tories had pursued a muddled Irish policy. They armed themselves with extraordinary powers, in the form of the fearsome Insurrection Act which the Talents had drafted shortly before their dismissal from office, reduced the grant to Maynooth, investigated the deficiencies of educational facilities, and promised reform of the magistracy. In short, the policy was neither genuinely conciliatory nor thoroughly coercive. Perceval's promotion brought an evangelical Protestant to the leadership of the government. He had discerned the hand of divine Providence in the French Revolution, directing Catholicism along the road to extinction. A Pittite, he had differed from the master on emancipation. His opposition to this concession acquired the strength of an article of faith following the Emmet rebellion. He fell under the influence of his brother-in-law, Lord Redesdale, who had introduced the relief bill for English Catholics in 1791 and had been appointed lord chancellor of Ireland in 1802. Redesdale concluded soon after his arrival in Dublin that the Catholic Irish harboured a deep enmity for the British connection and their Protestant fellow-countrymen, and only awaited a favourable opportunity to give it full rein. Therefore the Protestant Ascendancy had to be sustained if the connection with Britain was to be preserved and the work of civilization pursued.[72]

Redesdale's analysis confirmed Perceval in the opinion that the admission of Catholics to Parliament and the high offices from which they were still excluded would endanger the church and thus the Protestant state. He was convinced that to yield on these issues would not tranquillize Ireland but merely invite fresh demands. He agreed with Arthur Wellesley that concession "would only repeat 'the unfortunate lesson which has been too often and too successfully taught in Ireland, that, if discontent will but be turbulent enough, it will force its object from a yielding government'." Confronted by rural disorders in Tipperary and neighbouring counties, and by a resurgence of the agitation for emancipation, Perceval sanctioned a resort to stern measures. Special commissions handed down severe sentences in the disturbed counties and a convention summoned by the the leaders of the Catholic agitation was banned by the Irish executive under the provisions of the Convention Act. Sweeping aside doubts of the legality of this latter decision, and undeterred by the ineptitude with which it was implemented in Ireland, the prime minister was prepared to seek additional powers to prevent a Roman Catholic "*Representative Assembly*" from "*nosing*" the Irish government in its own metropolis. He was equally unbending in his response to the renewed appeals from the Catholic hierarchy for additional funding for Maynooth, prompting a disappointed Irish bishop to observe that it "is no small importance that the people should have a favourable opinion of their rulers. Our countrymen are high-minded & of warm hearts. He is a bad statesman who makes light of their affection."[73]

In 1812, after several weeks of political manoeuvring, Lord Liverpool succeeded the murdered Perceval as prime minister. He was well qualified for the office, almost uniquely so, having held the three major cabinet portfolios. As a statesman Liverpool was dogged rather than brilliant, even-tempered, serious, and conscientious. His ponderous and dour manner masked a high degree of political acuity. If slow to act, he had no fear of making decisions. A Pittite during his early career, he had supported the union with Ireland as a remedy for the "radical evils of the existing government" and had predicted that it would "allay the jealousies of the Catholics and Protestants, promote in every respect the prosperity of Ireland, and add to the strength and respectability of the whole empire." Later, as home secretary, he had been charged with the responsibility of supervising the administration of Ireland. His approach to that country's social problems reflected his faith in the new political economy which he later dubbed *laissez-faire*, while his inchoate opinions on Catholic Emancipation at the time of the union had slowly matured into firm opposition. The decisive influence was probably that of his father who in turn deferred to the hostility of the king.[74] The monarch's special relationship with the Church of England provided the core of Liverpool's argument that so long as "Roman Catholics refused to take the oath of supremacy, it was proper that they should be deprived of political power." But pragmatism buttressed principle, for Liverpool had the professional politician's taste for elevating expediency into policy. He simply did not believe that it would be possible to satisfy Catholics and afford "adequate security to the Established Church and Constitution." Nevertheless, faced in 1812 with an increasingly divided Parliament, the lower house being far more responsive to Catholic claims than the upper; aware of the divisions within Tory ranks and anxious to broaden and strengthen his administration through the introduction of moderates, Liverpool welcomed the expedient of leaving emancipation an open question.

Thus his cabinet included three ministers, among them Castlereagh, who sympathized with concessions to Irish Catholics. Moreover, the prime minister had hopes of adding George Canning to that number. The post of home secretary, however, went to a resolute foe of emancipation.[75]

Henry Addington, Viscount Sidmouth, was a man of middle-class origins, values, and attitudes, a lord of "dull respectability." His father had been a prominent doctor. The influence he had achieved attending the Elder Pitt was enhanced by a correct diagnosis of the transitory, though not the recurrent, nature of the king's madness. Sidmouth was never permitted to forget his background, being contemptuously named "Doctor" by aristocratic detractors, yet it endowed him with a powerful ambition to get ahead, a deep religious faith, a strong attachment to the Church of England, and a profound respect for the monarchy and the state. When he entered Parliament, the friendship of the Younger Pitt and the trust of the king were vehicles of rapid advancement. Elevated to the speaker's chair at the tender age of thirty-two, he was called upon to form a government following Pitt's resignation in 1801. As prime minister he helped advance the ministerial careers of Perceval, Liverpool, and Castlereagh. Although his administration was not a success and its fall was engineered by its creator, William Pitt, Sidmouth and his coterie of supporters remained a significant force in Parliament throughout the first two decades of the century. He helped to form and then to dissolve the Talents, and joined the Perceval ministry shortly before the prime minister's assassination. He and his followers then became an essential piece of the jigsaw which was the Liverpool administration.[76]

To the office of home secretary Sidmouth brought strong opinions on the problems of Ireland, a country that had already played a large role in his career. As speaker he had made a telling contribution to the union debate, while the issue of Catholic Emancipation had been the ostensible reason for Pitt's resignation and thus for his own promotion to the position of prime minister. Ireland had been a factor in the disintegration of his own government and had been at the centre of the collapse of the Talents. Sidmouth had greeted union as the only acceptable remedy for Ireland's ills, insisting that it would be a boon for Catholics even as he discreetly opposed emancipation. Yet in 1801 he had required no pledges on this subject from those invited to join his government, merely agreement that the time was not ripe to address it. On this basis Castlereagh had taken a seat in the cabinet. At the heart of his government's Irish policy, however, had been the conviction of Ireland's exceptionality. In the words of Redesdale, whom Sidmouth dispatched to Ireland as lord chancellor, "whoever looks to Ireland with English eyes only, and thinks of Ireland with English opinions only, will fall into many errors." The land forfeitures which had been a feature of Irish history were "the true source of all its misery," Redesdale reported. They had produced "that uncertainty of title, and still more of possession."

which had "rendered the people so savage." Resentful of those occupying lands they regarded as properly their own, Irish peasants were perpetually discontented. In short, discontent sprang not from religious but material grievances. Consequently, religious concessions would be of little avail. The correct policy for Ireland was to support the Established Church and reassure the Protestant population, thereby strengthening the connection to Britain; to suppress the rampant jobbery in the Irish administration, thereby persuading the Roman Catholic population of the government's commitment to fair dealing; and to seek to stimulate the island's economy, thereby creating the prosperity which would lessen the material grievances which were the root of the popular discontent. By creating confidence, security, and prosperity, the government would persuade the gentry to remain on their estates and forge those links with the lower orders "'so essential to a well-conditioned state of society'."[77]

There is little evidence that Sidmouth's instinctive conservatism, evident in his character and opinions, had undergone any radical modification by 1812. He remained, as even George Canning, the bitter critic who dubbed him "Captain Smallpox," admitted, an honest and well-meaning if vain man. His anxiety to promote fair dealing had not weakened, even if his desire to limit unnecessary suffering was being held more tightly in check by a strengthening ideological aversion to state intervention. Similarly, his obsession with the protection of property made him a stern enemy of the lawless. Nor had he grown any more moderate on the issue of emancipation. Ireland's need, he wrote shortly after taking office as home secretary, was "'emancipation from ignorance, poverty and bigotry'." And by bigotry he meant the "spirit of popery," for he no less than one of his correspondents was satisfied that its "'intolerant damnatory principles necessarily produce intolerance and cruelty in the bosom of its adherents'." Only a radical change in the opinions of the disaffected could reconcile them to the state, and this was not to be secured by conceding their claims. The only concession to Irish Catholics that Sidmouth envisaged in 1812, and on this point he and the prime minister were in harmony, was the implementation of that minor reform as initially proposed by the Talents five years earlier. He would afford "to the Irish R. Catholic officer serving in G. Britain the same exemptions from Penalties for not having taken the Oaths, which he enjoys under the Act of 1793, in Ireland." That act, he allowed, had made "the first & only formidable Breach" in the Ascendancy's protective wall, but he remained confident that by "steadiness & unbending firmness the fortress" might still be held.[78]

Preoccupied with the French war, to which had now been added the complication of the American, Liverpool and his colleagues were thankful for the comparative tranquillity of Ireland. For them, the essence of an Irish policy in 1812 was to keep the island as peaceful as possible while remaining vigilant for signs of rebellion or of conspiracy with the enemy. It was a policy which placed a premium on cooperation with the most evidently loyal section of the Irish population. Even had the prime minister been of a more liberal cast of mind, and his government united, there would have been little profit at this critical juncture in jeopardizing the support of the loyal by introducing measures which hoped to make loyal the disaffected. Yet as interested as he remained in what was happening in Ireland, the prime minister was able to give only limited attention to Irish policy and administration. The calls on Sidmouth's time and energies were equally diverse and demanding. His responsibilities included "'all Grants, Pardons and Regulations in all Civil Matters ...; Preferments in the Church, Matters of Police, the regular Army, Militia and Volunteers, Dispensations, Licences to Trade, Alien Regulations and all Correspondence regarding Ireland, Jersey, Guernsey, etc.'" To assist him to shoulder this crushing burden of work he had only a miniscule staff. Inevitably, therefore, much depended on the ability and good sense of those who administered Ireland. Indeed, the survival of a distinctive form of Irish administration was a prime example of Ireland's exceptionality.[79]

## CHAPTER TWO

# The Irish Executive Government

Unlike England's earlier union with Scotland, that of Great Britain and Ireland was legislative only. Ireland kept her separate administration headed by a viceroy. It was centred in the ancient but extensively remodelled castle on Cork hill in Dublin, and the name "Castle" continued to serve as the abbreviation for the Irish government. An Irish Privy Council, no longer a truly advisory body, retained a measure of functional significance insofar as it still gave expression to the executive will in the form of orders-in-council. Ireland preserved her own distinct legal structure, presided over by a lord chancellor. "An Englishman is generally appointed, from an idea, that having no family connexion in the country, his judgment will be more unbiased, and his decisions less subject to the influence of prejudice and partiality," Edward Wakefield observed. Yet there was no attempt to establish an English monopoly of "high prestige" positions. Those Irishmen who did occupy them, however, certainly belonged to a self-conscious and privileged minority which was unrepresentative of the Catholic majority of their fellow countrymen. Thus the two senior law offices, those of attorney general and solicitor general, were held by Irishmen. Ireland also boasted a Treasury, and there was an Irish chancellor of the exchequer to present an Irish budget to Parliament. The actual task of supervising the collection of taxes was entrusted to two boards, those of Customs and Excise. In all, there were more than twenty administrative departments of the Irish government employing a small army of public servants. A military department catered to the needs of a large garrison.[1]

Ireland's transparently anomalous position within the United Kingdom, for her integration was evidently less than complete, excited some concern. To an intelligent visitor, such as Wakefield, it was apparent that so long as the neighbouring island was administered like "a distant province" the intended benefits of union would be but "half effected." National spirit, jealousy, and prejudice were all too likely to be fostered, he warned. Instead of considering "themselves as members of one great family, all subject to the same laws," the Irish would conclude that they were regarded as a people "unworthy to be admitted to a participation in the benefits of the same government." There had been proposals shortly after union to dismantle this expensive administrative anomaly, for the annual cost of maintaining a separate civil establishment was some £145,000, but the limited achievements of the quest for economy and greater efficiency at a time of vast military expenditures did not include the complete assimilation of Ireland. The savings that were made there, through the abolition of a number of notorious sinecures and the dissolution of several departments, were merely reinvested in the distinct administration. Not that this had resulted in any significant improvement of the personnel staffing the boards which managed the majority of the departments. Wakefield's was a popular complaint: "One half of these boards answer no other purpose than that of extending patronage, strengthening parliamentary interest, and encouraging idleness." [2]

The task of directing "the whole of this separate colonial government" fell to handful of officials for whom one distinguished Irish historian, R. Barry O'Brien, constructed a nautical metaphor. The lord lieutenant wore the insignia of command and signed the log book, but the chief secretary was the captain of the ship and the under-secretary the helmsman. In 1812 this relationship of pomp to circumstance had not yet been fully established. The office of lord lieutenant or viceroy dated from the twelfth century, and the incumbent represented the Crown in Ireland. The fact that in 1782 he remained responsible to the British cabinet served to remind the Irish of the limited nature of the legislative independence they won that year. Moreover, so long as they acted with discretion, successive viceroys were able to pursue policies which conflicted with the wishes of their distant masters. Often it was a matter of balking at more liberal treatment of the Roman Catholic majority for fear of weakening or alienating the Ascendancy upon whom they depended for "loyal" support. Given the opportunities for independent action inherent in the viceroy's situation, which the union did little to alter, there was a need to select him with care. On the other hand, the considerable personal expense involved in maintaining a viceregal presence with all of its court trappings, and the rare combination of qualities sought in a lord lieutenant – honesty, patience, firmness, and skill – severely restricted the number of candidates available to any government and this discouraged confrontations over policy once a suitable man had been found. Fortunately, there was an alternative and more naturally pliable instrument of British policy at hand in the person of the viceroy's chief secretary. [3]

The chief secretary's responsibilities had grown even before the union, and with them his importance. One occupant of the office had listed in 1781 the demands upon his time. He superintended the administrative boards, was the channel for all military business, attended councils, maintained a large correspondence with the ports and the magistracy, dealt with the army of applicants for favours and patronage, regulated the revenue, and prepared legislation. Increasingly, the lord lieutenant's supreme executive authority was being exercised through his chief secretary. By 1800, in the person of Castlereagh, the junior officer had earned a full partnership in the business of government, while the British government had come to regard the post as a proving ground for future statesmen. The union set the chief secretary on the path of promotion to the senior partnership. For now, in addition to his administrative responsibilities in Ireland, he was required to travel to London for the parliamentary session, to answer Commons' questions on Ireland, and to pilot legislation through the lower house. He became a participating member of the British government, corresponding and consulting with the prime minister, the home secretary, and other cabinet members, on the formulation and implementation of Irish policy. Here was an office "important enough for the talents" of England's most talented men.[4]

The heavy burden of work had long since obliged the chief secretary to delegate some of his duties. In 1777 his office had been divided into the civil and military departments, each headed by an under-secretary. The more important office was that of civil under-secretary, and the quality of a succession of occupants during the late eighteenth century meant that it evolved into something more than a superior clerkship. Indeed, one visitor to Ireland in 1797 was led to believe that Under-Secretary Edward Cooke, the admitted master of every detail of administration, was the true governor of the kingdom. Nor was the potential influence of this subordinate official curtailed by the union. Much of his work remained the laborious routine which eventually prompted the weary Cooke's resignation in 1801.[5] He received and acknowledged much of the chief secretary's voluminous correspondence, including the reports on the state of the country, and shouldered the responsibility of distinguishing the matters of great consequence from the trifling. By 1828 almost 1,500 letters were arriving from local inspectors of police and stipendiary magistrates alone, and more than 1,000 required answers. Consequently, the motto of any under-secretary was "work, work, work," and one Irish newspaper readily conceded that this office was no sinecure. It demanded "incessant vigilance," "determination," and "a temperate and conciliatory nature." A gentlemanly bearing was no less important, given the daily communication with the lord lieutenant and the chief secretary whenever they were in Dublin. During the chief secretary's prolonged absences in London, the burden upon his under-secretary necessarily increased. He was responsible for bringing before the viceroy all matters of sufficient importance to require his personal attention, and for maintaining regular communications with the chief secretary and with public departments of government in both capitals. During the infrequent absences of both viceroy and chief secretary, the under-secretary "'was virtually the Irish

Government'." In the words of one Irish attorney general to a new viceroy, "'My Lord, [the under-secretary] will be your right eye, and if we have to spend our time plucking old beams out of it, your Government will not go straight'."[6]

The importance of the chief secretary, no less than the influence of the under-secretary, depended largely upon the character of the men who occupied those strategic positions. The first decade of the union witnessed a steady stream of chief secretaries, eight in all. Lack of interest, stamina, will, even health, explained their impermanence and consequent failure to establish their authority. Thus Arthur Wellesley, who possessed the necessary qualifications, was more concerned with the pursuit of his military career. The appointment in 1809 of his brother William Wellesley-Pole finally brought a degree of stability to the administration, in that he held the office for almost three years. But Pole's shortcomings – he was rash, vain, short-tempered, and preoccupied with his personal standing in Queen's County – diminished his effectiveness and heightened the government's unpopularity. Clearly, he had not answered. What Ireland required and deserved, Wakefield observed in 1812, was a man of "first-rate virtues and talents – a man of enlarged mind, and enlightened views; one who, looking forward to the future, can profit by the past; who is able to plan as well as to execute, and who, possessing sufficient penetration to discover the latent sources of national prosperity, has zeal and activity to turn them to advantage." Just such a man was appointed that very year.[7]

Robert Peel came from the ranks of the *nouveaux riches*. Wealth made in industry had purchased the status of gentry. The young Peel received a fashionable education, surviving Harrow before going up to Oxford where he enjoyed brilliant success. When he came of age in 1809 his father secured his entry to Parliament for a corrupt Irish borough, but in three years as their member Peel "found no occasion to visit his constituents or to hold communication with them." In the Commons he quickly attracted attention as a man of much promise and was appointed by Liverpool to serve as his under-secretary at the War Department. Like so many other products of the successful middle classes, he proved to be a natural conservative – prudent, cautious, and respectful of tradition. When in 1812 Prime Minister Liverpool began casting around for a chief secretary for Ireland to replace Wellesley-Pole, he soon settled on Peel. Here was a sensible, steady, and sober young man anxious to prove himself in that nursery of statesmen. "He has a particularly good temper, and great frankness and openness of manners, which I know are particularly desirable on your side of the water," the prime minister wrote to the duke of Richmond, the lord lieutenant. "He acquired great reputation, as you must have heard, as a scholar at Oxford, and he has distinguished himself in the House of Commons on every occasion on which he has had an opportunity of speaking.

I have the greatest hopes, therefore, that this appointment will prove acceptable to you and advantageous to the Government." Although the viceroy did cavil at the manner of the appointment, for he had not been consulted beforehand, he quickly suppressed his irritation. Peel, after all, did possess the viceroy's two indispensable qualifications for the office – he was neither timid nor a sympathizer with Catholic Emancipation.[8]

Peel arrived in Ireland to discover that his principal deputy, the civil under-secretary, had resigned. Of the three men who had held the post since 1801 not one of them had possessed sufficient self-confidence to fill the void in the office of chief secretary. Hard-working, even efficient, they had failed to stamp their personality on the administration in the manner of an Edward Cooke. This may explain Wakefield's jaundiced opinion of the office. Little was to be expected of such officials, he wrote, "since their subordinate situation precludes them from carrying any efficient measures into execution by their own authority alone." Moreover, they not only lacked personal political influence but also the talents to qualify them for promotion. Sentenced to secondary roles, ambition did not spur their initiative.[9]

Sir Charles Saxton, the serving under-secretary in 1812, had expected to be removed from office as a result of the ministerial skirmishing which followed the assassination of Perceval. Briefly, it had seemed possible that the prince regent might turn to men inclined to act liberally towards Ireland. After four years of "labour and anxiety" Saxton welcomed the prospect of his release. But the new government was of a more conservative complexion than he had envisaged and made no move to relieve him, much to the dismay of those Irish agitators for emancipation who denounced him as "an English drudge, without character or talents."[10] By the late summer he was determined to emancipate himself, and so advised the lord lieutenant. The obvious importance of this appointment for the smooth operation of the new chief secretary's office led the duke of Richmond to consult Peel. Both men were agreed on the wisdom of placing another Englishman in the position, one who had some knowledge of Ireland and was free of importunate Irish connections. Peel offered the post to his able and industrious friend, John Beckett, then an under-secretary at the Home Office. His refusal, and Peel's inability to think "of any other person fit for the office & who would consent to undertake it," prompted him to return the decision to the viceroy. There were reasons for urgency. It would obviously be better to have the new man "fairly in harness" before Peel was obliged to attend Parliament, and it was important that he be tutored in the arts of electoral manipulation by the experienced Saxton during the general election called for October. Unable to secure a qualified Englishman, Richmond recognized that his options had been reduced to a man who possessed both knowledge and connections or one who had neither. "I am convinced the former is the best," he confided to Sidmouth who was supporting a candidate of his own, "but it will be necessary to find a Man of the strictest Honor who will not allow his Irish connection to have undue weight with him." The man who he believed best met these requirements, and who had already sought the position, was William Gregory. "He was bred as a lawyer & has a sufficient knowledge of the law to be of use to him in this arduous office," Richmond explained to a home secretary disappointed that his own nominee had been passed over. "He has received the best English Education and has been accustomed to Business of some sort or other for a good while. His manners are very good, a material point in the absence of the Chief Secretary." Moreover, has was a man of very respectable and influential Irish connections.[11]

William Gregory was not a native Irishman. His family was Irish enough, having settled in Ireland in the mid-seventeenth century, but he had been born in India in 1762. His father had gone out to Bengal in 1746 to make his name and fortune and had certainly succeeded in the latter endeavour. On his return to Britain in 1766, Robert Gregory escaped the notoriety and contempt which was the lot of so many of those other Nabobs who returned from India laden with riches and stuffed with ambition. A free merchant, he had acquired his wealth "in a very honourable manner." He purchased social position, sinking much of his wealth in land ownership. The largest of his three country estates, and the only one he was to retain, covered 15,000 acres of his native Galway. In 1768 he entered Parliament and remained a member for sixteen years, loyally supporting the Rockingham faction but jealously guarding the appearance of independence. He found a friend as well as an ally in his fellow-Irishman Edmund Burke. They shared a concern for the security of the Indian empire and the well-being of its native population. In 1782, exhausted by overwork, debilitated by ill-health, and frustrated by a series of defeats in the byzantine politics of the East India Company, Gregory effectively retired from public life.[12]

William, the youngest of Robert Gregory's three sons, received the education befitting a gentleman – Harrow, Trinity College, Cambridge, and the Bar. In 1789 he married Anne, the third of W.P.K. Trench's eighteen offspring. The price of entry into one of Galway's great clans of ambitious families was his father's agreement to bequeath to him the vast estate of Coole. It was a decision made all the easier by the older boys' misconduct. One had disgraced himself in India and the other in the army. The Nabob also provided his youngest son with his principal means of support, supplementing a meagre income from the law with an annual allowance of £450 and securing his appointment to the Irish administration early in 1795, as surveyor of Skerries. William Gregory was therefore on hand to witness the extraordinary closing scenes of Lord Fitzwilliam's viceroyalty.[13]

Honourable and well-intentioned, Fitzwilliam had arrived in Ireland determined to emancipate the vast Catholic majority still shackled by the remnants of the penal laws enacted almost a century earlier. He believed that, once liberated, they would loyally serve in the war against revolutionary France. However, when he sailed for Ireland in January 1795 he did not carry the government's clear sanction for this bold policy. If anything was settled, it was that he should proceed cautiously. Instead, he acted precipitately and was recalled. He departed amid scenes of national mourning. His successor was Lord Camden, an amiable but indecisive man doomed to dash all the hopes Fitzwilliam had raised. The new viceroy was authorized to offer to Roman Catholics a state-supported seminary, and he promptly laid its foundation-stone in the small village of Maynooth a few miles west of Dublin, but he carried little else likely to appease middle-class radicals demanding political reform. His troubles were compounded by economic distress and sectarian violence. In the face of a mounting and subversive challenge Camden resorted first to draconian legislative measures and then to the sword.[14]

Among those Irishmen who favoured conciliation over repression were the Gregorys. They belonged to that conservative faction of Whigs whose fear of the French Revolution induced them to support liberal measures in Ireland. Edmund Burke was its most powerful spokesman, and Fitzwilliam had expected to be its instrument. Thus Robert Gregory lamented the recall of Fitzwilliam, denounced the Ascendancy Camden confirmed in power, and ridiculed the policy of repression. But father and son were eventually converted to Irish conservatism. They surrendered to the fear that a Jacobin conspiracy was already afoot in Ireland, and that its chosen instruments were the Catholic lower orders who had been excited by promises of the plunder of the rich and "taught to abjure all the restraints which divine or human laws" imposed on the passions of men. The enrolment of the Defenders by the United Irishmen lent credibility to this analysis. Equally, their employment heightened Protestant fears of a systematic campaign of sectarian revenge, fears that the rebellion of 1798 served to confirm.[15]

William Gregory did not personally experience the horrors of 1798. He served in Galway as a captain of militia, and Connaught, the most Catholic of Ireland's four provinces, proved to be the most loyal. Instead, it was his brief service in 1799 on the commission appointed to adjudge the claims for compensation made by loyalists who had suffered, which exposed him to the enormity of what had taken place elsewhere in Ireland. This, in turn, appears to have brought him to a conclusion similar to that which Sir Richard Musgrave was soon to draw in his *Memoirs of the Different Rebellions in Ireland from the Arrival of the English*. The "popish multitude" had been inspired from infancy by their clergy with an "envenomed hatred" for the "protestant state, their protestant fellow subjects," and the connection with England. No matter the name by which they called themselves, whether Levellers, Whiteboys, Rightboys, United Irishmen, or Defenders, they formed a link in the same chain "of barbarous practices peculiar to the savages of Ireland." Irish Catholics were a breed apart.[16]

In the rebellion's aftermath the Gregorys, father and son, emerged as ardent champions of union. In County Galway, Sheriff William Gregory was an important agent of Robert Stewart, Lord Castlereagh, who was charged as chief secretary with the management of the campaign to persuade the Irish Parliament to vote itself out of existence. Indeed, opponents argued that at the county meeting summoned to reconsider Galway's earlier declaration of opposition to union the sheriff had counted in the pro-union motion which his father had seconded. Subsequently, he was returned to the Irish Parliament for the borough of Portarlington and took his seat in time to cast his vote in the decisive division. His reward was less generous than that received by his wife's family, who had abandoned their earlier opposition to the measure – his father-in-law was promoted to an earldom and one of his brothers-in-law was elevated to the episcopal bench. Gregory was appointed secretary to the Board of Inland Navigation which Castlereagh had promoted as a means of completing the line of communication from Dublin to the Shannon and of opening that river to navigation from Lough Allen to the sea. The appointment gave a decisive fillip to his career, for he acquired valuable administrative experience coordinating the board's activities and supervising its staff. Then, in 1810, his opportunities to demonstrate his intelligence and ability were given wider scope with a further promotion. He was appointed one of the seven commissioners of His Majesty's Revenue, Inland Excise and Taxes.[17]

What then were the principal articles of faith of those Irish conservatives whose ranks William Gregory had joined at the turn of the century? The rebellion of 1798 had certainly deepened the conviction of the many Protestants among them that the great mass of Roman Catholics loathed their religion, lusted after their property, and looked only for an opportunity simultaneously to persecute and confiscate. But it had been the earlier horrifying events in France that had evoked a coherent defence of the existing order. Conservatives on both sides of the Irish Sea attributed the collapse of France into a state they could only view as both anarchic and savage to the dominance of the mob and the "pernicious" doctrine of equality. They determined to pick up the challenge thus thrown down to civilized life as they understood it, and elaborated a persuasive counter-revolutionary ideology. The fundamental purpose of government, they argued, was to prevent the rule of the anarchic masses. Equally, it was founded to preserve the natural hierarchy of classes so essential both for a well-regulated community and "'that reciprocity of good offices requisite to the general welfare'." Political authority properly belonged to that minority of men who possessed the independence and leisure needed to acquire the education and knowledge which gave insight into society's complexities. Not that this limiting of government to the upper classes implied a disregard of the peculiar problems of society's less advantaged members. To ignore the grievances of the poor would simply facilitate the work of those agitators ever ready to foment discord in order to effect radical change. Of course, whenever the lower orders succumbed to the blandishments of the mischief-makers, conservatives accepted the necessity for government to resort to harsh measures. "Misplaced leniency" was peculiarly ill-advised in a country such as Ireland, where "the elements of turbulence" were already rife; where the "path of sedition" had an "irresistible fascination to a large class of adventurers"; and where "a false, sickly sentiment" threw its "glamour over the most common-place and even the most contemptible of rebels."[18]

If this conservative ideology was transparently self-serving, for it justified continued rule by a miniscule elite, its tenets were nevertheless endorsed out of conviction rather than cynicism by the great body of its adherents. No less genuine was their oft-professed admiration of the British constitution. It was, for them, the finest example known to man of a government both mixed and balanced, of King, Lords, and Commons in a symbiotic relationship that served to preserve liberty, maintain stability, and secure property by ensuring the rule of law. In the minds of conservatives, the maintenance of order and the protection of property took precedence over the extension of individual rights. Convinced that true liberty was impossible without law and order, and that the British constitution guarded the interests of all men, conservatives opposed change in the name of a perfectibility itself unattainable.[19]

William Gregory's deepening conservatism complemented his evangelicalism. He had been an early member of the Philanthropic Society, and this youthful zeal to rescue children from crime had not diminished twenty years later. He recommended the provision of a basic education for the children of the ordinary soldiers of the Irish militia. Instruction in reading, writing, arithmetic, and "in the principles of the Christian Religion & duties of Morality," would not only rescue them from ignorance but also from "loose & idle habits" that would otherwise leave them "useless to themselves, & perhaps dangerous to the state." Progressive as it was, his belief in the social utility of education was tinged with proselytism. Gregory was to be encouraged farther in this dangerous direction by two of his brothers-in-law who had entered the Church of Ireland.[20]

This was the man who on 5 October 1812 noted in his diary: "appointed under secretary in the place of Sir Chas. Saxton – dined with Mr. Peel." Although Gregory was his new master's senior in age – more than twenty years separating them – this disparity was to prove less significant than those similarities of social background, temperament and attitudes which quickly bound them in friendship. They quickly established an intimate and efficient administrative partnership.[21]

The duke of Richmond, to whom Gregory owed his appointment, was no mere titular lord lieutenant. He was the dominant figure in the government. He had not been the Portland ministry's first choice as viceroy in 1807, nor its second, but had proven surprisingly successful in an always difficult and often thankless post. His was an engaging if slightly dissolute personality and he maintained a splendid court. Lavish expenditures enhanced his popularity among Dublin's merchants and vintners, while his catholic tastes in wines and women provided a rich source of gossip as did his wife's jealousy. A gregarious man, he was appreciated by a convivial people, though the costs of sociability, financial and physical, eventually necessitated a change in his life-style. Before the end of his term he had been obliged to economize in the face of mounting personal debts and was persuaded by friends to limit his prodigious consumption of claret. Writing to Peel early in 1813, the evangelical but far from abstemious Gregory reported that the duke had "lately quite altered his mode of living; I fervently hope it may continue; his want of resolution in that particular is his only fault."[22]

Richmond's political opinions were less liberal than his peccadilloes, and his policies more conservative than his lifestyle. He was instinctively intolerant of disorder. His response to the chronic unrest in Tipperary and the neighbouring counties had been harsh, as befitted a soldier by training. But it was the Catholic question which most exercised the viceroy. "No one is more strenuous against their Claims than I am," he later boasted. His opposition was rooted in principle as well as religious prejudice, but he was vehement in his denials of bigotry. "I have never shown any prejudice against the Catholics nor even inquired what religion a person was of provided the law did not insist on a Protestant holding the office," he commented on his own appointments to the Irish administration. Indeed, his fortuitous absences from Parliament during the debates on emancipation meant that he had never given his opinions a public airing. All of which fuelled his indignation when he found himself assailed in 1811 by Daniel O'Connell and the more radical elements of the Catholic Committee.[23]

The strong language employed by Catholic agitators helped to shape the viceroy's response. "These Violent People must cool before any thing can with safety be proposed in their Favour," he cautioned. It simply would not do to give the impression that the government was submitting to threats. Equally, the constitutional authorities could not tolerate the activities of a committee which had acquired a representative character. Once they had "ballotted for members and sent directors into the country to send up delegates, and all this contrary to existing law, to have hung back would have appeared like great weakness." He did acknowledge that the Castle's hamfisted efforts to suppress the committee under the terms of the Convention Act, without prior consultation with the "English Government," had been initiated at an "unlucky moment." Coming so soon after the appointment of the prince regent, who was popularly believed to be more sympathetic than his father to Catholic claims, the strong action of the Irish government was viewed in some quarters as a deliberate effort to forestall a more liberal policy.[24] Richmond welcomed the continuance in office of the Perceval ministry. Had the regent "allowed of any alteration to be originated in his Government in favour of people who met in open Defiance of the Law and also used Language nearly treasonable if not quite so, his throne would not have been safe a year, "he warned. For he and many of the Irishmen who recalled the events of 1798 detected a sinister purpose in the Catholic agitation. "If things go on as they have done, the Catholic emancipation will sooner or later take place, which Mr. O'Connell [sic] tells you is of no further consequence than that it leads to a repeal of the Union," he advised one cabinet minister. In short, the viceroy was convinced that the Irish Catholics organized first as the Committee and subsequently as the Roman Catholic Board were embarked upon an incremental strategy which looked ultimately to the separation of Ireland from Britain, if not to an alliance with France.[25]

Richmond sincerely believed that intimidation of the "loyal" Protestant minority was an integral part of the Catholics' strategy. "They bully and threaten the Protestants to sign their petitions, whilst many of the Protestants allow themselves to be bullied and none try to stop the current." He deplored the successful intimidation of Protestant members of Parliament by a Catholic electorate, which he naturally traced to the relief bill of 1793 and the enfranchisement of the forty-shilling freeholders. "In most counties people are a little afraid of their constituents, but here it is quite ridiculous and I must say disgraceful," he informed one Englishman. Accepting these developments as proof of a loss of heart among the Protestants, he emphasized the importance of the government offering public encouragement to them on the subject of Catholic Emancipation. "There are few Protestants here that wish the Claims to be considered even with Securities," he reported, "and still fewer who think any security strong enough for an alteration."[26] Hence his alarm when in June of 1812 the Commons, with several ministers voting with the majority, committed itself to take up the Catholic question early in the next session. This action threatened to deepen Protestant dismay and raise Catholic expectations. Unless the supporters of the motion were prepared to introduce and carry complete emancipation they were inviting greater difficulties in Ireland, he growled. For the Catholic population now believed that final victory was near and that success would bring a substantial improvement in their standard of living. Filled with anger and foreboding, he ridiculed the "extraordinary appearance" of a ministry which was founded on the understanding "that a measure relative to a material alteration in the Constitution should not have the decided approbation or disapprobation of the Cabinet as a body." It might well be impossible to form a government resolutely opposed to the claims of Catholics, "even when they are proposed with such violence and improper language," he conceded, but, if this was indeed the case, it was "most unfortunate for the country." For his own part, he declined to be a party to "the slightest even nominal advantage to people who chose to be led by those who in their hearts and very near if not quite in their speeches are decided rebels."[27]

Expecting to be relieved of his office, Richmond attemped to revive his military career. He offered to serve under Wellington whom he had long outranked. The government, however, urged him to remain in Ireland, at least until the spring of 1813. With a new chief secretary and under-secretary taking office this was not the moment to dispatch a novice as viceroy. "Indeed, it would be particularly awkward to make any change in the Government till the Catholic question is brought to some issue," the prime minister admitted to Peel, "and I am confident that, whenever a change is made, we may in vain look for a successor who will give equal satisfaction to all classes of the King's subjects."[28] Flattered, Richmond agreed to stay on in Dublin for a few more months. He realized that to do so would not involve any sacrifice of principle. "It is easier to talk of the emancipation than to put it [in] force," he reasoned. "A great variety of old acts must be repealed and new ones adopted." Then again, he might yet be of service to the Ascendancy. He bombarded the government with disptaches, urging the adoption of those measures he considered essential for Ireland. The Protestants "should know on whom they may depend," and he resented the cabinet's gagging of him. Silence was "hardly fair to the most loyal people of this country," he complained. He recommended that regiments not sent to bolster Wellington's force in the Iberian peninsula be transferred as a precaution to Ireland. "I certainly would much rather see a rebellion at once in consequence of Parliament refusing to do anything [on Catholic claims]. It would soon be put an end to and some of the most disaffected would fall." He also advocated the disfranchisement of the forty-shilling freeholders, presumably in the belief that this step would lessen the Catholic pressure on the Irish representatives at Westminster. But Liverpool's anxiety to maintain his ministry's fragile understanding on Ireland, and to preserve the relative tranquillity there, induced him to sidestep this controversial proposal. Richmond urged with no greater success the suppression of the Catholic Board.[29]

Although he failed to convince a divided British government of the wisdom of an aggressively Protestant Irish policy, Richmond had every reason to be confident that this objective would not be lost sight of following his departure from Dublin in June 1813. The attitudes of the most senior members of the Irish administration closely mirrored his own, as did those of his successor as lord lieutenant. Lord Whitworth was no stranger to difficult postings or to controversy. As a young commoner he had found a patron in the duke of Dorset, serving on his staff at the British legation in Paris during the last years of the *ancien régime*. His handsome features and winning manners had quickly made him a favourite of Marie Antoinette and his physical attributes may well have been his principal qualification for his promotion in 1788 to the rank of minister at the court of Catharine the Great. He remained in Russia for a dozen years, only to fall foul eventually of the unpredictable and unstable Tsar Paul, who demanded his recall in 1800. He returned to Britain a lord, having been ennobled partly as a result of the urgings of the tsar during happier days in their relationship. As a peer Whitworth would be a more appropriate suitor for the hand of his former patron's widow, a woman of extraordinary wealth and arrogance. When he was followed home by his Russian mistress, who allegedly came in search of respectability, the duchess of Dorset was obliged to purchase her silence, since the lady's claims on Whitworth were of "too delicate and serious a nature to be despised." Then, in 1802, after the Peace of Amiens, Whitworth was sent to France as his nation's representative. The reopening of hostilities between the two nations in 1803 was preceded by a legendary personal confrontation between Napoleon and the British minister at one of Josephine's receptions. In 1807 Whitworth had been the first choice of the British government to carry to Denmark the ultimatum which resulted in the bombardment of the Danish capital, but had declined the commission rather than serve under George Canning, then the foreign secretary and dubbed "*the Pope.*" Finally, in 1813, Liverpool turned to him – they were connected through their wives – to undertake the sensitive and difficult mission to Ireland. At a small reception in Whitworth's honour, the prince regent toasted a man "who is entitled to my praise, and that of his country, for his public-spirited and patriotic conduct, in sacrificing his own ease and convenience to the superior call of duty, by accepting the office of Lord Lieutenant of Ireland."[30]

Whitworth accepted the viceroyalty only after a full discussion with his wife, whose insistence on being addressed as the duchess of Dorset had caused confusion and misunderstanding during their sojourn among the French. After all, one understanding Irish visitor to the French capital recorded, "the new Ambassador has brought to Paris the same horses and the same wife and lives in the same house as the last Ambassador did eleven years ago." The new viceroy struck a conventionally humble pose in his letter of acceptance to the prime minister, trusting in Liverpool's kindness to compensate for his deficiency "in those qualifications which are requisite to fill so high a situation." In fact, he promised to be an astute choice. If at the age of fifty-nine he was no longer an Adonis, he remained a commanding figure with strong features and dark impenetrable eyes; his intelligence, guile, charm, and capacity to dissemble, a talent which his long service in Russia had fully developed, promised to stand him in good stead.[31]

Richmond's only concern was the sufficiency of Whitworth's rank for the viceroyalty, he being only a lowly Irish baron, but this difficulty was easily and promptly overcome by his elevation to an English viscountcy. More important to the departing lord lieutenant were his successor's religious loyalties. "I really believe he is as well calculated for the situation as any man can be," he responded, on first learning of the selection, "provided he is a firm Protestant which I believes he is." There was no problem on this score. "I am quite happy to find your Opinions and mine agree so much on the Catholic question," he was soon writing to Whitworth. "I am convinced you can give nothing to the Irish Catholic without endangering the English connection." Sharing this opinion, the home secretary was equally pleased with the appointment.[32]

Whitworth fatalistically accepted the inevitability of religious animosities in Ireland and was thankful that the means existed to maintain the Protestant Ascendancy. Convinced that "Reason [had] no Effect on such adversaries," he placed his trust in "nothing but a strong arm." "In God's name then let us strengthen ourselves by all the powers Civil & Military which can be given us – It is to that & that alone, we are to look for tranquillity in this Country." For those liberal Protestants who would concede emancipation he voiced only scorn. In the event of their triumph, it was his hope that they would "enjoy the fruits of their labours" by living in Ireland under a Catholic Ascendancy intolerant of all dissenters. "Convinced as I am that from the day [Catholic] Demands are complied with the Protestant Ascendancy may date its downfall," he informed Sidmouth, "I hope and trust that this will continue to be the opinion of all well-wishers of the Establishment." And when, soon after the new viceroy's arrival in Dublin on 26 August 1813, there was an "impudent attempt" by the *Dublin Evening Post* to persuade the Irish people that Whitworth intended to act upon "liberal principles," Robert Peel responded swiftly in order to prevent any further erosion of Protestant confidence. He drafted a statement correcting this "fabrication" and placed it in one of the newspapers supported by the government. Yet it was a mark of a more diplomatic viceregal style that Whitworth promptly donated £100 towards the construction of a Catholic chapel. "The Duke of Richmond never gave 100 shillings to any Catholic Chapel, or Catholic Charity, during his long viceroyalty," the *Dublin Evening Herald* commented.[33]

Unflinching opposition to Catholic claims united Richmond and Whitworth but not the administrations they headed. Nevertheless, those who disagreed with this policy were less numerous, less forceful, and less influential than its advocates. One of the viceroy's senior legal officers, Solicitor General Charles Bushe, was a moderate inclined towards conciliation but he was overshadowed by the attorney general. William Saurin lacked Bushe's wit and glittering turn of phrase but possessed in abundance the "stern and uncompromising" virtues of the Huguenots from whom he was descended. At the opening of the century he had opposed the union with such passion and indiscretion that the then lord lieutenant had given serious thought to depriving him of his silk gown. His appeal to "the right of resistance" seemed tantamount to "unfurling the bloody flag of rebellion." However, as attorney general, to which office he had been appointed in 1807 at the age of forty-nine, Saurin was quick to condemn the conduct of Catholic agitators. They were taking, he charged, "the essential first steps of revolution, against which, in its more violent and accelerated forms, it is the business of every wise and good man to guard." Standing rock-like on the permanency of the Protestant settlement of 1688, he was satisfied that the relief bill of 1793 had gone as far as was prudent towards levelling the distinction between Protestants and Catholics in Ireland. It was his conviction that the surviving restrictions on Roman Catholics, with respect to the crown, Parliament, and the highest offices of state, "merely and barely" preserved "the principle and the fundamental law on which the Constitution was settled at the [Glorious] Revolution." In Ireland the only protection for the Protestant Establishment was a Protestant government, for it was beyond the wit of man, in Saurin's opinion, to devise a scheme whereby that Establishment could be maintained if the government fell under the domination for Roman Catholics. Nor was the Catholics' exclusion from offices and Parliament either punishment or penalty. Only in an ideal democracy was the right of every citizen to share in government recognized, he argued. Elsewhere, it was confined to the few. Equally, the state must "insist on allegiance and obedience to the happiest and best government on earth."[34]

The harmony of Richmond's views and those of his attorney general, their common determination to ensure that "illegal combinations" did not "overawe all constituted authority," had given rise to the impression that Saurin dominated the administration. To the extent that his influence had predominated, it was a reflection also of a private personality which contrasted sharply with the public. This dour, inflexible, and harsh upholder of the letter of the law and the constitution of 1688 was known to his intimates as a man whose "temper was angelic, cheerful, and never ruffled," whose spirits were "playful," and whose conversation was "pleasing and instructive." In 1812 he was quick to recognize Robert Peel as a young man of similar opinions and much the same temperament. Not that this assessment tested Saurin's powers of perception, given the chief secretary's immediate declaration of unreserved support for the duke of Richmond and all his works. Having read the viceroy's recent dispatches to Sidmouth, Peel wrote to inform the lord lieutenant in August of 1812 of his complete accord "in the principles upon which the government of Ireland has been conducted."[35]

This private observation belied Peel's public protestations in the Commons that he had not pledged himself on the Catholic question. He shared the viceroy's opinion that yet another discussion of Catholic claims was pointless "unless it is to lead infallibly to something in their favour." As he prepared during the late autumn for the opening of the new Parliament, modestly accepting praise for the skill with which he had conducted the elections in Ireland and held off he government's opponents, Peel no less than Richmond expected the Catholics "to try how far intimidation" would succeed. He also found reason once Parliament met promptly to echo the lord lieutenant's complaint of the difficulty in which the Irish administration was placed as a result of the decision to make the Catholic question an open one within the British government. Thus another request from Maynooth for additional funding, in order to improve the quality of teaching there, threatened to expose the government's divisions. Important ministers lined up on both sides of the internal debate, and Liverpool proved to be more "liberal" than Peel had expected. For Peel, as for Richmond, the sum involved, a mere pittance, was unimportant. They wished to resist on principle an extension of the Catholic establishment in Ireland. Here was the rub. It would fall to Vesey Fitzgerald, the chancellor of the (Irish) exchequer and an advocate of concessions, to propose the motion. Peel was loath to parade their differences by moving a crippling amendment. Instead, once the additional sum had been voted, he gave his support to a successful but silly motion, one certain to irritate Catholics, which required the seminary to submit for parliamentary scrutiny a copy of the course of lectures on Divinity given to the students at Maynooth.[36]

If Peel quickly gained the viceroy's full confidence, Richmond found the company of William Gregory no less congenial. They dined together at least once, often twice, and occasionally three times a week. Not that the Gregorys had been strangers before William's appointment as under-secretary. Gregory subscribed to most of Richmond's articles of faith – that the Catholic Committee was a disloyal association; that the Roman Catholics were embarked on an incremental strategy with their own ascendancy if not the severance of the British connection as their ultimate aim; and that a genuine compromise with them was impossible. A devout Protestant and faithful in his attendance at annual yeomanry dinners, he withheld his signature from an anti-Catholic petition on one occasion only at the urging of Peel. In a land where appearances were almost as important as reality, the younger man cautioned, a signature might well be misunderstood and the effect prejudicial. "Your situation becomes more and more important every day – though ... all who know you are conscious of your impartiality – it is of great importance that the impression of the world should be in concurrence with that of your friends."[37]

The arrival of Lord Whitworth did not disrupt the harmonious working of the administration. He was soon bemoaning an unusual absence from Dublin of both Gregory and Peel because this exposed him to Edward

Littlehales, the aging and fussy military under-secretary, who unlike his civil counterpart was "rather inclined to attach more importance to trifles than they deserve." Self-assured, devoid of that punctilio for which diplomats are traditionally as notorious as soldiers, the new viceroy saw no reason for Peel to apologize for addressing to Gregory letters which ought properly to have been directed to himself. "I trust we are on such terms of perfect confidence," Whitworth replied, "that it is precisely the same thing." He extended the same latitude to Gregory, who on occasion sent off "long" letters to Peel without consulting him. Whitworth soon demonstrated his confidence in a more tangible way, by securing a pension of £500 a year for the under-secretary.[38] The viceroy was evidently aware that, for the smooth and effective daily functioning of the Irish administration, the pivotal relationship was that between the chief secretary and his civil under-secretary.

Similarity of background and identity of outlook were essential aspects of the Peel-Gregory partnership, but so also were the under-secretary's diligence, discretion, and steadiness. Peel had no fear of delegating to Gregory much of the daily and tedious routine of his office – the correspondence with supplicants and complainants, clergy, gentry, and nobility, sheriffs and magistrates. It was Gregory who dealt with those angry citizens who had run afoul of the bureaucracy, such as the Dublin alderman outraged by a summary order from the Paving Board to remove a projection in front of his house on Sackville Street. He it was who communicated with the Board of Inland Navigation on recommendations for increases in the salary of humble pay clerks, acknowledged the addresses from grand juries pleading the local and national benefit of an extension of canal navigation, and participated in the planning of new bridewells. He negotiated with the Board of Wide Street Commissioners over the siting of a new bridge over the Liffey, and was primarily concerned with "the beauty of the town." It fell to him to compromise the differences between factions feuding over the scheme to complete the lighting of Dublin with gas. Not a few of the opponents were governed by their animosity towards the project's principal spokesman, whose "coarseness" had made him "generally obnoxious." Others among them feared that gas lines would prove too vulnerable to attack during disturbances and that the capital might therefore be thrown into darkness in the midst of a crisis. Still others objected to the evil odour of the gas, and Gregory conceded the merit of their case.[39]

So persecuted had he been "by uninterrupted interruptions," Gregory once explained to Peel, that he had been unable to find time to write to him "on any point of Business." He was alive to the delicacy of his position, during the frequent and long absences of his superior. On the one hand he disliked "unnecessarily loading" the chief secretary with papers, but on the other was "equally averse to do anything" which might give "the appearance of assuming a Power" which did not belong to him. He did not fear that Peel would ever level this charge "but such have often been made on decisions of the under secretary without consulting the Chief." Moreover, a number of applicants or complaints simply refused to accept a reply from the under-secretary unless there had been "a Communication [with the chief secretary] on the subject." The refusal of some of those who had dealings with the chief secretary's office to acknowledge or accept Gregory's authority, and the trivial nature of many of the issues which absorbed much of his energy and monopolized so much of his time, were not the true indicators of his rapidly growing influence. Within two months of taking office he was writing to Peel: "I trust you will excuse my giving opinions freely on subjects as they arise, tho' my opinion may not be asked or required." The chief secretary's response could not have been more encouraging or flattering. "I hope I need not assure you," he wrote, "that nothing can be more satisfactory to me than the free communication of your opinions on any subject and that if communication is not at any particular time specially required it is only because it is at all times wished for and expected." Indeed, Peel invited his trusted subordinate to comment on his dispatches to the home secretary. "The letter to Lord Sidmouth is excellent," Gregory remarked of one such report, "and places our internal state in its proper view."[40]

Like every good "civil servant" Gregory sought to protect his minister from possible discomfiture in the Commons. He rushed information to Peel whenever questions on the administration of Ireland appeared to be imminent, explaining that though frequently of no real importance they "often embarrass a Minister if unprepared with an immediate answer." At times this necessitated the forwarding of voluminous papers since his "explanations might not be so clear or satisfactory in matters of detail, as the documents themselves." He also submitted a deliberate surfeit of documentation to Peel whenever they prepared the more detailed reports on affairs in Ireland which Parliament periodically demanded. It was better, he argued, for Peel to receive too much material "which you can according to your discretion curtail, than by scantiness of materials, give you the trouble of searching for, and supplying them." Gregory did make marginal comments for the minister's information, however. The chief secretary then returned the material with his own comments and instructions on what to include in the report. All of this Gregory submitted to the lord lieutenant for his opinion before composing the final draft. However, on the eve of any major debate on Ireland, Gregory preferred to withhold all minor matters and "unconnected correspondence" so as not to distract the minister from his preparations for the coming engagement.[41]

In the Commons Peel naturally looked for support to those Irish members who had been returned with the assistance of the government. Consequently, one of Gregory's more tiresome and frustrating tasks was to try and ensure their attendance at Westminster. He was particularly incensed at the un-cooperative conduct of one member, "as his being brought into Parliament saved him from being a fugitive, or incarcerated." Early in his career as chief secretary Peel complained to Gregory of the behaviour of the Irish members. "They treat us very ill and wring ten times as many favours [out of us] as English Members and do not give us one tenth of the support." For his part the under-secretary had quickly concluded that "Nothing will drive the Irish Members to Parliament unless convenient to themselves, and yet if they declare themselves for the Government, they think they are entitled to every branch of Patronage, as much as tho' they gave us useful support."[42]

Patronage was the essence of political management and eighteenth-century England had been awash in it. Ministries gathered and retained support in Parliaments devoid of disciplined political parties through the distribution of honours, pensions, preferments, and places. In turn, the control of minor offices made it possible for favoured members to secure their local interest. Thus was upper-class national power firmly rooted in a system of "clientage" in the localities. This "informal process," whereby men of political weight "fostered the careers of less powerful individuals who, in return, could be expected to uphold their patron's influence," has been adjudged "a natural development in the pre-meritocratic era. It was also the natural expression of a society where relationships even within the administrative machine were personal rather than official." That Ireland differed little from England in this regard is scarcely surprising. Indeed, offices were likely to be even more highly valued and avidly sought in a society where the opportunities for profitable employment were limited. Before the union patronage was the "link" which joined the legislature to the executive, thereby providing "the political cohesion essential for effective government." "'Your Excellency knowns'," one magnate wrote to a lord lieutenant, "'how useful and indeed necessary to one's importance in one's county the favour and countenance of government are'." After the union the control of offices, whether ecclesiastical, civil, legal, or military, was even more highly prized and tightly grasped by the executive. The patronage which had formerly been "dispensed to keep docile an Irish Parliament of 300 members and, basically, to maintain the British connection, survived to corrupt the 100 Irish members at Westminster, when the threat to the British connection could no longer be adduced in extenuation."[43]

A county member who supported the government was rewarded with "the patronage of the County," Wakefield reported. Appointments of excise and customs officers, and officers of the militia, were made with an eye to the creation of a nucleus of political allies who would bring out their freeholders to vote for him on election day. "Thus the fertile spring of corruption flows in a strong current," the critical Englishman moralized. There had been persistent calls for reform of the patronage system, in England as well as in

Ireland. A number of sinecures were abolished in both countries, and in Ireland the viceroy's generosity with pensions had been severely curtailed in 1793. Lords lieutenant, expected as they were to help return a manageable Parliament and to conduct a "'quiet and orderly government of the country,'" were quick to protest the reduction of the number of offices and favours at their disposal. The fewer the "jobs" in his gift the lesser the viceroy's "'means of obliging many Irish interests'." "Things are extremely changed in this Country since I first had the pleasure of knowing you," Richmond informed one female acquaintance who had sought a pension; "at that time there would not have been much difficulty in doing something for you but now I am sorry to report it is almost impossible." Three months later he was obliged to justify to his mother his refusal to find an ecclesiastical preferment for the son of one of her friends. Although "a considerable Degree of Church Patronage" remained in his hands, perhaps as much as formerly, "Patronage of every other description has diminished extremely," he informed her. Many of the sinecures which had survived were going to disappear with the death of the current holders. As a result, persons who had a strong claim on the government and had formerly sought a sinecure for themselves now applied for clerical livings for relatives or friends. "This makes the Demand on Ecclesiastical Preferment much beyond my means of satisfying." Indeed, the distribution of clerical patronage serves to illustrate the conflicting pressures under which viceroys operated, pressures which in turn heightened their apprehensions of the consequences of any departure from "the principle of leaving to the Lord Lieutenant the most unrestricted controul over all arrangements in the Law & the Church."[44]

Richmond and the cabinet had reached an understanding on the most important and valued form of church patronage, that of appointments to the episcopal bench. Instead of filling a vacancy with a rank partisan who held a good but lesser living which would then also be at his disposal, the viceroy would give preference to those friends of the government and its supporters who were of good character and "fitted for the Bench." As a result, he sometimes had "hardly a living to dispose of" when he recommended a bishop. However proud Richmond may have been of the quality of his episcopal appointments, the fact that they came almost exclusively from the ranks of the greatest families excited adverse comment in England and prompted the intervention of the prime minister. "It cannot be supposed for a moment that noble birth is a disqualification for the bench," the chief secretary reported after a discussion with Liverpool, "but it is perhaps desirable to make it less a recommendation to preferment than in former periods it has been in Ireland." On reflection, Richmond agreed that there were "a great many men of high Family on the Irish Bench and that it would be better to place there some who would keep us from the Imputation of promoting to that Bench from political motives."[45]

Further complicating this sensitive issue was a meddlesome prince regent. He repeatedly sought to advance the career of the bishop of Limerick, much to the embarrassment of the chief secretary and the viceroy. Alluding to one of the bishop's letters on an earlier patronage matter, Peel expressed his confidence that Lord Whitworth "would not see in the merits of the individual any particular ground for Royal Favour." "It is bad enough to let political influence interfere with promotion on the bench but present predilections are worse," he concluded. Meanwhile, the viceroy was still forced to contend with the insatiable appetite of the high families. In October 1814 the marquis of Ely sought the promotion of his brother from the see of Killaloe to that of Clogher, apparently in the belief that the archbishop of Dublin was about to expire and that this would trigger a chain reaction in the dioceses. Yet this candidate appeared to be a no worthier recipient of additional viceregal favour than was the bishop of Limerick. Whitworth, having conceded that he was an excellent man and truly exemplary in his private life, could not resist the opportunity to indulge his taste for irony. "It is however by such an example alone that he is calculated to render any essential service to the Church," he remarked to Sidmouth. "His habits of seclusion are such that he has not only, I believe, never yet been able to bring himself to ascend the pulpit but that he scarcely can be prevailed upon to see his clergy, or those whose business is to communicate with him on the concerns of his Diocese." Finally, the prospect of promotions brought the ordinary clergy to Dublin in large number. They sought to compensate for their lack of a powerful patron through the zealous persistence with which they lobbied on their own behalf. The task of dealing with them frequently fell to the under-secretary. Writing to Peel in the spring of 1813, Gregory reported that his office had been besieged by clerics fighting "their bye battles for inferior livings." It was also his duty to inform the unsuccessful, and there was little pleasure in its performance. "Nothing can be more irksome than addressing a letter to a Friend communicating to him the Disappointment of his Expectations," he opened one such missive.[46]

In his approach to the essential but often distasteful business of patronage, Robert Peel sought to be both systematic and principled. He found a faithful agent in William Gregory. He it was who suggested that all applications for civil patronage be channelled through the civil department so as to minimize the confusion which resulted from the personal applications made to the viceroy. Whitworth was only too willing to turn over to these two servants the bulk of this wearying and perplexing work. In the midst of one minor patronage squabble he informed Peel: "I have been talking it over with [Gregory] for this hour, but what with Longfields, the Longfords, the Rochforts and Robinsons, and all their friends, and the Mullingars and the Vicarages, my head is so confused that I scarcely know how to unravel them."[47]

As the principal negotiators with the patronage-mongers, such as Lord Waterford, Peel and Gregory showed themselves determined to resist all efforts at blackmail. When Waterford and an associate visited Gregory to demand two positions in their county, one clerical and the other civil, and threatened to withhold their support at the next election if denied, the indignant under-secretary gave a "decided and unqualified" refusal to this form of extortion. To their retort that the government was obliged to aid its friends, he urged "in vain" that such "a Compact was nothing short of the most gross Bribery." To the further suggestion that any arrangement might be informal, he confessed his "ignorance of a difference between an actual promise & an honourable Understanding, & of course declined entering into either." All he would promise was that, if a member friendly to the government was returned for the county, his recommendations for appointments would receive the same favourable considerations as those of other friends.[48]

Political loyalty also weighed heavily in the annual selection of sheriffs, frequently another source of contention between rival magnates. One recommendation for County Meath, submitted by Lord Headfort, was successfully blocked by Gregory with the argument that the candidate was "peculiarly objectionable," his having been the only dissentient voice at a county meeting which passed a resolution praising the conduct of the duke of Richmond. The principle Gregory now laid down was endorsed by the viceroy. The government "ought not to appoint a Person Sheriff who declares himself adverse to them on all occasions." At other times Gregory saw this essentially honorary but by no means powerless post, for the sheriff nominated the grand jurors, as a means of conciliating powerful families who were at odds with the administration. But efforts to extract unworthy concessions from the government as the price for accepting the position in those counties where there was an absence of volunteers were resisted with the same indignation as the other forms of attempted blackmail in patronage matters. In County Kildare, in 1815, one "gentleman" offered to accept the shrievalty in return for the government's payment of all his expenses; another wanted an appointment as a commissioner of revenue; a third demanded appointment as a landwaiter or some other situation worth £400 a year. "Any inconvenience is preferable to submitting to such propositions," Gregory observed, before adding: "what a ruinous system is the whole mode of naming sheriffs. How can Justice be rightly directed in such hands?"[49]

Where patronage had its most obvious, immediate, and damaging impact was on administrative effectiveness. Consequently, Peel and Gregory devoted much time and energy to the task of ensuring that persons appointed to positions of some responsibility possessed at least minimum qualifications for the office. Moreover, Peel believed that nothing was "half so disgusting as the personal monopoly of honours and offices by those to whom the distribution of them is entrusted." He scrupulously refrained from gratifying any private wish of his own "by the smallest Irish appointment" and vetoed an exchange of offices between Gregory's son Robert and one of his Trench relations. The first consideration in making appointments to posts that were not mere sinecures must be the competency of the individual, the chief secretary ordained. Gregory faithfully sought to enforce this rule, though he did ridicule a suggestion by the Customs Board that tide surveyors possess a degree of nautical experience since they had to board ships. A former surveyor himself, he pointed out that "their business is with the Cargo, and not the Navigation of the vessel." His response to recommendations for assistant barristerships was to demand proof of the candidates' eligibility, "as it is of the utmost consequence that those situations should be filled by Persons of professional knowledge, and good character." From personal experience he knew "the mischief which follows at sessions from an improper chairman." He set the same standard for the position of solicitor of the Board of Stamps, and the principle of appointing the most competent man was tested again when the first commissioner of the Board of Excise resigned.[50]

Peel's rejection in November 1814 of two schemes, one of superannuation and the other to revive certain fees which excise officers had formerly claimed, for he considered them "two of the most unwarrantable jobs that were ever intended," had brought the first commissioner's resignation. Gregory's influence upon the selection of a successor was considerable. A former commissioner, his assessment of the various candidates was especially valuable. He concluded that "every Candidate presents himself in the shape of a Difficulty." The second commissioner was a Roman Catholic. To appoint him would not conciliate Catholics, Gregory argued, for the promotion would be attributed by them to the man's seniority. On the other hand, it would alienate those Protestants who had no desire to see a Catholic in "such an important and confidential situation." Furthermore, he was "hardly fit to be at the head of the Board." Another of its sitting members was disqualified on the grounds of incompetency, while a third was able "but of low and vulgar habits, unfitting for such a situation." Two junior members were not "so gifted as to justify their superseding all their colleagues." In this quandary, Whitworth, Peel, and Gregory finally accepted William Hawthorne, who had been Sidmouth's nominee for the office of under-secretary in 1812 and whose availability the home secretary had again advertised. He had powerful enemies in Ireland, however. As a commissioner of enquiry he had enraged the legal profession, including Attorney General Saurin, by drawing unwelcome public attention to the fat fees paid by the Revenue Board to its legal advisers. But viceroy, Peel, and Gregory consoled themselves with the thought that the appointee had been the most highly qualified candidate.[51]

If the selection of competent men was essential for a more effective and efficient administration of Ireland, so also was a regular and diligent attendance to their duties by officeholders. Peel acted swiftly after his arrival to establish this test. When the Board of Stamps, perhaps hoping to profit from his youth and inexperience, requested additional staff, he and Gregory drafted a response shaped by the knowledge that many of its officers kept very short hours. They demanded from the board a statement of the hours of attendance of the present staff and made clear their opinion that a full working day ran for no fewer than eight hours. This was Peel's way of disabusing the entire administration of the notion that the new executive would be easily duped into creating unnecessary jobs. Instead, it expected its servants to earn their salaries. Thus Gregory informed one of his many brothers-in-law, who occupied his old place at the Board of Inland Navigation, that the secretary was expected to reside in Dublin and personally discharge his duties. The alternative was to relinquish the situation, he added meaningfully. Of course, some officeholders were able to resist such pressure if backed by a powerful patron. Edward Green had been appointed clerk of ship entries at Cork in 1779 at the request of the powerful Shannon family, but had always employed a deputy to perform his duties. Ordered by the Board of Customs in 1809 to assume them himself he had simply secured a series of leaves of absence, pleading "ill-health." Yet during this same period, Gregory noted, Green had been well enough to serve as mayor of Youghal, command an active corps of yeomanry, and serve as the principal agent of the Shannon political interest. In short, Green was undoubtedly useful to Lord Shannon but "most useless in his official capacity."[52]

The appointment of competent and diligent men went hand in hand with efforts to root out the corrupt. "There cannot in my opinion be a much greater offence than the improper use of public money" by those "entrusted with the government of the Country" and who are "particularly responsible for the due application of public funds," Peel declared. The reputation of the revenue departments, in particular, had long been tarnished by scandal. Gregory acted swiftly, therefore, when he received information from an inspector of taxes of improper procedures in the Hearth Money Office. He appointed a surveyor general to investigate, having first ordered that all of the papers in the office be sealed and secured. "I have no doubt that some very nefarious practices will be brought to light," he reported to Peel, for "during the time I was Commissioner [of Excise], I had strong suspicions of Jocelyn Waller the head of that office, as every Defaulter found a warm supporter in him." Consequently, the news that the surveyor general had found discrepancies in the accounts of thirty collectors, and that they had been ordered to offer reasons why they should not be dismissed, failed to satisfy the under-secretary. "I do not understand the reason of not extending the same order to the supervisors over those Collectors," he remarked, "who if they had done their Duty must have discovered the frauds, and not having made their own checks, are equally guilty." Nor did he applaud a move by the Excise Board to replace the discredited Waller and to censure him for "Inattention." He protested the glossing "over by mere censure either the Corruption or gross Misconduct of a Department which ought to make such a principal part of the Revenue."[53] Ironically, a parallel attempt by Vesey Fitzgerald, the Irish chancellor of the exchequer, to establish tighter control over the revenue departments was strenuously and effectively resisted by Peel.

In 1811 Wellesley-Pole had added the office of chancellor to that of chief secretary in order to prevent a recurrence of the friction within the Irish government which had been created by the abrasive personality and claims to independence of John Foster, who had occupied the Exchequer for six of the seven years between 1804 and 1811. Remembering these earlier difficulties, Richmond had suggested in 1812 that Peel also occupy both offices. Instead, Vesey Fitzgerald had been named to the lesser position. An intelligent as well as a liberal and ambitious man, he soon bridled at his virtual powerlessness. He discovered that he exercised little personal control over the revenue departments, in whose operations the lord lieutenant and his senior servants freely intervened. So, brandishing a threat of resignation, he sought from Liverpool an assurance of greater authority. In response, Peel admitted that had he been in Fitzgerald's place he might well have had a similar feeling. He conceded that the revenue might be increased by the arrangements which Fitzgerald proposed, and not the least of these involved the transfer of the patronage "to those who are directly and immediately responsible" for the collection of the revenue. But he strenuously opposed any change along those lines.[54]

Peel's resistance was not entirely disinterested. He had no wish to see the dignity and influence of his own office diminished. Having accepted it on the presumption that he would hold it on the same terms as had his predecessors, he "never could see with satisfaction a formal arrangement proclaimed by which a part of the duties and labours which had always been attached to it was to be transferred to another." His principal objection, however, and one which won the full support of the cabinet, was to any lessening of the viceroy's power. Not that this was unrelated to his concern to protect his own position. For in the prime minister's words, "The Chief Sec[retar]y is the Channel through which the Power and Patronage in Ireland must flow." Yet Peel steadfastly declined to assume the added responsibility of the Irish Exchequer, protesting that he had work enough already. Nevertheless, he repeatedly emphasized the need for a highly centralized administration. Situated as Ireland was, "there ought to be a paramount authority somewhere, an authority not merely superior to all others, but one upon which all others are dependent." Nothing could be worse there than the creation of "divided and independent authorities," and once a precedent was established by the Treasury where would it end? How long would it be before the military commander sought to assert his independence in all matters concerning the public peace? This same preoccupation with the dignity of his own office and the need for a highly centralized Irish administrative structure resurfaced when the idea was broached of extending the authority of the British Treasury into Ireland. He gave the proposal qualified support, arguing that "the advantages gained to the revenue will perhaps more than compensate the disadvantages which must and will arise from the necessary diminution of the authority of a Government, circumstanced as the Government of Ireland is." With that fundamental concern in mind, he urged that any residual authority which distance or delay obliged the British Treasury to leave in Ireland "should be devolved upon the Lord Lieutenant."[55]

Peel contended that it would be unwise and unsafe to deprive the government of Ireland of any of its existing instruments of influence, insufficient as he considered them already to be, unless a fundamental restructuring of that government was in prospect. "I shall be glad when the time arrives when the Government of this country can be concluded on different Principles from what it at present is," he added, "when you can look for support, and I do not mean merely Parliamentary support, but that effective support which active and loyal men can afford in this country, in an honest conviction of its necessity and a pure sense of duty." But that time had not yet arrived and until it did Ireland had either to be governed without such support or it had to be purchased. He was pleading the case of the island's exceptionality.[56]

CHAPTER THREE

# The Policy of Irish Exceptionalism

Robert Peel had landed in Ireland at a moment of dead calm. It was the conventional wisdom that this "extraordinary tranquillity" reflected the triumph of British arms in the Peninsula. Our "Rabble are all ears for news of Bonaparte's success," William Gregory was later to remark. Whatever the explanation, Peel was in the fortunate position of being able to concentrate his mind and energies on a number of urgent administrative problems. Not the least of these was the chaotic state of the island's finances. Ireland had retained a separate currency and the official exchange rate had been set at 12:13 – twelve British pence buying thirteen Irish. By 1812 the Irish currency was fluctuating wildly in value against the British in response to a shortage of both. Working closely with Vesey Fitzgerald, Peel managed to restore a measure of stability. A general recoinage and the "scraping together of everything from rupees to dollars" at least halted the drift to "financial chaos" but did not solve the fundamental problems of an economy under severe strain.[1]

Anxiety over the perilous state of Ireland's financial health encouraged Peel to resist the granting of pensions to persons who founded their claims on promises made at the time of the union. Similarly, it explained his enthusiastic welcoming of a scheme to unite the treasuries of Britain and Ireland and consolidate the debts and revenues of the two countries. For this step would not only complete the work of union and thus "efface every vestige of separation," but also facilitate the task of administering to the Irish the unpleasant medicine of direct taxation. He fancied that a land or property tax would be received "with better grace when considered as the act of a Board of Treasury which has a general superintendance over the whole financial concerns of the United empire, than as the act of a separate and inferior department." Nor was he unmindful of the odium which would otherwise fall upon the lord lieutenant and himself as the initiators of direct taxation. It might "create embarrassment in the conduct of the Government," he warned. Furthermore, a union of the exchequers would finally resolve that "conflict of authority" which had developed between chief secretary and Irish chancellor. Despite these advantages as seen from Dublin, the ever cautious Liverpool procrastinated. He insisted that the proposal first be submitted to the parliamentary committee on Irish finance, which had not sat for two years but was expected to be revived in the course of the next session. [2]

When Vesey Fitzgerald presented a number of Irish financial measures to the House in May 1813, he outlined the peculiar difficulties of his position as chancellor of the Irish exchequer. Four-fifths of Ireland's imports came from Britain but he was precluded under the terms of union from levying a duty on them of more than 10 per cent ad valorem. Moreover, he could only tax items which were taxed in Britain, and at no higher a rate. Therefore, almost in desperation, he proposed a duty of three shillings a barrel on Irish malt. Since this amounted to a tax upon Irish beer he was immediately assailed by spokesmen of the brewing industry. The surprised and bewildered chancellor heard himself denounced as a destroyer of the morals of the Irish people. Their sobriety and behaviour had improved, the House was informed, to the extent that they had been weaned from spirits and onto beer. [3] Yet only four months later Robert Peel successfully concluded a year-long campaign to end the ban on the distillation of spirits from grain.

The use of grains by distillers had been prohibited in the spring of 1812 by a government seeking to allay fears in Britain of a scarcity of provisions. The action had been opposed by the then Irish secretary, and shortly after settling into office Peel began pressing the British government to lift the ban. He put the value to the Irish Treasury of a duty on spirits at "nearly a million a year," and this was a revenue the financially troubled government could ill-afford to forgo. But England's "necessities" took precedence over Ireland's, and Peel's initial attack on the prohibition stalled. He continued to manoeuvre for position, however, harried as he was by a number of Irish distillers. Not that a deputation seeking an end to the prohibition and a reduction of the duty on spirits impressed Under-Secretary Gregory, who interviewed them in April 1813. "I know them well," he reported to Peel, "the present object is to alarm those who have engaged in the Distillation from sugar, and answer some corn speculation which is falling in price – the Persons who waited upon me have not as you may suppose engaged in the sugar spirit." [4]

To counter moral objections to the resumption of grain distillation, Peel made much of the stimulus prohibition gave to the illicit industry. In fact, it had expanded in response to several factors – the high cost and low quality of legal whiskey; increased demand from a population swelling in size and slightly more affluent; and the disinclination of landlords and magistrates to attempt to suppress an activity which put money into the pockets of tenants. The complicity of the landlordry had been apparent to William Gregory when, as a commissioner of revenue, he had travelled to Donegal and Derry in 1810 to investigate a thriving trade in illegal spirits. In his report, he recommended the establishment of a legal distillery. This would provide barley growers with a legal customer for their crops and reassure landlords that their incomes would not suffer as a result of their "Tenantry selling in obedience to the laws." To stimulate greater respect for those laws, and to obtain the assistance of local gentlemen and magistrates who "by their distance from each other, & from military aid," had been "unwilling to expose themselves to personal danger," Gregory advocated the stationing of a substantial body of regular troops in the area and the dispatch of a revenue cruiser to patrol loughs Foyle and Tilly. Finally, convinced that the illegal industry was one of Ireland's greatest "evils," he called for the continuation of the system of levying fines on the entire district or townland where an illegal still was discovered. He conceded that the fines were "excessive" and encouraged the "grossest perjuries," but saw no moral dilemma in choosing the lesser of two evils. The polluted means of correction were temporary but the evil of illegal distilling would become permanent unless checked. Nevertheless, Wellesley-Pole had subsequently secured the repeal of the fines, for he regarded them as "contrary to every principle of justice."[5]

In June 1813, over the protests of his predecessor in office, Peel secured the reenactment of the townland fines. After all, to the extent that they were collected the revenue would be benefited. During the debate he made telling use of a letter from the former commissioner of revenue who was now serving as under-secretary. Mr Gregory believed, he informed the House, "that if this Bill had been in force but six months longer, illicit distillation would have been put down in Ireland." Nor did he overlook the military implications of such an achievement. Once freed from the unsoldierly duty of searching for illicit stills, the discipline of the troops would improve, as would their relations with the community. "The people should learn to consider the soldiers as the protectors of the country, and ought not to be taught to view them in the light of enemies," Peel declared.[6] Three months later, in September, the ban on the distillation from grain was finally lifted. But this success could do little to ease Ireland's immediate shortfall in revenues.

Fitzgerald presented an Irish budget to the Commons on 1 July 1814. He forecast a substantial deficit (an Opposition member offered the more precise calculation of £2,400,000) and announced an increase in taxation. The duties on stamps and spirits were to be raised and new levies imposed on a number of articles ostensibly used in Irish manufacturing but whose importation was often fraudulent. Admitted to Ireland duty free, they were reshipped to English manufacturers. Unfortunately, these fresh impositions coincided with an acute crisis in Irish industry. Several woollen manufacturers had failed in December 1812, throwing hundreds of artisans out of work in Dublin. Their plight excited the under-secretary's sympathy but his desire "to alleviate their wants" was checked by the conviction that this task properly belonged to "the charity of individuals." As conditions worsened, so the appeals for "the succouring hand of Government" grew more shrill. A group of manufacturers called on Gregory in late July to complain of the "bitter effects of the union," the want of patriotism of the Irish gentry who preferred English clothes to Irish, and the scandalous conduct of the government in failing to outfit the Irish militia in uniforms cut from coarse Irish cloth. Cloth to the value of £10,000 was immediately available, they protested. "You may suppose what a set of opulent Manufacturers these must be, and how worthy of national encouragement," an ironic under-secretary remarked to Peel.[7]

Gregory did not scorn all public support for Irish industries. He considered the distressed cotton manufacturers significant enough to merit saving, and so he endorsed their appeal for £100,000 in state aid. But in London more cautious counsels prevailed. There, the worry was that depressed English manufacturers would demand that the government do no less for them than it had for the Irish. Peel therefore proposed that the Bank of Ireland extend credit to the cotton manufacturers ostensibly on the security of a deposit of their goods but with a confidential assurance that the government would make good any of the bank's losses. In this way the appearance of a purely private transaction would be preserved. Simultaneously, a small committee of respectable merchants should be struck to inquire into the industry's problems and draft a report which would establish the grounds "for the direct interference of the Government."[8]

The floundering textile industries constituted a minor sector of an economy which remained overwhelmingly agricultural. With an eye to the expansion of the market for Irish provisions, Peel proposed that violations of the restrictions on the export of grains be winked at. Sidmouth refused. English applications to the Privy Council for export licenses had recently been rejected, he explained, and it was inadvisable "to introduce into Ireland a course of Proceeding different from that which has been adopted in this part of the Kingdom."[9] In short, there were limits to Irish exceptionalism.

The danger of Ireland's economic interests becoming a hostage to Britain's, which had not escaped a number of vocal Irishmen, among them the woollen manufacturers, was illustrated anew by the Board of Trade. It recommended the removal of the 13 per cent duty levied on those foreign linens imported into Britain but earmarked for reexportation. The board feared that without this concession the Prussians, in particular, would attempt to penetrate Britain's valued South American market. Yet the proposal threatened to cripple an Irish linen industry already wounded in an American war which had interrupted its supplies of flaxseed. That trade was "now in a state of great improvement," Whitworth informed the home secretary. "All ranks are deeply interested in it; and I do believe that nothing would operate so fatally upon it, and at the same time upon the disposition of the public, as such a measure." His protest succeeded, supported as it was by Peel's warning that removal of the duty would certainly be opposed in the House by Irish members. Confronted by "clamour and general dissatisfaction" enough in Ireland already, the government had no wish to compound its problems. The "dead calm" of September 1812 had quickly given way to turbulence. [10]

Throughout the winter of 1812–13 the Protestant guard at the Castle had waited nervously for the opening of the new Parliament and the revival of the Catholic question under the terms of the motion passed in June 1812. As the day of the debate neared, Gregory worked frantically to orchestrate expressions of Protestant hostility to concession. He stopped short of providing the £500 the sheriff of Dublin requested to promote a petition of the capital's Protestants. But Parliament was inundated with petitions protesting against the removal of the disabilities, the great bulk of them English. This tide of sectarian opinion failed to sweep away the cause of conciliation, and Henry Grattan secured passage of his motion to go into committee. In the words of one of the most eloquent of his Irish fellow-liberals, it was something very like dishonesty, in the light of the assurances given to Irish Catholics at the time of the union, to press into service against their claims "the opinion of the people of England, and its authority with an English parliament." [11]

The news from London enveloped the Irish executive in gloom. Despair quickly gave way to anger which found a target in William Wellesley-Pole. He had announced his conversion to concession in June 1812, but it was his performance during the debate on Grattan's motion that moved his former colleagues in the Irish government to fury. Speaking with the authority of both a former chief secretary and a firm Protestant, he claimed that "a great proportion" of Ireland's Protestants now endorsed the claims. He dwelt upon the divisions in the cabinet and exposed those within the Irish administration. A moderate but weak Bushe was contrasted with a fanatical Saurin, "to whose intolerant opinions [the People] were indebted for the prosecutions against the Catholic Committee." He patronized Peel as a novice who exercised only half of the responsibilities he himself had shouldered in Ireland and then ridiculed his conduct. "He seems to think," he remarked of his young successor, "that the most effectual way of making the people quiet and happy, is to clap on a perpetual blister, to draw the bad humours of the country together, and to keep them in a state of continual irritation." [12]

If there was any consolation in all of this for the depressed members of the Irish executive it was the emergence of Peel as a formidable opponent of concession. He had crushed his supercilious predecessor in a few acidulous sentences before elaborating a reasoned defence of his own position. A conservative, he upheld the "fundamental law" of the constitution as drafted in 1688 and warned that Grattan's committee would seek its revision. He demanded assurances of loyalty from persons who recognized the spiritual supremacy of the pope and declined to define its meaning or give "voluntarily that security which every despotic sovereign in Europe" had received. Not that Peel genuinely accepted the worth of securities, such as a royal veto of Catholic episcopal appointments. What was at issue was not the loyalty and influence of individual bishops, he believed, but the probability that admission to full political rights was not the limit of Catholic ambitions. "What security have we that they or the great majority of them will not continue to act as a body, will not consider their interests distinct from those of the Protestant population in Ireland, and will not use every privilege they now receive to promote it," he asked rhetorically in a report to the lord lieutenant. And when the Catholic relief bill was taken up in May, Peel welcomed the securities Castlereagh attached to it – "to vest the nomination of Roman Catholics prelates virtually in the Crown, and to restrain intercourse with the see of Rome" – in the sure knowledge that they would be repudiated now as before by Irish Catholics. Even as he sought from Gregory chapter and verse of this hostility to securities, the bill unexpectedly came to grief in the Commons. The adoption of a crippling amendment moved by the speaker, which struck out the clause giving Catholics the right to sit in Parliament, caused its sponsors to abandon the measure.[13]

Within the Irish executive, pleasure at this unforeseen turn of events quickly gave way to apprehension. How would the bitterly disappointed Roman Catholics respond? The duke of Richmond, now in the last days of his lord lieutenancy, offered a soldier's judgment. The large and well-humoured crowd which attended the royal birthday parade was proof that the people were "not offended at the Catholic Bill being thrown out." Gregory was less sanguine. He had kept Peel advised during the spring of the growing control of the Catholic Board by the more "active spirits" led by Daniel O'Connell, and the withdrawal of aristocratic moderates. He reported an emerging alliance between these radicals and the priesthood, and noted the intimidation of those Protestants who had opposed Catholic claims. In Athy their names had been placarded on chapel doors throughout the town.[14] In Dublin the Guinnesses had been the victims. A false report that members of the brewing family had signed a Protestant petition, and malicious charges that they had given evidence against a rebel in 1798 and were involved in proselytizing activities, led to a boycott of their beer. Alarmed at the loss of trade, the brewers posted a reward of £500 for the apprehension of the authors of the reports, but it required a vote of confidence from the Catholic Board to end their suffering. This episode and the intervention of the "Inquisitorial Board" enraged William Gregory, who cited these developments as proof that "concession in its most unqualified sig- nification" would be "vain" so long as the connection with Britain was maintained and the Ascendancy upheld. The "Demagogues & the lowest Rabble of Dublin" carried everything at the board, he warned. This as- sessment did not augur well for a moderate response to the news of the defeat of the Catholic bill.[15]

Reports that at its meeting on 29 June the board had adopted a resolution calling for an Irish appeal to Britain's Catholic allies, Spain and Portugal, for assistance in persuading her to grant emancipation, created something of a sensation. A choleric Gregory claimed that there had also been talk of "an independent Ireland." He urged the immediate employment of a skilful propagandist to "expose" the board's proceedings. If ably done, an exposé might at least "satisfy the minds of the well disposed to any strong measures" which the government subsequently adopted against these "Rebels."[16]

Robert Peel forwarded a copy of the report of the Catholic Board's ex- traordinary action, together with Gregory's observations and recommen- dations, to the incoming viceroy. Whitworth seconded Gregory's suggestion of an exposé. It would provide an antidote to the poison constantly admin- istered to the public by the Irish government's enemies, he reasoned. Nor did he dispute the under-secretary's gloomy assessment that that govern- ment's options were being quickly reduced to a choice between pen and sword, but identified the latter as the last extremity. Both he and Peel continued to hope that the French military reverses in the Peninsula and Germany would still the agitation. Indeed, the chief secretary provided the home secretary with a more cheerful analysis of the situation.[17]

He divided the Catholic Irish into four classes – clergy, lower orders, the moderate and respectable elements, and the violent party headed by O'Con- nell and Denys Scully. Further, he noted the differences between the violent and "the great body of respectable Catholics," the alliance between that same party and the clergy, and the influence of both upon the lower orders. He assumed the basic disloyalty of the great mass of Roman Catholics, mordantly observing that in Ireland the "most effectual mode which a news- paper or any other publication can adopt to increase its circulation is to depreciate the victories gained by our arms, and to make out a case for the enemy." Nevertheless, he found comfort in the notion that O'Connell's influence was on the wane. Then again, he thought it likely that the clergy would eventually conclude that it was in "their interest to disavow any connection" with the O'Connellites. In this confident mood he exaggerated the significance of the defeat suffered by O'Connell at a meeting of the Catholic Board in November 1813. His motion recommending that Parlia- ment not take up any arrangements affecting the discipline of the Roman Church without first obtaining the approval of the Catholic prelates was successfully resisted by a priest who opposed all British meddling. From this one setback Peel unwisely deduced that O'Connell had lost all influence on the board.[18]

The urbane new viceroy also succumbed to optimism. In his dispatches to Liverpool and Sidmouth, he sought to smother with ridicule any lingering concern in Britain. The meetings of the Catholic Board were being "held in an unoccupied house about fourteen feet in front and twenty deep," he reported. "They nevertheless continue to make a great noise. I suppose from their being so compress'd." Contemptuously, he dismissed the proceedings as the "expiring effort of a desperate faction and no more the sense of the Catholics of Ireland than are the Toasts of a drunken dinner at the Crown and Anchor the sentiments of the people of England."[19] These were not opinions the under-secretary shared, and he had long since advocated decisive action.

Gregory broached the possibility of "putting down this Jacobin Club" early in June 1813, confident of the support of the departing viceroy. Surprisingly, William Saurin opposed its suppression. He was of the opinion that the board, by its "violent" proceedings, was still doing more harm than good to the Catholic cause. Peel agreed. He expected to take firm action at some stage, but for the time being was content to have the Irish government hold its hand. Confident that O'Connell was losing control of the Catholic Board and that the "extremists" he led were losing their influence among the larger Catholic Community, he saw no reason to move against them now. Moreover, he doubted whether the executive possessed the necessary powers to strike decisively. "We must have a law which shall not, like the Convention Act, enable those against whom it is directed to triumph over the Government by changing the letters of the name by which they are called," he observed. And the likelihood that ultimately he would have to seek additional "authority" for the executive government obliged Peel to give thought to the problems of parliamentary management. Would an application for broader powers at this moment be viewed as a rather tasteless act of triumph, an unnecessary humiliation of Catholics already smarting from the defeat of the relief bill? How would he explain the Irish government's long toleration of the board? Conversely, why not grasp this opportunity both to vindicate in Parliament the government's conduct and to convince "the most loyal and determined enemy of the board" that the reluctance to suppress it was a mark of "contempt" and not of timidity"? Peel sensed a growing despondency among the friends of emancipation in Britain, and therefore he had no wish to rekindle the issue.[20]

Sharing his chief secretary's opinions, Whitworth endorsed his recommendation that they "connive at the greatest absurdities" before seeking "to interpose the authority" of the government. But the viceroy soon made the discovery that ridicule provided no immunity to doubt. By December uncertainty infected his dispatches to the home secretary. Admitting that there could be no "permanent repose" in Ireland so long as demagogues were "suffered to inflame the minds" of the lower orders, he insisted that misgivings as to the adequacy of the law were the reason for his continued restraint. Yet he volunteered the information that the Irish lord chancellor and the attorney and solicitor general were as one in the legal opinion that the Catholic Board was liable to suppression under the terms of the Convention Act. Indeed, at a meeting on 28 December the viceroy and his principal advisers, although still by no means united on the wisdom of striking at the board, agreed to take the essential preliminary step of accumulating evidence of its proceedings.[21] These reports gave the home secretary the opening to press for decisive action.

For advice on Ireland, Sidmouth turned from time to time to the man he had sent there as lord chancellor a decade earlier. Redesdale was still preaching the word of Irish exceptionalism. "Falsehood and fraud are the marked features of the Irish character," he asserted. "Sincerity is rarely to be met with in an Irishman or woman." Warning that emancipation was no more than a stalking horse for separation from Britain and the creation of an Irish republic, he urged the government publicly to sustain the Protestant loyalists lest in the absence of such encouragement they emigrate. In much the same spirit Sidmouth applauded Peel's rebuff in October of a peace overture from Denys Scully, a leading figure on the Catholic Board and an intimate of O'Connell. "Any attempt, at any time, or under any Circumstances to conciliate a discontented Party by concession, is, I am confident, unwise," the home secretary declared. Then, early in the new year, he made plain his growing impatience with the Irish government's policy of "forbearance."[22]

Challenged, Whitworth composed a detailed defence of his conduct. He denied the existence of a direct "connection between the Board and the disturbed parts of the country," attributing local disorders to local causes of long standing. He emphasized the "turbulent spirit natural to this people" and the mischief produced by the publication in the press of the "inflammatory harangues" of the O'Connells and the Scullys. Nevertheless, he held fast to the opinion that the benefits of such verbal extremism – its alienation of moderate Catholic opinion – continued to outweigh the harm, and resorted yet again to the excuse that the government doubted its ability to launch an effective attack under the present law.[23] While paying lip service in his reply to a respect for the judgment of those on the spot, Sidmouth's mind had clearly not been altered by the viceroy's explanations. The "Existence, Proceedings, and Publications of the Catholic Board must be admitted to be a scandal, and a nuisance, and the late measures of levying a Tax upon the Catholic Population of Ireland, is of a tendency the most dangerous," he observed. He affected surprise over Whitworth's lingering "uncertainty" with respect to the reach of the law, having "previously supposed that the opinion of the Attorney and Solicitor General had removed all doubt of the sufficiency of your Powers under the Convention Act." His understanding had been that the only points to be decided were "where and under what circumstances" those powers were to be employed. However, he agreed that all uncertainty should be removed by Parliament.[24]

Sidmouth's unrelenting pressure, together with the demands of the Irish grand juries for the Catholic Board's suppression, eventually prompted the Irish government to seek an amendment of the Convention Act. In abandoning the policy of "forbearance" Peel appears also to have been influenced by the reports of the secret committees of the Irish Parliament on the United Irishmen. Led to them by his consuming passion for information and knowledge, he was struck by the "strong resemblance" between both the behaviour of the United Irishmen and that of the board and "the general disposition of the lower orders at that time & the present." Likening the board's ostensible aims of emancipation and reform to those avowed by the earlier society, he found other sinister parallels in its "inflaming" of popular opinion, its resort to the "most wicked and licentious abuse of the Press," and its frustration of "the administration of justice." From all of this he drew the conclusions that prevention was better than punishment and that it was "highly expedient" to put and end to all bodies "which whether delegated or not, or assuming to be representative or not, still professing to be of a permanent nature are inconsistent with the existence of a regular Government."[25]

There remained for Peel the problem of defending Irish policy in the Commons. How was he to answer interrogators who questioned the government's long delay in giving effect "to the wishes, so strongly expressed [in the resolutions of grand juries], of the loyal and suffering part of the Community?" An amendment of the Convention Act would permit him to finesse this potential embarrassment with the claim that the government required additional powers before it could strike down the board.[26] Hence his dismay when the English solicitor general offered the opinion that fresh legislation was both unnecessary and unwise, and in the form the Irish executive proposed constitutionally repugnant. This judgment promised to weigh heavily even with that zealot for firmness, Sidmouth. But it was the indecisiveness of the cabinet which most frustrated and worried the chief secretary. He feared that questions would be asked in the House before a policy decision had been made. "To tell you the truth," he reported to Whitworth towards the end of April 1814, "I am almost tired of speaking to Lord Liverpool & Lord Sidmouth on the subject." Clearly, the prime minister was "rather inclined to remain passive," being "always an advocate for not provoking discussion if it can possibly be avoided." On 7 May Peel was informed by Liverpool and Sidmouth that the government would not sanction an application to Parliament for amendment of the Convention Act. This decision left him with but one line of defence in the Commons – Ireland's "peculiar" circumstances. They would have to be pressed into service as the explanation of the Irish government's long toleration of the illegal activities of the Catholic Board.[27]

In refusing to sanction fresh legislation to deal with the board, Liverpool had not disguised his doubts as to the wisdom of any action at all. He was clinging to the hope that the defeat of Napoleonic France would discourage Irish agitation. This was not a belief either Whitworth or Peel continued to harbour. The "leaders of faction" would surely find "sufficient inducements to persevere in the agitating system," no matter what developments occurred on the Continent, they reasoned. So on 10 May the decision was finally taken in Dublin to suppress the board. Yet it was far from unanimous. During three hours of debate Gregory and Bushe advanced the argument that, if left to itself, the board would "sink quietly into a ditch," while Saurin now spoke powerfully for suppression. It was a stunning reversal of positions. Against this background of uncertainty and confusion, the news of the prime minister's misgivings took an immediate toll of the executive's confidence. The viceroy's principal advisers – he was absent with a cold – "unanimously" decided that it would be unwise to attempt to dissolve the board without the positive sanction of the British government. The chief secretary hurriedly reassured Whitworth that Liverpool "readily admits that the Irish Government are the best judges of the policy of the line of conduct to be pursued by them." In fact, Peel had already overcome the prime minister's reluctance by stressing the danger of parliamentary embarrassment. How would they respond, he asked archly, if, having discouraged the Irish administration from seeking to suppress the board, an MP called for the tabling both of the opinion of the Irish executive on its legality and of the resolutions of the grand juries? Not that the prime minister's endorsement of suppression ended the "hesitations" in Dublin.[28]

Whitworth and his advisers drafted a proclamation which included an "explanatory" paragraph justifying the long policy of forbearance. For a few days Peel resisted "an Apologetical Proclamation," but no sooner had he conceded the point to an adamant viceroy than the "leaders of faction" ceased to be cooperative. Indeed, there was an element of farce in the administration's growing suspicion that the Catholic Board had got wind of what was in the offing and had decided to cease assembling. In fact the board had suspended meetings until the Catholic bishops issued a formal response to a papal rescript, signed by Monsignor Quarantotti, the vice-prefect of propaganda, which endorsed the terms offered to Catholics in the recent relief bill, hedged as they had been with "securities." On 27 May the bishops announced that the rescript was not mandatory. Eight days later the dissolution of the board was proclaimed. Ironically, the Irish government's abandonment of forbearance after so long a trial passed without the serious parliamentary inquiry Peel had long feared. It was left to the *Dublin Evening Herald* to note the paradox. Tolerated throughout a period when its meetings had been marked by violent harangues, the board had been suppressed at a time of "moderation" in its language. "On the anniversary of the King – on the day when the peace of Europe was proclaimed," the newspaper sardonically observed, "it must seem to the people peculiarly ungracious to adopt a strong and questionable measure in reference to a body of men, which the correspondence of great men and long acquiescence of government had encouraged them to regard as a legal assembly."[29]

Peel hailed the "new era" in Irish policy. While the government had been acting "on the forbearing system" it had been "perfectly wise" to forbear "thoroughly," he mused in a private letter to the viceroy. Having adopted the "interfering system," they must now interfere "effectually." Those who violated the proclamation "should be treated with no more respect or ceremony than any other disturbers of the public peace." The Catholic Board ought to be considered as no more than "a meeting of 15 or 20 factious and seditious people," and should not be identified with the Catholics or accorded respect simply "because they profess to act for the Catholics." The lord lieutenant was in full agreement with his chief secretary and planned to make another request to Britain for additional powers in the event that the "august assembly" successfully evaded the present law. "If they were to evade us by artifice, it would be little less prejudicial to the Interests of good Government than if they were to overcome us by force," he remarked. Although a defiant O'Connell promptly summoned an "aggregate" meeting, and Gregory's most trusted informant reported a few days later the formation of an association with O'Connell acting as its secretary, the government paid little public heed. Catholics were reportedly divided over the wisdom of this response and a subscription of five guineas suggested that the new association would attract few members. One of those instructed to join was Gregory's informant.[30]

That the proclamation of suppression bore the date of the monarch's birthday, and arrived in London on the eve of an attempt by an Irish peer to reopen the Catholic question, Peel regarded as providential. Less fortunate was its appearance shortly after a sectarian affray in Shercock, County Cavan. Gregory quickly reassured Peel that Catholics had been the instigators as well as the principal victims of the bloody incident, but the conflict had opened with an attack on the house of a prominent Orangeman and the "Orange Party" was widely suspected of having frequently given "the original provocation." In the Commons, opponents of the Irish government's policies, who had withheld criticism of the action against the Catholic Board, now raised the cry of partiality. Why, they asked, had the executive left untouched the Orange associations?[31]

Both Peel and Gregory had long given thought to the problem. The proposal of a well-intentioned but politically naive military officer that the government ban in the name of public order all ceremonial pageantry at certain times of the year – for much of the violence was excited by triumphant Protestant celebrations of past victories – excited only an amused response. "To cure the distractions of Ireland by a public order," Peel remarked. "Why not order uniformity of religion by a circular from the Royal Hospital [the headquarters of the commander of the forces in Ireland]?" Neither he nor Gregory were able to distinguish between the Protestant commemorations and the gatherings of large numbers of Catholics, often in a remarkably well regimented way, for funerals and on saints' days. Furthermore, they were unsure of their legal authority to intervene and doubted the political wisdom of interference. Would they further inflame Protestants against Catholics and alienate the former from the government? If so, "the Government would lose a steady friend and the Catholics find a bitterer enemy." Nor was the chief secretary unaware of the prime minister's sympathetic interest in organizations that "had for their object the maintenance of the Protestant Establishment in Church and State."[32]

The complexity of the problem did not lessen the more deeply Peel examined it. He acknowledged the necessity to discourage behaviour that was intended "to irritate and insult others," or gave "*just* cause" for complaint, but accepted that "very ordinary & very inoffensive exhibitions of loyalty will give cause of offence in Ireland." In those instances the fault rested "with those who take offence." Nevertheless, he reissued in June of 1814 the instructions which had been dispatched the previous year to all northern brigade majors of the protestant yeomanry. They were to avoid provocative demonstrations and uniformed yeomen, including bandsmen, were not to participate in Orange processions. Yet Peel had no wish under existing circumstances to see the sectarian differences which divided the Irish lower orders entirely extinguished. Satisfied that the Protestants were "very loyal and the same class of Catholics to be very much the reverse," he preferred to foster the former's cultural consciousness so long as the latter continued to give grounds for suspicion. The "great art" was to maintain the divisions while preserving the peace, or at least keeping the two sides from going to war with each other. Further complicating Peel's response to the Orangemen, however, was his distrust of any political association with a military paraphernalia which was controlled by an authority other than the government. In Ireland, the toleration of such an institution promised to be peculiarly dangerous. Would a society "constituted in the same way" but organized to secure the repeal of the union be equally legitimate in the eye of the law? Suppressing his misgivings, he rallied to the defence of the Orangemen. Gregory had forwarded the information that they had abolished secret oaths, retaining only a secret recognition sign or word much like Masons, and Peel employed it to good effect in the House. He and the under-secretary were agreed that he ought to repudiate any comparison of the Orangemen and the "Ribbonmen," for the former were "truly loyal." He had to resist an inquiry into both, since such an investigation would imply "that they were equally dangerous."[33]

Throughout the deliberations concerning the Catholic Board, Whitworth and Peel had pointed accusing fingers at the popular press. A home secretary impatient for decisive action had been advised that unless the executive possessed powers "to control the licentiousness of the Press, the same mischief might, and would be effected, altho' it came no longer from the Catholic Board." The conviction, which viceroy and chief secretary shared, that the "factious prints" were a prime source of many of the government's difficulties, ensured that the curbing of the press would form an integral part of their Irish policy. Nor did they lack precedents. An exaggerated belief in the power of the press, and an excessive fear of its subversive potential, had prompted a series of extraordinary measures in Britain during the prolonged emergency of the French wars. Unable to resort to outright censorship in a nation boastful of its free press, successive governments had sought to intimidate critics and purchase friends. Heavy taxes guaranteed that all newspapers were expensive, while amendements to the law facilitated prosecutions for seditious libel and eased the task of securing convictions. Meanwhile, friendly newspapers and their publishers were secretly subsidized and favoured with the advance news of military and diplomatic developments which helped to boost their circulation.[34]

The rudiments of a similar policy of press management had existed in Ireland since 1784, but it was not until Camden's tension-filled lord lieutenancy that a systematic campaign was launched against those newspapers the administration perceived as enemies. With the outbreak of the rebellion, failure to support the government brought suppression. A decade later Wellesley-Pole relaxed the government's grip, and a critical press quickly reemerged, only for the chief secretary to resort to the traditional methods of control – increased taxation in the form of higher stamp duties and the prosecution of publishers.[35]

Initially, Robert Peel appeared to be content to follow in his predecessor's footsteps. The stamp duty was raised again and a prosecution launched. John Magee, the publisher of the *Evening Post*, was charged with seditious libel for printing an attack on the duke of Richmond. But the new chief secretary's unrelenting pursuit of Magee, who was subsequently indicted on two additional charges of seditious libel, was inspired by something other than the *Evening Post*'s enormous popularity and thus unusual capacity for mischief. What made it such a tempting target was the newspaper's close identification with the Catholic Board in general and Daniel O'Connell in particular. "All the influence they have is through the press," Peel believed.

It inflated a score of agitators into a "most numerous and respectable" body. Their speeches, he charged, were moulded by reporters "into sense and English." Consequently, even during that long period when the government refrained from direct action against the board, it had waged war on the press allies of the "leaders of faction." Indeed, in prosecutions of newspaper editors for publishing the speeches of O'Connell and his associates, Peel saw the wedge which would divide the leading agitators from their publicists. By prosecuting Magee the government expected either to oblige the speakers his newspaper had quoted to avow their remarks and thus expose themselves, or induce them "to leave to the press the punishment of their delinquency." They chose the latter course. In the words of the solicitor general, "they entered into a partnership with Magee, but left the gaol part of the concern exclusively to him." In this sense Peel's policy proved to be highly successful.[36]

O'Connell defended Magee in court, but scarcely in a manner consistent with his client's interests. Indeed, when the *Evening Post* published his speech for the defence, the attorney general sought an aggravation of the unfortunate publisher's punishment of fine and imprisonment. Nor was Magee assisted by O'Connell's vitriolic reply to Saurin at this second hearing. Pride, vanity, and perhaps sensitivity, for the figure he cut was less than heroic, excited an outburst which brought a reprimand from his uncle and benefactor for language "unbecoming the calm and intelligent barrister or the judicious and well-bred gentleman" and liable to expose him "to the reprehension, if not to the resentment, of the court." Angered by O'Connell's conduct, Magee and his brother soon broke with him and opened peace negotiations with the Castle which eventually saw the *Evening Post* accorded the privilege of a government organ. Others were to follow suit.[37]

The damage which Peel had inflicted on the Catholic cause was not limited to the alienation of those publishers and editors so cavalierly "sacrificed" by O'Connell. Disillusioned liberal Protestants also defected, some moving into the "orange camp." Other consequences were of more dubious value to the government. O'Connell's behaviour heightened Peel's contempt for him, a particularly dangerous sentiment given the ability and pride of the adversary. More ominous still was the strengthening popular conviction, which Peel discerned but dismissed as "absurd," that the prosecutions of such individuals as Magee demonstrated "the hostility of the Government to the Catholic Body at large."[38]

While with one hand the Irish government punished the press allies of its opponents, with the other it sought to manufacture friends. The tools at the disposal of the Irish executive were much the same as those employed by the British government. There were two secret service accounts – expenditures charged to the Civil List were limited to £5,000 a year but there was no ceiling to the monies devoted to the detection of treasonable conspiracies

– and additional subsidies were financed by the Proclamation Fund of £10,500 which Parliament voted annually. Moreover, the Castle could boost the circulation of friendly organs by giving them preferential access to the latest war news, by ordering government offices to subscribe, and by providing on occasion free distribution.[39]

On taking office Peel inherited a number of newspaper allies, or clients, but few could boast significant circulations, and all were excoriated in the more popular press. "The hireling Journals have got a general licence for all slander that is not directed against their masters," the *Evening Herald* charged, "and while every honest print that disdains the bribery of the Incapables is persecuted and goaded beyond the limit of human endurance, the licensed slanderer walks abroad in security and affluence." Peel resolved to put the press on a "better footing," and soon complained to Sidmouth that four-fifths on the sum nominally available as secret service charges on the Civil List was already earmarked for pensions. He exaggerated. An astonishing variety of expenses were paid out of this fund – the cost of renting boxes at the Theatre Royal on royal anniversaries; the payments to Dr Parkinson for his ceremonial odes; the small but regular payments in lieu of a pension to the housekeeper of Gregory's predecessor; even the Christmas gratuities to members of the Castle staff. Nevertheless, of the £4,500 expended in 1813 and 1814, and the amount rose to £5,600 in 1815, only in the first of these years did subsidies to the press fail to exceed one-half of the total. The *Dublin Journal*, the *Correspondent*, the *Patriot*, the *Belfast Newsletter*, the *Cork Advertiser*, the *Londonderry Journal*, the *Clonmel Herald*, and their several publishers, annually received payments which ranged from £100 to £500.[40]

Another lucrative mark of government favour were the payments ostensibly made for the publication of proclamations. The sums involved were often substantial. In 1813 the *Dublin Journal* and the *Patriot* were earning £800 a year in this way, while £500 went to the *Hibernian Journal*. The two owners of the *Hibernian* also occupied government places. Other newspapers, such as *Saunders's Newsletter* and the *Correspondent*, benefited on a smaller scale. Not surprisingly, the uses to which the proclamation fund was put attracted Opposition criticism in the Commons. Accusations that favoured newspapers received payment for proclamations they had not published, and charged the government for the publication of many that were several years old – Peel himself had noted in the *Patriot* a proclamation dated four years earlier – provided plenty of grist for the critics' mills. Apprehensively, Peel turned to Gregory for information on the procedures and for arguments he might employ to fend off attacks. The under-secretary assured him that the publication of proclamations was closely supervised, and that the printing of long outdated ones was simply a device of newspapers to fill space and did not involve a charge on the government. As for the

Opposition, he informed Peel that the Talents had spent a great deal more than £10,500 during their brief tenure. In the House, the chief secretary effectively silenced the Whigs with the reminder that their friends had spent as much as £18,000 a year. Fortunately, they failed to exploit a serious weakness in his defence – the fact that a number of departments, such as Ordnance and the Barracks, placed advertisements which were paid out of their own accounts. In short, the actual subsidies to the press in the form of government notices and advertisements exceeded £10,500 a year. Peel wearily admitted to Gregory that they had a very bad case to defend, but must do the best they could.[41]

In their use of these monies Peel and his able assistant Gregory were quite ruthless. When one of the publishers of the *Patriot* indulged his liberal views on the religious question, and printed "a long Eulogium" on a parliamentary supporter of emancipation, the newspaper was required as punishment to pay two guineas a week for the foreign intelligence provided by the government. But mindful of the miniscule circulation of the Castle newspapers Peel abandoned the practice of limiting this intelligence to them and often published it immediately in an *Extraordinary Gazette*. "I am sure the expediency of giving all the publicity possible to good news in Ireland far outweighs every other consideration," he observed to Gregory. Other recipients of government largesse paid an even higher price for acts of independence. Support of Opposition candidates in the election of 1812 cost George Grace of the *Clonmel Herald* his secret subsidy and then the proclamations. Indeed, 1813 saw the proclamations also withdrawm from the *Waterford Mirror*, *Wexford Journal*, and the *Southern Reporter*. What Peel secured in return was the support of a despised corps of "hirelings" who were often the cause of acute embarrassment. The crudity of their anti-Catholic campaigns, the vulgarity of their efforts to discredit opponents of the government, their excessive praise of their paymasters, and their feuding with one another put Peel and Gregory to endless trouble and did nothing to encourage popular acceptance of the executive's policies.[42]

The Irish government not only held the popular press to account for the mischief-making of the Catholic Board, but increasingly held them both responsible for rural disorders. The demagogues and their publicists, the argument went, had by "gross" falsehoods and misrepresentations" excited the lower orders to violence. This represented a significant change of position by the lord lieutenant, who had earlier denied the existence of any direct connection. One sure measure of the spread of disturbances throughout the country, and of the deepening unease at the Castle, was the sharp increase in secret service expenditures to detect treasonable conspiracies. Payments to policemen to cover their expenses, to informers, to men who had defended their property from attack, to the families of the victims of assassination, all multiplied in 1813. That year saw William Gregory account for £9,453.

In 1814 the amount exceeded £12,200.[43]

Serious disturbances had been reported from that perennial trouble-spot, Tipperary, in January of 1813. Already Peel had learned the lesson that local gentlemen were prone to exaggerate the peril to the state, though his criticism of them was tempered by sympathy for persons who "suffering from the excesses in the rebellion of 1798 are apt to view present dangers through a distorted medium." Nevertheless, he found no part of his official duties more "irksome" than the difficulty of reconciling contradictory reports and discovering "the real truth." By early spring he was in no doubt that several counties were disturbed, and while the list of disorders shortened as the days lengthened, individual acts of great savagery served both to alarm and to intimidate. An audacious attempt to assassinate a farmer who had defended his property and killed three of the attackers – the retaliatory assault took place outside his chapel on Palm Sunday – and the refusal of anyone to go to his aid or to give information to the authorities led Gregory to bemoan the "melancholy" condition of Irish society. Peel was moved to sarcasm on the state of Irish civilization. Later that year there was a second especially horrifying incident. An informant, named Connell, was taken from his home and brutally beaten until his body was almost flat. His corpse was then thrown onto a dunghill with a pitchfork through the heart. Not content, the enforcers of rough justice then turned on the man's wife. They reportedly left her dumb and blind. Such individual acts of barbarism were soon submerged in another tidal wave of disturbances as winter came on, and it proved to be a season of unusual severity. A hard frost which began on Boxing Day was followed early in the new year by heavy falls of snow. The weather conditions reminded Whitworth all too vividly of his years in Russia, while the oath-taking and disturbances in the countryside brought to some Irish minds memories of 1798. Gregory, for one, concluded that another attempt at a rising would be made even though the "rebels" knew they could not expect any foreign aid. The news from Europe was of a succession of French defeats. Indeed, the under-secretary puzzled over this seeming contradiction of the "common speculation on popular insurrection." How was the increased activity and audacity of the "malcontents," at a time when their hopes of success were diminishing, to be explained?[44]

The fact that the disturbances defied simple analysis heightened the sense of frustration within the Irish government. Throughout 1813 the executive struggled to comprehend what was happening in Ireland, and why. The Catholic press and the Catholic Board were still identified as villains. Several instances of a sectarianism which took the form of Catholics being discouraged from treating with Protestants excited additional suspicion of Catholic priests, but too many of them were seeking to restrain their parishioners to justify a general indictment. In several counties the sectarian clashes were attributed to Protestant provocations or a Catholic perception of partial justice administered by a Protestant gentry. Elsewhere, in Tipperary, Waterford, Westmeath, Roscommon, Kilkenny, the roots of the disturbances appeared to lie in the land. Many of the marauders bound together by secret oaths, whether Carders, Threshers, or Caravats, were evidently striving to regulate the price of land, especially the price of that in conacre, and to prevent tenants from being turned out or to dissuade others from taking their place whenever they were.[45]

Evidence that those involved in the disturbances lacked political aims and "respectable" leadership was welcomed by the government, but failed to allay all fears. Whitworth perceived among the lower orders such a deep and "rancorous hatred of Government, and such an open Defiance of Law, as [would] require all its Vigilance and Exertion to counteract." The disorders had revealed, he believed, an anarchic disposition "to attempt by force and intimidation" the redress of what the peasantry considered to be their grievances. No less worrisome, "the utmost alarm" had been excited among "the peaceable and well disposed" for the safety of their persons and property. Another concern, especially in the light of the success of the "banditti" in seizing arms from country houses and from yeomen, was the prospect of them becoming "engines which the designing and disaffected can readily employ in the furtherance of their political views" when some better opportunity presented itself. And when in November 1813 the frightened and beleaguered magistrates in County Westmeath urged the government to rearm itself and them with the extraordinary powers of curfew, suspension of trial by jury, and severe punishment of the convicted, they instigated a debate within the administration which resulted in an important policy decision.[46]

William Gregory sided with the magistrates. He recognized the geographically restricted nature of the unrest and the likelihood that any rising would be both localized and brief, but feared the loss of many "valuable" lives. The death of "one loyal Gentleman is poorly expiated by the blood of an Hecatomb of Rebels," he intoned. Beyond this, he claimed that those who knew Ireland best "must be satisfied of the necessity of always leaving in the hands of the executive a strong & efficient power to be called out when urgency & discretion requires." The argument was weakened by Gregory's inability to carry Saurin and Bushe with him. However, it was Peel who defined the policy the government now adopted.[47]

The chief secretary opposed a resort to the Insurrection Act which was what the Westmeath magistrates were urging. His resistance hinged in part on parliamentary strategy. The fact that in 1810 his predecessor had insisted on repealing the act only two months before it was due to expire, made the task of renewing it now that much more embarrassing. How would the Commons react to a proposal for renewal in the wake of the sweeping victories over the French, he wondered, when members recalled that repeal had taken place at a time of French triumphs? The Opposition would be quick to charge that Ireland must have been governed "very badly" in the interim. Loud would be the complaints against the sudden introduction of such an important measure at so late a period in the session, when many Irish members had already returned home. Would it not reflect poorly on Whitworth's viceroyalty if he applied for extraordinary powers within three months of setting foot in Ireland? Moreover, the Insurrection Act would do little "to conciliate the animosities" in the North or "to suppress the factious Demagogues" of the Catholic Board. Peel also questioned the necessity of the measure. Serious disturbances were confined to four counties, and only to parts of them, he pointed out. In short, he had no compunction about resorting to extraordinary measures whenever they were "imperiously called for by an extraordinary state of things," but was fully alive to the danger of doing so too readily. To get into the habit of suspending the constitution was to weaken "the effect of such suspension at those times when it becomes absolutely necessary." The chief secretary appears to have been anxious to prove his political mettle. "There is more boldness too in undertaking to carry on a Government with the ordinary powers of it, than in requiring to be entrusted with those which are extraordinary," he counselled Whitworth. He recommended that they continue as they were until the spring. Gregory quickly knocked under to Peel's arguments, while the viceroy, in reporting to Sidmouth his resolve to continue to govern Ireland without extraordinary powers, at least for several months, shamelessly plagiarized his chief secretary's arguments and language.[48]

In the front line of the struggle to enforce the laws and maintain order were the resident gentry and gentlemen. The British tradition was simply stated by Gregory. Local magistrates were "the properest authorities for putting down local disturbances." Nor did he believe that either "intimidation or unjust aspersion of partiality" should deter men from stepping forward to discharge their public duty. In an effort to assist them, the government offered substantial rewards for information. The Irish firearms bill, which had been renewed in May 1813, empowered them to search for and seize concealed weapons. Under the provisions of the Riot and Whiteboy Acts any lawbreaker who refused to surrender to a magistrate who had identified himself was fair game and magistrates might fire without warning at any person discovered committing a felony. It was the government's hope that the energetic utilization of these powers, backed by a bench determined to make severe examples of those arrested and convicted at the Assizes, would quieten the disturbed areas. But the ordinary process of the law was all too easily and successfully frustrated by the intimidation of informants, witnesses, and even magistrates. This in turn excited fresh charges of a supine magistracy. Whenever "Field Marshal Funck commands," Gregory observed, "the Enemy is certain of appearing formidable." Not that he was without sympathy for gentlemen personally confronting "the system of Terror" or believed that the powers granted to them under the Whiteboy Acts were adequate. To his mind, magistrates must be armed with the power to make "domiciliary visits" if those suspected of involvement in the disorders were to be kept at home.[49]

Behind the magistracy stood the military. In the absence of an effective police force, it had customarily been pressed into service to quell disturbances. The Irish government must depend upon "a vigorous exertion of our present powers and upon the cooperation of the Military force for the means of counteracting the spirit of outrage and disaffection which prevails," Whitworth reminded Sidmouth early in 1814. Similarly, Peel's proposal that they persevere with the effort to maintain order "by the common course of law" had been founded on an assurance of an ample supply of militiamen.[50]

The Irish military establishment had been reduced during 1813, in response to the demands of the several war theatres, and before the end of the year a bill was in preparation to permit "the Militia to volunteer their services & to act with the Line." Under pressure from Peel and Whitworth the British government agreed to make good any losses due to volunteering, and to add 3,000 men to Ireland's garrison. Nevertheless, the slow pace of the reinforcement and the extent of the volunteering threatened to effect a substantial reduction of the establishment. In the face of the insistent demands of the Irish executive, and by improvising in England, the army and the government scraped together the men promised earlier. At the same time, Sidmouth gave voice to the unease in British military and political circles at the way in which troops were employed in Ireland. Their division into small detachments to police the countryside was regarded as injurious to discipline. Another complaint was that the inhabitants of Ireland were being taught "to trust entirely to Military Aid, instead of placing their chief reliance on the Vigilance and Activity of Magistrates" and on their own prudence and exertions. Yet, as Peel had patiently explained, the troops were needed in Ireland to act as policemen.[51]

With the war in Europe at last drawing to a conclusion in the late spring of 1814, or so it seemed, viceroy and chief secretary were quick to call for the exception of Ireland from any reduction of the military establishment. Before the end of March Whitworth was complaining that, even after the long promised militiamen arrived, the force on hand would be smaller than when he had called for reinforcements in 1813. Two months later, Peel protested vigorously when he heard that a plan was afoot to set the Irish peacetime establishment at between 28,000 and 30,000 men. After all, the reports from across Ireland were alarming. The "lowest banditti" appeared to be in "full & undisturbed possession" of Queen's County and Kilkenny. Anarchy and confusion allegedly reigned in Tyrone and Donegal, where revenue officers and constables had been attacked in their homes and tithe collectors kidnapped and their houses demolished. There were also disturbances in Westmeath, Roscommon, Longford, and King's County, while in County Down a sectarian conflict had assumed the character of a pitched battle. No less dismaying was the evidence of "some dreadful apathy and Panic amongst the Gentry." The restoration of peace in Europe would have little impact upon such local and sectarian disorders, Peel observed. Moreover, to disband the Irish militia threatened merely to lengthen the Irish government's already daunting list of problems. Men who had made good soldiers when controlled by strict discipline might make bad citizens. On returning to their villages they would be pressed to place their military skills at the disposal "of their turbulent and disaffected neighbours."[52]

The executive summoned Sir George Hewitt, the military commander, to its aid. He agreed that a nominal establishment of 40,000 was required in Ireland and submitted a recommendation to that effect to army headquarters at the Horse Guards. Then, in June, the viceroy sent off to the Home Office an official dispatch, drafted by Gregory, which painted a suitably bleak portrait of Ireland. Its thrust was clear – that to repress the disaffected and "give confidence to the well disposed a larger military establishment must be maintained in Ireland than was thought necessary during the latter stages of the war." Furthermore, the Irish militia should be disbanded only gradually. Indeed, the dispatch called for the suspension of disbandments in or withdrawals from Ireland until regulars were available "to supply the deficiency." Whitworth also gave notice of his intention to make use of the Yeomanry Corps. Sidmouth responded encouragingly, informing the viceroy that he had forwarded the dispatch to the Horse Guards and had always succeeded in the past "in impressing on the mind of the Commander in Chief the necessity of adopting" the lord lieutenant's suggestions. Subsequently, he offered the somewhat more ambiguous assurance that Whitworth would have the military force the state of Ireland required. By that time Ireland had undergone such a transformation that the Irish executive took the news calmly.[53]

In April Whitworth and Gregory had been united in favouring renewal of the Insurrection Act, the viceroy now echoing the under-secretary's opinion that it ought never to have been repealed. But Peel continued to demur. He urged a further delay, at least until the effects of Napoleon's defeat and the severe punishments handed down at the Assizes could be assessed. In the meantime, the executive concentrated on securing the establishment of "an active and numerous Police" to cooperate with "a strong, efficient military Force" in the battle to restore and maintain order. Confronted by the traditional resistance to the creation of a formidable body of civilian guardians of law and order, which had been strengthened by distaste for the French gendarmerie, Whitworth emphasized Ireland's peculiarity. "The great object is not to lose sight of the Distinction to be made between England and this part of His Majesty's Dominions," he argued. Ireland was not to be governed in the same fashion as England. "The Character and Spirit of the governed are completely different," he reminded the cabinet. "It is only by a protecting force that the magistrates can be encouraged to do their Duty, and by an imposing one that the lower orders can be kept down." Indeed, meeting the opposition to a gendarmerie head on, and speaking with the authority of a former diplomat who possessed considerable knowledge of France, he likened the lower orders of Ireland to those across the English Channel. A resemblance so striking, he remarked, "must convince the common observer that good order is only to be obtained by the same means in both countries."[54]

Peel had long given thought to a reorganization of the Irish police which would lessen the government's dependence on the military for policing. He had alluded to the need for reform during the debate on the renewal of the firearms bill in May 1813, and had decided against a simultaneous renewal of the Counties Police Act because the entire system required revision. By February 1814 he had several proposals in mind. The lord lieutenant ought to be empowered to proclaim any district in a state of disturbance, and on the recommendation of a number of magistrates appoint any number of well-paid and thus more highly motivated special constables. The combination of flexibility and motivation promised to produce an effective police force. The viceroy should also possess the power to appoint a special stipendiary magistrate in the disturbed district. The expenses would be charged to the residents. This was the plan Peel carried in the spring to London, where crime on the Thames and the highways had already resulted in the formation of the river police and the horse patrol, and where stipendiaries had been operating successfully for a generation. It won the reluctant endorsement of such traditionalists as Liverpool and Castlereagh. Almost on the eve of its presentation to Parliament, however, Peel was tempted to respond to the continuing disorders in Ireland with a hybrid measure which would have added to these provisions some of the useful but transitory powers granted under the Insurrection Act – the ability to impose a curfew enforced by the right of magistrates to make domiciliary visits. Saurin counselled against this expedient, and on reflection Peel saw the parliamentary advantage in not entangling his new bill with the old act. "The truth is that by proposing this measure first, and getting so unanimous a concurrence in it," he reported to Whitworth after the successful introduction of the police bill, "I conceive the temporary reenactment of the Insurrection Act will be much facilitated should it be necessary."[55]

In the Commons Peel dwelt upon Ireland's unique problems. He made telling use of the accounts Gregory had forwarded of the savagery of the Carders, and described in some detail the torture of the informant Connell and his unfortunate wife, all of which produced the desired effect "upon the minds of the English country gentlemen" sitting in the chamber. He explained the peculiar obstacles to the "ordinary administration of the law" and the insufficiency of the "ordinary powers of the civil magistrates." Since the state of Ireland was so "essentially different" from that of England special measures were essential, he argued. So skilful and convincing was this presentation that two of the leading Irish spokesmen for the Opposition, Newport and Grattan, hailed the Peace Preservation Act for its "mildness." Then, on 1 July, Peel gave notice of the Irish assaults bill, which he justified as an attempt to persuade the victims of violent assault to appeal to the law for relief and protection "by enabling them to procure it more immediately, and without expence." Anyway, it was not unlike the measures long since adopted in England. Judges were to be empowered "to allow a compensation for expences to prosecutors," while the charging of the costs to the convicted offender "would be an additional security against the commission of the offence." Newport seconded the motion. One week later Peel moved the renewal of the Insurrection Act.[56]

Informed that Parliament was unlikely to meet again before the New Year, and fearing that the "bad disposition" of the lower orders would grow worse as the nights lengthened, Peel had sought cabinet sanction for the arming of the Irish executive with additional powers. He quickly discovered that the prime minister was "strongly inclined to do nothing," while the foreign secretary protested that any fostering of the impression that Ireland was "in a state of great agitation & disturbance" would have a "bad effect" upon Britain's bargaining position at the peace negotiations in Europe. This was not a concern which impressed the former ambassador now at the head of the Irish government. "I never yet met with any Minister at a Foreign Court who knew more of England than Japan," he observed to Peel. "We are considered as a distinct species, & the most extraordinary occurrences relating to us are considered as matters of course." Nevertheless, Castlereagh's objections prevented Peel from following his preferred course of action. He had hoped to secure a secret committee to examine the reports from Ireland and recommend renewal of the Insurrection Act. Instead, Liverpool invited him to go down to the House and seek renewal with whatever evidence he had at hand. In the event, the measure passed more easily than he had foreseen. On the decisive second reading only the legal reformer Sir Samuel Romilly, together with another prominent member and "a host of enlightened and philosophic Scotch lawyers," voiced opposition to the suspension of trial by jury. Significantly, "the Irish representatives with one single exception, Sir H. Parnell, seem[ed] to be of a different opinion."[57]

"If strong laws to repress the disaffected; every possible encouragement afforded to those who are in need of it; and a strict and impartial administration of justice, are not sufficient," Whitworth commented in mid-July,

"I am at a loss to devise how this country is to be governed." One month later he reported to Sidmouth that Ireland was "in point of Tranquillity in a state of amendment." He did regret that his plan "to try the effect of rigid severity towards offenders against the public peace, before we have recourse to the new powers with which the legislature has entrusted us," was impeded by judges who attached recommendations for mercy to capital sentences. His ruthlessness was also checked by William Gregory. A conservative who believed in the merits of exemplary punishment and deplored the fact that there was in Ireland "no crime so heinous but meets whith Advocates anxious to divert the Justice of Law," Gregory nevertheless strove to temper severity with humanity. Thus he urged transportation instead of execution for a youth of seventeen convicted of passing forged notes, a crime "which tho' very bad, does not partake of the ferocious atrocity of Burglary, or highway Robbery." He called for closer supervision of the practice of respiting, under which a man might postpone execution by offering information. Gregory considered inhumane the cruel "hopes, not promised, but insinuated" by unscrupulous officials, that if the doomed man's "Discoveries" proved to be true his life would be spared.[58]

"Since I have had any connection with this country I never recollect such a cessation of outrage and disturbance as there has been for the last three months: it might seem presumptuous if I said since the passing of the two Acts of last session," Peel reported to the speaker on the last day of September. Whitworth had ensured that abstracts of both measures were widely disseminated "so that offenders may know that we have the means as well of detecting as of punishing their misdeeds." Only in Tipperary had the new police bill been enforced, and by mid-October the viceroy was able to report to the home secretary that the county's most disturbed barony was at last in a state of "perfect Tranquillity." Indeed, he confidently predicted that peace would soon envelop the entire country as the people realized that good order was the only sure way to escape the costs of the new magistracy and police. As Peel explained to the speaker, "every peasant has his half acre, and thus every peasant has a direct pecuniary interest in keeping his district tranquil, and preventing it from being proclaimed." Likening the new law to that which imposed still fines on entire townlands, he considered it "the most effectual way" of keeping the country tranquil. Not that the more peaceful state of the country diminished the need for a powerful military establishment. Whitworth continued to warn that unless backed by a force which commanded respect "the wisest Institutions & Enactments" would be of no avail in Ireland. However, he did lower to 30,000 his estimate of the number of troops "indispensably necessary" for the maintenance of tranquillity and the protection of the well-disposed.[59]

When Parliament reassembled in November Peel took the opportunity to amend his police bill in a way intended to appease critics who argued that the costs of pacifying a disturbed district fell indiscriminately upon innocent and guilty. Thus he made it clear that there was no need to appoint a separate peace preservation force for adjoining baronies, and the government was given the power to narrow the operation of the law "strictly to the offending spot." But the omission from the throne speech of any mention of Ireland had already excited a belated Opposition attack on Irish policy, and Peel's amendments merely widened the front of the assault. The revelation that there had been little resort to the police bill and none at all to the Insurrection Act led to charges in both Houses that Peel had been duped by alarmists and bigots who sought extraordinary powers in order to administer partisan justice. He was also condemned for giving the lower orders the very "impolitic" impression "that nothing but the strong hand of the law could arrest the influence of their conduct." If Irish magistrates would but do their duty, George Ponsonby declared, and he spoke with the authority of a former leader of the Whig opposition in the Irish Parliament, as well as that of the current leader of the Opposition in the Commons, "the public peace could, in the ordinary way, be preserved without ulterior measures." This criticism of the policy of Irish exceptionalism was occasionally more explicit. Newport had challenged Peel in May 1813 to adduce more proof of the necessity of a firearms bill "which would completely distinguish the people of Ireland from those of England." Sir Frederick Flood had denied during the first reading of the police bill that Wexford was any more lawless than the counties of England and Wales. In the upper house, during the debate on the assaults bill, Lord Holland had remarked "upon the anomaly of applying these kinds of Bills to Ireland alone" and had argued that a full inquiry should precede any application of the principle of Irish exceptionality.[60]

There was an irony in the drawing of this particular parliamentary battle line; namely, the apparent reversal of positions when discussion turned from political to economic issues. Still searching for additional revenue, Vesey Fitzgerald introduced a duty on timber on 23 November 1814, and defended it as a step towards the assimilation of English and Irish duties. The abandonment of distinctly Irish duties was immediately assailed by Newport, who protested this would have the effect of "crushing Ireland." He denounced the timber duty as a peculiar injustice. English farmers had recourse to home-grown timber, but the Irish had to purchase theirs from timber yards and would thus pay this "extravagant duty." In turn, Ponsonby seized this opportunity to trace Ireland's financial problems to the union. He repeated the familiar charge that her contribution had then been set at too high a level. In rallying to Fitzgerald's support, Peel gleefully seized upon Newport's comment that the Irish peasantry were well fed but poorly housed, and Ponsonby's claim that the efforts of Irish landlords to improve the accommodation of their tenants would be discouraged by higher priced timber. The spokesmen for the Opposition had contradicted the oft-repeated assertion, he observed, that "the peasantry of Ireland were in a worse con-dition than English swine" and that Irish landlords "had no interest in the prosperity of their tenantry," and that their sole object was to "extract from the wretched peasant a rent which he cannot afford to pay." Nor was he merely scoring debating points. He had returned from a tour of western Ireland during the summer fully convinced that the Irish lower orders were "much better off in two essential points – food and fuel – than their brethren of the same class in many parts of England." And as a "friend of Ireland" he expressed the wish that the comforts of the peasantry would be increased. Similarly, in conceding that they were "badly lodged," he voiced "every hope that their condition was in this respect improving." In essence, Peel was claiming, as indeed had the prime minister several months earlier, that it was "the customs and disposition" of her people that set Ireland apart.[61]

## CHAPTER FOUR

# Exceptional Distress and Exceptional Measures

The death of the viceroy's stepson in a hunting accident in mid-February 1815 led to a temporary reorganization of the executive. Although Peel was already in London, attending the session of Parliament, a compassionate government granted the lord lieutenant's request for leave to accompany his distraught wife to England. With the Whitworths' departure in mid-March, the formal authority of the viceroy was transferred to three lords justices. The choice of the primate, the chief justice, and the commander of the forces was governed more by anxiety to avoid jealous bickering among the Irish nobility than by confidence in their particular abilities. Indeed, this "three-fold machine" quickly proved to be "a clumsy piece of workmanship." It met regularly enough but always in the late afternoon, by which time of the day two of the triumvirs had spent their energies attending to their "own distinct lines of business" and were in no condition to pay close attention to Edward Littlehales's interminable reports as military under-secretary. [1]

William Gregory emerged as the dominant figure. Patiently and discreetly, he guided the lords justices around a number of administrative pitfalls. When several important prosecutions at Mullingar were thrown into jeopardy by a witness's confession that his testimony had been fabricated, only for Saurin to suggest that the man had been induced to "unsay" his evidence and therefore recommend that the cases be continued, it was the civil under-secretary who halted this march to folly. He persuaded the lords justices that this course would expose the entire judicial system to justifiable criticism. What would be the advantage, he asked, in fostering an impression that the convictions had been obtained only because of paid witnesses and packed juries? But in the final analysis Gregory's dominance depended less on his powers of persuasion than on his command of the flow of information. He maintained a confidential correspondence with Peel of which the lords justices were ignorant. At other times he simply withheld intelligence from them. [2]

The prospect of both viceroy and chief secretary being absent from Ireland had not been a cause of concern in February when Whitworth's leave was granted. Abroad, the French had been defeated and the Americans had signed terms of peace. At home, there was "nothing alarming from the interior" nor any evidence of a revival of Catholic agitation for emancipation. But no sooner had the lord lieutenant departed than word arrived of Napoleon's escape from Elba and his landing in France. In London, Witworth and Peel hurriedly met with Sidmouth at the Home Office. They agreed that the government ought to maintain the military establishment in Ireland at its current level. Viceroy and chief secretary were also in agreement that in the event of a serious outbreak of disorder they would return to Dublin immediately. It was a measure of their confidence in Gregory that neither man hastened back to Ireland.[3]

The under-secretary was fearful that Bonaparte's successes in France would "revive the languid hopes" of Ireland's disaffected. Privately, he admitted that the kingdom was "full of mines" which might explode "in spite of the most vigilant care." The French consul, a Bonapartist, was placed under surveillance and his correspondence intercepted and opened, though Gregory ruefully acknowledged that the Irish were "not as expert in that business as they are in Paris." He ordered increased police vigilance in and around the capital, but instructed the officers to behave discreetly so as not to betray any lack of confidence on the part of the authorities. He studied closely the reports of disturbances in the countryside but discerned little evidence of political dissent. Rather, to his experienced eye, they contained the "usual details of Robberies and outrages" and sectarian animosities. Here was further proof of the "licentious folly" of the lower orders, of their wish to subvert "whatever is, to upset Law & Property, & substitute the wildest Anarchy." So, skilfully turning aside requests from magistrates in Westmeath and Limerick for the enforcement of the Insurrection Act, he persuaded the lords justices to give the Peace Preservation Act a fair trial.[4]

The decision of the British government in mid-April to withdraw more than 5,000 troops from Ireland to help meet the renewed challenge from Napoleon did cause consternation there. Hard-pressed by frightened magistrates, the lords justices officially placed on record their opposition to this action. In forwarding this dispatch, Gregory admitted that the troops could ill be spared but discounted the danger of an imminent general insurrection. Moreover, he accepted that the battle to restore order in Ireland might be won in Europe. If "we cannot keep down our own domestic Discontent when unassisted by Buonaparte," he observed, "what should we do to resist them when joined to him; which if he is susccessful they certainly will be."[5]

Peel applauded his deputy's steadiness and gave strong support to his unflinching opposition to the demands of the magistracy for the extraordinary powers of the Insurrection Act. Although he had come to share Gregory's opinion that this measure ought to be "the perpetual law" of Ireland, he was not a man to sanction its use without clear proof of the need. He dismissed as worthless the "unauthenticated statements of conspiracies and plots" made by frightened magistrates. He demanded facts not hearsay, remarking to Gregory that "you don't convict a man without evidence – and why should you convict a district without it." "If the Magistrates consent to the Peace Preservation Bill, and will cordially act under it, I would enforce it tomorrow," he advised in the immediate aftermath of the news of the troop withdrawals, and "if they do not consent to it, I think I should nevertheless enforce it, but with very diminished hopes of its complete success."[6]

Throughout this tense and difficult period Gregory had kept a wary eye on O'Connell and the Catholic Association he had formed following the suppression of the board. On 26 April he advised Peel that their informant had reported that Sir Henry Parnell was cooperating with the Association and planned to revive the Catholic question in the Commons. Tempted as he was by the thought of decisive action against the new body, Gregory was restrained by the need to protect his source of information. Peel and Saurin were more inclined to attack. They gave serious thought to ordering the arrest of O'Connell and his colleagues, and proceeding against them under the Convention Act. On reflection, however, the chief secretary concluded that it would be wiser "to allow Parnell to expose himself and his views first on the Catholic Question." Not that this prevented him from exploiting the Irish Whigs' dealings with the Association. In a long letter to Sidmouth voicing his objections to renewed discussion of the claims, Peel made much of the fact that Parnell would be acting at the "behest" of the most radical Catholic agitators. To adopt a bill framed in such circumstances would be to "abandon the functions of legislation to an Association in Ireland, every member of which glories in his avowed hostility to the connexion of the two countries," he argued. Besides, it would be the Association, not Parliament, which would receive the credit in the minds of Irish Catholics. When he repeated this same line of argument in the Commons, his satisfaction at the decisive defeat of the motion was tempered by a sense of personal injustice at the rough handling he received from some of its supporters.[7]

Daniel O'Connell had indeed been in correspondence with Parnell, feeding his vanity and striving to bolster his determination to reintroduce the Catholic claims unencumbered with Protestant securities. Further, he had drafted a pair of Catholic securities which he described as essential if the promise of reconciliation implicit in "*unqualified*" emancipation was to be fulfilled. First, several individuals would have to be removed from their positions in the Irish government. He proposed that the chancellor be promoted to England, Saurin elevated to the bench, Peel given a post in the diplomatic service or an undersecretaryship in England, and Gregory dispatched elsewhere. "He is in the constant habit of using foul language of the Catholics," he charged less than accurately, "and upon a system of conciliation he could not remain here with propriety." The second of O'Connell's demands was for the disciplining of the Irish government's *virulent, disgusting and inflammatory*" hired press. Ironically, Peel would have endorsed much of O'Connell's criticism and not least his observation that "Insulting language is very silly on the *part and behalf* of any government. It never convinces anybody. It excites insolence in the ruling party, hatred in the governed and *then* the reaction of those passions upon each other."[8]

Peel's growing disillusionment with several of his expensive and embarrassing press allies induced him to delegate to Gregory in 1815 the task of severing the connection. Unfortunately, it proved to be a difficult and protracted business. The government naturally moved cautiously lest it expose itself to the additional embarrassment of being vilified by erstwhile clients. In 1816 Gregory employed a carrot, in the form of a pension, to persuade the publisher of the *Dublin Journal* to discontinue his discredited newspaper. In other cases he resorted to the stick. Covert support, in the form of secret service funds, was withdrawn along with the benefits of the Proclamation Fund. Yet the campaign to disentangle the government from those relationships which cost a small fortune to maintain, "and in point of injury & discredit much more," enjoyed limited success at best. The *Hibernian Journal* continued to draw heavily from the Proclamation Fund in spite of the chief secretary's criticism of its readiness to inflame rather than allay religious animosities.[9]

Even as he strove to distance the government from worthless friends, Peel tempered the assault upon its enemies. He remained a supporter of prosecutions as an instrument for chastising that "infamous part" of the Dublin press "which never sought to enlighten the public mind, which never aimed at the dissemination of truth, which never endeavoured to correct the morals, or improve the happiness of the people." Nevertheless, he did require that the libel actions be carefully selected and with a scrupulous regard for the right of political criticism. Thus he acted swiftly in February 1817 to dissuade Whitworth from a prosecution of the *Dublin Chronicle* founded merely upon its call for a change of administration in London. "Now observe I do not say the article is not a libel," he commented to the viceroy, "but of all libels that one I would be most reluctant to Prosecute – is an attack on the Government in its capacity of a Government." As for the *Chronicle*'s charge that ministers had a direct interest in preventing reform, such a self-evident truth could scarcely constitute a libel. "They say every honest man with property and character has such an interest," he noted.[10]

O'Connell's acute criticism of the "hired press" was matched by his astute analysis of the disorders which increasingly preoccupied Gregory as they swept across Ireland during the spring and early summer of 1815. "The fall of prices has beggared the peasantry and ruined the farmers," he observed succinctly. It was a judgment issued with the authority of a lawyer who had recently been on circuit. Yet he was less than judicious when he went on to charge, in a letter to Henry Parnell, that "England is doing nothing for them. She gives them insults and taxes. Are you surprised that there should exist a frightful propensity to illegal combinations"? For Parnell had been at the centre of an effort to assist Ireland.[11]

The Liverpool ministry was given little time in which to savour the triumph of its foreign policy, which the decisive defeat of Napoleon in June of 1815 served to confirm, for peace was no harbinger of prosperity. Although it was at this moment that real growth began to accelerate, the economy and society experienced a painful period of postwar adjustment. The loss of war orders, and a labour force greatly swollen by a quarter of a million demobilized veterans, brought unemployment and a revival of the social tensions which had spawned Luddism only three years earlier. There was also a noticeable increase in crime. Another concern was a National Debt which was now approaching £750 million. The repayments due on enormous loans, for the interest on the debt exceeded one quarter of the expenditure, and the burden of taxation, excited concern for the fiscal health of the nation which the parliamentary opposition was quick to exploit. But no sector of the economy or segment of the population had greater reason to greet peace with mixed emotions than had the agrarian, especially the producers of cereals and those farmers working the clay-lands of the East Midlands and East Anglia where the resort to mixed farming required a substantial capital investment. The wartime prosperity had been unevenly distributed, and in many cases was more apparent than real. Some farmers had found their rents rising as fast as prices and, when the latter collapsed following the bumper harvest of 1813, theirs was an unenviable position. With the war's end the demand for food fell, as the government discharged soldiers and thus cut its purchases while adding to the ranks of the unemployed whose purchasing power was limited. Falling farm incomes were accompanied by rising costs, as the burden of poor relief necessarily grew heavier. Many farmers who had borrowed during the war to increase the size of their holdings, or had leased them a inflated wartime rents, were now unable to make their payments, and not a few were driven from the land. Inevitably, as much of agriculture felt the harsh grip of depression, and some farmers returned their lands to pasturage, the real wages of labourers fell and unemployment rose. Adding to their misery was a scarcity of homes, for desperate farmers destroyed cottages in an effort to lessen the burden of the poor rate. As a result, the end of the war was marked by growing agrarian as well as industrial unrest.[12]

In Ireland, given her greater dependence on agriculture and cereal production, the fall in prices was certain to be even more damaging. Any tendency on the part of landowners to follow the British in moving from tillage to pasturage, or to consolidate their holdings in an effort to work them more efficiently, would be pregnant with disaster in the peculiar circumstances of that country. The rapid growth of population had been especially marked among a rural poor who regarded possession of a plot of land as the only guarantee of survival. Consequently, disputes over access to land had sparked outrages even before plummeting prices after 1813 encouraged a contraction of the acreage given over to tillage, and the reversal of subdivision in the name of improvement. In short, trouble loomed in Ireland. Alarmed for the future, a group of Irish members of Parliament led by Henry Parnell had sought as early as 1813 to guard against a postwar agricultural depression.[13]

What Parnell and his allies wanted was the effective closing of Britain to foreign producers of grains, thus reserving the market for the Irish. The instrument was at hand in the Corn Laws, which regulated importations and had been under almost continuous debate since 1804. Naturally, the mutual benefits and national advantages in such an arrangement received a full airing from its sponsors. Irishmen flush with the profits of their sales to Britain would make excellent customers for English manufacturers. The Irish farmers' concentration on cereals would leave the market for dairy produce to their British counterparts. Moreover, the achievement of national self-sufficiency in food production would guarantee stable and moderate prices and would end the danger of famine. As an added safeguard on this score, however, foreign corn might be warehoused duty-free, and freely imported whenever domestic prices exceeded a level which roughly corresponded to the average of the war years. The Irish members also appealed for justice and generosity, and offered assurances that the action they advocated would finally erase their countrymen's ancient prejudices against England. Nor did they overlook the social implications of their proposal. Tillage was the form of agriculture to which Irishmen were "peculiarly disposed," John Newport informed the House, and was "more calculated than pasturage, or perhaps even manufactures, to promote morality, industry and good order."[14]

Parnell had secured a select committee in 1813 in order to promote the arrangement, but it did so with such crudity, calling only a handful of witnesses and all of them Irishmen, that the report was widely dismissed as an Irish "job." When the issue was revived the following year a number of Scottish members joined the Irish, for in their country the deepening distress threatened a deficiency of rents. No doubt some of them were also motivated by the thought that a new law "would do good in Ireland." Hence Peel's fury when few Irish members attended the House. "The Bill is attacked most vehemently as a measure intended exclusively for the benefit of Ireland, to the loss of England," he explained to Whitworth. Opponents of the measure charged that it was a scheme to raise the price Englishmen paid for their bread in order to prop up Irish rents, and that it would permit the Irish to capitalize upon their lower production costs to undersell English farmers. Such charges evoked the counter-accusation that Ireland was being spoken of as a foreign country. Although the measure was successfully blocked in 1814, Parliament settling for no more than the termination of the bounties on the export of grain, the government decided to take it up early in 1815. By this time English cereal farmers had added their powerful voices to the call for protection. The ministry was disposed to listen to the spokesmen for England's single most important industry, and one which was so well represented in Parliament. Furthermore, the prime minister and his colleagues appear to have harboured the hope that concession on the Corn Laws would not only make more palatable the medicine of continued heavy taxation but would also result in moderate and steady food prices. Last, but not necessarily least, any action which enhanced the attractiveness of investment in Irish agriculture would surely promote the civilizing and improvement of that "miserable and lawless country." To this end, the government sought not only to guarantee to the Irish profitable access to the British market but also to facilitate their capture of the West Indian. Hence the restrictions on exports were abandoned. The intent of the legislation, therefore, was not to increase Ireland's "dependency" on Britain, thereby maintaining her in an "underdeveloped" or "colonial" condition, but to promote economic growth along the lines Irishmen themselves had marked out. The experience of Scotland had demonstrated the benefits of complementary rather than competitive development, and suggested that only with time would they become manifest.[15]

"We are proceeding in the House of Commons most prosperously on the Corn Question," Peel reported to Whitworth on 25 February 1815. "The Opposition is very feeble and many who were enemies to the Principle of increased Protection to our own agriculture last year are now converted." His confidence that the measure would be enacted without "much Clamour" proved to be less justified. Instead, the prospect of dearer bread brought mobs into the streets around Parliament Square and from the War Office the young Palmerston issued advice to his colleagues on how to fortify their residences. But the crowds were easily dispersed by troops and there was little reason for the government to take alarm. The rioters "showed the same discrimination and moderation in their attacks that had been seen many times before."[16]

However "feeble" the opposition in the House to a measure seen as peculiarly advantageous to the Irish, the sense of national resentment was too easily exploited to be long ignored by politicians. The government's decision to extend the life of the income and property taxes in the wake of

Napoleon's escape from Elba sparked an English effort to extend them to Ireland. Over the objections of those Irish members who protested that their country was already being taxed too heavily, Vesey Fitzgerald compromised. He conceded that the taxes he had laid on Ireland since 1813 had come as an unpleasant shock to most Irishmen, but described additional sacrifices as the necessary price of peace, strength, security, and glory. Pointing to the economic benefits recently extended to Ireland – the Corn Laws, and grants for the improvement and extension both of inland navigation and Howth harbour – he moved the equalization of the British and Irish duties on silk imports and the raising of those on malt, spirits, and foreign hops. At the same time, he made an effort to appease his critics, especially those Irish Whigs who had broken with their English friends to support the government on the Corn Laws. He endorsed an investigation of the conduct of grand juries in levying and spending monies, called for the consolidation of the debts and exchequers of Great Britain and Ireland, and proposed a grant to promote the general education of the poor of Ireland.[17]

Ireland possessed a confusing variety of schools – parish, diocesan, royal, and charter – and, while many were supported by the state, most catered only to the wants of the Protestant minority. Those open to Catholic children were tainted with proselytism. Even more objectionable in Catholic eyes were the schools established by such evangelical organizations as the Hibernian Society. Yet the craving for education led Catholic parents to support the rudimentary "hedge" schools. In 1806, largely on the initiative of Sir John Newport, a commission of inquiry into Irish education was established and over the course of six years produced fourteen reports.[18]

The fourteenth report proposed the creation of a board of commissioners to rationalize and supervise the existing system, and to ensure that the current parliamentary grants were used to broaden the opportunities for an education purified of proselytism. These recommendations appeared to meet the demands of the Roman Catholic hierarchy for "a state system of schools that would be religiously neutral," but Peel's efforts to implement them were quickly frustrated. Before acting to establish a commission with such broad powers, including those to select teachers and texts, and one to which Catholics would have to be appointed if the schools it administered were to be acceptable to the hierarchy and the great mass of the Catholic population, he sought direction from Liverpool and Sidmouth. He wished to know whether the government was "disposed to sanction the institution of a system of general education in Ireland, of which institution the Protestant religion in Ireland is not to form (necessarily at least) a part." Wary of such a controversial issue, the prime minister and the home secretary took refuge in evasions and procrastination. For his part, Peel grew increasingly reluctant to jeopardize the "existing Protestant establishments." In the House he was quick to defend the contribution of the clergymen of the Established Church to the education of Irish children, and on one occasion even justified the expensive and notoriously ill-managed charter schools. Hence he soon came to favour the creation of two boards, an exclusively Protestant one "for the regulation of the present establishments, and the other for the control of such as may be founded upon the suggestion of the Fourteenth Report." He was further encouraged in this direction by his closest advisers in the Irish executive.[19]

William Gregory cautioned against an effort "to unite the Children of the two Religions in one System," however worthy the intent. To his mind, the obstacles were daunting. Not only had "many prejudices" to be conquered but the inevitable opposition of the Catholic clergy would have to be overcome. Saurin agreed with him, and their pessimism was seemingly confirmed by the virulent denunciation of the proposal by the titular bishop of Killala. So Peel did no more initially than form the first of the two boards he had envisaged – the one to supervise the existing Protestant establishments. As for the general education of the lower orders, both he and Whitworth concluded that "nothing would be more likely to impede its advance than the ostentatious interference of Government." Indeed, fearful that Catholics would join a mixed board only with the intention of eventually dominating it, the viceroy favoured a retreat from the "too liberal principle of the Fourteenth Report." It was an attitude at odds with his chief secretary's public professions of faith in the value of a religiously neutral system of general education.[20] "If the lower orders, instead of being kept in extreme ignorance, were allowed the means of obtaining information, they would not so easily be operated upon and misled," Peel declared in the House. Moreover, "the only rational plan of education in Ireland, was one which should be extended impartially to children of all religious persuasions – one which did not profess to make converts – one which, while it imparted general religious instruction, left those who were its objects to obtain their particular religious discipline elsewhere." Fortunately, there appeared to be an agent at hand through which the state might work without either compromising its relationship with the national religion or arousing the suspicions of the Catholic hierarchy. The Society for Promoting the Education of the Poor in Ireland, known as the Kildare Place Society, had been founded in 1811 to establish schools "divested of all sectarian distinctions in Christianity." Yet the fate of its endeavours in Cork, Ireland's second city, lent substance to Gregory's pessimistic predictions. There, both the Established Church and the Catholic hierarchy opposed a society school and education continued along sectarian lines. Ignoring or unaware of such reverses for the cause of religiously neutral education, Peel and Fitzgerald recommended in June 1815 that the society be partially funded by the state and it received a modest grant of £6,000 the following year.[21]

In the Commons, the Opposition ridiculed the government's deepening faith in education as the solution for Ireland's ills. Where was the utility of teaching Irishmen "reading and figures?" William Plunket asked, if only to "count the prosperity they did not possess, and to read about that liberty which they did not enjoy." Education would provide no cure for Ireland's political evils "unless accompanied by a radical reform of the present vicious system," Sir John Newport warned, and he spoke with the authority of the initiator of the investigation which had produced the fourteenth report. Although Peel was guilty of championing education almost as if it was a talisman, he knew that it did not possess magical powers. Moral habits would not be inculcated by the mere ability to read and write, he admitted privately. The lower orders who could not find employment "must be vicious." [22]

As the Irish executive struggled throughout the summer of 1815 to suppress the widespread disorders, William Gregory continued to play a large role even after Whitworth returned to Ireland in May. The viceroy no less than the under-secretary accepted that "the peace of Ireland must be fought for and maintained in France, and that it can never be firmly established, but by the destruction of Bonaparte and of the Revolutionary Government." Of course, the turbulence in Ireland compelled the government to fill up the military ranks thinned by the withdrawal of regulars for service in Europe. Fears of an insurrection might well be groundless, Gregory acknowledged, but in "the fever of disappointment" following the recent defeat of the Catholic claims in Parliament it was "impossible to say what mad enterprise may not be undertaken." He remembered all too vividly how the authorities had been taken by surprise by Robert Emmet in 1803. "The distance between a furious Demagogue, & a bitter Traitor is very short," he reminded Peel, "& we have never doubted the bad principles of our Irish Leaders to be deterred from any thing which could injure England even though their own Country." [23] The chief secretary's initial scepticism regarding serious danger did not survive this warning, and he immediately endorsed the under-secretary's precautions against "a sudden movement." With the backing of Whitworth and Peel, Gregory finally overcame the resistance of the commander of the forces to the calling out of some of the loyalists. Sir George Hewitt had a professional soldier's scorn for the yeomanry. Then, shortly before the end of June, a proclamation was issued embodying the militia. Nor did the news of Napoleon's final defeat, and the diversion to Ireland of troops returning from America and previously earmarked for Europe, bring any immediate change of course. The best plan, Peel advised the viceroy, was "to scrape together all the irregular force" they could in order to spare "the regular for services better suited to their distinguished gallantry than the pursuit of stills & the dispersion of Thrashers." [24]

In the war against the agrarian secret societies, the executive continued to look first to the local gentry and then to the Peace Preservation forces before resorting to the military. Whitworth shared the common belief that absentees bore a large share of the responsibility for Ireland's disorders. "It is a well known fact that the parts most disgrac'd by disturbances, are those which are abandoned by the Proprietors," he informed the home secretary. He therefore proposed that they be induced to return by "the certainty of being excluded by their absence from those Honours and distinctions to which they might otherwise fairly pretend." Characteristically, Gregory looked to sterner measures. The threat of the Peace Preservation Act, bringing as it did heavy charges on a disturbed district, would frighten the magistracy into exertion and the people into obedience. Instead, the threatened expense strengthened the magistrates' preference for the Insurrection Act. It then fell to Gregory to inform them that such extraordinary powers would only be sanctioned as a last resort, and to attempt to convince them that they were no more effective, and no less expensive to implement, than the provisions of the Peace Preservation Act. But the presence of a large force of policemen failed to pacify Tipperary, and by the end of August the government was obliged to dispatch a substantial military force to its aid. This in turn brought another appeal to the senior government for a larger garrison. "We have no apprehension whatever of any serious explosion," Peel reassured the home secretary, "but we cannot depend upon the ordinary civil powers of the country for the prevention of outrages of a very sanguinary character and for the protection of the well-disposed." Within a few days eight regiments of British militia were being readied for transport to Ireland.[25]

In the midst of this crisis the senior members of the executive were distracted by a dispute between those equally proud and mutually contemptuous men, Peel and O'Connell, which they agreed to settle on the duelling ground. Happily, the English authorities eventually intervened to prevent the Irishman from reaching the European site. In the meantime, Gregory had been obliged to return to Dublin from a well-earned leave in the country to fill the administrative void created by Peel's departure for Ostend. The chief secretary voiced complete confidence in his deputy. "You will have no scruple in acting upon everything of a public nature that occurs without reference to me – and you may be quite sure of my approbation," he wrote. Yet he was surely disappointed by the decision taken in his absence to resort to the Insurrection Act.[26]

The viceroy held the commander of the forces accountable for this unfortunate turn of events. Hewitt had not only prevented the effective employment of the yeomanry but had also responded lethargically to calls for the dispatch of additional troops to the disturbed areas. Reports from Tipperary and Limerick of large bodies of men operating in broad daylight as well as under cover of darkness, murdering, burning houses, seizing arms, and compelling the lower orders to take illegal oaths, had made Whitworth strive to rouse Hewitt from a state of "apathy and incredulity." The lord lieutenant angrily informed Sidmouth that the commander, as a result of age and poor health, was no longer equal to his duties and that a change of command was "absolutely necessary to the success of our measures." He was replaced the following year. Although Hewitt did belatedly order additional men into Tipperary and Limerick, bringing the total stationed in those two counties to almost 10,000, the viceroy no longer possessed either the will or the confidence to resist the appeals of local magistrates for enforcement of the Insurrection Act.[27]

By the end of October the strong military presence and the severe punishments handed down by the special commission sitting under the terms of the Insurrection Act appeared to have worked their intended effect. But Whitworth believed the tranquillity to be more apparent than real, for he had failed to detect any "solid or permanent improvement in the disposition of the People." William Gregory agreed. He undertook a working vacation in the West, stopping for several days in Athlone before travelling almost the length of Roscommon to visit one of his brothers-in-law, the bishop of Elphin, and from there moving across Galway. He was surprised by the extent and depth of distress on view, which drove peasants to acts of desperation. In Queen's County no magistrate could be found to assist in the collection of the tithe. Elsewhere, acts of vandalism were the most moderate form of protest against ejections and the reletting of the land. Far more unnerving was the murder of a magistrate who had been playing a prominent role in the special sessions in County Tipperary. "The law strong as it is, is unequal to such a Contest," a shaken viceroy reported to the home secretary, and "it is only by a strong military establishment that this country can be preserv'd."[28]

The brutality and savagery of the marauding bands also appalled and bewildered Peel, hardening his opinion that he was dealing with a people unlike others. "You can have no idea of the moral depravation of the lower orders," he wrote to the prime minister; "in fidelity towards each other they are unexampled, as they are in their sanguinary disposition and fearlessness of the consequences of indulging it." Increasingly, he identified religion as a source of this terrifying behaviour. Advisers such as Saurin and Gregory had long counselled that the Roman Catholic religion was the "grand cause" of their country's evils and disturbances. They were intensely suspicious of a priesthood, estimated to number well over 2,000, which was bound by an oath of celibacy and a strong esprit de corps, claimed to be the true and only church of Ireland, and exercised a powerful influence over millions of "ignorant and ferocious" peasants who evidently regarded the descendants of Protestant settlers as usurpers of their lands and enemies of their church and religion. The overthrow and massacre of Protestants was the essential if often unavowed object of the disturbances, the under-secretary charged. Peel was coming to a similar if less extreme conclusion. The "remorselessness" with which crimes were committed, "the almost total annihilation of the agency of conscience as a prevention of crime," and the "universal contempt in which the obligation of any but an *illegal* oath" was held by the mass of the people, satisfied him that "the prevailing religion of Ireland" operated as "an impediment rather than an aid to the ends of the civil government."[29]

The proposition that Ireland and most of her people were significantly different from other parts and peoples of the United Kingdom was one to which both the prime minister and the home secretary also subscribed. "In truth, Ireland is a political phenomenon – not influenced by the same feelings as appear to affect mankind in other Countries," Liverpool observed early in 1816, "and the singular nature of the Disorders must be the cause why it has hitherto been found impracticable to apply an effectual and permanent remedy to it." But the Irish policy which this sentiment had shaped was jeopardized by the welter of problems which came to the fore at the war's end.[30]

The standard of "economical government" was raised almost as soon as the imperial flag had been struck at Waterloo. Nor was it quickly to be lowered. "The state of the finances is very alarming," Peel was still writing to Whitworth early in 1817. "The great object of the Government at this moment is to reduce the expense to such an amount as to make the expenditure not exceed the revenue and sinking fund united, and thus shew that we are not plunging further into Debt."[31] In the battle for retrenchment neither government nor Parliament was likely to overlook Ireland, even had fate not intervened in the form of a dispute over an "exceptionally lucrative sinecure in the Irish Court of Exchequer." In response to the relentless pressure to economize, the Irish executive surrendered the expensive express system of communication with London; the budget for messengers was slashed; Whitworth, Peel, and Gregory cut their newspaper subscriptions; the pursuit of dishonest public servants was undertaken with fresh zeal; there was a more sparing distribution of the pension fund; and while Gregory's charges to the Treason Fund continued to grow – £13,900 in 1815, £14,500 in 1816, £15,100 in 1817 – he moderated the rise through a discreet use of patronage. Several persons who had aided government prosecutions and would normally have been moved to a place of safety and supported from the fund were now quietly appointed to distant ports as gaugers or tidewaiters. Yet none of these expedients reduced significantly the cost of governing Ireland. The principal target of the economists in Parliament and the economizers was the military establishment.[32]

Sidmouth had given notice in December 1815 that the Irish executive's pleas for the exemption of Ireland from the general postwar reduction of military forces were not going to be heeded. Indeed, some ministers suspected Whitworth of exaggerating the situation there. Consequently, the decision in February 1816 to cut the nominal Irish establishment to 25,000 men came as no surprise in Dublin. "It is vain for me to represent that 25,000 will not be sufficient," Peel informed the viceroy, for "it is said to be absolutely impossible to provide for more in the Estimates – whether more be neccessary or not." They would have "to prove not by general assertions but by minute calculations" that they could not safely govern with an even smaller force. This the chief secretary sought to do in a powerful speech during the debate on the Army estimates. He enlightened his listeners on the differences between Ireland and England, detailed the essential tasks assigned to the military, reminded members that out of a nominal force of 25,000 men there were rarely more than 20,000 effectives, and denied any preference for military over civil power. All too often in Ireland, the army alone was capable of executing justice and providing that measure of personal security without which the gentry would never take up residence. Moreover, by employing troops the government was often able to avoid resorting to the repugnant civil provisions of the Insurrection Act. Peel was satisfied that he had "told truth enough to alarm many an honest Englishman – and convince him that he knows about as much of the state of Ireland as he does of the state of Kamschatka."[33] Nevertheless, the pressure on the Irish government continued to increase. Its finances thrown into deeper confusion by the loss of essential sources of revenue, such as the income tax, the Liverpool government decided to reduce the establishment once again in 1817. Peel was pressed hard to accept the loss of another 5,000 men, and then to compromise on 4,000, but he doggedly held out for a cut of no more than 3,000. Still, the military budget remained so tight that Whitworth approved the recall of three of the major generals on the Irish staff and sought to save an additional £73,000 by not calling out the militia for its annual exercises.[34]

In waging a long rearguard action against troop reductions, Peel exposed himself to a counterattack which served to complicate the task of governing Ireland. His unflinching defence of a very large peacetime establishment provided the Opposition with excuses aplenty to debate the state of Ireland. It was in this context that he privately avowed his preference for a period of "honest despotic Government" in that country. He complained that people in Ireland were "very ignorant of the difficulties of managing business in the House of Commons." The fact that every member of that "deliberative assembly" was "at liberty to bring every subject under consideration" made the avoidance of discussion well-nigh impossible. Therein lay the danger. Englishmen who knew nothing of Ireland but investigated her grievances might not come to share the chief secretary's confidence in her present system of government. Then again, the divisions within the Liverpool administration on the Catholic question were an additional menace. Peel could not hope to exclude Castlereagh, Vesey Fitzgerald, and Wellesley-Pole from any select committee on Ireland. Nor had the ministry impressed him with its resolution in the face of wrong-headed demands. "Really the House of Commons is usurping the functions of the executive Government," he complained in the midst of the long campaign for economy. Moreover, in giving ground on this issue the prime minister managed to irritate those Irish members to whom Peel looked for support. Liverpool announced the surrender of a number of sinecures at a meeting of his supporters to which only two Irishmen had been invited. The majority of Irish members were understandably peeved by this slight, and their management was not simplified by the steady curtailment of patronage positions. Peel lamented his insufficient means to reward his allies, especially those whose conduct had been "exemplary." They "receive so little, their friendship does not remit," he wrote to Whitworth.[35]

Major debates on Ireland were scheduled for both houses early in April 1816. As the first neared, that in the Lords, the government plotted strategy. It was obvious that the Opposition would detail the Irish grievances against sheriffs, grand juries, magistrates, tithes, sectarian education, and heavy taxes. Peel suggested that any inquiry by a select committee be confined to an examination of the causes and progress of the disorders. He was confident that this would demonstrate "the hopelessness of any other immediate remedies than force." But Whitworth doubted that so limited an investigation would be acceptable to the Opposition, and on reflection Peel concluded that it would be too difficult to manage anyway. Instead, he belatedly sought to impress upon the prime minister the "extreme danger" and "embarrassment" of any parliamentary investigation. His was a forlorn effort, for the government elected the path of discretion. It resolved to resist a general inquiry but not the examination of specific problems. Nor did Peel enjoy greater success when he sought the exclusion of the tithe from any particular investigation. There were peculiar circumstances in Ireland which prevented equitable reform, he argued. He drew Liverpool's attention to the unusually high number of landholders there, and to the long undervaluation of tithes, or the exemption of certain crops, by forbearing or intimidated clergymen. When this appeal failed to move the prime minister, the young chief secretary changed tack and attempted to bind Irish tithes to English. In reply, Liverpool coolly insisted that they might be dealt with separately since they were as different as a sick man and a healthy one. All Peel secured was an assurance that, in expressing the government's willingness to examine any plan for commutation, the prime minister would voice the personal opinion that a scheme fair to the church and equitable to the payer would be extremely difficult to devise. On the day of the debate Liverpool was as good as his word, and the motion for a general inquiry into the state of Ireland was easily turned back. Yet Peel was filled with apprehension as he waited for the Commons debate two days later. Not only would the burden of defending the Irish executive and Irish policy now fall directly upon him, but he feared that the arguments used so successfully by the government in the Lords would be employed as ammunition by the Opposition in the Commons. Fortunately, the attendance in the House was so thin on 4 April that the debate was postponed for three weeks, giving him a valuable respite in which to strengthen his defences.[36]

Peel was all too aware of the vulnerability of his position. In Ireland the sheriff appointed the grand jury which taxed the county and he exercised considerable influence over elections. The information that he was often appointed on the recommendation of the sitting member of Parliament, if a government supporter, would shock Englishmen. Similarly, the magistracy did not bear too close an examination. Of the more than four thousand Irish magistrates fully one-third were absentees and less than one-half of them were active. Among this active minority, as even the lord chancellor of Ireland privately admitted, there were "monstrous abuses." "I wish to God it was possible to revise the Magistracy," the chief secretary privately remarked, "for half our disorders and disturbances arises from the negligence of some and corruption & party spirit of others." He turned to Gregory for the regulations governing their appointment. The under-secretary also received a request for a detailed report on the condition of the "common order of peasantry." Peel wished to be fully briefed in order to be able to counter the familiar charges that poverty and squalor lay at the root of Irish turbulence. He would suggest, instead, that the "real cause" of many of "the evils of Ireland" was "that infernal curse the forty shilling freeholds." The notorious fact that many voters had been fraudulently manufactured had promoted disrespect for the law.[37] But in line with the government's predetermined strategy Peel gave a little ground in the face of the Opposition's onslaught. As he explained to Whitworth, "it is expedient to yield something voluntarily and with good grace, in order to prevent the necessity of yielding much more by compulsion." Thus his rejection of demands for a general revision of the magistracy was softened by an undertaking to revive the "ancient mode" of appointing sheriffs – the judges at the Assizes would require each sheriff to provide the names of three persons qualified to fill the office. These returns would then be forwarded via the lord chancellor to the lord lieutenant who made the appointments. However, Peel was at pains to stress that in Ireland "Time alone, the prevalence of a kind and paternal system of government, and the extension of education, were the remedies which must be chiefly relied upon." He capped this skilful parliamentary performance less than a month later, when he artfully forestalled any separate investigation of Irish tithes. Describing the uncertainties of the tax as one of "the alleged causes of popular discontent in Ireland," he insisted that an inquiry into commutation in England should embrace Ireland too.[38]

Peel promptly honoured his commitment to purify the appointment of sheriffs, and before the end of the session he had quietly acquiesced in a reform of the much-abused grand juries. For more than a year critics of the administration of justice in Ireland had been demanding that grand juries be required to examine witnesses before finding bills of indictment, instead of proceeding on the strength of evidence presented only in the form of a deposition. On one occasion Peel had barely succeeded in dissuading a Commons' committee from declaring the Irish procedure illegal, which would have been "a fine topic for O'Connell and the Evening Post." At other times he had resisted change for fear it would dislocate upcoming meetings of the Assizes and in the knowledge that Irish judges opposed adoption of "the English practice." They worried that it would make more difficult the already formidable task of obtaining evidence, and interpreted the proposal as an implied censure of their past conduct. But the knowledge that the English law officers supported the measure, and that further resistance would be fruitless, convinced Peel to accept a seat on the committee drafting the bill. Its second reading, in June 1816, was welcomed by the Opposition. Equally gratifying to critics of the administration of Ireland was the news that the government intended to bring in a bill to regulate the presentments of grand juries. "The jobs and corruption of grand juries were well understood by the lower orders in Ireland," George Ponsonby remarked, "and had very much prejudiced them against the administration of the law in general." For all of the hyperbole the announcement inspired in the Commons, where one member hailed it as "one of the most important steps to restore tranquillity," it provided no solution to the chronic financial and economic problems of Ireland nor did it promise any immediate cessation of outrages.[39]

The year 1816 had brought even harder times to Britain and Ireland, ushering in as it did a prolonged period of distress. Industries dislocated by the inevitable problems of postwar adjustment were ill-equipped to absorb the additional shock of a contraction of overseas trade. On many English farms the crisis also worsened. Despite the passage of the Corn Laws, prices of grains had continued to fall and there were heavy falls also in those for livestock and wool. Unable to meet their high costs, tenants appealed to their landlords for aid. They sought rent rebates and the forgiving of arrears, but even these concessions could not save many of them from the loss of their farms. Then, in the spring, wheat prices began to recover, and by year's end they had reached famine levels. Welcome as this development was to landlords now able to let abandoned farms, the steep rise in the cost of food brought the expected popular response. Some of the disturbances gave the ministry cause for concern. In the capital, which had not escaped severe distress, there was evidence of a revival of political activity by radicals seeking parliamentary reform and universal suffrage. It culminated in the

Spa Field riots in December. Then, in January 1817, the prince regent's carriage was attacked by a mob as he left Westminster following the opening of Parliament. An alarmed government responsed with a series of repressive measures. Even more disquieting, however, for urban disorders had been common, was the spread of mob violence to long passive rural areas. In East Anglia, the few industries which might have provided supplementary employment for the "rural proletariat" were in decline. Their miserable plight and the terrifying prospect of even more expensive bread saw agricultural labourers go on the rampage in the spring in anticipation of greater suffering. Resorting to "the English prototype of the Irish Whiteboy acts," the government meted out severe punishment to the offenders.[40]

Ireland's plight was peculiarly worrisome, the prime minister publicly conceded. The long-depressed textile industries centred in Dublin had still not recovered, while in Belfast the rate of growth in employment was failing to keep pace with that in population. "There is the greatest distress and want of confidence in the commercial world," Peel reported to the Home Office in mid-summer, "and many serious failures have taken place lately." For the unemployed and increasingly restless artisans this meant reduction to a potato diet. In the dominant agricultural sector, meanwhile, an effort to promote improvements and thus productivity through the enactment of a measure designed to facilitate the eviction of unwanted small tenants threatened to heighten the tension in the countryside. Landless labourers had few if any rights on which they might rely for a measure of protection from the ravages of distress. Nor did the dark skies of early summer lighten the atmosphere of impending gloom. As the season wore on, wet weather played havoc not only with the crops in the ground but also the supply of fuel. Little peat had been cut by the second week of October. In the event of a severe winter, Peel warned, the want of fuel might emerge as a more critical problem than the shortage of food.[41]

To the relief of the Irish government, there appeared to be an inverse correlation between the depth of this depression and the incidence of outrage. Throughout the spring the executive had persisted with its deliberate policy of enforcing exemplary punishments. Convictions were too difficult to secure to permit a frequent resort to clemency, Peel had explained to a squeamish prime minister. In June Gregory reported that the people were at last "desisting from their lawless Courses." Against this more peaceful background the under-secretary refused a request from a group of magistrates in Roscommon for permission to search for arms. He sensibly concluded that it was better not to disturb the country with nocturnal visits by magistrates whose names he "never heard when Disturbances did exist".[42] In mid-August Peel informed Sidmouth that Ireland was "more tranquil" now than at any other period since his arrival there in 1812. Initially, he attributed this welcome calm not only to the absence of a Catholic Board or any "factious association," or aggregate meetings or itinerant orators, but also to the improved tone of a Catholic press chastened by prosecutions. For his part, Whitworth gave due weight to the effect of the "strict and severe execution of the Law." He did not believe that "the Disposition of the Lower Orders in favour of the Government [had] materially improved," an opinion Gregory seconded, but was satisfied that a people who had yet to learn to respect and venerate the law had finally been taught to fear it. From his vantage point in London, Sidmouth dwelt upon the impact of "the two powerful instruments" Parliament had placed in the viceroy's hands – the Peace Preservation Act and the Insurrection Act – and he expressed the hope that they would continue to be enforced as circumstances dictated. Whatever the explanation of Ireland's tranquillity, it enabled Peel to offer enthusiastic support to a magistrate in Wexford who was determined to maintain peace by the "unremitting exercise" of his "ordinary powers."[43]

Contemplating the welcome turn of events in Ireland, Peel concluded that distress had a different if not contrary effect there from what it had in England. Indeed, he speculated that severe distress "would rather tend to diminish than to increase" crimes and turbulence. Had policy been founded upon this assessment, the result ought to have been a greater effort to relieve the distress in England than to mitigate that in Ireland. Instead, the most radical departures from economic orthodoxy were to be restricted to the latter country. Not that the initial response of the British government violated any of the tenets of the new political economy. An increase in the duty levied on imported butter was explained as a boon to Ireland and especially to her poorest farmers, for it promised them an even greater share of the British market for a commodity which "constituted nearly 1-7th part of the whole amount of the exports" of the island. Two months later, in May, Parliament finally sanctioned the consolidation of the English and Irish Exchequers, and thus the debts and revenues, but there was as yet no assimilation of the currencies or uniting of the Bank of England and that of Ireland. Just how necessary this consolidation had been Vesey Fitzgerald detailed in the House. In the fifteen years immediately preceding the union Ireland's expenditures had amounted to £41,000,000, he reported, but in the fifteen subsequent to it that total had "swelled to the enormous size of £148,000,000." Despite "an advance in permanent taxation" which was "even greater in proportion to former revenues than that of Great Britain herself," Ireland was simply no longer able to carry alone the crushing burden of debt.[44]

Yet tinkering with customs duties and the prevention of Irish bankruptcy brought precious little immediate relief to the distressed peasantry. Peel had conceded in the House long before the failure of the crops that the food of the poor was inferior and that nothing "would be more calculated to seduce them from idle and vicious habits, and to inspire a relish for domestic comforts," than some means of giving them better food "and some better place in which to enjoy it." Significantly, no one proposed that the benefits of the English Poor Law be extended to Ireland. Instead, Ireland remained a weapon in the hands of those opponents of the English system whose demands that it be dismantled had become even more insistent as the costs of relief ballooned during the severe distress. They were to receive a timely intellectual fillip in 1817 from the fifth edition of Malthus's *Essay on the Principle of Population*, and also from the influential David Ricardo, but it was to Ireland that they turned for an example of the benefits abolition of the Poor Law would produce. Unlike the discontended, gloomy, and miserable English pauper, and no matter his perpetually "wretched state," the Irishman was "kind-hearted, affectionate, charitable in the highest degree; with the strongest sense of his duties as a son, a husband, and a parent, and happy in their execution." In short, he possessed that independence of spirit and warmth of feeling which the Poor Law was accused of destroying in Englishmen. The abolitionists triumphed on a select committee of the lower house, obliging a ministry preoccupied with the maintenance of order at a time of acute distress to conjure up a report from a Lords' committee which recommended that the laws be left as they were. This was not the moment "to overturn the paternalist order." And while Castlereagh admitted in the Commons that the government still shied away from any tampering with a system which the poor in England "considered as founded in right as well as in law," his effusive tribute to the virtues of his fellow countrymen made no less explicit its repudiation of any notion that such a system be extended to Ireland.[45]

One possible remedy for Irish distress, which Malthus's pervasive influence ensured would be widely attributed to an excess of population, was emigration. His pessimistic analysis did much to undermine the old notion that the exportation of people would fatally weaken the nation, though he disputed its adequacy as a remedy for the "miseries attending overpopulation." Many supporters of emigration still hoped to keep those people within the empire, where they would strengthen the colonies and help to create a market for British goods. In short, they thought in terms of colonization. In 1815 Peel drafted a plan which envisaged state assistance for Irish families willing to settle in Canada. At the Colonial Office, Bathurst and his deputy, Henry Goulburn, recognized the desirability of diverting to British North America the constant stream of British emigrants to the United States. The means both to convey and provide for them were fortuitously at hand. Transports required for the return of British regulars serving in North America would otherwise be making the westerly crossing empty while the simultaneous rundown of the naval forces made available substantial stores of provisions. In Ireland, Peel hoped to launch the scheme by offering assistance to persons who, having given evidence in criminal trials, needed a refuge. The project came to little in 1815. The Colonial Office delayed implementation of the scheme until the United States had ratified the Treaty of Ghent, thereby guaranteeing peace in North America. By the time the authorities were ready to act Napoleon had escaped from Elba. In this emergency there could be no holding of the transports while emigrants were collected, for the troops were required in Europe immediately. Although a number of Scottish and English families were subsequently carried across the ocean following Bonaparte's defeat, in Ireland the potential emigrants were too dispersed to be consulted in time to travel before the onset of the season during which the Atlantic is dangerous and the Canadian climate inhospitable. In 1816 the proposal for state assistance fell victim to the drive for retrenchment. Moreover, Peel's confidence in this remedy for Ireland's ills was shaken by the evidence that most of those making their own way to North America came from the Protestant population of the northern counties. He was loath to lose persons he regarded as both loyal and industrious. Unwilling to ban their departure, even when they were "mechanics and artificers" and therefore subject to restrictions, he was still keen to divert them to Canada. This was achieved to a substantial extent through amendments to the Passenger Act. Revelations of the appalling conditions aboard emigrant ships (the result of overcrowding, inadequate provisioning, and dishonesty), together, perhaps, with a desire in some quarters to impede emigration, had prompted the enactment of the bill in 1803. But its stringent provisions proved unenforceable. Now they were loosened and a differential introduced between ships sailing for the United States and those clearing for Canada. The latter were permitted to pack more passengers into the available space, thereby effectively reducing fares to British North America. This advantage was subsequently confirmed by an American law in 1819. The result was dramatic. In 1816, 75 per cent of emigrants took ship for the United States. By 1819, 70 per cent were landing in British North America. The rising tide of emigrants from the northern counties of Ireland, amounting to almost half the Irish total during the three decades following the French wars, may well have contributed to the greater tranquillity of Ulster, but this was the extent of the policy's success. Emigration offered no solution for the distress which afflicted the entire island in 1816-17. Relief was forthcoming, however.[46]

In England there were several thousand workhouses, excluding parish poorhouses, which provided paupers with food and shelter. In Ireland the Dublin House of Industry remained the only truly comparable institution. Complaints of poor management, specifically the mixing of inmates willing to work with those who were unwilling, prompted Peel to dispatch Gregory on a surprise inspection. The under-secretary considered "quite absurd" the claims of the governors that there was no work for the poor. He did not expect workhouse labour to be profitable in a commercial sense, but believed that the necessity to undertake it "would diminish the number of admissions" and thus lessen costs. Peel subsequently instructed the governors to require from the able-bodied inmates as much labour as was "'consistent with their health'." The House was already overcrowded, however, and it was at the suggestion of the governors themselves that he authorized them to exclude "Idiots, Lunatics and absolute Mendicants." Alive to the need to make adequate provision for the lunatic poor – only Dublin, Cork, and Tipperary maintained proper facilities – he subsequently secured the appointment of a select committee to investigate the problem. In 1817 Parliament authorized the viceroy to order the establishment of asylums for the lunatic poor, with the expenses being defrayed by the grand juries.[47]

The fact that the Irish poor were not entitled by law "to call for parochial assistance" led one Irish member of Parliament to declare early in 1816 that the "principle of benevolence" was therefore "more imperatively demanded from the House" for Ireland than for England. What he had in mind was another prohibition on distillation from grain. Peel had already examined this proposal with characteristic care, securing from distillers an accurate account of their weekly consumption of grain. He discovered that the actual quantity consumed was only one-half the widely reported figure. Then again, much of the grain used was unfit for human consumption, and by no means all of it was lost to the food chain. After the spirit had been extracted, the residue, perhaps one-quarter of the initial amount, provided meal for live-stock. If the apparent saving would therefore be far less than was popularly supposed, Peel feared the additional stimulus prohibition would give to the far more wasteful and inefficient illicit distillers. Besides, unless there was reciprocal action in Britain, the Irish market would simply be flooded with English and Scottish spirits. Neither Liverpool nor Sidmouth favoured re-strictions on the British industry or on the trade in spirits with Ireland. Furthermore, Peel could not ignore the revenue implications of prohibition. Nevertheless, he publicly denied that they were a decisive consideration. "The loss of revenue," he assured the House on 5 March 1816, "was not to be put in competition with the subsistence of the people." The following day, long before word of Peel's comments reach Dublin, William Gregory reopened the issue.[48]

The best information then reaching Dublin Castle indicated that before the end of the summer corn would be far too expensive to be purchasable by the poor. Already the traditional forms of food rioting had broken out across the island. Mobs sought to prevent corn and potatoes being shipped out of their localities. They attacked wagons on the roads and barges tra-velling the Grand and Royal canals, and even cut the canals' banks. In recommending a prohibition on grain distillation, together with a ban on the export of potatoes, Gregory and Whitworth were hoping both to appease popular opinion and to ease the shortage of these essential provisions. Peel was not a man to be hurried by a "great outcry," however. He counselled caution and ordered a dispassionate investigation of these expedients. On reexamination, the prohibition on distillation seemed a no more worthwhile response now than it had earlier, while the hastily compiled statistics of the potato trade disclosed that Ireland was a much heavier importer than exporter of the vegetable. Peel complained angrily to his colleagues in the Irish capital and Gregory apologized for his credulity in making the proposal. A man "jealous of his personal dignity" and "so self conscious as to be almost egotistical," the chief secretary was acutely sensitive. He did not relish the task of now admitting to senior members of government, with whom he had already discussed a possible ban on Irish potato exports, that the proposal had been an ill-considered one. Moreover, he grasped the narrowness of his escape from parliamentary ridicule.[49]

Peel did not scorn all opportunities to influence popular opinion. In London, the prince regent's bounty had been extended to the poor of Spitalfields and the chief secretary pressed the government to display a similar concern for the distressed residents of the Irish capital. He argued successfully that the comparatively small sum of £2,000 would "conciliate more good will than many acts of much more substantial benefit." Then, during a debate in the Commons on 5 March 1817, he revealed that "to obviate the dangers of scarcity" the Irish government had taken "on themselves the responsibility of admitting American flour, which the letter of the law did not admit." Nevertheless, the government sought to mask the full extent of its intervention. Publicly, the prime minister dutifully recited the creed of the new political economy with its avowal of faith in the marketplace. He attributed the distress in some parts of Ireland to the difficulty of transporting provisions from areas of plenty to those of scarcity, and insisted that the present high prices of foodstuffs would draw into British ports "whatever further supply was wanted." But in the privacy of the Board of Trade, where Liverpool and his senior ministers met with Peel to discuss the Irish crisis, more humanitarian concerns held sway. There was a general disposition, Peel reported to Dublin, "to put all considerations of general policy & principle aside – and a strong inclination to resort to any measure which whether wise or not under ordinary circumstances, could be shown to be applicable to the present emergency." In cases of "*extreme necessity*," where persons were "*actually starving & without the hope of relief from other quarters*," and so long as the districts involved were limited in number, Peel sanctioned direct intervention. It was fear of the precedent which might thereby be established, that of an almost limitless government obligation to afford relief in Ireland, which prompted him to urge that every precaution be taken to prevent the source of the assistance becoming known.[50]

Steps were taken to secure oats and seed corn for Ireland, and to ensure that they found their way to tenants and were not monopolized by landlords.

In addition, the government purchased unused stocks of corn held by distillers, suspended the duties on imported rice and Indian corn, and authorized the release onto the market of those stocks currently held in warehouses under bond. As for government importation of rice, the prime minister discouraged this form of direct action, not out of ideological conviction but on the basis of experience. He recalled that, during an earlier period of scarcity, merchants had been employed to import rice on the government's account only to exploit their position "shamefully," charging the highest price for rice unfit for human consumption. Even so, Peel was confident that the ministers would not veto any plan if it was shown to be "really necessary or likely to be useful."[51]

The demanding task of supervising the distribution and sale of the arriving supplies – Peel estimated the quantity of seed corn alone at 40,000 quarters – fell to William Gregory. He was instructed to ensure that they were disposed of impartially, efficiently, and on the most advantageous terms, but "at the same time at a rate that will not counteract the object we have in view." Subsequently, Peel's only cavil was that Gregory had been too conservative in setting the price. He authorized him to charge less, even much less, "if it would in a proportionate degree multiply the advantages of the supply." The government's discreet activity failed, however, to check the rising prices of corn, meal, and potatoes. Gregory reported to Peel at the end of May: "hunger is clamorous, & partial scarcity is soon magnified into general." In fact, the areas of distress had continued to enlarge. Scarcity was widespread in both the West and the midlands, and oats bought for seed were being sold for food. On the question of price, Gregory explained that unless he kept it near the market level, the provisions would simply be purchased by speculators and hoarded until they could be sold at an even greater profit. What could be done, then, for the poor who were clearly unable to buy food? First, to help maintain order and prevent the interruption of food shipments, Gregory proposed that elements of the yeomanry be used to reinforce the troops and the "peelers" in the most disturbed districts. Within two weeks yeomen were being employed on escort duty, and small bodies had been called out in Kildare, Meath, Carlow, and in the city of Dublin. Second, the under-secretary suggested that the lord lieutenant be authorized to issue "money to the Clergy and resident Gentry to establish Soup Shops, or any means of furnishing the Poor with any food to allay the calls of hunger." Finally, at a meeting held in Gregory's office at the Castle on 6 June, and attended by Whitworth, Saurin, and Solicitor General Bushe, a proclamation was framed calling on persons in "higher spheres of life" to discontinue their consumption of potatoes and to reduce the allowance of oats to their horses. The daily ration of cavalry horses was also cut.[52]

Peel applauded the creation of soup shops, considering them "the best and most economical" means of affording relief. He wisely recommended that local Catholic priests be invited to participate. Their involvement would tend to "repress turbulence and interest a powerful agent in repressing it." Initially, the Irish relief measures had been funded with money drawn from the Treasury but they were subsequently incorporated into the more comprehensive scheme which the government launched with a relief bill that provided up to £250,000 for Ireland. Thanks to an earlier and modest parliamentary grant, Gregory was already in the process of realizing his ambition to guarantee an adequate supply of good water to the poor of the Dublin Liberties. Much of the burden of superintending the administration of this substantial fund now fell upon him. A commission was appointed to consider applications for relief projects, one on which Catholics as well as Protestants were represented, but it was Gregory who controlled and directed affairs. "I propose all our Acts to be done in the name of the Lord Lieutenant," he advised Peel, "the letters to be written and to be signed by me; in short that the whole shall be a Government transaction, and others who act with me, only do so, to share a burden which I individually could not undertake." Not surprisingly, with his stamina undermined by "a little touch of gout," he was "much oppressed with business."[53]

The government's sudden display of its determination to ease the misery of the poor in Ireland, and Gregory predicted "much Good from the knowledge," marked a significant change of strategy. "We must repel force by force," Peel observed, "but the more we can soothe the better for the future at any rate. It will tend to prevent the future necessity of applying force." Not that the spectre of a dangerous precedent had ceased to frighten ministers. Public assistance was ostensibly to be restricted to those areas where private subscriptions had already been established. In short, the principle of self-help was to be both publicly reaffirmed and rewarded. Thus aid was given to local subscriptions and the soup shops set up. More discreetly, agents were dispatched to districts without either resident gentry or local means of relief. More innovative were the investments in "fisheries, mines and even communal resettlement projects" and the employment of the poor on the construction of roads and other public works. Here was a liberal departure from orthodoxy, but one a number of Tories had prescribed as "an antidote do distress." In order to maximize employment on these works, wages were to be low. The chief secretary drew the line at any advance of public money to individuals who promised to employ men in the construction of houses or some other "merely private undertaking." As he explained to the viceroy, who had considered this possibility, the applicant "will expect the money of course upon better terms than he can procure it elsewhere – and is there a man in Ireland who will not make any application for an advance on those terms?"[54]

Despite the comparatively small sum actually expended – no more than

£30,000 by the third week of July, although it eventually totalled almost £40,000 – and the fraud and incompetence which resulted in much of the seed oats arriving "in a rotten condition," Peel adjudged this experiment in relief an unqualified success. In many areas where the landowners were absentees "the inhabitants must have perished from want of food if they had not been assisted." Moreover, the intervention of the state and encouraging crop forecasts did lift the pall of despair which had long been hanging over the island. Food riots had ceased by late July, and Peel could never "recollect a period when there was less insubordination or secret confederacy." A modest public investment had not only supplied "the means of affording the most extensive relief" but also had "made a strong impression on the mass of the people in favour of the Government." Ruminating on all of this, he accepted it as confirmation of his opinion that in Ireland severe distress promoted peace and good order. "The lower classes became in many parts completely dependent upon the bounty of their wealthier neighbours, and soon found the policy of fortifying their claims to compassion by peaceable behaviour." It was equally important, and even more fortunate, that the Irish government had been presented with an all too rare and peculiarly well-timed opportunity "of coming into contact with the public through the medium of kind offices." "It was a short time before the season at which relief would be naturelly derived from the produce of the present year," he reminded Lord Liverpool in October. "The pressure was most severe because the supply was nearly exhausted, and when the new crop became available and the pressure was gradually relieved, the people attributed their relief in a much greater degree to the intervention of the Government than they ought to have done."[55]

## CHAPTER FIVE

# The Failure of a Liberal Chief Secretary

The agreed term of Whitworth's viceroyalty expired in 1816. The government pressed him to remain at least a little longer and the lord lieutenant considered himself duty-bound to continue in office. He was loath to quit his post at the very moment when the large military establishment which he considered so indispensable in Ireland was being significantly reduced. The additional year proved to be a difficult one, as the viceroy struggled with the widespread distress and a prolonged bout of ill-health. Nor was he greatly comforted by the eventual choice of his successor, Earl Talbot. Both he and Peel attempted to dissuade the prime minister from making this appointment. Whitworth had "long been on terms of great intimacy and friendship" with Talbot, the latter having served on his staff in Russia, and he avowed that "there does not exist a more honest and well intentioned individual," but he was alarmed by his "connexions." Lady Talbot, the daughter of a County Meath gentleman, had an "endless train of clamorous relations" who ill became a vicereine. Any favour shown to them would damage her husband's reputation. No less unwelcome were Talbot's kinsmen, the duke of Leinster and Lord Downshire, "two of the most important opponents of the Government." Neither Whitworth nor Peel was entirely confident that Talbot's personal commitment to the Protestant cause would withstand this family sympathy for Catholic claims. But in the absence of a more suitable candidate, Talbot received the appointment.[1]

Whitworth and Peel quickly reconciled themselves to the decision and cheerfully cooperated with the incoming viceroy. Peel even postponed his own resignation, which he had intended to synchronize with Whitworth's. Urged to remain by Liverpool, Talbot, and sixty of the Irish members of Parliament, he agreed to stay on until the new viceroy was securely in place and had gained some understanding of the character of those with whom he would have to deal. Here was one sure way to allay the misgivings he and Whitworth shared, and to ensure that the new administration held fast to the existing course.[2]

"We all like Lord Talbot very much," Peel reported to his former chief in mid-October 1817, barely a month after the transfer of government. Twenty years his predecessor's junior, Talbot was active, affable, personable, and convivial. He travelled extensively throughout the island and was soon boasting to friends that there had never been a "more moveable" viceroy than himself. His pleasures and tastes were those of the squirearchy – riding, shooting, and eating – and he was a dedicated agricultural improver. His political and religious opinions were fully in keeping with this life-style, and one critic was later to dismiss him as a "besotted predestinated" Tory. He was certainly a stalwart Protestant ever ready to raise his glass to "the glorious, pious and immortal memory" and resolutely opposed to concession on the Catholic question. As for his opinion of the Irish, that was characteristically genial, if patronizing. "They are a strange set of mortals," he remarked, "as mischievous and full of tricks as monkeys, and as little to be depended upon tho' they are good natured and very hospitable." Yet even those Irishmen who disagreed with him on the pivotal issue of emancipation considered him "honest" and "high-minded," and Daniel O'Connell described him as "impartial" and allowed that he was "not a bad man."[3]

An uncomplicated personality and limited administrative experience – apart from his brief diplomatic career he had helped to organize the Volunteers in Staffordshire and had been appointed lord lieutenant of the county in 1812 – led Talbot to accept gratefully guidance from the two commanding figures in the executive government. The self-assured Whitworth had willingly delegated responsibility to his capable subordinates, Peel and Gregory, and he had freely acknowledged his chief secretary as an indispensable "assistant" in the business of government. The success of the viceroyalty had been "mainly owing" to Peel's "inflexible integrity," "extraordinary and premature wisdom," and "ardent zeal," he admitted to the home secretary. As for Gregory, he had further consolidated his influence during Whitworth's illness. While the viceroy was confined to his lodge and with Peel absent in Britain, it was Gregory who supervised the administration. He had been "as rigid as a Methodist, & uncomplying as a Presbyterian" in fending off deputations seeking an audience with the ailing lord lieutenant. He alone was granted daily access to Whitworth, calling at the Viceregal Lodge as he returned each evening from the Castle to his own attractive residence in the Park. Indeed, he grew a little embarrassed by this singular mark of confidence. "I requested of him to see Littlehales," he reported to Peel; "such a preference to the civil Secretary would be Death to the Military."[4]

Talbot's dependence upon these two men was necessarily greater. No doubt, he was a little overawed by their knowledge of Ireland and he appears from the outset to have been content with a mere titular authority over Peel.

His relationship with Gregory was founded upon the realization that without a guiding hand he would quickly lose his way in the Irish maze. It was strengthened by the very high opinion he developed of the under-secretary's zeal and administrative ability, which encouraged him to extend to Gregory the privilege of speaking his mind "on all public matters without reserve," and by a deepening friendship which was long to survive their terms of office. Given this mutual respect and trust, the executive continued to function much as it had during Whitworth's time. "Every thing is going on smoothly," Gregory reassured Peel at the end of the year.[5]

The new viceroy wholeheartedly embraced not only the men he had inherited but also their measures. Yet important elements of the policy identified with Peel had already been called into question, or were undergoing significant modification in the face of continuing economic and political pressures. The British economy had picked up momentum in 1817, only to slow perceptibly in 1818. Prices of agricultural produce and manufactured goods began another long slide as supply exceeded demand, though government and Opposition disagreed over the cause. Ministers insisted that the problem was rooted in overproduction, thereby "exonerating themselves from blame for a failing economy [and] ... excusing themselves from the need to take action to correct it." The Whigs, meanwhile, argued that underconsumption had triggered the depression. They attributed the collapse of domestic demand first to excessive taxation, and subsequently to the deflationary consequences of the resumption of specie payments in 1819. It was a refrain the Irish among them took up with particular passion and vigour. They cited the decline in Irish purchases of English manufactured goods as irrefutable proof that an overtaxed people had been reduced to beggary. Their demand for a lightening of the tax burden was initially resisted by ministers worried by the parlous state of Irish finances. Peel advised Sidmouth in July 1817 that the government was in a "wretched state of Poverty" and that revenues were "declining at an alarming rate." Average weekly receipts in 1816 had been £90,000, but in the second week of July 1817 they totalled barely half that amount. "I never entertained very sanguine hopes of much improvement in the financial concerns of this part of the Empire," the chief secretary added. One year later he was warning the Opposition in the Commons that the cost of meeting their demands for tax relief in Ireland would be a substantial increase in that country's operating deficit; but the harassed government was obliged to give some ground. The window tax was reduced as were the luxury taxes on carriages, horses, and servants. The chancellor of the exchequer lamely explained that this general abatement was being granted in the hope that it "would operate as an inducement to gentlemen of property, now absentees, to reside at home." When all was said and done, however, Peel would be leaving the coffers of the executive government almost as empty as he had found them.[6]

The dismal state of the economy and of Irish finances ensured that there would be no slackening of economizing zeal, and cost-cutting and penny pinching continued to bear heavily upon policy. The severe restrictions earlier imposed upon the lord lieutenant's right to grant pensions were not relaxed, even though the annual expenditure had finally been reduced below the figure at which greater liberality would have been legal. Similarly, the pressure to reduce the military establishment was unrelenting. Peel ceased to talk of 25,000 men as the safe minimum force for Ireland. Instead, he suggested in November 1817 that it might ultimately be set at 18,000 men, and as an interim step proposed that the present garrison of 22,000 be cut by 2,000 men in March 1818. This was a recommendation the new viceroy dutifully endorsed. Another victim of the drive for economy was that system of education which Peel had described as central to his hopes of effecting Ireland's lasting tranquillization once a powerful army had overawed the unruly. Demands for savings were sent to the governors of the Protestant Charter Schools and to those of the Foundling Hospital. These institutions may have been of dubious value as educational instruments of social control, but this could not be said of the rapidly proliferating and far more promising schools of the Kildare Place Society, whose parliamentary grant was almost halved in 1818. More ominous still, sectarianism was jeopardizing this expriment in undenominational education. Roman Catholics were growing restless over the Protestant majority on the society's managing committee, and they disliked "the policy of reading the Holy Scriptures without note or comment." Their suspicion that education was really an instrument of proselytism was nourished by the increasingly aggressive activities of the London Hibernian Society, and the founding in 1818 of the Irish Society for Promoting the Education of the Native Irish through the medium of their own language.[7]

Emigration was another of Peel's long-term remedial measures, and like education it was continuing to show discouraging if not disappointing results. Of the 20,000 Irish who sailed for North America in 1818, an overwhelming majority were still Presbyterians or Anglicans from Ulster. Most of those who did leave the other provinces were also Protestants. In short, to the extent that it was having an impact upon Irish society, emigration was weakening that minority Peel was so anxious to protect. But 20,000 emigrants did little to ease the perceived problem of overpopulation, and even this modest figure was to fall dramatically with the news in 1819 of hard times in the United States. Ironically, the deepening depression in Britain, and with it rising unemployment and mounting unrest, led the cabinet to sanction in that year another modest emigration project.[8]

Peel's reforms of local government and of the administration of justice had not proven entirely successful either. The revised procedure for selecting sheriffs, which effectively gave the nomination to the outgoing officer, had failed to satisfy critics. Reluctantly, the chief secretary accepted the principle of judicial nomination. This he had earlier opposed because of his doubts of the wisdom and impartiality of the Irish judiciary. Even as the judges received instructions to take upon themselves the selection of "fit persons to serve the office of Sheriff," Peel and Vesey Fitzgerald were piloting through the Commons a measure designed to curtail the scandalous abuse of grand jury presentments. A qualified civil engineer was to be appointed in each Irish county to report on proposed works and to regulate and inspect those actually undertaken. The intent, as the prime minister explained in the Lords, was "to remove the opportunity of acting corruptly" without dismantling "the whole system, as it now existed." Six months later, in January 1818, the statute had to be suspended because of the Irish government's embarrassing inability to find thirty-two competent surveyors. The revised bill Fitzgerald introduced in May provided for the submission of all presentments for new works to a full attendance of magistrates at the quarter sessions previous to the assizes at which they were to be laid before the grand jury. Additional provisions required that greater publicity be given to intended projects, and empowered magistrates to call for evidence on the costs likely to be incurred. But a measure which relied upon the magistracy to check local corruption was unlikely to inspire confidence among the victims or critics of the grand jury "system of profligate jobbing and expense."[9]

Of all Peel's innovations in Ireland, the one most closely identified with him was the Peace Preservation Force. Yet in modifying the arrangements for defraying the costs of its employment he was making an implicit admission of failure. The "terror" of heavier taxes had been viewed by Peel as a vital stimulus to the higher orders to uphold the law, and an essential deterrent to the turbulence of the lower orders. Consequently, the amendments which he introduced in March 1817, under the terms of which a proclaimed district might secure relief from two-thirds of the costs involved, represented an important retreat. Nor was wide use made of the additional ordinary police powers which he had extended to grand juries. Only in County Longford had a jury acted. Furthermore, although he had secured a renewal of the Insurrection Act in 1817, and had privately expressed the opinion that it would be unfair to deprive a new executive of such an essential weapon, he moved its repeal shortly before his departure from Ireland in the summer of 1818. Overjoyed at his emancipation from duty and drudgery, he gave little thought to the ambiguous nature of his legacy as chief secretary. Free at last, he wrote to one friend as his Irish career came to an end; free of responsibility, anxiety, Ribbonmen, Orangemen, patronage mongers, and the daily trivia of Irish administration.[10]

Peel was succeeded by one of the "saints in politics." Charles Grant, Jr, was a child of the Clapham Sect. His family's evangelical ardour was reflected in the fifty-one subscriptions he, his brother Robert, and their father held in philanthropic societies. They were prominent in the British and Foreign Bible Society, and when he joined his father in the Commons in 1811 Grant quickly made his mark as a captivating speaker devoted to such Claphamite causes as the fostering of missionary activities among the natives of India and the promotion of education among the poor of Britain. While involvement in these crusades might well have been considered a fitting preparation for the office of Irish secretary, Grant had also been a consistent and eloquent champion of Catholic Emancipation. During the debate on Grattan's bill in 1813, he had denounced the Protestant Ascendancy as established in Ireland. It was "grounded on contempt and suspicion and hatred," and exalted "one class on the ruins of another," he had charged. Who could be surprised, therefore, that so many Irish possessed "no sense of the moral obligation of obeying the laws"? Of course, Charles Grant was offered the office despite his Catholic sympathies, not because of them. More than one stalwart Protestant had declined it before he had been approached. In short, Liverpool had turned to him for want of someone more attractive to the existing executive in Dublin. This information did not make the appointment any more palatable to Talbot, and from the outset of the partnership there was reason to fear that he and his chief secretary would fail to achieve that harmony so vital to successful government.[11]

Grant's friends were "not sanguine about his success" in Ireland, though their pessimism probably owed as much to their familiarity with his shortcomings as it did to an awareness of the distrust with which he was certain to be greeted at Dublin Castle. An amiable disposition and gracious manners did not compensate for absent-mindedness, unpunctuality, and indolence. One contemporary observed that if you invited Charles to "dine with you at six on Monday, you were very likely to have Robert at seven on Tuesday." "He thinks of nothing but devotion," another complained, "he is a saint, and can and will do no business whatever." He might have been rescued from the consequences of his administrative failings had he enjoyed the full confidence and support of the under-secretary. In background they were not dissimilar. Both were of middle-class origins; both were the sons of men who had not only made fortunes in India but had also risen high in the direction of the East India Company, and had entered Parliament and devoted themselves to the welfare of the natives of that part of the empire; both had been born in India; both had graduated from Cambridge and been called to the Bar; both were evangelicals. Nor was Grant an easy man to dislike, and Gregory did adopt a somewhat paternalistic attitude towards a superior who at the age of forty was sixteen years his junior. This sentiment never deepened into intimacy, however, and it failed to allay the suspicion with which the under-secretary regarded the chief secretary's policies. Where they differed most profoundly was on the Catholic question. The gulf that divided them on this fundamental issue was never to be bridged. As a result, from the day of his arrival, Grant found himself acting with a viceroy and an under-secretary who were united by friendship, by a determination to guard the Ascendancy, and by suspicion of him. Looking back on his experience a decade later, he warned another liberal about to set out for Dublin that William Gregory was the master of the "whole machine" of government. Undeniably, Grant's inability to wrest control of that machine from Gregory's grasp contributed to his failure as chief secretary.[12]

In one sense Grant was a victim of circumstance. He inherited an under-secretary already deeply entrenched at the Castle and enjoying the full confidence of the lord lieutenant. Moreover, Gregory conducted the entire business of the office during Grant's prolonged and unavoidable absences in London. Alive to the "peculiar difficulty" of the situation, Grant drew it somewhat tentatively and belatedly to the attention of the home secretary. "At present it is scarcely possible to follow out any systematic enquiry upon any important public subject connected with this people, or to mature and thoroughly canvass any proposition," he explained. "The train of thought & investigation is broken, and on every return to Ireland the process is to be recommenced." His suggestion that the chief secretary's obligation to attend Parliament be limited to every second year was impracticable, given the volume of Irish business in the Commons. Therefore, during his absence, and as a result of his administrative inefficiency and naiveté, William Gregory was able to exercise his discretion to the full. Indeed, the range of his activities expanded to embrace those of the military under-secretary in 1819. Time-consuming and trivial as many of these additional duties were, Gregory's shouldering of them saved the Exchequer £2,000 a year and made him an even more formidable figure. Little wonder that Peel assured him: "Your situation becomes more and more important every day."[13]

It was Charles Grant's added misfortune that his appointment was soon followed by renewed agitation of the Catholic question, for Talbot and Gregory linked this complication to his arrival. "We are thinking of starting again," O'Connell advised one friend early in 1819. The strategy called for a sympathetic lord mayor of Dublin to summon a meeting of the city's Protestants to petition for Catholic relief. In its aftermath, an angry Gregory instructed Grant that this "ill advised Meeting" had reawakened "that spirit of animosity" which had been dormant, and he warned that the "party violence" would "diffuse itself through the Country."[14] Meanwhile, Talbot was confiding in the sympathetic Sidmouth. He emphasized the embarrass-ment of his position in being yoked to Grant. "I must confess, that on the present occasion, I am totally at a loss how I ought to express myself," he wrote. "For situated as I am, the Representative of a Protestant Sovereign, holding as I most avowedly do the opinion that the present restrictions upon the Catholics should not be removed, how can I possibly reconcile the statements I am in duty bound to make to Government, with the sentiments of those with whom I have been recently politically connected, in this Country, whose Views & Opinions upon this vital question are in direct contradiction to my own?" He also appealed to the Almighty, seeking a providential parliamentary rejection of the claims sufficiently decisive to "allay the fears of the Protestants" and "put down the hopes and expectations of the Catholics." His prayers went unanswered. The Catholic bill was defeated in the Commons by less than a handful of votes, while the remarks of the prime minister in the Lords were less than reassuring to diehard Protestants. Having repeated his familiar objections to relief, Liverpool had gone on to declare that he would "be ready to abandon the considerations which theory and abstract reasoning suggested if a concession to those claims held out any prospect of practical good."[15]

Confident of the lord lieutenant's support, William Gregory obstructed Grant's well-intentioned efforts to appease Irish Catholic opinion. The under-secretary frustrated a proposal to appoint a Catholic as a fishery commissioner. He again intervened when the chief secretary attempted to put a stop to the provocative annual decoration of King William III's statue in College Green, to commemorate each July the victories of the Boyne and Aughrim, and the monarch's birthday every November 4. Although the state had "disassociated itself from active participation in Williamite celebrations" since 1806, and liberal Protestants had long denounced them, the under-secretary knew that Saurin and Talbot shared his concern that this action would alienate conservatives from the executive. Besides, the attorney general doubted the legality of any suppression of the event. "Suppose the lawyers you consult should differ in opinion with the Attorney General," Gregory cautioned Grant; "you could take no steps in your own name, no order would bear any Authority, unless issued in the name of the Lord Lieutenant, & you are aware, from what has already passed, how adverse he is to any *commands*, thinking them illegal."[16]

Grant's recommendation that the government stem the torrent of abuse one of its press allies – the *Hibernian Journal* – was pouring upon all sympathizers with the Catholic cause also failed to move the under-secretary to action. Although in this instance the proposal was merely an extension of the policy Gregory had executed for Peel, he now declined to go beyond an instruction to the newspaper's editor "to avoid Personalities." Unwilling to admit defeat, Grant tackled the problem indirectly. Over the course of the following two years he exploited the demand for economy to secure a significant reduction of the Proclamation Fund out of which the *Hibernian Journal* and other organs were heavily subsidized. For his part, even Gregory was anxious by 1821 to rid the Protestant cause of this particular liability. As he explained to Sidmouth, "being a Government Paper, and in very little circulation, the paragraphs of its columns were quoted by the opposition

Papers decidedly Catholic, and the Government (or rather the Protestant part of it) was constantly attacked for protecting and encouraging such violent principles." Yet this belated unity of purpose did not prevent disagreement over strategy, and the closing of the *Journal* illustrated anew the disunity within the Irish administration. Grant declined to endorse the terms which the under-secretary had offered to the newspaper's publisher with the lord lieutenant's full approval. Gregory surmised that Grant wished to leave himself free to declare in the House that the *Journal* had been suppressed without the government entering into any fixed arrangement with its proprietor. But when the disgruntled owner carried to Lord Sidmouth and the prime minister his complaint that the understanding he had reached with Gregory had been broken, the under-secretary took the opportunity to criticize his superior. "I regret very much that Mr. Grant is not aware of the great importance it is to the quiet administration of this country to keep the press on the side of the Government, or at least to prevent its hostility," he observed to the home secretary.[17]

The conciliation of Catholic opinion was only one aspect of Grant's policy. He was equally anxious to improve the quality of the Irish magistracy and to impress upon those persons connected with the administration of justice that their conduct was being closely watched. This latter concern was the larger intent of his bill to regulate fees in the Court of Chancery. Yet it paled into insignificance when compared to his ambitious scheme to seize the opportunity presented by George III's death to effect a thoroughgoing revision of the magistracy. He would have withdrawn all commissions of the peace and have reissued them to qualified persons only. The plan was frustrated by the lethargy of the Irish lord chancellor. Lord Manners still had not compiled the lists of suitable magistrates for each county by the time Grant left office in 1821. Nevertheless, by then this essential preparatory work was nearing completion.[18]

Charles Grant was also an advocate of the education of the lower orders. Having studied the problem, he calculated that as many as 400,000 Catholic children were receiving instruction in "hedge" schools. He feared it was of the worst kind, the masters being "active promoters of agitation" and the books in use the "adventures of notorious villains and profligates" which served "to cherish that disposition for enterprise and that passion for danger which constitutionally mark the Irish." All of which afforded, or so he believed, "strong proof" that education would be of little utility unless it embraced "the inculcation of moral and religious principle." In Ireland, however, that objective continued to pose peculiar problems. Indeed, they may well explain Grant's failure to bring before Parliament a promised bill to remove the obstacles to the implementation of the reports of the commissioners of education. He had concluded that a national educational system was certain to be bedevilled by controversy over moral and religious instruction, and came to favour a less ambitious scheme. State support ought to be offered to those individuals, whether Catholic or Protestant, who established schools in which "the true principles of Christian benevolence" were taught and "real moral and religious improvement" promoted. A small fund of £4,000 was therefore set aside for this purpose. On another vexed question, that of tithes, the devout Grant was admirably open-minded. He voiced a willingness to examine sympathetically any measure introduced by that indefatigable campaigner for reform, Sir Henry Parnell. His liberalism on this issue reflected his shock at the condition of the Irish poor. "They were obliged to feed on esculent plants, such as mustard-seed, nettles, potato-tops, and potato-stalks – a diet which brought on a debility of body, and increased the disease more than anything else could have done," he informed the House in explaining the fever epidemic which ravaged large areas of the island in 1818. In his opinion, "The patience with which they had borne that distress was truly admirable, and was not to be paralleled by anything in history."[19]

Grant's desire to aid the poor was restrained by the under-secretary and checked by those prevailing doctrines of political economy to which they both subscribed. Thus Gregory opposed his plan to purchase potatoes in the North in order to sell them cheaply in the South, "not from any doubt of the great partial Distress, but from the principle that the Government are not on all occasions to be the first resort when any pressure occurs, without the Gentry contributing to the relief of their impoverished Tenantry." How could the poor buy food unless they were provided with work, he asked? The government could not create employment, he added. Initially, the chief secretary uttered similarly orthodox sentiments. Speaking in the Commons in April 1819, he endorsed Newport's assertion that without additional employment "a great mass of the labouring poor must be reduced to absolute beggary," but cautioned "that though there might be some occasions in which the government might interpose to find employment for them, any permanent legislative enactment on such a subject would be nothing more than a delusion, and could not be attended with beneficial consequences." Not that this ideology withstood, in his case, further exposure to Ireland's chronic distress. Service on a select committee which under Newport's chairmanship inquired into the condition of the Irish poor persuaded him, as it did the other members, of the need to make exceptions to "'the un-questionable principle that legislative interference in the operations of human industry [ought] as much as possible to be avoided'."[20]

Writing to the prime minister in October 1819, Grant urged that serious consideration be given, for reasons of humanity and expediency, to a limited measure of public assistance for Ireland. "Want of work creates in this country a readiness to join any effort against the laws," he reported. "If some timely aid, rendered at small expense which, I am aware, is a consideration not to be lost sight of, should avert commotion, it would be well repaid." By the year's end he was privately pleading for a more ambitious measure of government intervention. He likened the position of Ireland to that of England in the seventeenth century, when state intervention had given "a prodigious stimulus to the national industry and prosperity." The development of Ireland's natural resources, especially those in the impoverished West, would bring rewards that would more than repay the government for its trouble and expense. As an initial, experimental step, he proposed that £100,000 of what remained of the £250,000 voted two years earlier be made available in the form of low interest or interest free loans, perhaps even as outright grants, to spur public works projects. These would afford "some vent" to the "superfluous activity of the unemployed and deeply distressed population," and produce "an excellent effect" on the minds of the Irish people. Here would be proof that the government was alive to their difficulties.[21]

The radical implications of Grant's proposal made its adoption unlikely, even had he not admitted the impossibility of a government creating "funds where a whole nation is in want." Furthermore, the chancellor of the exchequer, to whom it was forwarded by Liverpool, complained of the large amounts which had already been spent in Ireland, often on "'mere jobs'." Yet the proposal was not as striking a departure from recent practice as it seemed. Grant's scheme of public works was in a sense merely an extension of that of his predecessor. Peel had recognized that employment was essential if the Irish were to be rendered less "vicious," and he had overseen the modest program of public works during the crisis of 1817. Nor would he have disputed Grant's observation that "Temporary aid in a particular emergency may be afforded with advantage; but to provide that the population of a large country shall at all times be fully occupied and comfortably situated, is a task beyond the competence of human policy or power."[22] Moreover, Grant was appealing to that doctrine of Irish exceptionalism which had lain at the heart of Peel's policy. Nevertheless, in one important respect, he did intend his term of office to mark a sharp break with the past. Grant was determined to govern with the aid of the ordinary law only.

Grant had quickly formed a very high as well as a sympathetic opinion of the Irish. He admired "their genius and intelligence – their peculiarly sociable and affectionate natures – their disposition to give confidence where it is merited – their steadfast devotion to any cause which they have once heartily espoused – their patience under misfortunes – their constitutional hospitality – their romantic love of adventure – their passionate attachment to all the charities of blood and kindred." Not only had they lived up to their reputation for generosity in their dealings with him, but they had demonstrated a much greater "consideration and delicacy" than he had been led to expect. He was grateful that so few "mischief-makers" had sought to exploit his obvious differences with the viceroy on the Catholic issue, and he praised the popular newspapers for expatiating upon his appointment "with great ability and energy." On the strength of this brief personal experience he was soon drawing general conclusions about the state of Ireland. Not only were there "few materials for political agitation" left among the Irish but they were also "gradually settling down into peaceable habits," he advised Sidmouth in November 1818. He had come to believe that the incidence of serious crime was "not much worse" in Ireland than in "other parts of the Empire," and that a rapid improvement would result if gentry and magistrates were obliged to rely upon "their own exertions under the sanction of law, instead of flying for recourse on every occasion to military aid." [23]

To compel that self-reliance, Grant again exploited the desire for economy in government. He pressed for further reductions in the size of the military establishment, brushing aside the home secretary's caution that in the special circumstances of Ireland "the Magistrates, and other Civil Officers, cannot be brought, or perhaps reasonably expected, to act, without the certainty of immediate Support, and Assistance from the Military in case of Necessity." The chief secretary went directly to the prime minister with the welcome word that a garrison of 17,000 men would eventually suffice. He insisted that it was "really not doing justice to the people to represent them as in such a state of disturbance as can be encountered only by a large military force." Ireland's want was a good police force, he argued, again echoing Peel, and he predicted that it would never be supplied so long as there was a large military garrison. But what kind of police? A highly centralized gendarmerie controlled by the executive was constitutionally repugnant and would tend "to deteriorate, if not to extinguish what subsists of good magistracy in Ireland, and to degrade the gentry from their natural station." On the other hand, the existing ordinary police was "miserably defective." All too often baronial constables were the dependents of influential local figures "placed upon the police as on a superannuation list," and were "in every respect calculated to do more mischief than good." Nevertheless, impressed by the success of the regular force organized in County Longford under the additional powers extended to grand juries by Peel, Grant eventually plumped for reform of the existing constabulary. However, at the request of several ministers, he subsequently postponed introduction of the bill he had prepared. What the government did do was offer both to exempt from townland fines for illicit distillation any barony that established an effective force of "preventive revenue police," and to share the costs of maintaining them. [24]

Grant's repudiation of the military as an instrument of government, and his determination to bolster "the ordinary defences of society," was accompanied by an even more explicit repudiation of the doctrine of Irish exceptionalism. Magistrates denied a ready resort to military aid were also to be discouraged from applying for extraordinary civil powers. He despised the Insurrection Act as an invasion of fundamental rights and condemned it in the Commons as "contrary to that principle of which, in his opinion, the government of Ireland ought to be conducted." It was the essence of good government, he affirmed, that the excesses of the people – excesses he broadly attributed to illicit distillation, religious animosities, overpopulation, and widespread unemployment – be resisted by steady and constitutional rather than extraordinary measures. "The case of Ireland had always been considered as an exceptional case," he reminded the Commons in 1820. "This had been the unvaried tone – that such or such a particular measure might be very good for England, but that it would not be good for Ireland. The calamities by which Ireland had been most deeply afflicted, were to be mainly ascribed to their constant recourse to extraordinary measures." Her magistrates had thereby been encouraged to abandon their proper functions, and the mutual dependence and support which ought to exist between them and the people had been lost. Too often, in civil and political emergencies, "immediate recourse" had been had "to the agency of the government."[25]

"It was by a steady and inflexible adherence to constitutional principles that England had attained to her present prosperity, and by pursuing a similar course he hoped that Ireland would share the advantage," Grant announced to cheers in the Commons. Yet this was a strategy full of risk and fraught with danger, not least to its architect. Sidmouth questioned its wisdom, and the further reductions the chief secretary proposed to the garrison and staff in Ireland encountered strong opposition at the Horse Guards. In Dublin, Talbot offered grudging support at best. He leaned too heavily on Gregory for advice to accept the proposition that Ireland could be governed in the same manner as was England. Although he had outflanked the lord lieutenant in this opening skirmish over policy, with an appeal to the spirit of retrenchment, the test of Grant's experiment in "constitutional" government awaited the outbreak of widespread disorders.[26]

Fears that radicals such as "Orator" Hunt, who were exploiting in 1819 the misery the depression had brought to England's industrial cities to agitate for political reform, and had invited Irish Catholics to join the campaign, would find a responsive audience in Ireland proved to be groundless. Not that her farmers were faring any better than England's manufacturers, or her peasants suffering less than English operatives. The price of wheat continued to decline steadily throughout the year and the deepening distress was not eased by the deflationary fiscal policies of the Bank of Ireland and the partial failure of the potato crop. Talbot and Gregory watched carefully for any sign that the succession of large reform meetings being held in Britain, and which ended so tragically in St Peter's Square, Manchester, in August, were stirring Irish dissidents into activity. The viceroy admitted to

Sidmouth that there was reason to think that certain persons were merely awaiting the result of "the seditious proceedings in England to begin their own machinations," but he disclaimed any "apprehensions on the subject." There was no evidence that Ireland's Catholics would respond to Hunt's invitation to mix their claims with his "wild and wicked politics." Nor was Gregory surprised by this lack of Irish interest in the English agitation. The lower orders of Ireland "have no feelings in common with the same orders in England," he assured the Home Office, "tho' the national hatred is much too strong not to make them rejoice at any Disturbances in England, yet totally regardless whether People, or the Government, are successful. Parliamentary reform may catch the Presbyterians of the North, but the great Mass of the Catholic Population of Ireland, know nothing of it." This was not an analysis with which Charles Grant would have agreed, resting as it did upon a deep-seated conviction that the great mass of Irishmen were different from Britons and disloyal. Instead, he rested his hopes for the avoidance of commotion of the "earnest endeavours of the better sort of Catholics," including the priesthood, and the "peaceable disposition" of the people.[27]

The chief secretary's confidence in the Irish Catholic population was not shared by the lord lieutenant. In mid-November he advised the home secretary of the opinion of those, who, "from their long experience and acquaintance with Ireland," were the best judges of what was happening there. These experts, unnamed but presumably Gregory and Saurin, were sure that there was "a very bad spirit among the lower classes generally speaking, at least in five counties," and that many of them had enrolled as Ribbonmen. In short, there was a strong suspicion that the activities in the Irish countryside went beyond the traditional banding together by peasants to ensure the availability of land for tillage. Already, in Britain, the cabinet had responded to the perceived danger of radical revolution there with a fresh series of repressive measures. Talbot likewise responded to reports of nocturnal gatherings, the administration of oaths, and raids on houses of the gentry by peasants seeking weapons with the proclamation of districts in several counties. But it was in Galway, and to a lesser extent Roscommon, that Grant's liberal policies were put to the test.[28]

Responding to disturbances in the northern baronies of Galway early in October, the executive encouraged the magistrates to meet to consider whether "Military assistance in conjunction with the civil power might not tend to check the mischief," and instructed the general commanding the Connaught District to confer with them. The local gentlemen decided to establish a subscription, out of which to pay informants and reward peasants who refused to join the Ribbonmen, and requested the authority to search for arms. Although the request was immediately granted, they soon proved unequal to the task of restoring order. Few in number, they commanded a

"very inefficient" body of ordinary policemen. When small parties of soldiers were sent to their aid they were unable even to secure accommodation
for them in those towns where the need for a detachment was most urgent.
The nervous magistrates therefore made application for a force of "peelers."
Grant had not urged their employment because of his dislike for this harsh
"species of force." But the proclaiming of four of Galway's baronies on 21
December 1819, during the chief secretary's absence in London, failed to
check the disorder. Nor was this surprising, given the delay of three weeks
before the proclamation could take effect. The government found the selection of suitable men and their outfitting a frustratingly lengthy task, and
this "delay gave spirit to the disturbers and allowed an extension of their
efforts."[29]

In the midst of this crisis the executive was thrown into disarray by the
death of Lady Talbot. The viceroy, having already suffered the agony of
the death of his youngest son, who had died of "water on the Brain" in
April 1818, was prostrated by the loss of the mother of his ten children in
December 1819. Gregory hurriedly advised both Sidmouth and Grant that
the lord lieutenant was "totally incapacitated from the transaction of public
business," and on 11 January 1820 he sailed for Holyhead and a period of
leave in England. The primate and the chancellor were again sworn as lords
justices, as was the military commander when he recovered from an illness.
Grant had returned to Dublin shortly before Talbot's departure.[30]

The chief secretary's policy of lessening dependence upon the military
by cutting the establishment, thereby compelling magistrates to show greater
initiative and self reliance, had suffered a symbolic reverse even before he
left London. The cabinet had decided to reinforce the garrison, and it ordered
a regiment of infantry to Ireland. Despite Grant's objections, which he
repeated from Dublin on 10 January, the orders stood. No doubt it was in
an effort to forestall additional reinforcements that he now submitted a series
of optimistic reports to the Home Office. "The state of the country in general
is more tranquil than it was, or was represented to be, some weeks ago,"
he informed Sidmouth on 24 January. A fortnight later he reported an
enthusiastic popular response to the proclamation of George IV's accession,
and declared that "his Majesty has nowhere more loyal and faithful subjects
than in Ireland." He also discovered grounds for optimism in the news from
Galway, reporting that even in that county information was at last being
volunteered and that this was traditionally the first sign that the storm was
passing. It was an assessment the subsequent events in that county did little
to substantiate.[31]

The assassination of a prominent gentleman in broad daylight on a road
near Tuam in mid-January, and attacks on the homes of two magistrates by
men seeking weapons, had long since excited demands from the gentry for
additional policemen and for "a more direct interposition on the part of the

Government." By early February frightened magistrates were demanding the extension of the Peace Preservation Act to all but four of the county's baronies, the dispersal of the troops stationed there (many wanted small detachments for the protection of their own persons and properties), and the reintroduction of the Insurrection Act. The additional baronies were proclaimed, and the force of 1,000 troops and 300 "peelers" distributed across the county, but Grant had no intention of conceding the necessity of the Insurrection Act. Before this direct challenge to his policy of governing without resort to extraordinary powers, he stood his ground. The impossibility of securing passage of such a controversial piece of legislation during the coming abbreviated session of Parliament provided a convenient excuse. The act was "thus placed out of the option of the Government," the magistrates were officially informed by the lords justices.[32]

This stand moved the magistrates to a public condemnation of the lords justices and "A loyal inhabitant of Ireland" to denounce the chief secretary in a letter to the home secretary. Sidmouth discussed the charges made by this anonymous correspondent with Talbot, who was still in England and had made no secret of his distrust of Grant and disagreement with his policies. Rather than forward the letter to the lords justices or Grant for comment, they decided to ask Gregory to undertake the sensitive task of sounding out the former without the knowledge of the latter. Despite the viceroy's assurances that Grant was already "tottering," Gregory declined to engage in a form of "double dealing" which was "inconsistent with good feeling" and might well be interpreted as an effort to elevate himself at the expense of his superior. He did not deny that Grant had made many enemies "amongst the Gentry of Ireland by the difficulty of access to him, not from refusing to see them, but from neglecting to keep his own appointments, and putting them off from day to day;" and by his tardiness in answering letters. Equally, "his uncalled for and unfounded encomium on the Catholic priesthood" had created "an Host of Enemies" amongst the "well wishers to the Protestant Establishment." Even the Catholic gentry in Galway, Gregory added, attributed the chief secretary's opposition to the reenactment of the Insurrection Act to a concern that its passage "would falsify the supposed influence of a Popish clergy over the minds of an exclusively Catholic population." Although the under-secretary had long believed the act to be an essential weapon in the arsenal of the Irish government, he acknowledged the impossibility of getting it through a brief session of Parliament. Moreover, he suggested that Grant had a last recognized the seriousness of the crisis in Galway and neighbouring Roscommon, and that his general opinions on Irish government had undergone something of a transformation. He was now "sensible of the fatal error" which had influenced his behaviour since his arrival, that Protestant tyranny and Catholic slavery were the root causes of disturbances. In short, Gregory held out the possibility to Talbot and

Sidmouth that "the Tide of Popularity" might yet be turned in Grant's favour. Nor did he overlook the opportunity which would be presented to the viceroy to regain control of the government as a result of the accession of the new monarch. Grant would have to return to Scotland to seek reelection to a new Parliament.[33]

Gregory's impression that the chief secretary had finally grasped the extent of the evil at work in the West was soon confirmed. "The danger is lest the ribbonmen presuming on their numbers and impunity should attempt collectively some bold enterprise," Grant admitted in a report to Sidmouth on 21 February 1820. With this fear in mind, he abandoned his struggle to compel magistrates to shoulder their traditional responsibilities. Troops about to be shipped to Scotland were diverted to Connaught, and the force operating in Galway exceeded 3,000 men by the beginning of March. Owing to the lack of magistrates to lead troops serving as instruments of the civil authority, commissions of the peace were granted to all field officers in the disturbed districts, and to all captains commanding separate detachments, while a number of "peeler" constables were empowered to "call out and lead" the military. The most effective deployment of troops was initially hampered, however, by a wholesale change of commanders, including the commanding officer, at the height of the crisis. The ailing Sir George Beckwith, whom Gregory criticized for moving with "a lock step, when we require double quick time," resigned and was replaced by Sir David Baird. Of course, Grant's increased reliance upon the military exposed the foundations of his policy to further erosion. He was unable to prevent the addition of a major-general to the military staff and was threatened with "a further Augmentation of the Army" by a home secretary who did not disguise his irritation at the chief secretary's failure to keep him fully and regularly informed of developments in Ireland. Simultaneously, Gregory was discreetly questioning the wisdom of Grant's unflagging resistance to any resort to extraordinary powers.[34]

The under-secretary applauded the good sense of the sheriffs of Roscommon and Galway, whose "utmost attention" to the selection of juries had resulted in the conviction of a surprisingly large number of prisoners. He ridiculed those "foolish" magistrates who had administered the oath of allegiance to suspected Ribbonmen in the naive belief that this "flimsy test" would dissuade them from "Misdeeds." As worrying as the persistent disturbances were, it was the "bitter dregs" of the "existing evils" that most alarmed Gregory and hardened his conviction that the ordinary law would not answer. The ties which bound the orders of society together had evidently been broken. He foresaw the elapse of a lengthy period of time before the lower orders could be brought back to obedience to the laws, and confidence restored "between them and their landlords." Equally disconcerting was the evidence of sectarian persecution, which Gregory interpreted as proof that a Catholic revolutionary conspiracy was afoot. Reports that Ribonmen had compelled Protestants to swear on their knees that they would attend Mass, and had avowed a hatred of all Protestants and a determination to extirpate them, revived memories of 1798. Although he regarded this "diabolical wish" as "absurd and impracticable," Gregory deplored the possible loss of "many valuable lives" and dreaded the possibility of the Protestant lower orders arming themselves in self-defence. That would see the mass of the population arrayed "in open hostility against each other," he advised the absent lord lieutenant. And when Talbot returned to Ireland at the beginning of March he simply adopted the under-secretary's analysis as his own. Thus the abuse of Protestants by Ribonmen proved that "an attack on the Established religion" was one of the objects of the "miscreants," and that religion was "more or less" at the bottom of the disturbances. The more immediate danger, however, was the reaction of the Protestant lower orders and the likelihood of the two sects being "arrayed in open Hostility against each other." The situation demanded sustained vigilance, he informed the home secretary on 23 March 1820. He seconded the appeals of resident gentry for the Insurrection Act.[35]

In advocating strong measures Talbot was at pains to emphasize that the Irish peasantry were not without "great cause of complaint." The cost of the potato plots on which they were dependent for subsistence was fearfully high, he admitted. He complained of "a general neglect" of their moral culture and religious improvement. "Can it thus be wondered at," he asked "that a people so circumstanced, should be the ready instruments of every wicked scheme for the disturbance of the public peace?" He pointed to the consequences of the constant subdivision of estates by landlords whose anxiety to maximize the number of voters under their control also resulted in their involvement in the fraudulent swearing of many a forty-shilling freehold. "Thus the land is occupied by a crowded and indigent peasantry whose labour cannot produce their maintenance, and whose minds are demoralized by an open familiarity with perjury." If the implication of this observation was that the permanent tranquillization of Ireland awaited changes to the electoral law, a position Peel had held and which Gregory endorsed, the viceroy was rather more blunt in his warning that lasting peace and real security also depended upon the willingness of the gentry "to alleviate the pressure that weighs down the far greater part of [the] ... excessive population." Nor did he ignore the need for the reform of a magistracy whose failings had once again been exposed. Irish magistrates were, "generally speaking, very bad," he noted, and to the extent that they exceeded the bounds of law it was "with the view of procuring the escape, not the punishment, of offenders."[36]

At this "delicate" juncture Grant left Ireland to be present at his unopposed return for Inverness Burghs in the general election. From Scotland he waged a vigorous rearguard action to protect what remained of his policy. "All the Irish gentry are for the [Insurrection] Act," he remarked ironically to Sidmouth, "but the first thing to be decided is, how far circumstances have altered since the Repeal of the Act to Justify its Reenactment." Indeed, the fact that Peel had chosen to secure its repeal, rather than wait simply for the measure's expiration, enabled Grant to argue that his predecessor had thought "the means still left at the disposal of Government" would be sufficient to repress "future commotions." And the recent events in Ireland had vindicated this judgment, he observed. "A very extensive disturbance has been put down in Galway without the aid of the Insurrection Act. At the same time Clare has been rescued and Mayo preserved, and Roscommon restored, without the Insurrection Act – Is this then a crisis which calls for its reenactment?" He bolstered his position with a careful analysis of the disturbances which demonstrated both an impressive grasp of the history of agrarian disorders in Ireland and the depth of his liberal convictions. He placed the events in Galway and Roscommon in context, thereby demonstrating their similarity to the upheavals which had been a regrettable feature of Irish rural society since the middle of the eighteenth century. Artfully, he quoted extensively from the report submitted to Parliament in 1816 by his predecessor, but drafted by Gregory, to underscore the point. To the extent that the behaviour of the "Galway insurgents" had been exceptional, he observed, it was in their avoidance of the savagery which had marked the earlier lawlessness in Tipperary. He stressed the limited economic objectives of those involved and denied that there was any proof that they had been seeking radical political change or attempting to foment a "Popish insurrection." They had attacked Catholics and Protestants indiscriminately, he emphasized, had been "equally dreaded by both persuasions," and had been condemned by juries "partly composed of Catholics." As for those sectarian incidents which had taken place, they had been relatively few in number, had not occurred until "a late period in the troubles," and had been predictable. Since "the insurgents were chiefly Catholics, and though their passions were roused by other causes, it was natural to expect that in such a state of excitement their religious feelings would sometimes break out, and especially in a moment of success."[37]

In submitting a copy of this paper to Sidmouth, Grant was careful to describe it as a private communication. The home secretary showed it only to the prime minister before returning it. The chief secretary also sent a copy to Talbot. He forwarded it to the primate and the lord chancellor for comment – each of them had served as lord justice during the period to which it referred – and sought the formal opinion of the attorney general. To a man, they angrily challenged Grant's interpretation of the events, and the viceroy sent their acidulous responses on to the Home Office. The archbishop complained that Grant's remarks demonstrated a "manifest leaning to the Roman Catholics" and were "a laboured and artificial vindication of their character and conduct." He ridiculed the conclusion the chief secretary had drawn from the fact that Catholic jurymen had convicted Ribbonmen, pointing out that the juries had been selected "with great care, and probably with a reference to their opinions." Saurin mockingly remarked that he had never before heard it doubted "that the Ribbon Association was a Catholic Conspiracy and its primary object to exterminate Protestants and possess their Properties." No one suggested that all Catholics were involved, he declared, or that those who remained aloof or had property to protect "would not be obnoxious to those engaged in [the conspiracy] and as likely to suffer in their Properties as Protestants." Yet where was the inconsistency, he asked, between this undoubted fact and an appeal to religious hostility as "the primary and inciting principle" of the Ribbon Association? Although Grant made an effective rejoinder to most of these criticisms in a long private letter to the viceroy, and held fast to his contention that religious animosity had been a factor only in the sense that it had aggravated the "civil cause" of the disorders, he recognized the seriousness of the wound the Irish government had inflicted on itself. The divisions within the executive had now been paraded embarrassingly before the cabinet. And whatever satisfaction he derived from the viceroy's subsequent admission that "no change in the existing laws of the Country" was necessary, the cost of his successful opposition to the reenactment of the Insurrection Act continued to be a high one. The conflict with his colleagues, which this episode had unleashed and revealed, continued to fester and to impair the executive's effectiveness.[38]

Before Grant's arrival, Talbot and Gregory had conducted the often distasteful business of distributing patronage in that spirit of mutual confidence which had so quickly characterized all of their dealings with one another. From the beginning of his viceroyalty, the lord lieutenant had left the most irritating and wearying task, that of handling the incessant demands for local patronage, to the more knowledgeable under-secretary. He had kept largely in his own hands, however, the control of ecclesiastical appointments, and had quickly earned Peel's respect for the wisdom with which he made his arrangements. Even here he relied upon Gregory's experience and knowledge, consulting him about all vacancies on the episcopal bench.[39] But the distribution of church livings gave Talbot little pleasure. The monarch, first as prince regent and then as king, constantly demanded the advancement of the relatives or friends of his circle, while the prime minister also showed considerable interest in senior appointments. The lord lieutenant was repeating a familiar refrain when he protested that "the Irish Government must be subjected to very serious inconvenience if its recommendations in church patronage" were so often to be interfered with. Moreover, this delicate task saw him quickly foul the already tangled lines of authority which bound him to the British government. His failure to keep Sidmouth fully informed of the clerical arrangements he was discussing with the prime minister in September 1819 brought a sharp rebuke. "I have often been at a loss to know which of your Lordships I ought to address myself in my Communications from this Country," an exasperated Talbot replied. "If Your Lordship will have the goodness to give me any directions upon this point, it will afford me I assure you the greatest pleasure to conform to them." The directions Sidmouth subsequently provided did little to clarify the situation or lessen the administrative confusion. He laid claim to all official correspondence but did not "presume or desire to comprehend in this Rule and Practice such confidential communications, as may, and must, occasionally take place between the two persons respectively at the Head of the British and Irish Governments."[40]

Talbot's even less satisfactory relationship with his chief secretary added another snarl to the problem. When he turned reluctantly to the task of filling the archbishopric of Dublin in December 1819, the viceroy explored with Gregory the possibility of seeking an Englishman, and he carried the suggestion to London when he went on leave following the death of his wife. The news that an Englishman was likely to be appointed drew a strong caution from Grant. He warned both the prime minister and the home secretary that this was a subject on which the Irish were extremely sensitive, and he urged the appointment of a native Irishman. As a further discouragement to any English candidate, he reported that the archbishop's annual stipend of £8,000 was worth less than one might assume. Not only were his expenses very high, for he was one of Ireland's spiritual representatives in the House of Lords, and the demands of public charities very large, but he would need to spend considerable sums putting his palace in a state of repair. Eventually that "'most exemplary, pious and princely'" of Irish prelates, Lord John George Beresford, received the "Archiepiscopal Crozier," and two years later he was to become the first Irishman in more than a century to be appointed primate.[41]

At odds on the archbishopric of Dublin, viceroy and chief secretary also pulled in opposite directions when the death of the bishop of Cloyne opened that see in 1820. Talbot's recommendation that the bishop of Ossory be translated to Cloyne was resisted by Grant, who advised Sidmouth that this was an appointment "likely to bring disgrace on the Government." Not that this persuaded Talbot to alter his opinion. "The truth is that Dr. Fowler is not a popular person in manners," he explained to the home secretary, "but I cannot therefore refrain from expressing my conscientious conviction, that of the candidates for the vacant Bishopric, he is the most preferable." This lucrative living went, however, to the king's candidate, the bishop of Limerick. Another squabble resulted from Grant's support for the construction of a Methodist chapel in Belfast, though in this instance the primate was his principal adversary. Newspaper reports that the chief secretary had worn down Talbot's resistance to a grant of crown lands to these "enthusiasts" prompted the archbishop to carry to that faithful servant of the Established Church, Lord Sidmouth, his complaints against this form of encouragement to "dissent." Until now Belfast's dissenters had been quiet, he observed. "But Mr. Grant's enthusiasm sets at naught all human policy. I must add that it is now manifest the Irish Government affords no protection to the Church; but on the contrary countenances insidious measures which must ultimately prove the ruin of the Establishment."[42]

Religion and the defence of the Ascendancy lay at the heart of the dispute over a by-election in Dublin in the summer of 1820, which again pitted Grant against Talbot and Gregory. The election had been caused by the death of Henry Grattan, and Gregory persuaded Talbot, with Attorney General Saurin's assistance, to give official backing to Thomas Ellis, a former fellow of Trinity College and a master in Chancery. Grant dissented from this decision, for he regarded Ellis as "a furious Orange Partizan," but his objections carried little weight with his colleagues. Their overriding concern was to ensure the defeat of Grattan's son, who had also decided to stand. His Whig politics and "Catholic" sympathies made him anathema to Talbot and Gregory, the latter describing him as extreme a "Catholic" as Ellis was a Protestant. "Do not think I am activated by feelings for the Protestant cause alone," he added, "I feel much more for what I consider the Duty and Character of the Government." Grant's response to this rebuff was to secure Castlereagh's support for a proposal which would have seen the Irish government dissociate itself from Ellis's Orange principles and require him to disclaim them. Talbot would have none of this, and countered his chief secretary's alliance with Castlereagh with a claim to possess the full backing of Lords Liverpool and Sidmouth. It was at this moment that Grattan publicly asserted that he enjoyed the personal support of Grant and that the executive government was neutral in the contest. Indignantly, Talbot demanded from Grant an explanation of these statements. They proclaimed a deep division within the executive, he remonstrated. Unconvinced by Grant's account of his dealings with young Grattan, he subsequently sought from his chief secretary a public contradiction of the controversial remarks. This embarrassment Grant deftly avoided by threatening a greater one – a fuller disclosure of their differences. And while Talbot had the satisfaction of seeing Ellis returned for the city of Dublin, and Grattan issued a statement correcting the "misconstruction" placed upon his words on the hustings, the episode had deepened the distrust with which he and Gregory regarded the amiable and well-meaning chief secretary.[43]

The three men did cooperate to good effect, if briefly, in their response to the financial panic which in the summer of 1820 compounded Ireland's chronic economic troubles. In the Commons, an announcement of the government's intention to extend the life of the protective wall which the union had left around Irish industries for a period of twenty years, brought a sustained attack in June on the policy of protection. English manufacturers and English economists, and among the latter was David Ricardo, who had entered Parliament in 1819 for the Irish borough of Portarlington, called for the removal of the union duties. So also did a number of Irish Whigs, who insisted that the duties had been counterproductive. Resisting these demands, the chancellor of the exchequer argued that their continuation was rendered necessary by the "present state of Irish trade and manufacture." His principal consideration, however, may well have been the sorry state of the Irish government's income. The operating deficit seemed certain to exceed by a substantial margin that of the previous year, which had been large, and there were predictions that total revenues for the entire year would not reach £4 millions. Ireland's straitened circumstances were further grist for the Opposition's mills. Whigs had long argued that widespread corruption was the reason for Ireland's "excessive" taxation. Now they were able to secure the appointment of a commission to investigate abuses in the collection of revenue in Ireland. Then, in the midst of the debate on the union duties, Irish trade and manufactures were thrown deeper into turmoil by a rash of bank failures.[44]

Within a fortnight of the first failure, which occurred in Cork on 25 May, seven of the fourteen country banks in the southern provinces had collapsed. Even before the full extent of this disaster was apparent, a deputation of Cork merchants visited the Castle to appeal for government aid. What they sought was the exercise of the executive's influence with the Bank of Ireland to ensure that it advanced the loans which might yet save the situation. Founded in 1782, the bank's national domination had resulted as much from its intimate relationship with the government as from its many privileges. Indeed, the range of its functions and services was by 1820 so broad that it had already acquired some of the essential features of a central bank. During an earlier crisis, in 1814, it had staved off disaster by extending special drawing facilities to troubled smaller banks, and this it did again now. But the failure of one-half of the country banks and the decision, on 12 June, of a Dublin bank, Alexander's, to close its doors, demonstrated the partial success at best of the bank's intervention. Traders, merchants, and manufacturers continued to face ruin, for there was a real danger that they would be unable to convert their funds into money or negotiable securities in time to meet the immediate demands upon them. Equally chilling were the reports that food was being withheld from market by producers who feared that, in the absence of a circulating medium, it would be seized by a hungry and frightened people. Yet in this crisis the chancellor of the exchequer rejected calls in the Commons for direct intervention by the government of the United Kingdom. Two days later he was obliged to reverse himself.[45]

The British government's volte-face was forced by the actions of the Irish executive. In Dublin, Talbot and Gregory had responsed decisively and unilaterally to the crisis. They employed the unused portion of the £250,000 appropriated in 1817 to make loans to relieve the commercial distress. Moreover, as the chancellor admitted in the House, Gregory had also sanctioned the employment of "a certain sum upon the erection of public works." Making the best of this development, and citing historical precedents for the action, he announced that the government was going to increase the fund at the disposal of the lord lieutenant to £500,000. "The effect of this grant would be a most desirable one, the increase in the circulation," he explained. Furthermore, it would demonstrate "to the alarmed and anxious people of Ireland that parliament, in the consideration of their distress, had not lost sight of [its] duties." Although Grant had not been a party to the decision taken in Dublin, he made a timely intervention in the Commons debate. Having emphasized the limited and "circuitous" nature of the relief, he paid eloquent tribute to the patience of the destitute "inferior classes" of Ireland. Indeed, on his return to the Irish capital, he found reason to criticize the excessive caution with which the commissioners administering the fund were discharging their responsibilities. By November they had authorized loans which totalled a mere £99,000. The time had come, he suggested to Sidmouth, to instruct them to be more liberal, for the continuing currency crisis, together with an abundant harvest, were combining to drive agriculture deeper into depression. Ireland's distress was "infinitely worse" than that of England, one Irish member informed the Commons, "for there the agriculturists were reduced to the lowest state of depression; and as to manufactures, there was now left scarcely any thing which deserved the name, except one or two branches, and they also were under the greatest embarrassment." Distress on this scale seemed certain soon to exhaust the patience of the destitute, and in August reports from Kildare indicated that the labouring classes were combining "to prevent the hiring of strangers for the Harvest work and also to fix a Rate of wages." If there was little in this activity to alarm the government as yet, serious disturbances would almost certainly revive the unresolved conflict within the executive on how best to deal with them.[46]

Talbot and Grant both reported to Sidmouth in late summer that the country was in "a perfect state of tranquillity," and Gregory took advantage of this period of comparative peace to try and remove the principal objection to the employment of "peelers" in times of turbulence. Only in County Dublin, "where the District was very limited and the Population very thin and few," had the administration paid two-thirds of the costs as permitted under the amended Peace Preservation Act. In July the contribution from the consolidated fund was limited by proclamation to one-half the total, but Gregory had already acted to decrease the expense that would fall upon the counties.

He had, with the lord lieutenant's approval, reduced the annual pay of the "peelers" from £50 to £40. Many were pensioned soldiers, he reminded Grant, while those who came directly from the ranks of the peasantry would still be earning more than twice as much as were privates in the army. The savings to local taxpayers in the western counties, where detachments were stationed, he estimated at £4,000 in Galway, £3,000 in Roscommon, and £2,500 in Clare. Much as Grant disliked the force as a species of gendarmerie and preferred a reform of the ordinary police, and as deeply as he deplored the "frightful number" of "peelers" on duty in six western counties, he admitted that they tended to keep the country quiet and gave security to those who were disposed "to assist the authorities in keeping peace."[47]

Grant had long insisted that tranquillity depended upon the conduct of the established clergy, the magistracy, and the gentry. They were the essential instruments of the "local system of civil authority." He remained frankly scornful of them all, however, convinced as he was that in Ireland disorders were frequently rooted in "the oppression and unprincipled exactions of the higher orders." Sadly, the government was obliged to punish those driven to crime by "misery and oppression," but unable to touch "those whose conduct has really produced these calamities." He did take some comfort from the fact that the earlier disturbances had induced landlords to cut the ruinous rents charged for conacre, lowering them from twelve guineas to six in some areas. Nevertheless, in several midlands counties Ribbonism soon raised its ugly head and oaths were reportedly being administered close to Dublin itself. Inevitably, from the gentry there came a rising chorus of familiar praise for the Insurrection Act, but Grant hastened to assure the home secretary early in November that there was "nothing as yet to occasion serious alarm." At the opening of the new year he described an Ireland in her customary state of lawlessness – local outrages, robberies accompanied by brutal murders, vindictive excesses, burglaries in search of arms, faction fighting, "and many symptoms of the disorders incident to a country without an adequate local system of civil authority." This level of violence was not considered serious enough to prevent Talbot from exercising during the spring the discretionary authority which had been granted to him during the autumn, at a time when one of his daughters was seriously ill in England, to travel there on leave. In his absence, Grant again collided with the lords justices.[48]

Ireland's comparative tranquillity provided Grant with an opportunity to recover that initiative in policy matters which he had lost as a result of the earlier disturbances in Galway. Thus the proclamation by the lords justices of a number of baronies, implying as that action did a serious deterioration in the situation, brought a sharp response from the chief secretary at the end of May. From England, he wrote to Gregory to demand that before the proclamation of any additional districts the documents on which the action was to be founded be submitted to him. "He never cou'd have reflected on the insult such a proposal wou'd be to the Authority and Judgment of the Lords Justices," the under-secretary remarked to Talbot, "and how evidently they wou'd stultify their understandings and humiliate their power by submitting for his decision matters on which they may be presumed to be capable of forming at least as sound an opinion as himself." So, despite his many differences with Grant on policy, Gregory withheld the communication from the lords justices in order to give the chief secretary time to reflect on the wisdom of embroiling himself with them "on a point on which he must be considered decidedly wrong, and will inevitably subject himself to the most severe reprehension." Although Grant did concede, in reply, that it would be better to couch his demand in less pointed language, there was no weakening of his resolve both to "check this rage for proclaiming" and to gain "a veto" over the lords justices' proceedings. Nor was this his only ground of conflict with them. [49]

The debate on the army estimates in March had been enlivened by those calls for economy which Grant had always hoped to exploit in shaping Irish policy, and he had seized this opportunity to restate his determination "to recede from a system which in that country had been pursued to too great an extent." Sir David Baird had already advised the lord lieutenant that as his command shrank in size it would have to be concentrated. Facing the loss of 3,000 infantry, he objected to the continued dispersal of his force and urged the government to inform magistrates and gentlemen that they would no longer be able to secure permanent military protection. Talbot had elected to postpone giving them this unwelcome news, preferring to "let this part of the suggested arrangement rest upon eventual circumstances." Predictably, the lords justices coupled their proclamation of several districts in May with an official warning to the British government of the danger of proceeding with the reduction of the military establishment. Forwarding a copy of this dispatch to Talbot, Gregory pessimistically commented that he did not believe these representations would "augment or diminish the Army of this country to the amount of one Drummer." But Grant, who saw the dispatch for the first time when it arrived at the Irish Office in London for forwarding to Sidmouth, was not a man to ignore this challenge simply because it was likely to fail. He chose, instead, to dispute the lords justices' account of "the extent and degree" of the turbulence in Ireland, and formally dissociated himself from their recommendation. Further, he insisted that his letter accompany the dispatch of the lords justices when it was laid before the government. [50]

Talbot was both astonished and infuriated by Grant's conduct, and he again carried directly to the home secretary his complaints against the chief secretary. That no matter how "well disposed" he and Gregory were towards Grant "for his many private qualities," there existed "no point of union as

to the conduct of public affairs between him and the rest of the Government."
But there was no sign of the government responding to this elliptical plea
for Grant's removal from office.[51] Instead, Talbot learnt that the only change
in the offing was the replacement of William Saurin as attorney general by
W.C. Plunket. If the prime minister's principal motive in contemplating this
appointment was to strengthen the ministry in the Commons, the Irish implications promised to be far-reaching. Plunket was an ardent champion of
Catholic claims. His bill to concede emancipation with Protestant securities
had passed the lower House during the spring only to be defeated in the
Lords. During the debate in the Commons Grant had made an impassioned
plea for the measure's passage. Declaring that he appeared on behalf of
Ireland, he had implored the House "for the sake of Protestants as well as
Catholics – for the sake of peace, order and tranquillity – to adopt measures
that would be received with gratitude by a generous and suffering people."
Overly optimistic as this assurance was, for O'Connell remained unalterably
opposed to securities, though his one public comment on this bill was
ambiguous, Grant and Plunket would evidently form a powerful liberal
partnership in the executive. Further, the rumoured intention of Sidmouth
soon to surrender the seals of the Home Office threatened to weaken Protestant defences at that strategic point, for there was no certainty that his
successor would be as stalwart an ally of the Ascendancy as he had been.[52]

Gregory was dismayed by the word from London. His first, thought was
that there would be no place for him in any "new system of government"
and that he would either have to retire of his own choice "or be bowed, or
brow-beaten out of office." He decided against precipitate action, and within
a few days concern for his own future gave way to indignation at the treatment
in store for Saurin. It was scarcely credible to him that ministers could bring
themselves to remove "a faithful & invaluable Servant of the Crown, from
no other than the selfish motive of gaining the parliamentary support of a
powerful Advocate, who has for so many years been a powerful Antagonist."
Repeatedly, he urged Talbot to decline to be a party to this "dishonourable"
political arrangement. "In my mind you can at once put and end to this
disgraceful transaction," he wrote, "by declining to be the channel of any
communication whether official, or not; and by declaring that it cannot be
made so long as you remain Viceroy of Ireland." In fact, Talbot had already
attempted to dissuade Liverpool from making this change but the most he
had been able to secure was a delay until after the king's visit to Ireland.[53]

George IV landed at Howth on 12 August, but the news of the death of
the wife he detested obliged him to postpone his public entry into Dublin
and pass several days in relative seclusion and official mourning. Then, on
17 August, he made a triumphal entry to the Irish capital at the head of a
vast procession. The Irish, one sardonic observer noted, lacking "practice
in the expression of public joy," shouted rather than cheered. Despite the

inevitable incidents – the Catholic bishops presented an address that "talked too much politics" and was therefore considered in "bad taste," while at one official dinner an alderman offered the provocative toast to the pious and glorious memory – the visit had been adjudged a great success by the time the king embarked early in September. The demonstrations of Irish loyalty, which included Daniel O'Connell's presentation of "a crown of laurels à genoux to the monarch," gave grounds for the hope that this "spirit of loyal union" would survive "unabated and unimpaired" if every cause of irritation was "avoided and discountenanced" and "mutual forbearance and good-will" observed and encouraged. Within a few weeks, a fresh wave of disturbances was to demonstrate just how emphemeral that spirit was, and it produced changes in the Irish government that went far beyond those contemplated in June.[54]

Disturbances in Limerick had assumed "rather a serious character" by the end of September, and twenty-three magistrates, including the promiment Irish Whig, Thomas Spring Rice, appealed for military reinforcements. The immediate cause of the trouble was the conduct of a single agent for a large estate, but in the neighbouring counties of Clare and Kerry, to which the disorders quickly spread, the peasantry appeared to be anticipating scarcity if not famine. Weeks of incessant rain had given them every reason to fear for the potato crop. Indeed, the entire agricultural economy of the island remained mired in depression. The Corn Laws, whose passage had been sought as a boon for Ireland, had failed to produce the promised prosperity which would alleviate distress and end disorders. Irish corn exports to Britain had increased substantially. In the seven years since the enactment of the laws Ireland had sent to England, 2,500,000 quarters in excess of the quantity shipped there during the seven years before their passage, and fully 40 per cent of the greatly increased total had been exported between 1819 and 1821. But Ireland had not prospered, for the price of cereals had collapsed. A barrel of wheat which had once fetched five guineas now sold for a mere sixteen shillings.[55]

The depressed economy and the abject condition of the peasantry went far to explain, or so Charles Grant maintained, the recurring disorders. "I am apt to believe the Irish the most wretched peasantry of Europe, excepting perhaps the Polish," he later informed the House of Commons. He was convinced that neither force nor fear could "possibly long keep down such a mass of despair." Of course, after more than two years in Ireland, he acknowledged that this basic problem was exacerbated by other factors – the rapid increase in the population and the subdivision of property; a relationship between landlord and tenant in which the former escaped all of the responsibilities accepted by his English counterpart; excessive rents and local taxes; and the peculiar disposition of a people "easily excited, and above all things impatient of a continued course of fretful vexations." Nothing had occurred to shake his belief that the Irish had been conditioned to lawlessness by harsh and extraordinary legislation, such as the Insurrection Act, and by the failings of the traditional agents of good order. Too many of the gentry were absentees; the local police were inefficient and inadequate; the magistracy incompetent if not corrupt; and popular education deficient. "Such a gentry & so wretched a peasantry," he lamented. "The only wonder is that the machine works at all." If the correction of these many faults would take time, Grant continued to see in emancipation the means by which the attitude of the mass of Irishmen to the British legislature might be speedily improved and the Roman Catholic clergy conciliated. The latter he valued as a potential ally in the struggle to restrain the peculiarly excitable Irish.[56]

From London, Sidmouth demanded that the Irish government show "promptitude and vigour" in the face of "this incipient rebellion." He ordered the assembling of troops at convenient points in England for transportation if necessary to Ireland, and offered the opinion that insurrection could only be smashed by an overwhelming military force "instantly assembled, and instantly employed." Delay, compromise, or concession would be fatal, he added. The executive had responded with vigour to the disturbances, implementing the obvious strategy of attempting to confine them. Baronies were proclaimed and troops ordered into Limerick. The assassination of a police magistrate, whom Gregory had earlier reprimanded for permitting his men to wear Orange insignia, caused the government to put up a substantial reward for information concerning his murder and dispatch further reinforcements. Resorting to the expedient adopted in Galway, commissions of the peace were granted to officers leading troops operating in support of the civil power. Nor was Talbot loath to pick up the home secretary's suggestion that the Insurrection Act would be a useful weapon. "We must positively have some legislative enactment to enable the Executive Government to meet these deep and extensive combinations on something like fair terms," he replied. Distasteful as this recommendation was certain to be to the chief secretary, it was the lord lieutenant's decision to call out the yeomanry that led to a further parade of their differences.[57]

Informed by Sidmouth that the five regiments of the 29th Infantry were the only troops the Irish government could expect from Britain, where the number of infantrymen had shrunk to 9,000, Talbot turned to the yeomen. His order calling them out to service was countermanded by Grant, who had already questioned the wisdom of an action liable to create fresh irritation. Too many of these men, he explained to the home secretary, were Orangemen. Both Talbot and Gregory were outraged by the chief secretary's act. They had turned to the yeomen as a last resort, the under-secretary fumed, "when the military force was expended & they were not even intended to be employed against the Popish insurgents of the South." He conceded that any man of common sense and common feelings could not but deplore the poverty of the Irish peasantry, and that only a "Brute or an Absentee would refuse his money, his labour & his time, to promote any rational system for their amelioration," but he assailed Grant for his "sympathizing, philosophizing Prancing" at a moment when "bloody insurrection was in progress." He was appalled that "the Efforts of the Government (feeble as they are from the small means at their Command) should be paralysed by one, whose Duty it is to give Energy & spirit." It was a sentiment Sidmouth fully shared, and he now acted to end the immobilizing conflict within the Irish executive.[58]

The home secretary had long been irritated by Grant's administrative inefficiency. "His total neglect of his correspondence with this country, after repeated friendly admonition," wrote one observer of his fall, "was really inexcusable." Nor could there be any doubt of the intense suspicion with which the great majority of conservative Irish Protestants regarded Grant, or that they would welcome his departure. But it was Grant's response to the latest disturbances that moved Sidmouth to action. During his visit to Ireland as part of the king's entourage he had invited Gregory to write directly to him on Irish matters. Flattering as this invitation was to the under-secretary, it betrayed a lack of confidence in Grant which Gregory fully shared. And on 9 November he submitted his own report on the state of Ireland to the home secretary. Sombre in tone, it warned of a "very troublesome winter" ahead and urged the renewal of the Insurrection Act. It was a "wholesome and necessary Law for this Country," Gregory wrote, and had it been in force "the system of insurrection would never have risen to its present alarming heights." This implied criticism of Grant's evangelical faith in the ordinary law did not escape Sidmouth, whose own frustration had mounted as the chief secretary not only continued to set his face against this particular measure but also showed a reluctance to enlarge the area proclaimed under the Peace Preservation Act. Moreover, the home secretary considered his objections to the yeomanry "extremely futile." So, on 21 November, he informed the prime minister of his "painful apprehension" that the Irish government was not competent to meet the emergency it faced, and that "a partial change, at least," had become "indispensably necessary." It was a recommendation he repeated the following day, and the prime minister resolved to remove the lord lieutenant as well as the chief secretary.[59]

Talbot's recall came as a complete surprise, not least to the viceroy himself. After all, barely two months had passed since he had been informed of the "high sense" which the king entertained of "the ability, temper and firmness" with which he had "uniformly administered" the government of Ireland. But his latest dispute with Grant had served to remind disenchanted ministers of the lord lieutenant's lack of resolution. He had rarely exercised his authority to override those decisions of his chief secretary with which he strongly disagreed. He would have made a good lord lieutenant had he been coupled with an efficient secretary, Liverpool later observed, "but as it was he had no authority, and having lost his proper station, it would have been difficult to have propped him up by a new appointment in Grant's place, even if there were not other objections to it." Those objections were surely political. Although he had not carried it to the lengths Gregory had urged, the viceroy had made clear his opposition to that change in the executive, the easing out of Saurin to make room for Plunket, which the strengthening of the ministry in Parliament appeared to require. Moreover, the negotiations then under way to admit to the government the Grenvillite faction long identified with the cause of emancipation would have been impeded by the dismissal of Grant and the retention of Talbot. Liverpool could ill afford to create the impression that the new Irish government was going to be more hostile to the Catholic cause. Both men had to go, and the letters of recall were dispatched to Ireland on 29 November. Deeply wounded by this unexpected turn of events, Talbot protested to Sidmouth: "I cannot forbear expressing my regret at the *extreme suddeness of my Recal [sic]*, which *must* at this particular juncture of affairs in Ireland have an appearance of imputation on my public conduct." The Whigs, had they come into power, "could not have treated me more unceremoniously," he complained to Gregory. He had been dismissed with less consideration than a gentleman would show to a drunken butler. Grant, before whom Liverpool dangled the prospect of a renewal of their "official connexion," remained discreetly silent. It was left to one of his many admirers to compose an epitaph for the fallen evangelical constitutionalist. "His attachment to the Bible cause and to the Bible religion, his uncompromising purity of principle, and his paternal government of Ireland, raised up a host of enemies."[60]

## CHAPTER SIX

# The Failure of a Liberal
# Viceroy

Liverpool had long been keen to add William Plunket to the ministerial bench in the Commons. The Irishman's reputation for unmatched eloquence, which was patronizingly attributed to his English rather than Irish style, and administrative experience, for he had served as solicitor and attorney general of Ireland, made him a formidable parliamentary adversary and enhanced his appeal as an ally. More than once, during his years as chief secretary, the young Peel had offered up a silent prayer of thanks that this Irishman did not show greater interest in "Irish subjects." Although in 1820 he did inherit from Henry Grattan the mantle of spokesman for the Catholic cause in the lower House, he was a moderate on this issue. Thus the bill he introduced in 1821 was hedged with securities.[1] And it was shortly after the Commons adopted Plunket's motion for a committee to consider Catholic claims that the prime minister first broached the possibility of his rejoining the Irish government. He agreed to enter into discussions but soon grasped that the ministerial changes Liverpool had in mind extended beyond the Irish executive to embrace the "strengthening of the present Cabinet, by the accession of Persons favourable" to emancipation. It was for this very reason that some of the more stalwart Protestants in the government were coming to regard Liverpool with unease. His temporizing response to the Catholic bill when it eventually reached the Lords, at least until steadied by Sidmouth; his appointment of Catholic sympathizers to a pair of regius professorships and to a bishopric; his anxiety to bring Plunket into the administration; all had prompted the lord chancellor to question the depth of his commitment to the defence of the Protestant cause, even before the discussions with the Irishman were broadened to embrace the entire Grenvillite faction to which he adhered.[2]

With Lord Grenville's withdrawal from active public life in 1817 his followers had gone their separate ways. A number continued to act with the Whigs, a handful soon adhered to the government, while the remainder, led by the former leader's nephews, the marquis of Buckingham and Charles Wynn, attempted to steer an independent course. By 1821 the prime minister saw in this baker's dozen a means of shoring up a ministry weakened by its poor relations with the king and by internal dissension. Alive to the government's problems, the notoriously place-hungry Grenvillites drove a hard bargain. Buckingham obtained the dukedom he had long coveted, but not the lord lieutenancy of Ireland, which his father had twice held; Wynn secured the presidency of the Board of Control and with it a seat in the cabinet; while Plunket was to be appointed attorney general of Ireland, "forming a part of the Government as confidentially consulted as if he belonged to the Cabinet." The Grenvillites demanded and were conceded an extraordinary measure of independence with respect to Ireland. In Buckingham's words, "we acceded to the proposals made to us, in order and upon condition that we should have the measure through ... [Wynn's] seat in the Cabinet, of originating, and pressing either in Cabinet or in Parliament our views of Irish policy, at any moment which we in our discretion might think propitious to the attempt."[3]

Liverpool was equally determined to bring Peel and Canning back into office, the former generally recognized as the most impressive of the younger Tories and the latter the most formidable member of the lower House. The task was not eased by Castlereagh's jealousy of potential rivals and the king's detestation of Canning, but Sidmouth's surrender of the Home Office at least opened a suitable place for Peel. The prospect of his general supervision of Irish affairs was not welcomed by the Grenvillites, who correctly sensed his reciprocal distrust of them. They saw in George Canning, "slippery and uncertain" though he was, a potential ally in shaping a liberal Irish policy and were quick to support his return to government following Castlereagh's suicide in August 1822. With the chief of the "Catholic Tories" now taking over the vacant Foreign Office and leading the forces of the ministry in the Commons, the balance of power within the cabinet appeared to be tilting against the diehard Protestants.[4]

As he went about the work of reconstructing the administration the prime minister made astute use of the senior positions in the Irish government. Wellington had been Sidmouth's choice to replace Talbot, and he had been willing to return to Ireland, but Liverpool and Castlereagh flattered him that he was "too great a gun to fire." Similarly, the proposal that the civil and military commands in that kingdom be united in the person of Lord Hopetoun, a former commander of the forces there, was rejected on the grounds that his selection would create too great an "impression of alarm." A third candidate was Wellington's eldest brother, the Marquis Wellesley. His appointment would not only add another handful of parliamentary followers to the governing coalition but also assist the wooing of the Grenvillites.[5]

A native Irishman, Richard Wellesley had been educated in England.

Among the friendships of his formative years was one with William Grenville, and he it was who persuaded his cousin Pitt to bring the young Irishman into Parliament in 1784. Able, arrogant, ambitious, Wellesley's somewhat fortuitous promotion to the governor-generalship of India in 1797 provided him with a large stage on which to display his considerable talents. He succeeded in consolidating British control of the subcontinent but mishandled his relations with the directors of the East India Company, and his return to Britain in 1805 was neither a happy nor a triumphal one. Persecuted by enemies, and resentful of what he viewed as the ingratitude of his friends, he drifted away from Grenville. He drew closer to George Canning, and a brief but successful term as ambassador to Spain was followed by his replacement of Canning at the Foreign Office when Spencer Perceval formed his administration. He was soon isolated within the cabinet, for his colleagues were irritated by his surprising inefficiency as a minister, contemptuous of his vanity and pretensions, and distrustful of the reach of his ambition. His resignation early in 1812 proved to be peculiarly ill-timed, and his intrigues with Canning to replace the prime minister did little to enhance his chances of forming a government when Perceval was assassinated in May of 1812. His hopes of achieving the highest office dashed, Wellesley found himself banished to the periphery of public life, where he continued to sully his reputation. His licentiousness scandalized even that tolerant generation, while his creditors hounded him into bankruptcy. But on the subject of Ireland he continued to command respect, at least from the more liberal elements in Parliament.[6]

Relief for the dissenters of Ireland, Catholic and Protestant, had been consistently championed by Wellesley throughout his career. His appointment as lord lieutenant, together with that of Plunket as attorney general, would therefore go far to still the qualms of Grenvillites at entering a ministry led by Liverpool and containing so many high Tories. Charles Wynn welcomed this evidence that Ireland might fairly anticipate a "firm, impartial, and conciliatory" administration. However, familiarity with Wellesley's personal and administrative failings, and sensitivity to the alarm his appointment was certain to excite in many a Protestant breast, discouraged the prime minister and cabinet from offering him their complete confidence. "Vanity, dissipation, want of private and unsteadiness of public character, and a strong predilection for the Roman Catholic cause, are not the component parts which ought to constitute the Chief Governor for such a country in such times as these," one influential member of the Commons remarked. Wellesley's reputation as a man of exceptional ability but very defective judgment, his short temper and indolence, provided additional grounds for uneasiness. In these circumstances, it was essential that the new viceroy be accompanied to Ireland by "*a very capable secretary*."[7]

The Grenvillites had urged the retention of Charles Grant as chief secretary, and it was a decision Wellesley would have welcomed, but there was never any prospect of the prime minister hearkening to that suggestion. Instead, Liverpool first offered the post to William Huskisson as compensation for his failure to secure the presidency of the Board of Control. When he declined, it was proffered to Henry Coulburn, with the enthusiastic approval of the cabinet. The son of an absentee West Indian sugar planter, Goulburn had entered Parliament at the age of twenty-four in 1808. He adhered to Spencer Perceval and was appointed by him an under-secretary for the Home Department in 1810. Two years later he succeeded Peel as under-secretary for war and colonies, and for the next decade played an important role in colonial affairs. He was a natural choice as one of the three plenipotentiaries dispatched to Ghent to negotiate peace with the Americans in 1814. Goulburn was more than a little earnest, personally abstemious, and admirably devout, being a contributor to a number of evangelical causes and a member of the reformist group of High Churchmen. He was honest and efficient, "a man of business" who at the Colonial Office had shown himself to be an exceptionally able administrator. Morever, he was attractive and graceful. "His appearance is much in his favour," wrote one observer. A zealot in his defence of the Established Church, he was proud of its ability "to embrace in the same fold men who on minor points entertained different opinions," and was convinced that defects notwithstanding, it was the "best instrument for encouraging real piety & disseminating a pure religion throughout the world." For Roman Catholicism he entertained nothing but scorn. His opposition to Catholic claims was inflexible, hardened as it was by the belief that over the years Roman Catholics had, through an astute incremental strategy, secured an ever larger share of the full rights of citizenship. He feared that they would eventually be in a position, unless halted, to undermine the Establishment. Distasteful as such opinions were to the more liberal members of the government, they were a qualification in the prime minister's eyes. Grant "having done much mischief by the offence" he had given to the majority of Ireland's Protestants, it was "necessary" that either the new viceroy or the new chief secretary "should prefer the cause of that body." All in all, Goulburn was "not only invaluable in himself" but was the ideal man to accompany Wellesley to Dublin. "His purity & correctness of character [would] make amends for the defects of the other."[8]

Goulburn had first been tendered the office in 1818, at the time of Peel's resignation. But fearful of the expense involved, and of the contrast between the hospitality he would be able to afford and that extended by his wealthy predecessor; reluctant to leave his bed-ridden mother for extended periods; enjoying his service at the Colonial Office under Lord Bathurst, he had then declined the chief secretaryship. By 1821 much had changed. His mother had died; the evangelical Grant had terminated the largesse associated with the Peel years; and his financial concerns had been eased by the award of a pension for his long service as an under-secretary. Moreover, he was privately informed that Peel would soon be returning to office at the head of the Home Department. In any conflict with the "Catholic" lord lieutenant and the new attorney general he was assured of powerful support. To his post he brought not merely a determination to uphold the Ascendancy but also a belief in Ireland's exceptionalism. Before long, he was informing the Commons that "if gentlemen imagined that what was the rule in England, could be uniformly applied to Ireland, or that the difference of habits and situations of the people did not require a separate mode of conducting the affairs of each, they would grievously err." Such attitudes belied his assurances to Charles Grant, with whom he was on the best of terms, that he was not setting out for Ireland with any intention to reverse his policies.[9]

The "eastern ecstasy" with which Wellesley accepted the lord lieutenancy was a measure of his desperate need for its handsome salary and of his recognition that at the age of sixty-one this would surely be his last opportunity to establish a reputation for statesmanship. Yet to place him in harness with Goulburn promised an uncomfortable experience, and one fully as ineffective as the pairing of their ill-matched predecessors. "This balance & counterpoise of opinions is the very devil," Charles Saxton, the former Irish civil under-secretary, remarked. Lord Grenville was another who ridiculed this coupling together of "a friend and an enemy to toleration, like fat and lean rabbits, or the man and his wife in a Dutch toy," and he asked: "What is to result from this disheartening folly?" Wellesley hastened to reassure him that he would not be a "cypher" in his own government and was confident that neither Goulburn nor Peel would attempt to contravene a "liberal and benevolent" policy or seek to reverse the abolition of the system "by which the laws respecting the Catholics were administered in a spirit much more severe than their letter." Furthermore, he was to enjoy the "constant benefit" of Plunket's "council and assistance." But it was a measure of the Grenvillites' suspicion and discomfort that Charles Wynn secured the right publicly to dissociate himself from the appointment of Goulburn.[10]

The success of Wellesley's viceroyalty would obviously hinge in large part upon the conduct of Peel, and as late as the summer of 1822 Wynn suspected the home secretary of "lying back in order to make as strong a case as he can, before he attacks Lord Wellesley, after which he would more easily overturn us." Tension and distrust inevitably dogged Peel's relations with the viceroy, not least because neither he nor Goulburn was as familiar with the lord lieutenant's strengths as they were aware of his weaknesses. Unlike older members of the government, they could not see "that a man may be wise in some things & most foolish in others." Moreover, a home secretary with unrivalled experience and knowledge of Ireland, and given that country's disproportionate demands upon his time ("What a difference between Great Britain and Ireland," Peel was soon to sigh. "It frequently happens that a day passes without a single letter to the Secretary of State."), was certain to take an unusually keen interest in its affairs. Initially, he and the viceroy conducted a regular and full correspondence. Unfortunately, Wellesley was incapable of any sustained performance of laborious duties, and his detailed reports on the state of the country all too quickly became intermittent. The home secretary was swift to grasp this opportunity to assert his own authority over the government of Ireland. Of course, he was aided not merely by the viceroy's indolence but by his own intimate relationship with the chief secretary. Fast friends, each had discovered much to admire in the other. Peel described Goulburn as "one whose attachment I value as much as that of any *man* on earth, and for whom I have the sincerest regard and respect." Of all the men "with whom I was ever acquainted, he approaches the nearest to perfection." He had long considered him "admirably suited" for the Irish secretaryship. For his part, Goulburn acknowledged the younger man's intellectual superiority, precocious political skill, and extraordinary command of the intricacies and complexities of Irish administration. Not surprisingly, he welcomed his advice and deferred to his judgment.[11]

"Every consideration public & private makes me rejoice that you are going to Ireland and that thus I am to be in such constant intercourse with you," Peel wrote early in December 1821. They spent two days together at Lulworth Castle in Dorset, and during this extensive briefing Peel analysed the strengths and weaknesses of Gregory and Saurin, and assured the new chief secretary that both would "improve on acquaintance." Nor did Peel disguise his conviction that the imminent dismissal of Saurin was "a great mistake." It would be far better to make Plunket chief justice, he remarked. He was no less emphatic in his advice to Goulburn to resist any meddling by Plunket in the affairs of his office. "Put a stop to that at first," he enjoined. He was less forthcoming on the pivotal matter of relations with the viceroy. Indeed, he sought Goulburn's opinion on how to approach the lord lieutenant when he himself received the seals of the Home Department. "I merely wish to do what is most civil, & most likely to promote perfect harmony," he explained. A carefully phrased and graceful letter successfully gratified Wellesley's insatiable appetite for flattery. Goulburn's relationship with the viceroy was soon to be severely strained, however.[12]

Before setting out for Ireland, Wellesley had constantly referred to Goulburn as "My Secretary." Although by no means inaccurate, the persistent use of this description seemed to be a calculated attempt to emphasize the viceroy's supremacy. And ever mindful of the proprieties, Goulburn, having preceded Wellesley to Dublin, declined Talbot's offer formally to appoint him so that he could immediately set to work. He was Lord Wellesley's chief secretary, he explained. Indeed, as a much younger man he had stood in awe of the new viceroy's talents. It was not long, however, before a number of irritants began to poison their relationship. Energetic and efficient himself, Goulburn resented the viceroy's want of decisiveness and inattention to "business." Wellesley also wasted much time revising his dispatches in an effort to perfect their wording, such was his anxiety to guard his reputation as a stylist. As a result, requests for an opinion on important topics due to be raised in the House went unanswered, thereby exposing the chief secretary to possible embarrassment. Nor was the situation improved by Wellesley's subsequent decision to live several miles south of Dublin, because the mail from England did not reach there until evening by which time it was too late to send off a reply that night. Further aggravating these problems of communication was Edward Johnston, the viceroy's meddlesome and incompetent natural son, whom he had brought to Ireland as a private secretary. "Johnston is supposed to have more influence than ever," William Gregory reported in the spring of 1823, "& stories, strange in any Court but this, are repeated of [a] fracas during the last week between him & the viceroy, in which the Favourite was always triumphant."[13] Also, Wellesley's hypochondria, his habit of taking to his bed at the first hint of a cold, and he proved to be peculiarly susceptible to the virus, made access to him even more difficult. Such isolation contributed to that lack of consultation of which Goulburn also complained. His protests drew a lofty reply. Pleading the pressure of work, Wellesley added: "I think you will scarcely expect a very exact or punctual discharge of duties, which, in my unreserved sentiments towards you, I have imprudently considered, as merely formal." A promise "to endeavour for the future to have more early statements" forwarded to the chief secretary did not fully answer his complaint and was promptly broken anyway. Referring to a dispatch of such importance that by its argument he melodramatically declared his willingness to stand or fall before Parliament and the world, a supercilious Wellesley informed Goulburn that he had been greatly pleased to find that his opinions had so "exactly" if not "wonderfully" (given their lack of "previous concert") coincided with the chief secretary's. Nevertheless, whenever a frustrated Goulburn succumbed to the temptation to act independently he was liable to be rebuked and instructed to consult Plunket.[14]

The fifth figure in the new human equation of Irish government was William Gregory. At first, his future had seemed bleak. From England Talbot had sent word of authoritative reports that he was "off the stage" as well. Wellesley's frosty attitude on his arrival did nothing to extinguish the under-secretary's fears that he, like Saurin, was to be removed. Five weeks were to elapse before he was admitted to "any Communication" with the viceroy, and during this lengthy period Gregory drew his own conclusions. "I should be wounded to the quick, if I had received such treatment from a man I knew & esteemed," he wrote to Peel. From the home secretary he sought an assurance that he would be granted a pension commensurate with his long years of service. "When I leave office, I shall go away as poor as a Rat, without being one," he added by way of explanation.[15] Then, quite suddenly, and only two days after he had penned his pessimistic request, the atmosphere brightened. With Goulburn's departure for England on 4 February to attend Parliament, Gregory was invited to his first business meeting with the lord lieutenant, and they had "a great talk." Although another fortnight was to pass before he was invited to dine, the under-secretary concluded that he was secure. Do "not answer the letter I wrote a few days since," he hurriedly advised Peel. However, his injured feelings were slow to heal. When Wellesley explained airily that he had not met with the under-secretary sooner because he had been in daily communication with Goulburn and had no wish to take him out of his office, Gregory remained pointedly silent. Yet he was unable to suppress a growing respect for Wellesley's initial diligence "in minutely & attentively, reading every paper connected with the state of the Country, & never delaying to return them, beyond the time necessary for consideration." Nor did he hesitate to give his own opinion "without reserve," whenever it was requested. But the freedom and intimacy which had characterized his relationship with both Whitworth and Talbot were noticeably absent. The two men did not pass beyond "official acquaintance," and Gregory was ever careful not to vol-unteer opinions or intervene in any matter uninvited. Moreover, he resented the fact that the lord lieutenant's dispatches often by-passed his office. "I am ignorant of their contents, except the information supplied by the Precis," he reminded Goulburn. Another grievance was the interfering Johnston.[16]

When the position of third clerk in the under-secretary's office fell vacant in July 1822, Johnston first attempted to secure it for his brother. After Gregory had successfully resisted this proposal, Johnston pressed for the appointment of his own clerk. An exasperated Gregory informed Wellesley "that the civil office was one of great trust & confidence, into which none but young men of good connexion & considered as Gentlemen were admitted & that it was a matter of much importance to take care who came into it." As for Johnston's clerk, whose ability and respectability his patron now extolled, Gregory sarcastically disputed his claims to be a gentleman, ob-serving that he dined "with the Lord Lieutenant's servants." Of course, the under-secretary's principal concern throughout was to exclude from his staff an agent of the private secretary. Victorious in this instance, he observed with disgust the subsequent organization by Johnston of a "Corps d'espi-onage" recruited from the servants of families suspected of being critical of the viceroy. "To Lord Wellesley personally I owe nothing," he announced to Goulburn early in March 1823, but "to his Government, so long as I act under it, I am bound by every feeling of obligation and honor to give it

every support in my power by a faithful and diligent discharge of many &
varied duties attached to my office." Beyond that he declined to go until
satisfied that the "whole system of Espionage was abolished." The influence
of Plunket was another blow to Gregory, for he so detested and distrusted
the attorney general that he urged Goulburn to withhold from him all private
communications they exchanged.[17]

Despairing of his ability to put "this unfortunate man," the viceroy, "in
a right line of conduct," "heartily tired of the whole concern," Gregory
flirted with the idea of resignation in the spring of 1823. Begged by Goulburn
and Peel to remain at his post, he held on and slowly established a satisfactory
working relationship with the lord lieutenant. For as Wellesley's initial and
uncharacteristic diligence in attending "minutely" to his duties evaporated
so his reliance upon the under-secretary's mastery of administrative detail
increased correspondingly. By the summer of that year, Gregory was happily
reporting to the chief secretary that the lord lieutenant was now consulting
him with "less reserve" on all matters concerning the state of the country
and paying more heed to his opinions.[18]

Throughout the first difficult year of Wellesley's viceroyalty, Gregory's
friendship with Peel had served as a steadying influence. "Rely upon it,
Peel is as sincerely attached to you as either Lord Whitworth or myself,"
Talbot had reassured the nervous under-secretary during those especially
tense and painful first five weeks. From Peel himself came the assurance
that there would be "no half confidences" between them. When Gregory
visited England later in the year, he stayed not only with Whitworth in Kent
and Talbot in Staffordshire but also visited Peel in Dorset. The home secretary had also been at pains to ensure that Goulburn and Gregory cooperated
as closely and as successfully in the government of Ireland as had he and
the under-secretary. "He is prepared to give you his utmost confidence –
to consult you on everything – & I have assured him that you will give him
all the assistance in your Power," Peel had written of Goulburn in the letter
to Gregory announcing his own return to office.[19]

The knowledge that the new chief secretary came on a mission to defend
the Ascendancy guaranteed him a sympathetic welcome from the under-
secretary. Moreover, they were both Trinity men. It was with the Gregorys
that Goulburn put up while his own residence was being made ready for
him. Gregory was also relieved to be working again with a man of method
and intelligence in matters of business. Little wonder that he was soon
reporting to Talbot: "I like Goulburn very much." Attached to the chief
secretary by respect and friendship, he exhibited anew that anxiety to guard
the minister from possible embarrassment in Parliament which had been a
feature of his relationship with Peel, and had been so manifestly absent from
that with Grant. His wish, he assured Goulburn, who was unusually nervous
about the parliamentary management of Irish business, and therefore es-

pecially appreciative of aid, was to protect him "from being worried in the house by repeated Questions, without being able to return any answer from Authority." He volunteered advice on how to disguise potentially controversial expenditures. When he discovered an unspent appropriation which might be diverted with the consent of Parliament to public works, it was the chief secretary's attention that he discreetly drew to the possibility. "If any credit is to be gained by affording additional employment to the poor of Ireland," he explained, "I would rather it was given to you." Not surprisingly, when a fall from his horse disabled Gregory and kept him away from his office for much of the month of June 1822, he was sorely missed by Goulburn.[20]

The easy familiarity of their private dealings was reflected in their correspondence. Instructed by the lord lieutenant to submit to the chief secretary the former's nominee to administer the House of Industry, Gregory added that Wellesley's candidate, having long been the king of beggers, was well qualified and fit to rule over them. Although no one apart from Peel was aware that Goulburn had empowered the under-secretary even to amend his minutes, the chief secretary's evident dependence upon and confidence in the Irishman, his willingness to delegate to him many of his most wearying and tedious duties, and the lord lieutenant's notorious indolence and increasing remoteness, eventually fostered a public impression of an extraordinary concentration of power. "The petitioner at the Castle did not ask what the lord lieutenant thought but what the lord's lieutenant's secretary thought, or rather what his secretary's secretary thought," one contemporary commented. "It was not Lord Wellesley, nor even Mr. Goulburn, but it was Mr. Gregory who held in his hands the destinies of Ireland." Hyperbole aside, the appointment of Goulburn as chief secretary and Peel's return to office as head of the Home Department had opened the way for the under-secretary to exercise unprecedented informal influence.[21]

The task confronting Peel and the Irish government in 1822 was a daunting one, for after more than two decades of union Ireland remained an anomaly within the United Kingdom. In Britain there had been a partial economic recovery, led by the revival in commercial activity and manufacturing which had begun in 1819 and continued to gather pace. Agriculture was far less fortunate, and 1822 proved to be an especially cruel year for many English farmers. In Ireland, meanwhile, there was little evidence of industrial expansion. Admittedly, the textile industries were showing signs of renewed vigour, and fishing had benefited from one of Charles Grant's successful initiatives. Aid had been provided to spur the construction of piers and harbours together with the building of boats and the provision of curing facilities. Although these improvements had brought a modest growth in employment in some localities, the national impact was insignificant. The vast majority of Irishmen were still dependent upon the land. Another source of anxiety was the failure of the assured markets provided by the Corn Laws to stimulate the hoped-for investment in Irish agriculture. A Scottish aristocrat and large landowner remarked of the relatively prosperous area around Dublin that "The country appears to be cultivated without capital, and no good farm houses, nor any farm-yards or stock-yards are to be seen in this part of Ireland. The land appears to be let too high, to be very little manured, – ploughed, and when exhausted left to rest, but naturally productive and capable of improvement." Elsewhere, cottiers working small parcels of land "at the very margin of subsistence" were continuing to multiply. Throughout the year, one incredulous visitor recounted, they collect "dung and filth of every kind" in pits which they dig in front of their cabins. In the spring the man entered this reservoir of fecal matter to fill wicker baskets which had been clogged in order to prevent the "gullion" from escaping. The parents then spread it by hand upon the land while the children planted seed potatoes. Even on somewhat larger holdings, many farmers could afford neither plough nor draft animals. They were obliged to rent equipment at the end of the season, making payment with their labour, or were reduced to breaking up the ground with the three-pronged forks and iron rakes that were the tools of English gardeners. Nothing but "wretched crops can be expected to result from such a mode of culture," he concluded. Not surprisingly, that confidence in Ireland as the great British granary, which had underlain the Corn Laws, was being rapidly eroded. The island's economy appeared to have proven uniquely impervious to "progress" and improverishment had gone on apace. "The whole is a scene of idleness, laziness, and poverty, of which it is impossible, in this active and enterprising country, to form the most distant conception," one contributor to the *Edinburgh Review* asserted.[22]

The findings of the census of 1821, that the island's population was fast approaching seven millions, lent further currency to the Malthusian argument that her exceptional misery was the inescapable consequence. Moreover, the belief that the Irishman had brought much of his suffering upon himself continued to be reinforced by the indelible English assessment of his character. For many Englishmen, he remained a peculiarly feckless and reckless figure, one who was devoid of "skill in private or public economy" and despised the "slow and patient" virtues. As for his religion, its "debasing superstition" and "childish ceremonies" further contributed to national "backwardness and barbarism." Such rationalizations of nonintervention by the state did not go unchallenged. The notion that the Irish were incurably bad or vicious was vigorously disputed. They had the same feelings and expectations as the people of England and theirs was a "civilized barbarity," the counterargument went. It was not the want of civilization which had made them barbarous, but the existence of great social and political evils which would have produced this form of barbarism among the most cultivated people in the world. "Put the British peasantry into their situation, and see whether they will be more patient, and less criminal and cruel," suggested one sympathetic traveller. While these observations were not inconsistent with the theory of the island's overpopulation, there was criticism, both explicit and implied, of Malthusianism. Michael Sadler's systematic attack was only just beginning to take shape, with its "proof" that "human fertility fell as population density, urbanization and comfort increased," but the associated proposition that Ireland could sustain a much larger population if only her substantial areas of waste lands were brought into cultivation was scarcely an original one. The select committee which had reported in 1819 had estimated that two million acres of boglands could be reclaimed and a further one and one-half million acres of remote lands opened up by roads. Similarly, to attribute the heartrending plight of the Irish peasantry to rack-rents, vestry assessments or cesses, grand jury jobs and the exorbitant demands of tithe proctors, was to controvert Malthus and sound a clarion call for remedial action. [23]

Whatever their cause, Irish backwardness and poverty continued to serve as explanations of the disorders which in their frequency, extent and savagery still distinguished Ireland from the rest of the United Kingdom. Commenting on the disturbances that were sweeping across much of the countryside early in 1822, Gregory's predecessor as under-secretary, Charles Saxton, charged them to distress. "I do not mean absolute want, tho' I believe there is much of that in the South," he informed the new Grenvillite member of the cabinet, Charles Wynn, "but the consciousness which the majority of the population feel, that with the change of times, their hope of prosperity has been extinguished, & their subjection to a landlordry, not always the most merciful, been conclusively sealed." Who could think safe a society "where large bodies of men, in the extreme of poverty and want," and taught to reason as a result of the great strides made in elementary education, were left to contrast their condition with that of "bloated and overgrown wealth," and to ask themselves how this "enormous difference" was to be remedied? In short, the time had come to investigate and remove the causes of disorders instead of persisting in the failed policy of "endeavouring to suppress them by force." [24]

The government did not want for advice on how to proceed in Ireland. The commission appointed in 1821 to investigate the management of the Irish revenue proposed that Ireland be educated "to the institutions and usages of Great Britain." It recommended the "consolidation of Customs and Excise, and of the Irish and British Revenues: and fiscal unity of trade." But the implementation of these measures did not hold out any promise of a speedy improvement in the condition of the island. That was also true of large-scale emigration endorsed as it had been by the Poor Law committee in 1819 and for which there was growing intellectual support even among economists. Clearly more central to the country's immediate needs was agrarian reform. Select committees urged the reclamation of bogs and other waste lands, only to find legislative progress in this direction impeded by concern for the sanctity of private property. Other proposals looked to halt the splitting of farms into small inefficient parcels of land. Here again, possible encroachment upon the "right of property" presented a formidable obstacle to action. One possible solution was to resort to subterfuge, to stalk the problem in the guise of electoral reform. Why not remove the political inducement offered to landlords to divide and subdivide their property into forty-shilling freeholds? To restrict "the elective franchise to persons actually in possession of freehold or copyhold property of the real value of 10*l* or 20*l*" would surely facilitate that "replacement of the cottier system by a capitalistic agriculture" which classical economists recommended. But there was general recognition that "security" was the essential prerequisite for investment. "The whole population, high and low, rich and poor, Catholic and Protestant, must all be brought to obedience to the law," declared a former lord chancellor, and "all must be taught to look up to the law for protection and to treat it with reverence." How was this transformation to be effected?[25]

Critics of the administration of Ireland argued that respect for the law could be instilled only in those persuaded of its equity. The magistracy and the shrievalty had to be purged of the bigoted and the corrupt. Those harsh and ineffective laws designed to discourage illicit distillation, but which caused so much misery, disrespect for authority, fraud, and violence, had to be repealed. Further, the duty on spirits should be reduced in an effort to promote the expansion of the legal industry. Through a general lowering of all duties in Ireland, whether customs or excise, the government might "afford new motives to stimulate, and new comforts and conveniences to reward," the industriousness of the Irish peasantry. Once inspired with a taste for the enjoyments of hard work, the Irish would raise themselves from their "hopeless and wretched condition," and as consumption increased so would revenues. Equally important to the restoration of tranquillity, and thus of prosperity and "security," was the extension of education. Since Roman Catholics, clergy and laity alike, regarded the existing schools with suspicion, the time had come to establish Catholic parochial schools. The assumption was that such measures as these would persuade the peasantry that the government and the law were sensitive to their needs and concerns. In this regard, however, an end to the injustices of the tithe was considered essential. The outcry against the tax by the depressed farmers of England was but a muted echo of the enmity it excited among the impoverished Catholic peasants of Ireland. Where was the justice in their being required to maintain a Protestant clergy, and one far in excess of the spiritual needs of that minority of Irishmen who were communicants of the Established Church? At the very least, advocates of reform declared, this festering grievance ought to be dressed with some scheme of commutation. Of course, the "master grievance" of Ireland's majority was "the circumstance of the government of that country having been hitherto vested in, and administered for the particular advantage of, a small minority of her inhabitants." The sweeping away of the remaining restrictions on Roman Catholics, and thus the toppling of the Ascendancy, was the indispensable reform. The perpetuation of disabilities, themselves inconsistent with the modern civilized age, had fostered "feelings of insolent superiority" on the Protestant side "and of debasement and degradation" on the Catholic. It was this "real" inequality that had "rendered the letter of equal laws a mockery and an insult."[26]

When Parliament reassembled in February 1822 the Opposition promptly took up the cry of justice for Ireland. In the Commons, Newport and Spring Rice called for equality of political rights and the reform of the tithe and the revenue laws, while, in the Lords, Holland and Lansdowne added purification of the magistracy to the lengthening list of essential measures. By far the most trenchant analysis of Ireland's plight and of her needs came, however, from Charles Grant. Having detailed for his listeners the exceptional wretchedness of her peasantry, evident in their clothing, diet, and dwellings, he explained that in the face of even the most trivial reverse they had "nothing to fall back upon." Victims of their own fecundity and dispositions ("easily excited, and above all things impatient of a continued course of fretful frustration"); of the collapse in the prices of provisions since the end of the Napoleonic Wars; of absentee landlords and a landlordry less responsible for their welfare than was the English for its tenants; of excessive rents and excessive taxation, the latter levied by the landlord-controlled grand juries; the Irish peasantry had been further conditioned to insurrection by harsh and extraordinary legislation. What was required in Ireland, he declared, was emancipation to improve the attitude of the great majority of Irishmen towards the British legislature and to conciliate the influential Catholic priesthood; sectarian education; reform of the tithe; reform of the magistracy and the establishment of an efficient local constabulary.[27]

The anxiety and interest the state of Ireland now aroused, and the evident intention of the Whigs to exploit the question, placed an added burden on those responsible for the elaboration of Irish policy and its parliamentary management. As the 1823 session neared its end, Peel was to remind the House that of the eighty-four days of business no less than forty-nine had been "appropriated" to the discussion of Irish subjects. But neither he nor Goulburn trusted Wellesley. They were ever alive to the danger that the viceroy would parade his liberal sentiments, thereby exposing their parliamentary flank. The lord lieutenant's distribution of patronage without first consulting the chief secretary was another irritant. Finding himself opposed on Irish issues by members with whom he had long been personally and politically "connected," and expected by the government to maintain some "influence" over its Irish friends, Goulburn angrily demanded that the viceroy suggest how he might perform this duty once it got around that he was no longer consulted on "arrangements" in Ireland. The loyalty of the Irish members to the government was nourished on preferment, and Goulburn was soon complaining that it was "impossible to satisfy their appetite." Much as he deplored the practice of considering any judicial office as part of the patronage of county members, and despite his sympathy with Gregory's suggestion that the important post of assistant barrister be excluded from this form of political barter, his personal opinions were restrained by less elevated considerations. All forms of patronage had already been so curtailed that he feared it would be "hazardous" to make the experiment of withdrawing this office as well. Instead, he proposed that the nominees of loyal county members for assistant barristerships be submitted to Ireland's highest judicial figures for an opinion on their qualifications, so that the government might claim that the appointments had indeed been made on the grounds of superior legal fitness. The viceroy refused to be a party to this subterfuge, even when the county member in question was Vesey Fitzgerald, whom Goulburn was especially keen to conciliate. Wellesley insisted that vacancies be filled under the regulations which he had already drafted to guide promotions to the bench. Yet far-reaching compromises, including those of principle, promised to be necessary if the government was to develop a successful policy for Ireland. [28]

Wellesley's success in India had been founded upon "a definite, consistent, and coherent policy," which he had formulated and to which he resolutely adhered. He carried no similar blueprint with him to Ireland aboard the steampacket *Meteor* in late December 1821 – and the crossing proved to be the appropriately tempestuous – merely a set of admirably liberal, but less than precise, intentions. "My view of the present state of affairs in Ireland would lead me to think that an impartial, equitable, and mild administration of the law (of which the alteration cannot be effected or attempted by a Lord Lieutenant), is the only safe course which can now be pursued," he advised the then marquis of Buckingham. However, by removing "real or imaginary causes of distrust in the impartial administration of justice" he did expect "to induce the people to confide in the protection of the law, and to yield it a willing obedience." Moreover, "by showing an equal degree of personal civility, and of attention to individuals of every persuasion," he hoped to reconcile them to each other and to "the actual system of the Government." Nor was his attitude towards the pivotal issue of Catholic relief any more radical. Given the existing state of the law and of the country, he let it be known that he now believed that it would be "highly dangerous" to concede "further power" to the Catholics before they had learnt to conduct themselves with "more temper." It was an opinion his exposure to the Ribbon societies of Dublin quickly hardened. Within a month of his arrival in the Irish capital he had been convinced that the Ribbonmen were religious zealots whose object was "to inflame the Catholics to massacre & war against the Protestants, and to subvert the establishment of Church and State."[29]

"Lord Wellesley knows that he goes to administer the laws, and not to urge an alteration of them," a well-satisfied Sidmouth commented. Nevertheless, the notion that the "Catholic" Wellesley's appointment did indeed signify "a change of system" had been implanted in many Irish minds. The fact that it fell to the new viceroy to remove Saurin in order to make room for Plunket served to strengthen the impression that a more liberal system of government was about to be inaugurated, as did the old attorney general's graceless departure from office and withdrawal into embittered private life. Like Wellesley, however, Plunket took office quietly preaching caution on the Catholic question. He favoured its postponement until there was "some better prospect of good sense and good temper on the part of the Roman Catholic clergy." Another straw in the wind, or so Wellesley later boasted, was the removal of Sir David Baird as commander-in-chief. Here was an "intelligible notice that the sword of the executive was no longer to be unsheathed from its scabbard at the mere requisition of the ascendant party." But the viceroy's confidential correspondence at the time does not support this claim, and the larger significance of the change in command appears to have escaped even the most perceptive of Catholic observers. Indeed, Daniel O'Connell took less heart from the appointment of Plunket and the removal of both Saurin and Baird than he did from the presence of Anthony Blake among the viceroy's confidential advisers. A prominent London barrister, and an Irish Roman Catholic, Blake had helped to draft the Catholic bill in 1821. He and O'Connell were "particular" friends and the Catholic leader's introduction to the lord lieutenant was soon arranged. "Lord Wellesley is, I conceive, the harbinger of Emancipation and is determined to put down the Orange faction," O'Connell optimistically affirmed. Yet the new government's extreme caution on the issue of emancipation was swiftly exposed.[30]

The appointment of Plunket had been accompanied by the elevation of Bushe to the King's Bench and his replacement as solicitor general by Henry Joy. Joy made a "bad political second" to the new attorney general, being both a stern opponent of emancipation and a brilliant lawyer who took pleasure in embarrassing his colleague. How such a divided administration could be expected to function effectively on all matters related to Catholics few observers professed to understand. Plunket's faith in Wellesley's "energy and powers of business" to subdue all of the difficulties growing out of such a "mixed government" was as ill-placed as it was unique. Moreover, he and his Grenvillite associates were soon reminded of the awkwardness of their position. George Canning suddenly gave notice, at the end of March, of a motion to open the upper House to Catholic peers. At the time he was still earmarked for the governor-generalship of India, and there was a strong suspicion that he was bent merely on mischief. The response of the Grenvillites, who had traditionally supported emancipation, was transparently feeble. Divided on the wisdom of seeking to advance the cause in such a "piecemeal" fashion, and anxious not to jeopardize their handsomely rewarded alliance with Liverpool, they first equivocated. Then they turned to Plunket for guidance, only to discover that he also was wracked with indecision. "He is extremely distressed between the strong wish of [Castlereagh] to keep back," Charles Wynn noted, "and of the Opposition to force forward the question." Eventually both Plunket and Wellesley signified their desire that the issue of Catholic relief be delayed until the following year. But the attorney general's temporizing conduct, as Canning's bill made its way through the Commons, only to the thrown out of the Lords, did little to enhance his reputation. Those who had expected him to be "a Tower of Strength" to the government could only have been disappointed by his uncertain performance, while the sympathizers with Ireland who had envisioned his displacing Goulburn as the "House of Commons Minister for that country" had reason for dismay.[31]

The difficulties created by Canning's bill convinced Wellesley of the wisdom of Peel's suggestion that the issue of emancipation be kept separate from the island's many other complicated problems. This was the strategy adopted in Parliament, by Castlereagh and Goulburn in the Commons and the prime minister in the Lords. Ireland's turbulence, Liverpool asserted, was rooted in class and personal tensions, not in sectarian injustices. It was a war against property and landlords, a mass of private feuds between individuals. To those calling upon the government to go to the source of the problem, and enact a broad program of reform, he replied that this was a task for the future. "When a house was in flames, the first object was, to extinguish them; the next, to consider by what means a repetition of the conflagration was to be prevented." The correct order of business, Goulburn echoed in the Commons, was to control the disorderly, to root out the causes of evil, and then to ascertain if there were "real" grounds of complaint and to enquire as to their "proper remedy." Wellesley was in full agreement. "The confusion which now surrounds us must be dispelled, & some degree of order must be established, before the wisdom of Parliament can even approach the outline of any comprehensive plan for the permanent welfare of the country," he announced after only a week in Dublin. He accepted, willingly enough, that his first task was "to break the habit of crime, and to inculcate by close and hourly vigilance, a general sense of the difficulty and dangers of disobedience to the law."[32]

Several essential steps towards a reassertion of the government's authority had been belatedly taken by Talbot and Grant. To bolster the military force at their disposal they had called out a number of the pensioned veterans resident in Ireland, forming them into three battalions. Although criticised for acting without "the previous knowledge and sanction of the English Government," they had the satisfaction of seeing the orders approved. Talbot had moved with equal dispatch when the Ribbonmen of Dublin, whose Defender-like oaths and "overtly nationalistic or confessional sentiments" excited understandable alarm at the Castle, were reported to be plotting an uprising. The city's yeomanry were quickly called to duty, the several entrances to the capital soon bristled with palisades and cannon, barricades were erected on bridges, the gates to the Castle locked and the guard doubled, and stones carried to the roofs of public buildings to be rolled down upon assailants. In County Limerick, meanwhile, where "open acts of outrage" had been especially prevalent, a special commission was established to dispense swift and exemplary punishment.[33]

Wellesley had been startled by Dublin's fortified appearance. Determined to inspire confidence, he moved openly about the capital, ordered the Castle gates to be left open and the guard reduced, and had the barricades dismantled. He also commuted the capital sentences of two of the seven men awaiting execution. Both he and Goulburn had taken heart from the reports from several disturbed counties of a revival of the family feuds that were popularly regarded as "the pretty sure indications of returning peace." Only three days later Wellesley was composing a far more pessimistic assessment of the national situation. Seeking to explain this viceregal volte-face, Goulburn advised the Home Office that "the complexion of things varies so much from day to day that you will observe even the most intelligent officers on the spot [are] unable to form any correct opinion as to what is likely to take place."[34]

Before the month's end the disturbances long chronic in County Cork had assumed "a more decided appearance of insurrection," with ever larger bodies of so-called Rockites coming into more frequent conflict with troops. By the beginning of February some 300 prisoners were awaiting trial. Inevitably, alarming comparisons were drawn to the crisis in 1798. The level-headed Goulburn was far from satisfied that the country again stood on the brink of full-scale rebellion or civil war, but he and the viceroy were united in the opinion that they required additional powers. "If we can wait safely till Parliament can give those powers so much the better," the chief secretary advised his friend Peel on 26 January 1822; "if not they must be taken on the responsibility of the Government and Parliament can never withhold their approbation." However, in seeking renewal of the Insurrection Act, the executive suggested that it be modified. Plunket's proposal that it be shorn of such severe provisions as the harsh punishment for violators of the curfew was rejected by his colleagues. Nevertheless, there was agreement on the need to avoid any repetition of those notorious abuses which had marred the act's enforcement in the past, in particular, the employment of their vastly increased public authority by magistrates locked in personal conflict with difficult tenants. Peel deflected the proposal. He argued that charges of "gross acts of injustice" had not been recently levelled and that there were already adequate safeguards in the party feelings and personal animosities of the magistrates. These ensured that the government would not be long kept in ignorance of cases of abuse. In addition, he emphasized the danger of making cosmetic changes which neither increased the law's effectiveness nor lessened the "strong objections on the ground of its unconstitutional Principle." They would merely encourage a quicker resort to the law and a greater reluctance to dispense with it. And as introduced by Castlereagh on 7 February, for Goulburn had been delayed in Dublin, the Insurrection Act was modelled on the earlier version and its life limited to six months. It was accompanied by a suspension of habeas corpus. In the Lords, two days later, the prime minister voiced regret at the necessity of resorting yet again to powers that had never been entrusted to the government of Britain, and conceded that they demonstrated Ireland's exceptional status. Both measures were passed with a minimum of opposition.[35]

Reenactment of extraordinary legislation did not immediately calm the jittery magistrates and gentry of the most disturbed province, that of Munster, who feared that they stood in imminent peril of assassination. The clergy of the Established Church had also been unnerved. The firing of churches and glebe houses indicated a "malice" towards the ecclesiastical establishment. Not that Protestants exclusively were victimized by Rockites. In County Kerry, Daniel O'Connell's tenants "were actually leaders and principals among the infatuated wretches who composed *Captain Rock's Corps.*" The terms of peace which his brother negotiated on his behalf included an abatement of rents. Nor did Daniel O'Connell's claim that the people attacked only their enemies prompt him to travel at any time other than that at which "they never attack anybody."[36]

William Gregory read with a mixture of anger, dismay, and disgust the reports reaching his office of disturbances across the length and the breadth of the country. It was not only the number and extent of the outrages but also their character that moved him to fury. Evidence that elements of the army had been subverted and the magistracy intimidated was worrying enough, but the putting of Protestant churches to the torch touched the raw nerve of insecurity which the events of 1798 had exposed. No less disturbing was the exceptional brutality of the Rockites. An attack upon and rape of a group of wives of men serving in the Rifle Brigade, which had been operating very effectively in Cork, horrified and revolted an under-secretary all too familiar with descriptions of acts of almost unimaginable human cruelty. Moreover, there was some evidence of a sectarian animus, of a desire to single out Protestant women, in this appalling incident. Gregory marvelled that anyone who had access to the reports reaching the government could deny the religious and political motivation of the "rebels." Nor was this his only ground of difference with a viceroy who admitted that all of the offenders were Roman Catholics, but reasoned that this did not prove the sectarian purpose of the disturbances. The under-secretary was equally critical of other aspects of Wellesley's behaviour. His practice of holding large councils guaranteed that few deliberations remained confidential, while his indiscretion in naming persons who had volunteered information seemed certain to "deter many, not even of the timid class, from giving information which may make them the marked objects for assassination." Where he and the lord lieutenant did agree was on the need for exemplary punishments, though the executive was at pains to ensure that the death penalty was enforced only in cases of the most serious crimes. Even then Gregory had an uneasy conscience about Lord Norbury's sitting in judgment. His hearing of capital cases was "quite revolting to every feeling of Justice and Humanity," for "his Mind, or rather his Memory," had gone. Unfortunately, another five years were to pass before he could be induced to resign from the bench.[37]

Advised that whenever a detachment of troops evacuated a post the vicinity immediately "became the scene of the most brutal, and sanguinary excesses"; that when the special sessions in Limerick was briefly adjourned the crime-rate accelerated; and that few arms had been surrendered; the lord lieutenant concluded that this was not the time to dispense with extraordinary powers. "If the Terrors of the Insurrection Act, are to outdo the Terrors of Captain Rock," Gregory echoed in a report to Goulburn, "I would give no rest until the object was accomplished." Convinced that the state of Ireland remained "most perilous," the chief secretary secured from Parliament in July an extension of the act. On this occasion, however, the protests of the Whigs were somewhat louder and there were allusions to Wellesley's taste for despotic powers. "Let Parliament refuse me all Power," he peevishly remarked to Goulburn, whose own treatment at the hands of the Opposition had been far more severe, "& then determine (after the *long nights* etc.) whether I asked for powers on personal considerations."[38]

Early in the autumn Wellesley and Goulburn concluded that a strengthening of the military establishment was essential if the Insurrection Act was to be effectively enforced. Not that the chief secretary was more disposed now than earlier to credit most of the reports of attempted assassinations, or the warnings of a vast conspiracy. His scepticism was applauded by Peel. "I can only say that I have heard of more instances of shots through the hat in Ireland without the head being affected, than in any other country," the home secretary mordantly observed. Yet, although he "neither apprehended a very stormy winter nor a very tranquil one," Goulburn held out little hope

of "an early restoration of public tranquillity." Constant patrolling by the
military would at least permit a more rigid enforcement of the provisions
of the Insurrection Act.[39]

The events of the winter served to strengthen the impression that the
outrages were inspired by sectarianism. The dramatic increase in the number
of copies in circulation of Pastorini's Prophecy, with its promise to Catholics
of the imminent destruction of Protestantism, briefly unnerved the usually
steadfast under-secretary and conjured up in his mind the nightmare of a
massacre of the Protestant gentry. "Is it surprising that the Protestants are
alarmed, when the Papists are so confident," he asked Peel; "and will any
rational Man believe, that with such encouragement, & such hopes of an
early completion held out by these sanguinary prophecies, that the Ribbon-
man oath, to wade knee deep in Protestant blood until heresy shall be
extinguished, is the oath only of a few shoe blacks, Tailors, & coal porters?"
Nor were such fears entirely unreasonable. If economic distress, proselytism,
and Orange "triumphalism" contributed to the "great upsurge of millenar-
ianism and anti-Protestant feeling," that did not alter the fact that many
outrages were marked by sectarian animosity.[40]

On 12 May 1823 Goulburn announced to the Commons with "sincere
regret" that he was obliged to recommend a further continuance of the
Insurrection Act. One month later Gregory reported that the island remained
in a "frightful state," and this despite the fact that every regiment Britain
could afford to release had been sent there or was on the march. Wellesley
was by contract optimistic. He disputed the need for additional military
reinforcements and opposed Goulburn's proposal that greater use be made
of the yeomanry, describing as "perilous" any resort to that Orange-hued
body. And within a few weeks the number of incidents had declined markedly. A measure of the administration's growing confidence was Goulburn's
delaying of his return to Ireland. His wife had been unwell and was still
very weak, so he decided to remain with her in Britain until late August.
By mid-November both he and the viceroy were able to report to Peel that
the state of the country had at last improved considerably. Nevertheless,
convinced that in many districts "the spirit of insubordination" had been
repressed rather than subdued, they urged that there be no "abandonment
of precautionary measures" or any "diminution of that vigilance and force"
to which they ascribed the "present improvement." In short, both insisted
that the existing military establishment of some 21,000 men was essential
for the maintenance of order.[41]

Throughout the long struggle to suppress the disturbances, Wellesley had
also sought to identify their causes. He discerned among the turbulent an
instinctive union springing "from common habits, sentiments, prejudices
and errors, from the general accordance of ignorance, and the severe burthens
of universal Poverty and Distress." In different localities, and at different

times, this union struck to defend its members' interests. It punished, often savagely, those who had taken tenancies from which others had been ejected, and made war on the tithe. The depth of Irish enmity for the tithe went neither unnoticed nor unreported by Goulburn as well as by Wellesley. The resistance to tithe payments, he informed Peel in September 1822, "has become in some parts so general that the clergy who have not received in any instance a very active or cordial support from the gentry, are nearly in a state of ruin." If the chief secretary's sympathy was evidently for the clergy rather than the Irish peasantry, the viceroy was more impressed with the need to implement a broad range of "practical measures of a remedial nature" in the interests of public peace. Sound, sensible, and liberal as his position was, Wellesley's ability to shape a program of reform was seriously impaired by those foibles and administrative failings which quickly undermined his authority and realized all the misgivings harboured at the time of his appointment.[42]

Dubliners regarded with varying degrees of amusement the lord lieutenant's pretentious yet penurious regime. His administration was immediately dubbed that of "the needy man" and the city soon rife with rumours that he was repaying his creditors with offices. Even a local fishmonger was alleged to have been offered a "job" in settlement of an account. Whether true or not, such stories damaged the viceroy's "good fame and dignity." His failure to do justice to his annual salary of £30,000, by maintaining an impressive court and thus bolstering the income of local tradesmen hard-hit by the depression, excited a sharper-edged criticism. His "childish vanity" also exposed him to ridicule, and his taste for pageantry bordered on the ludicrous. He ordered a change in the dress of the viceregal suite, insisting that his attendants add richly embroidered silver lace to their waistcoats, while he decked himself out in ornate uniforms festooned with his orders and decorations. When he received the sacraments in the Viceregal Chapel the altar was flanked by horn-blowing heralds in full dress, while he wore the sword of state.[43]

Among Wellesley's sternest Irish critics were Orangemen, who had been angered by the dismissal of Saurin and were fearful that it signalled a "change of system." Alive to this distrust, and vain enough to believe that he was uniquely qualified to heal sectarian differences, he had lost no time following his arrival in making overtures to the Protestant Corporation of Dublin and in cultivating the lord mayor. A collision with the more extreme Protestants was inevitable, however, given Wellesley's belief that "Orange triumphalism" was an important contributory factor to Catholic disturbances. Not surprisingly, the annual dressing of King William's statue in College Green provided him, as it had Charles Grant, with a ready target for his good intentions.

Wellesley's failure to persuade Protestants to forgo their parades in July

1822, and the ignoring by the Dublin Orangemen of his wish that they discontinue the practice of decorating the statue, which resulted in a brief skirmish between them and some of O'Connell's supporters, induced him to recommend that such activities be prohibited by law. The cabinet declined to take up the issue, unwilling as it was to stir up a hornets' nest. It raised no objection, however, to Wellesley exercising the acknowledged authority of the municipality, through the agency of the compliant mayor, to ban demonstrations whenever there was reasonable grounds to fear a breach of the peace. Then, in September, the Orange lodges approached Wellesley. They presented him with an address and offered in return to discontinue their provocative processions. But the lord lieutenant declined to "notice" them, explaining to Goulburn that "whatever benefit may be expected from the declaration against the several irritating celebrations, I cannot agree to purchase it, at the expense of recognizing the Orange Corporation." Instead, armed with a fresh legal opinion from the attorney general and affidavits from residents of College Green who professed to apprehend a riot, and with the approval of Peel, the viceroy banned the traditional November decoration of the statue. Although a group of Orangemen attempted to ignore the order, and briefly confronted the police, the day passed without serious incident.[44]

Peel applauded the action as a demonstration of Wellesley's determination "to administer the Laws of Ireland with firmness and impartiality," and avowed that his own desire to exclude Roman Catholics "from any material share in the direction of public affairs," left him "anxious that the mortification inseparable from exclusion, should not be increased by any irritating ceremonies." Plunket was more effusive still, assuring the viceroy that his action had "carried with it the cordial approbation of nine out of ten of the respectable Protestant Inhabitants of the city of Dublin." Others were far less sure of the wisdom of Wellesley's conduct. They warned that he had given "umbrage to many a sturdy protestant" on whose loyalty the British connection rested, and that it was "madness to suppose that the Protestants of Ireland" would submit to be restrained from commemorating their deliverance by King William. A number of Orangemen took an early opportunity to give vent to their displeasure. When Wellesley attended a performance of *She Stoops to Conquer* at the New Theatre Royal on 14 December 1822, he was subjected to a barrage of insults. His response to this indignity was so excessive that he became a laughing-stock even in England and exposed the government to such embarrassment that there was talk of his being recalled.[45]

Catcalls were directed at the lord lieutenant from the moment of his appearance in the theatre, and Goulburn, attending his first Irish production, remarked that he had never before "heard so much of the audience and so little of the actors." The verbal abuse was followed by a number of missiles, including oranges, bottles, and a watchman's rattle, the last narrowly missing the wives of Goulburn and Gregory whose box was next to that of Wellesley. Whatever liberal Protestant sympathy the viceroy might have won by his courageous behaviour during the riot, he quickly sacrificed when it became known that he intended to prosecute the arrested men for treasonable conspiracy. Subsequently, at the urging of both law officers and Goulburn, who argued that there was little to be gained in charging the culprits with a capital offence on which it would be impossible to secure a conviction, Wellesley agreed that indictments should be sought on the lesser charges of riot and conspiracy to create a riot. On 2 January 1823 a grand jury almost certainly packed by an Orange sheriff effectively nullified the prosecutions. It simply ignored the charge of conspiracy and returned bills against two of the men for riot, knowing full well that two persons could not constitute a riot. Infuriated and frustrated, insistent that he was the victim of a plot to drive him from the government of Ireland, Wellesley sanctioned Plunket's decision to proceed directly against the rioters through the process of "*ex officio* information." In the meantime, he invited congratulatory adresses offering thanks for his escape from "assassination." In this activity O'Connell and other Catholics gleefully participated. "I do not think there ever was the least opportunity of putting down the Orange faction till now," the Catholic leader excitedly reported to his wife. "You may imagine what a curious revolution it is in Dublin when the Catholics are admitted to be the only genuine loyalists." He found himself invited to dine at the Viceregal Lodge and singled out for marked attention whenever he accompanied deputations carrying messages of sympathy and congratulation to the Castle. Certain as all of this was to alienate further even moderate Protestants, it strengthened the conviction in England that Wellesley was behaving "like a fool."[46]

Within the governing coalition the Grenvillites were peculiarly sensitive to the absurdity of Wellesley's behaviour in "aping half murdered Royalty," and they deplored his involvement of Plunket in this folly. However, they and the other members of the government saw no alternative but to offer support to an Irish administration publicly committed to prosecution by information. Not that their temper was improved when those prosecutions failed, the jury announcing it could not agree on a verdict even after the crown had employed the last resort of shutting the members up for twelve hours without food. Before word of this sensation had been fully digested there came that of another, and of the lord lieutenant's over-reaction to it. At a dinner of the Dublin Beefsteak Club attended by the lord chancellor, the commander-in-chief, and several members of the viceregal household, a series of toasts had been drunk which Wellesley interpreted, not without reason, as insolent if not offensive. By way of response, he dismissed the minor household officers who had been present, one of them a senescent and popular figure. His action in "having SWOOPED at such small birds, when the Chancellor and Commander-in-Chief crowed in his face" kindled considerable scorn and indignation in both London and Dublin. Among the fiercest private critics of this "barbarous Act" was the under-secretary. Gregory was another member of the Beefsteak Club, but one fortuitously absent on this occasion. A heavy cold had confined him to his residence. So vehement was his denunciation of "the Extravagance" of Wellesley's vanity that an alarmed chief secretary hastily advised him not to mix himself up "in any proceeding which could be justly objectionable" to the viceroy. Gregory had already decided not to attend the next gathering of the club, and he also absented himself from his glee club lest he give "an ill-timed sneeze, & be accused of disrespect." This "caution" might be termed "prudence," he admitted, but to his way of thinking it bordered "on base servility."[47]

Wellesley's inflaming of the Protestant minority, and the extent to which he had made himself a butt of general ridicule, were but two of the unwelcome features of his viceroyalty. His growing inattention to duty, not least that of keeping Peel fully informed of the state of the country, together with a deepening personal feud with the lord chancellor, were additional irritants to the ministers in London. Nor did they welcome his contribution to their parliamentary difficulties. For disapproval of the Irish government's response to the theatre riot, especially the prosecution by *ex officio* information, appeared to have helped reinvigorate a Whig opposition which had been conveniently languid.[48] Then, against its wishes, the cabinet found itself obliged to introduce a measure to suppress secret societies in Ireland.

There had been talk for some time of extending to Ireland the provisions of an English act designed to suppress societies established for "Seditious and Treasonable Purposes." It had promised to be a useful weapon in the struggle against the Ribbonmen. Wellesley now recommended its adoption as a means of disciplining the Orangemen. Peel demurred. He announced his support for the steady assimilation of the laws of the two countries, admitted that the Orange Lodges did foment religious discord, and denied that he had ever been a party to their activities. As chief secretary, he reminded the viceroy, he had neither countenanced them nor recognized an Orangeman in that capacity. But as much as he disapproved of "any confederacies of a political nature, not connected with the state," and wished for the dissolution of the Orange Lodges, Peel was struck by the inappropriate irony of applying to men long marked by their intense loyalty a law designed to check treason. Furthermore, this measure threatened to infuriate the already aroused Protestant population. Goulburn feared that it would be viewed as confirmation of the Irish government's resolve to depress Protestants in order to elevate Catholics. So the cabinet turned the question back to Wellesley, though he could have been in no doubt that it did not wish him to proceed. His reply was "rather an extraordinary one." He reaffirmed his belief in the act's necessity, but disclaimed an intention to have recommended any immediate alteration of the law. Instead, he announced that he was well satisfied by the news that the activities of the Orangemen were to be raised in Parliament by one of their inveterate critics, James Abercromby, and he urged a full parliamentary inquiry "into the condition of Ireland, the nature of the Orange societies, and of the impediments his Government had met with." Of course, that was the last thing the cabinet sought, with all of the inherent possibilities for political embarrasment, and Wellesley's enthusiastic advocacy of this dangerous course gave rise to suspicion of his motives. Unable to dissuade Abercromby from introducing his motion, which they decided to oppose, the government sought to head off a debate. They announced their intention to introduce after Easter the measure Wellesley had requested. In the Commons, Goulburn and Peel sought to soften the blow many Protestant Irishmen were certain to feel. They stressed that all secret societies were to be discouraged, acknowledged that Orangemen were bound together in loyalty, and emphasized the overriding need to assimilate the laws of the two countries. However, the unrestrained enthusiasm with which such campaigners against the Orangemen as John Newport welcomed the announcement sounded more convincing, and when Goulburn turned to Gregory for a frank assessment of Irist Protestant reaction he received a caustic reply.[49]

The under-secretary had long regarded the religious minority to which he proudly belonged as the very foundation of the British connection. Faithfully, he represented the Protestants' dissatisfaction "with the cold defense made for them against malignant and misrepresented statements," and sarcastically acknowledged their ignorance of the abhorrence in which Orangemen were held in the Commons. Men whose "only crime" was "Ultra Loyalty" were "represented by Whigs & Radicals as the most ferocious of Mankind, & at whose feasts popish Blood [was] the usual Beverage," whilst the "gentle Ribbonmen" escaped such censure. It was not easy "to teach prudence to a party, who think they are to be put down, who know the service they have done the state, & that if the state is again in danger, reliance can be placed only on them," he added. Responding to this bitter assessment, which had been forwarded to him, Peel urged Gregory to place the defence of the Ascendancy within a broader context. The real strength of Ireland's Protestants since the union was not any number of Orange lodges but the public opinion of England, the home secretary argued. Therefore the essential task was to convince the people of England that Catholic animosity towards the island's Protestant minority was the "result of sheer religious bigotry and hatred," exemplified by Pastorini's Prophecy, "and not the offspring of insulted and irritated feelings." If the battle to prevent emancipation was to be waged successfully "in this age of liberal doctrine," conservative Irish Protestants would have to exhibit "discretion, forbearance and moderation."[50]

Moderation or discretion was certainly the order of the day on 12 July 1823. There were few Protestant celebrations, even in the North, and only in Armagh was there any violence. In the capital, the Orangemen decided not to decorate the statue of their hero. Even so, it required the intervention of Gregory to prevent the viceroy from irritating them anew. He instructed the under-secretary to write to the mayor to thank him for the precautionary measures he had adopted, such as the stationing of substantial numbers of police in the area of College Green. Reminding Wellesley that this action had proven unnecessary, Gregory persuaded him that "such approbation" was both "unmerited and impolitic." One week later the unlawful oaths bill was passed by Parliament, and although the Orange Lodges evaded it, by dissolving themselves and then reorganizing, there was sufficient doubt as to the legality of this manoeuvre for them to keep their heads low.[51]

Wellesley could claim a victory, then, in his conflict with the Orangemen, but it had been purchased at a high price for his standing. Indeed, the embarrassment he had caused the government by his personal and political conduct briefly brought his future into question. His brother Wellington thought it impossible for him to remain in Ireland, because he had made himself so unpopular with the gentry. But the cabinet could ill afford to remove him. His recall would have been widely interpreted as a triumph of "Orangeism," and would almost certainly have led to resignations from, and perhaps the disintegration of, the Liverpool ministry. Nevertheless, in reaffirming the cabinet's support of him, Peel made clear to the viceroy its belief that he had contributed to Protestant irritability by his excessive response to the theatre riot. The home secretary also expressed the cabinet's hope that Wellesley would now endeavour "to secure the cooperation of persons of influence and consequence, whatever their persuasion or opinions might be."[52]

"W[ellesley] has again the cards in his own hand if he knows how to play them," Charles Wynn observed. The viceroy did move quickly to patch up his differences with the lord chancellor, for which he had not been entirely responsible, but hopes that he would mend his ways and exhibit more vigour and energy were shortlived. His complaints about his health were incessant. "He has had a very violent cold but has not been in that imminent danger which he has apprehended himself to be in," an ironic Goulburn remarked, after having been denied access to the lord lieutenant for thirteen days. This tiresome hypochondria served as an excuse for the continuing infrequency of the viceregal correspondence. As a result, the criticism of Wellesley was soon "universal." The cabinet continued to fume at his "unparalleled" silence; Goulburn protested the inconvenience of having an attorney general who resided out of Dublin and "a Lord Lieutenant who is so uncertain as to the days on which he can do business"; indeed, in Ireland it was said that he "does nothing & sees nobody, & the Wicklow retreat instead of being for his health is his Harem where he spends all his time." Far from seizing control of Irish policy, Wellesley virtually abdicated his responsibility for it. "There is little encouragement to me to attempt any course of a remedial nature, after the reception which has been given in the House of Commons to whatever I have done or proposed of that description," he sullenly informed Goulburn. The hope that Wellesley would inaugurate in Ireland a more liberal system of government had been quickly dashed, and his viceroyalty was to be marked by a fresh surge of conservative activism.[53]

## CHAPTER SEVEN

# The Limits of Conservative Reform

The conviction that Ireland "formed an exception to any general rule" served to justify not merely the suspension of traditional constitutional rights, and thus the resort to extraordinary instruments of social control, but also the introduction of a broad range of remedial measures. After all, Henry Goulburn traced much of Britain's difficulty in Ireland to the "embarrassment which the legislature had felt in applying laws, framed for the government of one country, to the peculiar circumstances of the other." Indeed, he drescribed the Insurrection Act as necessary in order to give the government time to mature and implement essential reforms. But the most pressing order of business was to seek to alleviate the distress which all observers recognized as either a causal or contributory factor in the disturbances. Wet weather during the autumn of 1821 severely damaged the potato crop. By the following spring there was evidence of much suffering, especially in western counties. In Clare, for example, the peasantry had lost their own crops and were too poor to purchase those potatoes on sale. In drawing their plight to Goulburn's attention, Gregory admitted that there were aggravating circumstances. The local gentry had failed to meet their obligations to provide for the distressed, while potential food supplies continued to be diverted to an extensive illicit distillation. Nevertheless, he posed the question: "yet with all these sins on their heads, are so many thousands to be left to the Chance of perishing for Want?"[1]

In London, there was alarm at the sums which might be involved. The executive had precious little money on hand to finance a large program of relief. Almost £42,000 remained of earlier parliamentary grants, and private subscriptions had raised an additional £6,875, but the total fell far short of what was needed, which Gregory conservatively estimated at more than £100,000. Moreover, relief for Clare would surely excite "clamourous Demands from other Districts." Reluctant for this very reason to seek a special appropriation, fearful of the discouragement parliamentary intervention might give to private charity, and ever mindful of the "mischievous results" of any "meddling with the natural means of supplying the market," the government's initial response was both discreet and cautious.[2] Wellesley was authorized to lay his hands on any available monies, and he promptly appointed a commission to administer their contribution. Gregory chaired its proceedings and supervised its activities. Evidently the model for this program of relief was that set up by Peel five years earlier. Thus Goulburn ordered that assistance be extended in the form of matching grants. It must be clearly understood, he instructed Gregory, that "unless sums are subscribed by the neighbouring proprietors (whether resident or absentee matters not) the Government will not give the money." Expenditures beyond the sums on hand he hoped eventually to cover through a general vote of credit. But the government's strategy of providing relief as unobtrusively as possible, and of compelling the gentry to make a substantial contribution, was soon frustrated by the loud cries in Parliament for assistance to Ireland in the form of advances to create employment. Its response came on 16 May 1822, when Goulburn introduced the Irish poor employment bill. The viceroy was empowered to advance out of the consolidated fund loans to grand juries equal to the presentments they had just voted at the Spring Assizes for the making or repairing of roads. The intent was to encourage an immediate start on such public works. Aware of the notoriety of these bodies, however, Goulburn hastened to reassure the House that the works would not be executed "under local authority, but by [Engineers] appointed immediately by government." In addition to these loans, £50,000 was placed at the lord lieutenant's disposal to finance public works. Warmly supported in both Houses, the bill was speedily passed. The only criticism was of the "paltry sum" involved.[3] Simultaneously, and surreptitiously, the government sought to guard against famine. Seed potatoes, and later biscuit, were quietly sent to the distressed districts. Another concern was the danger of a repetition of the disastrous fever epidemic of 1817, which had prompted Parliament to authorize the appointment of officers of health to enforce essential sanitary measures among the poor. With this peril in mind, the general Board of Health in Dublin established a correspondence with doctors in those districts "where disease might be expected first to shew itself." The members hoped, therefore, to receive timely warning of "any Epidemic malady" and to ensure prompt adoption of preventive and remedial measures.[4]

Private benevolence also came to Ireland's aid. Subscriptions were opened throughout England, and in the capital there was a remarkably successful charity ball held at the Opera House. Some 2,500 persons attended, each paying at least two guineas. Thomas Spring Rice, one of the sponsors of this event, admitted to a fellow countrywoman that he was "touched to the heart by the generous eagerness with which the English merchants and many of the city people whose names will ever be unknown to fame" had contributed to the fund for Irish relief. He recognized that the generosity of the British – in all more than £300,000 was raised – placed a heavy responsibility upon him and others to make sure that this money was "judiciously applied." Perhaps as a result, only £40,000 of the total was expended on immediate aid in the form of food and seed potatoes. The balance was invested in improvements and industries, such as fisheries and linens, which held out the promise of more permanent relief.[5]

Much the same resolve guided the viceroy's commissioners for relief of the poor. They concluded that the distress had arisen from a local scarcity in the midst of a more general abundance. The first duty of government, therefore, was to maintain the free movement of internal trade, for "local prejudice" had done much to prevent provisions being moved from one area to another. Beyond that, they recommended that grants be made to local relief committees to assist in building roads to potential coastal centres of a fishing industry; to improve the security of harbours used by fishing vessels; to drain bogs; and to improve the dwellings of the poor. Persons who found employment on these projects were to be paid at the lowest rate in order both to provide relief to the greatest number and to forestall accusations that the program was interfering with the ordinary labour market. And when the limited nature of this response attracted criticism from those who suggested that the problems of Ireland demanded a larger and more systematic make-work scheme, Peel was quick to protest that in giving "relief in every possible way" the Irish government had already deviated far fom the principles of political economy.[6]

Hopes rose in May that the worst was over, only to fade rapidly early in June. The archbishop of Tuam, Gregory's brother-in-law, warned of approaching famine in Galway and Mayo and described the £50,000 voted for public works as "*totally* inadequate." The worried under-secretary advised Goulburn that the money would give employment to a substantial number, but that they would not amount to "one twentieth" of those in need of assistance. The archbisphop dismissed the £1,000 urgently forwarded to him as a "literal drop in the Ocean." Alarmed by such reports, Goulburn ordered the dispatch of more biscuit from England. Expense must be a subordinate object of consideration, he instructed the under-secretary. Yet Gregory continued to counsel caution, as did Wellesley. Serious as they recognized the crisis to be, and heartrending the stories of suffering, they also agreed that the distress had been "most corruptly exaggerated." Gregory suspected the local gentry of planning to divert sums "from the Public Good to promote Party and local purposes." In an effort to counter the "system of jobbing," county relief committees were established to supervise those in the baronies. At the other end of the social scale were those peasants to whom "mendicity" brought no disgrace. If this class made the discovery that they could depend upon public assistance, the under-secretary warned, they would have an additional inducement to "their habitual idleness." Moreover, in many of the western districts it was customary for adult males, once the potatoes had been planted, to make their way to England in search of occasional work, leaving the women and children to take to the road as beggars. Those "ordinary habits are now added as items to swell the account of Extraordinary Distress," Gregory asserted. Hence "gratuitous relief" had to be avoided as far as was possible. Work was everything, he enjoined in a circular which was published by the press.[7]

Goulburn was quick to ridicule the notion that any government could provide food for an entire population, and was no less fearful than his colleagues of encouraging dependence upon public relief. Nevertheless, the gravity of the situation denied the Liverpool ministry the luxury of being governed by such concerns. The pressure to do more for suffering Ireland had continued to increase. Goulburn, in particular, heard himself traduced as "the most inhuman and unfeeling of men" because of his reluctance to commit the government to feed all the people. Privately, he instructed the executive to be liberal. "In the present state of things economy must be put out of the question," he informed the viceroy on 19 June 1822, "and I am sure that Parliament will not be satisfied unless every exertion be made to feed a starving population wherever it is to be found." Hounded and harassed, the minister decided to seek a grant of £250,000, to be advanced on public works, and an additional £100,000 to enable Wellesley to meet the applications for urgent relief. As a result by 17 July Parliament had voted £400,000 to support local relief efforts and to provide employment on public works. "We all agree that the more employment and the less gratuitous relief is given the better," Goulburn emphasized, "and if the Engineers [on public works] are active in their respective districts, which I have no doubt they will be, the people will be generally employed very soon if not at this very moment."[8]

A month later Gregory reported that no use had yet been made of the 2,500 bags of biscuit sent to Cork. Not that he was surprised, for he remained confident that there were provisions enough in Ireland to supply the needs of the distressed districts. There was much wheatmeal for sale, he assured Goulburn, "which tho' not so palatable to the taste of the Poor, is very good food, & £1 per ton cheaper than oatmeal." And soon after his return to Ireland in August, the chief secretary judged the worst of the crisis to be over. The claims of local gentry that their tenants were too poor to pay rent, and that the poor were still in desperate need of employment, he increasingly dismissed as self-serving. He did acknowledge the need to pursue public works in particular districts, but with the prospect of an excellent harvest, and thus a "superabundance of provisions," he soon discontinued the distribution of food relief.[9]

The decision to curtail public works was eased by the evidence that in

some areas they had been "infamously jobbed" or the aid "grossly mis-
applied." On the Aran Islands, thieving boatmen, islander ingratitude, and
the difficulty of monitoring the exchange of food for labour, had combined
to lessen the impact of relief. Archbishop Trench was enraged by the discovery that monies earmarked for a Protestant chapel had been diverted to
the construction of a Catholic one. Elsewhere, the recipients of relief were
reported to have exceeded the entire population as enumerated in the recent
census. Yet no one familiar with the report of the Board of Health on the
outbreak of a fever epidemic in Galway that autumn could doubt the existence
of abject poverty. The fact that by early October new cases were averaging
thirty each day, and this in a town of no more than 28,000 souls, lent itself
to ready medical explanation. The large number of mendicants and vagrants;
the overcrowded and inadequate accommodations of the poor, which were
invariably damp and usually windowless; the poor hygiene, for in the absence
of sewers there collected before almost every door and at the foot of every
set of stairs "a compost of the most offensive kind" which the feet of pigs
and children constantly carried into the dwellings; the lack of adequate
supplies of fresh water, despite the presence of the river carrying the waters
of Lough Corrib to the sea; a diet "miserable and insufficient," and a want
of clothing and night-time coverings which compelled healthy and sick to
huddle together for warmth; all helped to provide a natural breeding ground
for disease.[10]

In all, ten counties had received grants from the lord lieutenant in 1822,
with Cork, Galway, Clare, and Mayo leading the list of beneficiaries. But
the total expenditure had been less than £27,000, and caution continued to
be the administration's watchword throughout 1823. The chief secretary
reacted sharply when one of the engineers supervising relief works exhibited
a taste for "great national improvements," while nothing came of a recommendation made by a Commons committee on the employment of the
Irish poor that a general drainage act be introduced. Instead, there were
piecemeal efforts to promote economic development and thus create long-
term employment. Gregory urged that a vacant textile factory in Kilkenny
be leased to an English company (others wished simply to dispose of the
property), recalling that during its earlier operation there had been local
prosperity and tranquillity. "One gleam of comfort in the dark shade of
misery which clouds this unhappy land, ought not to be neglected however
short may be [its] duration," he advised Goulburn. Nevertheless, conservative to a fault, and pessimistic of the state's ability to effect permanent
improvements, he was quick to deny that he was an "Owenite." Similarly,
Peel was willing for the state to offer encouragement to the linen industry
in the southern provinces. He had not undergone a change of heart on the
wisdom of government intervention in the economy, but was prepared to
concede that in Ireland "if it would practically do no harm, it would be

useful as evincing a disposition to do good."[11]

Pragmatism did not always override ideology. The home secretary discouraged the stockpiling of provisions on the government's account to meet any shortages that might develop during the winter. Whatever protection this precaution would afford the ministry from the "attacks of foolish people in the House of Commons" was more than outweighed in his mind by the danger of encouraging "improvident consumption" by persons "who will be taught to rely on the Assistance of Government in the time of necessity." He also feared that the government's entrance into the market would drive up the price of corn, encourage "ruinous speculation," and even trigger the reopening of the ports to foreign produce at a time of acute agricultural distress.[12]

Another concern was that to which William Gregory gave expression when reports of famine in Connemara, in the areas around Moycullen and Oughterard, reached the Castle during the spring of 1824. Appeals from local priests on behalf of the starving poor were greeted sceptically by an under-secretary who recalled that one of the priests in question had been employed the previous year distributing food, and had then excited suspicions "of not having forgotten the shepherd." More important, however, was the dangerous precedent which might be established by sending supplies to a distressed district in three successive years. If there was compliance with the demands for food on this occasion, Gregory reasoned, "the Government must be prepared to pay annually for any local, or partial failure of any crop." So, instead of dispatching food for "present maintenance," the administration forwarded seed potatoes which had been cut in order to prevent their use for any purpose other than planting. Subsequent reports from Moycullen that some of these potatoes had gone to persons who had enough of their own to sell, and that the price of this essential foodstuff had fallen, merely strengthened a determination to respond with greater caution to future requests for direct relief. Yet as Gregory acknowledged, no matter how cheap potatoes were in Galway, it might well be said "that if the price was 1$^d$ [a stone], the poor could not buy as they had not the money." The problem was less one of scarcity, therefore, than of "a want of employment" for the "labouring classes." Gregory's insistence that this was a question distinct from the want of food did not blind him to the fact that it was "not perhaps less serious, as affecting this Country, and will ere long produce afflicting circumstances."[13]

However conservative the government's response to Irish distress ultimately proved to be, and by 1824 its principal concern was to oblige the gentry to shoulder their responsibilities, the anodyne of relief was a more progressive prescription for Ireland's chronic malady than the purgative so frequently administered under the provisions of the Insurrection Act. Of course, a simple combination of even these two powerful physics was never expected to effect a complete cure. Instead, Ireland clearly required a complexity of remedies. And one of the most important ingredients of this therapeutic concoction was a "vigorous, effectual & impartial" enforcement of the law and of the administration of justice. To this end, much thought had already been given to the improvement of the police and the magistracy.[14]

Both of Goulburn's immediate predecessors had sought to reform the police, though Charles Grant had repudiated the species of gendarmerie associated with Peel. Not surprisingly, with Peel at the Home Office, and still deeply interested in the matter, it was just such a force that the administration now envisaged, though prudence dictated the use of "some less startling name." Indeed, Goulburn initially planned to use the Peace Preservation Force as his model and to make it permanent and national. But the concept of a national police force promised to encounter strong resistance from local gentry, who in their capacity as magistrates controlled the existing baronial constabulary. So the chief secretary incorporated the county organization which Peel had sketched out but never implemented during his years in Ireland. Each detachment, of which there would be several in a county, was to be composed of constables and sub-constables commanded by a chief constable. Nevertheless, Goulburn still intended the new force to be under the control of the executive. The government would appoint the men and be empowered to appoint a police magistrate to command them whenever, in the opinion of the lord lieutenant, it was expedient to do so. In short, although the scheme did not provide for the "immediate and absolute supercession" of the local magistracy, the government was to possess the discretionary power to install stipendiaries.[15]

The chief secretary's confidence that these provisions, with their cosmetic features, would be carried "without serious difficulty" proved misplaced. The Irish members balked at the threatened loss of influence and patronage, while Irish Whigs insisted that, if only the magistracy was first reformed, then the nomination and control of the police might safely be left in traditional hands. Charles Grant also made a telling intervention in the debate, protesting the sacrifice of "constitutional freedom" involved in placing all of Ireland under an armed police and by rendering "the whole magistracy of the country liable to the control of the Lord Lieutenant." Notwithstanding powerful support from Peel and Plunket, who dwelt upon the desirability of lessening the expensive dependence upon the military for law enforcement, and "the saving of public morals, and the probable restoration of peace, obedience, and sober habits to the country," which did see the measure through second reading, an uneasy chief secretary elected to compromise with the critics of his proposals. The appointment of the senior officers – the four provincial inspectors-general and the chief constables commanding the individual detachments – remained firmly in the grasp of the viceroy, but local magistrates were granted the right to appoint the constables and were conceded their traditional control over the constabulary's operations. Equally significant was his deletion from the bill of the government's discretionary authority to install stipendiaries. Instead, they would only be appointed at the request of at least seven local magistrates. Finally, the expenses of the new County Constabulary were to be borne by both levels of government, local and executive.[16]

Angered by the criticism of the original bill, and the retreat from complete government control of "a really efficient police," Wellesley dismissed as worthless the amended version that was speedily enacted into law. As ever, he overstated the case. Alive to the need to ensure that the police force was composed of "honest hands as well as honest chiefs," the executive enjoyed some success in its subsequent efforts to persuade magistrates to surrender to the inspectors-general the nomination of constables, or at least sub-constables. In short, this "clumsy compromise between centralization and local autonomy" was not as awkward as it seemed nor were the results as valueless as Wellesley feared they would be. Together with the Peace Preservation Force, which continued to operate, the County Constabulary provided the means for a more effective policing of Ireland. And "due obedience" to the law was widely regarded as inseparable from its impartial administration. But if justice was ever to be perceived as even-handed, and the police effectively employed, a thoroughgoing reform of the magistracy was no less essential.[17]

The executive had inherited from Charles Grant a process for purifying the magistracy. However, several months passed before the indecisive Wellesley endorsed the cancellation of the existing commission of the peace and the issuance of another only to men qualified to serve as magistrates. The viceroy soon noted that as word of this plan of revision spread the existing magistracy exhibited greater diligence in the performance of their duties. Not content, he pressed for the institution of petty sessions. By requiring public hearings before more than one magistrate he hoped not only to check abuses which had all too often resulted from solitary and private exercices of authority, but also to guarantee a "more systematic and regular course of action." Further, he proposed at the under-secretary's urging that the chairmanship of the quarter sessions be removed from the gift of the county MPs. "They are judicial situations and the poor Man never should be taught to believe that the Chairman of the Sessions is appointed by any local Influence," Gregory observed, for that notion "tends to empeach [sic] the fair administration of Justice, and induces a suspicion on the Decrees." The upshot was the decision to appoint the salaried and professionnally trained assistant barristers as chairmen, which amounted to "a considerable encroachment on the peculiar jurisdiction of the magistrates." Subsequently, the administration also turned its attention to the sub-sheriffs, who were widely regarded as venal. Charged with the duty of arresting debtors and enforcing judgments against property in satisfaction of debts, they did not scruple to oblige plaintiffs to outbid defendants before they would perform it. The commissioners of law inquiry were instructed to investigate their conduct, and they eventually recommended that the functions of the sub-sheriffs be transferred to a permanent official like the sheriff-depute in Scotland who was under their control.[18]

The assurance of more impartial and honest administration of justice was unlikely to pacify Ireland, even when backed by a more effective constabulary. Recognizing this, the government responded to the evidence from Ireland, and the cries of the critics of its policies, that the tithe was the prime cause of the recurring waves of disturbances. Thus the prime minister again breached the defence-work Peel had earlier attempted to erect around the property of the Established Church in Ireland. He informed the Lords that this was "purely an Irish question." Not that it was one the executive was keen to tackle. Characteristically, Wellesley let it be known in February 1822 that his opinion was "no opinion at all," and he exhibited a strong desire to shirk responsibility for policy in such a controversial field. "I am inclined to hope, that some proposition on the subject might be made by Mr. Peel, & the Government during the Session," he informed Goulburn, before placing firmly upon the chief secretary's shoulders the burden of preventing parliamentary agitation of such a "delicate, intricate, & perilous question at the present time."[19]

Goulburn was in no haste to act. He deplored any concession to the disaffected and was loath to tamper with property rights. Interference ought to be "as delicately & as carefully measured by the necessity of the case when tithes are concerned as it would be if the landed property of certain Country Gentlemen were the object of it," he observed sardonically. Convinced that the hope of the Catholic majority of Ireland was to "defraud" the church of its due, his overriding concern was to protect it from "plunder." Moreover, he was assured by Gregory that the tithe was not the load under which the poor man sank. Rent charges were "tenfold more oppressive," the under-secretary observed, especially those demanded for the small plots of land held in conacre. Thus to the extent that a tithe proposal did take shape in Goulburn's mind at this early stage, it amounted to nothing more than a voluntary transfer of payment from occupier to proprietor. The landlord would recover the sum involved in the form of a higher rent. Such an arrangement promised at least to dull the sharp edge of peasant resentment of the Protestant clergy. But Goulburn's vague assurances that "some proposition" was in preparation failed to satisfy the House, and the repeated demands for action strengthened the prime minister's determination to have a measure introduced.[20]

Liverpool, Peel, and Goulburn had already sought to impress upon the representatives of the Irish prelacy assembled in London to attend Parliament the advantages of the government taking the issue in hand. Wellesley had been urged to sound out the bishops remaining in Ireland. Although in his dealings with the Irish primate the prime minister had raised the possibility of compulsory commutation, he was prepared to accept a modest interim measure. For the time being, at least, he would be satisfied with the exemption of potato plots from a tithe (only in certain areas were potatoes liable to the tax), and the provision of "adequate" compensation for the clergy in the form of an acreable assessment on other lands in the parish, including pasturage at present exempt from the tithe. The supposed advantages of this plan were explained to Wellesley by Peel. The actual losses suffered by the church would be inconsiderable, and friction between clergy and tithe payers prevented. Indeed, both payer and receiver would benefit if law charges were avoided, proctors dispensed with, and tithes no longer farmed. But in a further effort to place a buffer between Protestant clergy and Catholic peasantry, the government also intended to encourage the leasing of tithes for periods of up to twenty-one years. Landlords would take the charge upon themselves and recover it through higher rents.[21]

The scheme was supported by Plunket, and presumably by Wellesley, for it did not differ markedly from proposals the attorney general had finally brought over from Ireland, but their Grenvillite associates were less enamoured of it. Wynn feared that landlords would encounter serious difficulties when they sought to increase rents "by the amount of what will be payable for tithes." Buckingham was more scornful. Why would landlords "take a loan" of tithes the parson had found so difficult if not impossible to collect? "Where is the policy of throwing upon the 'landlords' the odium of a vile system, even if the 'landlords' were foolish enough to give in to the plan?" he asked Wynn. "It is not by half measures such as these that Ireland is to be tranquillized and the Empire benefited." And when Goulburn finally introduced the tithe bill in mid-June all that remained of the original measure was the proposal to enable incumbents to lease their tithes to the proprietors of the soil. He did offer assurances that a plan of commutation was under consideration, and attributed the delay in bringing it forward to the complicated nature of the question. How, for example, was a "fair equivalent" for the tithe to be established, given the clergy's disinclination or inability to levy more than a fraction of their tenth? But none of this satisfied the Opposition. Nor was Wellesley impressed by the bill, informing Goulburn early in July that it seemed to him "very unimportant" whether it passed or not. Enacted it was, but by the autumn there were claims that not a single lease had yet been signed. The viceroy ascribed this lack of interest to the widespread belief that a general commutation was in the offing.[22]

"I think it will be quite impossible not to do something more effectual on this subject, than what was intended to be done by the Bill of last session," the prime minister informed Peel in October, before instructing him to advise both Wellesley and Goulburn that the government was "really in earnest." The lord lieutenant had in fact been amassing information on the subject, in the form of detailed statements from the various dioceses of the tithe assessments for 1822, while the revival of anti-tithe disturbances served to concentrate his mind. By the third week of November his proposals were at last ready. "The word commutation is (I find) unpleasing to a Churchman's ear, so I have commuted it for composition," he observed facetiously to Peel. The "composition" was to be for a period of twenty-one years, revisable every seventh, and based on the average yield and value of produce over the preceding seven years. In the event of disagreement, the assessment might be arbitrated. Wellesley also revived the proposal that proprietors effectively pay the parson's stipend and then reimburse themselves through increased rents. In cabinet, this last provision was rejected by ministers convinced that it would be stoutly resisted by the powerful landed interest. Any arrangement was to be between the clergy and the occupiers of the soil. Another concern was the conduct of arbitration. Ought not the arbitrators to be provided with a "general rule or instruction for their guidance," lest different principles and practices be adopted and followed in adjoining parishes? Indeed, would the lord lieutenant be able to find a sufficient number of properly qualified persons "to act as final Judges upon considerations so complicated, rights so various, and interests so important?" In addition, there was some support for the extension to Ireland of that form of commutation which had already taken place in parts of England – land in exchange for tithes. Although the prime minister had appeared to exclude this arrangement during the debate on the leasing bill, when he made the valid point that such commutations tended to transform a resident clergy into a nonresident landlordry, it formed part of the radical measure which Goulburn introduced in March 1823.[23]

Wellesley's failure to consult the Irish clergy about his plan, and rumours that it had been drafted by the Catholic barrister Anthony Blake, guaranteed an indignant if not furious response from the Protestant hierarchy when they finally learned what exactly was in prospect. Almost to a man, the prelacy assailed the proposals as a violation of the solemn terms of union which had united the Church of England and that of Ireland. Why, they asked, was the Established Church to be destroyed in Ireland through a raid on its property and "consequent subversion" of its independence? Before this clerical onslaught, Wellesley's nerve again showed signs of failing him. Perhaps the introduction of tithe reform should be delayed, he observed to Goulburn, before making the foolish suggestion that the question be sent to committees of both Houses. Shrugging off these viceregal misgivings, and convinced that he was protecting the property rights of the church from more radical invasion, the chief secretary announced two bills in the Commons on 6 March. One sought to effect temporary compositions while the other allowed for permanent commutations for land. Despite the welcome given to the latter measure by several prominent Whigs, among them the tithe reformer Henry Parnell, it soon disappeared from sight, leaving only the composition bill on the agenda. This provided a formula for the summoning of special vestries to initiate compositions, and specified the complicated procedures which had to be followed in order to complete them. Wherever they were adopted, the exemption of pasturage from the tax was to cease. [24] "The bill's chief merit was that it simplified the tithe system by substituting a single money payment for the myriad small calculations on each type of produce. Further, it made the tithe both as a tax and a source of revenue more predictable. At the same time the three-year re-evaluation provision meant that the tithe revenue would be reasonably reflective of the national economic condition." [25]

Most objections to the bill turned on the basis of the valuation on which composition was to be made – was it to be the full tenth, the value recorded in the proctors' books, or the actual receipts of the clergy? Goulburn stoutly defended the principle of full compensation whenever there was a resort to compulsion. In those instances where someone was compelled to surrender his property for the public good it was only just, he argued, that the party receive "full value of the property surrendered." If this was an artful tactic designed to defeat the principle of compulsion, which he had never favoured, it succeeded. The House demanded the deletion of the compulsory clause, and the chief secretary beat a painless retreat. Far better to trust initially to voluntary cooperation, the prime minister declared in the Lords. [26]

"The Government has amply proved its sincerity on this most arduous question, & if the plan should fail the blame must fall on the country," Wellesley remarked in September. Before the year's end 966 vestries had given notice of their intention to assemble to consider the question, but by the time Parliament reassembled in February 1824, only 216 had taken advantage of the provisions of the act. Analysing this very limited success, Goulburn concluded that a number of parishes were waiting to see how composition worked elsewhere, and that others had been so successful in evading tithes that they were under no pressure to reform. Yet there could be no hiding from the fact that the bill's effectiveness had been much impaired by the absence of compulsion, which vindicated those "economists" in the Commons who had opposed it on this very ground. Either incumbent or vestry could veto the process at the outset, but relatively few clergymen had exercised this power. Instead, the larger landowners whose pasture lands were presently exempt from the tithe used their domination of the vestries to protect that favoured position. To overcome such resistance Goulburn introduced a number of amendments to his bill. He tinkered with the formula in order to make the prospect of composition even more attractive to the parson, and extended the interval between revisions. He sought to circumvent the obstructive grassland interest by making alterations to the vestry regulations in an effort to lessen the influence of the large landowners, and through the reintroduction of a degree of compulsion which might be exercised at the viceroy's discretion. Within a decade the average cost of the tithe had been reduced, and its payment rationalized, in more than half of Ireland's parishes. Thus the composition bills did apply balm to a long-festering grievance. [27]

If the burden of the tithes had both fostered and deepened the popular Catholic antipathy to the Protestant clergy, as even the most blinkered of Tory defenders of the Establishment acknowledged, the nonresidence of much of the clergy provided critics of the Church of Ireland with a broader field of fire. Determined to protect the church, if only from itself, Peel and Goulburn resolved to require from the clergy "a strict discharge of the duties which they ought to perform, and a rigid fulfillment of the conditions on which they hold their Property." Drawing his friend's attention to one reprobate who was spending his enormous income from Irish livings "on profligate life at Boulogne," Peel avowed that such men were "the real enemies of the Establishment." To check the abuses, Goulburn introduced a bill in February 1824 which enlarged the powers extended to Irish bishops in 1808 to enforce residence, and curtailed their ability to grand exemptions. "Adequate provision" had also now to be made for the performance of the incumbent's duties whenever his absence was "strictly unavoidable." Conservative in intent, the bill nevertheless eventually helped to work a radical change in the pattern of residence. [28]

Another controversial issue, and one even more damaging to the Church of Ireland's reputation within the larger Catholic community, was that of burials. Under the law, interment in churchyards was controlled by the local parson, and the service of committal was to be that of the Established Church. Over the years, however, a *modus vivendi* had been achieved. Ordinary Catholics were buried without ceremony, while the better orders were laid to rest in the simplest of ceremonies by a priest attired in no more than a simple form of clerical dress. But the possibility of conflict with a rigid Protestant clergyman determined to enforce the letter of the law was ever present, and in 1819 the bishop of Ossory had only been restrained by the "good sense and good feeling of Charles Grant." Then, in September 1823, the issue was thrust to the fore as a result of a public accusation that the archbishop of Dublin had prohibited the offering of Catholic prayers over a grave. At the Castle, there was a strong and not entirely groundless suspicion that the incident had been manufactured by a priest anxious "to inflame the Roman Catholic Body" against the archbishop. For on his elevation the year before, William Magee had declared religious war on Nonconformists and Roman Catholics. Although Wellesley concluded that it would be as well to consider this "very delicate subject," nothing more had been heard from him by the time Parliament met in February 1824.[29]

When John Newport raised the matter in the Commons the government decided to take it into its own hands, only to discover that the law officers could not agree on the best mode of proceeding and that Wellesley was anxious to cavort before the gallery. The lord lieutenant, in a dispatch marked secret but which he urged be published, proposed that every Protestant minister "be enjoined" to license the burial of the Roman Catholic dead at those times which did not interfere with the services of the Established Church. Moreover, he urged that the legislation define the acceptable "rites and ceremonies." The cabinet had no intention of being drawn into such "very embarrassing details" as the precise rules of performance; the vestments of priests; and whether the right to perform the ceremony belonged to a priest of a particular parish or to all priests. Nor was it willing to accept the most obvious solution, that of separate burial grounds, which "the most vehement of each side – the antipodes of every other point of the circle of opinion" appeared to coalesce in. For such an arrangement would strengthen rather than weaken sectarian differences. "I wish we could say of them that like Saul and Jonathan they were lovely & pleasant in their lives," an ironic Peel wrote to the viceroy, "but we may yet say, and I hope shall continue to say 'that in death they are not divided'."[30]

The news that the cabinet had decided merely to empower Anglican ministers to license Catholic burial services brought an angry protest from a viceroy who had already placed on record his opposition to any discretionary arrangement which depended for its effectiveness on the good sense of the established clergy. However, when the government added a clause which required from every parson who refused to sanction a Catholic service a full written explanation to his bishop and the lord lieutenant, he gracelessly withdrew his objection to the bill. But when the cabinet continued to refuse to authorize the publication of his original proposals, Wellesley relapsed into embittered self-pity. "It is a sequel of the same plan of extinction, which, on the questions of the Statue, the Riot, the Orange, the Ribbon confederates, by concealing my opinions, reduced me to the condition of a villain and slave on a mock throne," he complained to Plunket, "and rendered me an object of ridicule and contempt to a country which would have hailed me with respect and gratitude if I had not been crushed by pretended candour at Whitehall."[31]

Wellesley had indeed been "vilified" and "degraded." The founding of the *Dublin Evening Mail* soon after his arrival – he suspected Saurin of having set it up – saw him mercilessly assailed by a Protestant organ which proved to be astonishingly and distressingly popular. Nor was it alone in its hostility, although the conversion of the *Patriot* to the cause of Catholic relief ensured that Goulburn was attacked with equal vigour. The divisions within the ranks of the Castle press, reflecting those within the executive itself, were a further measure of the decay of the administration's system of press management. In part, the malaise was a mark of the deepening disillusionment of the would-be managers of opinion with the work-force at their disposal. Thus Peel admitted that his faith in Irish newspapers remained "far felow zero." "I disbelieve what they assert, because they assert it." Similarly, Gregory denounced as "scandalous" the attacks on the magistrates of the disturbed county of Cork by the *Correspondent* at a time when the newspaper was receiving £1,200 a year from the government in direct and indirect subsidies. Another problem was the steady contraction of the means of influence at the disposal of the Castle. The pressure for economy was relentless, for almost two-thirds of the revenue was still committed to the servicing of the debt, and Goulburn acted promptly in 1822 to cut the subsidies to the press. By 1826 the proclamation fund had shrunk to £6,000, and fully one-third of that was earmarked for the official *Dublin Gazette*. Moreover, Goulburn had little taste for the task of scrutinizing the press and less time to devote to it. His aversion appears to have infected Gregory, who, since his shouldering of the additional duties of the military under-secretary, had more than enough work to fill his days.[32]

The decline of the Castle press was accompanied by a revival of the Catholic organs of opposition, for the arrival of Wellesley and the appointment of Plunket led to a further relaxation of those measures of intimidation which had been another feature of the policy formulated by Peel. The home secretary watched this development with concern, for his conviction had not weakened that the Roman Catholic leaders exercised all their influence by means of the press. Nor was his belief an entirely unfounded one. Daniel O'Connell recognized the need to purchase support and publicity for the cause of Catholic relief and identified the press as "an agency of mass propaganda." The success of this strategy was limited only by his intolerance of independence as well as of criticism.[33]

Among those who fell victim to O'Connell's talent for abuse was the hapless viceroy. Their honeymoon, following Wellesley's conflict with the Orangemen, did not long survive the Catholic leader's failure to secure that mark of professional distinction as a lawyer to which he believed himself eminently entitled. Although the lord lieutenant proposed to the cabinet that a number of Catholic barristers be extended the privileges of King's Counsel, his suggestion never embraced O'Connell and he lacked the will to persist with it in the face of ministerial resistance. Nor was he more energetic in responding to the private pressure of his Grenvillite supporters that he appoint Catholics to any office from which they were not excluded by law, and specifically to that of assistant barrister. Of the ten vacancies that occurred during his term of office, only three were filled by Catholics. Where Roman Catholics did make significant gains was in the new police force, receiving half the places, including a number of chief constableships. But this was not a record which inspired confidence in Wellesley's impartial administration of the patronage.[34]

Blind to his own failings and deaf though not impervious to criticism, Wellesley composed a glowing tribute to his regime's achievements as 1824 neared its end. "Every measure, insurrection act, police, tithe bill, revisions of the magistracy, petty sessions, better administration of law, has succeeded beyond my most sanguine hopes," he proclaimed in a report to the prime minister. "The general prosperity of the empire begins to reach Ireland. Prices have improved, rents and even tithes are better paid, and in the districts which had been most disturbed the people are turning their attention to pursuits of industry and honest labour, instead of plotting or executing schemes off outrage and violence." These claims were echoed by the provincial inspectors-general of police in their year-end reports. Even in the most disturbed province, that of Munster, the situation appeared to have improved dramatically. Yet elements of the Protestant population became hysterical as the appointed time for the fulfilment of Pastorini's Prophecy neared. Although he discounted such fears, for he saw no evidence of an "insurrectionary movement," Wellesley was reluctant to dispense with those extraordinary powers which had remained in his arsenal as a result of Parliament's extensions of the Insurrection Act, but Peel and Goulburn, the two ministers who would have to go down to the House and defend yet another continuance bill, now insisted upon the act's repeal. However, the picture of an increasingly tranquil and prosperous Ireland did not bear too close an examination. In the opinion of one perceptive and knowledgeable visitor to the island, Charles Abbot, the "apparent *comparative* quiet" would not long survive, for what had been done "under the idea of conciliation" had merely "produced increased irritation."[35]

The viceroy's boastful optimism was also contradicted by the island's endemic poverty, upon which the recovery of the prices of provisions, and thus of some farmers' incomes, made little obvious impact. Witnesses appearing before a Lords' committee on Ireland testified to the unimaginable wretchedness of the population and identified the "reduntant population," the want of manufactures, and the subdivision of property as the principal causes of such misery. In England there was a growing awareness that self-interest, if nothing else, dictated further intervention. A nation of paupers threatened Britain with bankruptcy. "They pay no revenue, have no taxes, & [during] the year of scarcity [1822] had between two & three millions [of pounds] from England," observed the duke of Wellington of his fellow-countrymen. His brother the viceroy had long since pointed to the lack of employment and the related want of "active capital" as the chronic problems.[36]

The select committee on the Irish labouring poor which had been set up in 1822 under the chairmanship of Thomas Spring Rice to investigate the famine had reached the same conclusion. Similarly, the demands for an end to the malpractices of the sub-sheriffs had been linked to Ireland's chronic shortage of capital. Capitalists would never invest in a land where the recovery of debts was so uncertain. Others, such as Robert Wilmot Horton, who had succeeded Goulburn as the under-secretary for colonial affairs, reasoned that little capital would flow to Ireland until the existing surfeit of labour had been reduced. Indeed, the possibility of tackling Ireland's perceived ills of overpopulation, unemployment, and pauperism through schemes of state-assisted emigration helped revive an interest in Britain's overseas possessions which had flagged since the end of the French wars. Peel had long advocated this policy, providing the emigrants were recruited from the ranks of Roman Catholics. Goulburn, while more sceptical of the value of emigration as an instrument of relief, fancied that "the hope of being conveyed to Canada as a reward for good conduct" might induce the lower orders "to adopt a more peaceable line of conduct." Spring Rice also offered support, arguing that something must be done "to give increased means of employment to the people, or they must be entitled to emigrate to seek employment elsewhere." At the request of the government, Parliament appropriated in the two years of 1823 and 1825 £56,000 to finance the emigration to Canada of 2,500 cottiers and smallholders. Unfortunately, no one thought to consult the viceroy whose first knowledge of the scheme was the appearance of the government agent charged with the recruitment of emigrants. Indignantly and unavailingly, Wellesley protested that the punishment of transportation would hold little terror for the guilty if a similar fate was offered as a reward to the innocent. A few hundred Irishmen were also to take advantage of the system which had been in place since 1814 to encourage men of substance to remove to Australia. But the success of the schemes of state-assisted emigration paradoxically illustrated their limited remedial significance. No sooner did the Catholic poor reveal their willingness to emigrate – in 1825 there were more than 50,000 applicants – than Parliament drew back, alarmed by the escalating costs.[37]

David Ricardo, the leading political economist of his day, had sanctioned emigration as an experiment, albeit with misgivings. To his mind, the answer to Ireland's problems was capital. And as a member of Spring Rice's committee, he acknowledged that it would not be forthcoming until that country was tranquil and investments therefore more secure. Of course, he also recognized that public order would never be securely established until the people were employed. This was the conundrum which eventually led him to admit "that the behaviour of the Irish quite defeated him." Thus the committee was reduced to pleading Ireland's "exception to the general rule" of laissez-faire. It recommended limited government intervention to encourage the fisheries, improve communications, and instruct the peasantry in more advanced agricultural techniques.[38]

There were calls for a much more substantial public investment in the island's industrial development. Robert Owen made the case during his appearance before the committee. Subsequently, William Maberly, MP, a member of the Political Economy Club, proposed in the Commons that £1 million be advanced in the form of low-interest loans to entrepreneurs willing to set up works in Ireland. Although Spring Rice, among others, spoke up in support of the proposal, the government rejected it. Goulburn declared that such an expedient would never succeed but would provide unfair competition for those businessmen who had not obtained this form of assistance. The only measure to make its way through Parliament was Spring Rice's bill to promote the establishment of textile factories "'by means of British capital and to regulate a joint stock company for that purpose'," but the results were negligible.[39]

In truth, the government was convinced that it had already done as much as was wise, or necessary. It had implemented the proposals of the commission appointed to investigate the collection of revenue in Ireland, and at great cost to the executive's "influence"; it had removed or sharply reduced many of the assessed taxes, such as those on windows, servants, and four-wheeled carriages; it had lowered significantly the distillery tax on spirits, which was generally held responsible for producing "in a large class of persons a habit of insubordination, and of open resistance to the law," while discouraging honest toil; it had abolished the countervailing duties and drawbacks on the trade between the two countries, an action which even Whigs had praised as one "calculated to produce a very extensive improvement in the condition of Ireland" and to foster manufacturing there, but had maintained the linen trade's favoured position; it had assimilated the currencies, though the continuing circulation of notes of small denomination in Ireland prevented the creation of a common currency for the United Kingdom; it was even prepared to tackle the knotty problem of subdivision in order to promote agricultural reform. A Subletting Act was in preparation which would neatly sidestep the treacherous issue of trespass on the rights of property by granting to landlords the right to veto subleases. Lastly, the restoration of tranquillity promised to loosen the purse strings of private capital.[40]

There were cheering reports of "an influx of English capital" at last "communicating activity to the manufactures of the south." Charles Wynn received a very encouraging account of conditions in Ireland from Frankland Lewis, one of the commissioners on education. He described an encounter with an agent of a Manchester cotton factory who was distributing yarn to Irish weavers and already had 2,000 looms at work in Drogheda alone. Attracted by the cheapness of Irish labour, such English concerns appeared to be ready to employ all who could find looms. Lewis was equally optimistic about the prospects of Irish industries in general. In Belfast a decline in cotton spinning resulted merely from the decision of a number of manufacturers to invest in the more profitable spinning of flax. Similarly, the landlords' desire to eject small tenants in order to consolidate their holdings suggested that at last capital was being invested in agriculture. Evidence such as this made much easier strict adherence to the first principles of political economy. Any manufacture dependent upon artificial stimulation would not succeed, Liverpool instructed one delegation which visited him in search of governemnt aid. In fact, investment was not increasing nor was manufacturing expanding in the southern provinces. Rather, those moribund domestic industries which had once provided an impoverished peasantry with an essential supplementary income were now decaying at an alarming speed. The further contraction of employment opportunities at a time of swelling population and restrictions on the subdivision of land was a recipe for turbulence.[41]

Unaware of the true situation, the government was inclined to follow the example of the viceroy and recite the litany of its achievements. Impressive as the list was, containing as it did the far-reaching measures to improve the administration of justice, lessen sectarian animosities, and spur economic development, the ministry would have been well advised to pay more heed to those critics who detailed the limitations of many of the remedial measures. Not that Peel and Goulburn were blind to the political danger of resting on their laurels. The reports of the several parliamentary committees on Ireland were certain to provoke debate. But the chief secretary's conservative aversion to haste and the elusiveness of his legal advisers prevented him from drafting a legislative bill of fare which would have satisfied the Opposition's appetite for reform. Additional measures were under consideration, and the conduct of sheriffs was being investigated, while the troublesome question of grand jury presentments appeared to require a committee, but little was in hand. "You may think we have been dilatory in not having more bills actually in a state to be presented to you," an apologetic Goulburn wrote to the home secretary in November 1825, "but until the lawyers assemble in Dublin, it is scarce possible to get any legal assistance, and even now it is next to impossible to get an hour's conversation with the Attorney or Solicitor General."[42]

Making full use of the evidence gathered by the parliamentary committees on Ireland, Whigs sought to expose the "fatal limits" to "ministerial liberality." The constabulary bill, "though perhaps bordering too closely on the *gendarmerie* system," was admitted to have been "productive of the greatest advantage," but the accompanying reform of the magistracy was found to have fallen far short of its goal. The revision had failed to remove from the commission of the peace many of those unqualified for the responsibility. In the Commons, Henry Brougham claimed that of 152 persons removed in twelve counties, only fourteen had been found unsuitable; the remainder having been absentees or militia officers. "Numbers of improper persons have been left in the Commission," the *Edinburgh Review* charged, "many good magistrates removed, and several bad ones, after being removed, have been restored." Too many of them were still open to "solicitation," received "presents," and acted on "partial principles." Nor had the valuable innovation of the petty sessions been permanently established. The public had no security that magistrates would continue to attend them and "abstain from their old habits of hall-door justice." Therefore the sessions ought to be placed on a secure footing, and their regularity guaranteed. The fate of the earlier efforts to reform grand jury presentments by requiring their prior submission to a full attendance of magistrates had already demonstrated how easily good intentions were vitiated in Ireland. The fact that the grand jury was not obliged to accept the recommendation of the magistrates discouraged them from attending in number, one unimpeachable witness testified before a select committee. Another problem was the very short time that grand jurors had to consider the presentments brought before them. As for conclusive proof that expenditures had not been brought under control, that was to be found in the reports of the engineers who supervised the road works undertaken with relief funds in 1822. They had discovered that these works could be completed on average for less than half the amount appropriated by the grand juries.[43]

The charge of insufficiency was also levelled against the reform of the tithe. The Church of Ireland was too large and far too expensive to maintain, critics protested. Why did Ireland's 500,000 Anglicans require an establishment comparable in size and cost to that which catered to the spiritual needs of 9 millions of British Anglicans? Surely "the numbers of the Established clergy, and the revenues destined for their support, ought to bear some reasonable proportion to the number of their flocks and the extent and laboriousness of their duties." It was not enough "to palter with the Irish tithe system" as Goulburn had done. And the evidence that composition had failed to appease influential voices of Catholic opinion was too obvious to be ignored. Members of the Roman Catholic priesthood, led in this instance by the titular bishops of Cork and Cashel, had attacked it as "adverse to their interests." Moreover, to the extent that the reform was adopted, thereby extending a tithe charge to pasturage, it paradoxically added larger farmers, many of them Protestants, to the ranks of the measure's critics. Nor had the attempted liberalization of the regulations governing burials proven any more successful as an instrument of sectarian conciliation. By the summer of 1824 it was clear that the Roman Catholic clergy had settled among themselves not to apply to Protestant parsons for permission to officiate at Catholic funerals. Instead, with few exceptions, burials followed the pattern established before passage of the act.[44]

Whigs also sat in judgment on the government's struggle to come to grips with Irish "ignorance." Education had long been a hobby horse of theirs, and one most frequently mounted by John Newport. There were confident predictions that its progress would have a peculiarly beneficial effect upon the great mass of Roman Catholics by emancipating them "from blind submission to the authority and dictates of their priests," and by removing their "prejudices and animosities." In short, it "would amend their moral feelings." Conversely, there were fears that children left "*wholly destitute of education,*" or at best enrolled in "hedge" schools, would turn, unless properly taught, to that "great national instructor – Captain Rock." A properly instructed Irishman would be both more pliable and more passive. Faith in education as a means of social control had long made its promotion a feature of Peel's policy towards Ireland. Yet, if they were all agreed, as Newport asserted in the Commons, "that general education was the most certain mode by which the situation in Ireland could be ameliorated," there were important differences on how best to approach the task.[45]

Peel had promulgated "two great rules: first, to unite as far as possible, without violence to individual feelings, the children of protestants and catholics under one common system of education; and secondly, in doing so, studiously and honestly to discard all ideas of making proselytes." Not surprisingly, he remained an admirer and supporter of the Kildare Place Society whose activities he had so energetically fostered as chief secretary. He credited it with the dramatic expansion of Irish elementary education, pointing to the existence by 1824 of 1,100 schools. But the society had long since become another source of sectarian controversy, its largely Protestant management tainted with proselytism and a target for the Catholic clergy. The financial support it extended to the schools of such frankly proselytizing agencies as the Association for Discountenancing Vice and the London Hibernian Society deepened Catholic suspicions, as did the actitivies of a number of over zealous masters in its own schools. At the urging of their priests, therefore, Catholic parents were beginning to withdraw their children from mixed schools. They enrolled them instead in the denominational institutions being established by their clergy. This in turn spurred complaints by the hierarchy over the distribution of public monies in support of education – three essentially Protestant societies were being subsidized, and there was the annual grant placed at the disposal of the lord lieutenant. In 1824, in order to educate the Catholic poor under the superintendance of the Catholic clergy, they demanded a share of the £70,000 that had been appropriated for that year. Although Peel and Goulburn conceded in the Commons that the Kildare Place Society had made mistakes, neither of them contemplated for a moment either the abandonment of it or public support of separate education. Instead, the chief secretary successfully moved a substantial increase in the society's annual parliamentary grant, raising it to £22,000.

However, the government did agree to the appointment of another commission to investigate Irish education.[46]

Peel encouraged the commissioners, one of whom was the ubiquitous Anthony Blake, to expose the negligence of the established clergy in the matter of education and to recommend that all children "take at least one daily draught from the common fountain of their religious creeds." In their first report, which they submitted in May 1825, the commissioners documented the sad number of parish and diocesan schools, and the deplorable conditions which had been tolerated in the Charter Schools. They proposed that elementary schools be established in each benefice, supervised by a government board, and that Catholic and Protestant pupils receive joint "literary instruction." Those extracts from the Scriptures read daily, and any explanatory notes, were to be "unobjectionable" to Catholics, for whose separate religious instruction portions of one or two days of each week were to be set aside. Finally, they recommended the withdrawal of public support from the overtly proselytizing agencies, and the imposition of severe restrictions on the Kildare Place Society's use of its grants.[47]

Few of these proposals held any appeal for the chief secretary, although in his initial comments to the lord lieutenant he offered a tepid endorsement of "the principles of the Plan" and warmly supported the pursuit of those persons guilty of cruelties in the Charter Schools. With Peel he was more forthright. He had met no one in Ireland who approved of the report, he wrote in September. Protestants complained that the Catholic veto over the common daily readings from Scripture would place them at a peculiar disadvantage during the periods set aside for religious instruction, because the foundation of proper Scriptural knowledge had not been laid beforehand, while the critical comments of the influential James Doyle, the titular bishop of Kildare, did not bode well for Catholic acceptance of the report. Intensely suspicious of the Catholic clergy, convinced that the priests' principal concern was to keep their flocks in ignorance, Goulburn despaired of ever gaining their support for any system which did not concede to them "a separate and complete" control. Consequently, he was doubly determined to maintain the societies' schools until the new plan had been successfully implemented. To do otherwise might merely be clearing the ground for sectarian education. He was willing to sacrifice, however, the discredited Charter Schools and the Lord Lieutenant's Fund, which had not escaped religious controversy. But the fact that the grants from the fund had been announced before the report was issued meant that they were continued through 1826. For they were matching grants, so that private parties had already laid out their own monies in expectation of assistance in the funding of schools.[48]

It was less the continuation of the Lord Lieutenant's Fund than the other education items included in the Irish Estimates for 1826 that caught the eye of the Opposition. A vote of £2,000 for the schools of the Association for Discountenancing Vice, one of £25,000 for those of the Kildare Place Society, and the sum of £19,500 for the Charter Schools excited strong protests. And if Goulburn's defence of the Kildare Place Society proved difficult to fault, critics did not spare those other schools which were of "a character exclusive and objectionable." Fortunately, for Goulburn, the evidence of sodomy in a handful of the Charter Schools was kept confidential by the commissioners. But the critics did not want for ammunition. The statistical fact that of more than 400,000 Catholic children being educated in Ireland no more than 31,000 were benefiting from public assistance lent weight to accusations of religious discrimination. Much the same figures were cited by the Catholics of Ireland, "in aggregate meeting," who petitioned in April 1825 "for a grant of money for the Education of Catholics in Ireland in their own way." Ireland's Catholic hierarchy had already submitted a list of five requirements to the commissioners on education, together with a warning that they would not endorse any educational system which did not include these guarantees of the protection of Catholic sensibilities. The sectarian disputes clearly detracted from the therapeutic value of education in the treatment of Ireland's ailments, and its effectiveness as an opiate of the Catholic masses had been brought seriously into question.[49]

No program of reform could ever succeed, Whigs warned, which did not correct the "Centuries of oppression and misgovernment" which had generated "a deep-rooted and cordial hatred of the English name and nation in the minds of the vast majority of the Irish people," had "depraved and vitiated their characters," and had "fitted them for the commission of every crime." Moreover, one preliminary measure was indispensable – emancipation. Without emancipation in the broadest sense of the word, "without emancipation in *law* and in *fact* – without the abolition of every existing legal disability, and the adoption of a system of the most rigid impartiality on the part of the Government," the *Edinburg Review* sermonized, "it would be worse than absurd to suppose that the spirits of discord should depart from the land, and that the foundations of national wealth or prosperity should be laid." This argument had long been advanced by many of Parliament's "economists," while the same message was carried to the hearings of the parliamentary committees on Ireland by a number of the witnesses called to give evidence. But this was one policy the Liverpool ministry could not adopt, its members having agreed to stand collectively neutral on emancipation. As for the tension inherent within a government many of whose members were so much at odds on so fundamental an issue, it briefly found release in a common hostility to the aggressive Irish agitation organized so brilliantly by Daniel O'Connell. Even Wellesley, who had long worn his sympathies on his sleeve, had qualified his boastful assessment of his own achievements as viceroy with the observation that Ireland would have been completely tranquillized had not "the general prosperity and happiness" been "disturbed by the noisy fury" of the Catholic Association.[50]

## CHAPTER EIGHT

# The Catholic Association

The Catholic Association was formed during the spring of 1823, the choice of name harking back to 1816 and hinting at a rejection of "moderation." The Catholic nobility and gentry who initially lent it respectability soon withdrew, leaving control firmly in the grasp of a group of barristers and ensuring a heavily middle-class complexion. Lawyers, merchants, and journalists, whose rise in society, advancement in their professions, or entry into political life had been frustrated by religious discrimination, all had an axe to grind. Their "thwarted mobility and professional discontent" made them a potentially potent force for change if they could recruit vast numbers to march under that banner. To the extent that peasants require the leadership of an "urban intelligentsia" if they are to be fashioned into a powerful instrument of radical social change, these were men ideally suited for that role. Moreover, they possessed in Daniel O'Connell a demagogue of extraordinary power. This complex, vain, ambitious, and sensitive man, full of national and personal resentment and pride, had at last found a vehicle worthy of his charismatic personality and political skills. He intended to unite the Catholic Irish across those divisions of class which had seen him as a landlord victimized by Rockites. He would emphasize their common "nonprivileged" status, their common suffering at the hands of a privileged minority, and their ethnic distinctiveness. The Association would agitate not only the issue of emancipation but also those more immediate concerns of the peasantry – the provocative and often violent conduct of Orangemen; tithes and vestry cess; unequal administration of justice; burials and sectarian education; and the rise of proselytism as a Protestant crusade gathered momentum. No less important in the successful conversion of the Association into a mass movement was the innovation of offering associate membership to persons who paid a small regular subscription. "All I ask is one farthing a week from one-sixth of the Catholics. Who is it that cannot afford a farthing a week," O'Connell observed. "Yet it would make more than

£50,000 if collected."[1]

For assistance with the essential tasks of organizing the peasantry, encouraging them to pay the "rent," and discouraging them from that traditional lawlessness which was usually visited on fellow Catholics and facilitated the executive's resort to repressive measures, O'Connell turned to another important section of the professional middle class – the Roman Catholic clergy. Thus Bishop Doyle's open letter to the viceroy – *A Vindication of the Religious and Civil Principles of the Irish Catholics* – aroused many of those O'Connell was seeking to organize. Parish priests served as agents of the Association, and O'Connell was careful to allocate a portion of the "rent" to sectarian education and to the construction of chapels and houses for priests. He also used it to employ the press, pay the legal expenses of Catholics, finance parliamentary lobbying, and establish in Dublin a headquarters which quickly took on many of the forms and much of the paraphernalia of a representative assembly without evidently violating the Convention Act. There was to be no repetition of the mistake made in 1811, when the Catholic Board invited Catholics in every county to elect ten members to a "General Committee." Naturally, the radical means of agitation, the unprecedented politization of the country, and the undercurrent of national hostility towards England, no less than the end in view, obsessed and frightened many among the Protestant minority and tended to obscure O'Connell's conservative features – his attachment to the crown, acceptance of the traditional class structure, and rejection of violence.[2]

Gregory had reported to Goulburn on 2 May 1823 that the Catholics, disappointed by yet another parliamentary setback for the cause of emancipation, intended to reestablish a "Board." Eventually he found or placed an informant within its ranks. At first, the chief secretary and the lord lieutenant were content merely to observe developments "very narrowly" and "weigh well" whether there was in its proceedings "when combined with the professed object of the board" sufficient grounds for formally dissolving the new organization. The under-secretary was somewhat less phlegmatic. He was satisfied that the Association was making a mockery of the Convention Act, and was certain that in playing upon grievances the government was already seeking to redress it was deliberately fomenting disaffection. Peel and Goulburn responded to these concerns and gave every indication of not permitting the viceroy to take refuge in his customary inactivity. The chief secretary wrote from London, on 18 June 1823, to request the opinions of Plunket and Joy, the Irish law officers, as to whether the Association's present course was likely to bring it within reach of the act. If not, there remained the possibility of the legislature amending that measure. Assured that the Association had not contravened the "existing Provisions of the Law," and surely noting that Wellesley had qualified his support for their enlargement with a recommendation that the government resort to the less controversial law controlling political debating societies, the ministers in London held their hand.[3]

By the year's end the uneasy Gregory had detected the alliance between the Association and elements of a Catholic clergy he had long regarded with profound distrust. Bishop Doyle's efforts to inspire the Catholic masses with renewed faith in the "truth of miracles" alarmed the under-secretary. He interpreted "all these tricks" as but the "different parts" of "grand melodrama" which sought "to excite the minds of the lower orders of Catholics against the protestant State" and might rapidly be transformed from farce into "deep tragedy." At a time when Pastorini's Prophecies were proving so captivating to those same lower orders, he was not alone in the belief that hatred of Protestantism was a driving force among the hierarchy and that the applause with which Doyle's *Vindication* had been greeted in the "popish Parliament" was proof that it declared "the sentiments of their whole Body." Then, early in 1824, the Association instituted the "Catholic Rent" and most members of the hierarchy voluntarily provided it with the returns of priests in their respective dioceses, thereby much facilitating the collection of this "parochial tax." "The collectors of this Tax will know in what manner to address the lower orders to induce them to contribute," Gregory warned Peel; "they will not tell them that it is to procure Catholic Emancipation, but that it is to enable them to carry into effect that prophecy the fulfillment of which they have so long & so anxiously expected." Suddenly the Association had acquired an "authority and power" which Goulburn for one had not foreseen. For as the under-secretary was quick to observe, the Association's system for raising funds had established direct communication between the "popish Parliament" and the "popish Population." Furthermore, the appointment of "County Secretaries" who were to be responsible for the collection of the rent promised to strengthen the popular impression that a parallel administration had indeed been established. The time had come, Gregory advised in mid-May, to stifle this attempt "to usurp the executive Government."[4]

Peel responded immediately to Gregory's prompting. He urged Goulburn to confer with Wellesley and Plunket, emphasizing his own concerns in language reminiscent of the under-secretary's. "It is notorious that there is a Body in Dublin regularly constituted, adjourning its Meetings from Time to Time – imitating the Forms of Parliament – commenting upon the Speeches and Conduct of Members of the Legislature, and upon the public Measures of the Legislature – and to crown all, levying a Rent or Tax, or whatever it may be called, upon the mass of the Roman Catholic Population, for very indefinite public objects." Moreover, the system for collecting the "rent" could all too readily be adapted to other purposes. He therefore revived the question of the Association's legality. Did it offend against "the Letter and Spirit of the Convention Act?" If the answer to this question was yes, would it be prudent to enforce the law? If no, would they not be well advised to amend and strengthen the act? But Wellesley, convinced as he was at this time that he was surrounded by enemies in the Castle and had been betrayed "by pretended candour at Whitehall," was in no mood to follow the lead of Gregory and Peel. He had an ally in Plunket, who was averse to any move against the Catholic Association which did not embrace the Orange societies. The viceroy quickly adopted the same position.[5]

Within the Liverpool ministry the Grenvillites, while privately deploring the Association's conduct as folly, because it threatened to play into the hands of the anti-Catholics by goading the government into a prosecution, opposed any "*ultra proposition.*" The cabinet's failure to respond decisively to the challenge thrown down by the Association, and the striking of a parliamentary committee on Ireland which, as the Grenvillites gleefully pointed out, was dominated by liberals, surely contributed to Peel's "excessive ill humour" early in June. He unburdened himself to Wellington, voicing regret at his decision to accept office, resentment of those of his colleagues who thwarted him on Ireland, and indignation at being "obliged to remain silent when he heard Papists praised and Orangemen abused." Nor was his temper improved by the news that George Canning planned to visit the island during the summer. "What takes him to Ireland I know not," he commented to Goulburn. "It cannot be really to see Lord Wellesley's plush breeches. The newspapers say that his daughter is going to be married to Lord Clanricarde, but even if that be true, why should Canning go to Dublin? I have no doubt there will be speculation enough as to the causes and consequences of the visit." This same question was asked by others, even though in this instance the newspaper reports were accurate. Canning's daughter was to wed his under-secretary at the Foreign Office whose estates covered 56,000 acres of County Galway. Rumours persisted, however, that Canning's real purpose was to consult Lord Wellesley about the eventual succession to Lord Liverpool, for there was also talk that the prime minister was giving thought to his retirement. None of this speculation quietened fears that the leader of the "Catholic" Tories would commit "indiscretions" during his visit. But enjoined by the king himself to be "very careful what sentiments he expressed in public" and not to make "declarations of the intentions and opinions of the Government," Canning pledged to behave with discretion and was as good as his word.[6]

Even before Canning sailed from Ireland in September Peel and Goulburn were giving fresh thought to the problems posed by the activities of associations, both Orange and Catholic. As another season of Protestant triumphalism neared, the cabinet was united in the wish that "all Party confederacies in Ireland (whether they be actually illegal or not), and all offensive displays, should be discontinued." Peel desired quietly to discourage the Orangemen, for differences among the law officers as to the illegality of their processions did not augur well for a successful prosecution. He was also anxious not to cut off the retreat from the lodges of a number of public figures whose "retirement" would "bring these associations into more discredit." His attitude towards the Catholic Association was far less considerate. Nor was this surprising, given the traditional loyalty of the Orangemen and his deepening conviction that the Association was a sinister force. The fact that a handful of members of Parliament had been added to its membership, while many of the Catholic upper classes had returned to its ranks, was a source of regret and additional concern. The enrolment of the former indicated the burgeoning political influence of the Association, while the behaviour of the Catholic nobility and gentry was interpreted as a further illustration of the sway of the priesthood.[7]

In Goulburn's opinion, a Catholic clergy which considered their "whole importance to depend upon retaining their command over the people" would never jeopardize that influence by opposing anything that had even the appearance of being popular. Disconcerting as was the prospect of demagogues setting the pace, and inflaming the minds of a mushrooming membership drawn largely from the ranks of the lower orders, the chief secretary's anxiety was heightened by the accompanying success of the "rent." The collectors were reported to be forwarding as much as £300 each week to Dublin. The sums in the Association's coffers, he concluded, were sufficient "to abet any purpose of mischief" and to interrupt "the administration of the Law & the ordinary function of Government." He had come to share fully William Gregory's three fears; first, that through their elaborate organization the Association's leaders had already acquired the power "of addressing themselves directly by means of their own Agents to most parts of the country, and directing simultaneously to one object the great mass of the people"; second, that widely disseminated speeches "in which the destruction of the established Church, the dissolution of the Union, and every other inflammatory and revolutionary doctrine is inculcated" would encourage the enrolment in the Association of the vengefully anti-Protestant Ribbonmen; and third, that it was systematically undermining the regularly established institutions of justice. Thus whenever a sectarian affray took place a barrister was retained by the Association to defend the Catholics involved. He either procured or fabricated evidence, Goulburn charged, invariably threatened and insulted the authorities, made violent speeches, and then submitted a detailed written report which received great publicity. As a result, the police had become objects of popular enmity, the magistracy had already been cowed and juries would soon be intimidated.[8]

What was to be done? The recent creation by the Association of a number of standing committees offered some hope that its representative character could be established. Another possibility was the enactment of new measures specifically to suppress the Association. But they promised to be ineffective so long as "extensive charitable Associations" were permitted to function, for Goulburn supposed that all of its objects might be advanced "under the cloak of charity." The prosecution of the editors of the publications in which the Association's "inflammatory proceedings" were circulated might serve a purpose. "A conviction would do much to discredit the body with the better part of the Roman Catholics," the chief secretary hopefully predicted to Peel, "and it would remove the foolish impression which exists that the Government either approves or are afraid of it." Uncertain how to proceed, he sought guidance from the home secretary.[9]

Peel opposed "forbearance and passiveness." Any hint of government connivance at the activities of the Association would dismay some Irishmen and dishearten others, he argued. "The bold will attack us for our want of energy, and the timid will commit themselves to the Association. In the meanwhile the system of correspondence and combination will be gradually improving, and a change of name will be almost sufficient to develop, on the proper occasion, a formidable and traitorous confederacy." So, while acknowledging the difficulties, his inclination was to seek fresh legislation framed broadly enough to control all such societies but specifically directed against the Association. As a preparatory step, he pressed the executive to investigate the Association thoroughly, and to obtain from the Irish law officers a formal opinion as to its legality. Clearly he was determined to flush Wellesley and Plunket from cover on the issue of suppression. Profoundly suspicious of them both, irritated by the viceroy's prolonged silence on this as on every other subject, he resolved to obtain an official statement of Wellesley's opinion. The lord lieutenant's practice of submitting a series of complicated draft proposals, accompanied by a statement leaving entirely to the government the responsibility for their adequacy and the wisdom of proposing them to Parliament, would not suffice on this occasion. Neither "manly nor straightforward," Peel scornfully remarked, the course was a convenient one for those who adopted it. In the event that a bill was introduced and failed, the "immediate proposers" would be held accountable, while a refusal to act would leave the author of the draft in the enviable position of being able to appeal to it should subsequent events bring the wisdom of that inaction into question.[10]

While Peel waited for a dispatch from the viceroy, the pressure for action increased. The king's indignation at the proceedings of the Association, together with his conviction that they were little short of "intended rebellion," and his apprehension that he was widely believed to be sympathetic to Catholic relief, now prompted him to threaten that a continuation of the agitation would induce him to withdraw his consent "to Catholic Emancipation being left as an open question in his Cabinet." From Ireland, meanwhile, came reports of mounting suspense as an explosion in the Association's membership coincided with the imminent arrival of the year in which Partorini's Prophecy was to be fulfilled. Hysterical Protestants, led by two of William Gregory's brothers-in-law, the earl of Clancarty and the archbishop of Tuam, vehemently protested the misguided policy "which in defiance of the lessons of all history, has, under the false name of Conciliation, – been latterly adopted towards the ultra-Montane Romanists of Ireland." They demanded the suppression of the Association and the fortification of cities and strong points. Clancarty volunteered to raise his own force to defend his property and the adjacent territory, and applied to the Horse Guards for hand grenades and Congreve rockets. Although Goulburn and Wellesley were agreed that there was little likelihood of any immediate crisis, the chief secretary did not entirely discount the possibility of "an indiscreet or wicked priest" igniting a localized and "sudden ebullition of fanactical fury." For his part, Peel attributed the peculiar anxiety of Clancarty and his brother to the fact that they had been singled out for attack by the Association. Nevertheless, the publicity given to the "inflammatory proceedings" of the Association, and the evidence of deepening sectarian animosity, convinced him that there was "great risk of even immediate danger" and he advised the executive to prepare for the worst.[11]

On 10 December 1824 Wellesley forwarded to London his long-awaited advice on how to proceed against the Association. The dispatch was artfully constructed, and surely strengthened Peel's distrust of him. The viceroy reported that the Irish law officers were of the opinion that the Association had still not exposed itself to prosecution under the Convention Act, but offered his own judgment that it had clearly violated the spirit of that law. He conceded its representative character, the active participation of priests in its deliberations, and thus the mixing of the Roman Catholic Church in political contests and animosities, and surmised that the consequences of the enrolment of so many Catholic freeholders would be counted at the next general election. He deplored the rhetoric of the Association's spokesmen. "The dissolution of the unity of the British Empire, the alteration of the frame of Parliament, the degradation and ultimate ruin of the Protestant Established Church have been the themes of earnest and applauded agitation, if not positive recommendation." But his recommendation with respect to new legislation to deal with this menace remained infuriatingly ambiguous. He voiced the fear that no law would be effective which did not provide him with discretionary powers greater than those with which any virtuous public officer would wish to be endowed. He insisted that no regulation could be adequate which did not apply equally to the Orangemen. "It is evident that a reaction exists between those bodies," he wrote, "and that, unless both be restrained within due bounds of law, it will be hopeless to attempt to restrain either." Finally, he urged a full parliamentary investigation of the necessity of additional legislation, thereby preempting Peel's suggestion that Parliament be called into special session to deal with the

Association. [12]

In London, the members of the cabinet had been impatiently awaiting word from Dublin. Although satisfied that the executive was sufficiently well-armed to resist any physical challenge to its authority – the 20,000 regulars still stationed in Ireland were no longer dispersed in small detachments; the police numbered almost 5,000 and 900 of them were mounted; and there was also the yeomanry – ministers did not minimize the potential danger posed by a body as "formidable" as the Association. Even the Grenvillites, who still flattered themselves that they formed "the link in the Government between it and the Catholics," feared that, unless the Association was suppressed, Irish Catholics would seek nothing less than the subversion of the Established Church, the restoration of their bishops to their estates, and the abrogation of the king's Coronation Oath. "What excuse can we frame to ourselves for not resisting demands thus held out to us at the point of a bayonet, and thus enforced by threat of rebellion, and the exercise of power beyond the law, in defiance of the law, and commensurate only with the powers of Parliament," Buckingham asked Wynn? If the duke's support for emancipation wavered in this crisis that of the president of the Board of Control did not. Meanwhile, the prime minister was talking of there being but two possible solutions to the Catholic question – "either to give up the Church to the Catholics, or, that the dispersion of the Bible should convert the population." For the present, however, he seemed to favour passage of a "strong law" to put down all societies. The lord lieutenant's refusal to provide the cabinet with an unequivocal recommendation led it to endorse Peel's proposal that a measure be introduced, though ostensibly out of deference to the viceroy there was to be no summoning of Parliament into an early session. [13]

One week later the news reached London of the executive's decision to prosecute O'Connell on a charge of sedition. Reporters had long been attending the meetings of the Association, and some of them were in the employ of the authorities, making a record of its proceedings for their newspapers but one which they would be prepared to verify under oath in court. Wellesley maintained that he had read these reports and submitted to the law officers those passages which appeared to him to be objectionable. Having read on 17 December a speech delivered by O'Connell on the previous day, and considering it to be seditious, he reported that he had ordered the charging of the Catholic leader as soon as the law officers substantiated his opinion. Not that the chances of securing a conviction were good. Protestant jurors would be too frightened, and Catholics too involved, to render an impartial verdict, Goulburn feared. Of course, failure would at least strengthen the government's case for a stronger law, insofar as it demonstrated that the executive had acted to the extent that the present law allowed. With this thought in mind he ensured that O'Connell was quickly brought to trial and thus a verdict rendered before Parliament met.[14]

The prosecution was soon the cause of unexpected political embarrassment. The "ravings" of a prominent Orangeman, Sir Harcourt Lees, who called upon the Protestants of Ulster to arm against the Catholics, could not be ignored even though many persons regarded him as "half mad." A failure to prosecute in this case would expose the government to accusations of "partiality" and excite sympathy for O'Connell. Even more awkward was the fact that the Irish government had chosen to prosecute O'Connell for invoking the name of Bolivar at the very moment that the cabinet had decided to recognize the South American state of which he was the liberator. The king seized upon this apparent contradiction to attempt to frustrate his government's recognition of the American rebels, and only with difficulty did his ministers convince him that the national interest could not be impeded by an Irish prosecution. Yet there was little alternative to "decided support" of the Irish executive, least of all for Peel who he had prodded it into action. Writing to Goulburn on 6 December, he had emphasized the importance of seizing any "fit opportunity" to prosecute members of the Association. Moreover, he had promptly promised, once informed of the charging of O'Connell, to "give the measure every support that it is possible for me to give it." Not that he entertained high hopes of success in any case which rested upon reports published in Irish newspapers. Indeed, there were five accounts of O'Connell's speech, each differing from the others in certain particulars. And when the grand jury convened on 3 January 1825 the journalists who were called to give evidence proved most unhelpful to the crown. The principal witness testified that he had fallen asleep during the speech and had based his report upon the uncertain recollections of those of his colleagues who had remained awake. Goulburn speculated that bromides taken in the form of liberal doses of the "rent" had induced this narcosis, but he agreed with Wellesley that the endeavour had not been entirely fruitless. The Association's demagogues had at least been put on notice that they had better choose their words more cautiously.[15]

Peel had written to Wellesley on 18 December to inform him of the cabinet's decision to introduce legislation, and to request that he direct the Irish law officers to prepare a bill which would "guard against the artifices by which legal subtlety and skill might attempt to defeat the provisions of an ordinary law." Further, the measure was to be a temporary not a permanent inroad upon the constitution, and ought to be general enough to extend to all societies, including the Orange. By the same token, Peel made clear his belief that the law "must be a very strong one." The time had passed for "complimenting people who [avowed] their hostility to the British name and connexion into loyalty and submission to the law." He even forwarded his own ideas on what the bill should contain, refusing to be "so terrified by the technical difficulties" or by the clamour against "sweeping clauses, as to overlook the benefit of a parliamentary declaration against the Catholic Convention." Action would "cheer the well affected, perhaps detach some timid dependants on the Association," and rescue the government "from the disgrace of remaining passive, while a confederacy" was being formed which might at any moment be turned against the "English."[16]

Predictably, neither Wellesley nor Plunket evinced much enthusiasm for legislative action. Yet the evidence from the Irish countryside pointed to the seriousness of the challenge to established authority posed by the Association. Provincial inspectors-general of police, and assistant barristers, not only warned that the current efforts of priests and the Association to impress upon the peasantry "the necessity of peace and submission to the laws" might not survive another parliamentary setback for Catholic claims, but they also dwelt upon the "mischief in allowing any irresponsible body to arrogate to itself the right or power to have in its keeping the peace of the country." Seemingly oblivious to this fundamental question of principle, both the attorney general and the viceroy insisted that through "Admonition and private remonstrance" the Catholics could yet be persuaded voluntarily to repress the Association. Moreover, although the draft of a bill was forwarded to London in time to meet the deadline which Peel had set for its receipt, Wellesley and Plunket sought to draw a distinction between this performance of their *"ministerial"* duty and their continued personal aversion "to coercive measures by legislation." In another cunningly constructed dispatch, Wellesley revived his earlier demands that a parliamentary inquiry precede action and that the law refer specifically to the Orangemen. At the same time, he protected himself from any prospective accusation that he had been blind to the menace of the Association with language which was also calculated to convince the cabinet of the folly of further delay. He reported that it now included "nearly the whole Roman Catholic Population of Ireland, rather than a mere representation of that numerous and powerful body," and added that over the leadership of this united force of laity and clergy the government exercises precious little influence.[17]

The efforts of the viceroy and the attorney general to evade responsibility for the suppression of the Association did not sit well with their colleagues in London. Privately, the Grenvillites demanded to know Plunket's "sincere opinion." Looking to him for advice and even for *"direction"* on Irish affairs, they believed that they had a right to know long before the meeting of Parliament whether he approved or disapproved of the bill. Similarly, the cabinet sought to pin Wellesley down. Fastening upon a phrase in his dispatch, in which he appeared to suggest that no coercive statute should be introduced unless Catholics were to be given "some expectation" of a "more favourable issue than has hitherto attended the discussion of their Claims," it demanded a clarification. The viceroy quickly denied that he had ever intended to imply that such an assurance ought to be offered. As for the draft bill which had been sent over from Ireland, the cabined feared that it would arouse more opposition in Parliament than was necessary for the accomplishment of the object. So, in its place, the ministry eventually substituted a modified version of the earlier measure controlling secret societies in Ireland. The task of remodelling the bill, "so as to make it effectual for the suppression of the Association without any unnecessary severity of restriction," was handed to Plunket and his English counterpart. What emerged was a measure which made no mention of either the Association or the Orange Order by name, but contained provisions applicable to them both. When printed, the bill was forwarded to Dublin, and Wellesley returned a copy with marginalia signifying his approval. "Our Bill will, I think, effectually prevent the collection of rent, and give a fair way out for all those who became members from intimidation; and, indeed, for all the cautious and *moderately violent*, though it may be impossible to prevent repeated meetings to petition against repeated grievances," Charles Wynn reported to Buckingham. "The Orange lodges will, I think, find it more difficult to evade."[18]

Goulburn introduced the bill on 10 February 1825, just one week after the government had given notice of its intention to suppress the Association in the Speech from the Throne. Among those of his colleagues who spoke in support of the measure were Plunket, Wynn, and Canning, the last castigating this "Self-elected, self-constructed, self-assembled, self-adjourned" body. All were careful, however, to draw a distinction between it and the cause of emancipation and to reaffirm their backing for the latter. This did not save them from Opposition ridicule, while Peel made something of a fool of himself. The nub of the Opposition's argument was that the Association had grown out of a solid grievance, and that the proper way to put it down and thus check the growth of Irish nationalism was to grant emancipation. Moreover, there was a strong and widespread suspicion, which Goulburn shared, that the law had not been longer delayed (the bill received royal assent on 9 March and the Catholic Association promptly disbanded, while the grand lodge of the Orange Order held a final meeting on 18 March and issued a circular informing all lodges meetings were now illegal) because of the desire of the supporters of emancipation to have it out of the House before they revived that issue.[19]

On 1 March Sir Francis Burdett moved for a Committee of the Whole to consider the claims of Roman Catholics for relief from the remaining disabilities. His speech was "not of the highest class" but it proved to be "well fitted for the purpose" and the motion was carried with a majority of thirteen in a full House. Among the members named to assist in the preparation of the bill were Plunket, Canning, Wynn, and Charles Grant, but it was soon clear that Burdett was consulting most closely with the Irish attorney general and the leader of the Catholic Association. Daniel O'Connell had arrived in London some time earlier as a member of an Irish Catholic delegation. No less disturbing to stalwart Protestants were the persistent reports that Lord Liverpool "was giving way on the question," for this encouraged the more sanguine supporters of emancipation to speculate openly that it would at last be carried in the Lords.[20]

William Gregory greeted the news of the developments in the capital with anger and dismay, having long since accepted Peel's argument that on "England alone must We rest our hope for continuance of our Establishment in Ireland." The course of events in 1825 had not been kind either to him or to the cause he epitomized. He had shrugged off the reports early in the year of his being replaced as under-secretary by Thomas Spring Rice, but his relations with the lord lieutenant and the chief secretary had recently been less than satisfactory. He had again been denied ready or regular access to the viceroy, whose pleas of ill-health did not ring entirely true, and had been wounded deeply by Goulburn's failure to consult him fully on the provisions of the bill to suppress the Association. "To say that I was not much annoyed by your want of confidence, would be a gross falsehood," he wrote on 9 February; "and perhaps my annoyance was not diminished by hearing the provisions of your bill spoken of the day before yesterday at dinner, and being obliged the acknowledge that I was ignorant of every part of it." If quickly mollified by Goulburn's frank admission of error, which he attributed to pressure of work and forgetfulness, and the assurance that he had missed nothing in not seeing the bill in its original form, Gregory's frustration and tension found a release in his response to the chief secretary's warning that the House of Commons was likely to endorse emancipation.[21]

The conduct of the Association and the demagoguery of its leaders had seemed certain to diminish the chances of emancipation. The denunciations "held out against the Protestant Church," and thinly veiled "threats of separation from England by means of foreign Aid;" the "foul calumny uttered against the Heir Apparent to the throne," the duke of York, who had paraded his ultra-Protestant sentiments; the organization of Ireland "by the agency of a bigotted and relentless Priesthood;" all these developments had led Gregory to the comforting conclusion that the "Catholic Cause" must have lost support in England. Instead, it now appeared that the leaders of the Association would be able to boast that they had "extorted their demands from the fears of England." For Gregory, as for other Irish Protestants, the attacks upon their church threatened "a whole way of life," and the consequences of a Catholic triumph were therefore chilling. "Every Irish Protestant who has property he can remove, must look out for some other country," he remarked darkly to Golburn; "the young will emigrate; the hapless residue, whose ages or circumstances compell them to remain, must await their fate."[22]

Many advocates of emancipation had long coupled it with Protestant "securities," and among the six resolutions passed at the end of the debate on Burdett's motion had been one calling for such guarantees. Although the bill he introduced on 23 March concentrated on the eradication of most of the remaining Catholic disabilities (he proposed that the Declaration against Transubstantiation be dispensed with as a qualification for all but a few offices, that the Oath of Supremacy be modified, and that a board of bishops be created to advise the monarch on episcopal appointments), two "securities" had been generally settled upon as the desirable "wings" to this measure. The vast mass of Catholic voters were to be disfranchised by raising substantially the freehold property qualification from forty shillings to at least £10, and the Roman Catholic clergy were to be paid by the state. These measures had already been widely touted in Ireland as means both of eliminating the "beggarly burlesque on legitimate constituency," and of converting priests "from factious politicians into quiet ministers of Religion." In short, the "wings" appeared to safeguard a Protestant culture in Ireland. Nevertheless, in the House, Peel announced that neither measure would diminish his resistance to emancipation and he reserved his position on their worth. He turned to Ireland, and particularly to Gregory, for advice on the matter.[23]

The under-secretary was scornful of all "securities," dismissing them as "downright nonsense" and certain ultimately to be removed for the very reason that the claims were now to be admitted – "to satisfy the Catholics." The two specific proposals which had been advanced he spurned as worthless guarantees, if not sources of even greater danger. Although he had already advised Goulburn that many priests were themselves opposed to state stipends, "knowing that any connexion with Government would destroy their influence over the lower orders," a response which appeared to lend some weight to the arguments of the sponsors of the measure, Gregory was convinced that it would be "madness" for the state to pay and thus to acknowledge a clergy which did not acknowledge it in return. The crown, after all, would not possess the right to nominate them. Indeed, "an independent income" would give them "the means of exercising greater influence over their flocks, without relieving the Poor from their exactions." He, for one, did not believe that Catholic priests would cease to accept the dues which had frequently been a cause of peasant disorders.[24]

The disfranchisement of the forty-shilling freeholders was a reform he had earlier endorsed, though more for moral than political reasons. To the extent that it terminated the wholesale perjury committed by men who swore to freeholds they did not occupy it would reduce the "depravity" which the higher orders had encouraged among the lower. Evidently a sharp increase in the property qualification would also produce a "better description" of elector than the "present wretched, famished, perjured" freeholders. Yet where was the "real security" in this, for the electorate in large areas of the country would still be overwhelmingly Catholic? For him, therefore, the value of this "security" was as a weapon to disrupt the serried ranks of emancipation's supporters, and he later urged Goulburn to support or oppose the abolition of the freehold qualification "as may best serve the protestant cause by dividing the ranks of the Enemy on the question."[25]

Contemptuous of the supposed "securities," disgusted by "the mutual language of the versatile herd" in Parliament, the under-secretary repeated his warnings of the "horrors" which "must be the consequence of popish supremacy," because "an equal division of power between rival parties who have so long been opposed hating each other is contrary to human nature; one Party must have the ascendancy." Catholics would expect to fill the offices for which they were eligible, and before long their religion would become the qualification for appointment. Only a "popish Government" would be obeyed by the great mass of the peasantry, he predicted, and once its supremacy had been established the connection to England would be in peril. Even the Protestants of the North would in these circumstances become alienated from the state which had failed to protect them. They would emigrate in large numbers and "leave the best part of Ireland to the possession of the R. Catholic population." In short, the Ascendancy was but the first in a row of dominoes which emancipation would topple. Who could tell what would finally be left standing?[26]

Several of the witnesses appearing before the select committees on Ireland, which had been set up by both houses and whose hearings were under way, expressed similar fears. John Leslie Foster, the MP for Louth, an education commissioner and a friend of Peel, proved an impressive witness. He did not seek to gloss over the "vicious structure" of Irish society, "the extreme physical misery of the peasantry," or their wealth of grievances, but disputed the utility of emancipation as a solution for these problems. He emphasized the fears of most Irish Protestants that it would be followed by the fall of the Established Church. There was a general impression among them, he declared, that Catholics would never "allow of any compromise." Representatives of the Church of Ireland, among them one of Gregory's clerical brothers-in-law, the archdeacon of Ardagh, also appeared. They warned that the equalization of civil rights would "unavoidably lead to an endeavour to overturn the Protestant Establishment in Ireland," and protested the peculiar inappropriateness of this action at a time when a missionary work was at last bearing fruit. "In truth, with respect to Ireland," declared William Magee, the controversial archbishop of Dublin, "the Reformation may, strictly speaking, be truly said only now to have begun."[27]

Second reading of Burdett's bill began on 19 April and was carried with a majority of twenty-seven two days later. The "wings" were introduced without delay. The elective franchise bill was presented by a son-in-law of

Wellesley, while the resolution calling for state payment of the Catholic clergy was moved by a friend of Canning but was widely believed to be the handiwork of the viceroy's intimate – Anthony Blake. On 10 May the relief bill was read for a third time, though the majority had shrunk slightly. "The minority cheered, and well they might," commented one sympathizer, "for we have fallen off woefully in our numbers." Here was proof that the "wings," which had been attached in order to "get over many enemies," were alienating as many if not more friends. Some Whigs had opposed the reduction of the electorate, while the conservative Goulburn had taken Gregory's advice to heart and had voted against disfranchisement of the freeholders in the belief that defeat of this "security" would erode support for emancipation. Progress on these measures was suspended, however, until the Lords passed judgment on the main bill. The Commons "stared me very impudently in the face, when they delivered to me the Catholic Bill at the bar of the House," the lord chancellor growled to one friend, before predicting that they would not see it again.[28]

In the Lords, the duke of York had already created a sensation with his declaration as heir apparent that he would never assent to the Catholic claims, and that no monarch could assent to them, "so long as the Coronation Oath stood as it did on the Statute Book." Nevertheless, the prime minister was expected to play the decisice role. "Without Lord Liverpool we could not succeed," O'Connell repeatedly advised his wife. "With him we should drive every opposition out of the field." As the day for the decisive test in the upper House neared, O'Connell's confidence in the prime minister's support melted away. He mistook his man, however, when he contemptuously dismissed him as "too much of an old woman to take any active or decided part" in the debate. Liverpool confounded most observers by intervening powerfully and decisively.[29]

The prime minister had long shown signs of inclining towards compromise, but his will to resist concession was stiffened in this instance by the danger of his ministry's disintegration. The differences between moderates, moderate anti-Catholics, and extremists quickly surfaced, and the debate was enlivened by the spectacle of ministerial colleagues embarrassing one another. Then, following his defeat on this issue in the lower House, and acutely conscious of his and Goulburn's isolation on the Treasury Bench, Peel had indicated his intention to resign. If the home secretary resigned so must he, Liverpool concluded, despite the efforts of their colleagues to draw a sharp distinction between their relative situations in the two Houses. Both of them did at least agree to suspend their decisions until after the debate in the Lords, and there, on 17 May, following Liverpool's "first violent speech against the measure," emancipation was decisively rejected.[30]

O'Connell reacted angrily to the defeat, which was all the more bitter given his acquiescence in the "securities." He commented darkly to his wife that Ireland had been condemned "to more tyranny and distraction," and his undisguised bitterness led the English friends of emancipation to ponder apprehensively "the consequences of all this in Ireland." The immediate crisis, however, was within the ministry. As the danger of Peel and Liverpool resigning receded so that of defections by disappointed supporters of emancipation appeared to loom larger. During the debate in the Lords the discord within the ministry had been illustrated by Plunket, who had stood throughout on the steps of the Throne and had at one point audibly dismissed as "altogether false" an assertion made by the prime minister. For his part, Liverpool considered disgraceful the conduct of those supporters of the measure in the lower House who had attached the "wings" in order to catch a few extra votes. Yet neither Plunket nor Wynn, nor the other Grenvillites, were sufficiently indignant or embarrassed to feel called upon to resign. They persuaded themselves that their departure from office would merely open "the way to the formation of an exclusive & bigotted" government. It was a decision the lord lieutenant applauded from Dublin. "Firmness, calmness, perseverance, and (for the present) *steady inaction*, are the true principles of policy, justice, and honour, towards ourselves, our friends, and the country," Wellesley wrote to Plunket; "and you may rely on my strict observance of these principles in *word* as well as in *deed*." Temperamentally suited as the viceroy was to a policy of "steady inaction," George Canning was more of a meteor. He insisted on a meeting of the cabinet to thrash out a positive policy on the Catholic question. "The Catholic Association, Lord Wellesley's despatches, and the various occurrences of the last twelve months, give Canning a plausible pretence, if not a full justification, for the course he has adopted," the prime minister wearily conceded. But after three meetings the cabinet agreed to muddle on as before, for Canning had sensed a willingness on the part of his fellow "Catholics" to let him depart alone if he pushed the issue to a decision.[31]

In Dublin, Gregory greeted the news with a sigh of relief. He had already played a minor role in the distant ministerial drama. The Irish lord chancellor, angered by O'Connell's attacks upon him in his evidence to the parliamentary committees, and profoundly resentful of the failure of anyone present to challenge or contradict the Catholic leader, had threatened to resign. The obvious candidate to succeed him was Plunket, but a cabinet already riven had no wish to open another conflict between "Protestants" and "Catholics." Fortunately, Lord Manners was dissuaded from quitting office immediately, and for this success the under-secretary could claim a substantial portion of the credit. Far more important in Gregory's own eyes, however, was the assurance that Peel and Goulburn would continue to supervise and administer Irish affairs. "I am fully sensible of the Difficulty of restraining the feelings that arise from acting with any Man, or set of Men, whose principles & actions you detest, and also the danger to which an honest Man is liable by such an association," he remarked pointedly. But Peel had an obligation to place national interest before personal convenience. Were he to leave the Home Office and be succeeded by a "Papist," it was certain that "the Policy [would] be rather to inflame, than to allay, popish discontent, and to endeavour by every jesuitical artifice to make it supposed that the disappointment of the Roman Catholics, [was] the sole cause of all the woes of Ireland." As for Goulburn, whose removal or transfer had been widely rumoured, with Robert Wilmon Horton and Frankland Lewis spoken of as likely successors, Gregory looked to his return "with the greatest anxiety; partly from interested & selfish motives," but more from the conviction that his continued presence in Dublin was essential in order to conteract the "many proceedings" that his removal would have promoted.[32]

A violent popular response to the defeat of the relief bill had been a widely anticipated "proceeding," but it failed to materialize. Gregory did predict that the leaders of the former Association would now seek to evade the law, and O'Connell subsequently organized the New Catholic Association. Not that this prospect disturbed him unduly. The under-secretary was content to request the services of "an intelligent [English] shorthand writer to take accurate notes" of what was said at Catholic meetings. "No such person can be engaged in Dublin," he reminded Goulburn. Another encouraging sign was the removal of the Insurrection Act from three baronies in Cork and two in Tipperary, though in mid-June, perhaps with the traditional marching season of the Orangemen in mind, the counties of Down and Louth were placed under the Peace Preservation Act. And Gregory went to some lengths to publicize the illegality of Orange demonstrations and impress upon magistrates their duty to discourage illegal activities. "All those, who were formerly [the Orangemen's] Leaders, and with whom I have communicated, are very anxious to keep them quiet, & to let the whole order be abolished," he reported encouragingly to the chief secretary.[33]

Free of major worries, Gregory threw himself into the renewed campaign to persuade Lord Norbury to retire from the bench. The knowledge that O'Connell was showing an interest in the case, and might even be planning to launch a petition seeking the chief justice's removal on grounds of incompetence – he continued to fall asleep during trials and rarely took a note when awake – had served to concentrate some minds in the executive, but it had discouraged others from taking any action which might be construed as evidence of the agitator's ability to get rid of the most senior of judges. The under-secretary was not a man to be guided by such considerations, observing to Goulburn that "much as we might regret any triumph of O'Connell, how much more must We regret the injury sustained by the public by Norbury continuing on the Bench." He could not be dislodged, however, not even by the threat of a Commons petition. The chief justice "does so cling to his sordid avarice," Gregory explained to Peel, "that it is not possible to anticipate what he will hazard rather than diminish any part of his income."[34]

The personal conduct of the viceroy was yet another source of acute embarrassment. Wellesley had decided to remarry and the woman of his choice was a youthful American widow of great beauty. Related by marriage to a brother of Napoleon, she now accepted the proposal of the brother of the late emperor's military nemesis. Not that Wellington, who had himself been captivated by the lady, considered her choice a prudent one. He warned Mrs. Paterson that his brother was financially ruined, but she ignored this cautionary advice, sharing as she apparently did her family's fondness for the British aristocracy. Two of her sisters turned to English noblemen for husbands. "'It is a singular instance'," one diarist noted, "'of three sisters, foreigners, and of a nation hitherto little known in our aristocratical circles, allying themselves to such distinguished families in England'." Indeed, Maria Edgeworth considered the bride "rather too English" and waspishly dismissed her reputation for remarkably good manners. "Perfect good manners should never be remarkable." Most comment centred, however, on the lady's religion and her intended's age. "The thing is absurd enough in itself," Goulburn commented. "Her being a Roman Catholic & a bigotted one will prove I apprehend a serious inconvenience here as he will I presume be as much under her influence as he has heretofore been under that of Mr. Johnston." Despite these fears, and the O'Connellites' hopes that a devout "Catholic vice-queen" would be a constant irritant to the sensitive "*Orangeists*," the marriage was celebrated discreetly (although the fact that the Anglican ceremony was followed by a private Catholic one at which the archbishop of Dublin officiated in full vestments did excite Protestant indignation) and subsequently failed to effect any marked change in the viceroy's attitudes or policy. Nor did it precipitate the expulsion of those "worthless minions," led by Johnston, who in Gregory's opinion had "seriously injured" the lord lieutenant's reputation. Dublin was soon rife with rumour of a bitter domestic struggle for influence between Lady Wellesley and Johnston in which the latter had emerged victorious, at great cost to the marriage.[35]

Throughout the summer and autumn of 1825 friends of emancipation counselled Irish Catholics to be patient and to remain calm if not inert. Canning set the tone. Speaking in the Commons, he warned that if anything could retard the progress of relief "it would be an expression of violence, or any interruption of tranquillity, on the part of Irish Catholics." Satisfied that "a furious zeal against the Catholic question" only awaited a suitable opportunity to erupt in Britain, he convinced the prime minister of the wisdom of delaying the general election until the following year. If the conduct of the "Catholics" within the government was evidently self-serving, for they had no desire to place at risk the ministry's recently repaired but still fragile unity, their temporizing policy won broad support. Initially an advocate of a September election, for he was certain it would return a greater number of friends of emancipation from Irish constituencies, Wellesley eventually endorsed the delay as "judicious." Most Whigs were also preaching patience. Thomas Spring Rice privately agreed with Charles Wynn that "no rational man" could doubt that the most sensible strategy in the coming session of Parliament was to preserve silence on the Catholic question, if only to assist those English friends of the cause whose seats had been endangered by their votes for it. Yet he feared that the peculiar situation within Ireland would frustrate good sense. Those leading Catholics who had cooperated with them last session, he warned Wynn, had found on their return home that all their concessions had been turned against them. Fearful for their political influence and sectarian importance, they were all too likely to support active measures in an effort to preserve their authority. "If O'C called upon them to hold back, I doubt but the enragés would beat him, & that we should in that case see the cause more mischievously handled," he speculated. Nor was a complete cessation of agitation in the form of meetings and petitions desirable. The continued exertion of traditional and constitutional pressure would be helpful, Plunket mused, but the revived Catholic Association was a liability. Not only was it certain to be identified with the language of violence and intimidation but it also appeared to be making a mockery of the Unlawful Societies Act.[36]

The Irish law officers concurred in the opinion that the regular gatherings of the new Association, and the annual meeting set for 16 January 1826, were contraventions of the law. As ever, Wellesley procrastinated and sought to evade personal responsibility either for action or inaction. He suggested that the Catholic gentry be approached privately in an effort to persuade them to discountenance the Association's activities. Goulburn disputed the wisdom and propriety of this recommendation. Ought the governement to deal with the members of an illegal body merely on the score of their rank and station, he asked? Would not the only likely result be a change in the Association's proceedings calculated to make more difficult its suppression? Although the cabinet endorsed the chief secretary's objections to any communication with the higher orders prior to action, Wellesley's inactivity proved in this instance to have been fortunate. The English law officers did not share the opinion of their Irish colleagues that the Association's meetings had placed it in conflict with the law, and in the face of this advice the government welcomed the viceregal procrastination. By the end of January Wellesley was able to report that the annual meeting had passed off without serious incident. The debates had been marked by a "censurable spirit" but nothing had occurred which in his opinion demanded intervention, and he fancied that "symptoms of internal weakness and natural decay" were already detectable. Peel was well content with this outcome. The new Association had been given a full opportunity to exercise the constitutional right to petition the legislature, there had been no flagrant violation of the law, and peace had been maintained.[37]

Wellesley had greeted 1826 with another example of that hyperbole he reserved for descriptions of his own achievements. He assured the prime minister that Ireland had "not enjoyed such a state of tranquillity for Centuries, & that general prosperity was advancing in all quarters." Even in Munster, he boasted, that great source of all the administration's woes, there was a state of "perfect tranquillity." Nevertheless, persistent sectarian clashes in several northern counties prompted Peel to suggest to Goulburn that perhaps the time had arrived to prohibit all processions by law. The chief secretary demurred, unable as he was to see how fresh legislation would solve problems which resulted from a dependence upon local magistrates to enforce the present law. Moreover, he was acutely sensitive, and by no means unsympathetic, to the deepening Protestant resentment of the apparent "partiality & unfairness" of a government which had made no move to suppress the new Catholic Association. If the condition of several of the northern counties fell short of the viceroy's boast of "perfect tranquillity," that also held true of the Province of Leinster. In County Longford four capital sentences and seven of transportation for life had been imposed at the spring assizes on persons convicted of "Whiteboy offences." Gregory trusted that these exemplary punishments (two of the capital sentences were commuted) would convince "deluded Peasants" that the law was "too much for them," and he took some comfort in this regard from the willingness of witnesses to come forward and of juries to discharge their duties. The fact that they had not been intimidated gave reason to hope that the system of terror was neither so great nor so general as had been feared.[38]

Wellesley's confidence that Ireland had escaped the ravages of the financial panic which had struck Britain in December 1825, as banks which had speculated in the South American marked failed, also proved to have been misplaced. His predictions of prosperity were no less inaccurate. Dublin's declining textile industries were visited by a crippling depression during the spring, which threw much of the remaining work-force out of employment, and the distress rapidly spread to the cotton weavers of Drogheda. Private subscriptions in the capital and the provinces were poorly supported. In truth, "we are not wealthy, & not disposed to relieve *distant* objects of charity – one hundred yards is a considerable space for the range of *our* benevolence of a practical description," Wellesley observed. Others attributed the want of charitable zeal to a belief that the crisis had resulted from the activities of trades unions which ought to be broken up. Ever the realist, the under-secretary reminded Goulburn that the trade of "this never flourishing City" had long been contracting. Serious unemployment was a persistent problem he added, and those long out of work had been added to the more recent victims of the depression to create the impression of an acute emergency. He denied, however, that he wished "to shut the hand against affording relief to the distressed for hard must be the heart to whose humanity numbers alone are accessible." [39]

The crisis in Irish manufacturing had not as yet developed when Parliament reassembled for the last time before the general election. "Ireland appears to be generally admitted as the bright part of the picture," Goulburn reported to Wellesley early in February. In this relaxed frame of mind, the government gave notice that its program of reform had almost run its course. Liverpool and Goulburn advised their respective houses that the problem of grand jury presentments was still being investigated, and that the prevalence of sectarianism had dissuaded the government from seeking to implement generally the proposals of the education commissioners. Instead, they would be experimented with in those places where resistance was unlikely. The government did commit itself to submit an amended version of the bill which had been introduced the previous session to regulate relations between landlord and tenant, and the Subletting Act was subsequently passed. Similarly, the ministry was prepared to tackle a number of the abuses involved in the disbursement of the vestry cess. Evidence that funds had been used for such questionable purposes as the building of houses for parish clerks, and even the stocking of rectors' wine cellars, necessitated action. The church rates (Ireland) bill broadened the powers of the vestry, to include the building and enlarging of churches, as well as their restoration and repair. In addition, it required the itemization of the projects for which taxes were to be levied, and provided that the accounts be open to inspection by all payers. Further, it granted the right of appeal against the total sum to be raised, or a particular assessment, and transferred the hearing of appeals from ecclesiastical tribunals to the magistracy. The bill did permit the use of the vestry cess for purposes other than the construction and repair of churches, but in a circular letter Goulburn was careful to detail them – the provision of wines for communion, chests for alms, and "decent" surplices. But these improvements, important as they were, did not silence critics of the vestry cess. After all, Catholics formed the vast majority of cess-payers yet they were still effectively excluded from all decisions of the vestries, "except in voting for coffins." And only the insistent demands of the Whigs drove Goulburn to make explicit the discretionary power of vestries to provide for the building and repair of Catholic chapels. Even more disquieting to the government was an effort to empower the vestries to assess parishes for relief of the poor. The notion that Ireland required a poor law system appeared to be gaining a parliamentary toehold. [40]

The general election of 1826 confirmed the apprehensions voiced during the previous year that it would be fought under the no-Popery banner in much of England and would demonstrate the burgeoning political influences of priests in Ireland. Landlord control of freehold electors had never been absolute. The Catholic clergy had interfered in a handful of elections before 1826, but proving their involvement had been difficult. As Gregory explained to Goulburn after a by-election in 1823, "the Parties influenced, who from fear have deserted their landlords, will be equally afraid to shew up the Priests by whom they were seduced." Now there was no concealment of their intervention, while its scale was unprecedented. In Louth (where John Leslie Foster came within a whisker of defeat), Cavan, Monaghan, Waterford, Westmeath, Galway, and Kerry, priests and Association agitators led by O'Connell were reported to be urging tenants to go against their landlords. Gregory held a meddling clergy responsible for much of the violence which erupted, and it had been most savage in those places where no religious differences existed. In Catholic Kerry, for example, twenty-six people were killed. "I am very glad you have at last had your eyes opened to some of the Knavery of popery," wrote one unsympathetic correspondent to a resident of that distracted county. "The mob, the priests & the gentlemen – all seem worthy of each other," Peel sourly remarked.[41]

Among the handful of defeats inflicted upon representatives of the Ascendancy, one stood out. In Waterford, the victim had been a member of the Beresford family and the campaign had been waged with calculated sectarian enmity. The Beresfords, who epitomized the Ascendancy, had been excoriated as "'Orange Blood-suckers'." For those in the Irish administration, such as Goulburn and Gregory, who believed sincerely that the "protestant interest" was the only true support of both the government and the British connection, these were not results to be taken lightly. Unless swiftly checked this "the popish Supremacy" would see the return of members of Parliament transferred from landed proprietor to the priesthood, Gregory warned Peel. It was an analysis his most trusted informer confirmed. "You'll perceive sir," he wrote to the under-secretary, that "the landlords [sic] no matter how indulgent can have not [sic] influence of his Roman Catholic Tenantry if his opinions differ in Politics from the Priest of the Parish – there is certainly something necessary to check the growing evil." This was a point the chief secretary had already made forcefully in a letter to Peel. He complained that in many parts of the country the sermons of the priests were "purely political," and instead of disseminating Christian doctrines they were declaiming upon Catholic grievances, denouncing Protestants, and exhorting their parishioners to pay the "new Catholic rent" which O'Connell had established to compensate freeholders punished by their landlords for their conduct during the elections. They had also devised a new form of sectarian economic pressure. They were discouraging their parishioners from patronizing Protestant shopkeepers. Indeed, he advised the home secretary, it was impossible to detail in a letter the extent of priestly interference and influence. "How they rule the mob, the gentry and the Magistracy – How they impede the administration of Justice – To my mind their conduct presents a foretaste of what we may expect, when those who are their puppets (for after all the first Roman Catholics in the Country are nothing more) shall have all the power they desire."[42]

Much as he deplored the events in Ireland, gloomily observing to Wellington that "party animosities" had never been higher "in spite of conciliation," Peel had no immediate countermeasures in mind. Significantly, neither he "nor any member of the Castle administration considered for a moment encouraging the Orangemen as a counterweight" to the alliance of the priests and O'Connell. He voiced the hope, at least to nervous Protestants, that eventually a reaction would develop against clerical political meddling, and as the year wore on and the nights lengthened he advised Goulburn to be on guard against a resurgence of peasant violence. But the prospective political dangers in Ireland were a less pressing concern than was the prevailing economic crisis in both countries.[43]

Summer had brought no seasonal relief for an ailing Irish economy. This year, there was scant demand for occasional labour in Britain. In Dublin and elsewhere conditions had worsened, especially for those persons involved in the woollen and cotton industries. Many were dependent on charity, and by the third week of July the never ample supply of funds was nearing exhaustion. But other workmen in the capital and vicinity compounded the crisis by organizing a "general turn out" to enforce their demand for increased wages, and the streets were all too frequently filled with "idle mobs not disinclined to riot." Early in August a crowd five thousand strong came storming out of the "Liberties" to attack food stores, "declaring they would not starve." Outraged by this episode, and fearful that if the unruly were not "completely reduced" the "most dreadful consequences must ensue," Wellesley turned to the military as the instrument of "rigorous & vigorous coercion." Even more alarming was the outbreak of an epidemic of typhus. Misery and filth had combined to breed disease, Goulburn concluded.[44]

The executive exhibited little compassion for strikers, and was willing to repress by force "those who having the means of employment will not avail themselves of it." But its response to the industrial depression was shaped by an ideological aversion to the "quackery" of state intervention; by a pragmatic recognition of the need to resort to "a little oil" whenever industries appeared to be grinding to a halt; and by a humanitarian concern with the plight of the helpless. Hopeful that industrial production in Britain, at least, would soon pick up, for the stocks of manufactured goods on hand were extremely low, Peel was disposed only to tinker with stalled machinery. He did advance £4,000 to the Irish administration to cover fever expenses, and made clear that more was available. "Of course absolute necessity must overrule every minor consideration," he instructed Goulburn on 31 July, "and if fever spreads, and more money is indispensably necessary, you may inform us and we shall contrive to send you more." An additional £3,000 was forwarded to assist in the relief of the unemployed. Goulburn wished to distribute these monies, or at least a portion of them, in the king's name. He believed that an earlier royal donation to Irish relief committees in Dublin and Drogheda in May had had a very good effect upon popular opinion. Peel was reluctant to repeat the gesture and limited to £500 the sum which might be ascribed to the monarch's largesse. So much had recently been given in Britain in the king's name, he explained, that there was a danger of one of two unwelcome inferences being drawn. "Either these advances do not come out of the Privy Purse, or the Privy Purse is vastly too large."[45]

The executive contributed small sums to local subscriptions in those towns embarrassed by an unemployed manufacturing population, for it still held to the principle that the state ought to help those who were already endeavouring to help themselves. In Dublin, meanwhile, the administration devoted much of its energies and allocated most of its funds to the amelioration of the fever epidemic. Accommodation was provided for victims in hospitals, sheds, and even tents; houses and streets were cleaned; nevertheless, by late August death was claiming one patient in forty, and the epidemic continued with unabated severity throughout September and into October. By the second week of the latter month the government's daily expenses were averaging £120, and appeals to the city for assistance, either in the form of a special assessment on residents or voluntary contributions, went largely unheeded by a people whom Goulburn suspected reposed a "careless confidence" in the government's willingness to provide succour. Moreover, he was hesitant to encourage too many public meetings for fear they would be diverted into discussions of the Association or Ireland's need for a poor law. Nor was he responsive to the argument that as the fever originated by common consent in extreme poverty and want the only solution was for the government to distribute food. He regarded this course as one "pregnant with great evils & liable to great abuse," but in shunning it he excited charges of government indifference to suffering. It was partly in an effort to counter these accusations that he made "more ample provision for those who [were] absolutely sick than might on the whole appear reasonable," for generosity in the treatment of the ill promised to satisfy the public that the administration's "resistance to the plan of feeding the poor was founded on principle & not on indifference to their suffering."[46]

The scorching summer, which in the opinion of many had facilitated the spread of disease, played havoc with the crops. The damage was neither general nor universal. Some crops weathered the drouth and the lowlands and boglands naturally proved far more productive than limestone soils where moisture drained quickly away. Ominously, potatoes had suffered the most severely. But it was clear that oats would also be in short supply. They were another of the basic goodstuffs of the lower orders, including those of industrial Britain. These reports, and those of food riots in Lancashire, galvanized Peel into action. He returned to London from his summer retreat to consult with Liverpool, and the cabinet was summoned to meet during the first week of September. The home secretary saw little prospect of another outpouring of private generosity towards Ireland, such as that during the famine in 1822. This year there were poor enough in Scotland and England to absorb charitable energies. Moreover, many in Britain were convinced that Irish proprietors were escaping "their fair share of the Burthen." He could see no other remedy than the importation of provisions, and the cabinet ordered the opening of the ports of the United Kingdom to those foods in which the Irish harvest was most deficient. Further, Peel was authorized to provide additional "pecuniary aid" to help defray the costs of relieving the suffering, but he made plain to Goulburn his wish that the distribution of government funds be supervised by its own agents and not left in the hands of "jobbing local committees." The government had little alternative but to summon the new Parliament into session in mid-November to seek indemnity for its reopening of the ports which contravened an act passed earlier in the year. Well before that date, however, there had been resurgence of Irish peasant violence. Visiting his estates in the disturbed county of Sligo in mid-October, Lord Palmerston, the secretary of war, attributed much of the "animosity & ferment" to the recent elections and "that detestable Catholic Question." "I wonder whether the Govt & Parliament will ever find out that so long as people think only of quarrelling & fighting between themselves they cannot advance in industry & prosperity," he commented to friends, "& that internal concord is necessary for national wealth as well as foreign peace."[47]

When the two Houses gathered on 21 November to listen to the Speech from the Throne they heard neither mention of nor allusion to Ireland. Henry Brougham likened this astonishing omission to the failure a half-century earlier of the government of that day to mention the outbreak of the American Revolutionary War. In the face of criticism and studied disbelief, Canning informed Parliament that it was not the government's intention to bring in "any specific measure respecting Ireland," though he invited individual members to agitate the subject. Subsequently, Henry Grattan, Jr, reopened the question of an Irish poor law and drew support from several English and Scottish members who complained of the cost to their counties of returning Irish vagrants to their native land. Robert Wilmot Horton successfully moved for the renewal of the Emigration Committee. Thomas Spring Rice and Grattan dwelt upon the complaints of the Roman Catholic hierarchy that their flocks had not benefited from the parliamentary grants in aid of education, and that these public monies were being used to promote proselytism. And to Peel's protests against any plan of separate education,

Spring Rice replied that "A system of divided education was certainly a great evil; but it was the necessary consequences of a divided people and divided institutions." Only emancipation, in other words, could preserve the joint instruction of Roman Catholic and Protestant children. Indeed, it remained the indispensable step along the road to Irish prosperity and tranquillity. The great problem was a degree of poverty "which might be banished, if the people of Ireland were put into a situation, that they could enjoy the benefit of British enterprise, British industry, and British capital," Grattan had declared during the debate on the Speech from the Throne; "but that they could not enjoy without the adoption of such measures as would ensure conciliation and peace between the two countries."[48]

The certainty that the Catholic question would be reopened as soon as Parliament reassembled after this brief emergency session, mixed, perhaps, with uneasiness at a call on Ireland for troops to form an expedition to Portugal, may well have persuaded Peel to attempt to preempt the discussion by suppressing O'Connell's new instrument of agitation. He surely sensed the Catholic leader's intention to exert more pressure on the legislature. "From our members, our combination and the continued expression of our discontent something *may* be attained," O'Connell was writing to one sympathetic MP, "especially if we ourselves keep within the law and succeed in procuring the people to avoid illegal excesses." He was planning a massive, simultaneous assembling of Catholics "in every parish of Ireland" to petition for relief, calculating that "there would appear such a union of physical force with moral sentiment that Mr. Peel would be insane if he continued his opposition." But when the home secretary turned to the executive for an opinion on the legality of the new Association, he encountered once again that infuriating Wellesley proclivity officially to "throw the responsibility of acting or of forbearing on any one besides himself." Privately, however, the lord lieutenant informed his chief secretary that he did not think a successful prosecution could be launched and that the attempt would only aggravate the existing evils. He had resorted to much the same rationale two months earlier to discourage the prosecution of one of the Association's most formidable demagogues, Richard Lalor Sheil, for a scurrilous attack upon the character of the duke of York.[49]

Provoking though it was, the viceroy's response to Peel's approach could scarcely have taken the home secretary by surprise. Far more unexpected was Goulburn's rejection of suppression. He was not sanguine about the state of Ireland. "No country can be satisfactory to the Government in which a power exists stronger than that of the Government, independent of the Government, and in which that power can at any moment direct against the Government a mass of poor, ignorant, unemployed & discontented population," he had admitted to Peel in October. It was his opinion, however, that this "power" was less the new Association than it was the newly politicized priesthood. The Association's meetings were not impressively attended nor its new "rent" well supported, he reported in December. There was no evidence that its suppression would cool the excitement created in the countryside by Protestant proselytizers and a series of parochial meetings dominated by the Catholic clergy. Priests who had originally entered the fray as supporters of the Association were now operating independently of it, he warned. "They are a body more fitted for business, admirably disciplined & acting more secretly & whether the Association exists or not they will as I believe continue to direct Roman Catholic affairs in the Country with more mischievous effect and with equal unity of object." The only consolation he could subsequently offer the disappointed Peel was the news that Sheil had made another indiscreet speech which in the opinion of the law officers exposed him to prosecution on a charge of sedition. But Plunket's impulse to evade responsibility for actions which might be denounced as illiberal was almost as strong as Wellesley's, and it was not until the English law officers and cabinet seconded the decision that the prosecution was launched.[50]

On 5 March 1827 Francis Burdett again moved a motion in the Commons calling for emancipation. The following day it was defeated by a handful of votes out of the 548 which were cast. "I am well satisfied with the majority of 4, considering the trying circumstances under which the Catholic question has been brought forward," a relieved under-secretary wrote to Goulburn. But the slim margin of victory after an election which had been fought in a number of English constituencies under the standard of "No Popery" had disappointed other die-hard Protestants, and the debate had reopened those deep cracks in the ministry which the year before had merely been papered over. Indeed, the chief secretary now wrote to Gregory in a vein which he interpreted to mean that compromise was in the offing, and that his opinion was being solicited on what concessions might safely be made to Roman Catholics. As the most powerful voice of the Ascendancy within the Irish administration, Gregory warned that none could be granted with safety. Concessions could not produce "even temporary tranquillity," he protested, and would probably "be attended with ruin of our protestant Establishment, & British connexion." On the presumption that the cabinet had already decided the fundamental question, he argued that "the fewer restrictions that are left, the better." He was willing to open Parliament to Catholics, since the "elective franchise" was already in their possession. "I agree with Brougham," he explained, "that they are likely to act with more honesty, than those Protestants, who are indebted for their seats to popish Influence." He did expect them to be excluded from the Privy Council and the lord lieutenancy. He urged their exclusion from the Bench, but warned that this bastion would eventually fall if they were not denied silk growns and thus such positions of eminence in their profession as the offices of attorney and solicitor general. Similarly, he would not allow them to be sheriffs or to hold any situation of authority or influence in the university "or in any Seminary for Education, supported by protestant Endowment." In short, far from recommending the fewest restrictions, Gregory was proposing that the most eye-catching concession be granted in order that a Protestant redoubt be more tightly drawn around the senior positions in the administration, the law, and education. Not that he ever wished to find himself barricaded within a circle of such small circumference. Consequently, he welcomed with a heavy sigh of relief Goulburn's assurance that he had misunderstood his remarks about a possible "treaty" with the Catholics. But the inscrutability of Providence prevented Gregory from relaxing. Even before the debate on emancipation, Lord Liverpool had been felled by a stroke and his ability to continue in office brought seriously into question. "We should pray that this severe visitation to an Individual, may not by his loss, affect our protestant Establishment," the anxious under-secretary observed to Goulburn. His prayers went unanswered.[51]

The news that Canning had been commissioned by the king to form a ministry, and that Peel, Goulburn, and several other "Protestants" had declined to join it, prompted a disheartened Gregory to announce to the viceroy his own intention to resign. Wellesley greeted the news graciously. He praised Gregory for acting so honourably and decidedly, promised to seek a generous retirement allowance for him, and raised the possibility of some additional mark of favour, such as a knighthood or privy councillorship. "It was impossible for me not to express, & to feel much obliged by his kindness," a flattered and surprised under-secretary reported to Goulburn. No sooner had Gregory made up his mind to bring his public career to an end than the decision was unmade by his friends. Led by Saurin, they chastised him for acting hastily and instructed him in his duty to soldier on as long as possible in defence of the Ascendancy. Perhaps recalling his own reproof of Peel in 1825, for thinking of placing personal considerations before the interests of the Protestant cause, Gregory seized an opportunity which fortuitously and immediately came his way ro rescind a resignation of which he had given the viceroy only verbal notice. Informed by the solicitor general that Wellesley had expressed deep regret at the under-secretary's imminent departure, Gregory wrote to the lord lieutenant to request that he ignore his earlier statement of intent. Once again a cooperative Wellesley responded with striking generosity and uncharacteristic dispatch. He assured him that he had employed no "flattery" in speaking to the solicitor general. "I expressed the strongest approbation of your integrity, industry, knowledge, honour, zeal, & impartiality (notwithstanding your avowed principles on the question, which distracts this Country); I added my sense of your personal assistance to me; above all in the most arduous part of my duty, the exercise of the Royal Prerogative of Mercy; in which I have been greatly aided by your active spirit of humanity & benevolence." Finally, he applauded Gregory's "just and wise decision, not to resign *now*; It would be (what you would most lament) injurious to the Public Service, it would also (I would not urge this consideration, if it were not for your honour, as well as your interests) be injurious to yourself." Basking in the warmth of this lavish praise, and flattered by the approval voiced by Peel and Goulburn of his resolve to carry on, Gregory had reason to be "very much obliged to the Lord Lieutenant for his conduct on this occasion."[52]

## CHAPTER NINE

# Catholic Emancipation

George Canning spent several gruelling weeks of manoeuvre and negotiation constructing his administration. Almost six elapsed before he received the commission from the king in April 1827, and several more were to pass before he completed the task by bringing in a group of office-hungry Whigs led by Lord Lansdowne to fill a void created by the retirement of the coterie of "Protestants." Their departure may have illustrated the growth of party spirit in an age when patronage was being reduced and royal power was in decline, for they suspected Canning of habitually flirting with the Whigs. Of course, by their action this group of Tories forced him to turn to the Opposition benches for allies. Although the breach was ostensibly over Canning's commitment to emancipation, and this provided the basis of the alliance with Lansdowne, here was one question the new prime minister had no intention of quickly bringing forward. The king had made plain the rigidity of his anti-Catholic position, while the recent defeat of the claims in the Commons provided the premier with another reason, and excuse, to consider the matter closed at least for the remainder of the session. He announced that he would not raise hopes which he did not see any "immediate means" of realizing. Instead, his cabinet, despite a heavy preponderance of "Catholics," intended to adhere to the neutrality identified with the Liverpool administration. Simultaneously, Daniel O'Connell was being deluged with pleas to forbear from further agitation, so as not to embarrass a ministry friendly, however circumspectly, to the Catholic cause. His agreement to do so saw him inundated with expressions of appreciation. For his part, Canning quietly halted the prosecution of Sheil. [1]

The new government's politic discretion naturally excited some ridicule in the Commons, where Sir Henry Hardinge, a Tory sympathetic to emancipation, but no Canningite, mockingly observed that the Catholic question was *sine die* rather than the *sine qua non* of the coalition. After all, the arguments in favour of concession remained as strong as ever. Indeed, as

Sir John Newport pointed out, the failure of the reforms enacted by the late government to tranquillize the island proved that palliatives would not suffice, while the alleged lack of interest of the Irish lower orders in this issue had been contradicted by their ballots during the recent general election. Nevertheless, the Canning government continued to steer a non controversial course. It introduced legislation to make secure the innovation of petty sessions and set a select committee to work on the task of devising effective controls on grand jury presentments.[2]

Throughout the delicate manoeuvrings and tortuous negotiations, the composition of the Irish government had been a central concern. Peel had given as a reason for his retirement the fact that as home secretary he was responsible for the supervision of Irish affairs. He avowed that he could not in good conscience continue to exercise that responsibility in an administration led by a "Catholic." The king had insisted that the Irish executive reflect a distinctly Protestant hue, while Lansdowne's opening gambit had been a demand for a purely "Catholic" tandem at the Castle. Canning's rejection of the Whigs' ultimatum led to its withdrawal, but the irony of all of this posturing was that the Whigs, by accident rather than design, eventually obtained an Irish government much to their taste. To mollify the king, Canning did seek to replace Wellesley as lord lieutenant. The viceroy pleaded for time. It was of the "highest importance" to his "interests and his honour" that he remain at his post at least until January, Wellesley informed Canning. "To remove me before that period of time (whatever may be the motive) would bear all the appearance of a recall, and would expose me to great inconvenience." Even offers of the lucrative governor generalship of India and of the Austrian embassy failed to entice him away. Reluctantly, Canning consented to Wellesley's remaining in Dublin until the end of the year but to forestall royal complaints he announced the name of his successor – the marquess of Anglesey. He had served under Wellington at Waterloo and had just succeeded him as master general of ordnance, entering Canning's cabinet as one of its three "Protestants." His best-remembered remarks on the Catholic question had been uttered in 1825. Speaking in the Lords debate, he had excoriated the Catholic Association and had challenged Irish Catholics to rebel. So extreme had his position then seemed to be that Dublin's Protestant newspapers had merrily printed false reports of his imminent appointment as viceroy merely to alarm Catholics. The king welcomed the nomination of a man he regarded as a stout Protestant. Yet Anglesey had earlier supported concessions, and following the announcement of his appointment as head of the Irish government he did not disguise the fact that his conduct in 1825 had been an aberration.[3]

Canning had also gone in search of a "Protestant" to succeed Goulburn as chief secretary. He had rejected Robert Wilmot Horton on the grounds that he had "'spoilt himself'" by his pamphlets in support of emancipation.

Eventually, in frustration, he turned to the moderate "Catholic," William Lamb. Happily, he proved acceptable to the king, who liked him, and provided the Lansdowne Whigs with an excuse to enter the government. Similarly, Canning's inability to persuade a "Protestant" to replace Peel at the Home Office, for this had been another of the conditions the monarch had sought to impose upon his choice as prime minister, resulted in the selection of Lansdowne to fill that vacancy. He then appointed another advocate of emancipation, Thomas Spring Rice, as his under-secretary. Reflecting on these arrangements, as they were finalized in July 1827, Lord Talbot as a former viceroy found little reason for "Protestant" optimism. "With a Catholic Home Secretary, & do Irish Secretary, with Mr. Spring Rice for an under secretary. With a L[ord] L[ieutenant] who always has been a Catholic [and] who remains [until Christmas], and is to be succeeded by one who tho' he has voted ag[ain]st emancipation, is not a decided Protestant, I lament & grieve from my very soul for poor dear Ireland."[4]

Within the Irish executive only the law officers and the under-secretary remained as pillars of the Ascendancy. Plunket's claims to the Irish lord chancellorship were vetoed by the king, and Canning's attempt to compensate him for this disappointment with the mastership of the Rolls was frustrated by an English Bar hostile to the appointment of an Irishman. He had to be content with the chief justiceship vacated by Norbury, who was at last "bought off" the Bench. The appointment to the Great Seal, which Manners now surrendered, went to Sir Anthony Hart, "a sound lawyer, a painstaking judge," and an Englishman "without either religion, or politics, and therefore safe in Ireland." Or as Goulburn observed more succinctly to Gregory, "I presume he is a Protestant, but he may be quite the contrary." That determined Protestant Henry Joy did succeed Plunket as attorney general, but the office of solicitor general went to yet another "Catholic," John Doherty. Clearly, William Gregory was now something of a political anomaly in the Irish executive, and it was not surprising that an effort was made to remove him.[5]

Several of Gregory's confidential letters to Talbot were misdirected to a solicitor, whose clerk opened them. Convinced that he had stumbled upon a conspiracy against Wellesley, he forwarded the correspondence to Canning. The prime minister responded as a gentleman ought, reprimanding his informant for opening another's correspondence and returning the letters, but within a few weeks he was dead. His successor was Frederick Robinson, the former chancellor of the exchequer in Liverpool's cabinet, who had been elevated to the peerage as Lord Goderich when he threw in his lot with Canning and accepted the Colonial Office. The new prime minister was an amiable, ineffectual, indecisive, and lachrymose man. His alliance with the Whigs was tenuous from the start, since they were united chiefly by a common support for emancipation. Although, in deference to the monarch, the new ministers agreed to continue the policy of collective neutrality, they did assert the cabinet's claim to take up the issue at its discretion. Perhaps for this reason the dismissal of Gregory as under-secretary seemed all the more appealing as a public vindication of their liberal principles. It would ease relations with O'Connell and encourage him to maintain his cooperative attitude. Anglesey, the viceroy-designate, was also agitating for the removal of this "violent Anti-Catholic – a furious Tory – and quite ready to betray the secrets of any one whose confidence he obtains." He had no intention of harbouring a known "spy" in his camp. Moreover, Charles Grant, who had joined the government as president of the board of trade, recalled all too vividly his own experience as chief secretary. He predicted that Lamb's liberal policies would inevitably be vitiated, as had his own, during those unavoidable absences in London. Remember, he warned, that Gregory would then be master of the whole machine of government. The cabinet decided to ease him gently out of office, only to encounter unexpected resistance from Lamb. Although several attempts had already been made to prejudice him against the under-secretary, and Gregory had returned prematurely from a vacation in England in order to conduct his own defence against the charge that he was secretly in league with the *Dublin Evening Mail*, a newspaper bitterly hostile to the new liberal regime at the Castle, the "Catholic" chief secretary protected his "Protestant" deputy. In part, his reluctance to see Gregory ousted was motivated by political prudence. "Nothing must be attempted, if it is not sure of succeeding," he cautioned an impetuous Spring Rice. "Nothing must de done harshly or so as to wear the appearance of decided proscription & exclusion – that would be most prejudicial here & would, I should think, be capable of being much misrepresented elsewhere." A "Catholic" government could ill-afford to provide ammunition to suspicious Protestants in either country. Equally important, however, in explaining the chief secretary's conduct, was the very satisfactory working relationship he had quickly established with the under-secretary.[6]

On appointment, Lamb immediately wrote a gracious letter to Gregory expressing satisfaction that the country was to continue to enjoy the benefit of his experience and abilities. "I shall be glad to hear from you personally & to have my attention called to any matters, which you may think require it," he wrote on 3 May, and "you may depend upon it your communications shall receive immediate attention and reply." The under-secretary lost no time responding to this overture, offering his frank opinion on a number of pressing issues. Their official relationship was further assisted by those sensible friends of Gregory, such as Goulburn, who did not relay to Dublin rumours soon circulating in London that Lamb planned to dismiss him. As Gregory conceded later, "had I harboured such a thought, I certainly should not have acted with the same unreserved freedom as I have done, in giving my opinions on any matter of Information he required. The Book of Wisdom has been read to little purpose, if We forget 'consult not with one that suspecteth thee'." Inevitably, he did get wind of the anxiety of "some of the ci-devant Whigs" to remove him from office, but he was assured by other sources that Lamb had expressed a determination to form his own opinion of the under-secretary. In this regard, their happy personal relationship lent added security to Gregory's position.[7]

Both were Trinity men, both had been called to the Bar, both had briefly represented the borough of Portarlington in their respective Parliaments, and Gregory was soon captivated by Lamb's charm, apparent openness, "love of honour," good humour, engaging cynicism, and evident moderation on the Catholic question. On his side, Lamb valued the under-secretary for his unmatched knowledge of Ireland and the intricacies of its administration, the importance of which he did not underestimate in the light of his own comparative ignorance of the land whose affairs he was to administer. As he ruefully admitted, he had hitherto failed to pay "the least attention to any of the reports or debates upon Irish subjects." But utilitarian attachment was strengthened by a personal fondness for an aging public servant devoted to what he genuinely believed to be the best interests of the kingdom and its union with Britain.[8]

The new chief secretary proved to be no less confident, or adept, in his handling of the prickly lord lieutenant. "Lord Wellesley is of a very susceptible temperament," he speedily judged, "but with patience and observance anything may be done with him." Thus he was careful to exhibit a scrupulous attention to etiquette. When Spring Rice initiated an official correspondence with him, Lamb hastened to remind Lansdowne's junior minister that all such communications were technically the province of the lord lieutenant. Not that established procedures proved either satisfactory or efficient. The viceroy's laziness and indecision were still compounded by his physical isolation. Indeed, the prolonged ineffectivenes of viceregal government, as first Talbot and Grant, and then Wellesley and Goulburn, had been yoked in uncomfortable harness, and the heavy expense of maintaining it, generated discussion of the direct administration of Ireland from London. The completion of the new road through Wales, characteristically described by one British traveller as the "finest" in "England," and the construction of "that wonderful work of human ingenuity," the great suspension bridge across the Menai Straits which separate Anglesey and thus the harbour of Holyhead from the mainland, together with the introduction of steam packets to ferry passengers to Dublin, appeared to have lessened the need for "a colonial establishment in Ireland." The distance between the two capitals was now measured in hours rather than days. In the Commons, Joseph Hume, a Radical, had long denounced the expensive paraphernalia of executive government that survived in Dublin. He put the annual cost to Britain at £3 million. The cause was taken up by a number of Whigs, including several of the Irish variety. "It was necessary, in respect to Ireland, not merely to give to it the whole of the English constitution, but the whole system which existed in England for administering it," Henry Parnell insisted. Thomas Spring Rice had reopened the question of the executive's abolition in the spring of 1827, and Wellesley responded to his own forthcoming retirement with a similar proposal. Nor did William Lamb dispute the "anomalous & unsatisfactory state of the Irish government," at least as then structured. "Without the supreme authority & yet subject to all the responsibility," subject to the "animadversions of a free press, without a Parliament in which publicly to explain its conduct," he observed, "it stands exposed to every attack & at the same time deprived of all means of defence." His own mind concentrated by the difficulties the formation of an Irish government had created in his dealings with the king and negotiations with the Whigs, Canning may also have given serious thought to the abolition of the viceroyalty. If so, the scheme died with him. Nevertheless, after only a few months in Dublin, Lamb wearily remarked to Spring Rice, that if the office could expire with Wellesley, "so much the better."[9]

The Irish problems that confronted the "Catholics," who for the first time in two decades dominated both the British government and the Irish executive, were much the same as those that had plagued their "Protestant" predecessors in office. There was, however, one significant difference. Thanks to O'Connell, they enjoyed a respite from agitation of the central issue of emancipation. Not that religious controversy and conflict lay dormant. "This is a most curious country, a most strange people," one bemused Whig visitor noted. "Amongst other things they are all quarrelling about religion." The regular members of the Established Church appeared to be content to collect their tithes, eat and drink at Orange dinners and abuse Catholics, but the "New Light people," whom he identified as a "Calvinistic sect," were far more active and aggressive. Their growing popularity within the Protestant community inspired jealousy if not hatred among High Churchmen, while their challenging of Catholic priests to theological jousts did little to calm sectarian passions. The Presbyterians were also divided, some being sympathetic towards Catholic claims and others hostile. Even more disruptive of social peace were the "Bible People," especially the converts from Catholicism. They made "dreadful dissensions" among the Catholics, even tormenting the dying and then fighting for "the dead body." As for the Catholics themselves, while "not good for much" they were the victims of oppression and insults. But Catholic priests were not blameless. The redoubtable Father Tom Maguire was a peculiarly controversial figure, falsely accusing Archbishop Trench of attempting to bribe him into a conversion. A group of visiting Quakers, interested in prison reform and seeking to carry the Word, but not distributors of provocative tracts, were surprised both by the depth of priestly hostility they encountered and the bar Popery presented to "free and fair religious instruction" in schools and in prisons. "It may be said," one of them sadly recorded, "that the blind teachers of this blind people, prefer darkness to light." Surveying the situation, one Irishman was moved to lament "how prone the contending sects are rather to nourish all the bad passions than to cherish the kindly feelings which such a state peculiarly calls for."[10]

Important as the sectarian animosities inflamed anew by the Protestant crusade were in fomenting the persistent disorders which bedevilled Ireland, acute distress continued to stand forth as their fundamental cause. The seemingly inexorable contraction of the island's already small industrial base was heightening a mushrooming population's excessive dependence upon the land. The endemic violence in Tipperary was manifestly related to the quest of the poor for plots on which to grow the mainstay of their diet. The persons who turned up eighty acres of Lord Llandaff's desmesne left a notice indicating that this was the quantity of land required by the poor as potato patches. A scarcity of provisions in Wexford, and parts of Waterford and Kilkenny, saw large bodies of the unemployed lower orders tour the region in search of work or food. Much the same behaviour was reported from Carlow and Louth, while in areas where there was an adequate supply of provisions the poor attempted to prevent any being sent away. Predictably, fever soon compounded the misery. Summarizing his country's predicament, and its relevance to Britain, John Newport wrote: "We pass year after year in the alternations of extreme misery from failing crops of Potatoes with lesser misery in larger crops so as to ensure somewhat more & cheaper food but too often with no means whatever of purchase. The wretchedness of this Island will very speedily pauperize England & Scotland also."[11]

To the challenge of devising a remedy for a chronic malady which William Gregory diagnosed as "Starvation from want of employment," the new home secretary brought an inquiring and sympathetic mind. The owner of vast estates in County Kerry, Lansdowne had long since dissociated himself from the English notion that "there was something in the soil and climate of Ireland which necessarily tended to produce a semi-barbarous race, incapable of improvement, and insensible to the advantage of civilization." He did concede that Ireland's plight "was one of peculiarity." The use of public money to provide work or food for the poor proved the point. He had endorsed, however reluctantly, the furnishing of direct relief in 1822. The root of Ireland's misery, Lansdowne believed, lay in the connection between the system of government and the state of society. A Malthusian, he accepted that an excess of population had produced not only massive degradation but also a people indifferent to comfort and content to eke out a bare existence. The pressure of population, together with the enfranchisement of the forty-shilling freeholders, had fostered the disastrous division of property into unproductive smallholdings. But of all the evils under which the Irish laboured, the system of government remained the foremost. The discrimination against Catholics; "the most extraordinary misapplications of the principles of taxation that had ever been made in any country"; the partisan administration of justice, and the imposition of heavy stamp duties on legal proceedings which "shut out from the protection of the law" the impoverished mass of the population; the hardship of the tithe, which might be equitably eased by a scheme of commutation; and the absence of a resident gentry; all these had combined to produce the peculiar state and condition of the Irish people.[12]

For detailed knowledge of Ireland, Lansdowne turned to his undersecretary. A small, dandified figure, rather prim in manner, who was cruelly dismissed by the acerbic Thomas Creevey as "the least-looking shrimp," Spring Rice was generally regarded as a man of "considerable talents, but more showy than solid." He was convinced of the justice and expediency of giving "marks of attention to the fair & equitable claims of Roman Catholics," and consequently advocated their appointment as King's Counsels. But Spring Rice's influence did not rival that of Lamb, who brought to the office of chief secretary a reputation for cleverness and of being a consistent champion of concessions to the Catholics. Yet for all his Whiggish connections, Lamb had found the liberal Toryism of Canning somewhat more appealing. On Ireland, his views had been much influenced by William Plunket, whose conditional liberalism was much to his taste. Thus Lamb's support for Catholic relief was qualified. His concern for the safety and superiority of the Protestant establishment had caused him to endorse the "wings" in 1825 and support the suppression of the Catholic Association. Similarly, his acknowledgment that the "first duty of every citizen" was to "acquiesce in the law as it stood at the time" led him to ridicule the notion that the Catholics were conferring "'great obligation upon the government by their tranquillity and forbearance'." Disorders which erupted out of disputes over land he laid at the door of extortionate middlemen, who interposed themselves between landlord and occupier, or at that of a politically ambitious gentry. "If Irish gentlemen were so anxious to sit in parliament that they cut up their properties into forty-shilling freeholds to create votes, and thereby surrounded themselves with paupers, how were the legislature or the government of this country [Britain] to blame," he asked in the House? Here was an analysis which encouraged caution to the point of inaction, a strategy well suited to Lamb's indecisive personality and his personal distaste for the Irish. Perhaps as a result of his service on the Irish Committee in 1825, or of his "Sensitive and fastidious" nature, he had formed a very low opinion of this "very violent," "very noisy," and "most conspiring" people. In short, he was not a chief secretary who wished to stir up the Irish "hornests' nest." Instead, Lamb was inclined to substitute style for substance, affability for action.[13]

He did sponsor the worthwhile cause of prison reform. The visiting Quakers had discovered at the Newgate "an awful scene of multitudinous wickedness and misery! Vast crowds of criminals, without occupation, without instruction, without any provided clothing, and therefore half-naked, herded together in great dens; for such was the character of some of their day rooms." The conditions at the two debtors' prisons were if anything worse. To his credit, Lamb responded. He abolished the system whereby debtors were required to pay rent for their rooms, which had the desired effect of forcing the authorities to classify them. He called a halt to the growing practice among magistrates, many of them landlords and some of them parsons, of employing the police in the execution of civil process, whether distraining for rents or to enforce payment of tithes. No longer were constables to double as bailiffs, for such activities both heightened their unpopularity and diverted them from their proper function of preserving the peace. In short, they threatened to render them "utterly useless." Not content, Lamb gave thought to the "more economical management" of a force which numbered 5,310 by the time he arrived at the Castle. Costs were cut, without reducing the establishment, at the expense of police mounts and uniforms. An even greater proportion of them now travelled on foot, while all of them lost their undress jackets and flannel drawers. The annual savings amounted to almost £11,000. In a parallel effort to increase effectiveness, Lamb introduced the principle of rotation. Chief constables were not to remain at the same station for more than one year. However worthwhile and desirable, these comparatively insignificant measures were as unlikely to arouse controversy as they were to advance a solution to the Irish problem.[14]

When Gregory reported to Goulburn in July that the new chief secretary had not as yet disclosed "his views or intentions respecting the intended policy to be pursued towards Ireland," he assumed that he had still to win Lamb's full confidence. Instead, it was less a matter of him being kept in the dark than of there being little about which to enlighten him. The arrival of Lansdowne and Spring Rice at the Home Department did infuse the Irish administration with somewhat more energy, at least in its response to sectarian violence. The Whigs had long held Orangemen responsible for much of the animosity and conflict in Ireland. Consequently, the home secretary seized upon the reports of a riot in Tipperary on 12 July, allegedly provoked by a group of Orange yeomen, to insist that provocative Protestant behaviour be more effectively restrained and participating yeomen disciplined. If those in the pay of the government and supposedly under military discipline behaved in a fashion "calculated to irritate others & to endanger that peace in the neighbourhood which they are specially intended to observe," Lansdowne remarked, it was vain to expect the Catholic lower orders to abstain from tumult.[15]

Another preoccupation of the new team at the Home Office was the Castle's manipulation of the Irish press, but it was now no more than a bugbear. The Peel system had long been in decay, while O'Connell's was in robust health. Keen to complete the work of demolition, Spring Rice argued that the executive's involvement with the press was dishonourable, expensive, and a source of "mischiefs infinitely greater than any it seeks to avert." For newspapers excluded from the public trough were driven into "furious discontent." The home secretary enthusiastically endorsed his deputy's suggestion that in the name of retrenchment and sound policy they abolish the proclamation fund and discontinue subsidies. Prudently, Lamb announced his assent but little was done. The fact that neither the viceroy nor his confidential adviser, Plunket, was persuaded of the wisdom of withdrawing support from the press, the chief secretary explained, necessitated that he proceed "with a little caution."[16]

At the end of August, with the upcoming session of Parliament in mind, Lansdowne forwarded to Dublin the outline of a comprehensive program of legislative action. He envisaged a codification of the numerous statutes prescribing and regulating public works, the reform of the prisons, the reformation of abuses in the office of the registration of deeds, the regulation of tolls and customs, the further reform of the system of grand jury presentments, of the corporate magistracy, of the sheriffs, and of the tithes, the further promotion of education and the removal of the obstacles of sectarian prejudice and jealousy. In reply, Lamb urged that they proceed with the "greatest caution & deliberation." These worthy measures and those inherited from the previous administration – a jury bill, the general paving and lighting bill, the renewal of the Insolvents' Act, bills for the consolidation and amendment of the criminal law, and the prevention of malicious injuries – were all matters of great importance and interest but also of divided opinions and great complexity, the chief secretary cautioned. Be more deliberate, he counselled the especially frenetic Spring Rice. "Let one measure be adopted & settle down a little before you bring on another. If you dash at the whole at once, you run the risk of provoking confusion & discrediting your own reformations." Lamb did take up the education question but he was motivated less by remedialism than retrenchment. Insensitive to the passionate longing of the Catholic poor for education, sceptical of the worth of any "neutral scheme of primary instruction," he was perfectly content to allow Roman Catholics to attempt to finance sectarian schools. "Everything of this sort is better done by private exertion than by public institution," he commented to Spring Rice. Similarly, he wished to reduce public support of the societies active in education and transfer a larger share of the financial burden to an amply endowed Established Church. Lansdowne's views did not entirely coincide with those of the chief secretary. He desired to establish some recognized connection between the government and the Presbyterians' Belfast Institution, and did favour a "general scheme of education," but precious little had been settled before he left office in January 1828.[17]

By the year's end it was painfully evident that government of Ireland by "Catholics" had not ushered in an era of tranquillity. The situation in Tipperary remained serious and chilling. "The prevalence of a general disposition to lawless outrage; the traversing of the Country by large bands of armed men at night; the abetting and assisting of these proceedings by farmers of property; a compleat despair of any successful resistance, and an established and universal system of terror with respect to giving information or evidence. These are the acts which are generally done and the feelings which generally prevail," Lamb reported to the Home Office in mid-October. He was at a loss to devise effective countermeasures in a country "where no person will stir a hand to prevent a crime beforehand or to apprehend the criminal, & where no person can be induced to give any information afterwards." He could think of no more innovative response than to attempt to make the constabulary even more active and efficient, and to order the accumulation of evidence with a view to bringing offenders before a special commission. No less troubling than the violence in Tipperary was the growing evidence that O'Connell's patience with the government was wearing thin.[18]

Lamb's conduct towards leading Roman Catholics, his limiting "all intercourse of opinion" to "great attention and civility," had been applauded by Lansdowne. "Let us be responsible, as we must be, for our own conduct upon their question when it presents itself," he wrote to the chief secretary, "but not for the consequences which must attend either too much or too little activity in passing it." Expedient as this strategy was, it was unlikely to satisfy O'Connell. "I think the Roman Catholics have sufficiently declared what their expectations are from their friends in power, and they will not be put off, by being told that this is not the time for bringing forward their claims," Gregory predicted in mid-October. "If they are not brought forward, & strenuously supported, their annoyance to the Government will be proportionate to their disappointment."[19]

Ironically, Gregory's retention as under-secretary had been one of the first sources of O'Connell's disappointment and annoyance. He had placed great store in Lansdowne as a conciliator of Ireland, but had made no bones of his conviction that Gregory's removal was an "*indispensable*" concession to Catholic opinion. He excoriated him as one of the triumvirs (Manners and Saurin were the others) who had governed Ireland for twenty years and had brought it "to the very verge of a sanguinary struggle." Thus the first step towards lasting tranquillity was the removal of those who "were the prime movers of discontent and the most prominent causes of irritation." Frustrated in the matter of Gregory, O'Connell's temper was not improved

by an embarrassment he suffered at the hands of Bishop Doyle. Drawing
attention to the "deeds and omissions on the part of the New Administration," Doyle warned that he and those with whom he had consulted believed
that Catholic disappointment ought to be drawn to the attention of the
government, and that no person was better entitled to make the representations than was O'Connell. After all, the bishop added pointedly, he had
taken upon himself the responsibility of giving to the ministry "the sanction
of our general approbation." "I have already had my head nearly broke for,
as they say, suppressing the public voice," O'Connell ruefully observed to
one friend. To calm the increasingly restless agitator the government dangled
before him the prospect of a "patent of precedence," fully aware of his
ambition for the silk gown, yet the pressure upon him to revive the agitation
continued to mount. He was pressed to stop fretting about his claim to be
appointed King's Counsel and to ponder the current paradox. With friends
rather than "decided antagonists" in power, the popular and priestly sense
of indignation was waning. In this sense, one leading fellow-agitator mused,
it would be almost better "to have our open enemies than either our lukewarm
and impotent advocates in office." At the very least, they must "make double
exertions" and "bring the priests into efficient and systematic action." Perhaps it was no coincidence that O'Connell's anger over the Whigs' failure
to secure for him the professional recognition he deserved and desired was
accompanied by a decision to implement the strategy which he had first
considered as a means of pressuring the Tories – "to hold a meeting for
petition in every parish in Ireland." A Sunday in mid-January 1828 was
selected for this massive demonstration. "The whole plan on the part of the
Roman Catholics is to act by menace & intimidation," Lamb angrily reacted.
"Nothing can be more unfair or ungracious than that they should assume a
sterner tone towards us, than they did towards the former government."
Even as the Catholics gathered, however, a significant political development
was taking place in London. The Goderich coalition fell apart and the
government which replaced it was dominated by two men O'Connell despised – the "Odious" Peel and Wellington.[20]

The king commissioned the duke rather than Peel, and probably did so
because he considered the latter too closely identified with the "Protestant"
Tories to hold the Canningites in a ministry from which the Whigs were to
be excluded. There was general agreement that the "Ultra" Protestants lacked
men of talent in sufficient number to form an administration. The monarch
instructed Wellington to maintain cabinet neutrality on the Catholic question,
and he insisted that "Protestants" hold both lord chancellorships and the
lord lieutenancy, but these were minimal conditions. Accorded a broad
measure of freedom of action, Wellington, in consultation with Peel, excluded all "Ultras" in order to facilitate a union with the Canningites which
would provide the Treasury bench with needed debating talent. Charles

Grant, William Huskisson and Lords Dudley and Palmerston became the holdovers from the Goderich government, helping to give the new cabinet a pro-Catholic majority. It was also one which possessed unrivalled experience of Ireland. For, with Peel's return to the Home Office and Goulburn's appointment as chancellor of the exchequer, four of its members, among them the prime minister, had served as chief secretary. Indeed, the Irish government was again central to the task of cabinet building. Wellington rejected the appeal of his brother that he be restored to the viceroyalty, and his retention of the Canningites induced Anglesey not to withdraw his acceptance of the lord lieutenancy and led Lamb to continue as chief secretary. Had Anglesey declined to go to Ireland under the new government, Wellington would have appointed Lord Aberdeen, a moderate "Catholic."[21]

What could be expected of this new government? The "New" Association received a pessimistic assessment from a parliamentary sympathizer. The situation was "a hopeless one," Lord Duncannon wrote. For the "best intentions" of Lamb and Anglesey were certain to be stultified by Peel, who as home secretary would claim "complete control of Ireland." Left unasked, and therefore unanswered, was an important question. What was the attitude of the new prime minister towards the central problem of his native land? Although Wellington had quit his cabinet post of master general of the ordnance and resigned his command of the army in 1827, declining to serve under Canning in a "Catholic" government, he was in truth even less of an "Ultra" than was Peel. Indeed, his resignation probably owed less to their disagreement over emancipation than to a long conflict with Canning over foreign policy and a deep personal dislike of the new prime minister. As for Ireland, Wellington freely acknowledged that conquest and confiscations were the means by which Protestantism had been established there. These in turn had provided the well-springs of a popular resentment and bitterness which showed no signs of drying up with the passage of time. He believed that Ireland might eventually be tranquillized – if landlords were induced to reside on their estates, serve as magistrates, and treat their tenants paternalistically; if the Anglican clergy was required to live in their parishes and pluralism was ended; and if materialism was encouraged and early marriages discouraged among labourers by payment in wages rather than with a plot of land. In the meantime, however, to concede full political rights to Roman Catholics was to invite them to seek to restore their religion to its former supremacy and to attempt to recover possession of the land. Yet in 1825 he envisaged the repeal of Catholic disabilities in return for a concordat with Rome which would afford security against foreign and papal meddling in the United Kingdom. And soon after taking office as prime minister he initiated a discreet inquiry of the terms under which emancipation might be acceptable to "Protestants." Yet publicly he appeared to be a resolute defender of the Protestant constitution.[22]

The King's Speech opening Parliament on 29 January 1828 made no mention of Ireland and gave not a hint of the new prime minister's sentiments on the fundamental problem of emancipation. Then, on 11 February, in reply to a question about the unsettled state of the island, and the government's willingness to make concessions to Roman Catholics, Wellington declared that "he had no intention of bringing forward any measure of the description alluded to," but that other measures would be brought forward during the course of the session in the Commons. Little of substance was subsequently introduced, however. Demands for radical changes to, if not outright repeal of, the Sub-Letting Act, which O'Connell retitled "An Act to render it impossible for a labourer to become a farmer, to prevent a farmer from becoming a gentleman, to prevent a gentleman from acquiring Property, to purchase an estate," were opposed by Lamb. The act was "grounded on right principles" and was essential for the reform of Irish agriculture, he responded. He would agree to do no more than investigate the possibility of modifying it in a way consistent with its main principle and object. An attempt to stir debate on the need for an Irish poor law was resisted by Peel, who warned in Malthusian language that the introduction of the English system to Ireland would encourage earlier marriages, and thus an even faster rate of increase in the population, and further subdivision of landholdings. Moreover, the absence of a resident gentry left the island devoid of the human material out of which to fashion the administrative tools necessary to maintain such a system. For his part, the chief secretary recommended to the Irish a regimen of "patience, perseverance, rigid economy, strict punctuality, determined enterprise and unwearied labour." Nor was the government any more sympathetic to a more limited proposal, one which would have provided public assitance to the sick. The prime minister feared that his fellow countrymen would refuse work in order to induce sickness brought on from want of sustenance, and thus be eligible to "come on the rates." Nevertheless, Peel did betray the government's growing sensitivity to the mounting indignation in England at the high cost of returning Irish vagrants to their native land. The number had risen steeply, from 1,337 in 1823 to almost 8,000 in the thirteen months beginning June 1826.[23]

One alternative to a poor law was the employment of the impoverished on public works. Advocates of this form of relief urged the government to make generous advances of public monies to spur such familiar projects as the expansion of the fishing industry, the construction of roads, and the reclamation of a substantial portion of the estimated four million acres of uncultivated lands. Although he acknowledged that in Ireland assistance of this kind might be usefully and profitably advanced, for industry promoted tranquillity and this form of investment was probably less expensive and certainly more productive than a large military garrison, Peel voiced the familiar reservations and restated the obvious difficulties. Expenditures of public monies had to be undertaken with extreme caution, so as to prevent waste and to guard against the danger that individuals would consider themselves freed from their responsibilities. And just as "private rights" created an obstacle to the introduction of a general drainage act so the customary rights of the peasantry stood in the path of the enclosure of boglands. [24]

Another alternative, and one to which Peel had long given at least qualified support, was state-assisted emigration. During the final year of the Liverpool administration the cabinet, confronted by yet another recession and mounting unemployment in England, had returned to this proposal. But the prime minister and his colleagues had drawn back from the massive and permanent scheme envisaged by that enthusiast Robert Wilmot Horton. Peel and Goulburn saw emigration more as a means of strengthening the colonies than of removing an excess population in Britain and Ireland. Similarly, Frederick Robinson and Wellington, both of whom disputed the notion that England was overpopulated, favoured only a limited program which might afford some temporary relief to Ireland. And with Liverpool's retirement even that prospect had receded for Canning exhibited little interest in the subject. Not that Wilmot Horton abandoned the cause, for he had in the Emigration Committee of the Commons a vehicle for reviving it. Although he was the driving force on the committees of 1826 and 1827, they had a powerful membership which included Peel, Goulburn, and Spring Rice. They devoted much time to the task of finding a source of funding other than a continuing parliamentary grant, having agreed to make Ireland "the focus of any extensive system of emigration." Eventually the committee recommended a three-year experiment which would see almost 100,000 emigrants assisted. The costs of their passage were to be met by parishes and landlords while the emigrants would be required to repay with interest the monies advanced to them after they landed. Subsequently, impressed by the fact that a number of English parishes, especially in Kent, had been sending paupers out to North America, Horton introduced a bill which sanctioned the mortgaging of the rates for this purpose. Here was one way to tackle indirectly the problems created by the arrival in England of large numbers of impoverished Irish who stood accused of depressing wages and whose return home had become a heavy charge on the rates. In 1826 alone, Manchester had spent over £1,100 returning Irish vagrants to their native land. But critics argued that the subsidized transportation of 100,000 paupers, who Horton calculated through imaginative arithmetic could be dispatched to Canada at handsome savings to the rates, would simply create a population vacuum which nature would rapidly fill. Yet Peel, having carefully separated himself from the more controversial features of this plan, did reaffirm his faith in emigration as one of a number of responses which together might alleviate Ireland's chronic poverty. Moreover, he insisted that if as a result of emigration the sphere of civilization was enlarged, a body of industrious labourers settled abroad, unproductive ones removed from home, and new markets created for British manufactures, then the benefits would long survive even the filling of the vacuum.[25]

Horton's committee had greater success when it turned to the promotion of unsubsidized emigration. The Passenger Act had been revised in 1823. Evidence of the hardships suffered by emigrants and the growing popularity of the doctrine of free trade saw the reimposition of a higher but common standard for all vessels, no matter their destination. When shipowners complained that this had driven up fares, with a consequent decline in the numbers of emigrants, the Board of Trade relaxed the new measures for vessels sailing from Ireland to North America, while a number or archaic legal restrictions on emigration, such as the ban on artisans, were finally removed. Then in 1827, at the suggestion of the Emigration Committee, but not of its chairman, Parliament repealed the Passenger Act. The response of the Irish to the lower fares was dramatic. Some 20,000 left for the New World that year alone. Unconvinced of the wisdom of an unregulated trade, Horton took care to ensure that he was speedily informed of its consequences. The reports he received were of unsound vessels putting to sea and of acute suffering during the voyage, for some emigrants carried typhus aboard and others arrived in Canada in a state of near starvation. Naturally, the colonials resented their exposure to epidemics of disease. Horton recognized the need to reintroduce at least some regulations, but by this time he had been reduced to the rank of private member. He had retained his post at the Colonial Office when Canning formed his government, only to resign shortly before the Goderich ministry collapsed. Unlike the other prominent Canningites he was not initially offered office by Wellington, but the new colonial secretary, Huskisson, sponsored a moderate reform. Over the protests of John Newport, among others, whose free trade principles happily coincided with the interests of the shipping industry with which he had long been associated, the Passenger Act of 1828 restored a measure of government control over the trade in order to afford a minimum level of protection to emigrants.[26]

An important measure, ostensibly unrelated to Ireland, though that kingdom was never very far from anyone's mind during the debate, was the repeal of the Test and Corporation Acts. Lord John Russell, the sponsor of this measure to make permanent the annuel exemption of Protestant dissenters from the laws, pointed to Ireland as proof that the acts were not necessary to protect the Established Church. There, he asserted, the Corporation Act had not been enforced and the Test Act had been abolished almost fifty years earlier. For opponents of the measure, however, it was merely a stalking horse for Catholic Emancipation. Foreseeing this, Russell insisted that this issue be kept quite separate from the Catholic one. This sensible strategy was successful in Parliament, where the government first opposed and then acquiesced in the bill's passage, but, as his opponents suspected,

Russell was indeed seeking to turn their flank on the larger question. He had been exhorted by a member of his august family to take up the Irish question in order to make a greater mark in the Commons. Thus he calculated that repeal of the Test and Corporation Acts would enhance his reputation by advancing the cause of emancipation. For this success weakened "the principle that the State and the established Church were co-extensive, and, once commenced, the process of encroachment might continue more easily."[27]

Unimaginative, cautious, and hesitant as the government's general course had been during the session, the stance of its two leading figures on the specific topic of Catholic Emancipation appeared to be unflinchingly "Protestant." Wellington had boasted during the debate on the repeal of the Test and Corporation Acts that no member of the Lords had a more decided opinion on the Catholic question than did he, and he had announced that until he saw a decided change among the Roman Catholics he would continue to oppose their claims for relief. In the Commons, a fortnight later, during debate of yet another Burdett motion for a committee, Peel had sounded no less intransigent. He spoke, he declared, for those "in whose mind no disposition for change existed," and he concluded "that, in the present balanced state of the government and of Parliament, it was not just or expedient that the Roman Catholics and the Protestants of Ireland should stand, in respect of civil offices, on precisely the same footing." But the carrying of the motion by six votes, and this was the first time that the supporters of emancipation had secured a majority in the Commons returned in 1826, induced a pragmatic Peel to counsel the prime minister not to set his face against concession when the motion was debated in the Lords. Wellington hearkened to the advice, founding his opposition on the shifting sands of expediency. Undetected by most observers, Wellington and Peel were inching towards a dramatic reversal of policy. Their pace was soon to be forced by developments in Ireland.[28]

Wellesley had sailed from Ireland in December 1827, his departure unmourned and little noticed. His successor did not arrive until 29 February 1828, and chose to enter the city the following day. Anglesey settled his family in an unpretentious villa in Kingstown, overlooking the Irish Sea, and thus several miles from the centre of Dublin. Nonetheless, he did not repeat the mistakes of his predecessor. His was a conspicuous presence in the capital. He rode daily through its streets and placed orders with local tradesmen for vast quantities of provisions. He reinstituted a lavish court, not only to distinguish his regime from that of the parsimonious Wellesley, but also to serve a political purpose. Having enticed absentees back to the capital he planned to send them down to their counties to fulfil their obligations to their tenants. He made a great parade of his desire to conciliate Catholic opinion, for he had arrived "with a much stronger feeling of Catholicism upon him then he ever before displayed." The sporting of a sham-rock during the celebrations of St Patrick's Day, and his constant drawing of the crowd's attention to the emblem, won popular applause. He fished for O'Connell's support with the bait of patronage. The year before the agitator had recommended one of his particular friends – the foreman of the grand jury which had thrown out the indictment in 1825 – for a vacancy on the Paving Board. He had assured the "Catholic" government that from this position his nominee would be able to manage the Dublin Corporation, but there had been no response. Anglesey made the appointment. Nor were their relations harmed by the apparently accidental attendance of the viceroy's son at an Association meeting in April. Equally helpful was the news that Anglesey had turned to Catholic partisans, such as Lord Cloncurry, for advice on forming a "private cabinet" which would free him from depend-ence upon "the bloated staff of lawyers, jobbers, and privy councillors" who formed the Castle administration. [29]

Inevitably, the viceroy's relations with the under-secretary who supervised that administration, for Lamb was in London attending Parliament, were formal and not a little uneasy. Anglesey had, as Gregory knew, attempted to secure his removal. There was the added complication of the Gregorys' puritanical abhorrence of the vicereine, who had conducted a notorious liaison with Anglesey before either of them had been divorced by their respective spouses, her first husband having been another of the Wellesleys. Moreover, the under-secretary surely resented the lord lieutenant's turning to others for advice, implying as this did a lack of confidence in him and the other senior members of the executive. His indignation was heightened by the Catholic persuasion of these unofficial advisers. Nevertheless, he cooperated with Anglesey and surprised him by his "fair and candid" opin-ions and "agreeable disposition." [30]

Anglesey pressed the policy of conciliation with a recommendation that the law to suppress unlawful societies, which Parliament had enacted in 1825 for a limited period, be permitted to expire on time at the end of the session. He considered it a double liability, being an ineffectual instrument of suppression whose renewal was certain to inflame Catholic opinion. Lamb seconded the proposal. He and Lansdowne had agreed that the measure should be allowed quietly to expire and no doubt it was with that decision in mind that he had already drawn the prime minister's attention to the approaching deadline. But Peel was not so easily persuaded of the merits of expediency in this instance, and several weeks of investigation and debate elapsed before he acquiesced in the decision. Even then, he exhibited a marked lack of enthusiasm and emphasized the necessity "to watch with increased vigilance all assumptions of authority or violations of the ordinary law by the Roman Catholic Association if we are to part with the temporary enactments which are intended to be a check upon them." The cabinet agreed that in the event of a deterioration of public order during the autumn it would be in a stronger position to request new and more effective powers.[31]

Satisfied that there was little of a political or religious nature in the "daily atrocities" reported from the countryside, but rather "a great restlessness of character & general spirit of insubordination," Anglesey urged the adoption of policies which would impress the Irish with Britain's deep interest in their welfare and advancement. The time had come "to call forth the energy of the People & to divert it from its present idle & dissolute habits." Hence he endorsed a plea by Dublin's principal manufacturers and merchants for the remission of all duties on imported coal. Inexpensive fuel would go far to assist Irish industries to compete with those in Britain, he reasoned. To illustrate the benefits of thriving industries, he pointed to a successful Clonmel manufacturer. "The improvements in the habits, the industry & the morals of the people around his works is prodigious," he noted. "Party and religious disputes no longer occur." He envisaged a similar pacification of turbulent Tipperary, and proposed that industrialists be induced to locate there with a promise of government compensation for any losses they suffered as a result of local violence. Although controversial, his proposal won Gregory's backing. But the centre-piece of the viceroy's plan to rescue Ireland from misery was the familiar nostrum of public works. He claimed that the comparatively "trifling" sum of £10,000 would enable him to set men to work building roads and police barracks, thereby providing employment while facilitating the maintenance of law and order. And well aware of the extent to which earlier grants and advances to Ireland had been tainted with "jobbing," Anglesey pledged to supervise personally the distribution of monies.[32]

Peel's response, which was uncharacteristically long in coming, disappointed the viceroy. The home secretary declared that he possessed too much personal experience of Ireland and its government "not to feel very strongly the Policy of strict inquiry and mature deliberation before any Proposals are adopted." Thus the government declined to sanction the offer of guarantees to manufacturers who set up business in Tipperary. The dangerous precedent which would be established by this degree of state intervention, the fact that the victims of the Luddites had not received this form of aid, and the ineffectual safeguards against fraud, were adduced as reasons for its unwillingness to depart from the "general principle" upon which British trade and manufacturing had long been conducted. As for the coal duties, Peel promised that they would undergo "deliberate investigation" during the parliamentary recess, and one guided by a desire to promote industrial expansion. On the subject of public works, he stressed the amount of aid which had already been extended to Ireland and disputed the oft-repeated contention that Scotland had been dealt with more generously. The five years ending in January 1828 had seen £2,149,000 advanced from public funds to assist Irish public works, he informed Anglesey, while an additional £251,000 had been forwarded as outright grants. Moreover, he disputed the wisdom of attempting to solve chronic unemployment through continual applications of large sums of public monies. Might not government largesse discourage the exertions of local persons of influence and wealth on whom hopes of a permanent improvement rested? So, in sanctioning an expenditure of £10,000 to spur road works in Tipperary, the government required the local grand juries to vote at least an equal sum.[33]

Even as Anglesey waited impatiently for a reply from London several of his political friends departed the cabinet. A dispute over the allocation of the two parliamentary seats removed from the corrupt borough of East Retford was only the latest in a series of disagreements over policy and it ended with Huskisson submitting a resignation which much to his surprise Wellington accepted. The prime minister's action may have been inspired by weariness in dealing with the difficult Canningites or by a desire to appease "Ultra" peers alienated by his government's acquiescence in the repeal of the Test and Corporation Acts, but the consequences of forcing Huskisson and his associates (for they quickly resigned) out of the government surely exceeded anything Wellington had contemplated. Although the continued exclusion of "Ultras" and the appointment of "Catholics" to a pair of the vacant seats ensured that the cabined acquired only the faintest of Protestant hues, the delicate shading of the Irish executive had been jeopardized by the ministerial changes. William Lamb had followed his political friends out of the government. He would soon have been obliged to resign, in any case, for his aged father was nearing death and Lamb would then be elevated automatically to the House of Lords. Also, his quitting of office may not have been entirely unconnected to the inconvenient consequences of his alleged philandering. Yet Lamb's loss was regretted by several of his colleagues. "He is a man of perfect honour and frankness and you will not find another who in these times will impartially administer the difficult office of Chief Secretary," Goulburn commented to Gregory. The under-secretary agreed.[34]

The events in London caused Anglesey to reflect upon his position, but, satisfied that Huskisson had acted precipitously in tendering his resignation, and assured by Wellington that Lamb would be replaced by someone who held similar opinions on Ireland, the lord lieutenant deferred to his own strengthening sense of mission. He believed himself to be uniquely popular, fully trusted by both Catholics and Protestants. His resignation "might produce much mischief" and "recreate an irritation" that he had had "some success in allaying." The messianic viceroy was convinced of "the necessity of bringing to a satisfactory & speedy conclusion the great question" of emancipation, and "also of effecting by every possible means an amelioration of the condition & habits of its people." He was less than satisfied, however, with the moderate "Catholic" named by Wellington as Lamb's successor. He understood that he had been given a veto on the appointment and his objections doomed the candidacy of Wellington's Irish friend, John Wilson Croker. Yet his opposition to Lord Francis Leveson Gower was disregarded. Dismissed by Creevey as an "offensive, inefficient sprig of nobility," Leveson Gower was in fact widely admired as a "very superior, clever man," his romantic good looks matching his taste for poetry, prose, and drama. He also had a reputation for extreme caution, and a coldness of manner, which the extroverted Irish were unlikely to find attractive. Conversely, his wife, Harriet Greville, the sister of the diarist, and daughter of one of the duke's former mistresses, was noted for a "total want of natural tact and feeling," and was cruelly characterized by Maria Edgeworth as a "sharpish tartish looking" person. More important to Wellington, however, was Leveson Gower's steady support of emancipation, his moderation on the issue – he had been selected to introduce one of the "wings" in 1825 – and his willingness to go to Ireland even though he had resigned an undersecretaryship at the Colonial Office when his fellow Canningites departed the government. Indeed, his father had written that Wellington ought to be impeached for easing Huskisson out of cabinet, but ambition overcame this awkward obstacle. "He leaves a worse place upon principle to accept a better," an observer cynically remarked.[35]

The appointment served to heighten the distrust with which Anglesey had always regarded the Wellington ministry. In Leveson Gower, he grumbled to his brother Arthur, "I have a Man whose Manner is so cold, so rebuffing, so distant that it will be impossible to establish free & familiar intercourse, & then His Wife's Connexions are alone sufficient to make his appointment disagreeable, embarrassing, & even unsafe to me." Her family were "intriguing, mischievous, gossipping & busy about the affairs of others," he growled. Nor could he have been reassured by the cautious Leveson Gower's determination to steer clear of the Catholic question while in Dublin, "reserving the expression of his opinion" to the House of Commons. This ambitious young man subsequently assured the prime minister that he was too well aware of the differences between the duty of making or altering the law, and that of administering it, ever to allow himself as chief secretary to be influenced by any consideration of Roman Catholic claims. And it was to Peel rather than to the lord lieutenant that he looked for guidance. Not surprisingly, when Palmerston visited Ireland later in the year he was informed that the two men did "not quite harmonize." Anglesey "wants to act without check or control," he noted, and Leveson Gower "considers himself as more immediately in the confidence of the Duke." But the distrust which increasingly distorted the viceroy's view of Wellington and Peel was mutual, and for the deterioration in relations he bore a full share of the responsibility. His lukewarm response to Peel's invitation to enter into a private correspondence was evidence of a lack of confidence in the minister, about which he was less than discreet. Equally unwise was his correspondence with Lord Holland, a leading member of the Opposition. Although its extent was unknown to the prime minister and the home secretary, they were not unaware of its existence.[36]

The cabinet shuffle, and the defeat shortly thereafter of the Catholic motion in the Lords, brought a predictable response from sectarian forces in Ireland. "The Orange party is elated with what they call a triumph," Anglesey reported to a brother, but "the Agitators are furious & are using very unmeasured language." O'Connell was determined to embarrass a government led by two men he despised. To the extent that this possibility had entered the duke's mind at the time he ousted the Canningites, he surely foresaw only an irritating increase in the level of agitation and perhaps a more combative Twelfth of July than of late. Although the Association had committed itself to oppose any Irish MP who supported the government, Wellington appears to have been oblivious to the danger or even ignorant of the threat. Certainly he was unconcerned, for in promoting Vesey Fitzgerald to the cabinet he seemed to have skilfully forestalled an effective challenge in the by-election which the new minister was required by law to fight. A steady friend of emancipation, and a respected landlord, Fitzgerald was such a genuinely popular figure in County Clare that the Association was unable to persuade another liberal Protestant – it approached the viceroy's son, among others – to contest the seat. More in desperation than by design, therefore, O'Connell determined to stand himself. The law permitted him to run and to be returned but not to sit in Parliament. "O'Connell *may*, and probably will, succeed, and He will just sit until there is a Call of the House," Anglesey predicted. "In the meantime there will be rare work at Ennis [the county town of Clare], and I must look about me." He ordered military and police reinforcements into the area, to guard against disorders and to attempt to prevent the intimidation of voters, but these precautions were either unnecessary or ineffectual. Contrary to Gregory's expectation, O'Connell did choose to act "by those rules which would guide other men." He discouraged tumult and disorderly behaviour in order to prove that he had not been returned by violence and intimidation, but was the "quiet and peaceable choice" of the people. Not that his overwhelming victory was achieved without a species of intimidation, as scores of demagogic priests summoned Catholic freeholders to vote their religion and even escorted them to the polls to ensure they did so.[37]

Anglesey had concluded even before the result was declared that if O'Connell "could be fairly seated, it would be a perfect Godsend, & would get rid of the odious question," but he lacked confidence in Wellington's readiness either to confront the issue himself or to grant him the discretion to tackle it. "I have the game in my hand, if I am allowed to play it," he boasted to his brother Arthur. "But I sadly fear the D. of W. has not the nerve to let me play it. He is temporazing, vacillating, & every minute lost is an advantage thrown away." These convictions may well have prompted his curious decision to forward his solution to the cabinet via the newly appointed chief secretary. In a letter to Leveson Gower shortly before O'Connell's victory in Clare, he declared his abhorrence of the Association, its agitators, the priests, and their religion. He warned that the power of the Association was such that it could, if it so chose, lead a formidable rebellion, and he affirmed his belief that the continuance of peace rested upon O'Connell's conviction that his object was within reach. "I believe their success inevitable," he added. Therefore the only sensible course was to deprive the demagogues of the power of directing the masses by taking such leading lights as O'Connell and Richard Lalor Sheil out of the Association and putting them into Parliament. "I abhor the idea of truckling to overbearing Catholic Demagogues," he concluded. "To make any movement towards conciliation, under the present excitement, and system of terror, would revolt me, but I do most conscientiously, and after the most earnest consideration of the subject, give it as my conviction, that the first moment of compromise and tranquillity should be seized, to signify the intention of adjusting the Question, lest another period of calm should not present itself." No doubt the viceroy expected the inexperienced chief secretary to defer to his judgment and accept his leadership, and may have hoped that their united representations would induce the Wellington government to act or to give him free rein. But Leveson Gower was too detached and calculating a young man to be so easily led into possible conflict with superiors whose public opinions were so at variance with the viceroy's suggested course of action. At first, he forwarded only extracts of the letter to the prime minister and to Peel, omitting the controversial references to O'Connell's admission to Parliament. Even then, he carefully distanced himself from the contents. Subsequently, at the viceroy's insistence, the entire document was submitted to Wellington. On 12 July he sent it on to Peel, who promptly read it to the cabinet. They decided to bring it to the attention of the king, who, Wellington predicted, would not be impressed but would "swear a little."[38]

The events in Ireland were pushing Wellington and Peel in the direction towards which they had turned in May. The prime minister detailed the developing crisis for the king in a memorandum on 1 August, and sought his permission to enter into confidential discussions with the lord chancellor and Peel. The first hurdle in the way of emancipation was successfully cleared, though from the king's attitude it was evident that this had been the smallest of the royal obstacles. George emphatically denied that he was in any sense committing himself to emancipation. The proposal which the prime minister described to Peel in a memorandum a week later included the annual suspension rather than the repeal of the exclusion of Catholics from Parliament, the disfranchisement of the forty-shilling freeholders, and the payment and licensing of the Catholic clergy. The home secretary's response revealed the depth of his personal embarrassment at being forced to acknowledge the expediency of a measure he had always stoutly opposed on principle. The problem, one of his colleagues observed, "was not with Peel's real opinions, but with his position and reputation, which may throw great difficulties in the way." He spoke of withdrawing from the government and giving the measure his support as a private member. Further, he made clear his aversion to partial concessions, suggested that Wellington's new franchise qualifications might be found to be too high, and questioned the wisdom of the state entering into a more formal relationship with the Catholic clergy.[39]

It was his determination to find a solution to the crisis in Ireland along these lines which prompted the duke to veto the holding of a by-election in Galway, where a sitting member had been promised promotion to the peerage. Peel, encouraged by information from Gregory that an alliance with the Roman Catholic gentry of that county gave grounds for optimism about the result, was tempted by the propect of inflicting a dramatic reverse on the Catholic Association and priesthood. Although the prime minister was less sanguine of success in such a contest, the probability of defeat was a less important consideration with him than was the possibility of victory. The return of a candidate supported by the government would almost certainly cause people "to waver, and to think that after all the influence of the Association and of the Roman Catholic clergy is not quite sufficiently established to induce them to depart from principle so far as to legislate upon franchises, and to make further concessions to Roman Catholics," he observed.[40]

One of the multiplying ironies of the progress towards emancipation was the extent to which it was impeded by the mutual distrust and hostility of companions on that journey. Discretion, if not suspicion, discouraged Wellington and Peel from disclosing too much of their hand to the viceroy. They did offer strong hints, however, that change was in the wind. Peel had emphasized in mid-July the "utmost promptitude" with which he had submitted Anglesey's views "with respect to the present state of Ireland and the only effectual remedies for it, to those to whom they ought to be made known." Then, only a few days after his exchange of memoranda with the prime minister, he advised the lord lieutenant "that the advisers of the King will continue to direct the most serious consideration to the whole state of Ireland, will weigh most maturely all the circumstances connected with its present condition, and determine some time before the commencement of the next Session of Parliament what advice it may be proper to offer his Majesty as to the course fitting to be pursued, and the declarations to be made when Parliament shall assemble." "What more can I say to him?" an exasperated home secretary later asked Wellington. An even broader hint was given by the prime minister himself in late September, but the inebriants of popularity and messiahship rendered Anglesey insensible to subtleties. He angered both men by continually harping upon the need for emancipation, while his arrogance was insufferable. All that they required of him for the time being was quietly to administer the island. More provoking, still, were those actions of the lord lieutenant which seemed perversely if unknowingly well calculated to make an already daunting task more difficult and hazardous. The king had yet to be persuaded to allow the cabinet to consider emancipation, for Wellington had failed to recognize the precedent the Goderich ministry had established the year before. No less important, uneasy Protestants needed to be reassured and pacified lest they explode in protest or flee in fear.[41]

The king suggested in August that Anglesey be recalled. Fearful that this move would inflame popular opinion in Ireland, Wellington declined to act. Peel agreed with him. "It would be very easy to get a much better man," he remarked, "but I think we should take no step at the present moment, which will prevent the excitement in Ireland from gradually subsiding." As autumn wore on and the reports from Ireland were of ever bolder agitation by the Association, the king grew even more irritated with the apparent "passiveness and want of energy in the Irish Executive" and even less disposed "to recede from his delared resolution to maintain inviolate the existing law." Wellington persistenlly emphasized the weakness of this defensive position. The army had been much reduced, the ever-swelling ranks of Catholics were united, and British opinion was divided. Hence the prime minister's mounting displeasure with a lord lieutenant seemingly blind to the obvious necessity to appease a monarch whose consent had to be obtained if emancipation was to be made a cabinet question.[42]

Protestant alienation was equally unwelcome and embarrassing. William Gregory's first concern after the Clare election had been the likelihood of a Protestant outburst on 12 July, and a "Collision between the contending parties." That was one danger for which the viceroy prepared with admirable level-headedness. He ordered magistrates to make whatever arrangements were necessary to preserve the peace, but also to exhibit "the greatest forbearance and moderation" in their employment of the police or the military. The day passed without serious incident. Nor was he entirely responsible for the "sullen indignation" of the Protestant community in the face of "the spirit of triumph on the part of the Catholics." George Dawson delivered an astonishing speech indicating his own conversion to concession on the occasion of the dedication of a memorial pillar commemorating the proud defence of Londonderry during the siege by the forces of James II. The sensation was exceeded only by "the rage and fury" of the Orangemen at this act of "apostasy" and "desecration." In the words of one of Dawson's ministerial colleagues, Henry Hardinge, "a more extraordinary piece of indiscretion never was committed," for his words, uttered as they were by a treasury secretary who was a brother-in-law of Peel, gave "an appearance to the intentions of the Ministry as if they were ready to concede everything in fright." Privately, Peel denounced Dawson's conduct as "unfair and impolitic in the extreme," while Wellington muttered that he was fit only for a straitjacket, but the public damage had been done. Fresh alarm had been excited among Irish Protestants and the hopes of Catholics raised. Despite this unfortunate episode, the premier had reason enough to regard the viceroy as the principal cause of Protestant estrangement.[43]

Anglesey's well-intentioned efforts to conciliate and cultivate Catholics, his turning to Catholic advisers, his administration's toleration of the propaganda organs of the Association, his meeting with O'Connell after the Clare election, all contributed to Protestant suspicion of his intentions. This distrust was heightened by his evident dislike of Orangemen, the continued withdrawal of government support from Protestant newspapers, and by his choosing to reply to a loyal address from Northern Prebyterians with an ambiguous reminder of their own "past privations." More unfortunate still was his decision to treat with silent contempt the published reports that he planned to disarm the yeomanry. Many Protestants were alarmed by the thought that they were to lose their weapons, and especially at a moment when large numbers of flag-bearing Catholics were parading in the South and John Lawless was with O'Connell's endorsement threatening to march into Ulster at the head of another Catholic parade. Contemplating these two developments, Wellington surmised that the Southern demonstrations were "a notification to the Protestants of the north that their scattered brethren in the south will be massacred some Sunday, if Mr. Lawless's progress should be impeded." Although Lawless was to be quickly seen off by the Orangemen, there was no shortage of evidence of Protestant anxiety throughout the South. One rector, writing to Henry Goulburn from Roscrea, urged that action be taken quickly to restrain the Association before Protestants, especially tradesmen, sought asylum from perpetual harassment. Few men wished to remain in the midst of "open and avowed contempt for every thing protestant – the execrating even the very name, and the holding out retribution threats of a coming day of justice." Goulburn forwarded the letter to Wellington, as an indication of the state of the Protestant mind, only to learn that the prime minister had already heard "from all quarters of the Emigration to the United States of the Protestants from the South of Ireland," and that "nobody can be surprised that they do so.[44]

"The feelings which have been excited amongst the Protestants, by the threats & arbitrary measures of the Papists are stronger than I had supposed," Gregory advised Peel on 12 August, "and the Belief that they are deserted by the Government, is driving them into Clubs & Associations amongst themselves, which will soon spread through the Country, and there will be a regular line of demonstration between the Opposite parties, which tho' tacitly existing at present, will then be openly maintained." These Brunswick clubs were modelled on the electoral or Liberal clubs which had been established by the Association in a number of counties during 1827, including Clare, and they even sought to collect a Protestant "rent." Their principal objective was to discourage any movement towards emancipation. "The Orange faction is endeavouring to beard the Government," O'Connell observed to Lord Cloncurry, before expressing the hope that every liberal Protestant would now join the Association. "There is in Ireland no neutral ground," he continued darkly, "whatever is not with us is, in reality, against us." Even as he penned these lines the existing polarization was being sharpened in a more sinister way by priests, who in a number of localities were successfully seeking to exclude liberal Protestants from the Association. The cause of emancipation was being converted in Ireland into an exclusively Catholic movement, at least at the grassroots level, and this was not a development calculated to lessen sectarian tensions. Although the Brunswick clubs, both those in Ireland and the less successful duplicates established in Britain, received no encouragement from the government, and Wellington and Peel had long been hostile to political associations, the prime minister was in this instance not without some sympathy. He believed that Anglesey had driven the Protestants to extreme measures, and Leveson Gower admitted the depth of their suspicion when he formally pledged himself "for the entire falsity" of the Protestants' belief that there was an "underhand communication between the Ld. Lieutenant & the Agitators." Indeed, as the viceroy himself admitted, it was impossible to persuade them that the executive government was "watchful to protect their interests, their persons & their property." As subsequently summarized by Vesey Fitzgerald, the sentiment was one of universal "disgust, indignation, and alarm at the proceedings of Lord Anglesey's Government, and at the tone of his partisans and his press." In these circumstances, Wellington discouraged Leveson Gower from making any move to halt the establishment of the clubs. "They may do good by saving lives and properties," he observed to the chief secretary, "and if there should be mischief in Ireland, they will add greatly to the force at the disposition of the government to put an end to it."[45]

By the end of August the "feverish" condition of the country was "very alarming," and Gregory feared that the seeds of civil war were being sown in a soil that was all too fertile. Nor did the situation improve during September. A nervous Leveson Gower urged the British government, when making its military arrangements, "to consider Ireland on the eve of Rebellion, or civil war, or both." But the viceroy continued to insist that he knew of no other "mode of proceeding" than that which he was already following – "of keeping a good look out – of avoiding the evil moment as long as possible, but of being ready to act, and of acting vigorously if necessary." He inclined to the belief that the Catholics were persuaded that Brunswickers were scheming to bring on a clash simply to commit the government against the former, and that the Catholic leaders could therefore be relied upon to avoid a conflict. Moreover, he doubted the reliability of the Catholic members of the police and the military. If this was a concern the prime minister shared, Wellington nevertheless had by now lost all confidence in Anglesey. He complained that the viceroy was "conducting himself in a very extraordinary manner," that he took every opportunity to criticize the government for tying his hands, and had declared that he would neither have accepted the office nor remained in Ireland had not prominent members of the Opposition advised him to do so. Furthermore, he had permitted two of the Irish government's senior legal officers to go off on European vacations. Under increasing pressure from London to act, if only to give confidence to the "Protestants and well affected of all classes;" at last acknowledging the terrifying effect of the vast Catholic demonstrations in the South, and fearful that the restraining influence of the priests was waning; Anglesey finally recommended that a proclamation be issued declaring the gatherings illegal. It was drafted by the English law officers and the Irish lord chancellor, who happened to be in Kent. To ensure it was obeyed, Anglesey sought military reinforcements. Troops were dispatched to Ireland and others ordered to hold themselves in readiness to respond immediately to a summons from Dublin. Then, at the last minute, Anglesey again began to drag his heels on the proclamation, and when it was finally published, at the beginning of October, the viceroy contrived to frustrate its political purpose.[46]

By forewarning the Roman Catholics he induced them to halt their agitation before the proclamation appeared. As a result, the king and the Irish Protestants were denied the pleasure of seeing the "Papists" bow to the authority of the state or being prosecuted. Anglesey issued the document in his own name instead of following the traditional procedure of securing the signatures of as many privy councillors as possible. To many observers, including Wellington and Peel, this action seemed to be a calculated slight to the Privy Council, or at least to those members living in the neighbourhood of the Irish capital. The prime minister speculated that as old servants of the crown, and thus probably Brunswickers and Orangemen, these men were anathema to the viceroy. Much as he disliked Anglesey's cavalier violation of tradition, Wellington was more exercised by the evidence that this latest viceregal indiscretion had made the king even more obdurate on the subject of emancipation. Thus the monarch's renewed demands for Anglesey's recall were in this sense less worrisome than his proposals that the former lord chancellor and prominent "Ultra," Lord Eldon, be invited to join the cabinet, and that Parliament be dissolved in order to secure a more Protestant Commons. What the prime minister required from the Irish executive, therefore, were measures which would appease the king and conciliate the Protestants. "I am for the prosecution of everybody that can be prosecuted," he informed Peel in mid-October. In turn, the home secretary urged the Irish government "to enforce the law against seditious acts, seditious speeches, and sedition in every shape. The enforcement of the law compromises no opinion on political questions," he added, "and it enables the government to speak with a tone of authority, not only to the party against whose acts the law may be immediately directed, but to other parties who may be carried beyond due bounds in their preparation for resistance or self-defence." In particular, he and the prime minister sought the prosecution of the provocative John Lawless, the prosecution and dismissal from the commission of the peace of two controversial Catholic magistrates, O'Gorman Mahon and Thomas Steele, and the dissolution of the new Catholic Association.[47]

Although the viceroy did order the arrest of Lawless, confident that it would eventually enable him to serve the Brunswickers with "the same sauce," he cited the opinions of the law officers to justify his failure to move against the magistrates and the Association. The prime minister angrily protested to Peel that viceroy and chief secretary "have no notion how much they increase my difficulties with the King by their unwillingness to carry into execution the measures necessary to show that the government will preserve the peace of the country; by the partiality to everything that is connected with opposition to the government; and by the company they keep, and the society in which they live in Ireland, such as Lord Cloncurry." Nor was Wellington's predicament eased at this sensitive moment – on 16 November he applied for royal permission to bring emancipation before the cabinet – by the reports that the viceroy had again met with O'Connell and had paid a visit to Cloncurry immediately after which the peer had attended a meeting of the Association. When Wellington's fury spilt over into a long letter of remonstrance and reproach – "I cannot express to you adequately the extent of the difficulties which these and other occurrences in Ireland create in all discussions with his Majesty" – he found himself engaged in a sarcastic correspondence which was rendered all the more unpleasant by the viceroy's getting the better of the exchange. "Lord Anglesey certainly writes plausibly, and well for his purpose," one of Wellington's senior cabinet ministers remarked. "He intends, and intended from the beginning, to take a popular course. It gratifies his vanity, of which he has an abundance; and his spleen against a government which he dislikes. Evidently there was scant prospect of securing his cordial cooperation.[48]

Anglesey's refusal to cater to the government's political needs dictated his recall. Learning of his dismissal as the old year expired, he wrote to Huskisson: "You was caught in a trap. I would not be driven to resign.

Indeed I have too much identified myself with the People to abandon Them in a difficulty. I bore much & would have borne more for their sake, but I have been delivered from a distressing dilemma." It was this belief in his personal popularity which prompted him to publish a letter which he had written to the titular archibishop of Armagh in response to a correspondence between the archbishop and Wellington on the subject of emancipation, copies of which had been shown to him. Interpreting the duke's remarks to mean that there was no chance of the question being solved during the upcoming session of Parliament, but that the prime minister was not personally averse to the measure, Anglesey counselled Catholics against falling in with Wellington's recommendation that they suspend all agitation. Nonetheless, he did recommend that they confine themselves to constitutional means, as distinct from legal, shun intemperate language, show "patient forbearance," and submit obediently to the laws. Clearly, Anglesey was anxious to calm a public certain to be outraged by his recall, but the probability that his conduct would add to Wellington's embarrassment must surely have added a little spice to the otherwise bland flavour of such a responsible admonition.[49]

The care Leveson Gower had taken since his appointment to separate his administrative duties from his political opinions, and to keep his distance from the viceroy, ensured that he would be asked to continue in office and would agree to do so. But the choice of a successor to Anglesey had to be weighed carefully, given the likelihood of an imminent change of course on emancipation. Several candidates were considered, either to refuse or to be rejected, before the cabinet settled on the duke of Northumberland. Disparaged as a verbose, "very weak, silly man," with the peculiarly inconvenient failing of a "proning to toadies," his attractions for the government were his vast wealth, which promised the kind of glittering court in Dublin the Irish appeared to relish, his moderate politics, and his willingness to do anything it asked. "I have hitherto, by my vote in Parliament, opposed any concession to the Roman Catholics when such concession was sought by persons unauthorized by the crown to make such a proposition," he wrote to Wellington, "but I confess that I shall rejoice to see a settlement of the question originating with your Grace, as Prime Minister, in the House of Lords."[50]

It was inevitable, however, that the dismissal of Anglesey and his replacement by an avowed Protestant, and one widely rumoured "to be ruled in all things" by a duchess who was regarded as "a great anti-Catholic vixen as ever breathed," should be generally misconstrued as evidence of Wellington's unflagging resistance to concessions to Catholics. This was certainly how William Gregory read the changes. He had spent the autumn in England, visiting Talbot and Peel, and being consulted by the latter on developments in Ireland. As intimate as his relations with Peel and Goulburn still were – they had quickly advised him of the government's formation in January 1828 and of its reorganization in May – he received not a hint of what might now be in the offing. At the time of Dawson's indiscretion Peel did dwell upon the difficulties of a situation in which both cabinet and legislature were divided on Catholic claims, and had complained to the Irishman of the paralysis of government. The prospect of the Association duplicating the Clare result in a host of Irish constituencies discouraged any appeal to the country to break the deadlock. But the implied warning, that this state of affairs could not continue indefinitely, was obscured by the apparent constancy of Peel's own views. "I have not trusted myself to say so much to any other person," he wrote to his Irish friend of Dawson's conduct. "You will not have believed it possible – that I could employ such an agent directly or indirectly to further any purpose of mine. I am a man, to whom of all others his proceedings in 1825 [inflaming Orangemen] and his Proceedings recently have been the most revolting." When Gregory returned to Ireland at the beginning of December he had no reason to suppose, therefore, that Peel was entertaining thoughts of concession or that their personal relationship was any less intimate. Quite the reverse, for Peel had pressed him to write "in confidence." He watched the departure of Anglesey without regret and soon had cause to misinterpret its meaning. "The appointment of the Duke of Northumberland gives a fair promise of a better order of things and I trust the King's Government will be the same in Ireland as in England," he wrote to Goulburn on 29 January 1829. Thus he was stunned by Peel's belated disclosure, on the very eve of the new session of Parliament, that he and his colleagues intended to introduce emancipation. The despair he experienced at the almost certain enactment of a measure which he feared would destroy the Ascendancy and eventually the union, and had long resisted, was intensified by a sense of personal betrayal. Unlike other Protestants who had long looked to Peel for leadership of the forces opposed to emancipation, he did not bring the charge of apostasy. It was the failure of his friends, Peel and Goulburn, to prepare him for this development which inflicted a wound that was never completely to heal.[51]

The government formally announced its intentions in the Speech from the Throne on 4 February 1829. Emancipation was to be granted. The Catholic Association was to be suppressed by a law which temporarily conceded large discretionary powers to the lord lieutenant in an effort to defeat the fertile ingenuity of O'Connell. The forty-shilling freeholders were to be disfranchised, and the new qualification set at £10. The dramatic reduction in the size of the electorate would presumably make it more amenable to landlord influence. This measure had the added attraction of discouraging the proliferation of small freeholders, who were generally regarded as an obstacle to agricultural improvements. At Peel's urging, supported by a majority of the cabinet, Wellington reluctantly abandoned his schemes for the state licensing and payment of the Catholic clergy. The safeguards of the establishment, now that Catholics were to be admitted to Parliament, were to be found in a new parliamentary oath abjuring the pope and pledging full allegiance to the Protestant monarchy, and the continued exclusion of Catholics from the highest offices of state, including the viceroyalty. As additional sops to Protestant opinion, the Catholic clergy "were forbidden to wear clerical dress in public," and Catholic bishops "were prohibited from assuming existing territorial titles," while religious orders and Catholic bequests were to be closely regulated and scrutinized. As for O'Connell, he would have to win Clare once again before he could take his seat. He was not to be the first Catholic readmitted to Parliament. The progress of the bill was not without drama, outside Parliament as well as within. Wellington fought a duel with one "Ultra;" the man who had thrown the rattle at Wellesley during the theatre riot in 1822 was reported to be in London lying in wait for his brother; and Peel lost his Oxford seat. Moreover, the king's willingness to sign the law was frequently in doubt. By mid-April, however, all of the hurdles had been cleared. Emancipation had finally been enacted, though only with the aid of the Opposition and in the face of popular resistance to the concession. Yet there had been subtle changes of opinion over the past decade and a half. Once a bulwark of the anti-emancipation cause, the Methodists as a body declined to take a stand in 1829. There was simply too great a difference of opinion on the subject, one leader explained. Other evangelicals were similarly at odds. But had concession come in time? Was emancipation on these terms likely to pacify Ireland? O'Connell's attitude did not encourage optimism. He had lobbied the Whigs unavailingly on behalf of the forty-shilling freeholders. They had, after all, made a vital contribution to the triumphant struggle. Moreover, he was still demanding the removal of Gregory as an essential Catholic "wing" to emancipation. If Ireland was to be tranquil and productive, the government had to follow up the bill by discountenancing "*all* partisans" and employing "only the efficient and useful, no matter what party they may have belonged to," he warned. "There *must* be a grant for public works." Scotland had been "*quieted* by just laws of religious liberty and afterwards by lavish expenditures *in waste*," he noted. All Ireland sought was one or two grants of money. "The people will be taken out of *our* hands by Emancipation as we took them from Capt. Rock by *our* agitation. They may fall back into Rock's hands unless the government have the common sense to take them into their own." This could easily be done, he argued, by giving them "present employment and taking the simple precaution of not making a hatred of the people one of the qualifications for office according to the hitherto approved practice." In short, the Liberator acknowledged the limits of emancipation.[52]

## CHAPTER TEN

# The Failure of Emancipation

Many liberal-minded or pragmatic Britons had advocated or embraced emancipation in the belief that it would solve the Irish problem. Thus, in the midst of the long debate in the Commons, Joseph Hume had predicated that "The country would become tranquil, capital would flow in, and permanent employment would be afforded to the people at home." Others had always been less sanguine, arguing that the problem was not to be summarily solved. It was "idle to expect tranquillity in Ireland so long as its inhabitants [were] the poorest and most oppressed people in Europe." That had been the thrust of O'Connell's comments in the immediate aftermath of emancipation. Similarly, die-hard Protestants did not expect this large concession to satisfy the Catholic Irish. "We always said that C[atholic] Emancipation was only a pretence, a stepping stone for ulterior objects," Lord Talbot observed to his Irish friend, William Gregory, in June of 1829. Of course, "Catholics," such as Thomas Spring Rice, retorted that the government had contrived to do a good act in so mischievous a manner that half its benefits had been neutralized. "The agitators are informed that their violence has succeeded & triumphed. The protestants are therefore outraged & alarmed." Indeed, an evidently uneasy Peel had written to the new viceroy late in March seeking information on the minority's state of mind. "I suppose the intelligent part of the Protestant community is quiescent if not entirely contented," he wrote without conviction, "and I hope the lower classes of the North are not outrageous."[1]

The task of handling the delicate situation in Ireland fell to the executive government headed by the duke of Northumberland. He arrived on 6 March, stepping ashore at Kingstown to be greeted by the lord mayor, aldermen, sheriff, and commons of Dublin. Accompanied by these dignitaries, and escorted by a squadron of dragoons, he travelled through streets that lacked the crowds which had so enthusiastically greeted his predecessor just one year earlier, and had mournfully bid him farewell in mid-January. At the

Castle, he was introduced to the Privy Council, his commission was read, the oaths administered, and he was invested with the collar of the Most Illustrious Order of St Patrick before receiving the sword of state from the lords justices.[2]

"The Duke's character was soon developed: magnificent in his habits, charitable in his disposition – a disposition in which his benign and sympathizing consort shewed a brilliant participation" – he set a munificent example in his extensive support of private charities and a noble one in his "pure and unostentatious attention to the Scriptural forms" of the Established Church. Given his determination "to assume the state of a sovereign, keeping himself aloof from politics and parties," his relationship with the senior officers in the executive appeared to be no less formal than that which had marked Anglesey's brief tenure. Leveson Gower made the discovery that the lord lieutenant was "justly punctilious as to any improper interference in a Branch of his official duty, to which he invariably devotes his most scrupulous attention." Moreover, although "totally ignorant of Ireland," he was prolix to a fault. "I trust you will have no difficulty in inducing him to take your opinion on all matters of business," the chief secretary wrote to Gregory from England, following an introduction to the new viceroy, "but the great difficulty you will find is to *give* it, for it is necessary previously to hear him out, and *on this point* I Tremble for you and myself." Gregory's own relations with the duke seem to have been cordial rather than intimate. The under-secretary was impressed by the Northumberlands' sumptuous style, which included "gold service of Plate," but his diary suggests that he dined less frequently with the duke than he had with Anglesey. His association with the chief secretary was no closer.[3]

Although Spring Rice subsequently described the Irish government as the weakest he could remember, "the whole power being considered to be exercised by Gregory," the under-secretary's influence was on the wane. Age and infirmity were taking their toll, for he had become a martyr to gout. He was no longer able to carry the administrative burden which had been greatly increased by the union of the civil and military offices in 1819. So, in February, he had requested the appointment of "one efficient person" to examine and arrange" the extensive correspondence with inspectors of police and stipendiary magistrates. Instead of the clerk whose aid he had sought, he received an assistant under-secretary to superintent all communications with the constabulary establishment. Whatever the significance of this senior appointment, Gregory's dealings with Leveson Gower lacked that mutual unreserved confidence which had been a feature of those with Peel and Goulburn. He regarded the chief secretary as "a manly, honourable Man," but a little naive. Not only had he made some unfortunate "acquaintances," who would strive to "give unfavourable prejudices to his mind," but he appeared to be oblivious to "the apparently open, but insidiously secret counsel" they would insinuate. Significantly, Leveson Gower described John Doherty, the "Catholic" solicitor general and fellow former Canningite, as the only official character in Dublin to whom he considered himself indebted for advice and assistance. Nor did his aloof personality encourage intimacy, least of all with a dyed-in-the-wool conservative Protestant. Further, as an ambitious and clever young man, he lacked the maturity and humility necessary to defer willingly and regularly to the judgment and experience of a much older man who was officially his junior. He resented the lord chancellor's action in calling upon the under-secretary instead of the chief secretary to discuss a pair of controversial nominations to the magistracy, and he appears to have suffered little embarrassment in rejecting Gregory's request for the advancement of his elder son in the Irish administration. Moreover, he was surely aware of the decline in Gregory's informal influence. Emancipation had severely strained the relationship with Peel, and that with Goulburn.[4]

An immediate concern of both the British government and the Irish executive was the danger of Protestant eruptions during the annual celebrations in July and August of past victories over the ancient foe whose cause had so recently triumphed. Leveson Gower proposed that a circular be sent to all brigade majors instructing them to take the appropriate steps to ensure that no uniformed or armed yeomen participated in processions. In addition, he scouted the possibility of Orange demonstrations being banned by the lord lieutenant. Gregory preferred a more discreet approach. He drew the chief secretary's attention to the "very strong orders" which had long since been issued to yeomen on the subject of participation in Orange parades, and suggested that the brigade majors be confidentially reminded of them. After all, "nine-tenths of the northern Yeomen" were Orangemen. It would not be wise, he cautioned, to irritate further a formidable body already in a state of great excitement. Yet Gregory's caution reflected his own ambivalence towards these men. However wrong "they may be considered by some in their principles, and too often in their proceedings," he pointedly remarked to the "Catholic" chief secretary, "every kind allowance should be made for them, the more especially as they were for so many years cherished by the Government. The most gentle means should be used to endeavour to check their excesses before others are tried." Similarly, he was in two minds on how to respond when men of standing came to him for advice on whether they should resign from positions of leadership in the Orange societies. Admittedly, he observed, such men lent strength and respectability to these associations, but they also served to restrain the lower orders who constituted almost the entire membership. If the gentlemen resigned, their successors as leaders were sure to be men of greater prejudices and deeper passions "who instead of endeavouring to suppress, [would] join in the general excitement." As for a proclamation prohibiting processions, the under-secretary argued that it would be self-defeating. Orangemen would almost certainly disobey it and Catholics would then attack them on the ground that their parades were illegal.[5]

Having consulted Peel, as Gregory had counselled, Leveson Gower replied that the connection of men of high rank and character with political associations produced "more permanent evil" than was likely to result from the transfer of their influence to more dangerous men; nevertheless, he disclaimed any intention of obtruding "advice or interference upon men of character and education" in Ireland and he withdrew his proposals in favour of Gregory's confidential caution to the yeomen. No doubt he was influenced by the fact that the attorney general had seconded the under-secretary's recommendations, while the lord lieutenant was insistent only that the brigade majors be reminded in some way of the law and of their duty to uphold it. Leveson Gower was also alive to the suspicion with which he, as a "Catholic," was already regarded by many Irish Protestants. A little boastful of the fact that he had so far escaped criticism by either side of the sectarian divide, he surely knew that he would be a principal target of Orangemen enraged by efforts to suppress their celebrations. But the violence and deaths which accompanied the parades, held this year on 13 July, as an estimated 50,000 Orangemen marched, and skirmishes broke out between them and Ribbonmen, brought the executive to the unanimous decision to forbid the second round of processions in early August. Ironically, although action now seemed politically safe to the ambitious chief secretary, the proclamation which he advised the lord lieutenant to issue infuriated the prime minister.[6]

Wellington was angered by "the particular notice of Orange processions in the Proclamation and the absence of all notice of the Ribbon processions." He feared that the government would be obliged to adopt additional measures of dubious merit and legality in support of the executive's action, and would find itself in conflict "with the best and only loyal part of the population or Ireland." What Leveson Gower ought to have done, he complained to Peel, was issue a proclamation "including every description of illegal meeting." The suggestion that meetings of unarmed men who gathered to sing songs, drink toasts, make speeches, and denounce ministers be suppressed excited scorn in the cabinet. To limit the damage of this "partial" measure, the Irish government ought to "take some steps to manifest their determination to put down the Roman Catholic as well as the Protestant party." Dutifully, Peel so instructed the chief secretary. More important than the prime minister's flare of temper, however, was his loss of confidence in the Irish executive.[7]

Wellington considered Northumberland "a very good kind of man & very well disposed," but one sadly deficient in knowledge of Ireland or experience of government. As for Leveson Gower, he was inexperienced, immature, and proving to be "vastly too liberal" for the Iron Duke's taste. The chief secretary laboured under the palpable error, the prime minister charged, "that this mischief in Ireland originates with the Orangemen." His visiting of only "the most Catholic and liberal" of houses during a tour of the island, and his apparent support for the disbanding of the yeomanry did nothing to dispel the suspicion which had formed in Wellington's mind that Leveson Gower regarded the Catholics as an oppressed race. He would do better, the duke's confidante Mrs Arbuthnot noted, to look upon them as merely the most numerous, barbarous, and turbulent of Ireland's residents, who had to be coerced if that kingdom was ever to be civilized. But as Peel was quick to remind the prime minister, having conceded that the proclamation might have been "more happily worded," Leveson Gower had conducted Irish business in the Commons "perfectly well," and they would be hard pressed to find an adequate replacement. He urged Wellington to offer "a few encouraging words" to the chief secretary. Nevertheless, it was unfortunate that the prime minister's distrust of the capabilities and reliability of the commanding officers of the Irish executive coincided with a prolonged debate over post-emancipation policy.[8]

The discussion was launched by Northumberland. He had drafted a long and powerful analysis of Ireland's problems within two months of taking office. His principal concern was to counter the potentially disastrous social consequences of the disfranchisement of the forty-shilling freeholders in a land where so large a proportion of the population was already impoverished. No doubt, his anxiety on this score was aroused by Gregory. The undersecretary watched with dismay the sharp rise in ejectments, as landlords who no longer had any political need of uneconomic tenants sought to convert their lands to pasture. "The 40 s[hilling] freehold slavery is happily abolished, and [as] the wretched slave is no longer an article for sale, a profitable stock must take his place, and the ejected biped, must make room for the more valuable quadruped," Gregory wrote to Leveson Gower. "It is not possible to contemplate without horror the misery into which the poor wretched People will be driven, and the Evils which must necessarily follow. Where is the remedy?" Northumberland did not expect to find it in a poor law. He disliked the "perversion" of the Elizabethan statute which had taken place in England, to which the Speenhamland magistrates had given their name. He emphasized also, as had Peel in Parliament, the peculiar Irish obstacle to any duplication of the English system. The want of sufficient independent magistrates, intelligent churchwardens, and trusty overseers to administer it, ensured that the Poor Law could "never be introduced with a tolerable prospect of success." Subsequently, he did acknowledge the responsibility of all societies to make provision for those "infirm by the act of God, by the decay of age or the helplessness of infancy," and admitted that the voluntary relief extended in Ireland amounted to an unequal tax upon the good and the generous. What he proposed was the construction of additional asylums and hospitals, and their support by a general county assessment. If to these institutions "a system of general and gratuitous education" was added, "neither the rich nor the poor of Ireland would have any fair ground of complaint."[9]

Northumberland also discounted the value of emigration. It would simply be too expensive to implement on the massive scale which alone could have a measurable impact upon Irish living standards. He worried that the wrong persons would leave – "the industrious & provident man of small capital" – and the wrong would remain – "the idler and the Bigot." Instead, he proposed a program of public employment and economic development not unlike that sketched out by his predecessor. A "narrowly watched and limited disbursement for Public Works would be the least objectionable method of meeting this exigency," he argued, for the building of roads into the island's remote and inaccessible regions would facilitate both trade and law enforcement. An Irish equivalent to the English Commission of Sewers would be a useful instrument through which to promote the drainage of central Ireland, and while the government would provide the initial funding, the expense ought ultimately to be borne by those who benefited. Nor was he unmindful of the need to promote industrial development, and thus permanent employment off the land. Reviving another earlier proposal, he urged the government to permit Ireland to capitalize upon her great advantage, the abundance of inexpensive labour, by removing the duty on the coals required to power manufacturing industries. Not that he contemplated with equanimity the concentration of the Irish in manufacturing towns. Although they possessed "many high and estimable qualities," he considered them "for the most part irritable, untaught – addicted to the use of maddening spirits, and not as yet accustomed to acknowledge an unbending and equal law."[10]

The troubling and vexatious obstacles to the administration of justice and enforcement of the laws were never far from the lord lieutenant's mind. He deplored the difficulty of bringing culprits to trial, of securing their conviction by jurors immune neither to sympathy nor intimidation, and of keeping the convicted in jail. It seemed to him that judges were too lenient, and doctors too free with medical certificates of release. He advocated "firmness" as an essential qualification for all judicial appointments. Similarly, he called for constant vigilance to ensure that the "admirable" police system did not "degenerate" as had so much else in Ireland. "I more than suspect that in many Districts the Police Barracks is made appendant to the State and Security of the great landlord," he reported, "and that Old and inefficient men are borne upon the Establishment."[11]

One other pillar of the Establishment attracted the viceroy's attention – the church. He fully expected it to come under attack both in Parliament and in post-emancipation Ireland. That it had to be defended despite its many and glaring shortcomings he did not question. For the Irish Church was a "great auxiliary, if not essential to [the] British connection." But he was anxious to correct some of its defects, such as "too many instances of personal extravagance and Professional meanness – too many evils of enormous Unions – of Non-residence – of unseemly traffick and chaffing for preferment." Consequently, he considered the appointment or recommendation of persons to ecclesiastical office as one of his "most fearful" responsibilities. He was determined to nourish the "spirit of improvement" which had already taken root among the junior clergy, to advance men of "enlarged views and parochial experience," and to exclude those "tinctured with the forbidding gloom of fanaticism." The dominance of this last consideration was evident in the rejection of Archdeacon Trench's application for promotion. Devout though the under-secretary's brother-in-law was, and extensive his parochial experience, Northumberland was wary of a man who was "mixed up with a party who by blending secular & spiritual polemics together have become, for the moment at least, distasteful to the people of Ireland."[12]

The pressure on the Wellington government to devise a policy for Ireland, pressure to which Northumberland had been so prompt to respond, was sustained by the growing alarm in Parliament at the breadth and depth of Irish poverty. After all, the Sub-Letting Act had provided landlords with a ready means by which to rid themselves of tenants no longer politically useful. The anxiety of some Irishmen was shared by Englishmen who feared that ever larger numbers of the dispossessed would migrate to their shores. Representatives of the landed interest were perturbed by the thought of an increase in the poor rates to cover the cost of shipping the vagrants home, and complained that the absence of such rates in Ireland already gave the producers there an unfair price advantage by depressing wages. Landlords were thereby enabled to "screw extortionate rents from the miserable tenantry, whom they thrust upon England for maintenance." Others were responding to the sad decline in the condition of British agricultural labourers. "If they did not raise the condition of Irishmen in particular, but left inducements for them to leave their own country, and come over to compete with Englishmen in labour, working at least as hard, and able to live on one half, they could not raise the condition of the English." Proposals that the Irishman be accorded the advantages of a poor law – "the opportunity of obtaining the comforts and luxuries of life, by raising the price of his labour," and the erection of a safety net which would prevent him "from falling into a state of abject poverty, in which all a man's feelings were absorbed in thinking of the means by which he should get a bare subsistence" – were passionately opposed, especially by representatives of the Irish landed interest. Thomas Spring Rice railed against the "vicious," "indefensible" system which had failed in England and would surely "inflict deep injury"

on Irish landholders. Emigration, public works, and the removal of the
burdens which fell on the occupiers of the land, these were the true remedies
for Ireland's ills, he declared.[13]

If the public calls for action lent urgency to the policy debate within the
government, so did the continuing violence in Ireland. The disturbances in
the Protestant North were matched by those in the Catholic South. Fears
that O'Connell's second election for Clare would be accompanied by massive
disorders proved to be groundless, but there was trouble enough there and
elsewhere. Mobs gathered to expel magistrates from the bench and to intimidate witnesses in cases of ejectment. In Tipperary, the "unquiet temper"
demanded constant vigilance. Informed that the county's peasants were
among the most affluent in all of Ireland, Northumberland attributed the
lawlessness to "a fierce and vindictive temper, and a barbarous union for
mischief and revenge which it seems impossible to account for." Leveson
Gower believed that the peasantry was united in a conspiracy against the
police which was designed to force them to concentrate, thereby lessening
their effectiveness. "The only remedy," the lord lieutenant concluded, was
to "endeavour to bring all offenders, great and small, to justice by diligence,
by reward, and, above all, by the full indemnification of witnesses who
give evidence against delinquents at the imminent hazard of their lives."
Not that this plodding course was likely to satisfy a frightened gentry. The
Insurrection Act was "constantly clamoured for by honest men, but bad
lawyers," while Leveson Gower called for additional troops.[14]

The more the prime minister reflected upon Ireland, "its history, its present
state, its absentees, its parties, its natural riches and productiveness, and
the poverty, misery, excessive numbers, ignorance and bigotry of its people," the more deeply confirmed has was in the long-held opinion that separation from Britain was the ultimate objective of Catholic clergy and
demagogues. "Much time will elapse, and much labour, good will and good
sense must be applied to the government of Ireland, before we can expect
to alter men's views of the connexion," he cautioned Leveson Gower. "They
must be made sensible by experience of the practical benefits resulting from
the British connexion, before they can be driven from the pursuit of objects
calculated to flatter their vanity and ambition, to gratify their desire to avenge
former defeats and misfortunes, and to hold out hopes of ease, comfort,
and riches."[15]

Northumberland's proposals to aid the poor won only limited support
from Wellington and his cabinet. The prime minister and his colleagues
were sceptical of the value of poor laws and public works. They agreed with
the viceroy that it would be impossible to transfer to Ireland the British
system of poor relief. Indeed, the escalating costs of that system continued
to dictate its revision not expansion. Yet they acknowledged the need "to
improve the laws establishing houses of industry, asylums, dispensaries,

etc., in counties." Further, in granting that something might be done to provide employment for the poor, Wellington envisaged nothing more than "an improved system of conducting works" undertaken by the grand juries. Similarly, in conceding that there was "a great deal to be amended in the Church of Ireland," he laid emphasis on the constraints of the Act of Union "which provides for keeping the Church in both countries on the same footing." Here was an excuse for virtual inaction. He proposed that the geographic scope of the commission already at work in Britain, investigating ecclesiastical law and possible improvements, be widened to embrace Ireland.[16]

Two concerns above all others governed the prime minister's response to the continuing problems of Ireland and the task of formulating a policy for the post-emancipation era. First, Roman Catholics must be left in no doubt that that they had received all that they could expect. "We have done everything for them," he remarked to Northumberland; they now possessed every political privilege they could require. "There remains no concession to be made excepting our religion, our properties, and our lives." In this mood he attempted, informally and indirectly, to influence the pope's episcopal appointments in Ireland. He also rejected Leveson Gower's recommendation that the government seek to exploit the breach which appeared to have opened in the ranks of lay Catholics. O'Connell's advocacy of repeal of the union had led to differences between him and Sheil. The chief secretary proposed that overtures be made to the latter in the form of a silk gown. "I don't believe that in this country it has ever been the practice to appoint demagogues to be King's Counsel," Wellington acidly observed to Peel, who favoured the idea. Another six months were to pass before the prime minister and the cabinet were to sanction this strategy.[17]

Wellington's aversion to making "any further approaches to the Roman Catholics, and particularly to any leading individuals among them," was closely allied to the second of the concerns which determined his attitude towards his native land. Political considerations demanded that his ministry seek to regain the confidence of those friends lost as a result of emancipation. Government with "vigour and decision" was the order of the day, for the restoration of tranquillity in Ireland was the only way to persuade conservative Irish Protestants and English conservatives that emancipation had not been the first in a row of dominoes. Such a course would also demonstrate a determination to protect the rights of property and thus induce the gentry to hang together "and to adhere to the government." Beyond this, Wellington was hoping to impress Irish gentlemen with the fact that the conflict in their country was now between "Robbers and Murderers on the one hand, and those who have something to lose on the other." If in these circumstances they failed to act to "preserve peace and good order in their several capacities of magistratres," then the government would be obliged to resort to stipendiaries and the police and charge the full expense to the counties.[18]

Peel, no less than the prime minister and their cabinet colleagues, was weary of the problems of Ireland. The "violence and Barbarity" appalled him, especially that in Tipperary, for he firmly believed that it had become "habitual" and arose out of "sheer wickedness," and he favoured the suppression of the "insurrectionary spirit" there "by any means." "The quieting of Tipperary will have a powerful influence on other parts of the Country," he argued. Yet he was contemptuous of the local gentry as the agents of law and of order. He accused them of having encouraged the violence either by their apathy as magistrates or by their "half connivance" at it. "I am quite sick of Communications from Irish Gentlemen. They do nothing except abuse the Government which does everything," he later wrote to Gregory. "I have come to the conclusion that there is less moral courage in Ireland than in any Country on the Face of the Earth." Cowardice gave "Captain Rock all his power." Peel was passing a final sentence of failure on all of the earlier efforts to reform and strengthen the ordinary Irish magistracy.[19]

The task of coercing Tipperary, and of permanently administering "some severe discipline" to all of Ireland, would have to be given, therefore, to the stipendiaries and the police, though the home secretary emphasized the need for a more efficient force of the latter. He agreed with the prime minister that England should no longer bear the costs of "civilizing" her sister kingdom. Indeed, to the extent that Ireland was obliged to pay "the charge of suppressing her own disorders" so would she have "an inducement to keep the peace." In short, he wished to reintroduce that fiscal discouragement of lawlessness which he had originally intended to be an important ally of his Peace Preservation Force. "It appears to me that we ought to consider the policy of greatly extending the police system, and levying the expense of it on the land," he informed Wellington. That the constabulary as presently organized would not answer was evident from Gregory's response to the home secretary's request for nominees to fill senior positions in his new police force for the capital. The four inspectors-general inspired little confidence, the under-secretary replied. One was "a pen and ink man", another "fond of his ease with not much intelligence & a grumbler," and a third unfit for his office. Leveson Gower, meanwhile, suggested that an inspector-general be appointed for each of the six circuits instead of the four provinces. This arrangement "would enable each Inspector to attend personally at the Assizes, & afford facilities, not merely for the better regulation & supervision of the Police, but fot the Prosecution of offenders." Peel's ideas, however, went beyond this form of tinkering. He envisaged a truly national force, with an *esprit de corps* that would obliterate local or religious distinctions. Appointments would be taken out of the hands of the local gentry and placed firmly in the grasp of the viceroy. A highly centralized and efficient force would be capable "of compelling for ten years to come obedience to the law." [20]

The home secretary also gave thought to the introduction of other remedial measures. He despaired of "making any essential changes in the Grand Jury system," though his pessimism may in this instance have reflected a pragmatic reluctance further to provoke the local gentry at a time when he was planning finally to remove the police from their control. Another question "full of difficulties" was that of the Poor Laws. Peel was not insensitive to the plight of English agricultural labourers, whose impoverishment had been effected by forces not unlike those at work in Ireland. The labourers' condition had deteriorated sharply following the enactment of another Corn Law in 1828. Contrary to the intent of its framers, the new law resulted in the worst of all price combinations – farmers were forced to sell low and consumers to pay high. As they struggled with great difficulty "against merely domestic evils," English labourers were ill-equipped to compete with "a host of ragged Irishmen," "strong," "patient of labour," and with "fewer wants and fewer charges." Yet Peel hesitated to obstruct the inflow of Irish labour, for as the son of an industrialist he recognized the advantages of maintaining a deep pool of "cheap labour." While he shared the resentment of the landed interest at the "increasing tendency on the part of Ireland to make the English poor laws subservient to the maintenance of the Irish paupers," he disputed the effectiveness of those limited proposals advanced by Northumberland and endorsed by the prime minister. An increase in the number of infirmaries and dispensaries to care for the truly helpless in Ireland would not solve England's problems with the Irish poor, he observed, for it was the healthy and the strong who made the journey. Moreover, some of his cabinet colleagues were not unmindful of the fact that many of those payers of poor rates who complained of the cost of sending Irish vagrants home had already derived advantage from their labour. [21]

With Wellington and Peel committed to the strengthening of the civil arm of the state in order to teach the Irish a lesson in obedience to the law, Leveson Gower prudently delineated the limits of his liberalism. He was one of those, he hastened to assure the home secretary, who believed "that we have granted all we can grant to Catholics, with safety," for their ultimate purpose was to subvert the Protestant church and establish their own in its place. He avowed a profound regard for "the value of the support of the Protestant opinion in this Country," although he stressed the "great difficulty" of preventing them from "vitiating their own cause, & making the cooperation of the Govt. in their endeavours, difficult if not impracticable, by a stupid aimless violence and injustice." The agents of this folly lived in a region of the country where they outnumbered the Catholics, the chief secretary remarked, and they never wasted a thought "on the situation of [fellow Protestants], who reside in parts, where the rascally Papists outnumbered them." As for the "Rockite outrages," they were in some sense inevitable in a land "cursed with poverty, population, & absenteeism, or what is worse a bad resident gentry." He believed that these chronic social problems went far to explain the deeply rooted sentiment, which he shared, in favour of a poor law. Finally, he reaffirmed his enthusiastic support for the improvement of the police. He now urged that inspectors be appointed for every county and that they, rather than the magistrates, control the appointment of their men. [22]

The background to the debate on policy, and the developing consensus that police reform ought to be the first order of business, was the continuing violence in Tipperary. "The state of society there is such as cannot be paralleled in any country which has any pretensions to civilization," Leveson Gower reported in mid-August. After some discussion and disagreement, the latter principally between the lord lieutenant and Sir John Byng over the viceroy's wish to disperse troops in small detachments (Wellington resolved the argument in favour of the civil authority), the executive settled on a number of temporary measures – the dispatch of stipendiary magistrates to disturbed baronies, the doubling of the police force in the county, the placing of the area under an inspector-general, and the appointment of military officers to commissions of the peace. The additional expense was initially to be financed out of the Secret Service Fund, but eventually it was to be borne by the occupiers of the land. The prime minister gave his "unqualified concurrence" to all of these measures, though he did caution the viceroy to select with great care those soldiers to be entrusted with commissions of the peace. "They all mean well," he remarked of the members of his profession, "but I don't think that all of any rank could be trusted to act as magistrates." [23]

These actions notwithstanding, the crisis in Tipperary continued to worsen thoughout the autumn. The dolorous effects of the Sub-Letting Act helped to spark an increase in crimes which even the Catholic clergy seemed powerless to prevent. Then, in October, a welcome calm was shattered by the brutal murder of the Reverend Mr Going, the brother of the Major Going assassinated several years earlier. He had been a magistrate as well as a clergyman. It soon emerged that Going had refused a "fair" composition for his tithe and had insisted on taking it in kind, including potatoes, but the horror of this crime brought renewed demands from frightened if not cowardly gentry for the reenactment of the Insurrection Act. Northumberland and Leveson Gower stoutly refused to recommend a resort to this extraordinary measure. Instead, rewards were offered fo the detection of Going's murderers and other criminals, exemplary punishments were enforced, the military patrolled more actively, and searches for arms were instituted. But ordinary measures such as these had not proven effective in the past. Although Wellington now began to lean towards reintroduction of the Insurrection Act, Peel aligned himself with Northumberland and Leveson Gower.

The act "produces no permanent effect, as is proved by its frequent application to Tipperary," he reminded the prime minister. "It leaves the people at least as had as it found them; it rather weakens the energy of the regular law, upon the due exertion of which, after all, the main reliance must be placed." The decisive consideration, however, was a sudden and astonishing improvement in Ireland which held out the unexpected hope of genuine tranquillity. By the third week of January 1830 a far more confident and relaxed viceroy was reporting a decline in religious animosity and a level of resistance to ejectments which the police and gentry were well able to counter. Incidents were still being reported from Tipperary, Clare, and Roscommon, but Northumberland took reassurance from the fact that they resulted from particular and readily identifiable causes. In Tipperary, the curse of rack-renting continued to embitter relations between proprietors and occupiers of the soil; in Clare, two elections had served to alienate landlords from tenants; while in Roscommon, the source of the trouble was the proselytizing by zealous Protestants. In these circumstances, he concluded, there was no need for any extraordinary parliamentary enactment. What Ireland required was a national police with more extensive powers and firmly under the control of the executive.[24]

The government had looked to the approaching session of Parliament in the confident belief that with the Catholic question out of the way the "discretion," "good sense," and "personal interests of all Men of Education & Property" assured it of broad support for "such measures as shall dry up the sources of Tipperary unruliness & disorder." During the autumn and into the winter there were lengthy discussions of a possible legislative program. Leveson Gower repeatedly suggested that they grapple with the subject of the tolls imposed by corporations at fairs and markets, but in return for which no services were rendered. In one of the largest counties, they were levied on potatoes, corn, oatmeal, fresh butter, coarse woolens, flannel, friezes and linens. Indeed, they were frequently levied again on these items when sold by retail. Moreover, exemptions on turf and timber were often disregarded. The annual cost was conservatively estimated at £500,000, but to this charge had to be added the discouragement these "outrageous" tolls offered to industry, and especially to the industry of the poor. "If something be not done," Leveson Gower warned, "we shall shortly have throughout the whole of Ireland a system of public resistance to the execution of laws which are so ill defined & doubtful as almost to justify such resistance." There was renewed interest in the popular opiate of education. To the several reports of the most recent Commission on Education had now been added that of the parliamentary committee struck in 1827 and chaired by Spring Rice. It endorsed the familiar principles – the joint education of Protestant and Catholic children in literary and moral subjects; their separate religious instruction; and the prohibition of proselytism – called for the establishment of a government commission to administer closely state-supported schools, and recommended a number of stringent conditions under which parliamentary grants ought in future to be made. Acknowledging the failure of the Kildare Place Society, Peel sought Leslie Foster's opinion of his own modified version of this plan. The former education commissioner was pessimistic of the Catholic hierarchy ever accepting any scheme which they did not control. Furthermore, he feared that action would revive sectarian animosities at a time when they appeared to be "in a sort of sullen torpor," and warned of the political consequences of further exasperating Protestant "feelings of hostility to the Administration, which are already so prevalent." It was a concern shared by members of the cabinet. Foster's analysis impressed the young chief secretary, to whom Peel forwarded it for comment, though Leveson Gower observed "that renewed agitation of the Question can no more be prevented than any other Visitation from Heaven upon those who have to manage the affairs of this Country."[25]

The meagre results of both the long debate on Irish policy and the extensive preparations for the session were reflected in the Speech from the Throne. There was no mention of Ireland nor any hint of prospective legislation. Of course, the encouraging reports recently received from Dublin not only permitted ministers to indulge a taste for indecision but also afforded timely evidence of the "success" of emancipation as an instrument of tranquillity. Peel explained to the Commons that, with the placing of Ireland on a footing of equality with the rest of the empire, "there existed no necessity for making special mention of a part of the Kingdom which had no longer anything to distinguish it from the remainder." Thus did an architect of the policy of exceptionalism avow that in future Ireland would be "looked upon as England or Scotland." When Daniel O'Connell protested the omission of all reference to such a distressed region as his homeland, it was the Knight of Kerry who insisted that not even Ireland's suffering could be regarded any longer as exceptional. "There was certainly great distress in Ireland, but nothing equal to the extent in which it pervaded England." It was the distress in England's manufacturing cities, as well as that in her countryside, which preoccupied government and Parliament.[26]

Henry Goulburn, as chancellor of the exchequer, responded to falling revenues and a rising deficit with a series of expenditure reductions. The cuts in the military estimates were facilitated by the withdrawal of 3,000 men from Ireland. Simultaneously, he sought "to afford the utmost relief within our power to the lower orders of the agricultural and manufacturing classes," by repealing taxes on beer, cider, and leather. To cover some of the losses of revenue, Goulburn raised the duty on spirits, though the fear of stimulating illicit distillation ensured a much smaller increase in Scotland and Ireland than in England. He also imposed a tax on tobacco and announced the assimilation of the stamp duties in the different parts of the United

Kingdom. But this amounted to a sharp increase in taxation in Ireland, where the duties had been lower. Irish members angrily protested the taking of a further £150,000 in taxes from their country while Britain enjoyed the benefits of substantial remissions,. They appealed for the removal of the coal duty, but not even their assurances that the resulting stimulation of Irish industries would provide employment at home for those Irishmen so unwelcome in Britain brought the desired action. The government blithely ignored all warnings, private as well as public, that the taxes were extremely unpopular and were uniting Ireland against Britain, for it was infected with a new spirit. "The time is come when it is unnecessary any longer to pet Ireland," Peel had informed Leveson Gower several months earlier. "We only spoil her by very undeserved flattery, and by treating her to everything for which she ought to pay herself." In future, Ireland would have to bear "the burthens of the country more proportionate to her real means."[27]

The Opposition had little difficulty illustrating the limits to assimilation, and the persistence of exceptionalism. When John Newport and Thomas Spring Rice remounted an old hobby horse, and sought reform of the Irish First Fruits – "or the first year's revenue of all vacant benefices" – which, were they properly collected and expended, would relieve the occupiers of the land of much of the burden of the vestry cess, they insisted that they were only seeking to apply to Ireland a principle already adopted in England. Responding for the government, Goulburn declined to accept a measure which would divest the Irish clergy of a full year's income. When Daniel O'Connell launched a direct attack upon the vestries, seeking the admission of Catholic ratepayers as equal members fully entitled to vote on assessments, he declared "that the Churches in England and Ireland should be put on the same footing." In reply, Peel protested that to "admit 1,000 Catholics to be on a level with twelve Protestants in parishes where the population was so unequally divided between the religions, would be to make the Church establishment in Ireland a mere mockery." Joseph Hume's renewed campaign against the viceroyalty, which was an expression of Irish exceptionalism, was also successfully opposed by the ministry. However, talk of assimilating the provisions for relief of the English and Irish poor brought a bipartisan response. The government welcomed Spring Rice's motion for a select committee to investigate the problem, providing as it did a convenient excuse for avoiding a decision on this complicated question. Michael Sadler's long and classic restatement of the argument in favour of an Irish poor law was easily deflected by Leveson Gower, who remarked that the House should come to no resolution until the committee had made its report. Privately, Wellington was setting his face ever more sternly against the poor law and applauding Northumberland's refusal to give public monies to relieve the distress in Ireland. Publicly, he rejected the proposal that a land tax be assessed "to be disposed of on the spot in the general employment of the poor," fatalistically observing that however much "any privation of suffering among any class was to be regretted, it was frequently the fact, and almost unavoidable. It arose out of the state of the country." He then sidetracked a bill which, by seeking to promote the drainage of bogs, much as Northumberland had earlier proposed, would have improved land and provided employment. Such projects were more properly left to individuals or private companies, he declared. The unspoken reason for this opposition, one Irishman later claimed, was fear "lest the extension of arable territory should so cheapen food in England, as to force the lowering of agricultural rents."[28]

The fate of the bog drainage bill was symptomatic of the government's dismal legislative performance. It offered few Irish measures of substance and none was enacted. Leveson Gower introduced amendments to the Sub-letting Act, which were intended to clarify its meaning and not to tamper with the principle. His "Bill to provide for the maintenance of illegitimate children in Ireland," by extending to that country the bastardy provisions of the English Poor Law, was promptly assailed by O'Connell as "a temptation to vice" which threatened to expose the Catholic clergy to the "vile perjury of any strumpet in the pay of an Orange or Biblical miscreant." This measure lapsed at the end of the session. Another casualty was the constabulary bill, which proposed to vest the appointment of officers in the executive government, establish the new rank of sub-inspector whose authority was to be county-wide, and provide the means to rid the force of many of the chief constables, an office which Peel discovered had become a refuge for "distressed Gentlemen." Although long regarded as the centre-piece of the government's new policy, it simply disappeared from the order paper. The same fate befell two minor measures designed to improve the administration of justice by more closely regulating both sheriffs and the compilation of jury lists.[29]

Long before the demise of the bills for whose parliamentary management he was primarily responsible, Leveson Gower had indicated to the prime minister his wish to relinquish his office but not to leave the government. He was responding less to political disappointment than to the personal inconvenience of annually shipping a young, large, and growing family across the Irish Sea. The death of the king in June 1830 and the subsequent dissolution of Parliament gave Wellington an opportunity to engage in a minor ministerial shuffle, which saw Leveson Gower exchange positions with Sir Henry Hardinge, the secretary at war. A retired soldier, Hardinge was closely associated with Wellington, having served with distinction in the Pensinsula and as a liaison officer at Blücher's headquarters during the Waterloo campaign, and had acted as his second in the duke's duel with Lord Winchilsea in 1828. Entering Parliament in 1820, he proved to be an effective speaker. Wellington had first considered him for the post of Irish secretary when he formed his administration in January 1828 and had long since regretted his decision to send Leveson Gower instead. He brought to the office in 1830 a reputation as "plain, straight-forward, and just, and an excellent man of business," though Daniel O'Connell was later to describe him as "'a one-handed miscreant'." This was a tasteless reference to his war injury. It was believed that he and his Irish wife would prove to be popular. Hardinge knew little of Ireland but following his arrival in August he drove energetically into the "labyrinth" of Irish affairs, and encountered an "extra-ordinary people" who had "no more peculiarity of character" than any he had yet mixed with. Greeted by the news of a bloody sectarian affray in Cavan, he noted that the "facility of suddenly assembling without any ostensible leaders in the worst feature of these affairs," and bemoaned the "selfish cowardice of the upper classes" which gave "to the turbulent rascals the power which they possess." Nevertheless Ireland "w[oul]d shortly be quiet & happy," he observed sympathetically, "if the poorer classes could be relieved from the squalid misery & want in which they barely exist." His horror of famine was twofold. It sprang from a gentlemanly and soldierly distaste for the employment of force against "starving depredators," and from an ideological aversion to the provision of aid out of the public purse. He was much relieved, therefore, by the reports of a "large & good" potato crop. He was soon "going on well" with both Northumberland and Gregory. "I like the office much better than the War Office," he reported to one friend at the end of his first month in Ireland.[30]

Hardinge methodically set about the task of analysing the sources of tension and disturbance, political and social. He traced much of the instability to demagogues, and especially to O'Connell and his agitation for repeal of the union. The revolution in Belgium, which had seen a Catholic population establish its independence of foreign Protestant rulers, had given a fillip to the movement, he observed, exciting "a restless expectation throughout the lower classes, that they can by similar means overpower the Military & dissolve the Union." That same class promised to respond also to O'Connell's exploitation of the fear of the Sub-Letting Act, for Hardinge recognized that ejections converted men into Ribbonmen. The condition of the mass of the people "is so deplorable," he noted, "that having so little to lose they are recklessly ready to rush into any attempt for a change, & are only withheld by a want of Arms & of Leaders." Nor was he devoid of sympathy for their plight, as his questioning whether agricultural improvement had not been purchased at too high a social price implied. He dissuaded the Beresfords from ejecting 500 Catholics from their property in Wicklow, but expected the sorry work to be pushed to completion in the spring. Could it be a matter of wonder, he asked, "that young men, whose fathers for 3 or 4 generations have lived on the Estate, & who have punctually paid their rents, should become Ribbonmen & Outlaws?" Like his predecessors, he attributed much of the evil to "the want of a proper manly spirit" among the gentry which had led them to delegate to stipendiaries their responsibilities for the maintenance of order. Furthermore, he deplored "the mischief attending the system of Stipendiary Magistrates." It worked "so much better than the local Magistracy" that a temporary expedient became "a confirmed habit, rendering the resident gentry more inert than they were before."[31]

To counter O'Connell's activities, the executive utilized the discretionary power granted to the lord lieutenant at the time of emancipation to suppress dangerous associations. The Society of Friends of Ireland of all Religious Persuasions, which O'Connell had formed in April, to protest Goulburn's budgetary measures, together with the Sub-Letting and Vestry acts, and to agitate for repeal of the union, had been promptly suppressed. "We must be prepared for every trick and evasion which will of course be tried," the experienced Gregory had then written to Leveson Gower, "but they must also be met by the same steady determination not again to suffer this Hydra to raise its head." And in mid-October Hardinge acted with dispatch to suppress the Irish Society for Legislative Relief. He did not stand upon the constitutional nicety of waiting for an opinion from the Irish law officers before issuing a proclamation over the viceroy's name. "I think it fortunate that O'Connell & his Associates have given the Government an early opportunity of evincing their determination to meet them at the outset with all the rigour of the law," Peel wrote approvingly. But little had been gained, as Northumberland soon had reason to report. O'Connell simply re-formed his association under another name. The viceroy envisaged "a series of proclamations by the government, and counter-proclamations by the agitators" until the law expired at the end of the coming session of Parliament, when he hoped it would be reenacted "with a kind of suspension of 'Habeas Corpus' so far as regards conveners, orators, and secretaries reappearing at such meetings."[32]

The ineffectiveness of the weapon of suppression caused Hardinge to endorse the strategy of seeking to subvert O'Connell's influence. Now that Sheil's silk gown had "covered his former enormities" he would make a more presentable ally. The chief secretary assiduously cultivated the Catholic lawyer and demagogue, as had his predecessor, inviting him to his residence. What Sheil sought was the assistance of the government to get into Parliament, and he offered in exchange vague assurances of limited personal support within the House and the promise that other leading Catholics would follow his example of support for the government and opposition to repeal of the union. That question, "by mere brute force & mob numbers will under present circumstances require to be met by Irish partizans of all parties," Hardinge observed to Peel, and "I cannot but consider this opening as affording a practical proof of the benefits of Emancipation by dividing the Catholic leaders, & enlisting those who hitherto have been opposed to the Government, and of acquiring useful aid at a moment of need." But just as he had balked initially at wooing Sheil with a silk gown, and had rejected an earlier suggestion by the viceroy that the Catholic's admission to Parliament be quietly assisted, so did Wellington again shun any connection with the Irish demagogue. Together with Peel, he feared that the qualified nature of the support Sheil was prepared to promise, in particular his reserving his independence on the potentially "all-important vital question" of parliamentary reform, might lead to the government's acute embarrassment in the Commons. By all means show Sheil every civility, and comply with "any reasonable wish on his part," Peel instructed to Hardinge, "but be very cautious how you undertake to be sponsor for his parliamentary conduct." Undismayed, the chief secretary doggedly strove to overcome the resistance in London to an informal alliance with Sheil, but the government was to fall before his endeavours could make much of an impact.[33]

There was no disagreement between Dublin Castle and the British government on the need for the executive to launch a propaganda campaign of its own to counter that of O'Connell. Hardinge was dismayed by the discovery that the government was bereft of press allies. "There is not at this moment one paper which advocates our side," he informed Peel on 12 October. "Exaggeration & Falsehood are boldly put forth in popular forms calculated to mislead – the uncontradicted lie daily circulated ends by having the effect of truth, & the well disposed are seduced as well as the evil minded to have a contempt for the laws & a hatred for their rulers." Anxiously, the home secretary pressed Hardinge to open "the Press upon the subjects of the Union and employ all the argument, but above all – all the Ridicule you can command against the project of dissolution." He recommended the establishment of a weekly modelled upon the *Anti-Union* put out by Plunket and others in 1799. In its columns the fallacy of the parallel to Belgium should be exposed, and attacks launched against the leaders of dissolution. "Hold up O'Connell and his Partizans weekly to cutting sarcasm and Ridicule. Confirm the just fears that are entertained on account of the predominancy of a set of sanguinary lackland bankrupt agitators, backed by a mob. Give a picture of Liege, of Brussels [and] of Paris and Bourdeaux [*sic*], under an established Government and compare it with the effects of Revolution." Further, Peel employed Gregory in the collection of the materials of propaganda, turning to the under-secretary for proof that the value of land had increased since the union. Above all, he emphasized the need to win the backing of the Protestant community. To that end, he suggested that Hardinge convince it that repeal of the union meant repeal of the Act of Settlement.[34]

The chief secretary enjoyed some success. He solicited and obtained the support of the *Evening Mail* and the *Evening Post*, and by way of reward proposed that they be taken by government offices and London clubs. He had hopes of enlisting the *Evening Packet* and the *Warder* before he departed to attend the opening of Parliament, but he prudently kept his distance from the "ragamuffins" who edited all of these newspapers. He exhibited a similar prudence and good sense in seeking to unite Catholics and Protestants in opposition to repeal. The Protestants "are so thoroughly alarmed," he advised Peel, "that whilst we must look to them as our strength & garrison in case of crisis, we have the opportunity I think of preventing a relapse into party animosities, by the desire of leading men of both parties, and creeds, to coalesce on this occasion – in short to give effect to the relief bill." No doubt he was responding also to the unrelenting opposition to the government by a group of Protestants embittered by emancipation, whom he dismissed as "obstinately bigotted to Orangeism," and among whom three of William Gregory's brothers-in-law were all too prominent – the earl of Clancarty, the archibishop of Tuam, and Archdeacon Trench. As for the under-secretary, he professed himself "happy to believe that the Protestant feeling [was] becoming every day more strongly against a repeal of the Union," and that "the wish to unite with the Government in resisting the attempts of the Rebels [was] more cordially expressed." From all of this Hardinge deduced that there was little likelihood of an imminent uprising in Ireland. Nevertheless, before leaving for London, he gave thought to arming the students of Trinity College and he took a series of soldierly precautions. Munitions stored in exposed depots were quietly removed to more secure locales, the Pigeon House was garrisoned, and a number of towers around the coast were provisioned so that they could be occupied in an emergency by the 1,600 strong coastguard and could serve as places of refuge. Indeed, he was so active that Peel began to fear that this old soldier was too lively. Even cabinet admirers of his "promptitude" questioned the wisdom of his attempting to call out O'Connell over one of the Irishman's disparaging comments.[35]

Among the pieces of propaganda whose circulation Hardinge had assisted was the Anti-Repeal Declaration. It warned not only of the dangers of the repeal agitation (the undermining of confidence in tranquillity and thus the frightening away of the private investment the island's economy so desperately required) and the perils of its success (civil war and the dismemberment of the empire), but called on Parliament speedily to adopt measures which would improve the condition of the peasantry by alleviating their distress and preventing the periodic recurrence of famine. The need for action had been underscored by Spring Rice's committee on the Irish poor, which issued a report in July. It disclosed that estimates of unemployment ranged from one-fifth to one-quarter of the population, and that the resultant distress, together with the movement towards the consolidation of landholdings, had produced "'misery and suffering which no language [could] possibly describe, and which it [was] necessary to witness in order to estimate'." By way of recommendations, it urged the extension of public works projects and further amendments to the laws concerning grand juries and vestries. In response, Maurice Fitzgerald, an Irish member and one of the government's minor officers, drafted a paper and forwarded it to Wellington and Peel. He recommended the establishment of a commission to ensure that presentments for public works were properly accounted for and wisely expended, and the expediting of such works through advances of public monies. The certainty that Irish poverty would loom large in the approaching session saw Wellington and Peel give a qualified assent to this scheme. Further, reports of serious distress in Limerick, Tralee, and other places, as the supplies of potatoes were exhausted, and of attacks on stores, led the government to authorize Northumberland to spend £3,000 on food should this form of direct assistance become necessary. But the government did not long survive in the new Parliament returned in the general election following the accession of William IV. Although the miniscule electorate created by the disfranchisment of the forty-shilling freeholders had ensured that there would be no mass return of O'Connellites, a pair of government stalwarts, George Dawson and John Wilson Croker, had gone down to defeat as had two of Peel's brothers in England. Marginally weaker after the election, Wellington's overtures to both conservative and liberal Tories were rebuffed. The "Ultras" had neither forgotten nor forgiven emancipation. The Canningites, on the other hand, had little reason to think kindly of a ministry which had undertaken a determined campaign against those of them sitting for boroughs where government influence was strong. Instead, this merely strengthened their attachment to parliamentary reform against which the duke had set his face. Meanwhile, outside the House, distress and agitation had combined to produce a volatile situation to which the government appeared peculiarly insensitive. But defeat on the Civil List on 15 November brought the announcement on the following day of its intention to resign.[36]

The responsibility of governing Ireland now fell to the Whigs, who were at last ready and able to take power. Earl Grey accepted the monarch's commission. He entrusted William Lamb, Lord Melbourne, with the portfolio of home secretary. It was a challenging assignment, for the new government was confronted by industrial and agricultural unrest in Britain as well as by agitation and disturbance in Ireland. To implement its policy in the latter country, Grey sent Anglesey back to Dublin accompanied by one of the party's cleverest and most promising young men, E.G. Stanley. Liberal ideas balanced by devotion to the Established Church and a faith in strong government appeared to be the ideal qualifications for the post of chief secretary and to guarantee effectiveness in dealing with both sides of the sectarian divide. The two men carried with them instructions to pursue a policy of conciliation by exhibiting impartiality in the administration of justice, in the conferral of honours, and in appointments to places of trust and power. They were directed to consider fully all measures which promised to diminish the suffering and raise the condition of the peasantry, and to give particular attention to the education of the poor, but to bear in mind at all times the government's commitment to economy, Their principal tasks, however, were to preserve public peace and to discourage and discountenance "in the strongest manner" the notion of repeal of the union. To assist the executive in this last endeavour the government was willing to purchase O'Connell's moderation with the "rustling of a silk gown" or an appointment to the bench, but Anglesey soon discovered that the Irishman was "*not to be had.*"[37]

"If we can allay the present fermentation upon that sadly pungent question [repeal] – If we can soften down a few of the desperate agitators (& I think we can) – If we can engage the Government at once to shew an anxious & a pressing desire, not merely to have *reports* on the wants of Ireland, but vigorously to act upon those that we already possess – If we can get a good grant to set the People to work," Anglesey wrote to Spring Rice early in December, "Then will Ireland ... set an example of industry & good humour & *true loyalty*, that shall put her neighbours to shame. But we must not lose time. She has been waiting too long." It was a tall order. Practising what he taught, Anglesey expended a great deal of energy cultivating the most important agitator. He had carefully maintained contact with O'Connell following his return to Britain from his first viceroyalty, flattering him with "the kindness of attention." So ephemeral a sentiment as gratitude did not survive the brief retention of John Doherty, an effective parliamentary tormentor of O'Connell, as solicitor general in the new executive. Anglesey quickly packed Doherty off to the bench, thus removing him "from under [O'Connell's] nose" in the Commons, and he dismissed Gregory. His removal had long been demanded by O'Connell as the "indispensable" Catholic "wing" to emancipation. "I think the sending me to Ireland (forgiving the impudence), the removal of Gregory, the displacement of the two law advisers, the one (Joy) being an Orangeman & the other (Doherty) being in personal hostility with the Arch[fiend?], will be sufficient boon to the Catholics for a time," Anglesey had optimistically written to the prime minister. He soon discovered otherwise. The popular anger O'Connell continued to direct at Doherty obliged the viceroy to place a guard on the new judge's house, while the decision to remove Gregory was the only one the great demagogue considered worthy of applause.[38]

Anglesey had sent a terse and far from gracious note of dismissal to the under-secretary on 7 December. Friends quickly wrote consolingly to the aged public servant, and Charles Flint, who administered the Irish Office in London, penned a heartfelt letter of regret at the loss of "a kind Friend and a most able Colleague." There was a question in the House, for the dismissal violated the tradition that, while removable, an under-secretary was generally retained as a matter of public convenience and because he was not supposed to be influenced by political partiality. When in reply Whigs referred to the necessity to clean out an office which "had long been a nest of partiality and party spirit," and alluded to Gregory's earlier sabotaging of liberal measures, Peel rose and made a dignified defence of his old Irish friend. From the Whigs, however, there was no mark of respect for his long years of service, and he was granted no more than a modest pension. When Peel sought to make belated amends in 1835 by appointing him an Irish privy councillor, O'Connell seized upon this minor honour to launch another personal attack on Gregory and to accuse the Tory ministry of being Orange-hued.[39]

No doubt Gregory welcomed retirement. He was nearing the end of a biblical life-span and had held demanding offices for more than thirty years. He was tired, and like Henry Goulburn, his time and thoughts had been "too much engrossed by the routine & anxieties of business." Moreover, he was surely afflicted with a sense of failure. The Ascendancy he had long personified, represented, and defended was evidently crumbling. Yet he would have been less than human had he not derived malicious pleasure from the immediate collision between Anglesey and O'Connell, which made the viceroy first attempt to suppress the repeal organization by proclamation, and then, in desperation, order the arrest of the agitator. Gregory surely interpreted O'Connell's behaviour as vindication of his own dogged opposition to emancipation. Here was proof that it had been a "stepping stone for ulterior objects." Had he known the extent of the Liberator's lengthening list of demands he would have been alarmed. By December 1830 Daniel O'Connell had informally itemized his policial agenda. He sought the repeal of the Sub-Letting and Vestries Act as well as of the union; the abolition of tolls and customs, of the Protestant monopoly of municipal corporations, and a strict inquiry into corporate property; the termination of the Charter Schools and a distribution of education grants to the different sects in proportion to their numbers; the disarming of police, except when under attack, and their gradual reduction "with a view to their total abolition"; grants of public monies for public works; and the exoneration of "the Protestant Dissenters and Catholics from the burden of the Established Church" through the reform of its temporalities.[40]

If the evident failure of emancipation to usher in an era of constitutional harmony and social peace confirmed conservatives such as William Gregory in their darkest suspicions of the ultimate aims of the Irish leaders and supporters of that cause, it also stood as an indictment of their government of Ireland. After three decades of union, the island remained an anomaly within the United Kingdom. The report of the select committee on the Irish poor provided Britons with a timely reminder of the dimensions of that problem. Ireland's economy had proven peculiarly and discouragingly resistant to that form of "progress" which held out the promise of greater prosperity, although well-informed observers may have derived some comfort from the knowledge that the Scots had taken three-quarters of a century to capitalize upon the advantages extended to them in 1707. In this sense, the hope that Ireland would also eventually prosper from an economic development which complemented Britain's was not entirely illusory. Her abundant supply of cheap labour was a valuable industrial asset, one which offset her shortage of certain raw materials, and Belfast continued to expand as a manufacturing centre. The prospects in the southern provinces were far less cheering, however, and some Irishmen attributed the erosion of the industrial base there to the progressive loss of protection from British competition which was one consequence of union. Alternatively, it has been suggested that an industrial revolution was frustrated by the survival of a peasant society "still half immersed in tribalism, dominated by near-feudal or alien landlords, remote and often absentee, and almost completely without the varied prosperous, energetic 'middle ranks' which characterized Anglo-Saxon society in England, the Scottish Lowlands and the Ulster plantation."[41]

Recognizing the crucial importance of agriculture to the Irish economy and society, the central government did attempt to foster its development and improvement. The Corn Laws sought to prolong the boom of the war years by providing producers of cereals with a guaranteed market, thereby making investment in farming an attractive proposition. But prosperity proved elusive in a period of depressed prices. Another problem was the fragmentation of landholdings, which at the time was generally equated with inefficiency. More small farmers survived the agricultural revolution in England than contemporaries assumed, and the argument for consolidation did not go unchallenged, but the degree of subdivision in Ireland was exceptional. The cure prescribed by Parliament was the Sub-letting Act. Inevitably, it heightened tensions in a society where access to land had always been an explosive issue. How would the dispossessed support themselves given the limited employment opportunities off the soil? There were calls for massive public investment in economic development. Robert Owen, William Maberly, and to a lesser extent Charles Grant, the marquess of Anglesey, and the duke of Northumberland, advocated an extraordinary measure of state intervention in Ireland. That such proposals were not adopted is scarcely surprising. Economical government was a cause whose time had come.[42]

An obsession with the size of the debt accumulated during a generation of warfare, and a determination to escape the heavy taxes of the war years, dictated a reduction in expenditures. Soon after Bonaparte's defeat, the Liverpool ministry was acutely embarrassed by Parliament's withdrawal of the income tax. Moreover, to the extent that the government's activities were limited by a contraction of the financial means at its disposal, so would the doctrines of political economy be faithfully adhered to. The avoidance of state intervention was the very basis of the creed, as was the inutility of artificial stimulation of the economy. This was the gist of the reply Liverpool gave to an Irish delegation which came to London in search of assistance. Nor were he and his ministers unmindful of the British implications of extending aid to Ireland. During the recurrent depressions which afflicted industry, British manufacturers might demand the same treatment for their ills. In any event, the government believed that Ireland had been treated with generosity. One commentator estimated that during the first sixteen years of the union parliamentary grants to encourage manufacturing and industry, and in aid of public works and employment, had totalled almost £2,500,000. And Peel later documented for Anglesey a record of public investment in Ireland which to his mind disproved the charge that she had been treated less generously than had Scotland.[43]

The impossibility of a government creating "funds where a whole nation is in want" had been acknowledged by the liberal and sympathetic Charles Grant, and fear of the expense which would be incurred helped to discourage thoughts of erecting in Ireland a safety net for the poor similar to the one which was in place in Britain. But inaction had found powerful intellectual support in the Malthusian analysis of poverty. Convinced that Ireland was already overpopulated, politicians feared that the Poor Law as then administered would only produce an even more abject poverty. A possible solution, though Malthus was sceptical of its value, was state-assisted emigration. Here again, expense quickly emerged as a restrictive factor. Significantly, the most consistent champion of such schemes argued that removal of a portion of the island's redundant population was an essential preliminary to the investment of capital. For there was broad agreement that private capital was the only key which would unlock the door to development and prosperity. Capital "to till the soil ... to clear the bogs, to convert its wastes into valuable flax fields, to drain its morasses and lakes, to render its water-power available to manufactures, to work its rich mines, to obtain from the ocean stores of food, [and] to provide remunerative employment for labour." And one reason for the government's swift resort to coercion to suppress Irish disorders was its anxiety to convince capitalists that their investments would be secure.[44]

The exceptional lawlessness and savagery of Irish society was a British conviction by 1830. Ironically, that year saw English industrial workers and agricultural labourers engage in another wave of demonstrations against their conditions. Striking spinners paraded through the streets of Manchester carrying arms and clubs. In southern and eastern counties, farm workers protested the competition of cheap Irish labour, depressed wages, and tithe charges with threatening letters, cattle houghings, arson, and attacks on Irishmen. Yet as extensive and persistent as these particular disturbances proved to be, disorders on this scale remained in England the exception whereas in Ireland they appeared to be the rule. Indeed, the essential passivity of the English smallholder in the face of his reduction to the rank of labourer has been explained in terms of the "evolutionary nature" of a process which had resulted by 1800 in the virtual disappearance of the subsistence or near-subsistence farmer from the English countryside. Was the violence in Ireland attributable to the fact that a large peasant population, and even the growing numbers of labourers, had a much stronger concept of having owned land?[45]

The British have been accused of misreading Irish economic and social resistance as a political challenge, but those persons responsible for Ireland's government early in the nineteenth century ought, perhaps, to be forgiven this error. The rebellion of 1798 and Emmet's conspiracy of 1803, the activities of the Ribbonmen, the adoption of Ribbon-like oaths by some of the agrarian secret societies, even the Catholic Association's frankly nationalistic appeal and strong undercurrent of hostility towards England, all encouraged this misinterpretation. Further, it made more palatable the employment of extraordinary measures of control which few Britons regarded with pride. Charles Grant both expressed and tapped a longing to see Ireland administered under the ordinary law only. The resort to coercion reflected a conviction that the first duty of government was to assert the authority of the law. Beyond this, only if assured of their personal safety could Irish gentlemen be expected to reside on their estates. Many conservatives attributed to the influence of the resident gentry the "moral superiority" of the English countryside over that of Ireland. A peaceful Ireland would be more readily "civilized." Thus the government not only made use of such traditional weapons as the Insurrection Act and the military but also experimented with a powerful police and stipendiary magistrates.[46]

Coercion was often a preliminary to rather than a substitute for conciliation. At times of acute distress and threatened famine the government shrugged off the restraints of political economy. In 1817 and 1822 substantial relief programs were organized, while recurrent epidemics of fever led to the introduction of measures to improve public health. A number of the grievances of the Irish poor were redressed. Visitors to Ireland, and select committee investigations of the state of the island, stressed the necessity to convince the peasants that the law was not their enemy. That endeavour involved the reform of a system which all too often had been administered in a partisan, bigoted, or corrupt manner. The magistracy was purged but not purified, petty sessions established, assistant barristers appointed as chairmen of quarter sessions, the apointment of sheriffs better regulated, and the misconduct of sub-sheriffs investigated. Simultaneously, public support for education was increased in the belief that Irishmen could be taught docility. Unhappily, the schools became another battleground of sectarianism. Steps were also taken to control grand jury presentments, check abuses of the vestry cess, and lighten somewhat the burden of the tithe. Significant as several of these measures were, and they did amount to a distinctive regional policy for Ireland, the conduct of the central government had clearly been reactive rather than deliberate. Not that its failure to formulate a coherent social policy was in any sense remarkable. Although much was known about the condition of her people, there was at this time no "systematic collection of social facts." Select committees were developing into powerful vehicles of reform but neither the Home Office nor that of the chief secretary possessed the personnel to comb the parliamentary papers for the wealth of evidence they contained, and then to correlate it. The bureaucracy was rudimentary at best. Furthermore, the traditional notion that measures of social policy were the province of individual members of Parliament rather than of the government still held sway. Nevertheless, one perceptive contemporary analyst of that country's disturbances was of the opinion that "the plan of administration pursued since the Union has at least prevented the existence of such widespread discontent and disaffection as prevailed in Ireland at the end of the last century."[47]

Unfortunately, the confusion over policy was most evident on the fundamental issue of emancipation. Royal hostility to any concession, and internal differences, obliged the cabinet to take refuge in a collective neutrality which permitted individuals to speak and vote their consciences in Parliament. This expedient was the source of some embarrassment to an Irish executive whose senior officers were united in opposition to Catholic claims, at least until 1818. From that date the central government experimented with unmatched pairs of liberal and conservative viceroys and chief secretaries. What would result from this "disheartening folly" of coupling together "a friend and an enemy to toleration, like fat and lean rabbits, or the man and his wife in a Dutch toy," Lord Grenville asked? Disagreement on so important a question naturally fostered mutual distrust which impaired administrative effectiveness.

The government's inability to take a stand meant that the crucial question of emancipation would fester for more than a decade. During that period the arguments of die-hard Protestants were held up to inspection and not infrequently to ridicule. They were accused of having in their minds "an indistinct feeling" that Catholics were dangerous persons, who, because of their alleged divided allegiance, would if given the opportunity subvert the Established Church. "That six millions of persons, not having the powers of government in their hands, should convert or conquer twelve millions, does not seem a very probable contingency," one radical critic mockingly observed. This commentary did less than justice to the case of those opponents of emancipation who were concerned that the admission of Catholics to the full rights of citizenship would eventually lead to an erosion of the Protestant foundations of the State. The fear of Catholics was most marked among the Irish fraction of the Protestant majority. Difficult and even embarrassing allies, they were encouraged to look to the British connection rather than to themselves for protection and security. But attachment to the union served only to widen the gulf which already separated them from the mass of their countrymen. For one consequence of the delay in conceding emancipation was the creation in Ireland of a new spirit of nationalism. By the 1830s a group of Gaelic revivalists was beginning to emerge, whose purpose was to redefine "Irish identity in uncompromising anti-British terms." The more moderate O'Connell, meanwhile, was continuing to agitate for repeal of the union. How different was this situation from that in Scotland, where not even the Jacobins of the 1790s had adopted a nationalist position. Thus Peel's claim that the enactment of relief had completed Ireland's assimilation into the United Kingdom, that in future she would be looked upon "as England or Scotland," did not bear close examination. Irish exceptionalism continued to shape policy long after the era of emancipation.[48]

# Notes

## INTRODUCTION

1 Karl S. Bottigheimer, *English Money and Irish Land: The 'Adventurers' in the Cromwellian Settlement of Ireland* (Oxford 1971), 7, 11.
2 Patrick O'Farrell, *England and Ireland since 1800* (London 1975), 5.
3 *Speeches of William Pitt*, 4 vols. (London 1806), 3: 402, 394–5.
4 *Ibid.*, 354, 379, 396.
5 George Cornewall Lewis, *On Local Disturbances in Ireland and on the Irish Church Question* (London 1836), 39; W. Kirk, "Cores and Peripheries: The Problems of Regional Inequality in the Development of Southern Asia," *Geography* 66 (1981): 190; Brian W. Ilbery, "Core-Periphery Contrasts in European Social Well-Being," *Geography* 69 (1984): 290; see also Robert J. Hind, "The Internal Colonial Concept," *Comparative Studies in Society and History* 26 (1984): 543–68; Michael Hechter, *Internal Colonialism: The Celtic Fringe in British National Development, 1536–1966* (London 1975).
6 Hechter, *Internal Colonialism*, 73, 9, 33, 43; A.W. Orridge, "Uneven Development and Nationalism: 2," *Political Studies* 29 (1981): 188; Colin H. Williams, ed., *National Separatism* (Vancouver 1982), 159; J.A. Froude, *The English in Ireland in the Eighteenth Century*, 3 vols. (London 1974), 3: 497–8; Michael Hechter, "Internal Colonialism Revisited," in Edward A. Tiryakian and Ronald Rogowski, eds., *New Nationalism of the Developed West* (Boston 1985), 21; see also Colin H. Williams, "Cultural Nationalism in Wales," *Canadian Review of Studies in Nationalism* 4 (1976): 15–37.
7 Hind, *Comparative Studies in Society and History* 26: 553; for a recent examination of regional complexities see Munroe Eagles, "The Neglected Regional Dimension in Scottish Ethnic Nationalism," *Canadian Review of Studies in Nationalism* 12 (1985): 81–98; J.C. Beckett, *The Anglo-Irish Tradition* (London 1976), 85–9; Homer L. Catkin, "For and Against the Union," *Eire-Ireland* 13 (1978): 22–33; G.C. Bolton, *The Passing of the Irish Act of Union: A Study in*

*Parliamentary Politics* (Oxford 1966), 78–81, 67.

8 Oliver MacDonagh, *Sates of Mind: A Study of Anglo-Irish Conflict 1790–1980*, pb ed. (London 1985), 38, 90; Oliver MacDonagh, *Ireland: The Union and Its Aftermath*, rev. ed. (London 1977), 33.

9 MacDonagh, *Union*, 18; Froude, *English in Ireland*, 3: 490; Patrick O'Farrell, *Ireland's English Question: Anglo-Irish Relations 1534–1970* (London 1971), 69–70; Redcliffe N. Salaman, *The History and Social Influence of the Potato*, rev. ed. (Cambridge 1985), 288; J.W. Croker, *Commentaries on National Policy and Ireland* (Dublin 1831), 55–9.

10 Norman Gash, *Aristocracy and People: Britain 1815–1865*, rev. ed. (London 1983), 53.

CHAPTER ONE

1 See John Bohstedt, *Riots and Community Politics in England and Wales 1790–1810* (Cambridge, Mass. 1983); R. Quinault and J. Stevenson, *Popular Protest and Public Order: Six Studies in British History 1790–1920* (London 1974); John Stevenson, *Popular Disturbances in England 1700–1870* (London 1979); Roy Porter, *English Society in the Eighteenth Century* (Harmondsworth 1982), 116–17.

2 Stevenson, *Popular Disturbances in England*, 105; Ian R. Christie, *Stress and Stability in Late Eighteenth Century Britain: Reflections on the British Avoidance of Revolution* (Oxford 1984), 35–6; James Walvin, *English Urban Life 1776–1851* (London 1984), 124; Clive Emsley, *British Society and the French Wars 1793–1815* (London 1979), 13; R.W. Harris, *Romanticism and the Social Order 1780–1830* (New York 1969), 67–9; George Rudé, *Ideology and Popular Protest* (New York 1980), 135–8; P.J. Corfield, *The Impact of English Towns 1700–1800* (London 1982), 86–7, 130–4, 165; see also E.P. Thompson, "The Moral Economy of the English Crowd in the Eighteenth Century," *Past and Present* 50 (1971): 76–136; E.J. Hobsbawm, *Primitive Rebels: Studies in Archaic Forms of Social Movements in the 19th and 20th Centuries*, pb ed. (New York 1965), 108–25.

3 Emsley, *British Society*, 43–9, 85; Christie, *Stress and Stability*, 154–5; Porter, *English Society*, 336; Corfield, *Impact of English Towns*, 145; George Rudé, *Criminal and Victim: Crime and Society in Early Nineteenth-Century England* (Oxford 1985), 10, 28–30; Clive Emsley, *Crime and Society in England 1750–1900* (London 1987), 27–31, 52–3, 158–9, 170–80; L.G. Boyd, "The Role of the Military in Civil Disorders in England and Wales, 1780–1811," (PHD thesis, University of Tennessee, 1977); Stevenson, *Popular Disturbances in England*, 142; see also Malcolm I. Thomis and Peter Holt, *Threats of Revolution in Britain 1789–1848* (London 1977); J.M. Beattie, "The Pattern of Crime in England 1660–1800," *Past and Present* 62 (1974): 47–95.

4 Glenn R. Hueckel, *The Napoleonic Wars and Their Impact on Factor Returns*

*and Output Growth in England 1793–1815* (New York 1985), vii–xi; W.H. O'Neill, *The Pursuit of Power: Technology, Armed Force, and Society since A.D. 1000* (Chicago 1982), 211–13; A.D. Harvey, *Britain in the Early Nineteenth Century* (New York 1978), 334; Pamela Horn, *The Rural World 1780–1850: Social Change in the English Countryside* (London 1980), 13; Corfield, *Impact of English Towns*, 2; see also N.F.R. Crafts, "British Economic Growth, 1700–1831: A Review of the Evidence," *Economic History Review* 36 (1983): 177–99.

5 See John Rule, *The Labouring Classes in Early Industrial England 1750–1850* (London 1986), 76–81; Horn, *Rural World*, 32; Phyllis Deane, *The First Industrial Revolution* (Cambridge 1969), 10; Roger A.E. Wells, "The Development of an English Rural Proletariat and Social Protest, 1700–1850," *Journal of Peasant Studies* 6 (1979) 117; Eric J. Evans, *The Forging of the Modern State: Early Industrial Britain 1783–1870* (London 1983), 9, 138–9; Salaman, *History of the Potato*, 462.

6 See Christie, *Stress and Stability*, 94–116; Anne Digby, *The Poor Law in Nineteenth-Century England and Wales* (London 1982), 6–8; Horn, *Rural World*, 48–9; the extent of the "Speenhamland system" remains a matter of historical dispute; see also J.D. Marshall, *The Old Poor Law, 1795–1834* (London 1968); J.D. Chambers and G. Mingay, *The Agricultural Revolution 1750–1850* (London 1966); 119–20; see Peter Dunkley, "Paternalism, the Magistracy and Poor Relief in England, 1795–1834," *International Review of Social History* 24 (1979): 371–97; Oliver MacDonagh, *Early Victorian Government 1830–1870* (London 1977), 98; David Roberts, *Paternalism in Early Victorian England* (New Brunswick, NJ 1979), 5–6; Porter, *English Society*, 110; Harold Perkin, *Origins of Modern English Society*, pb ed. (London 1985), 22.

7 See E.R. Norman, *Church and Society in England 1770–1970* (Oxford 1976), 16–19, 21–3, 36; Donald Greene, "The Via Media in an Age of Revolution: Anglicanism in the 18th Century," in Peter Hughes and David Williams, eds., *The Varied Patterns: Studies in the Eighteenth Century* (Toronto 1971), 297–320; S.C. Carpenter, *Church and People 1789–1889* (London 1933), 27; L.E. Elliot-Binns, *Religion in the Victorian Era* (Greenwhich, Conn. 1953), 39–43; W.R. Ward, *Religion and Society in England 1790–1850* (London 1972), 9–10; Eric J. Evans, "Some Reasons for the Growth of English Rural Anticlericalism c1750–c1850" *Past and Present* 66 (1975): 94–100; Peter Mandler, "The Making of the New Poor Law *Redivivus*," *Past and Present* 117 (1987): 140; Evans, *Forging of the Modern State*, 48–9; Corfield, *Impact of English Towns*, 139.

8 Norman, *Church and Society*, 38; Harris, *Romanticism*, 127, 141; F.K. Brown, *Fathers of the Victorians* (Cambridge 1961), 26–7, 37; see also G.F.A. Best, "The Evangelicals and the Established Church in the Early Nineteenth Century," *Journal of Theological Studies* n.s. 10 (1959): 63–78.

9 Brown, *Fathers of Victorians*, 7; Ernest Marshall Howse, *Saints in Politics: The*

'Clapham Sect' and the Growth of Freedom (Toronto 1952), 7, 127–9; Carpenter, Church and People, 42; Harris, Romanticism, 129–30.

10 Harvey, Britain in Early Nineteenth Century, 106, 76–7; Elliot-Binns, Religion in Victorian Era, 23; Porter, English Society, 313; Howse, Saints in Politics, 114.

11 Brian Simon, Studies in the History of Education 1780–1870 (London 1960), 45–6, 136, 126; Howse, Saints in Politics, 95–7; Porter, English Society, 314–16; Brown, Fathers of Victorians, 123–34, 134–5; Rule, Labouring Classes, 232; Frank Witson Fetter, The Economist in Parliament 1780–1868 (Durham, NC 1980), 137; Sydney Checkland, British Public Policy 1776–1939: An Economic, Social and Political Perspective (Cambridge 1983), 99.

12 Ford, Fathers of Victorians, 230–1; David Hempton, Methodism and Politics in British Society 1750–1850 (London 1984), 15, 48–9; Hobsbawm, Primitive Rebels, 129; V. Kiernan, "Evangelicalism and the French Revolution," Past and Present 1 (1952): 54; see also Christie, Stress and Stability, 187–213; J.M. Golby and A.W. Purdue, The Civilization of the Crowd: Popular Culture in England 1750–1900 (London 1984), 51ff.

13 Emsley, British Society, 153–5; Frank Ongley Darvall, Popular Disturbances and Political Order in Regency England (reprint, New York 1969), 3–7, 260; Donald Low, 'That Sunny Dome': A Portrait of Regency Britain (Toronto 1971), 52–9; for the modern debate on the revolutionary motivation of the English lower orders see E.P. Thompson, The Making of the English Working Class, rev. ed. (London 1968), and Craig Calhoun, The Question of Class Struggle: Social Foundations of Popular Radicalism during the Industrial Revolution (Chicago 1982).

14 R.B. McDowell, Ireland in the Age of Imperialism and Revolution 1760–1801 (Oxford 1979), 330–7; Canning's Speeches, 1: 119–51, 202–37.

15 See T.C. Smout, "The Anglo-Scottish Union of 1707: 1. The Economic Background ," Economic History Review 2nd ser. 16 (1963–4): 455–67; R.H. Campbell, Scotland since 1707: The Rise of an Industrial Society, 2nd ed. (Edinburgh 1985), 6ff; L.E. Cochran, Scottish Trade with Ireland in the Eighteenth Century (Edinburgh 1985), 8, 1; Checkland, British Public Policy, 35; T.M. Devine and David Dickson, Ireland and Scotland 1600–1850: Parallels and Contrasts in Economic and Social Development (Edinburgh 1983), 12–14.

16 Hind, Comparative Studies in Society and History 26: 548; Devine and Dickson, Ireland and Scotland, 14–18; for a radical analysis of Ireland's colonial economic relationship to Britain see Colm Anthony Regan, "Colonialism and Dependent Development in Ireland," (PHD thesis, McGill University, 1980).

17 See McDowell, Ireland in Imperialism and Revolution, 4–5, 14–15, 18–20; L.M. Cullen, An Economic History of Ireland since 1660 (London 1972), 90–7; L.M. Cullen, "Eighteenth-Century Flour Milling in Ireland," Irish Economic and Social History (4 (1977): 5–25; thesis abstract, Irish Economic and Social History 7 (1980): 93–4; L.M. Cullen, "Problems in the Interpretation and Re-

vision of Eighteenth-Century Irish Economic History," *Transactions of the Royal Historical Society* 5 ser. 17 (1967): 1–22; L.M. Cullen, *Anglo-Irish Trade 1660–1800* (New York 1968), 56, 206; David R. Schweitzer, "The Failure of William Pitt's Irish Trade Propositions 1785," *Parliamentary History* 3 (1984): 129–45; Patrick Flanagan, "Markets and Fairs in Ireland, 1600–1800," *Journal of Historical Geography* 11 (1985): 373.

18 Kerby A. Miller, *Emigrants and Exiles: Ireland and the Irish Exodus to North America* (New York 1985), 32; Cochran, *Scottish Trade with Ireland*, 42–9, 162; Cullen, *Anglo-Irish Trade*, 214; James D. Cockcroft, André Gunder Frank, and Dale L. Johnson, *Dependence and Underdevelopment: Latin America's Political Economy* (New York 1972, 12; for a brief but extreme statement of the dependency conspiracy see Richard Ned Lebow, *White Britain and Black Ireland: The Influence of Stereotypes on Colonial Policy* (Philadelphia 1976), 89, 96.

19 James Warner O'Neill, "Popular Culture and Peasant Rebellion in Pre-Famine Ireland," (PHD thesis, University of Minnesota, 1984), 57–8, 108; Cullen, *Anglo-Irish Trade*, 67, 47; Cochran, *Scottish Trade with Ireland*, 98–9; see also K.H. Connell, *The Population of Ireland 1750–1845* (Oxford 1950); D. Grigg, "Modern Population Growth in Historical Perspective," *Geography* 62 (1982): 97–108; L.A. Clarkson, "Irish Population Revisited, 1687–1821," in J.M. Goldstrom and L.A. Clarkson, *Irish Population, Economy, and Society Essays in Honour of the late K.H. Connell* (Oxford 1981): 13–35; N.L. Tranter, *Population and Society 1750–1940: Contrasts in Population Growth* (London 1985), 50; Stuart Daultry, David Dickson, and Cormac O'Grada, "Eighteenth-Century Irish Population: New Perspectives from Old Sources," *Journal of Economic History* 41 (1981): 601; B.R. Mitchell, *Abstract of British Historical Statistics* (Cambridge 1962); Rule, *Labouring Classes*, 8.

20 Samuel Clark and James S. Donnelly, Jr, eds., *Irish Peasants Violence and Political Unrest 1780–1914* (Manchester 1983), 29; Joe Mokyr, *Why Ireland Starved: A Quantitative and Analytical History of the Irish Economy 1800–1850* (Boston 1983), 114, 287; McDowell, *Ireland in Imperialism and Revolution*, 10–11; Cullen, *Economic History since 1660*, 52–4; Edith May Johnston, *Ireland in the Eighteenth Century* (Dublin 1974), 87; Salaman, *History of the Potato*, 286.

21 F.M.L. Thompson, *English Landed Society in the Nineteenth Century*, pb ed. (London 1980), 215; Cullen, *Economic History since 1660*, 100–101; O'Neill, "Popular Culture and Peasant Rebellion," 40, 80.

22 Grattan quoted by George O'Brien, *Economic History of Ireland from the Union to the Famine* (New York 1921), 569; Lord Cloncurry, *Personal Recollections of the Life and Times* (Dublin 1849), 216–17; McDowell, *Ireland in Imperialism and Revolution*, 34–5; *Quarterly Review* 15 (1812): 185.

23 Edward Wakefield, *An Account of Ireland Statistical and Political*, 2 vols. (London 1813), 1: 38–43; O'Brien, *Economic History from Union*, 453; R.M.

Martin, *Ireland before and after the Union with Great Britain*, 3rd ed. (London 1848), 85.

24  W.H. Lecky, *A History of Ireland in the Eighteenth Century*, 5 vols. (reprint, St. Clair Shores 1972), 5: 106–7; Clark and Donnelly, *Irish Peasants*, 58–9; McDowell, *Ireland in Imperialism and Revolution*, 499–501; O'Brien, *Economic History from Union*, 459.

25  O'Brien, *Economic History from Union*, 419, 343–9; R.B. McDowell, *Public Opinion and Government Policy, 1801–1846* (London 1952), 36; Hind, *Comparative Studies in Society and History* 26: 556–8; Patrick Lynch and John Vaizey, *Guinness's Brewery in the Irish Economy 1759–1876* (Cambridge 1960), 119–24; Martin, *Ireland before and after Union*, 78, 158; Mokyr, *Why Ireland Starved*, 289.

26  O'Brien, *Economic History from Union*, 44–9; McDowell, *Ireland in Imperialism and Revolution*, 501; Joseph Lee, "The Dual Economy in Ireland, 1800–50," in T.D. Williams, ed., *Historical Studies* (Dublin 1971), 197; O'Neill, "Popular culture and Peasant Rebellion," 81, 90; Marianne Elliot, *Partners in Revolution: The United Irishmen and France* (London 1982), 354.

27  Cullen, *Anglo-Irish Trade*, 22; Connell, *Population of Ireland*, 86–8; Terence Burke, "County Cork in the Eighteenth Century," *Geographical Review* 64 (1974): 64; McDowell, *Ireland in Imperialism and Revolution*, 38; S.J. Connelly, *Priests and People in Pre-Famine Ireland 1780–1845* (New York 1982), 25–8; Maureen Wall, "The Rise of a Catholic Middle Class in Eighteenth-century Ireland," *Irish Historical Studies* 11 (1958): 91–115; Clark and Donnelly, *Irish Peasants*, 27; Regan, "Colonialism and Dependent Development," 213.

28  James Hall, *Tour through Ireland*, 2 vols. (London 1813), 2: 288; Cullen, *Economic History since 1660*, 71; M.R. Beames, *Peasants and Power: The Whiteboy Movement* (New York 1983), 2–3; Mokyr, *Why Ireland Starved*, 6; Cochran, *Scottish Trade with Ireland*, 38; J.C. Curwen, M.P., *Observations on the State of Ireland Principally directed to its Agriculture and Rural Population*, 2 vols (London 1818), 1: 110–11.

29  Clark and Donnelly, *Irish Peasants*, 6–7; Mokyr *Why Ireland Starved*, 123, 140; Kevin O'Neill, *Family and Farm in Pre-Famine Ireland: The Parish of Killashandra* (Madison 1984), 15; Roger Wells, *Insurrection: The British Experience 1795–1803* (Gloucester 1983), 4.

30  *Edinburgh Review* 20 (1812): 354; see also Gale E. Christianson, "Landlords and Land Tenure in Ireland, 1790–1830," *Eire-Ireland* 9 (1974): 25–58; O'Neill, "Popular Culture and Peasant Rebellion," 245, 266; David Large, "The Wealth of the Greater Irish Landowners, 1750–1815," *Irish Historical Studies* 15 (1966): 21–45.

31  McDowell, *Ireland in Imperialism and Revolution*, 105–7; Curwen, *Observations*, 1:152.

32  Travis L. Crosby, *English Farmers and The Politics of Protection* (Hassocks 1977), 15; Eric J. Evans, *The Contentious Tithe: The Tithe Problem and English*

*Agriculture, 1750–1850* (London 1976); W.R. Ward, "The Tithe Question in the Early Nineteenth Century," *Journal of Ecclesiastical History* 15 (1964): 67–81; Evans, *Past and Present* 66: 90–1; Fetter, *Economist in Parliament*, 168; Donald Harmon Akenson, *The Church of Ireland: Ecclesiastical Reform and Revolution, 1800–1885* (New Haven 1971), 102; Clark and Donnelly, *Irish Peasants*, 30; McDowell, *Ireland in Imperialism and Revolution*, 167.

33 Akenson, *Church of Ireland*, 5, 10, 60, 81, 89; McDowell, *Ireland in Imperialism and Revolution*, 161, 169–70.

34 McDowell, *Ireland in Imperialism and Revolution*, 201, 204–5; Akenson, *Church of Ireland*, 132–9; Desmond Bowen, *The Protestant Crusade in Ireland, 1800–70* (Montreal 1978); McDowell, *Public Opinion and Government Policy*, 30–1; Connolly, *Priests and People*, 75.

35 McDowell, *Ireland in Imperialism and Revolution*, 194–5; Connolly, *Priests and People*, 9, 34–5, 69–71, 149, 155–61, 226–56.

36 Connolly, *Priests and People*, 244–8; J.A. Murphy, "The Support of the Catholic Clergy in Ireland, 1750–1850," in J.L. McCracken, ed., *Historical Studies* 5 (London 1965): 103–16.

37 Curwen, *Observations*, 1: 301; Murphy *Historical Studies*, 5: 110; Connell, *Population of Ireland*, 59; Hall, *Tour through Ireland*, 2: 268–9; O'Brien, *Economic History from Union*, 139; Mokyr, *Why Ireland Starved*, 116.

38 McDowell, *Ireland in Imperialism and Revolution*, 53, 58–9; R.B. McDowell, *The Irish Administration, 1801–1914* (Toronto 1964), 165; O'Brien, *Economic History from Union*, 162–4; Christie, *Stress and Stability*, 118–20.

39 See T. Desmond Williams, ed., *Secret Societies in Ireland* (Dublin 1973); Clark and Donnelly, *Irish Peasants*, 144–7; Samuel Clark, *Social Origins of the Irish Land War* (Princeton 1979), 66–85; Beames, *Peasants and Power*, 24ff; Gale E. Christianson, "Secret Societies and Agrarian Violence in Ireland," *Agriculturel History* 46 (1972): 369–84; David Leahy, *An Abstract of Evidence taken before the Committee of the House of Lords upon the State of Crime in Ireland* (London 1839), 76, 3; Lewis, *On Local Disturbances*, 99, 124, 250, 78, 49–50, 307, 90; for definitions of peasantry see Wells, *Journal of Peasant Studies* 6: 115, and Golby and Purdue, *Civilization of the Crowd*, 20–1; Carlo Geneletti, "The Political Orientation of Agrarian Classes: A Theory," *Archives: European Journal of Sociology* 17 (1976): 67; D. Frances Ferguson, "Rural/Urban Relations and Peasant Radicalism: A Preliminary Statement," *Comparative Studies in Society and History* 28 (1976): 106–18.

40 Lewis, *On Local Disturbances*, 307, 154; see also David Fitzpatrick, "Unrest in Rural Ireland," *Irish Economic and Social History* 12 (1985): 98–105.

41 Defender oath quoted by Miller, *Emigrants and Exiles*, 184; *Reports from Committees of the House of Commons*, 10: 1785–1801 (London 1803): 833; Tom Garvin, "Defenders, Ribbonmen and Others: Underground Political Networks in Pre-Famine Ireland," *Past and Present* 34 (1982): 143; Tom Garvin, *The Evolution of Nationalist Politics* (Dublin 1981), 27–9; Connolly, *Priests and*

*People*, 12; Lecky, *Ireland*, 4: 434; see also Marianne Elliott, "The Origins and Transformation of Early Irish Republicanism," *International Review of Social History* 23 (1978): 405–28.

42 Garvin, *Evolution of Nationalist Politics*, 33–5, 36, 16–17; Lewis, *On Local Disturbances*, 161; Leahy, *Abstract of Evidence*, 74–5; T. Brown, "Nationalism and the Irish Peasant 1800–1848," *The Review of Politics* 15 (1953): 423–4; Garvin, *Past and Present* 34: 144–5; Elliot, *Partners in Revolution*, 341; see also Clark and Donnelly, *Irish Peasants*, 64–99.

43 Hereward Senior, *Orangeism in Ireland and Britain, 1795–1836* (New York 1966), 188.

44 Thompson, *English Landed Society*, 111; L.P. Curtis, jr, ed. W.H. Lecky, *History of Ireland in the Eighteenth Century* (Chicago 1972), 214; Beames, *Peasants and Power*, 167–8, 140–1; Williams, *Secret Societies*, 24; McDowell, *Ireland in Imperialism and Revolution*, 62–3, 66–7, 77; Fitzpatrick, *Irish Economic and Social History* 12: 100.

45 Christie, *Stress and Stability*, 156; A.W. Smith, "Irish Rebels and English Radicals 1798–1820," *Past and Present* 7 (1953): 78–85; Emsley, *British Society*, 95; McDowell, *Ireland in Imperialism and Revolution*, 494–5; Evans, *Forging of the Modern State*, 72–3; Darvall, *Popular Disturbances*, 52.

46 David Hay, Peter Linebaugh, E.P. Thompson, *Albion's Fated Tree: Crime and Society in Eighteenth-Century England* (London 1975), 55; see also Wells, *Journal of Peasant Studies* 6: 115–39; Kenneth Logue, *Popular Disturbances in Scotland 1780–1815* (Edinburgh 1979); Quinault and Stevenson, *Popular Protest*, 75; John Prebble, *The Highland Clearances*, pb ed. (Harmondsworth 1982); Thompson, *English Landed Society*, 203; Rosalind Mitchison, "The Making of the Old Scottish Poor Law," *Past and Present* 63 (1974): 58–93; R.A. Gage, "Debate: The Making of the Old Scottish Poor Law," *Past and Present* 69 (1975): 113–18; and Rosalind Mitchison, "A Rejoinder," *Past and Present* 69 (1975): 119–21.

47 John McLeish, *Evangelical Religion and Popular Education: A Modern Interpretation* (London 1969), 84, 8, 29; Salaman, *History of the Potato*, 412, 416–17; David J.V. Jones, *Before Rebecca: Popular Protests in Wales 1793–1835* (London 1973), 30, 63; Corfield, *Impact of English Towns*, 14; David W. Howell, *Land and People in Nineteenth-Century Wales* (London 1977), 10; David W. Howell, "The Agricultural Labourer in Nineteenth Century Wales," *Welsh History Review* 6 (1972–73): 275–6; R.J. Colyer, "The Gentry and the County in Nineteenth-Century Cardiganshire," *Welsh History Review* 10 (1981): 497–8; see also B.F. Howells, "Society in Early Modern Wales," in S. Dyrvik, K. Myklund, and J. Oldervold, eds. *The Satellite State in the 17th and 18th Centuries* (Bergen 1979): 80–98.

48 Charles Townshend, *Political Violence in Ireland: Government and Resistance since 1848* (Oxford 1983), 22; William N. Sloan, "Ethnicity or Imperialism? A Review Article," *Comparative Studies in Society and History* 21 (1979): 124;

Connolly, *Priests and People*, 219; Tocqueville quoted, ibid., 1; Wakefield, *Account of Ireland*, 2: 760; Curwen, *Observations*, 1: 4; *Edinburgh Review*, 20 (1812): 349.

49 Wakefield, *Account of Ireland*, 1: 836–7.

50 George Nicholls, *A History of the Irish Poor Law in connexion with the Condition of the People* (London 1856), 82, 73–5; Mokyr, *Why Ireland Starved*, 6; O'Brien, *Economic History from Union*, 164–5; MacDonagh, *Early Victorian Government*, 185.

51 Mokyr, *Why Ireland Starved*, 7–10, 291; Connell, *Population of Ireland*, 60; Curwen, *Observations*, 2: 39.

52 Porter, *English Society*, 110; Crosby, *English Farmers*, 14; Marshall, *Old Poor Law*, 23; J.R. Poynter, *Society and Pauperism: English Ideas on Poor Relief, 1795–1834* (London 1969), 17, 25, xvi; A.W. Coats, "Economic Thought and Poor Law Policy in the Eighteenth Century," *Economic History Review* 2nd ser. 13 (1960–1): 41; Gertrude Himmelfarb, *The Idea of Poverty: England in the Early Industrial Age* (New York 1984), 37–41.

43 Robert L. Heilbroner, ed., *The Essential Adam Smith* (New York 1986), 166, 206; Himmelfarb, *Idea of Poverty*, 66–73; Coats, *Economic History Review* 13: 42.

54 Poynter, *Society and Pauperism*, 45–6; quoted in Himmelfarb, *Idea of Poverty*, 108, 101, 107, 114–15; Evans, *Forging of the Modern State*, 41.

55 Quoted in Himmelfarb, *Idea of Poverty*, 106, 112, 118; William Petersen, *Malthus* (Cambridge, Mass. 1979), 48, 118, 4; Poynter, *Society and Pauperism*, 156–7.

56 Poynter, *Society and Pauperism*, 173–5, xviii, 109–10; Harris, *Romanticism*, 265; George Spater, *William Cobbett The Poor Man's Friend*, 2 vols. (Cambridge 1982), 2: 553; Christine Colvin, ed., *Maria Edgeworth Letters from England 1813–1844* (Oxfrod 1971), 331; Himmelfarb, *Idea of Poverty*, 126; Howse *Saints in Politics*, 128.

57 Richard Thompson, *The Charity Commission and the Age of Reform* (London 1979), 22; Checkland, *British Public Policy*, 48; Mandler, *Past and Present* 117: 143–4; Poynter, *Society and Pauperism*, 114, 163–4, 170; Harris, *Romanticism*, 87.

58 Himmelfarb, *Idea of Poverty*, 70, 120, 130; Poynter, *Society and Pauperism*, 117, 195; Checkland, *British Public Policy*, 16–17; Evans, *Forging of Modern State*, 39; see also Arthur J. Taylor, *Laissez-faire and State Intervention in Nineteenth-century Britain* (reprint, London 1968).

59 *Edinburgh Review* 20 (1812): 360, 366; Petersen, *Malthus*, 108–9; Harris, *Romanticism*, 53; see also James O'Neill, "The British Quarterlies and the Religious Question, 1802–1829," *Catholic Historical Review* 52 (1966–7): 350–60; Ursula Henriques, *Religious Toleration in England 1787–1833* (Toronto 1961), 32–9.

60 Henriques, *Religious Toleration*, 146, 220–2; Howse, *Saints in Politics*, 132; D.N. Hempton, "The Methodist Crusade in Ireland, 1795–1845," *Irish Histor-*

*ical Studies* 22 (1980–1): 33–9; Ward, *Religion and Society*, 117–19; Hempton, *Methodism and Politics*, 36–9, 120; see also David Hempton, "Methodism in Irish Society, 1770–1830," *Transactions of the Royal Historical Society*, 5th ser., 36 (1986): 117–42.

61 See A.D. Gilbert, *Religion and Society in Industrial England: Church, Chapel, and Social Change 1740–1914* (London 1976), 27ff; John Bossy, *The English Catholic Community 1570–1850* (London 1975), 287ff; M.R.D. Leys, *Catholics in England 1559–1829: A Social History* (New York 1961), 140, 143–50.

62 O'Neill, *Catholic Historical Review*, 52: 360–1; Henriques, *Religious Toleration*, 68–82, 100–6, 133–4; G.I.T. Machin, *The Catholic Question in English Politics 1820 to 1830* (Oxford 1964), 7–9; see also G.F.A. Best, "The Protestant Constitution and Its Supporters, 1800–1829," *Transactions of the Royal Historical Society* 5th ser. 8 (1958): 105–28.

63 See Dale T. Knobel, *Paddy and the Republic Ethnicity and Nationality in the Antebellum America* (Middletown 1986), 37–40; Walter L. Arnstein, "Victorian Prejudice Reexamined," *Victorian Studies* 12 (1969): 452–7; S. Gilley, "English Attitudes to the Irish in England 1780–1900," in Colin Holmes, ed., *Immigrants and Minorities in British Society* (London 1978), 84–5, 93; Emsley, *British Society*, 67.

64 Ned Lebow, "British Historians and Irish History," *Eire-Ireland* 8 (1973): 18, 8.

65 Corfield, *Impact of English Towns*, 103–4; Senior, *Orangeism*, 156; P.D. James and T.A. Critchley, *The Maul and the Pear Tree: The Ratcliffe Highway Murders 1811* (New York 1971), 189, 200; Bohstedt, *Riots and Community Politics*, 172–3; Spater, *William Cobbett*, 2: 442; Salaman, *History of the Potato*, 121, 455; Prebble, *Highland Clearances*, 67; see also M.A.G. O'Tuathaigh, "The Irish in Nineteenth-Century Britain: Problems of Integration," *Transactions of the Royal Historical Society* 5 ser. 21 (1981): 149–83; Gilley, *Immigrants and Minorities*, 81–110.

66 See P.N. Jupp, "The Irish M.P.s at Westminster in the Early Nineteenth Century," in J.C. Beckett, ed., *Historical Studies* 7 (London 1969): 65–80.

67 Henriques, *Religious Toleration*, 138; McDowell, *Public Opinion and Government Policy*, 17, 20–1; Senior, *Orangeism*, 140; Murphy, *Historical Studies*, 5, 117–18; Oliver MacDonagh, "The Politicization of the Irish Catholic Bishops, 1800–1850," *Historical Journal* 18 (1975): 41.

68 Lecky, *Ireland*, 5, 277–9; W.M. Torrens, *Memoirs of the Right Honourable William Second Viscount Melbourne*, 2 vols. (London 1878), 1, 75; Dunn to Newport, 8 December 1806, Newport Papers, M 483/12, Public Record Office, Ireland (PROI), Dublin.

69 Bossy, *English Catholic Community*, 331–2; Elliot, *Partners in Revolution*, 354; Garvin, *Evolution of Nationalist Politics*, 46; Macdonagh, *Historical Journal* 18: 38–9; Gerard O'Brien, "The Beginning of the Veto Controversy in Ireland," *Journal of Ecclesiastical History* 38 (1987): 94; *Quarterly Review* 3 (1810): 129.

70 See Donald Groves Barnes, *George III and William Pitt, 1783–1806* (Stanford 1939), 334–69; Richard Willis, "William Pitt's Resignation in 1801: Reexamination and Document," *Bulletin of the Institute of Historical Research* 44 (1971): 239–57; Norman Gash, *Lord Liverpool* (London 1984), 37; Piers Mackesy, *War without Victory: The Downfall of Pitt 1799–1802* (Oxford 1984), 200; James J. Sack, *The Grenvillites, 1801–29: Party Politics and Factionalism in the Age of Pitt and Liverpool* (Urbana 1979), 116–19; E.A. Smith, *Whig Principles and Party Politics: Earl Fitzwilliam and the Whig Party 1748–1833* (Manchester 1975), 310–1; A.D. Harvey, "The Ministry of All the Talents: The Whigs in Office, February 1806 to March 1807," *Historical Journal* 15 (1972): 646; Ilchester, ed., *The Journal of Lady Holland (1791–1811)*, 2 vols. (London 1860), 1: 212–26; Leveson Vernon Harcourt, ed., *The Diaries and Correspondence of the Right Hon. George Rose*, 2 vols. (London 1860), 2: 324–33; Peter Jupp, *Lord Grenville 1759–1834* (Oxford 1985), 399–410; Michael Roberts, *The Whig Party, 1807–12* (London 1939), 2–3, 41–73.

71 See Frank O'Gorman, *The Emergence of the British Two-Party System 1760–1832* (London 1982), 44–60; Machin, *Catholic Question*, 13–14; Wendy Hinde, *George Canning* (New York 1973), 189–91; Emsley, *British Society*, 130.

72 Castalia, Countess Granville, ed., *Lord Granville Leveson Gower (First Earl Granville) Private Correspondence 1781 to 1821*, 2 vols. (London 1916), 2: 329–30, 336–7; Roberts, *Whig Party*, 35–9; Spencer Walpole, *The Life of the Rt. Hon. Spencer Perceval including His Correspondence with Numerous Distinguished Persons*, 2 vols. (London 1874), 1: 81; Denis Gray, *Spencer Perceval: The Evangelical Prime Minister 1762–1812* (Manchester 1963), 46–7, 49, 19; Henriques, *Religious Toleration*, 140–3; Twiss, *The Public and Private Life of Lord Eldon*, 3 vols (London 1844), 1: 432–3.

73 Gray, *Spencer Perceval*, 20–1, 146; *Life of Lord Eldon*, 2: 179–80; Power to Newport, 24 March 1812, Newport Papers, M 483/14.

74 Gash, *Lord Liverpool*, 60; see also W.R. Brock, *Lord Liverpool and Liberal Toryism 1820 to 1827*, 2nd ed. (Hamden 1967), 26–39; Charles Petrie, *Lord Liverpool and His Times* (London 1954), 56; Francis Plowden, *An Historical Review of the State of Ireland*, 3 vols. (London 1803), 3: 900.

75 R.J. White, *Waterloo to Peterloo* (London 1957), 86; Gash, *Lord Liverpool*, 63, 94–5; Charles Stuart Parker, ed., *Sir Robert Peel from His Private Papers*, 3 vols. (reprint, New York 1970), 1: 68.

76 Petrie, *Liverpool and His Times*, 63; Philip Ziegler, *Addington: A Life of Henry Addington Viscount Sidmouth* (London 1965), 28–38, 43, 52, 111, 303, 307.

77 Ziegler, *Addington*, 85–6, 157, 281–2; *Life of Eldon*, 1: 431, 435.

78 *Dublin Evening Herald*, 16 March 1812; George Pellew, *Life and Correspondence of Henry Addington 1st Viscount Sidmouth*, 3 vols. (London 1847), 3: 100–2, 109–111; Sidmouth to Richmond, 19 November 1812, Home Office (HO) 100/168, Public Record Office (PRO), London; Lord Charles Colchester, ed., *The Diary and Correspondence of Charles Abbot, Lord Colchester*, 3 vols.

(London 1861), 2: 440.

79 J.E. Cookson, *Lord Liverpool's Administration: The Crucial Years 1815–1822* (Edinburgh and London 1975), 4; Ziegler, *Addington*, 315; Townshend, *Political Violence in Ireland*, 51–2.

## CHAPTER TWO

1 G. Shawe Lefevre, *Peel and O'Connell: A Review of the Irish Policy of Parliament from the Act of Union to the death of Sir Robert Peel* (London 1887), 7; McDowell, *Irish Administration*, 72, 2–4; H. Montgomery Hyde, *The Rise of Castlereagh* (London 1933), 231; see also Wakefield, *Account of Ireland*, 2: 332ff.

2 Wakefield, *Account of Ireland*, 2: 325–7; the cost of the civil establishment in 1807 is to be found in Withworth Papers, U269/0217, Kent Archives, Maidstone; Harvey, *Historical Journal* 15: 639.

3 Wakefield, *Account of Ireland*, 2: 332; R. Barry O'Brien, *Dublin Castle and the Irish People* (Dublin 1909), 33; David R. Schweitzer, "The Whig Connection between Great Britain and Ireland, 1784–1801," (PHD thesis, University of London, 1983), 7, 335ff; McDowell, *Irish Administration*, 54; see also Edward Brynn, *Crown and Castle: British Rule of Ireland 1800–1830* (Dublin 1978).

4 See Edith M. Johnston, *Great Britain and Ireland 1760–1800: A Study in Political Administration* (St Andrews 1963), 35–54; McDowell, *Irish Administration*, 56–7; R.B. McDowell, "The Irish Executive in the Nineteenth Century," *Irish Historical Studies* 9 (1954–5): 264–80; C. Bartlett, *Castlereagh* (London 1966), 18.

5 See Johnston, *Great Britain and Ireland*, 57–61; A.P.W. Malcomson, *John Foster: The Politics of Anglo-Irish Ascendancy* (Oxford 1978), 193; Hyde, *Rise of Castlereagh*, 219; McDowell, *Irish Administration*, 63.

6 Gregory to Leveson Gower, 18 February 1829, British Library (BL) Add. Ms. 40336; see also John F. M'Lennan, *Memoirs of Thomas Drummond Under Secretary to the Lord Lieutenant of Ireland 1835–1840* (Edinburgh 1867), 184, 252, 250–2; S.M. Houghton, "The Civil Administration of Ireland 1801–1846," (MA thesis, University of Manchester, 1924); R. Barry O'Brien, *Thomas Drummond Under Secretary in Ireland 1835–1840: Life and Letters* (London 1889), 75.

7 Wakefield, *Account of Ireland*, 2: 328–9.

8 Parker, *Peel*, 1: 35, 33; for Peel's background see Norman Gash, *Mr. Secretary Peel: The Life of Sir Robert Peel to 1830* (London 1961).

9 Wakefield, *Account of Ireland*, 2: 331.

10 Saxton to C. Wynn, 22 May 1812, Coed-y-Maen [Wynn] Papers, National Library of Wales, Aberystwyth; *Dublin Evening Herald*, 24 August 1812.

11 Ziegler, *Addington*, 316; Peel to Whitworth, 19 August 1814, Whitworth Papers; Richmond to Gregory, 30 August 1812, Richmond Papers, 74, National Library

of Ireland, Dublin; Richmond to Sidmouth, 17 September 1812; Sidmouth to Richmond, 20 September 1812, Richmond Papers.

12  Rockingham to Newcastle, 4 March 1768, BL Add. Ms. 32989; James M. Holzman, *The Nabobs in England: A Study of the Returned Anglo-Indian 1760–1785* (New York 1926), 49; Gregory to Burke, 3 February 1783, Edmund Burke Papers, 1/1760, Sheffield Central Library; Gregory to Burke, 3 March 1786, Burke Papers, 1/2015.

13  Large, *Irish Historical Studies* 15: 39; William Gregory's Account Books, William Gregory Papers, Woodruff Library, Emory University; see also Richard, 2nd Earl of Clancarty, *Memoir of the Le Poer Trench Family* (Dublin 1874).

14  Smith, *Whig Principles*, 175, 210; Malcomson, *John Foster*, 71; Hyde, *Rise of Castlereagh*, 134; John Erhman, *The Younger Pitt: The Reluctant Transition* (Stanford 1983), 405; see also R.B. McDowell, "The Fitzwilliam Episode," *Irish Historical Studies* 16 (1966): 115–30.

15  Gregory to Fitzwilliam, 18 September 1795, Fitzwilliam Papers, F30/46, Sheffield Central Library; Gregory to Fitzwilliam, 7 June 1797, F30/158; Smith, *Whig Principles*, 231; Albert Goodwin, *The Friends of Liberty: The English Democratic Movement in the Age of the French Revolution* (London 1979), 416; *Parliamentary Papers*, 1801 (1st series), 10: 829; *Reports from Committees of the House of Commons*, vol. 10, *Miscellaneous Subjects 1785–1801* (London 1803) 790.

16  See, for example, the Petition of Suffering Loyalists, 23 June 1800, Official Papers (OP), State Paper Office (SPO), Dublin, OP 80/3; Commissioners to Castlereagh, 10 December 1799, OP 61/4; Sir Richard Musgrave, *Memoirs of the Different Rebellions in Ireland from the Arrival of the English* (Dublin 1801), 67; Hill, *Past and Present* 118: 127.

17  Bartlett, *Castlereagh*, 5–6; G.C. Bolton, *The Passing of the Irish Act of Union: A Study in Parliamentary Politics* (Oxford 1966), 104, 126–7; W. Gregory to Castlereagh, 3 September 1799, Castlereagh Papers, Public Record Office of Northern Ireland, Belfast, D3030/962; Charles Ross, ed., *Correspondence of Charles, First Marquis Cornwallis*, 3 vols. (London 1859), 3: 278–9; Gregory to Cooke, 12 March 1801, OP 99/10, SPO.

18  See R.B. McDowell, *Irish Public Opinion 1750–1800* (London 1944), 10, 33–5, 168–71, 220–37; McDowell, *Ireland in Imperialism and Revolution*, 353–9; H.T. Dickinson, *Liberty and Property: Political Ideology in Eighteenth-Century Britain*, pb ed. (London 1979), 270ff; Curtis, *Lecky, Ireland*, 403.

19  Dickinson, *Liberty and Property*, 290, 312, 317.

20  Circular addressed "To the Officers of the Irish Militia," 10 January 1807, Gregory Papers.

21  Gregory Diary, Gregory Papers.

22  Granville, *Private Correspondence of Lord Granville*, 2: 243, 333; Cloncurry, *Memoirs*, 253; Charles O'Mahoney, *The Viceroys of Ireland* (London 1912), 213–16; R. Warwick Bond, ed., *The Marley Letters 1778–1820* (London 1937),

128–31, 153; Lord William Pitt Lennox, *My Recollections from 1806 to 1873*, 2 vols. (London 1874), 2: 185–6; Gregory to Peel, 12 April 1813, BL Add. Ms. 40196.

23 Richmond to Peel, 9 March 1813, Richmond Papers, 61; Richmond to Lady Connolly, 20 March 1812, Whitworth Papers, U269/0214; *Report on the Manuscripts of Earl Bathurst Preserved at Cirencester Park*, Historical Manuscripts Commission (London 1923), 155; Senior, *Orangeism*, 191.

24 Richmond to Lady Connolly, 29 March 1812, Whitworth Papers, U269/0214; *Bathurst Manuscripts*, 154–5.

25 *Bathurst Manuscripts*, 180–1; Richmond to Sidmouth, 13 March 1812, HO 100/169; Richmond to Peel, 6 May 1813, Richmond Papers, 61.

26 *Bathurst Manuscripts*, 180–1, 185–6; Richmond to Peel, 5 March 1813, Richmond Papers, 61.

27 *Bathurst Manuscripts*, 182, 185, 181; Richmond to Peel, 7 March 1813, BL Add. Ms. 40185.

28 Richmond to Torrens, 24 September 1812, Whitworth Papers, U269/0214; Parker, *Peel*, 1: 37.

29 *Bathurst Manuscripts*, 215, 186; Parker, *Peel*, 1: 71; Richmond to Sidmouth, 28 July 1813, HO 100/171; Richmond to Sidmouth, 31 May 1813, HO 100/170.

30 Granville, *Private Correspondence of Lord Granville*, 2: 289; V. Sackville-West, *Knole and the Sackvilles* (London 1922), 202; Petrie, *Liverpool and His Times*, 77; *Report on the Manuscripts of J.B. Fortescue, Esq. Preserved at Dropmore*, Historical Manuscripts Commission, 10 vols. (London 1892–1907), 10: 343; see also Norman E. Saul, *Russia and the Mediterranean 1797–1807* (Chicago 1970), 137–53; K. Waliszewski, *Paul the First of Russia the Son of Catharine the Great* (London 1913), 63, 249–53, 308–10, 326–33, 412–15; John Goldsworth Alger, *Napoleon's Visitors and Captives 1801–1815* (Westminster 1904), 22–3, 175–6; *Notes and Queries* 5 (April 3, 1852): 313–14.

31 Christian Colvin, ed., *Maria Edgeworth in France and Switzerland: Selections from the Edgeworth family Letters* (Oxford 1979), 35; Whitworth to Liverpool, 14 May 1813, Whitworth Papers, U269/0225; see also James J. Kenney, Jr, "Lord Whitworth and the Conspiracy against Tsar Paul I: The New Evidence of the Kent Archive," *Slavic Review* 36 (1977): 205–19.

32 Brynn, *Crown and Castle*, 32; Richmond to Peel, 18 May 1813, BL Add. Ms. 40185; Richmond to Simouth, 19 May 1813, HO 100/170; Peel to Richmond, 15 May 1813, Richmond Papers, 69; Richmond to Whitworth, 8 June 1813, Richmond Papers, 69; Sidmouth to Whitworth, 12 August 1813, Whitworth Papers, U269/0218.

33 Whitworth to Peel, 11 April 1814, Whitworth Papers, U269/0218; Parker, *Peel*, 1: 105–6; Whitworth to Peel, 3 May 1814, BL Add. Ms. 40188; Whitworth to Sidmouth, 5 May 1814, HO 100/178; *Dublin Evening Herald*, 20 May 1814.

34 Bolton, *Act of Union*, 78–80; *Cornwallis Correspondence*, 3: 29; Plowden, *An Historical Review*, 3: 1039–42; James Willis, ed., *Lives of Illustrious and Dis-*

*tinguished Irishmen*, 6 vols. (Dublin 1847), 6: 328–47; Saurin to Peel, 21 February, 16 March, 1813, BL Add. Ms. 40211.

35 Willis, *Lives*, 6: 346–7; W. Torrens McCullagh, *Memoirs of the Right Honourable Richard Lalor Sheil*, 2 vols. (London 1855), 1: 179; O'Brien, *Dublin Castle*, 106; Parker, *Peel*, 1: 34.

36 *The Speeches of the Late Right Honourable Sir Robert Peel, Bart. Delivered in the House of Commons*, 4 vols. (London 1853), 1: 11–12; Parker, *Peel*, 1: 72, 64; Peel to Richmond, 20 February, 6 March 1812, BL Add. Ms. 40281; *Parl. Deb.*, 1st ser. 25: 811.

37 William Gregory's Diary, October, November 1812, Gregory Papers; Gregory to Liverpool, 24 December 1812, OP 380/3, SPO; Gregory to Peel, 28 November 1812, 23 March 1813, BL Add. Ms. 40195; Peel to Gregory, 2 March 1819, BL Add. Ms. 40334.

38 Whitworth to Peel, 20 June 1814, BL Add. Ms. 40188; Peel to Whitworth, 11 June 1814, Whitworth Papers, U269/0225; Whitworth to Peel, 15 June 1814, U269/0218; Whitworth to Sidmouth, 17 August 1814, U269/0218.

39 Gregory to Peel, 1 June 1813, Gregory Papers; Gregory to Peel, 22 April 1813, BL Add. Ms. 40196; Gregory to Peel, 28 April 1817, BL Add. Ms. 40204.

40 Gregory to Peel, 6 June 1815, BL Add. Ms. 40201; Gregory to Peel, 31 March 1813, 10 December 1812, BL Add. Ms. 40195; Gregory to Peel, 21 March 1816, BL Add. Ms. 40202; Peel to Gregory, 15 December 1812, OP 375/8, SPO; Gregory to Peel, 17 January 1814, BL Add. Ms. 40198.

41 Gregory to Peel, 8 April 1813, BL Add. Ms. 40195; Gregory to Peel, 25 May 1814, BL Add. Ms 40198; Gregory to Peel, 7, 10 May, 25 April 1816, BL Add. Ms. 40202.

42 Whitworth to Peel, 20 April 1814, BL Add. Ms. 40188; Gregory to Peel, 6 April 1813, BL Add. Ms. 40195; Peel to Gregory, 16 February 1813, Gregory Papers; Gregory to Peel, 30 March 1816, BL Add. Ms. 40202.

43 Porter, *English Society*, 124ff; Harvey, *Britain in Early Nineteenth Century*, 12–13, 25; McDowell, *Ireland in Imperialism and Revolution*, 129; Johnston, *Great Britain and Ireland*, 30; McDowell, *Irish Public Opinion 1750–1800*, 32; Malcolmson, *John Foster*, 244.

44 Wakefield, *Account of Ireland*, 2: 320–1; Jupp, *Historical Studies*, 7:75; McDowell, *Public Opinion and Government Policy*, 48; Richmond to Lady Frances Beresford, 1 December 1812, Whitworth Papers, U269/0214; Richmond to Mother, 7 March 1813, U269/0214; Peel to Whitworth, 2 December 1813, U269/0255/1.

45 Richmond to Mother, 7 March 1813, Whitworth Papers, U269/0214; Peel to Richmond, 8 June 1813, Richmond Papers, 71; Richmond to Peel, 10 June 1813, Richmond Papers, 71.

46 Peel to Whitworth, 2 December 1813, Whitworth Papers, U269/0255/1; Whitworth to Sidmouth, 7 October 1814, HO 100/181; Gregory to Peel, 31 May 1813, BL Add. Ms. 40196; Gregory to Vesey Fitzgerald, 12 August 1819,

Gregory Papers.

47 Gregory to Peel, 2 April 1815, BL Add. Ms. 40200; Whitworth to Peel, 12 November 1813, BL Add. Ms. 40187.

48 Gregory to Peel, 4 April 1814, BL Add. Ms. 40198.

49 Gregory to Peel, 8 February 1813, BL Add. Ms. 40195; Richmond to Gregory, 7 February 1813, BL Add. Ms. 40195; Gregory to Peel, 17 November 1813, BL Add. Ms. 40197; Gregory to Peel, March 1815, Gregory Papers.

50 For a full discussion of patronage see Robert Shipkey, "Problems of Irish Patronage during the Chief Secretaryship of Robert Peel, 1812–18," *Historical Journal* 10 (1967): 41–56; see also his PHD thesis, "Robert Peel's Irish Policy" (Harvard University, 1962); Parker, *Peel*, 1: 60; Peel to Gregory, 24 February 1813, Gregory Papers; Gregory to Peel, 23 February 1816, BL Add. Ms. 40202; Gregory to Peel, 6 April 1813, BL Add. Ms. 40195; Gregory to Peel, 30 December 1813, BL Add. Ms. 40197.

51 Peel to Whitworth, 15, 16 November 1814, Whitworth Papers, U269/0255; Gregory to Peel, 21 November 1814, BL Add. Ms. 40199; Gregory to Whitworth, 23, 25 November 1814, U269/0255; Whitworth to Sidmouth, 23 November 1814, HO 100/182.

52 Peel to Gregory, 15 December 1812, OP 375/8, SPO; Gregory to Peel, 3 November 1813, BL Add. Ms. 40197; Gregory to Peel, 13 May 1813, BL Add. Ms. 40196.

53 Peel to Whitworth, 20 June 1814, Whitworth Papers, U269/0255; Gregory to Peel, 17 March 1813, BL Add Ms. 40195; Gregory to Peel, 17, 28 April, 22 May, 1813, BL Add. Ms. 40196.

54 Malcomson, *John Foster*, 108; Gash, *Mr. Secretary Peel*, 111; *Bathurst Manuscripts*, 193; Peel to Richmond, 16 July 1813, Richmond Papers, 71; Parker, *Peel*, 1: 110–12.

55 Parker, *Peel*, 1: 111–12; Liverpool to Peel, 4 October 1813, BL Add. Ms. 40181; Peel to Richmond, 16 July 1813, Richmond Papers, 71; Peel to Liverpool, 25 August 1815, BL Add. Ms. 40289.

56 Peel to Liverpool, 20 October 1813, BL Add. Ms. 40285.

CHAPTER THREE

1 Peel to Liverpool, 14 September 1812, BL Add. Ms. 40280; Gregory to Peel, 16 March 1815, BL Add. Ms. 40200; G.L. Barrow, *The Emergence of the Irish Banking System 1820–1845* (Dublin 1975), 25; Shipkey, "Robert Peel's Irish Policy," 99.

2 Peel to Sidmouth, 10 January 1813, HO 100/169; Peel to Whitworth, 9 November 1813, Whitworth Papers, U269/0225; Peel to Whitworth, 8 December 1813, U269/0225/3.

3 *Parl. Deb.*, 1st ser. 26: 255.

4 Peel to Sidmouth, 14 September 1812, HO 100/168; Peel to Sidmouth, 21 November 1812, BL Add. Ms. 40280; Gregory to Peel, 12 December 1812, BL

Add. Ms. 40195; Gregory to Peel, 6 April 1813, BL Add. Ms. 40195; seel also Robert Shipkey, "Problems in Alcoholic Production and Controls in Early Nineteenth-Century Ireland," *Historical Journal* 16 (1973): 291–302.

5 K.H. Connell, *Irish Peasant Society* (Oxford 1968), 1ff; Gregory to Excise Board, 19 December 1810, Gregory Papers; Gregory to Peel, 6 June 1813, BL Add. Ms. 40196.

6 Peel to Gregory, 2 June 1813, Gregory Papers; Shipkey, *Historical Journal* 16: 298–9; *Parl. Deb.*, 1st ser. 26: 703, 795–6; *Peel's Speeches*, 1: 23; Peel to Sidmouth, 21 August 1813, HO 100/171; Sidmouth to Peel, 4 September 1813, HO 100/172.

7 *Parl. Deb.*, 1st ser. 28: 493–502; Gregory to Peel, 12 December 1812, BL Add. Ms. 40195; Gregory to Peel, 23 July 1814, BL Add. Ms. 40199.

8 Peel to Gregory, 20 July 1814, BL Add. Ms. 40287.

9 Sidmouth to Peel, 26 January 1814, HO 100/176.

10 Trustees of Linen Board to Gregory, 9 December 1812, HO 100/168; Gregory to Peel, 10 December 1812, BL Add. Ms. 40195; Whitworth to Sidmouth, 10 October 1812, HO 100/173; Peel to Beckett, 28 January 1815, HO 100/183.

11 Gregory to Peel, 10 December 1812, BL Add. Ms. 40195; Gregory to Peel, 22 February 1813, BL Add. Ms. 40195; Benjamin Ward, *The Eve of Catholic Emancipation*, 3 vols. (London 1911), 2: 22; *Parl. Deb.*, 1st ser. 24: 224–64, 692, 811.

12 Parker, *Peel*, 1: 78–82; Gregory to Peel, 5, 8 March 1813, BL Add. Ms. 40195; *Parl. Deb.*, 1st ser. 24: 894–7.

13 *Parl. Deb.*, 1st ser. 24: 908–15; Parker, *Peel*, 1: 74–6; Peel to Richmond, 27 February 1813, BL Add. Ms. 40281; Peel to Richmond, 21 May 1813, BL Add. Ms. 40283; Peel to Richmond, 14 May 1813, Richmond Papers, 69; Peel to Gregory, 22 May 1813, Gregory Papers; *Colchester Diary*, 1: 446–7; Pellew, *Sidmouth*, 3: 99; Ward, *Eve of Catholic Emancipation*, 2: 48–9.

14 Richmond to Peel, 5 June 1813, Richmond Papers, 71; Gregory to Peel, 19 April, 8, 27, 29 May 1813, BL Add. Ms. 40196.

15 Lynch and Vaizey, *Guinness's Brewery*, 142–3; Gregory to Peel, 22 May 1813, BL Add. Ms. 40196; Gregory to Peel, 16 June 1813, BL Add. Ms. 40197.

16 Gregory to Peel, 30 June 1813, BL Add. Ms. 40197.

17 Whitworth to Peel, 4 July 1813, BL Add. Ms. 40187.

18 Parker, *Peel*, 1: 123; Peel to Richmond, 20 November 1813, Richmond Papers, 60.

19 Whitworth to Liverpool, 16 October 1813, Whitworth Papers, U269/0218; Whitworth to Sidmouth, 17 October 1813, U269/0218.

20 Gregory to Peel, 8, 9 June 1813, BL Add. Ms. 40196; Peel to Gregory, 3 July 1813, BL Add. Ms. 40284; Parker, *Peel*, 1: 119; Peel to Gregory, 13 November 1813, Gregory Papers.

21 Peel to Gregory, 13 November 1813, Gregory Papers; Peel to Whitworth, 18 November 1813, Whitworth Papers, U269/0225/2; Whitworth to Sidmouth, 20,

28 December 1813, HO 100/175; Whitworth to Sidmouth, 28 December 1813, U269/0218.

22 Redesdale to Sidmouth, 24 September 1813, HO 100/172; Peel to Sidmouth, 7 October 1813, HO 100/173; Sidmouth to Peel, 18 October 1813, HO 100/173; Sidmouth to Whitworth, 30 January 1814, HO 100/176.

23 Whitworth to Sidmouth, 5 February 1814, Whitworth Papers, U269/0218; Whitworth to Sidmouth, 24 February 1814, HO 100/177.

24 Sidmouth to Whitworth, 17 February, 5 March 1814, HO 100/177.

25 Peel to Whitworth, 11 April 1814, Whitworth Papers, U269/0225.

26 Whitworth to Sidmouth, 13 May 1814, HO 100/178; Peel to Whitworth, 25 April 1814, Whitworth Papers, U269/0225.

27 Peel to Whitworth, 25 April, 7 May 1814, Whitworth Papers, U269/0225.

28 Peel to Whitworth, 7, 13, 18 May 1814, Whitworth Papers, U269/0225; Gregory to Peel, 10 May 1814, BL Add Ms. 40198; Whitworth to Peel, 10, 16 May 1814, BL Add. Ms. 40188.

29 Gregory to Peel, 21, 23 May, 4 June 1814, BL Add. Ms. 40198; Peel to Whitworth, 24 May 1814, BL Add. Ms. 40286; Peel to Gregory, 25 May 1814, BL Add. Ms. 40286; Gash, *Mr. Secretary Peel*, 160–1; Ward, *Eve of Catholic Emancipation*, 2: 71ff; *Dublin Evening Herald*, 15 June 1814.

30 Peel to Whitworth, 8 June 1814, BL Add. Ms. 40286; Whitworth to Sidmouth, 13 June 1814, HO 100/178; Gregory to Peel, 9, 14 June 1814, BL Add. Ms. 40198.

31 Peel to Whitworth, 8 June 1814, BL Add. Ms. 40286; Gregory to Peel, 2 June 1814, BL Add. Ms. 40198; Baron Smith to Gregory, 4 September 1813, Gregory Papers; *Parl. Deb.*, 1st ser. 28: 34–5, 245–6.

32 Gregory to Peel, 27 June 1813, BL Add. Ms. 40197; Peel to Gregory, 1 July 1813, BL Add. Ms. 40284; Liverpool to Peel, 21 October 1813, BL Add. Ms. 40181.

33 Peel to Whitworth, 16 June, 23 July 1814, Whitworth Papers, U269/0225; Gregory to Peel, 19 July, 11 June 1814, BL Add. Ms. 40199.

34 Whitworth to Sidmouth, 5 February 1814, HO 100/177; Peel to Whitworth, 11 April 1814, Whitworth Papers, U269/0225; Parker, *Peel*, 1: 123–4; Harvey, *Britain in Early Nineteenth Century*, 47; Low, 'That Sunny Dome,' 31; Harris, *Romanticism*, 70–1; A. Aspinall, *Politics and the Press c. 1780–1850* (London 1949), 33, 38–40, 66–9, 126–7.

35 Brian Inglis, *Freedom of the Press in Ireland 1784–1841* (London 1954), 24–5, 128–31; Brian Inglis, "O'Connell and the Irish Press 1800–42," *Irish Historical Studies* 8 (1952): 1–2.

36 Inglis, *Irish Historical Studies* 8: 2–3; Aspinall, *Politics and the Press*, 107; Inglis, *Freedom of Press*, 137; *Colchester Diary*, 2: 470–1.

37 Parker, *Peel*, 1: 104; Maurice R. O'Connell, ed., *The Correspondence of Daniel O'Connell*, 8 vols. (Dublin 1972–81), 1: 347, 349–52, 367–8; Aspinall, *Politics and the Press*, 122.

38 Inglis, *Irish Historical Studies* 8: 4–5; L.J. Jennings, ed., *Correspondence and Diaries of J.W. Croker*, 3 vols. (London 1884), 1: 89; Peel to Sidmouth, 21 October 1813, HO 100/173.

39 See Aspinall, *Politics and the Press*, 108–9, 138–9, 148–9, 179–81, 183; A. Aspinall, "The Irish Proclamation Fund, 1800–1846," *English Historical Review* 56 (1941): 265–9.

40 Inglis, *Freedom of Press*, 116–17, 123–5, 154–5; *Dublin Evening Herald*, 10 February 1813; Peel to Liverpool, 14 September 1812, BL Add. Ms. 40280; A. Aspinall, "The Use of Irish Secret Service Money in Subsidizing the Irish Press," *English Historical Review* 56 (1941): 641; copies of the secret service account books are to be found in the Gregory Papers.

41 Gregory to Peel, 8 May 1813, BL Add. Ms. 40196; Peel to Gregory, 5 May 1813, Gregory Papers; Peel to Richmond, 14 April 1813, Richmond Papers, 69; *Parl. Deb.*, 1st ser. 25: 791–2.

42 Gregory to Peel, 28 April 1813, BL Add. Ms. 40196; Peel to Gregory, 3 July 1813, BL Add. Ms. 40284; Peel to Gregory, 14 May 1813, Gregory Papers; Peel to Gregory, 12 March 1813, Gregory Papers; Gregory to Peel, 16 March 1813, BL Add. Ms. 40195; Peel to Gregory, 10 June 1814, BL Add. Ms. 40286; Parker, *Peel*, 1: 114–15.

43 Whitworth to Sidmouth, 5 January 1814, Private and Official Correspondence, 1811–23, Chief Secretary's Office (CSO), SPO; secret service accounts, Gregory Papers.

44 Peel to Sidmouth, 8 January 1813, HO 100/169; Gregory to Peel, 14 April 1813, BL Add. Ms. 40196; Gregory to Peel, 24 November 1813, BL Add. Ms. 40197; Peel to Gregory, 17 April 1813, Gregory Papers; Whitworth to Sidmouth, 18 January 1814, HO 100/176; Gregory to Tighe, 3 December 1813, HO 100/175.

45 Gregory to Peel, 10 March 1813, BL Add. Ms. 40195; Whitworth to Peel, 13 October 1813, BL Add. Ms. 40187; Gregory to Peel, 15 October 1813, BL Add. Ms. 40197; Richmond to Sidmouth, 15 June 1813, HO 100/169; Willcocks to Peel, 23 March 1814, HO 100/177; Wills to Peel, 26 March 1814, HO 100/177.

46 Whitworth to Peel, 7 May 1814, Whitworth Papers, U269/0218; Whitworth to Sidmouth, 13 December 1813, HO 100/175; Whitworth to Sidmouth, 5 June 1816, *Parl. Papers*, 1816, 9: 582.

47 Gregory to Peel, 1 December 1813, BL Add. Ms. 40197; Gregory to Tighe, 3 December 1813, HO 100/175.

48 Peel to Gregory, 23 November 1813, Gregory Papers; Parker, *Peel*, 1: 125; Peel to Whitworth, 2 December 1813, Whitworth Papers, U269/0225; Gregory to Whitworth, 12 December 1813, U269/0225; Whitworth to Sidmouth, 13 December 1813, HO 100/175.

49 Gregory to Hill, 12 November 1813, HO 100/174; Gregory to Granard, 18 November 1813, HO 100/174; Peel to Castlemaine, 27 October 1813, HO 100/173; Gregory to Peel, 16 June, 1 December 1813, BL Add. Ms. 40197.

50 Whitworth to Sidmouth, 5 January 1814, Private Official Correspondence 1811–

23, CSO, SPO.

51 Galen Broeker, *Rural Disorder and Police Reform in Ireland 1812–36* (Toronto 1970), 30–1; Peel to Whitworth, 10 November, 2 December 1813, Whitworth Papers, U269/0225; Sidmouth to Peel, 19 January 1814, HO 100/176; Peel to Sidmouth, 6 January 1814, HO 100/176.

52 Whitworth to Sidmouth, 25 March 1814, HO 100/177; Whitworth to Peel, 8 May 1814, BL Add. Ms. 40188; Peel to Sidmouth, 18 May 1814, HO 100/178, Gregory to Peel, 8 May 1814, BL Add. Ms. 40198.

53 Peel to Sidmouth, 18 May 1814, HO 100/178; Whitworth to Sidmouth, 27 June 1814, Private Official Correspondence 1811–23, CSO, SPO; Sidmouth to Duke of York, 3 July 1814, HO 100/179; Sidmouth to Whitworth, 4 July 1814, Private Official Correspondence 1811–23, CSO, SPO; Sidmouth to Whitworth, 11 August 1814, HO 100/180.

54 Gregory to Peel, 16 May 1814, BL Add. Ms. 40198, Whitworth to Sidmouth, 21 April 1814, HO 100/177; Peel to Whitworth, 25 April 1814, Whitworth Papers, U269/0225; Broeker, *Rural Disorder and Police Reform*, 60; Whitworth to Sidmouth, 16 June 1814, HO 100/178.

55 Peel to Gregory, 9 May, 7 June 1813, Gregory Papers; *Peel's Speeches*, 1: 22; Parker, *Peel*, 1: 142–3; Peel to Gregory, 11 June 1814, BL Add. Ms. 40287; Peel to Saurin, 18 June 1814, BL Add. Ms. 40287; Peel to Whitworth, 24 June 1814, BL Add. Ms. 40287; see also J.J. Tobias, *Crime and Police in England 1700–1900* (Dublin 1979), 51–3; David Ascoli, *The Queen's Peace: The Origins and Development of the Metropolitan Police 1829–1979* (London 1979), 56–7.

56 Peel to Gregory, 24 June 1814, BL Add. Ms. 40287; Emsley, *Crime and Society in England*, 24; Beattie, *Past and Present* 62: 56; *Parl. Deb.*, 1 st ser. 28: 163–74, 502–3.

57 Peel to Whitworth, 7 July 1814, BL Add. Ms. 40287; Whhitworth to Peel, 13 July 1814, Whitworth Papers, U269/0218; Peel to Whitworth, 14 July 1814, U269/0225; *Parl. Deb.*, 1st ser. 28: 646–9, 693.

58 Whitworth to Peel, 12 July 1814, BL Add. Ms. 40189; Whitworth to Sidmouth, 15 August 1815, HO 100/180; Gregory to Whitworth, 22 August, 24 November 1814, 22 April 1815, Whitworth Papers, U269/0255; Gregory to Peel, 29 March 1813, BL Add. Ms. 40195; Gregory to Mooney, 23 March 1820, Private Official Correspondence 1820, CSO, SPO.

59 *Colchester Diary*, 2: 515, 517; Whitworth to Sidmouth, 15 August 1814, Whitworth Papers, U269/0218; Whitworth to Sidmouth, 14 October 1814, HO 100/181.

60 *Peel's Speeches*, 1: 35–9; *Parl. Deb.*, 1st ser. 29: 516–17, 522–3; ibid., 26: 369; ibid., 28: 259–61, 824; see also T. O'Ceallaigh, "Peel and Police Reform in Ireland, 1814–18," *Studia Hibernica* 6 (1966): 36–9.

61 *Parl. Deb.*, 1st ser., 29: 484–7, 489–91; Peel to Whitworth, 31 August 1814, Whitworth Papers, U269/0225; *Parl. Deb.*, 1st ser. 28: 862.

## CHAPTER FOUR

1 Whitworth to Peel, 15 February 1815, BL Add. Ms. 40190; Gregory to Peel, 24 February 1815, BL Add. Ms. 40200; Gregory to Whitworth, 28 April, 17 March 1815, Whitworth Papers, U269/0255.

2 Gregory to Peel, 18, 15 March, 26 April 1815, BL Add. Ms. 40200.

3 Sidmouth to Whitworth, 27 December 1814, HO 100/182; Gregory to Peel, 15 February 1815, BL Add. Ms. 40200; Lady Gregory, ed., *Mr. Gregory's Letter-Box*, 2nd ed. (Gerrards Cross 1981), 47–8.

4 Gregory to Peel, 25 March, 5, 9 April 1815, BL Add. Ms. 40200; Gregory to Whitworth, 27, 29 March 1815, Whitworth Papers, U269/0255; Gregory, *Letter-Box*, 52.

5 Gregory to Peel, 19 April 1815, Private Official Correspondence 1811–23, CSO, SPO; Whitworth to Sidmouth, 23 April 1815, HO 100/183; Gregory to Peel, 19, 17 April 1815, BL Add. Ms. 40200.

6 *Colchester Diary*, 2: 517; Parker, *Peel*, 1: 178–9; Peel to Gregory, 18 April 1815, BL Add. Ms. 40288.

7 Gregory to Peel, 26 April 1815, BL Add. Ms. 40200; Gregory to Peel, 8 May 1815, BL Add. Ms. 40201; Peel to Saurin, 3 May 1815, BL Add. Ms. 40288; Peel to Gregory, 11 May 1815, BL Add. Ms. 40288; Peel to Sidmouth, 23 May 1815, BL Add. Ms. 40289.

8 O'Connell, *O'Connell Correspondence*, 2: 35–6, 48–9, 40.

9 Peel to Saxton, 5 February 1815, BL Add. Ms. 40288; Peel to Gregory, 10 April 1815, BL Add. Ms. 40288; Peel to Gregory, 29 March 1816, BL Add. Ms. 40290; Gregory to Peel, 26 March, 9 April 1816, BL Add. Ms. 40202; Gregory to Peel, 20 February 1817, BL Add. Ms. 40203; Whitworth to Peel, 21 February 1817, BL Add. Ms. 40193; Inglis, *Freedom of Press*, 160; secret service account books, 1816–18, Gregory Papers; Gregory to Peel, 30 March 1818, BL Add. Ms. 40205; Aspinall, *Politics and the Press*, 142; Aspinall, *English Historical Review* 56: 272.

10 Peel to Whitworth, 1 February 1817, Whitworth Papers, U269/0225.

11 O'Connell, *O'Connell Correspondence*, 2: 49.

12 Hueckel, *Napoleonic Wars*, xxxiv; A. Mitchell, *The Whigs in Opposition 1815–1830* (Oxford 1967), 60; Emsley, *British Society*, 165–75; Emsley, *Crime and Society in England*, 29; Checkland, *British Public Policy*, 23; Leonard P. Adams, *Agricultural Depression and Farm Relief in England 1813–1852* (reprint, London 1965), 64–75; Thompson, *English Landed Society*, 231; Evans, *Forging of the Modern State*, 132; Glenn Hueckel, "English Farming Profits during the Napoleonic Wars, 1973–1815," *Explorations in Economic History* 13 (1976): 331–45; Salaman, *History of the Potato*, 462.

13 Cullen, *Economic History since 1660*, 100–101; O'Brien, *Economic History from Union*, 52–5, 9–15; Mokyr, *Why Ireland Starved*, 114; Beames, *Peasants and Power*, 4, 11, 118–19; Connolly, *Priests and People*, 238.

14  Adams, *Agricultural Depression*, 17–20, 38–42, 46–8, 56–8; *Parl. Deb.*, 1st ser. 27: 716, 893–7, 940–1, 963–7; ibid., 29: 803, 1059, 1079; ibid., 30: 125–39.

15  Muriel E. Chamberlain, *Lord Aberdeen: A Political Biography* (London 1983), 177; Peel to Whitworth, 31 May 1814, BL Add. Ms. 40286; Peel to Gregory, 31 May 1814, BL Add. Ms. 40286; see also Boyd Hilton, *Corn, Cash, Commerce: The Economic Policy of the Tory Governments 1815–1830* (Oxford 1977), 8–23; Fetter, *Economist in Parliament*, 34–6; Crosby, *English Farmers*, 27; Chambers and Mingay, *Agricultural Revolution*, 123–4; R.H. Campbell, "The Anglo-Scottish Union of 1707: II. The Economic Consequences," *Economic History Review*, 2nd ser. 16 (1963–4): 468–77.

16  Peel to Whitworth, 23 February 1815, Whitworth Papers, U269/O225; Parker, *Peel*, 1: 168–9; Stevenson, *Popular Disturbances*, 192.

17  *Parl. Deb.*, 1st ser. 30: 956–8; ibid., 31: 871.

18  See Donald H. Akenson, *The Irish Education Experiment: The National System of Education in the Nineteenth Century* (Toronto 1970); McDowell, *Ireland in Imperialism and Revolution*, 92–5; James Johnston Auchmuty, *Irish Education: A Historical Survey* (London 1937), 16–17; Akenson, *Church of Ireland*, 134–9.

19  Akenson, *Irish Education*, 77–8, 80; Parker, *Peel*, 1: 87–9; Peel to Sidmouth, n.d. [January 1813] BL Add. Ms. 40280; Peel to Richmond, 8 May 1813, BL Add. Ms. 40282; *Parl. Deb.*, 1st ser. 25: 260; Peel's *Speeches*, 1: 94.

20  Gregory to Peel, 30 April 1813, BL Add. Ms. 40196; Parker, *Peel*, 1: 91, 93; Whitworth to Sidmouth, 14 March 1814, HO 100/177; *Colchester Diary*, 2: 519.

21  *Parl. Deb.*, 1st ser. 21: 879; Akenson, *Church of Ireland*, 141; see also Peadar McCann, "Charity Schooling in Cork City in the late 18th & early 19th centuries. Part 4: The Lancasterian Committee," *Cork Historical and Archeological Society* 87 (1982): 133–41.

22  *Parl. Deb.*, 1st ser. 34: 43, 23; Parker, *Peel*, 1: 232–3.

23  Whitworth to Sidmouth, 20 June 1815, HO 100/184; Gregory to Peel, 15 June 1815, BL Add. Ms. 40201.

24  Peel to Gregory, 17 June 1815, BL Add. Ms. 40289; Gregory to Whitworth, 26 April 1815, Whitworth Papers, U269/O255; Peel to Whitworth, 23, 30 June 1815, BL Add. Ms. 40289.

25  Whitworth to Sidmouth, 13 November 1815, HO 100/187; Gregory to Peel, 29 May 1815, BL Add. Ms. 40201; Peel to Gregory, 17 May 1815, BL Add. Ms. 40289; Peel to Sidmouth, 28 August 1815, Private Official Correspondence 1811–23, CSO, SPO; Sidmouth to Whitworth, 31 August 1815, HO 100/184.

26  Peel to Gregory, 11 September 1815, BL Add. Ms. 40201.

27  Whitworth to Sidmouth, 18 September 1815, HO 100/185; Gregory to Peel, 25 September 1815, BL Add. Ms. 40201.

28  Whitworth to Sidmouth, 27 October 1815, HO 100/186; Gregory to Whitworth, 10 November 1815, Whitworth Papers, U269/O255; Gregory to Peel, 17

November 1815, BL Add. Ms. 40201; Hamilton to Peel, 2 November 1815, HO
100/187; Willcocks to Gregory, 14 December 1815, HO 100/188; Whitworth to
Sidmouth, 30 November 1815, HO 100/187.

29 *Croker Papers*, 1: 91; Peel to Sidmouth, 1 November 1816, HO 100/191; C.D.
Yonge, *The Life and Administration of Robert Banks, 2nd Earl of Liverpool*, 3
vols. (London 1868), 2: 250; Saurin to Peel, 12, 24 April 1816, BL Add. Ms.
40211; Gregory to Peel, 4 May 1816, BL Add. Ms. 40202; *Colchester Diary*,
2: 591.

30 Liverpool to Peel, 28 January 1816, BL Add. Ms. 40181; Sidmouth to Dean of
Cork, 4 April 1816, HO 100/189; Fetter, *Economist in Parliament*, 115–16.

31 J.E. Cookson, *Lord Liverpool's Administration: The Crucial Years 1815–1822*
(Edinburgh 1975), 21–2; Peel to Whitworth, 29 January [1817], Whitworth
Papers, U269/0225.

32 Cookson, *Liverpool Administration*, 124; Peel to Beckett, 3 October 1816, Private Official Correspondence 1811–23, CSO, SPO; Gregory to Peel, 25 April
1817, BL Add. Ms. 40204; Gregory to Peel, 29 March 1817, BL Add. Ms. 40203;
Gregory to Peel, 30 March, 14 February 1816, BL Add. Ms. 40202.

33 Whitworth to Sidmouth, 30 November 1815, HO 100/187; Sidmouth to Whitworth, 8 December 1815, HO 100/188; Whitworth to Sidmouth, 19 January
1816, HO 100/189; Peel to Whitworth, 14, 18, 29 February 1816, BL Add. Ms.
40290; *Parl. Deb.*, 1st ser. 32: 922–9.

34 Fetter, *Economist in Parliament*, 125–7; Peel to Sidmouth, 10 November 1816,
HO 100/191; Peel to Whitworth, 29, 2 January [1817], Whitworth Papers, U269/
0225; Whitworth to Sidmouth, 28 January 1817, HO 100/192.

35 Parker, *Peel*, 1: 215, 220; Peel to Whitworth, 12 February [1817], Whitworth
Papers, U269/0225; Peel to Liverpool, 20 February 1817, BL Add. Ms. 40292;
Peel to Whitworth, 4 June 1817, BL Add. Ms. 40293.

36 *Parl. Deb.*, 1st ser. 33: 64–6, 84–6, 158, 193, 314–50, 871; Peel to Whitworth,
11, 18, 30 March, 2 April 1816, BL Add. Ms. 40290; Peel to Liverpool, 30
March 1816, BL Add. Ms. 40290.

37 Peel to Gregory, 2, 9 April 1816, BL Add. Ms. 40290; Peel to Saurin, 8 April
1816, BL Add. Ms. 40290; Report on Irish Magistracy, November 1815, HO
100/189.

38 Peel to Whitworth, 8 April 1816, BL Add. Ms. 40290; *Parl. Deb.*, 1st ser. 34:
31; *Peel's Speeches*, 1: 67.

39 Peel to Gregory, 27 April 1816, BL Add. Ms. 40290; Peel to Whitworth, 22
May 1815, BL Add. Ms. 40289; Peel to Manners, 29 May 1815, BL Add. Ms.
40289; Peel to Sidmouth, 20 February 1816, HO 100/189; Peel to Saurin, 15
February 1816, BL Add. Ms. 40290; *Parl. Deb.*, 1st ser. 34: 1043–5, 1007.

40 Horn, *Rural World*, 76; Quinault and Stevenson, *Popular Protest*, 63; Adams,
*Agricultural Depression*, 86; Stevenson, *Popular Disturbances in England*, 193–
5; see also A.J. Peacock, *Bread and Blood: A Study of the Agrarian Riots in
East Anglia in 1816* (London 1965), and Richard Hawkins's review of *Captain*

*Swing* by E.J. Hobsbawm and George Rudé in *Historical Journal* 12 (1969): 717.

41 Geary, *Irish Economic and Social History*, 8: 36; O'Brien, *Economic History from Union*, 421, 157; O'Neill, *Family and Farm in Pre-Famine Ireland*, 99; Peel to Beckett, 26 July 1816, HO 100/189; Peel to Liverpool, 9 October 1816, BL Add. Ms. 40291.

42 Gregory to Peel, 18 June 1816, BL Add. Ms. 40203.

43 Peel to Sidmouth, 17 August 1816, HO 100/190; Whitworth to Sidmouth, 5 October 1816, HO 100/191; Sidmouth to Whitworth, 20 December 1816, Whitworth Papers, U269/0218; Gregory to Peel, 15 December 1816, BL Add. Ms. 40203; Parker, *Peel*, 1: 231.

44 Parker, *Peel*, 1: 235, *Parl. Deb.*, 1st ser. 33: 710; *Peel's Speeches*, 1: 55; *Parl. Deb.*, 1st ser. 34: 601.

45 O'Brien, *Economic History from Union*, 459; *Parl. Deb.*, 1st ser. 34: 32; Poynter, *Society and Pauperism*, 223ff; "Malthus on Population," *Quarterly Review* 17 (1817): 369–403; Perkin, *Origins of Modern English Society*, 191; Mandler, *Past and Present* 117: 145; *Parl. Deb.*, 1st ser. 35: 509–10, 523.

46 Poynter, *Society and Pauperism*, 267; Shipkey, "Robert Peel's Irish Policy," 91; Peel to Whitworth, 2 January 1815, Whitworth Papers, U269/0225; Peel to Goulburn, 7 February 1815, Goulburn Papers, Surrey Record Office, Acc. 319/35; Peel to Gregory, 13 April 1815, BL Add. Ms. 40288; Peel to Goulburn, 26 April 1815, BL Add. Ms. 40288; Peel to Liverpool, 24 June 1816, BL Add. Ms. 40291; Parker, *Peel*, 1: 257; Peel to Whitworth, 17 June [1816], U269/0225; see also H.J.M. Johnston, *British Emigration Policy 1815–1830: 'Shovelling out Paupers'* (Oxford 1972), 2–25, 51; Oliver Macdonagh, *Pattern of Government Growth 1800–1860: The Passenger Acts and Their Enforcement* (New York 1961), 22–65; Klaus E. Knorr, *British Colonial Theories 1570–1850* (Toronto 1944), 223–7, 277; Peter Dunkley, "Emigration and the State, 1803–1842: The Nineteenth Century Revolution in Government Reconsidered," *Historical Journal* 23 (1980): 356; Clark and Donnelly, *Irish Peasants*, 150.

47 Poynter, *Society and Pauperism*, 15; McDowell, *Irish Administration*, 169–70; Peel to Gregory, 15 May 1815, BL Add. Ms. 40289; Gregory to Peel, 3 June 1816, BL Add. Ms. 40203; *Parl. Deb.*, 1st ser., 35: 881; Nicholls, *Irish Poor Law*, 78.

48 *Parl. Deb.*, 1st ser. 35: 309; Peel to Liverpool, 9 October 1816, BL Add. Ms. 40291; Peel to Sidmouth, 10 October 1816, HO 100/191; Peel to Whitworth, 11 October [1816], Whitworth Papers, U269/0225; *Peel's Speeches*, 1: 72; Sidmouth to Peel, 19 October 1816, BL Add. Ms. 40182; *Parl. Deb.*, 1st ser. 35: 886.

49 Gregory to Peel, 25 February, 2, 3, 6, 7, 11 March 1817, BL Add. Ms. 40203; Peel to Whitworth, 8 March 1817, Whitworth Papers, U269/0225; Peel to Gregory, 14 March [1817], Gregory Papers; J.P. Thursfield, *Peel* (London 1893), 40–1.

50 Peel to Sidmouth, 5 December 1816, HO 100/191; Sidmouth to Peel, 9 December

1816, HO 100/191; *Parl. Deb.*, 1st ser. 35: 888, Peel to Whitworth, 8 March 1817, BL Add. Ms. 40292; Peel to Whitworth, n.d. [March 1817], Whitworth Papers, U269/0225.

51  Peel to Whitworth, n.d. [March 1817], Whitworth Papers, U269/0225.

52  Peel to Gregory, 15 March 1817, Gregory Papers; Peel to Gregory, 30 March 1817, BL Add. Ms. 40292; Gregory to Peel, 30 May, 5, 9, 21 June 1817, BL Add. Ms. 40204; Whitworth to Sidmouth, 22 June 1817, HO 100/192.

53  Peel to Whitworth, 9 June 1817, BL Add. Ms. 40293; R.D. Collinson Black, *Economic Thought and the Irish Question 1817–1870* (Cambridge 1960), 171; Gregory to Peel, 20 May 1817, Whitworth Papers, U269/0255; Gregory to Peel, 19 June 1817, BL Add. Ms. 40204; Whitworth to Peel, 11 June 1817, BL Add. Ms. 40194.

54  Gregory to Peel, 19 June 1817, BL Add. Ms. 40204; Peel to Whitworth, 12, 25 June 1817, BL Add. Ms. 40293; Peel to Gregory, 22 June 1817, BL Add. Ms. 40293; Poynter, *Society and Pauperism*, 254.

55  Peel to Sidmouth, 21 July 1817, BL Add. Ms. 40293; Cookson, *Liverpool Administration*, 93; Peel to Sidmouth, 21 July 1817, HO 100/192; Parker, *Peel*, 1: 257.

CHAPTER FIVE

1  Whitworth to Peel, 20 March 1816, BL Add. Ms. 40191; Liverpool to Whitworth, 14 August 1816, Whitworth Papers, U269/0218; Whitworth to Sidmouth, 10 July 1816, HO 100/190; Whitworth to Sidmouth, 24 March 1817, HO 100/192; Peel to Liverpool, 31 October 1816, BL Add. Ms. 40292.

2  Peel to Whitworth, 8 July 1817, Whitworth Papers, U269/0255.

3  Peel to Whitworth, 4 November 1817, BL Add. Ms. 40193; *Cloncurry Memoirs*, 267; J.F. Bagot, *George Canning and His Friends*, 2 vols. (London 1909), 2: 90; Philip Whitwell Wilson, *The Greville Diary Including Passages Hitherto Withheld from Publication*, 2 vols. (New York 1927), 2: 246; Gregory, *Letter-Box*, 73; Talbot to Gregory, October 1819 (Talbot Papers) Shrewsbury Mss., Staffordshire Record Office; Talbot to Gregory, 6 February 1819, Gregory Papers; O'Connell, *O'Connell Correspondence*, 2: 229.

4  Whitworth to Sidmouth, 22 September 1817, HO 100/193; Gregory to Whitworth, 24 December 1816, Whitworth Papers, U269/0255; Gregory to Peel, 19 November 1816, BL Add. Ms. 40203.

5  Gregory to Talbot, 7 July 1821, Talbot Papers; Talbot to Sidmouth, 29 April 1819, HO/196; Talbot to Peel, 13 May 1818, BL Add. Ms. 40193; Gregory to Peel, 29 December 1817, BL Add. Ms. 40204.

6  Hilton, *Corn, Cash, Commerce*, 72; *Parl. Deb.*, 1st ser. 36: 579–87, 592–4; Peel to Sidmouth, 2 July 1817, HO 100/192; *Parl. Deb.*, 1st ser. 38: 248–58, 631–46.

7  Peel to Liverpool, 24 September, 31 October, 21 November 1817, BL Add. Ms. 40294; Talbot to Sidmouth, 24 November 1817, HO 100/193; Parker, *Peel*, 1:

262–4; Akenson, *Irish Education*, 82–7; Bowen, *Protestant Crusade*, 96–7.

8 Miller, *Emigrants and Exiles*, 194–5; Johnston, *British Emigration Policy*, 32–56.

9 Peel to Saurin, 28 March 1817, BL Add. Ms. 40292; Whitworth to Lord Chancellor, 9 May 1817, BL Add. Ms. 40204; Gregory to Lord Chancellor, 5 July 1817, OP 479/18, CSO, SPO; *Peel's Speeches*, 1: 86–7; *Parl. Deb.*, 1st ser. 36: 117, 565, 959–60, 1267–77, 1369; ibid., 37: 113; ibid., 38: 535–7; ibid., 39: 394–6; Peel to V. Fitzgerald, 22 November 1817, BL Add. Ms. 40294; Peel to Gregory, 3 February 1818, BL Add. Ms. 40294.

10 *Parl. Deb.*, 1st ser. 34: 854; Gregory to Peel, 17 March 1818, BL Add. Ms. 40205; *Parl. Deb.*, 1st ser. 35: 980–3; Peel to Gregory, 30 April 1817, BL Add. Ms. 40293; *Parl. Deb.*, 1st ser. 38: 567; *Croker Papers*, 1: 116.

11 Brown, *Fathers of Victorians*, 357; *Parl. Deb.*, 1st ser. 26: 129–32; Liverpool to Peel, 18 June 1818, BL Add. Ms. 40181.

12 *Fortescue Manuscripts*, 443; *Greville Memoirs*, 1: 356; Gregory, *Letter-Box*, 77; Henry Morris, *The Life of Charles Grant* (London 1904); Brynn, *Crown and Castle*, 70.

13 Grant to Sidmouth, 4 November 1820, HO 100/199; Peel to Gregory, 2 March 1819, BL Add. Ms. 40334.

14 O'Connell, *O'Connell Correspondence*, 2: 186; Gregory to Grant, 23 February 1819, Gregory Papers.

15 Talbot to Sidmouth, 25 February 1819, HO 100/196; *Parl. Deb.*, 1st ser. 40: 437.

16 Peel to Gregory, 4 May 1819, Gregory Papers; Grant to Gregory, 4 October 1819, Gregory Papers; Jacqueline R. Hill, "National Festivals, the state and 'protestant ascendancy' in Ireland, 1790–1829," *Irish Historical Studies* 24 (1984): 41; Gregory to Grant, 3 November 1821, Gregory Papers.

17 Gregory, *Letter-Box*, 80–1; Gregory to Grant, 19 March 1819, Gregory Papers; Grant to Gregory, 20 March 1819, Gregory Papers; *Parl. Deb.*, 2nd ser. 5: 1446; Sidmouth to Gregory, 9 May 1821, HO 100/200; Gregory to Sidmouth, 11, 12 May 1821, HO 100/200; Gregory to Liverpool, 11 May 1821, Gregory Papers.

18 *Parl. Deb.*, 1st ser. 40: 846–7; ibid., 2nd ser. 6: 1529; Grant to Sidmouth, 4 November 1820, HO 100/199.

19 Grant to Sidmouth, 4 November 1820, HO 100/199; *Parl. Deb.*, 2nd ser. 7: 152ff; ibid., 1st ser. 39: 1430–1.

20 Gregory to Grant, 10 March, 9 June 1819, Gregory Papers; *Parl. Deb.*, 1st ser. 39: 1432; Nicholls, *Irish Poor Law*, 87–8.

21 Grant to Liverpool, 16 October 1819, BL Add. Ms. 38280; Grant to Liverpool, 28 December 1819, BL Add. Ms. 38280.

22 Grant to Liverpool, 28 December 1819, BL Add. Ms. 38280; Hilton, *Corn, Cash, Commerce*, 85; *Parl. Deb.*, 2nd ser. 6: 1525.

23 *Parl. Deb.*, 2nd ser. 6: 1524; Grant to Sidmouth, 3 November 1818, HO 100/

195.

24 Sidmouth to Grant, 28 November 1818, HO 100/195; Grant to Sidmouth, December 1818, HO 100/195; *Parl. Deb.*, 2nd ser. 6: 1522; Parker, *Peel*, 1: 232; *Parl. Deb.*, 2nd ser. 6: 1528; ibid., 1st ser. 40: 593–4.

25 *Parl. Deb.*, 2nd ser. 6: 1527; ibid., 2: 96–100.

26 Ibid., 101; Grant to Sidmouth, 18 March 1819, HO 100/196; Duke of York to Sidmouth, 15 April 1819, HO 100/196.

27 Reinhard Cassirer, "The Irish Influence on the Liberal Movement in England 1798–1832" (PHD thesis, London, 1940), 83; Cullen, *Economic History since 1660*, 104; Talbot to Sidmouth, 4 August 1819, HO 100/197; Gregory to Hobhouse, 22 August 1819, HO 100/197, Grant to Sidmouth, 6 September 1819, HO 100/197.

28 Talbot to Sidmouth, 17 November 1819, HO 100/197; Broeker, *Rural Disorder and Police Reform*, 110–11.

29 Grant memorandum, n.d., HO 100/198; Talbot to Sidmouth, 4 December 1819, HO 100/197; Talbot to Gregory, 7 December 1819, Gregory Papers; Grant to Sidmouth, 24 January 1820, HO 100/198.

30 Gregory to Peel, 21 April 1818, BL Add. Ms. 40205; Gregory to Sidmouth, 30 December 1819, Gregory Papers; Gregory to Grant, 29 December 1819, HO 100/197; Gregory Diary, 11, 12 January 1820, Gregory Papers.

31 Sidmouth to Grant, 7, 23 January 1820, HO 100/198; Grant to Sidmouth, 10, 24 January, 4 February 1820, HO 100/198.

32 Grant memorandum, n.d. HO 100/198; Grant to Sidmouth, 16 February 1820, HO 100/198.

33 Anon to Sidmouth, 11 February 1820, Sidmouth Papers, Devon Record Office; Gregory to Talbot, 22 February 1820, Talbot Papers.

34 Grant to Sidmouth, 21 February, 22 March, 1820 HO 100/198; Grant memorandum, n.d., HO 100/198; Gregory to Talbot, 26 February 1820, Talbot Papers; Sidmouth to Grant, 27 March 1820, HO 100/198.

35 Gregory to Daly, 14 March, 23 February 1820, Private Official Correspondence, CSO, SPO; Gregory to Talbot, 20 February 1820, HO 100/198; Talbot to Sidmouth, 13, 17, 23 March 1820, HO 100/1980.

36 Talbot to Sidmouth, 8 April 1820, HO 100/198.

37 Grant to Sidmouth, 7 April 1820, HO 100/198; Grant memorandum, HO 100/198.

38 Grant to Sidmouth, 18 April 1820, HO 100/198; Talbot to Sidmouth, 15, 23 May 1820, HO 100/198; Armagh to Talbot, 3 May 1820, HO 100/198; Manners to Talbot, 6 May 1820, HO 100/198; Saurin to Gregory, May 1820, HO 100/198; Grant to Talbot, 2 June 1820, HO 100/198.

39 Peel to Gregory, 12 February, 14 March 1818, BL Add. Ms. 40294.

40 Sidmouth to Talbot, 10 September 1819, HO 100/197; Talbot to Sidmouth, 8 March 1820, HO 100/198; Talbot to Sidmouth, 7 September 1819, HO 100/197; Sidmouth to Talbot, 19, 29 September 1819, HO 100/197.

41  Gregory, *Letter-Box*, 87; Grant to Liverpool, 27, 31 January 1820, BL Add. Ms. 38282; Grant to Sidmouth, 27 January 1820, HO 100/198; Bowen, *Protestant Crusade*, 44.

42  Grant to Sidmouth, 1 August 1820, HO 100/199; Talbot to Sidmouth, 14 August 1820, HO 100/199; Armagh to Sidmouth, 17 January 1821, HO 100/200.

43  Grant to Gregory, 6 June 1820, Gregory Papers; Talbot to Grant, 30 June, 15, 20 July 1820, HO 100/199; Grant to Talbot, 12, 14, 15, 24 July 1820, HO 100/199.

44  *Parl. Deb.*, 2nd ser. 1: 802–3, 1005, 1033, 1053, 1106–10; ibid., 5: 1193, 1314–15.

45  See Barrow, *Emergence of Irish Banking*, 4, 17ff; C.W. Munn, "The Emergence of Central Banking in Ireland: The Bank of Ireland 1814–1850," *Irish Economic and Social History* 10 (1983): 19–32; Grant to Gregory 12 June 1820, Gregory Papers.

46  *Parl. Deb.*, 2nd ser. 1: 1106, 1110; Grant to Sidmouth, 28 September, 4 November 1820, HO 100/199; *Parl. Deb.*, 2nd ser. 4: 571; Gregory to Bagot, 22 August 1820, Private Official Correspondence, CSO, SPO.

47  Talbot to Sidmouth, 25 August, 29 September 1820, HO 100/199; Grant to Sidmouth, 1, 28 September 1820, HO 100/199; Gregory to Grant, 28 April 1820, Gregory Papers; O'Connell, *O'Connell Correspondence*, 2: 288.

48  Grant to Sidmouth, 28 September, 4 November 1820, HO 100/199; Grant to Sidmouth, 2 January 1821, HO 100/200; Talbot to Sidmouth, 23 August 1820, HO 100/199.

49  Gregory to Talbot, 3 June 1821, Gregory Papers; Grant to Gregory, 6 June 1821, Gregory Papers.

50  *Parl. Deb.*, 2nd ser. 4: 1208; Sorell to Gregory, 14 February 1821, Private Official Correspondence, CSO, SPO; Gregory to Sorell, 23 February, 1821, General Private Correspondence, CSO, SPO; Gregory to Talbot, 22 May 1821, Gregory Papers; Grant to Sidmouth, 26 May 1821, HO 100/200.

51  Gregory, *Letter-Box*, 83–5.

52  Talbot to Gregory, 4 June 1821, Talbot Papers; *Parl. Deb.*, 2nd ser. 4: 1426–7; Ward, *Eve of Catholic Emancipation*, 3: 69.

53  Gregory to Talbot, 6, 8 June, 7 July 1821, Talbot Papers; Talbot to Gregory, 2 July 1821, Talbot Papers.

54  Gregory, *Letter-Box*, 99–100; *Croker Papers*, 1: 203, 214–15; William John Fitzpatrick, *The Life, Times and Contemporaries of Lord Cloncurry* (Dublin 1855), 335; Ziegler, *Sidmouth*, 397.

55  Talbot to Sidmouth, 13 October 1821, HO 100/201; Warburton to Gregory, 7 October 1821, HO 100/201; Adams, *Agricultural Depression*, 154–7; *Parl. Deb.*, 2nd ser. 6: 495.

56  *Parl. Deb.*, 2nd ser. 6: 1505–14; Grant to Sidmouth, 28 November 1821, HO 100/202.

57  Sidmouth to Talbot, 19, 23 October 1821, HO 100/201; Gregory to Going, 12

August 1820, Private Official Correspondence, CSO, SPO; Talbot to Sidmouth, 6, 7 November 1821, HO 100/202.

58 Gregory, *Letter-Box*, 104–5; Grant to Sidmouth, 19 November 1821, HO 100/ 202.

59 Buckingham and Chandos, *Memoirs of the Court of George IV 1820–1830 from Original Family Documents*, 2 vols. (London 1859), 1: 317–18; Gregory to Sidmouth, 9 November 1821, Sidmouth Papers; Sidmouth to Gregory, 18 November 1821, Sidmouth Papers; Sidmouth to Talbot, 20 November 1821, HO 100/202; Sidmouth to Liverpool, 21, 22 November 1821, Sidmouth Papers.

60 Pellew, *Sidmouth*, 3: 369, *Bathurst Manuscripts*, 525; Liverpool to Talbot, 29 November 1821, BL Add. Ms. 38290; Talbot to Sidmouth, 3 December 1821, Sidmouth Papers; Gregory, *Letter-Box*, 108; Goulburn memoir, Goulburn Papers, Acc 319/68; Liverpool to Grant, 29 November 1821, BL Add. Ms. 38290; Viscountess Knutsford, *Life and Letters of Zachary Macaulay*, (London 1900), 376–7.

CHAPTER SIX

1 Sidmouth to Talbot, 16 January 1821, Sidmouth Papers; Yonge, *Liverpool*, 3: 158; *Quarterly Review* 22 (1820): 497; Lefevre, *Peel and O'Connell*, 38; *Colchester Diary*, 2: 439–40; Peel to Whitworth, 2 July 1814, BL Add. Ms. 40287; Peel to Gregory, 8 April 1815, BL Add. 40288; Sack, *Grenvillites*, 107–8, 175, 178, 184, 186; David Plunket, *The Life, Letters and Speeches of Lord Plunket*, 2 vols. (London 1867), 2: 7; Buckingham and Chandos, *Memoirs of the Court of England during the Regency*, 2 vols. (London 1856), 2: 357.

2 Buckingham, *Memoirs of Court of George IV*, 1: 241; Plunket to Wynn, 2 May [1821], Coed-y-Maen Mss; *Life of Eldon*, 2: 418.

3 Peel to Whitworth, 19 March 1817, Whitworth Papers, U269/0225; Sack, *Grenvillites*, 222–4, 186; Mitchell, *Whigs in Opposition*, 168–9; Wynn to Buckingham, n.d., Coed-y-Maen Mss; Liverpool to Wynn, 12 December 1821, BL Add. Ms. 38290; Buckingham to Wynn, 2 October, 29 September 1822, Coed-y-Maen Mss.

4 Cookson, *Liverpool Administration*, 309; Buckingham, *Memoirs of Court of George IV*, 1: 353; Henriques, *Religious Toleration*, 159.

5 Gash, *Mr. Secretary Peel*, 367; Mitchell, *Whigs in Opposition*, 76; *Bathurst Manuscripts*, 522; A. Aspinall, ed., *The Diary of Henry Hobhouse (1820–1827)*, 80.

6 Wellesley Memoir, BL Add. Ms. 37416; see also John Kenneth Severn, *A Wellesley Affair: Richard Marquis Wellesley and the Conduct of Anglo-Spanish Diplomacy, 1809–1812* (Tallahassee 1981), 39–42, 88–99, 204–9; P.E. Roberts, *India under Wellesley* (London 1929), 258–9, 269–72; Harvey, *Britain in Early Nineteenth Century*, 264–7; Iris Butler, *The Eldest Brother: The Marquis of Wellesley the Duke of Wellington's Eldest Brother* (London 1973), 479–80, 491–

2.

7 Roberts, *India under Wellesley*, 19; *Parl. Deb.*, 2nd ser. 8: 1145; Buckingham, *Memoirs of Court of George IV*, 1: 250; *Colchester Diary*, 3: 241; *Hobhouse Diary*, 80; *Random Recollections of the House of Lords 1830–1836* (London 1836), 115; *Bathurst Manuscripts*, 522.

8 Buckingham, *Memoirs of Court of George IV*, 2: 50; *Liverpool and Liberal Toryism*, 152; Goulburn Memoir, Goulburn Papers, Acc 319/68; Gash, *Mr. Secretary Peel*, 80; Saxton to Wynn, 15 December 1821, 13 January 1822, Coed-y-Maen Mss; Gillian Sutherland, ed., *Studies in the Growth of Nineteenth-Century Government* (London 1972), 140; Johnston, *British Emigration Policy*, 15; Goulburn to Ripon, 16 December 1850, BL Add. Ms. 40877; *Random Recollections of the House of Commons from the Year 1830 to the Close of 1836* (London 1837), 123; *Hobhouse Diary*, 81; A. Aspinall, ed., *Correspondence of Charles Arbuthnot, 1808–1850*, Royal Historical Society, Camden, 3rd ser. 65 (1941): 45.

9 Goulburn Memoir, Goulburn Papers, Acc 319/68; Liverpool to Goulburn, 26 November 1821, Acc 426/6; *Parl. Deb.*, 2nd ser. 9: 1283.

10 *Bathurst Manuscripts*, 524; Saxton to Wynn, 19 December 1821, Coed-y-Maen Mss; Buckingham, *Memoirs of Court of George IV*, 1: 235, 239–40.

11 Buckingham, *Memoirs of Court of George IV*, 1: 351; *Arbuthnot Correspondence*, 45; Peel to Goulburn, 26 December 1821, Goulburn Papers, Acc 319/36; George Peel, ed., *The Private Letters of Sir Robert Peel* (London 1920), 32; Peel to Whitworth, 19 March 1817, Whitworth Papers, U269/0225.

12 Peel to Goulburn, [December 1821], Goulburn Papers, Acc 319/35; Peel to Goulburn, 2 January 1822, Acc 319/35; Parker, *Peel*, 1: 305–6.

13 Ilchester, *The Journal of the Hon. Edward Fox (afterwards fourth and last Lord Holland) 1818–1830* (London 1923), 90–1; Goulburn to Sidmouth, 21 December 1821, Sidmouth Papers; Goulburn to S. Goulburn, 27 November 1809, Goulburn Papers, Acc 319/61; Goulburn Memoir, Acc 319/68; Wellesley to Goulburn, 22 February 1822, Acc 319/44; Wellesley to Peel, 15 November 1823, BL Add. Ms. 37301; Butler, *Eldest Brother*, 503; Gregory to Goulburn, 7 May 1823, Acc 319/71.

14 Goulburn to Peel, 24 March 1823, BL Add. Ms. 40329; Wellesley to Goulburn, 9 July, 1823, 5 March 1824, 15 May 1823, Goulburn Papers, Acc 319/44.

15 Talbot to Gregory, 10 January 1822, Talbot Papers; Gregory to Peel, 2 February 1822, BL Add. Ms. 40344.

16 Gregory to Peel, 5 February 1822, BL Add, Ms. 40334; Gregory to Goulburn, 6, 16 February, 22 March, 26 April 1822, Goulburn Papers, Acc 319/69.

17 Gregory to Goulburn, 21 July 1823, Goulburn Papers, Acc 319/70; Gregory to Goulburn, 16 February 1823, Acc 319/69; Gregory to Goulburn, 9 March, 20 February 1823, Acc 319/71; Gregory, *Letter-Box*, 54.

18 Gregory to Peel, 31 March 1823, BL Add. Ms. 40334; Gregory to Goulburn, 30 July 1823, Goulburn Papers, Acc 319/72.

19 Gregory, *Letter-Box*, 109, 131; Peel to Gregory, 28 January 1822, 5 April 1823, BL Add. Ms. 40344; Gregory to Peel, 4 October 1822, BL Add. Ms. 40334; Peel to Goulburn, 7 April 1823, BL Add. Ms. 40329; Peel to Gregory, n.d. [December 1822], BL Add. Ms. 40344.

20 Saxton to Wynn, 13 January 1822, Coed-y-Maen Mss; Gregory, *Letter-Box*, 111; Gregory to Goulburn, 3, 22 April 1822, Goulburn Papers, Acc 319/69; Goulburn to Gregory, 26 February 1822, Gregory Papers; Goulburn to Gregory, 27 February 1822, Acc 319/69; Gregory to Goulburn, 22 April 1822, Acc 319/69; Gregory to Goulburn, 23 April, 18 May 1823, Acc 319/71; Goulburn to Wellesley, 1 June 1822, Acc 319/43.

21 Gregory to Goulburn, 10 April 1823, Goulburn Papers, Acc 319/71; D.A. Chart, *Ireland from the Union to Catholic Emancipation* (London 1910), 181; Thomas Wyse, *Historical Sketch of the Late Catholic Association of Ireland*, 2 vols. (London 1829), 1: 357.

22 Gash, *Mr. Secretary Peel*, 355; Gash, *Lord Liverpool*, 183; Peter Quennell, ed., *The Private Letters of Princess Lieven to Prince Metternich 1820–1826* (New York 1938), 154; *Colchester Diary*, 3: 241; Black, *Economic Thought and Irish Question*, 143, 141; O'Brien, *Economic History from Union*, 310, 289–90, 294. Thomas Reid, *Travels in Ireland in the Year 1822* (London 1823), 153–5; *Life of Eldon*, 2: 434; Hilton, *Corn, Cash, Commerce*, 111; John O'Driscol, *Views of Ireland Moral, Political and Religious*, 2 vols. (London 1823), 1: 230; *Edinburgh Review* 34 (1820): 335.

23 *Edinburgh Review* 43 (1826): 198–9; *Edinburgh Review* 34 (1820): 335; Reid, *Travels in Ireland*, 325–6; *Edinburgh Review* 38 (1822): 62; O'Driscol, *Views of Ireland*, 2: 226; *Memoirs of the Life and Writings of Michael Thomas Sadler* (London 1848), 51; Perkin, *Origins of Modern English Society*, 241; Nicholls, *Irish Poor Law*, 88; *Parl. Deb.*, 2nd ser. 6: 12–13.

24 Reid, *Travels in Ireland*, 325–6; Saxton to Wynn, 15 February 1822, Coed-y-Maen Mss; *Quarterly Review* 43 (1830): 243; *Edinburgh Review* 37 (1822): 61.

25 C.B. Fay, *Huskisson and His Age* (London 1951), 114; Johnston, *British Emigration Policy*, 14; Black, *Economic Thought and Irish Question*, 203–6; O'Brien, *Economic History from Union*, 123, 131, 139–40, 144; *Edinburgh Review* 37 (1822): 103, 106–7; *Life of Eldon*, 2: 443.

26 See *Edinburgh Review* 21 (1819): 445; *Edinburgh Review* 37 (1822): 64–105; Ward, *Religion and Society*, 112–13; *Edinburgh Review* 34 (1820): 61–79; 324–6; Wray Vamplew, "Tithes and Agriculture: Some Comments on Commutation," *Economic History Review* 2nd ser. 34 (1981): 115–19.

27 *Parl. Deb.*, 2nd ser. 6: 114–15, 126–30, 201–8, 213, 1505–34.

28 *Peel's Speeches*, 1: 263; Peel to Wellesley, 12 April 1822, BL Add. Ms. 40324; Johnston to Peel, 15 April 1822, BL Add. Ms. 40324; Goulburn to Wellesley, 5 July 1823, BL Add. Ms. 37301; Goulburn to Wellesley, 2 July 1823, BL Add. Ms. 37299; Goulburn to Gregory, 12 March 1822, Gregory Papers; Goulburn to Wellesley, 20 March 1822, BL Add. Ms. 37298; Goulburn to Wellesley, 3

June 1822, Goulburn Papers, Acc 319/43; Wellesley to Goulburn, 5 July 1822, Acc 319/44.

29 Roberts, *India under Wellesley*, 10; Buckingham, *Memoirs of Court of George IV*, 1: 239; A. Aspinall, ed., *The Letters of King George IV 1812–1830*, 3 vols. (Cambridge 1938), 3: 297; *Hobhouse Diary*, 81; Wellesley to Peel, 3 February 1822, BL Add. Ms. 40324.

30 Pellew, *Sidmouth*, 3: 381; Wellesley to Sidmouth, 12 January 1822, Sidmouth Papers; Goulburn to Peel, 24 March 1823, BL Add. Ms. 40329; Grenville to Wynn, 11 January 1822, Coed-y-Maen Mss; Buckingham, *Memoirs of Court of George IV*, 1: 242; R.R. Pearce, *Memoirs and Correspondence of the Most Noble Richard Marquis Wellesley*, 3 vols (London 1846), 3: 336; Wellesley to Goulburn, 5 July 1822, Goulburn Papers, Acc 319/44; O'Connell, *O'Connell Correspondence*, 2: 347.

31 Saxton to Wynn, 28 January 1822, Coed-y-Maen Mss; Plunket to Newport, 5 January 1822, Newport Papers; Gregory, *Letter-Box*, 113; Buckingham to Wynn, 31 March, 2, 5 April 1822, Coed-y-Maen Mss; Buckingham, *Memoirs of Court of George IV*, 1: 307–11; 351; Machin, *Catholic Question in English Politics*, 36; Sidmouth to Manners, 12 December 1821, Sidmouth Papers.

32 Peel to Wellesley, 12 April 1822, BL Add. Ms. 37299; *Parl. Deb.*, 2nd ser. 6: 186–7; 1479; Wellesley to Sidmouth, 3 January 1822, BL Add. Ms. 37298; Wellesley to Peel, 22 May 1822, BL Add. Ms. 37299.

33 Talbot to Sidmouth, 1, 5 December 1821, HO 100/202; Clive to Grant, 6 December 1821, HO 100/201; Grant to Sidmouth, 12 December 1821, HO 100/202.

34 Wellesley to Sidmouth, 29 December 1821, Sidmouth Papers; Aspinall, *Letters of George IV*, 3: 300; Goulburn to Sidmouth, 2, 5 January 1822, HO 100/203.

35 Wellesley to Peel, 29 January 1822, BL Add. Ms. 37298; Goulburn to Peel, 26 January 1822, HO 100/203; Goulburn to Hobhouse, 1 February 1822, HO 100/203; Peel to Goulburn, 21 January 1822, Goulburn Papers, Acc 319/35; *Parl. Deb.*, 2nd ser. 6: 105–10, 185.

36 James W. O'Neill, "A Look at Captain Rock: Agrarian Rebellion in Ireland, 1815–1845," *Eire-Ireland* 17 (1982): 25; Wellesley to Peel, 16 February 1822, BL Add. Ms. 37298; O'Connell, *O'Connell Correspondence*, 2: 356–7, 359.

37 Gregory to Goulburn, 27 February, 5, 1 March 1822, Goulburn Papers, Acc 319/69; Clark and Donnelly, *Irish Peasants*, 135; Gregory to Goulburn, 25 February, 2 March, 26 April 1822, Acc 319/69; Wellesley to Peel, 31 January 1822, BL Add. Ms. 37298; Plunket to Wellesley, 26 February 1822, HO 100/203; Wellesley to Peel, 26 February 1822, HO 100/203; Talbot to Gregory, 16 April 1824, Talbot Papers.

38 Wellesley to Peel, 1 May 1822, BL Add. Ms. 37299; Gregory to Goulburn, 20 April 1822, Goulburn Papers, Acc 319/69; Wellesley to Goulburn, 16 June, 5 July 1822, Acc 319/44; *Parl. Deb.*, 2nd ser. 7: 1525–36.

39 Wellesley to Goulburn, 13 September 1822, Goulburn Papers, Acc 319/44; Goulburn to Peel, 25 October, 19 September 1822, HO 100/206; Peel to Goulburn,

6 November [1822], Acc 319/36.

40 Gregory to Goulburn, 16 April 1823, Goulburn Papers, Acc 319/71; Gregory to Peel, 31 March 1823, BL Add. Ms. 40344; Clark and Donnelly, *Irish Peasants*, 102–37.

41 *Parl. Deb.*, 2nd ser. 9: 218–20; Goulburn to Wellesley, 18 June, 1823, BL Add. Ms. 37301; Wellesley to Peel, 29 June, 15 November, 1823, BL Add. Ms. 37301; Goulburn to Peel, 15 November 1823, BL Add. Ms. 37301.

42 Wellesley to Peel, 1 May 1822, BL Add. Ms. 37299; Goulburn to Peel, 19 September 1822, HO 100/206; Wellesley to Peel, 15 November 1823, Goulburn Papers, Acc 319/43.

43 Saxton to Wynn, 28, 8, 13 January, 3 November, 16 December 1822, Coed-y-Maen Mss; McCullagh, *Sheil Memoir*, 1: 280; *Colchester Diary*, 3: 271–2.

44 Wellesley to Sidmouth, 5 January 1822, Sidmouth Papers; Wellesley to Peel, 15 July, 27 October 1822, BL Add. Ms. 37299; Peel to Wellesley, 21 July 1822, BL Add. Ms. 40324; Wellesley to Goulburn, 15 September, 4 October 1822, Goulburn Papers, Acc 319/44; Peel to Wellesley, 2 November 1822, HO 100/207; Peel to Goulburn, 6 November 1822, BL Add. Ms. 40328.

45 Peel to Wellesley, 11 November, 1822, BL Add. Ms. 37300; Plunket to Wellesley, 9 November 1822, HO 100/207; Saxton to Wynn, 13 November 1822, Coed-y-Maen Mss; *Colchester Diary*, 3: 265.

46 Hunter to Sidmouth, 18 December 1822, Sidmouth Papers; Goulburn to Peel, 15 December 1822, BL Add. Ms. 40328; Peel to Goulburn, 26 December 1822, Goulburn Papers, Acc 319/36; Goulburn to Peel, 1 January 1823, BL Add. Ms. 40329; Wellesley to Goulburn, 1 January 1823, Acc 319/44; *Colchester Diary*, 3: 267; O'Connell, *O'Connell Correspondence*, 2: 412–13; *Lieven-Metternich Letters*, 225.

47 Buckingham to Wynn, 26 January 1823, Coed-y-Maen Mss; Buckingham, *Memoirs of Court of George IV*, 1: 425; 416; *Lieven-Metternich Letters*, 236; O'Connell, *O'Connell Correspondence*, 2: 435; Herbert Maxwell, ed., *The Creevey Papers*, 2 vols. (New York 1903), 2: 63; Gregory to Goulburn, 17, 26; February 1823, Goulburn Papers, Acc 319/71; Goulburn to Gregory, 21 February 1823, Acc 319/71.

48 Gregory to Goulburn, 16 February 1823, Goulburn Papers, Acc 319/69; Goulburn to Wellesley, 17 February 1823, BL Add. Ms. 37300; Machin, *Catholic Question in English Politics*, 39; Mitchell, *Whigs in Opposition*, 177.

49 Buckingham, *Memoirs of Court of George IV*, 1: 401, 436; 440–41; Wellesley to Peel, 20 February, 1 March 1823, BL Add. Ms. 37300; Peel to Wellesley, 22 February, 6 March 1823, BL Add. Ms. 37300; Goulburn to Wellesley, 23 February 1823, BL Add. Ms. 37300; *Peel's Speeches*, 1: 220–2; *Parl. Deb.*, 2nd ser. 8: 461, 465.

50 Gregory to Goulburn, 14 March 1823, Goulburn Papers, Acc 319/72; Parker, *Peel*, 1: 341.

51 Goulburn to Wellesley, 27 June 1823, BL Add. Ms. 37301; Gregory to Goulburn,

30 July 1823, Goulburn Papers, Acc 319/72; Senior, *Orangeism*, 206–7.

52 Buckingham to Wynn, 4 March 1823, Coed-y-Maen Mss; Buckingham, *Memoirs of Court of George IV*, 1: 432–5; Peel to Wellesley, 10 March 1823, BL Add. Ms. 37300.

53 Buckingham, *Memoirs of Court of George IV*, 1: 443; 317–18; Gregory Diary, 4 April 1823, Gregory Papers; Goulburn to Peel, 14 January 1823, BL Add. Ms. 40329; Buckingham to Wynn, 8 October 1822, Coed-y-Maen Mss; Wellesley to Goulburn, 6 June 1823, Goulburn Papers, Acc 319/44.

CHAPTER SEVEN

1 *Parl. Deb.*, 2nd ser. 7: 473; 1529; ibid., 6: 1483; Gregory to Goulburn, 28 March 1822, Goulburn Papers, Acc 319/69.

2 Goulburn to Wellesley, 16 April 1822, BL Add. Ms. 37299; Gregory to Goulburn, 17 April 1822, Goulburn Papers, Acc 319/69; *Parl. Deb.*, 2nd ser. 7: 472.

3 Goulburn to Wellesley, 2, 15 April 1822, BL Add. Ms. 37299; Goulburn to Gregory, 20 April 1822, Gregory Papers; *Parl. Deb.*, 2nd ser. 7: 147; 670–3, 698, 726–7.

4 Peel to Gregory, 13 May 1822, BL Add. Ms. 40334; Peel to Goulburn, 18 May 1822, BL Add. Ms. 40328; Goulburn to Gregory, 21 May 1822, Gregory Papers; Nicholls, *Irish Poor Law*, 78; Connell, *Population of Ireland*, 221ff; Board of Health to Wellesley, 25 May 1822, HO 100/204.

5 *Maria Edgeworth's Letters from England*, 400–1; *Memoirs of Michael Sadler*, 55; Yonge, *Liverpool*, 3: 168.

6 Commissioners for Relief of Poor to Gregory, 16 May 1822, HO 100/204; Black, *Economic Thought and Irish Question*, 172; Commissioners for Relief of Poor to Gregory, 13 June 1822, HO 100/205; *Peel's Speeches*, 1: 208.

7 Wellesley to Peel, 24 May 1822, HO 100/204; Gregory to Goulburn, 21 May, 8, 18 June 1822, Goulburn Papers, Acc 319/70; Tuam to Gregory, 5, 12 June 1822, Gregory Papers; Goulburn to Gregory, 10 June 1822, Gregory Papers; Wellesley to Goulburn, 16 June 1822, Acc 319/44; Gregory to V. Fitzgerald, 11 June 1822, Gregory Papers; Stephen Royle, "Irish Famine Relief in the Early Nineteenth Century: The 1822 Famine in the Aran Islands," *Irish Economic and Social History*, 11 (1984): 45–6.

8 Fitzgerald to Gregory, 4 June 1822, Gregory Papers; Gregory to Goulburn, 22 June 1822, Goulburn Papers, Acc 319/70; Goulburn to Wellesley, 15, 19 June 1822, BL Add. Ms. 37299; Goulburn to Gregory, 18 June 1822, Gregory Papers; Peel to Wellesley, 19 June 1822, BL Add. Ms. 37299.

9 Gregory to Goulburn, 16 July 1822, Goulburn Papers, Acc 319/70; Goulburn to Peel, 7 September 1822, HO 100/206.

10 Royle, *Irish Economic and Social History* 11: 50–4; Buckingham to Wynn, 8 October 1822, Coed-y-Maen Mss; Gregory to Goulburn, 22 June 1822, Goulburn Papers, Acc 319/70; Board of Health to Wellesley, 14 October 1822, HO 100/

205.

11 *Parl. Deb.*, 2nd ser. 8: 3; see list of grants made by the lord lieutenant in 1822, HO 100/192; Black, *Economic Thought and Irish Question*, 172, 174; Gregory to Goulburn, 4 May 1823, Goulburn Papers, Acc 319/71; Peel to Goulburn, 28 October 1823, Acc 319/36.

12 Peel to Goulburn, 19 November 1823, Goulburn Papers, Acc 319/36.

13 Gregory to Goulburn, 18 March, 1 April, 28 May, 13, 20, 22 June 1824, Goulburn Papers, Acc 319/73.

14 Goulburn to Gregory, 7 June 1824, Gregory Papers; Wellesley to Peel, 27 April 1823, BL Add. Ms. 37301.

15 Peel to Wellesley, 12 April 1822, BL Add. Ms. 37299; Broeker, *Rural Disorder and Police Reform*, 142–3; Goulburn to Wellesley, 15 April 1822, BL Add. Ms. 37299.

16 Goulburn to Wellesley, 15 April 1822, BL Add. Ms. 37299; *Parl. Deb.*, 2nd ser. 7: 853–4, 863–7, 855–7; Broeker, *Rural Disorder and Police Reform*, 146–7; McDowell, *Irish Administration*, 136.

17 Wellesley to Goulburn, 5 July 1822, Goulburn Papers, Acc 319/44; Saxton to Wynn, 3 November, 15 December 1822, Coed-y-Maen Mss; Broeker, *Rural Disorder and Police Reform*, 155, 158; Wellesley to Peel, 27 April 1823, BL Add. Ms. 37301.

18 Wellesley to Peel, 27 September 1822, BL Add. Ms. 37299; quoted in McDowell, *Public Opinion and Government Policy*, 81; Wellesley to Peel, 18 May 1823, HO 100/209; Gregory to Goulburn, 8, 15 March 1822, Goulburn Papers, Acc 319/69; *Edinburgh Review* 41 (1825): 369, 371; *Parliamentary History and Review for 1826* (London 1827), 609–10.

19 *Parl. Deb.*, 2nd ser. 6: 1169; Wellesley to Goulburn, 23 February 1822, Goulburn Papers, Acc 319/44.

20 Akenson, *Church of Ireland*, 103; Goulburn to Wellesley, 13, 23 February 1822, BL Add. Ms. 37298; Goulburn to Peel, 16 October 1822, BL Add. Ms. 40328; Gregory to Goulburn, 12 April 1822, Gregory Papers.

21 Goulburn to Wellesley, 26 February, 25 March 1822, BL Add. Ms. 37298; Liverpool to Wellesley, 22 March 1822, BL Add. Ms. 37298; Peel to Wellesley, 12 April 1822, BL Add. Ms. 37299.

22 Buckingham, *Memoirs of Court of George IV*, 1: 313–14; Buckingham to Wynn, 17, 24 April, 8 October 1822, Coed-y-Maen Mss; *Parl. Deb.*, 2nd ser. 7: 1030–41; Wellesley to Goulburn, 5 July 1822, Goulburn Papers, Acc 319/44; Wellesley to Liverpool, 18 November 1822, BL Add. Ms. 37300.

23 Liverpool to Peel, 9 October 1822, BL Add. Ms. 40304; for Wellesley's material on tithe payments see BL Add. Ms. 37299; Pearce, *Wellesley Memoirs*, 3: 350–1; Wellesley to Peel, 21 November 1822, BL Add. Ms. 37300; Liverpool to Wellesley, 9 December 1822, BL Add. Ms. 37300; Wynn to Plunket, 4 December 1822, Coed-y-Maen Mss; Saxton to Wynn, 2 December 1822, Coed-y-Maen Mss; *Parl. Deb.*, 2nd ser. 7: 1065.

24 *Colchester Diary*, 3: 285; Irish Archbishops and Bishops to Wellesley, [7] March 1823, HO 100/208; Wellesley to Goulburn, n.d. February 1823, Goulburn Papers, Acc 319/44; Goulburn to Wellesley, 8 March 1823, BL Add. Ms. 37301; Akenson, *Church of Ireland*, 107; *Parl. Deb.*, 2nd ser. 7: 495–500; 1132–3.

25 Akenson, *Church of Ireland*, 108.

26 *Parl. Deb.*, 2nd ser. 8: 499; ibid., 9: 366, 1454–5, 373; 1453–4; Goulburn to Wellesley, 7 June 1823, BL Add. Ms. 37301.

27 Wellesley to Goulburn, n.d. September 1823, Goulburn Papers, Acc 319/44; Goulburn draft report on Tithe Composition Act [January 1824], BL Add. Ms. 37302; Fetter, *Economist in Parliament*, 169; *Parl. Deb.*, 2nd ser. 10: 852–7; ibid., 11: 425; Akenson, *Church of Ireland*, 105, 109; Clark, *Social Origins of Land War*, 91.

28 *Quarterly Review* 31 (1825): 496, 509; Peel to Goulburn, 28 October 1823, Goulburn Papers, Acc 319/36; Akenson, *Church of Ireland*, 125–7; *Parl. Deb.*, 2nd ser. 10: 183–7.

29 Plunket to Wynn, 18 November 1823, Coed-y-Maen Mss; Goulburn to Wellesley, 24 September 1823, Goulburn Papers, Acc 319/43; Bowen, *Protestant Crusade*, 88–9, 93–5.

30 Peel to Wellesley, 7 February, 10 March 1824, HO 100/209; Plunket to Wynn, 10 February 1824, Coed-y-Maen Mss; Buckingham, *Memoirs of Court of George IV*, 2: 48–9; Wellesley to Peel, 1 March 1824, HO 100/210.

31 Peel to Wellesley, 7 March 1824, HO 100/209; Wellesley to Goulburn, 5 March 1824, Goulburn Papers, Acc 319/44; Goulburn to Wellesley, 16 March 1824, BL Add. Ms. 37302; Plunket, *Life and Correspondence of Plunket*, 2: 145–6.

32 Aspinall, *Politics and Press*, 143n1; Inglis, *Freedom of Press*, 170–1, 175, 181; Peel to Gregory, 18 November 1823, BL Add. Ms. 40344; Peel to Goulburn, 4 January 1825, Goulburn Papers, Acc 319/37; Gregory to Browne, 30 June 1822, Private Official Correspondence, CSP, SPO; Gregory to Goulburn, 4 April 1822, Acc 319/69; Goulburn memoramdum, 17 March 1824, Acc 319/69; *Parl. Deb.*, 2nd ser. 15: 542.

33 Inglis, *Freedom of Press*, 173; Peel to Goulburn, 29 November 1825, Goulburn Papers, Acc 319/37; Aspinall, *Politics and Press*, 319–24; Inglis, *Irish Historical Studies* 8: 6–9, 15–17.

34 Peel to Wellesley, 8 July 1824, HO 100/211; Wynn to Plunket, 1 November 1823, Coed-y-Maen Mss; Aspinall, *Letters of George IV*, 3: 297, 299; *Parl. Deb.*, 2nd ser. 11: 686–7; Buckingham, *Memoirs of Court of George IV*, 2: 46.

35 Quoted in Broeker, *Rural Disorder and Police Reform*, 157; *Parl. Papers* 9 (1825): 15–16; Wellesley to Peel, 20 December 1824, BL Add. Ms. 37302; Broeker, *Rural Disorder and Police Reform*, 140–1; *Colchester Diary*, 3: 341.

36 *Parl. Papers* 7 (1825): 8; F. Bamford and Duke of Wellington, eds., *Journal of Mrs. Arbuthnot 1820–32*, 2 vols. (London 1950), 1: 311, 317–18; Wellesley to Sidmouth, 5 March 1824, BL Add. Ms. 37302.

37 Barrow, *Emergence of Irish Banking*, 53–4; Nicholls, *Irish Poor Law*, 91ff;

*Parliamentary History and Review for 1826*, 609–10; Donald Winch, *Classical Political Economy and Colonies* (London 1965), 48ff; Peel to Goulburn, [May 1823], Golburn Papers, Acc 319/36; Goulburn to Wellesley, 13 May 1823, BL Add. Ms. 37301; See also Johnston, *British Emigration Policy*, 69–90; Wendy Cameron, "Selecting Peter Robinson's Irish Emigrants", *Histoire Sociale/Social History* 9 (1976): 29–46; David S. Macmillan, "Commercial and Industrial Society in Great Britain and Ireland 1814–1824: A Study of Australian Immigration Applications, "*Histoire Sociale/Social History* 6 (1973): 181–201; Black, *Economic Thought and Irish Question*, 206–9; Miller, *Emigrants and Exiles*, 196.

38  Gordon, *Political Economy in Parliament*, 183, 233; Nicholls, *Irish Poor Law*, 95.

39  Ford, *Social Theory and Social Practice*, 26; Barry Gordon, *Economic Doctrine and Tory Liberalism 1824–1830* (London 1979), 82; *Parl. Deb.*, 2nd ser. 11: 450–77; Kenneth Charlton, "The State of Ireland in the 1820s James Cropper's Plan, "*Irish Historical Studies* 17 (1970–1): 335.

40  Charlton, *Irish Historical Studies* 17: 334–5; 335; *Parl. Deb.*, 2nd ser. 8: 204–12, 227–8; ibid., 11: 596, 707–8; *Peel's Speeches*, 1: 225; *Parl. Papers* 9 (1825): 27ff; Barrow, *Emergence of Irish Banking*, 25.

41  Lewis to Wynn, 13 January 1825, Coed-y-Maen; Geary, *Irish Economic and Social History* 8: 47; *Parliamentary History and Review for 1826*, 601; O'Brien, *Economic History from Union*, 160; Buckingham, *Memoirs of Court of George IV*, 2: 40, 47; *Parl. Papers* 5 (1826): 662; Mokyr, *Why Ireland Starved*, 281; Black, *Economic Thought and Irish Question*, 156.

42  *Parl. Papers* 5 (1826): 661; Yonge, *Liverpool*, 3: 351–4.

43  *Edinburgh Review* 41 (1824): 152; see also 41 (1825): 356–410; *Edinburgh Review* 43 (1826): 461–94; *Parl. Deb.*, 2nd ser. 9: 1264–7; *Parl. Papers* 9 (1825): 172, 176–7.

44  *Edinburgh Review* 41 (1825): 376; *Edinburgh Review* 43 (1826): 483; Buckingham, *Memoirs of Court of George IV*, 2: 14; Peel to Goulburn, 6 November 1823, Goulburn Papers, Acc 319/36; Clark, *Social Origins of Land War*, 92; Goulburn to Peel, 24 July 1824, HO 100/212.

45  *Edinburgh Review* 42 (1825): 404; *Edinburgh Review* 43 (1826: 199; *Parl. Papers* 9 (1825): 111; *Parl. Deb.*, 2nd ser. 9: 1241.

46  *Peel's Speeches*, 1: 293; 308; Akenson, *Irish Education*, 90, 94; *Parl. Papers*, 9 (1825): 373–7; *Parl. Deb.*, 2nd ser. 10: 838; 1476; Goulburn to Wellesley, 3 February 1824, BL Add. Ms. 37302; McDowell, *Irish Administration*, 242.

47  Parker, *Peel*, 1: 344; Akenson, *Irish Education*, 96–8.

48  Goulburn to Wellesley, 6, 10 June, 18 August 1825, Goulburn Papers, Acc 319/43; Goulburn to Peel, 19 September 1825, Acc 319/43.

49  *Parl. Deb.*, 2nd ser. 15: 3–25, 81, 227; Akenson, *Church of Ireland*, 99.

50  *Edinburgh Review* 41 (1825): 356–7, 368; Fetter, *Economist in Parliament*, 23; *Parl. Papers* 9 (1825): 111, 305; Wellesley quoted in Broeker, *Rural Disorder*

*and Police Reform*, 159.

## CHAPTER EIGHT

1 D. George Boyce, *Nationalism in Ireland* (London 1982), 140–1; Williams, *National Separatism*, 30–1; D. Frances Ferguson, "Rural/Urban Relations and Peasant Radicalism: A Preliminary Statement, *"Comparative Studies in Society and History* 28 (1976): 115–17; Michael Hechter, "Group Formation and the Cultural Division of Labor, *"American Journal of Sociology* 84:2 (1978): 297, 299; *O'Connell Correspondence*, 3: 31–2; See also Denis Gwynn, *Daniel O'Connell: The Irish Liberator* (London 1929); Charles Chevenix Trench, *The Great Dan: A Biography of Daniel O'Connell* (London 1984); Maurice O'Connell, "Daniel O'Connell and the Eighteenth Century," *Studies in Eighteenth-Century Culture* 5 (1976): 475–95.

2 For the organization of the Association and the relative importance of the clergy see James A. Reynolds, *The Catholic Emancipation Crisis in Ireland 1823–1829* (reprint, Westport 1970); and Fergus O'Ferrall, *Catholic Emancipation: Daniel O'Connell and the Birth of Irish Democracy 1820–30* (Dublin 1985); Ward, *Eve of Catholic Emancipation*, 3: 112–16; Boyce, *Irish Nationalism*, 139.

3 Gregory to Goulburn, 2 May 1823, Goulburn Papers, Acc 319/71; Goulburn to Wellesley, 5 May 1823, BL Add. Ms. 37301; Gregory to Peel, 11 May 1823, BL Add. Ms 40334; Peel to Wellesley, 16 May 1823, BL Add. Ms. 37301; Goulburn to Wellesley, 18 June 1823, BL Add. Ms. 37301; Wellesley to Peel, 22 June 1823, BL Add. Ms. 37301.

4 Gregory to Streatfield, 13 April 1823, BL Add. Ms. 40334; Bowen, *Protestant Crusade*, 63, 19; Gregory to Peel, 22, 14 November 1823, 11 April 1824, BL Add. Ms. 40344; O'Ferrall, *Catholic Emancipation*, 54, 59–61; Goulburn to Wellesley, 26 March 1824, BL Add. Ms. 37302; Gregory to Goulburn, 20 March, 16 May 1824, Goulburn Papers, Acc 319/73.

5 Peel to Goulburn, 14 April 1824, Goulburn Papers, Acc 319/35; Plunket, *Life and Letters of Plunket*, 2: 145–6; Goulburn to Peel, 20 April 1824, BL Add. Ms. 40330; Buckingham, *Memoirs of Court of George IV*, 2: 79, 89.

6 Buckingham, *Memoirs of Court of George IV*, 2: 79–80, 76; Buckingham to Wynn, 7 May 1824, Coed-y-Maen Mss; *Journal of Mrs. Arbuthnot*, 1: 331; 337; Peel to Goulburn, 31 July 1824, Goulburn Papers, Acc 319/37; Peel to Goulburn, 14 September 1824, Acc 319/35; *Colchester Diary*, 3: 343; *Lieven-Metternich Letters*, 328–9; Brock, *Liverpool and Liberal Toryism*, 246.

7 Peel to Goulburn, 24 September 1824, Goulburn Papers, Acc 319/35.

8 Goulburn to Peel, 27 October 1824, Goulburn Papers, Acc 319/35.

9 Goulburn to Peel, 27 October 1824, Goulburn Papers, Acc 319/35.

10 Parker, *Peel*, 1: 346; Peel to Goulburn, 2 November 1824, BL Add. Ms. 40330; Peel to Goulburn, 22 November 1824, Goulburn Papers, Acc 319/35.

11 Parker, *Peel*, 1: 349; Gash, *Mr. Secretary Peel*, 401–2; Clancarty to Liverpool,

18 November 1824, BL Add. Ms. 40304; Clancarty to Goulburn, 5 December 1824, HO 100/212; Goulburn to Peel, 16 November 1824, HO 100/211; Wellesley to Peel, 2 December 1824, HO 100/211; Goulburn to Peel, 14 December 1824, BL Add. Ms. 40330; Peel to Goulburn, 7 December 1824, BL Add. Ms. 40330; Peel to Goulburn, 6 December 1824, Goulburn Papers, Acc 319/35.

12 Wellesley to Peel, 10 December 1824, BL Add. Ms. 37303.

13 Buckingham, *Memoirs of Court of George IV*, 2: 166; 171; Buckingham to Wynn, n.d. [23 November 1824], Coed-y-Maen Mss; Peel to Wellesley, 18 December 1824, BL Add. Ms. 37303.

14 Wellesley to Peel, 2 November 1823, BL Add. Ms. 37301; Parker, *Peel*, 1: 355; Wellesley to Peel, 20 December 1824, BL Add. Ms. 37303; Goulburn to Peel, 20 December 1824, BL Add. Ms. 40330.

15 Parker, *Peel*, 1: 355, 367; Peel to Liverpool, 30 December 1824, BL Add. Ms. 40304; Liverpool to Peel, 31 December 1824, BL Add. Ms. 40304; Peel to Goulburn, 6, 27 December 1824, Goulburn Papers, Acc 319/35; Goulburn to Peel, 14 December 1824, BL Add. Ms. 37303; Plunket to Wellesley, 2 January 1825, BL Add. Ms. 37303; O'Connell, *O'Connell Correspondence*, 3: 90; Wellesley to Peel, 30 December 1824, HO 100/211; Goulburn to Peel, 5 January 1825, BL Add. Ms. 40330.

16 Peel to Wellesley, 18 December 1824, BL Add. Ms. 37303; Peel to Goulburn, 15, 30 December 1824, BL Add. Ms. 40330; Parker, *Peel*, 1: 369.

17 Peel to Wellesley, 27 December 1824, HO 100/211; Warburton to Wellesley, 26 January 1825, BL Add. Ms. 37303; *Parl. Papers* 9 (1825): 15–16, 18–19; Buckingham, *Memoirs of Court of George IV*, 2: 194, 199, 202; Wellesley to Peel, 19 January 1825, BL Add. Ms. 37303.

18 Grenville to Wynn, 26 January 1825, Coed-y-Maen Mss; Peel to Wellesley, 31 January, 1 March 1825, BL Add. Ms. 37303; Wellesley to Peel, 3 February 1825, BL Add. Ms. 37303; Goulburn to Wellesley, 1 February 1825, BL Add. Ms. 37303; Goulburn to Wellesley, 7 February 1825, Acc 319/43; Buckingham, *Memoirs of Court of George IV*, 2: 207.

19 *Parl. Deb.*, 2nd ser. 12: 185, 318, 200; Lord Broughton, *Recollections of a Long Life*, 5 vols. (London 1909–10), 3: 85–6, 88–9; *Canning's Speeches*, 5: 332; Senior, *Orangeism*, 215; Gash, *Mr. Secretary Peel*, 394; Buckingham, *Memoirs of Court of George IV*, 2: 215; *Hobhouse Diary*, 113; Robert Stewart, *Henry Brougham 1778–1868* (London 1985), 210; Goulburn to Wellesley, 3 March 1825, BL Add. Ms. 37303.

20 Broughton, *Recollections*, 3: 92–3.

21 Gregory to Peel, 25 February 1824, BL Add. Ms. 40344; Gregory to Goulburn, 1, 7, 9 February 1825, Goulburn Papers, Acc 319/74; Goulburn to Gregory, 12 February 1825, Acc 319/74.

22 Gregory to Goulburn, 6 March 1825, Goulburn Papers, Acc 319/74; Bowen, *Protestant Crusade*, 26.

23 John Biggs-Davison and George Chowdharay-Best, *The Cross of St. Patrick:*

*The Catholic Unionist Tradition in Ireland* (Abbotsbrook 1984), 135; Tuam to Wellesley, 25 November 1824, HO 100/121; Peel to Gregory, 21 March 1825, BL Add. Ms. 40344.

24 Gregory to Peel, 25 March 1825, BL Add. Ms. 40344.

25 Gregory to Peel, 25 March 1825, BL Add. Ms. 40344; Gregory to Goulburn, 24 April 1825, Goulburn Papers, Acc 319/74.

26 Gregory to Peel, 25 March 1825, BL Add. Ms. 40344.

27 *Parl. Papers* 9 (1825): 35ff., 439–50, 386; Bowen, *Protestant Crusade*, 50.

28 *Parl. Deb.*, 2nd ser. 13: 229, 308, 325, 329; Broughton, *Recollections*, 3:98; O'Connell, *O'Connell Correspondence*, 3: 153; *Parliamentary History and Review for 1825*, 621–2; *Life of Eldon*, 2: 548–9.

29 *Life of Eldon*, 2: 546; Broughton, *Recollections*, 3: 96–7; O'Connell, *O'Connell Correspondence*, 3: 159, 161, 165, 172; *Canning and His Friends*, 2: 251.

30 See G.I.T. Machin, "The Catholic Emancipation Crisis of 1825," *English Historical Review* 78 (1963): 458–82; Machin, *Catholic Question in English Politics*, 42–4; Liverpool to Peel, 10 March 1825, BL Add. Ms. 40305; *Canning and His Friends*, 2: 279; *Life of Eldon*, 2: 552.

31 O'Connell, *O'Connell Correspondence*, 3: 176–7; *Canning and His Friends*, 2: 281; Broughton, *Recollections*, 3: 102; Grenville to Wynn, 19 May 1825, Coed-y-Maen Mss; Plunket, *Life and Letters of Plunket*, 2: 207; *Bathurst Manuscripts*, 583; *Hobhouse Diary*, 115.

32 Gregory to Goulburn, 17, 23, 7, 29 May 1825, Goulburn Papers, Acc 319/74; Goulburn to Gregory, 27 May 1825, Gregory Papers; O'Connell, *O'Connell Correspondence*, 3: 173.

33 Gregory to Goulburn, 29 May, 10, 6, 17 June, 5 July 1825, Goulburn Papers, Acc 319/74; Gregory to Peel, 10 July 1825, BL Add. Ms. 40344.

34 Gregory to Goulburn, 24, 30 June 1825, Goulburn Papers, Acc 319/75; Gregory to Peel, 10 July 1825, BL Add. Ms. 40344.

35 Wellesley to Goulburn, 27 June 1825, Goulburn Papers, Acc 319/44; Pearce, *Memoirs of Wellesley*, 3: 387–8; Albemarle, *Fifty Years of My Life*, 2 vols. (London 1876), 2: 227–32; Warrene Blake, *An Irish Beauty of the Regency* (London 1911), 279–80; Neville Thompson, *Wellington after Waterloo* (London 1986), 51; Butler, *Eldest Brother*, 497; *Maria Edgeworth's Letters from England*, 486–7; O'Connell, *O'Connell Correspondence*, 3: 193–4, 197; Goulburn to Peel, 13 October 1825, BL Add. Ms. 40331; Gregory to Peel, 14 October 1825, BL Add. Ms. 40344.

36 *Canning's Speeches*, 5: 428; Augustus Granville Stapleton, *George Canning and His Times* (London 1859), 253–6; Wellesley to Peel, 26 September 1825, HO 100/214; Stewart, *Brougham*, 211; Spring Rice to Wynn, 13 October 1825, Coed-y-Maen Mss; Plunket to Wynn, 2 October 1825, Coed-y-Maen Mss.

37 Gregory to Peel, 12 December 1825, BL Add. Ms. 40344; Wellesley to Peel, 30 December 1825, BL Add. Ms. 37303; Goulburn to Peel, 31 December 1825, BL Add. Ms. 40331; Peel to Wellesley, 5, 3 January, 3 February 1826, BL Add.

Ms. 37304; Wellesley to Peel, 29 January 1826, BL Add. Ms. 37304.

38 Wellesley to Liverpool, 12 January 1826, BL Add. Ms. 38301; O'Connell, *O'Connell Correspondence*, 3: 237–8; Peel to Goulburn, 26 March 1826, BL Add. Ms. 40332; Goulburn to Peel, 1 April, 25 July 1826, BL Add. Ms. 40332; Gregory to Goulburn, 6 March 1826, Goulburn Papers, Acc 319/75.

39 Wellesley to Liverpool, 12 January 1826, BL Add. Ms. 38301; Cullen, *Economic History since 1660*, 105; Wellesley to Peel, 13 May 1826, HO 100/216; Gregory to Goulburn, 4, 5, 12 May 1826, Goulburn Papers, Acc 319/76.

40 Goulburn to Wellesley, 4 February 1826, BL Add. Ms. 37304; Goulburn to Wellesley, 25 June 1825, Goulburn Papers, Acc 319/43; *Parl. Deb.*, 2nd ser. 14: 129, 426–7, 544–9, 718; ibid., 24: 89, 91, 198, 201.

41 Gregory to Goulburn, 14 February 1823, Goulburn Papers, Acc 319/71; Gregory to Goulburn, 22, 24, 26 June 1826, Acc 319/76; K. Theodore Hoppen, *Elections, Politics, and Society in Ireland 1832–1885* (Oxford 1984), 391; Hunt to Fitzgerald, 7 August 1826, Letters of Sir Peter Fitzgerald, Spring Rice Collection, Rylands Library, Manchester; Peel to Gregory, 3 July 1826, BL Add. Ms. 40344; see also J.A. Whyte, "The Influence of the Catholic Clergy on Elections in Nineteenth-Century Ireland," *English Historical Review* 75 (1960): 239–59; O. MacDonagh, "The Politicization of the Irish Catholic Bishops, 1800–1850," *Historical Journal*, 18 (1975): 37–53; J.A. Whyte, "Landlord Influence at Elections in Ireland, 1760–1885," *English Historical Review* 80 (1965): 740–60; Reynolds, *Catholic Emancipation Crisis*, 87–100.

42 O'Ferrall, *Catholic Emancipation*, 130–1; Machin, *Catholic Question in English Politics*, 84; Gash, *Mr. Secretary Peel*, 395; Gregory to Peel, 29 June 1826, BL Add. Ms. 40344; Gregory to Goulburn, 18 November 1826, Goulburn Papers, Acc 319/76; Goulburn to Peel, 13 September 1826, BL Add. Ms. 40332.

43 Peel to Wellington, 31 July 1826, BL Add. Ms. 40306; Senior, *Orangeism*, 221; Gash, *Mr. Secretary Peel*, 397; Peel to Goulburn, 20 October 1826, Goulburn Papers, Acc 319/38.

44 Goulburn to Peel, 25 July 1826, BL Add. Ms. 40332; Hunt to Fitzgerald, 7 August 1826, Spring Rice Collection, Manchester; Goulburn to Wellesley, 6 August 1826, Goulburn Papers, Acc 319/43; Wellesley to Goulburn, 7 August 1826, Acc 319/43.

45 Goulburn to Peel, 25 July 1826, BL Add. Ms. 40332; Goulburn to Peel, 29 July 1826, Goulburn Papers, Acc 319/43; Peel to Goulburn, 31 July 1826, Acc 319/38; Peel to Wellesley, 11 August 1826, Acc 319/38.

46 Goulburn to Wellesley, n.d. August 1826, Goulburn Papers, Acc 319/43; Wellesley to Peel, 27 August 1826, HO 100/216; Goulburn to Peel, 11 October 1826, HO 100/216.

47 Goulburn to Peel, 25 July 1826, BL Add. Ms. 40332; Goulburn to Peel, 25 August 1826, Goulburn Papers, Acc 319/38; Peel to Goulburn, 17 August 1826, Acc 319/38; Wellesley to Peel, 4 September 1826, HO 100/216; Hilton, *Corn, Cash, Commerce*, 277; Goulburn to Peel, 10 October 1826, HO 100/216; Bourne,

*Palmerston-Sulivan letters*, 185.

48 *Parl. Deb.*, 2nd ser. 16: 39, 48, 1086, 485–94, 1261–6, 89.

49 Gash, *Mr. Secretary Peel*, 398; O'Connell, *O'Connell Correspondence*, 3: 283; Peel to Goulburn, 15 December 1826, BL Add. Ms. 40332; Goulburn to Peel, 17, 23 December 1826, BL Add. Ms. 40332; Aspinall, *Letters of George IV*, 3: 174, 176–7.

50 Goulburn to Peel, 10 October 1826, HO 100/216; Goulburn to Peel, 20 December 1826, 24 January 1827, BL Add. Ms. 40332.

51 *Parl. Deb.*, 2nd ser. 16: 825; Gregory to Goulburn, 9, 14, 18 March, 19 February 1827, Goulburn Papers, Acc 319/77.

52 Gregory to Goulburn, 14, 17, 20 April 1827, Goulburn Papers, Acc 319/77; Peel to Gregory, 20 April 1827, BL Add. Ms. 40344; Goulburn to Gregory, 14 April 1827, Gregory Papers; Wellesley to Gregory, [17 April 1827], Acc 319/ 77; Gregory to Peel, 25 April 1827, BL Add. Ms. 40344.

CHAPTER NINE

1 See Wendy Hinde, *George Canning* (New York 1973), 437ff; Robert Stewart, *The Foundation of the Conservative Party 1830–1867* (London 1978), 3–5; Machin, *Catholic Question and English Politics*, 94ff; Mitchell, *Whigs in Opposition*, 195ff; Peter Dixon, *Canning Politician and Statesman* (London 1976), 266–7; *Parl. Deb.*, 2nd ser. 17: 441; O'Connell, *O'Connell Correspondence*, 3: 370.

2 *Parl. Deb.*, 2nd ser. 17: 578, 501–2.

3 See Gash, *Mr. Secretary Peel*, 433ff; Parker, *Peel*, 2: 485–6; *Hobhouse Diary*, 133; Arthur Aspinall, ed., "The Formation of Canning's Ministry February to August 1827," *Camden*, 3rd ser. 59 (1937); Aspinall, *Letters of George IV*, 3: 245–6, 252; Editor of *The Windham Papers, The Wellesley Papers*, 2 vols. (London 1914), 2: 190–2, 199–200; 159–64; Yonge, *Liverpool*, 3: 331; Peel to Goulburn, 29 November 1825, Goulburn Papers, Acc 319/36; Machin, *Catholic Question in English Politics*, 74.

4 D.M. Young, *The Colonial Office in the Early Nineteenth Century* (London 1961), 107; Mitchell, *Whigs in Opposition*, 200; Talbot to Gregory, 14 July 1827, Talbot Papers.

5 Machin, *Catholic Question in English Politics*, 105; *Hobhouse Diary*, 132; *Camden*, 3rd ser. 59: 234–6, 255; *Melbourne Memoirs*, 1: 221, 272–3; Gregory, *Letter-Box*, 147.

6 Gregory to Talbot, 23 July 1827, Talbot Papers; for Goderich's account of the formation of his government see his memorandum, 17 August 1827, BL Add. Ms. 40862; R.W. Davis, "The Tories, the Whigs, and Catholic emancipation, 1827–1829, "*English Historical Review* 97 (1982): 95; Philip Ziegler, *Melbourne* (London 1976), 92; Anglesey, *One-Leg: The Life and Letters of Henry William Paget First Marquess of Anglesey 1768–1854* (London 1961), 188; W.D. Jones,

*Prosperity Robinson: The Life of Viscount Goderich 1782–1859* (London 1967), 175; Lloyd C. Sanders, ed., *Lord Melbourne's Papers* (reprint, New York 1971), 105–6; Gregory to Goulburn, 10 October 1827, Goulburn Papers, Acc 319/77; Lamb to Spring Rice, 27 September 1827, Monteagle Mss. 13368, National Library of Ireland.

7 Gregory, *Letter-Box*, 155; 146; Lamb to Gregory, 3 May 1827, Gregory Papers; Gregory to Lamb, 6, 21 May 1827, Gregory Papers; Gregory to Goulburn, 12 November 1827, Goulburn Papers, Acc 319/77.

8 Gregory to Goulburn, 26 July 1827, Goulburn Papers, Acc 319/77; Augusta Gregory, ed., *Antobiography of the right Honourable Sir William Gregory* (London 1894), 11; *Melbourne Memoirs*, 1: 280; Goulburn to Gregory, 10 February 1828, Gregory Papers.

9 *Camden*, 3rd ser. 59: 276; Lamb to Spring Rice, 11 November 1827, Monteagle 13368; Joseph Bevan Braithwaite, ed., *Memoirs of Joseph John Gurney*, 2 vols. (Philadelphia 1854), 1: 330–1; *Edinburgh Review* 41 (1825): 373–5; *Parl. Deb.*, 2nd ser. 9: 1212–26, 1232; Wellesley to Goulburn, 25 March 1827, Goulburn Papers, Acc 319/44; Lamb to Wellesley, 7 June 1827, BL Add. Ms. 37305; Brynn, *Crown and Castle*, 155.

10 Rollo Russell, ed., *Early Correspondence of Lord John Russell 1805–40*, 2 vols. (London 1913), 1: 260; Bourne, *Palmerston-Sulivan Letters*, 202; Bowen, *Protestant Crusade*, 107–8; *Memoirs of Gurney*, 1: 354; Newport to Spring Rice, 6 October 1827, Monteagle 13368.

11 Gregory to Goulburn, 21, 22 March, 4 April 1827, Goulburn Papers, Acc 319/77; Newport to Spring Rice, 6 October 1827, Monteagle 13368.

12 Gregory to Goulburn, 4 April 1827, Goulburn Papers, Acc 319/77; *Parl. Deb.*, 2nd ser. 6: 12–13; Fetter, *Economist in Parliament*, 69; *Parl. Deb.*, 2nd ser. 7: 1046–52.

13 *Random Recollection of Commons*, 201–3; Maxwell, *Creevey Papers*, 2: 180; Spring Rice to Lamb, 10 December 1827, Monteagle 548; *Camden*, 3rd ser. 59:206; *Melbourne Memoirs*, 1: 91, 95, 162, 165; Sanders, *Melbourne's Papers*, 100; Ziegler, *Melbourne*, 91–2; *Parl. Deb.*, 2nd ser. 6: 179; Bertram Newman, *Lord Melbourne* (London 1930), 77.

14 *Memoirs of Gurney*, 1: 334; *Melbourne Memoirs*, 1: 252; Lamb to Gregory, 14 May 1827, Gregory Papers; Gregory memorandum, n.d., Gregory Papers; Lamb to Spring Rice, 18 September 1827, HO 100/218; for police returns see *Parl. Papers* 20 (1826–7): 27–9.

15 Gregory to Goulburn, 26 July 1827, Goulburn Papers, Acc 319/77; Lansdowne to Wellesley, 30 July 1827, Monteagle 548 (see also HO 100/217).

16 Spring Rice to Lamb, 12 September 1828, Monteagle 548; quoted in Inglis, *Freedom of Press*, 185; *Melbourne Memoirs*, 1: 249–50; Aspinall, *English Historical Review* 56: 645; Lamb to Spring Rice, 14 September 1827, Monteagle 13368.

17 Lamb to Lansdowne, 19 September 1827, HO 100/220; Lamb to Spring Rice, 7

January 1828, Monteagle 13368; *Melbourne Memoirs*, 1: 278–82; Sanders, *Melbourne's Papers*, 112–13.

18 Lamb to Lansdowne, 18 October, 11 November 1827, HO 100/219; Lamb to Spring Rice, 22 November 1827, Monteagle 13368; Wellesley to Lords Justices, 14 December 1827, HO 100/219; Lamb to Wellesley, 2 January 1828, HO 100/ 219.

19 Sanders, *Melbourne's Papers*, 111; Gregory to Goulburn, 16 October 1827, Goulburn Papers, Acc 319/77.

20 O'Connell, *O'Connell Correspondence*, 3: 287, 291–2, 312, 316, 318–20, 322–3, 326, 346–7, 358, 372–3; Lamb to Spring Rice, 24 December 1827, 4 January 1828, Monteagle 13368; O'Connell, *O'Connell Correspondence*, 3: 341–2.

21 Gash, *Aristocracy and People*, 131; Mitchell, *Whigs in Opposition*, 208; Thompson, *Wellington after Waterloo*, 71; Elizabeth Longford, *Wellington Pillar of State* (London 1972), 152–4; Lord Mahon and Edward Cardwell, eds., *Memoirs of The right Honourable Sir Robert Peel*, 2 vols. (London 1856), 1: 11–15; Machin, *Catholic Question in English Politics*, 110; Chamberlain, *Lord Aberdeen*, 194.

22 *Parl. Deb.*, 2nd ser. 18: 1050; ibid., 1st ser. 40: 446; Thompson, *Wellington after Waterloo*, 44–5, 48–9, 62–3; Longford *Pillar of State*, 138, 118–19; Davis, *English Historical Review* 97: 96; Stewart, *Foundation of Conservative Party*, 34; Johnston, *British Emigration Policy*, 154.

23 *Parl. Deb.*, 2nd ser. 18: 2–4; 574; 1417, 1422, 1126; O'Connell, *O'Connell Correspondence*, 3: 377; *Melbourne Memoirs*, 1: 311; *Parl. Deb.*, 2nd ser. 19: 259.

24 *Parl. Deb.*, 2nd ser. 19: 1045; *Peel's Speeches*, 1: 642–4.

25 See Johnston, *British Emigration Policy*, 150–9, 91–5, 104–5, 116, 100; Young, *Colonial Office*, 107; Gordon, *Economic Doctrine and Tory Liberalism*, 74–9; Black, *Economic Thought and Irish Question*, 214–15; *Parl. Deb.*, 2nd ser. 18: 961–2, 1214–17, 1547–54; Miller, *Emigrants and Exiles*, 197.

26 Johnston, *British Emigration Policy*, 118–26; Miller, *Emigrants and Exiles*, 197; Macdonagh, *Pattern of Government*, 65–73.

27 *Parl. Deb.*, 2nd ser. 18: 691; *Early Correspondence of Lord John Russell*, 1: 253; G.I.T. Machin, "Resistance to Repeal of the Test and Corporation Act, 1828," *Historical Journal* 22 (1979): 119; see also R.W. Davis, "The Strategy of 'Dissent' in the Repeal Campaign, 1820–1828, *"Journal of Modern History* 38 (1966): 374–93.

28 Longford, *Pillar of State*, 166; *Peel's Speeches*, 1: 612, 622; Gash, *Mr. Secretary Peel*, 514; *Croker Papers*, 1: 115.

29 R.E. Tighe, "A Brief Sketch of the Marquis of Anglesey's Administration," pamphlet (Dublin 1829), 7–8; 9, 22; Reginald W. Jeffery, ed., *Dyott's Diary 1781–1845*, 2 vols. (London 1907), 2: 32–3; Anglesey, *One-Leg*, 184–5, 191–2; Sanders, *Melbourne's Papers*, 170; Buckingham, *Memoirs of Court of George IV*, 2: 369; O'Connell, *O'Connell Correspondence*, 3: 332–3; *Cloncurry*

Memoirs, 331–2; Gregory, Letter-Box, 149; Fitzpatrick, Life and Times of Cloncurry, 381.

30 Gregory to Goulburn, 3 July 1827, Goulburn Papers, Acc 319/77; O'Mahoney, Viceroys, 230; Gash, Mr. Secretary Peel, 509.

31 Peel Memoirs, 1: 23–8; 29–34, 38–55, 56; Melbourne Memoirs, 1: 307; Sanders, Melbourne's Papers, 107, 114; Edward Law, Lord Ellenborough, A Political Diary 1828–1830, ed. Lord Colchester, 2 vols. (London 1881), 1: 96–7.

32 Anglesey to Huskisson, 3 April 1828, BL Add. Ms. 38756; Anglesey to Peel, 18 May, 5 June, 16 May, 2 June 1828, HO 100/222.

33 Peel Memoirs, 1: 166–77; Peel to Anglesey, 14 August 1828, HO 100/224.

34 Chamberlain, Lord Aberdeen, 194; Thompson, Wellington after Waterloo, 79; Ellenborough, Diary, 1: 76, 107; G.I.T. Machin, "The Duke of Wellington and Catholic Emancipation," Ecclesiastical History, 14 (1962): 199; Melbourne Memoirs, 1: 315; Goulburn to Gregory, 26 May 1828, Gregory Papers, Gash, Mr. Secretary Peel, 516; Gregory to Peel, 3 February 1828, BL Add. Ms. 40344.

35 Anglesey to Huskisson, 28 May 1828, BL Add. Ms. 38756; Duke of Wellington, ed., Despatches, Correspondence, and Memoranda of Field Marshall Arthur Duke of Wellington, 2nd ser., 8 vols. (London 1871), 4: 478–9; Anglesey to Peel, 2 June 1828, HO 100/222; Maxwell, Creevey Papers, 2: 160; Journal of Mrs. Arbuthnot, 2: 48; Gervas Huxley, Lady Elizabeth and the Grosvenors: Life in a Whig Family, 1822–1839 (London 1969), 16–17; Thompson, Wellington after Waterloo, 25; Maria Edgeworth's Letters from England, 158, 491; Ellenborough, Diary, 1: 145–6; F. Leveson-Gower, ed., Letters of Harriet Countess Granville 1810–1845, 2 vols. (London 1894), 1: 19; 2: 23.

36 Augustus Paget, ed., Paget Papers, 2 vols. (London 1896), 2, App. 2: 392–3; Gregory, Letter-Box, 167; Wellington Correspondence, 2nd ser. 4: 420; 5: 148; Peel Memoirs, 1: 149, 36–7; Leveson Gower to Peel, 26 June 1828, BL Add. Ms. 40335; Gash, Mr. Secretary Peel, 518–21, 509–10; Longford, Pillar of State, 163.

37 Paget Papers, 2, App. 2: 393, 395; O'Ferrall, Catholic Emancipation, 178; Anglesey to Gregory, 27 June 1828, BL Add. Ms. 40344; Anglesey, One-Leg, 199.

38 Paget Papers, 2, App. 2: 396, 398; Anglesey, One-Leg, 201; Anglesey to Leveson Gower, 2 July 1828, BL Add. Ms. 40355; Peel Memoirs, 1: 146–7; Gash, Mr. Secretary Peel, 525–6; Parker, Peel, 2: 51; Ellenborough, Diary, 1: 161.

39 Longford, Pillar of State, 169–70; Gash, Mr. Secretary Peel, 528–31; Wellington Correspondence, 2nd ser. 4: 254–68; Ellenborough, Diary, 1: 182; Parker, Peel, 2: 54–60.

40 Peel to Wellington, 11 September 1828, BL Add. Ms. 40307; Parker, Peel, 2: 62–4; Wellington Correspondence, 2nd ser. 5: 42–3.

41 Parker, Peel, 2: 52, 61, 68; 76–7; Gash, Mr. Secretary Peel, 541; Longford, Pillar of State, 173; Paget Papers, 2, App. 2: 399; Davis, English Historical

*Review* 97: 97.

42 Wellington to Peel, 6 August 1828, BL Add. Ms. 40307; Parker, *Peel*, 2: 67; Best, *Transactions of Royal Historical Society* 5 ser. 8: 118; Ellenborough, *Diary*, 1: 209.

43 Gregory to Peel, 7 July 1828, BL Add. Ms. 40344; Gregory to High Sheriff of Leitrim, 8 July 1828, Country Letters, 4 March 1828–20 October 1828, CSO, SPO; *Wellington Correspondence* 2nd ser. 4: 604–10, 633–4; 622–63; *Correspondence of Arbuthnot*, 108; Ellenborough, *Diary*, 1: 199, 203.

44 Parker, *Peel*, 2: 67–8; Anglesey, *One-Leg*, 206; O'Ferrall, *Catholic Emancipation*, 211; *Wellington Correspondence*, 2nd ser. 5: 91–3; Higgin to Goulburn, 17 September 1828, Goulburn Papers, Acc 319/34; Wellington to Goulburn 24 October 1828, Acc 319/34.

45 Gregory to Peel, 12 August 1828, BL Add. Ms. 40344; Senior, *Orangeism*, 225–6; O'Connell *O'Connell Correspondence*, 3: 403–4; Bowen, *Protestant Crusade*, 136; Wellington to Peel, 31 August 1828, BL Add. Ms. 40307; Leveson Gower to Peel, 27 September 1828, BL Add. Ms. 40335; Anglesey to Peel, 2 October 1828, BL Add. Ms. 40326; *Peel Memoirs*, 1: 263; *Wellington Correspondence*, 2nd ser. 5: 154; see also G.I.T. Machin, "The No-Popery Movement in Britain in 1828–9," *Historical Journal* 6: (1963): 195–211; O'Ferrall, *Catholic Emancipation*, 170–3.

46 Gregory to Peel, 30 August 1828, BL Add. Ms. 40344; Leveson Gower to Peel, 24 September 1828, HO 100/223; Ellenborough, *Diary*, 1: 226; *Peel Memoirs*, 1: 207, 209; 218–22, 230–5; Broeker, *Rural Disorder and Police Reform*, 178–9; *Wellington Correspondence*, 2nd ser. 4: 666.

47 *Paget Papers*, 2, App. 2: 401; *Wellington Correspondence*, 2nd ser. 5: 105, 111; 133–7; Wellington to Peel, 14 October 1828, BL Add. Ms. 40308; Peel to Leveson Gower, 17 October 1828, BL Add. Ms. 40336.

48 *Paget Papers*, 2, App. 2: 407; *Peel Memoirs*, 1: 246–61; *Wellington Correspondence*, 2nd ser. 5: 214, 252–3, 240–1, 287; Ellenborough, *Diary*, 1: 281.

49 Leveson Gower to Peel, 2 December 1828, BL Add. Ms. 40336; Anglesey to Huskisson, 3 January 1829, BL Add. Ms. 38757; Anglesey, *One-Leg*, 213–16; *Paget Papers*, 2, App. 2: 407.

50 Gregory to Peel, 6 December 1828, BL Add. Ms. 40334; *Wellington Correspondence*, 2nd ser. 5: 289–90, 463; 453; *Lady Holland to Her Son 1821–1845*, 88; *Journal of Mrs. Arbuthnot*, 2: 231–2; Bourne, *Palmerston-Sulivan Letters*, 227; Ellenborough, *Diary*, 1: 310.

51 Wynn to Spring Rice, 8 January 1829, Monteagle 13370; *Lady Holland to Her Son 1821–1845*, 94; *Greville Memoirs*, 1: 241–2; Ellenborough, *Diary*, 1: 312; Peel to Gregory, 26 August 1828, BL Add. Ms. 40344; Gregory to Peel, 6 December 1828, BL Add. Ms. 40344; Gregory to Goulburn, 26 January 1829, Gregory Papers; Gregory to Peel, 30 January 1829, BL Add. Ms. 40344; Peel to Gregory, 1 February 1829, BL Add. Ms. 40344; Goulburn to Gregory, 6 February 1829, BL Add. Ms. 40344; Gregory to Goulburn, 4, 9 February 1829,

BL Add. Ms. 40344.

52 See Machin, *Catholic Question in English Politics*, 159ff; Ellenborough, *Diary*, I: 308; Ward, *Religion and Society*, 82–3; *Greville Memoirs*, I: 279; David M. Thompson, *Nonconformity in the Nineteenth Century* (London 1972), 10, 68; Hempton, *Methodism and Politics*, 135–40; O'Connell, *O'Connell Correspondence*, 4: 27, 35, 39; O'Ferrall, *Catholic Emancipation*, 267.

## CHAPTER TEN

1 *Parl. Deb.*, 2nd ser. 20:542; *Parliamentary History and Review for 1825*, 606; Talbot to Gregory, 1 April 1829, Talbot Papers; Spring Rice to Wynn, 25 July [1829], Coed-y-Maen Mss; Peel to Northumberland, 25 March 1829, BL Add. Ms. 40327.

2 Government Correspondence, 6 March 1829, CSO, SPO.

3 E. Tighe Gregory, "Ireland in 1829; or, the First Year's Administration of the Duke of Northumberland," pamphlet (Dublin 1830), 15–16; Leveson Gower to Peel, 19 April 1830, Leveson Gower Mss., M738, PROI, Dublin; Ellenborough *Diary*, I: 310; Gregory, *Letter-Box*, 164–5.

4 Spring Rice to Wynn, 7 January 1830, Coed-y-Maen Mss; Gregory to Peel, 8 August, 6 December 1830, BL Add. Ms. 40344; Gregory to Leveson Gower, 18 February 1829, Gregory Papers; Flint to Gregory, 27 February 1829, Gregory Papers; Leveson Gower to Peel, 26 January 1829, BL Add. Ms. 40336; Leveson Gower to Peel, 14 November 1829, Leveson Gower Mss., M737; Leveson Gower to Gregory, 31 March 1829, M736.

5 Leveson Gower to Gregory, 26 May 1829, Leveson Gower Mss., M736; Gregory to Leveson Gower, 29 May 1829, Gregory Papers.

6 Leveson Gower to Gregory, 4 June 1829, Leveson Gower Mss., M736; Gregory to Leveson Gower, 13 June 1829, Gregory Papers; Leveson Gower to Peel, 31 July 1829, M736; Senior, *Orangeism*, 240–1; Leveson Gower to Peel, 18 July 1829, HO 100/227.

7 *Wellington Correspondence*, 2nd ser. 6: 33; 62–3, 47, 52–5; Wellington to Peel, 25 July 1829, BL Add. Ms. 40308; Ellenborough, *Diary*, 2: 79; Peel to Wellington, 27 July 1829, BL Add. Ms. 40308.

8 Ellenborough, *Diary*, 2: 79, 82, 207, 221; *Journal of Mrs. Arbuthnot*, 2: 301–2, 308; *Wellington Correspondence*, 2nd ser. 6: 37–8.

9 Gregory to Leveson Gower, 9 May 1829, HO 100/226; Northumberland to Peel, 4 May 1829, HO 100/226; *Wellington Correspondence*, 2nd ser. 6: 244–6.

10 Northumberland to Peel, 4 May 1829, HO 100/226.

11 Northumberland to Peel, 4 May 1829, HO 100/226.

12 Northumberland to Peel, 4 May 1829, HO 100/226; *Wellington Correspondence*, 2nd ser. 6: 244–6; Singleton to Leveson Gower, 25 May 1829, BL Add. Ms. 40336.

13 *Parl. Deb.*, 2nd ser. 20: 542; *Quarterly Review* 43 (1830): 245–6; *Parl. Deb.*,

2nd ser., 21: 1125–7, 1142.

14 Leveson Gower to Gregory, 19 June 1829, Leveson Gower Mss., M736; Leveson Gower to Peel, 22 July 1829, BL Add. Ms. 40337; Leveson Gower to Peel, 2 August, 2, 23, 28 July 1829, M736; *Wellington Correspondence*, 2nd ser. 6: 53–4.

15 *Wellington Correspondence*, 2nd ser. 6: 121–3; Longford, *Pillar of State*, 164.

16 Ellenborough, *Diary*, 2: 64, 68; Macdonagh, *Early Victorian Government*, 96; *Wellington Correspondence*, 2nd ser. 6: 262–3.

17 *Wellington Correspondence*, 2nd ser. 6: 262, 241–2, 254.

18 Ibid., 239–40; 262–3; 12, 16, 19–21; 70–1; 5: 615; Wellington to Peel, 29 October, 1829, BL Add. Ms. 40308.

19 Peel to Leveson Gower, 14 August 1829, BL Add. Ms. 40337; Peel to Gregory, 20 January 1830, BL Add. Ms. 40344.

20 Ellenborough, *Diary*, 2: 80; Peel to Wellington, 27 July 1829, BL Add. Ms. 40398; *Wellington Correspondence*, 2nd ser. 6: 47; Gregory to Peel, 1 June 1829, BL Add. Ms. 40344; Leveson Gower to Peel, 28 July 1829, Leveson Gower Mss., M736; Parker, *Peel*, 2: 122–4; Peel to Leveson Gower, 14 August 1829, BL Add. Ms. 40337.

21 Parker, *Peel*, 2: 116–17; Stevenson, *Popular Disturbances in England*, 237–8; Hilton, *Corn, Cash, Commerce*, 291; Ellenborough, *Diary*, 2: 64.

22 Leveson Gower to Peel, 5, 15 August, 15 September 1829, Leveson Gower Mss., M737; Leveson Gower to Peel, 31 July 1829, M736.

23 *Wellington Correspondence*, 2nd ser. 6: 88–90, 93; 86–8, 180–1.

24 Leveson Gower to Peel, 4, 25, 26 October 1829, Leveson Gower Mss., M737; *Correspondence of Arbuthnot*, 120; Leveson Gower to Gregory, 8 September 1829, M737; *Wellington Correspondence*, 2nd ser. 6: 256–7, 267–8, 282, 288–9; Northumberland to Peel, 23 January 1830, BL Add. Ms. 40327.

25 Peel to Northumberland, 5 October 1829, BL Add. Ms. 40327; *Wellington Correspondence*, 2nd ser. 6: 312, 316–17; Leveson Gower to Peel, 11 December 1829, 13 January 1830, 16 November 1829, Leveson Gower Mss., M737; *Parliamentary History and Review for 1826*, 612; Akenson, *Irish Education*, 102–3; Nicholls, *Irish Poor Law*, 112–13; Ellenborough, *Diary*, 2: 203; Parker, *Peel*, 2: 127–32; 133–7.

26 Parker, *Peel*, 2: 144; *Parl. Deb.*, 2nd ser. 22: 103, 118.

27 *Parl. Deb.*, 2nd ser. 22: 778; ibid., 23: 301–22; 798, 1417, 458–60; ibid., 24: 34, 532, 698; Ellenborough, *Diary*, 2: 275; Parker, *Peel*, 2: 122–3; *Wellington Correspondence*, 2nd ser. 7: 73.

28 *Parl. Deb.*, 2nd ser. 24: 838–58, 84–104; 555–79; ibid., 25: 190–210; ibid., 22: 574; ibid., 23: 183–220; ibid., 24: 1294–329; Thomas G. Conway, "The Approach to an Irish Poor Law 1828–33, "*Eire-Ireland* 6 (1971): 72–3; *Wellington Correspondence*, 2nd ser. 7: 111–12, 210; *Parl. Deb.*, 2nd ser. 25: 713–14; Gordon, *Economic Doctrine and Tory Liberalism*, 83; Croker, *Commentaries*, 48.

29 O'Connell, *O'Connell Correspondence*, 4: 127, 141–2; *Parl. Deb.*, 2nd ser. 23: 1110–14; Peel to Goulburn, 25 December 1829, Goulburn Papers, Acc 319/39; Broeker, *Rural Disorder and Police Reform*, 200–1; McDowell, *Public Opinion and Government Policy*, 77.

30 Leveson Gower to Singleton, 21 May 1830, Leveson Gower Mss., M738; *Wellington Correspondence*, 2nd ser. 6: 534–5; 7: 57–8, 104; Leslie Stephen and Sydney Lee, eds., *Dictionary of National Biography*, 22 vols. (London 1908–9), 8: 1227; Ellenborough, *Diary*, 2: 260; *Correspondence of Arbuthnot*, 129, 131–2.

31 Hardinge to Peel, 19, 12, 13 October, 23 September 1830, BL Add. Ms. 40313; O'Connell, *O'Connell Correspondence*, 4: 226n1.

32 O'Connell, *O'Connell Correspondence*, 4: 161n6; Gregory to Leveson Gower, 30 April 1830, BL Add. Ms. 40338; Ellenborough, *Diary*, 2: 398; Peel to Hardinge, 21 October 1829, BL Add. Ms. 40313; *Wellington Correspondence*, 2nd ser. 7: 313.

33 Hardinge to Peel, 13, 21 October 1829, BL Add. Ms. 40313; *Wellington Correspondence*, 2nd ser. 7: 43–4; Peel to Hardinge, 16 October 1830, BL Add. Ms. 40313.

34 Hardinge to Peel, 12 October 1830, BL Add. Ms. 40313; Peel to Hardinge, 20 October 1830, BL Add. Ms. 40313; Peel to Gregory, 30 October 1830, BL Add. Ms. 40344.

35 Hardinge to Peel, 22, 13, 20 October 1830, BL Add. Ms. 40313; Gregory to Hardinge, 7 November 1830, Gregory Papers; Ellenborough, *Diary*, 2: 391–2, 402.

36 Anti-Repeal Declaration, 1830, Hardinge Papers, McLennan Library, McGill University; Nicholls, *Irish Poor Law*, 95, 107–8; *Wellington Correspondence*, 2nd ser. 7: 305–6, 314–15, 317–18; Ellenborough, *Diary*, 2: 288; Gash, *Mr. Secretary Peel*, 636; Anglesey, *One-Leg*, 238–9; O'Gorman, *Emergence of British Two-Party System*, 112–13; Thompson, *Wellington after Waterloo*, 101.

37 Mitchell, *Whigs in Opposition*, 216; Ziegler, *Melbourne*, 151; *Memoirs of Melbourne*, 1: 336–7, 354–5; Melbourne to Anglesey, 18 December 1830, BL Add. Ms. 38103; Sanders, *Melbourne's Papers*, 167–9; *Maria Edgeworth's Letters from England*, 440.

38 Anglesey to Spring Rice, 3 December 1830, Monteagle Mss., 13370; O'Connell, *O'Connell Correspondence*, 4: 41, 47, 73, 228–38; Anglesey, *One-Leg*, 245; Anglesey to Grey, 25 November 1830, Grey of Howick Mss. (microfilm), National Library of Ireland.

39 Anglesey to Gregory, 7 December 1830, Gregory Papers; Flint to Gregory, 8 December 1830, Gregory Papers; *Parl. Deb.*, 3rd ser. 1: 1369–82; ibid., 26: 629.

40 Goulburn to Gregory, 3 December 1830, Gregory Papers; *Greville Diary*, 1: 432–4; O'Connell. *O'Connell Correspondence*, 4: 244–5.

41 Perkin, *Origins of Modern English Society*, 97.

42  J.V. Beckett, "The Debate over Farm Sizes in Eighteenth and Nineteenth-Century England," *Agricultural History* 57 (1983): 308–25.

43  Martin, *Ireland before and after Union*, 158.

44  Ibid., 85; Perkin, *Origins of Modern English Society*, 223.

45  See Stevenson, *Popular Disturbances in England*, 234ff; E.J. Hobsbawm and George Rudé, *Captain Swing*, pb ed. (Harmondsworth 1985); Wells, *Journal of Peasant Studies* 6: 120.

46  Townshend, *Political Violence in Ireland*, 7–8; Boyce, *Nationalism in Ireland*, 141; Perkin, *Origins of Modern English Society*, 275.

47  Ford, *Social Theory and Social Practice*, 10; Macdonagh, *Early Victorian Government*, 5, 24; Checkland, *British Public Policy*, 2; Lewis, *On Local Disturbances in Ireland*, 39.

48  *Parliamentary History and Review for 1825*, 605; John Hutchinson, *The Dynamics of Cultural Nationalism: The Gaelic Revival and the Creation of the Irish Nation State* (London 1987), 71; Roger A. Mason, ed., *Scotland and England 1286-1815* (Edinburgh 1987), 247–62.

# Bibliographical Essay

There is a wealth of source material on British government of Ireland in the early nineteenth century. The principal governors have left important collections of private papers. In terms of bulk and value, three are particularly noteworthy. The Peel Papers in the British Library have been well mined by historians, and extensive use has been made of the Goulburn Papers. Equally important but little used, and in need of cataloguing, are the Whitworth Papers. They form part of the Sackville Mss. on deposit in the Kent Archives, Maidstone. The original Peel correspondence which forms a large portion of the Whitworth collection reveals the inadequacy of the copybooks in the Peel Papers. Another central figure, and one well represented in the Peel and Goulburn Mss., is William Gregory. His papers, which include copies of the secret service account books, have recently been purchased from the family by the Robert W. Woodruff Library, Emory University. Public papers are another treasure trove, especially the Home Office 100 (Ireland) series, containing sixty-four volumes for the period of this study. The records of the Chief Secretary's Office proved to be less helpful.

There are several excellent introductions to the political and social history of Britain during the early nineteenth century. *The Age of Improvement 1783–1867* (1959) by Asa Briggs, and *The Age of Reform 1815–1870* (2nd ed. 1962) by Sir Llewellyn Woodward have long been standard works. More recently, two volumes in "The New History of England" have together provided an account of a peculiarly testing century for the British. Ian R. Christie's *Wars and Revolutions Britain, 1760–1815* (1982) and *Aristocracy and People Britain 1815–1865* (1979) by Norman Gash are lucid works of synthesis. Another worthy volume, in yet another series, is Eric J. Evans's *The Forging of the Modern State: Early Industrial Britain 1783–1870* (1983), though its "limited treatment" of Ireland is not entirely convincing. In *Romanticism and the Social Order 1780–1830* (1969) R.W. Harris interprets the era through its literature. H.T. Dickinson has emphasized the importance of ideology in determining political action in *Liberty and Property Political Ideology in Eighteenth-Century Britain* (1977). His short study of *British Radicalism and the French Revolution 1789–1815* (1985) is a valuable summary of a topic which has received fuller treatment from others, including Albert Goodwin in *The Friends of Liberty: The English Democratic Movement in the Age of the French Revolution* (1979). Britain's avoidance of revolutionary upheaval is the theme of Ian R. Christie's persuasive essays, *Stress and Stability in Late Eighteenth-Century Britain: Reflections on the British Avoidance of Revolution* (1984). Two other important works are *Britain in the Early Nineteenth Century* (1978) by A.D. Harvey, and Clive Emsley's *British Society and the French Wars 1793–1815* (1979).

The political history of the first three decades of the nineteenth century may also be followed through the lives of the principal figures. John Ehrman's massive biography of the younger Pitt is still incomplete. Piers Mackesy emphasizes the failure of the war policy in *War without Victory: The Downfall of Pitt 1799–1802* (1984). Pitt's successor was Henry Addington. George Pellew's *Life and Correspondence of Henry Addington 1st Viscount Sidmouth*, 3 vols. (1847), contains much useful information but must be supplemented by Philip Ziegler's modern interpretation, *Addington: A Life of Henry Addington Viscount Sidmouth* (1965). Similarly, Spencer Walpole produced a Victorian tribute to Spencer Perceval, *The Life of the Rt. Hon. Spencer Perceval including His Correspondence with Numerous Distinguished Persons*, 2 vols. (1874), while Denis Gray has offered a more critical analysis of his career and greater insight into his character in *Spencer Perceval: the Evangelical Prime Minister 1762–1812* (1963). Lord Liverpool has attracted greater attention, which the length of his term as prime minister fully justifies. C.D. Yonge's *The Life and Administration of Robert Banks, 2nd Earl of Liverpool*, 3 vols. (1868), does contain a wealth of material but it is not a joy to read. The three modern studies are much shorter. The second edition of W.R. Brock's *Lord Liverpool and Liberal Toryism 1820–1827* (1967) perhaps makes too much of the liberalism, while Charles Petrie's *Lord Liverpool and His Times* (1954) is thin and has recently been replaced by Norman Gash's stylish *Lord Liverpool* (1984) which lays due weight upon the subject's abilities and political acuity. A detailed examination of the problems which confronted Liverpool and his ministers at the end of the French wars is to be found in *Lord Liverpool's Administration: The Crucial Years 1815–1822* (1975) by J.E. Cookson. George Canning remains a compelling figure, given his extraordinary career and its premature end. Arthur Aspinall has edited a documentary account of his brief government, *The Formation of Canning's Ministry February to August 1827* (1937) and Augustus Granville Stapleton's *George Canning and His Times* (1859), J.F. Bagot's *George Canning and His Friends*, 2 vols. (1909), and H.W.V.

Temperley's *Life of Canning* (1905) are of value. Of the modern biographies, which include Peter Dixon's *Canning Politician and Statesman* (1976), that by Wendy Hinde, *George Canning* (1973), is the most thorough. The prime ministerial career of Lord Goderich (later Ripon) was both brief and undistinguished. W.D. Jones has written an adequate biography of him, *Prosperity Robinson: The Life of Viscount Goderich 1782–1859* (1967). Elizabeth Longford's substantial biography of Wellington provides insight into his character, with the second volume, *Pillar of State* (1972), chronicling his postwar political career. An alternative interpretation of the same period is offered by Neville Thompson in his *Wellington after Waterloo* (1987). Additional light is thrown on Wellington's personality and attitudes by an intimate in the *Journal of Mrs Arbuthnot 1820–32*, 2 vols. (1950), edited by F. Bamford and the duke of Wellington. The second series of the *Despatches, Correspondence, and Memoranda of Field Marshall Arthur Duke of Wellington*, 8 vols. (1871), is an essential source for his political career, while Lord Ellenborough's *A Political Diary 1828–1830* (1881), edited by Lord Colchester, remains a valuable account of his administration. *The Public and Private Life of Lord Eldon*, 3 vols. (1844), edited by H. Twiss, is valuable not merely for its documenting of the sentiments of a prominent "Ultra" Protestant but also for its extracts from the correspondence of the former Irish lord chancellor, Redesdale. Similarly, *The Diary and Correspondence of Charles Abbot, Lord Colchester*, 3 vols. (1861), edited by Lord Charles Colchester, is significant both because of Abbot's position as speaker of the Commons and because of his correspondents, such as Peel. Other published manuscript collections and diaries worth consulting are those of *Earl Bathurst* (1923), *Charles Arbuthnot* (1941), *Henry Hobhouse* (1952), and the Dropmore Mss. of *J.B. Fortescue* (1892–1907).

The performance of the Whigs, briefly as a government and then in opposition, was less than impressive. A.D. Harvey offers a critical assessment of "The Ministry of All the Talents: The Whigs in Office, February 1806 to March 1807,"*Historical Journal* 15 (1972). Peter Jupp, *Lord Grenville 1759–1834* (1985), is more sympathetic but admits the prime minister's failure in the field of human relations. Grenville's subsequent career and life are not dealt with at any length, but his leadership of the Opposition was not a success. Michael Roberts, *The Whig Party 1807–12* (1939), and A. Mitchell, *The Whigs in Opposition 1815–1830* (1967), explore the divisions and difficulties which helped to delay their return to power. Two other important modern studies of prominent Whigs are E.A. Smith's *Whig Principles and Party Politics: Earl Fitzwilliam and the Whig Party 1748–1833* (1975) and Robert Stewart's *Henry Brougham 1778–1868: His Public Career* (1986). For those Whig allies who defected to the government in 1821 see James J. Sack, *The Grevillites, 1801–29: Party Politics and Factionalism in the Age of Pitt and Liverpool* (1979). Equally important as a source on this office-hungry faction are the memoirs of the duke of Buckingham and Chandos – *Memoirs of the Court of England during the Regency*, 2 vols. (1856), and *Memoirs of the Court of George IV 1820–1830 from Original Family Documents*, 2 vols. (1859).

The standard work on economic policy in the postwar era is that of Boyd Hilton, *Corn, Cash, Commerce: The Economic Policies of the Tory Governments 1815–1830* (1977). His emphasis is on Huskisson as was that of Alexander Brady a half-century earlier in his *William Huskisson and Liberal Reform: An Essay on the Changes in Economic Policy in the Twenties of the Nineteenth Century* (1928). He concentrated on the currency question, the Corn Laws, and the dismantling of the remnants of the old navigational system. Frank Whitson Fetter has focused on sixty-two parliamentarians, whom he identifies as economists, in *The Economist in Parliament 1780–1860* (1980). The rise and decline of David Ricardo's influence in Parliament, which after the arrival of the Grenvillites was strengthened within the government, are the themes of the two volumes by Barry Gordon, *Political Economy in Parliament 1819–1823* (1976), and *Economic Doctrine and Tory Liberalism 1824–1830* (1979). Arthur J. Taylor has witten a brief survey of *Laissez-Faire and State Intervention in Nineteenth-Century Britain* (reprinted 1968). For a further discussion of that tension see Oliver Mac-Donagh, *Early Victorian Government 1830–1870* (1977), while Sydney Checkland has stressed the weak central control of the early nineteenth-century polity in *British Public Policy 1776–1939: An Economic, Social and Political Perspective* (1983). For an introduction to Adam Smith see Robert L. Heilbroner, ed., *The Essential Adam Smith* (1986), while William Petersen's *Malthus* provides a sympathetic analysis of his subject's thought and impact. The effect of economic theory on Irish policy is a major theme of R.D. Collinson Black in *Economic Thought and the Irish Question 1817–1870* (1960). Additional light is thrown on theory and policy by students of the Poor Law. A.W. Coats, "Economic thought and Poor Law Policy in the Eighteenth Century," *Economic History Review*, 2nd ser. 13 (1960–61), provides an introduction to Gertrude Himmelfarb's penetrating analysis of the new political economy in *The Idea of Poverty: England in the early Industrial Age* (1984). Also important is J.R. Poynter's *Society and Pauperism: English Ideas on Poor Relief, 1795–1834* (1969). J.D. Marshall's short account of *The Old Poor Law, 1795–1834* (1968) is useful, while Mark Blaug in "The Myth of the Old Poor Law and the Making of the New, "*Journal of Economic History* 23 (1963) concludes that the policy was by "no means unenlightened." Similarly, Peter Dunkley in his article "Paternalism, The Magistracy and Poor Relief in England, 1795–1834," *International Review of Social History* 24 (1979) suggests that it provided the landowners in their capacities as magistrates with an instrument for reinforcing deference in rural society. Peter Mandler, "The Making of the

New Poor Law *Redivivus*," *Past and Present* 117 (1987) reasons from the failure to initiate reform in 1817 that "middle-class liberalism" was the catalyst in 1834.

The problems confronting policy-makers figure large in the second volume of George Spater's *William Cobbett: The Poor Man's Friend* (1982). Those of farmers in particular were examined from a strictly economic standpoint by Leonard P. Adams in *Agricultural Depression and Farm Relief in England 1813–1852* (reprinted 1965). Travis L. Crosby in his methodical *English Farmers and the Politics of Protection 1815–52* (1977) has sought to show how farming pressure groups originated and how they in turn contributed to the development of the farming community as an active political force. Welsh farmers, apart from those in the Vale of Glamorgan, were principally pastoral and thus little interested in the campaign for protection of the producers of cereals. The problems of Welsh agricultural society in the eighteenth century are discussed in one of the essays in *The Satellite State in the 17th and 18th Centuries* (1979), edited by S. Dyrvik, K. Myklund, and J. Oldervold. The story is one of increasing population pressure, land subdivision, and a steady deterioration in the condition of the peasantry. Welsh labourers continued to suffer during the Napoleonic Wars, as a result of the inflation in food prices, and their plight was evident in the scramble for plots of mountain land and the rise in the poor rates. See David W. Howell, "The Agricultural Labourer in Nineteenth Century Wales," *Welsh History Review* 6 (1972–3). But as R.J. Colyer explains in "The Gentry and the County in Nineteenth-Century Cardiganshire," *Welsh History Review* 10 (1981), a rift between the gentry and the other elements of rural society had barely developed by the beginning of the century and was retarded by the tradition of deference. For an economic history of the farming community over the course of the century, which seeks to emphasize human factors, see David W. Howell's *Land and People in Nineteenth-Century Wales* (1977).

In an evocative account of *English Society in the Eighteenth Century* (1982) Roy Porter focused upon the "fundamental strength and resilience of its social hierarchy," the "continual adaptiveness to challenge and individual mobility," and the attempts to secure consensus. Nevertheless, social tensions were mounting towards the end of the century. It was the unique character of the society, the existence of an "open dynamic aristocracy based on absolute property and linked vertically by patronage," that Harold Perkin stressed as a cause of a "spontaneous industrial revolution" in his *Origins of Modern English Society* (1969). Phyllis Deane's *The First Industrial Revolution* (1969) is but one of several excellent conventional introductions to the subject. In an article, "British Economic Growth, 1700–1831: A Review of the Evidence," *Economic History Review*, 2nd ser. 36 (1983), N.F.R. Crafts argues that the rate of industrial growth was slower than economic historians once surmised, that the acceleration came later than they had previously believed, and that living standards as measured by personal consumption were therefore little changed between 1760 and 1820. In short, that the high rate of growth which overcame "Malthusian" problems was a nineteenth-century phenomenon. Peter H. Lindert and Jeffrey G. Williamson, "English Workers' Living Standards during the Industrial Revolution: A New Look," *Economic History Review*, 2nd ser. 36 (1983), have also dated the improvement after 1820. In the introduction to *The Napoleonic Wars and Their Impact on Factor Returns and Output Growth in England 1793–1815* (1985), Glenn R. Hueckel has summarized recent interpretations in a way which is intelligible to nonspecialists. The standard works on the accompanying agricultural revolution, and on landowners, are those of J.D. Chambers and G. Mingay, *The Agricultural Revolution 1750–1850* (1966) and F.M.L. Thompson, *English Landed Society in the Nineteenth Century* (1963). J.V. Beckett in "The Debate over Farm Sizes in Eighteenth and Nineteenth-Century England," *Agricultural History* 57 (1983), has shown that consolidation of landholdings was a contentious intellectual issue, and Roger A.E. Wells in "The Development of an English Rural Proletariat and Social Protest 1700–1850," *Journal of Peasant Studies* 6 (1979) has offered an explanation of the passivity of the smallholder in the face of his relegation to the rank of labourer. W.A. Armstrong has examined "The Influence of Demographic Factors in the Position of the Agricultural Labourer in England and Wales, c1750–1914," *Agricultural History Review* 29 (1981), and he finds little evidence of the improvement in real wages that "optimists" date from the 1820s. Glenn Hueckel has reported the uneven distribution of "English Farming Profits during the Napoleonic Wars, 1793–1815," in *Explorations in Economic History* 13 (1976).

For modern discussions of the quality of urban and rural life see P.J. Corfield, *The Impact of English Towns* (1982); James Walvin, *English Urban Life 1776–1851* (1984); and Pamela Horn, *The Rural World 1780–1850: Social Change in the English Countryside* (1980). R.J. White describes his *Waterloo to Peterloo* (1957) as a study in social transition and an essay in "suspended revolution." A broader work of synthesis, one which summarizes both the ongoing debate between "optimists" and "pessimists" on the effects of industrialization on living standards and the academic dispute over the revolutionary character of lower-class protest, is John Rule's *The Labouring Classes in Early Industrial England 1750–1850* (1986). The challenge to traditional interpretations of working-class disturbances, such as Frank Ongley Darvall's *Popular Disturbances and Political Order in Regency England* (1934, reprinted 1969), was thrown down by E.P. Thompson in *The Making of the English Working Class* (revised edition 1968). The existence of a secret revolutionary underground in England continues to excite argument among historians of Britain. Roger Wells's *Insurrection: The British Experience 1795–1803* (1983) is one of the later arrivals on the field of battle. Thus when J.R. Dinwiddy questioned the existence of an underground in Yorkshire at the turn of the nineteenth century, J.L. Baxter and F.K. Donnelly replied in the same issue of *Past and Present*, 64 (1974), that Thompson's only mistake had been to understate the case. A persistent critic of the radical view has been Malcolm Thomis, who with Peter Holt published *Threats of Revolution in Britain 1789–1848* (1977). More recently, Craig Calhoun has argued in *The Question of Class Struggle: Social Foundations of Popular Radicalism during the Industrial Revolution* (1982) that the popular protest was the work of "reactionary radicals" seeking to defend traditional values against industrial change. This defensive rather than progressive motivation was consistent with that which Thompson himself had described in a seminal article, "The Moral Economy of the English Crowd in the Eighteenth Century," *Past and Present* 50 (1971). He found that the participants in disturbances subscribed to the "legitimizing notion" that they were defending "traditional rights and customs" and were in general "supported by the wider consensus of the community." Subsequently, in *Albion's Fatal Tree: Crime and Society in Eighteenth-Century England* (1975), he, together with Douglas Hay and Peter Linebaugh, extended the argument to embrace many of the traditional criminals, such as poachers and wreckers. A recent scholarly analysis is Clive Emsley's *Crime and Society in England 1750–1850* (1987), but as the title indicates it does not embrace Ireland. A similar study, if less general and somewhat less satisfying, is George Rudé's *Criminal and Victim: Crime and Society in Early Nineteenth-Century England* (1985). Their conclusions do not differ significantly from those of J.M. Beattie, "The Pattern of Crime in England 1660–1800," *Past and Present* 62 (1974). Of course, Rudé remains the dean of the historians of the crowd and most of those who have analysed the turbulence of British society have emphasized the limited ends and means of the rioters. Thus in addition to the *Crowd in History* (1964) and Rudé's *Ideology and Popular Protest* (1980), see R. Quinault and J. Stevenson, *Popular Protest and Public Order: Six Studies in British History 1790–1820* (1974); John Stevenson, *Popular Disturbances in England 1700–1870* (1979); John Bohstedt, *Riots and Community Politics in England and Wales 1790–1810* (1983); David J.V. Jones, *Before Rebecca: Popular Protests in Wales 1793–1835* (1973); Kenneth Logue, *Popular Disturbances in Scotland 1780–1815* (1979). Only rarely were there serious rural disturbances in early nineteenth-century England. A.J. Peacock has described the riots in East Anglia in 1816, in *Bread and Blood* (1965), while George Rudé and E.J. Hobsbawm have offered a modern study of the more extensive upheavals of 1830–31 in *Captain Swing* (1969).

As J.M. Golby and A.W. Purdue demonstrate in *The Civilisation of the*

*Crowd: Popular Culture in England 1750–1900* (1984), the effort to tame an undisciplined and disorderly society included an assault upon the underlying popular culture. It was led by secular radicals anxious to redeem the populace through reason, and by evangelicals, especially Methodists, who taught redemption through Christ. The role of religion in British society, the problems of the State Church, the rise of evangelicalism and its impact upon society have been much discussed. See, for example, Donald Greene, "The Via Media in an Age of Revolution: Anglicanism in the 18th Century," in *The Varied Patterns: Studies in the 18th Century* (1971), edited by Peter Hughes and David Williams; V. Kiernan, "Evangelicalism and the French Revolution," *Past and Present* 1 (1952): G.F.A. Best, "The Evangelicals and the Established Church in the Early Nineteenth Century," *Journal of Theological Studies* n.s. 10 (1959); F.K. Brown, *Fathers of the Victorians* (1961); Ernest Marshall Howse, *Saints in Politics: The 'Clapham Sect' and the Growth of Freedom* (1952); E.R. Norman, *Church and Society in England 1770–1970* (1976); W.R. Ward, *Religion and Society in England 1790–1850* (1972); S.C. Carpenter, *Church and People 1789–1889* (1933); L.E. Elliot-Binns, *Religion in the Victorian Era* (reprinted 1953). John McLeish, in *Evangelical Religion and Popular Education: A Modern Interpretation* (1969), probes the motivation of the evangelical leaders of popular education in England and Wales. Alan D. Gilbert, *Religion and Society in Industrial England: Church, Chapel, and Social Change 1740–1914* (1976) emphasizes the extent to which the Established Church found itself early in the nineteenth century in danger of being relegated to a minority position. The growing resentment of the tithe, as an excessive and inequitable tax which impeded agricultural improvements has been discussed most fully by Eric J. Evans, *The Contentious Tithe: The Tithe Problem and English Agriculture 1750–1850* (1976). In his article "Some Reasons for the Growth of English Rural Anti-Clericalism c 1750–c1850," *Past and Present* 66 (1975), Evans also dwells on the consequences of the enclosure movement. No less helpful are articles by W.R. Ward, "The Tithe Question in the Early Nineteenth Century," *Journal of Ecclesiastical History* 15 (1964), and Wray Vamplew, "Tithes and Agriculture: Some Comments on Commutation," *Economic History Review* 2nd ser. 34 (1981).

The most controversial religious question of the early nineteenth century was that of Catholic Emancipation. Benjamin Ward's detailed study of the Catholics in Britain remains an important work, with the three volumes entitled *The Eve of Catholic Emancipation* (1911) being particularly relevant. M.R.D. Leys's *Catholics in England 1559–1829: A Social History* (1961) is a brief survey but *The English Catholic Community 1570–1850* (1975) by John Bossy departs from the traditional view. He makes a convincing case that the community had already recovered its vigour before the arrival of refugee priests from France and the large numbers of immigrants from

Ireland. In *Religious Toleration in England 1787–1833* (1961) Ursula Henriques observes that the permanent repeal of the restrictions on dissenters slipped through under cover of the government's embarrassment during the final stages of the Catholic struggle. R.W. Davis has discussed "The Strategy of 'Dissent' in the Repeal Campaign, 1820–1828," *Journal of Modern History* 38 (1966). The opposition to Catholic Emancipation has been analysed by G.F.A. Best in "The Protestant Constitution and Its Supporters, 1800–1829," *Transactions of the Royal Historical Society*, 5th ser. 8 (1958). In his *Methodism and Politics in British Society 1750–1850* (1984, 1989), David Hempton has carefully examined the movement's anti-catholicism and emphasized Ireland as a factor in the evolution of Methodist political attitudes. G.I.T. Machin has examined both the unsuccessful "Resistance to Repeal of the Test and Corporation Acts 1828" by those who feared that this was the stalking-horse for emancipation, *Historical Journal* 22 (1979), and the effort to revive "The No-Popery Movement in Britain in 1828–9," *Historical Journal* 6 (1963). Machin's account of "The Duke of Wellington and Catholic Emancipation," *Ecclesiastical History* 14 (1962), should be read in association with R.W. Davis's "The Tories, the Whigs, and Catholic emancipation, 1827–1829," *English Historical Review* 97 (1982). Davis contends that the royal veto on cabinet discussion of emancipation had been rejected by the Canning-Goderich administrations, but Wellington failed to grasp that fact when he formed his government in January 1828. Henriques and Machin are agreed that emancipation was a victory of expediency rather than of principle, though the latter in his detailed discussion of *The Catholic Question in English Politics 1820–1830* (1964) does describe its passage as a great liberal achievement of English statesmanship.

Catholic relief was complicated by its identification with Ireland and thus with a people for whom many Britons harboured a strong measure of disdain. Much of the work on anti-Irish prejudice has concentrated on the Victorian era, though the difficulties of the Irish who settled in Britain during the earlier period are touched upon by M.A.G. Tuarthaigh, "The Irish in Nineteenth Century Britain: Problems of Integration," *Transactions of the Royal Historical Society*, 5th ser. 21 (1981). S. Gilley has stressed the complexity of "English Attitudes to the Irish in England 1780–1900," in *Immigrants and Minorities in British Society* (1978), edited by Colin Holmes. Ned Lebow discovered less complexity. In "British Historians on Irish History," *Eire-Ireland* 8 (1973), he explored some of the literary sources of a national disdain. Subsequently, Richard Ned Lebow published *White Britain and Black Ireland: The Influence of Stereotypes on Colonial Policy* (1976).

Emancipation had been intended by Pitt to serve as a handmaiden of the union which resulted from the rebellion of 1798. The background to the rebellion has been extensively discussed by two historians whose works also rank as literature: James Anthony Froude's *The English In Ireland in the*

*Eighteenth Century*, 3 vols. (1872–4), and W.E.H. Lecky's *A History of Ireland in the Eighteenth Century*, 5 vols. (reprinted 1972). R.B. McDowell is the modern historian of this era. In *Irish Public Opinion 1750–1800* (1944) he analysed the response of liberals/radicals and conservatives to the political and social problems of the late eighteenth century. Then, in *Ireland in the Age of Imperialism and Revolution 1760–1801* (1979), he surveyed Irish politics, economic development, social problems, administration, and intellectual life. The best study of the system of Irish government during this period remains Edith M. Johnston's *Great Britain and Ireland 1760–1800: A Study in Political Administration* (1963). The crucial failure of the Fitzwilliam viceroyalty has been described by McDowell in "The Fitzwilliam Episode," *Irish Historical Studies* 16 (1966). On the rebellion itself Lecky provides a wealth of information and Thomas Pakenham's *The Year of Liberty: The Great Irish Rebellion of 1798* (1969) is a solid narrative. The most satisfying investigation of the United Irishmen's conspiracy is Marianne Elliot's *Partners in Revolution: The United Irishmen and France* (1982). She observes that their legacy included the myths of the noble failure and the sanctity of the hopeless struggle. The legend that they were the first champions of Irish nationalism in arms, for few of them were doctrinaire Republicans, she lays, in part, at the door of O'Connell. He depicted them as violent Republicans in order to distinguish his own advocacy of moral force. The legend was also fostered by Sir Richard Musgrave in his *Memoirs of the Different Rebellions in Ireland from the Arrival of the English* (1801). For links between "Irish Rebels and English Radicals 1798–1820," see A.W. Smith's article in *Past and Present* 7 (1953).

The negotiation of the prior union, that between England and Scotland, is discussed by William Ferguson in *Scotland's Relations with England: A Survey to 1707* (1977). The economic background and consequences of that arrangement, and its success by the end of the eighteenth century, are summarized by T.C. Smout, "The Anglo-Scottish Union of 1707: I. *The Economic Background*," *Economic History Review* 2nd ser. 16 (1963–4); R.H. Campbell, "The Anglo-Scottish Union: II. *The Economic Consequences*," *Economic History Review* 2nd ser. 16 (1963–4); and R.H. Campbell, *Scotland since 1707: The Rise of an Industrial Society*, 2nd ed. (1985). The enactment of the union with Ireland has been much written about, often with a heavy emphasis on the extensive use of bribes to persuade the Irish Parliament to vote itself out of existence. Castlereagh was the central figure. H. Montgomery Hyde described his Irish career at some length in *The Rise of Castlereagh* (1933) and in *Castlereagh* (1976) John Derry concludes that his Irish experiences reinforced his scepticism about idealism as a political force for good and tutored him in the complexities of political motivations. C.J. Bartlett, *Castlereagh* (1966), depicts him in domestic affairs as "undogmatic" and "essentially uncreative," a politician whose skills were the executive ones of the management and manipulation of people. In the most impressive account of *The Passing of the Irish Act of Union: A Study in Parliamentary Politics* (1966) G.C. Bolton had modified the traditional interpretation of venal men selling their national identity. Homer L. Catkin provides a useful synopsis of the contemporary arguments "For and Against the Union," *Eire-Ireland* 13 (1978). P.N. Jupp has scrutinized the first Irish representatives sent to the Parliament of the United Kingdom, "The Irish M.P.'s at Westminster in the Early Nineteenth Century," *Historical Studies* 7 (1969). The failure of Parliament to follow union with three measures of Catholic relief – emancipation, commutation of tithes, and payment of the clergy – went far to explain the alienation of the great majority of the Irish people, Lecky argued. McDowell has also fastened upon the "fatal" failure to enact emancipation quickly, arguing that the delay destroyed any hope of an alliance between Catholic Church and State. Froude, who asserted that the union was essential for Britain's security, and that the integrity of her existence could not be sacrificed to "the pleasure of a numerical majority of the Irish people," insisted that it was the employment of Ireland as a pawn in British party politics which prevented her full integration into the United Kingdom.

There are several excellent introductions to Ireland under the union. Oliver MacDonagh's two analytical studies, *Ireland: The Union and Its Aftermath* (revised and enlarged 1977), and *States of Mind: A Study of Anglo-Irish Conflict 1780–1980* (1983) are rich in insights. Patrick O'Farrell, *Ireland's English Question: Anglo-Irish Relations 1534–1970* (1971) emphasizes religious differences. Gearoid O Tuathaigh, *Ireland before the Famine 1798–1848* (1972), and Lawrence J. McCaffrey, *Ireland from Colony to Nation State* (1979) are both sound surveys. In *Public Opinion and Government Policy 1801–1846* (1952) R.B. McDowell examines the Irish reaction to British rule.

The administrative structure of the Irish government after union has been most methodically studied by R.B. McDowell in *The Irish Administration 1801–1914* (1964), though R. Barry O'Brien's *Dublin Castle and the Irish People* (1909) is a little more entertaining. *The Viceroys of Ireland* (1912) by Charles O'Mahoney is superficial and Edward Brynn's *Crown and Castle: British Rule of Ireland 1800–1830* (1978) is a disappointing work despite the solid research upon which it is founded. The office of the under-secretary has been examined biographically by R. Barry O'Brien in *Thomas Drummond Under-Secretary in Ireland 1835–1840: Life and Letters* (1889), and John F. M'Lennan's *Memoirs of Thomas Drummond Under-Secretary to the Lord Lieutenant of Ireland 1835–1840* (1867) contains some useful information. Robert Shipkey has highlighted one of the difficulties of the Irish executive in exerting influence in his article "The Problems of Irish Patronage during the Chief Secretaryship of Robert Peel, 1812–18," *His-*

*torical Journal* 10 (1967).

The personalities who directed the Irish government between 1812 and 1830 have not proven especially attractive to historians. James J. Kenny, Jr, has thrown some light on the character of Lord Witworth in his article "Lord Whitworth and the Conspiracy against Tsar Paul I: The New Evidence of the Kent Archive," *Slavic Review* 36 (1977), and Vita Sackville-West has briefly commented upon his domestic life in *Knole and the Sackvilles* (1922). Richard Wellesley, who bore a newly illustrious name and was a major political figure in his own right, has received somewhat more attention. His career as governor general of India has been favourably appraised by P.E. Roberts in *India under Wellesley* (1929), and his involvement in foreign policy assessed by John Kenneth Severn, *A Wellesley Affair: Richard Marquis Wellesley and the Conduct of Anglo-Spanish Diplomacy 1809–1812* (1981). *The Eldest Brother: The Marquis of Wellesley, the Duke of Wellington's Eldest Brother* (1973) by Iris Butler stresses the problems of his private life. The *Memoirs and Correspondence of the Most Noble Richard Marquis Wellesley*, 3 vols. (1846), by R.R. Pearce is a panegyric. More critical and more helpful is the Marquess of Anglesey's *One-Leg: The Life and Letters of Henry William Paget First Marquess of Anglesey 1768–1854* (1961). Of the chief secretaries, Peel and Melbourne, who went on to become prime ministers, have been well served by historians. The first of Norman Gash's two volumes on Peel, *Mr. Secretary Peel: The Life of Sir Robert Peel to 1830* (1961) remains the standard work, just as the condensed version of the complete work, issued as *Peel* (1976), is now the standard short biography. *Sir Robert Peel from his Private Papers*, 3 vols. (reprinted 1970), edited by Charles Stuart Parker, is a significant source but one marred by editorial deficiencies. More accurate and complete are the letters published in the two volumes of *Memoirs of the Right Honourable Sir Robert Peel* (1856), edited by Lord Mahon and Edward Cardwell, the first of which is a justification of Peel's controversial conduct as home secretary during the emancipation crisis. There is precious little on Charles Grant in the biography of his father, *The Life of Charles Grant* (1904) by Henry Morris. David Cecil's two extended essays, *The Young Melbourne* and *Lord M*, were reissued as one volume in 1955 under the title *Melbourne*, and they offer an engaging portrait of the man. More substantial is Philip Ziegler's *Melbourne* (1976), which concludes that in public or private "a thin streak of indifference ran pallid" through his life. There is a substantial body of material on Lamb's term as chief secretary in W.M. Torrens's *Memoirs of the Right Honourable William Second Viscount Melbourne*, 2 vols. (1878), and a little useful information in *Lord Melbourne's Papers* (reprinted 1971) edited by Lloyd C. Sanders. Another important collection of correspondence is Lady Gregory's selection of material from the Gregory Papers, *Mr. Gregory's Letter-Box* (1898, 1981). There is some interesting anecdotal comment on Gregory in Vere R.T. Gregory's *The House of Gregory* (1943). Another important secondary figure was William Plunket, the Irish attorney general. See David Plunket, *The Life, Letters and Speeches of Lord Plunket*, 2 vols. (1867).

Contemporary accounts abound of the economic and social problems of Ireland in the early nineteenth century, but two are of particular value. Edward Wakefield provided his readers with a mine of detail in *An Account of Ireland Statistical and Political*, 2 vols. (1813), while John Curwen, MP published his sympathetic *Observations on the State of Ireland Principally directed to its Agriculture and Rural Population*, 2 vols. (1818). In the modern era the study of the Irish economy following the union long reflected a nationalistic belief that development had been deliberately frustrated by Britain. The classic statement of that case was George O'Brien's *Economic History of Ireland from the Union to the Famine* (1921). Over the past two decades a more sophisticated analysis has held sway. L.M. Cullen, in a series of studies and essays – *Anglo-Irish Trade 1660–1800* (1968); *Economic History of Ireland since 1660* (1972); "Problems in the Interpretation and Revision of Eighteenth-Century Irish Economic History," *Transactions of the Royal Historical Society* 5th ser. 17 (1967); "Eighteenth-Century Flour Milling in Ireland," *Irish Economic and Social History* 7 (1980) – argued that Britain had not pursued a deliberately colonial policy towards Ireland and that the interpretation of colonial nationalists, depicting an economy and society characterized by depression, stagnation, and poverty, required modification. Industrialization was taking place and it was characterized by innovation, both in the use of technology and in business organization. An expanding commercial sector was suggested by Patrick Flanagan's study of "Markets and Fairs in Ireland, 1600–1800," *Journal of Historical Geography* 11 (1985), and Terence Burke emphasized the regional variations in Cork, as south Cork was drawn into the commercial systems of the European economy, in his article "County Cork in the Eighteenth Century," *Geographical Review* 64 (1974). Maureen Wall documented "The Rise of a Catholic Middle Class in Eighteenth-Century Ireland", *Irish Historical Studies* 11 (1958). Additional light has been thrown on Irish developments as a result of the rise of comparative history. See, for example, L.E. Cochran's *Scottish Trade with Ireland in the Eighteenth Century* (1985) and *Ireland and Scotland 1600–1850: Parallels and Contrasts in Economic and Social Development* (1983) edited by T.M. Devine and David Dickson. As for the immediate post-union era, F. Geary in an article on "The Rise and Fall of the Belfast Cotton Industry: Some Problems," *Irish Economic and Social History* 8 (1981), has suggested that the decline during the 1820s resulted not from an inability to compete with British industry but from a logical decision by manufacturers to invest in a more profitable flax spinning. Equally important are Joseph Lee, "The Dual Economy in Ireland, 1800–

1850," *Historical Studies* (1971), and Patrick Lynch and John Vaizey, *Guinness's Brewery in the Irish Economy 1759–1876* (1960). For the development of the Irish banking system see C.W. Munn, "The Emergence of Central Banking in Ireland: The Bank of Ireland 1814–1850," *Irish Economic and Social History* 10 (1983), and G.L. Barrow, *The Emergence of the Irish Banking System 1820–1845* (1975).

Important aspects of the backwardness of Irish agriculture are treated by David Large, "The Wealth of the Greater Irish Landowners, 1750–1815," *Irish Historical Studies* 16 (1966), and Gale E. Christianson, "Landlords and land tenure in Ireland 1790–1830," *Eire-Ireland* 9 (1974). R.D. Crotty's *Irish Agricultural Production: Its Volume and Structure* (1966) has been carefully and sympathetically criticized by Joseph Lee in the *Agricultural History Review* 17 (1969). A recent study of one parish but with broad implications is Kevin O'Neill's *Family and Farm in Pre-Famine Ireland: The Parish of Killashandra* (1984). Joel Mokyr has sought to explain why Ireland was so poor in *Why Ireland Starved: A Quantitative and analytical History of the Irish Economy 1800–1850* (1983). He concludes that the real problem was not that Ireland's integration into the British Empire had imposed its economy upon her but that integration did not go far enough.

The backwardness of Irish agriculture was associated by many contemporaries with the dramatic growth in the Ireland's population. The factors behind that growth have provided historians with another field of battle. D. Grigg has briefly summarized the principal explanations for what was a general phenomenon in "Modern population growth in historical perspective," *Geography* 62 (1982). In *The Population of Ireland 1750–1845* (1950) K.H. Connell advanced the theory that the peculiarly rapid growth in Ireland, which he dated from the 1780s, had resulted from increased fertility rather than a decline in mortality, which was itself the product of younger marriages made possible by an ample diet of potatoes. All the essential aspects of this explanation have been challenged. Michael Drake disputed the accuracy of the literary and nonstatistical sources upon which Connell had relied for evidence of earlier marriages, and he questioned Connell's conclusions on the spread of the potato culture and the sharpness of the population increase from the 1780s. See "Marriage and Population Growth in Ireland, 1750–1845," *Economic History Review* 2nd ser. 16 (1963–4). L.M. Cullen argued in the article on eighteenth-century Irish economic history noted above that the potato had been the cart not the horse of population growth. Stuart Daultry, David Dickson, and Cormac O Grada, in their article "Eighteenth-Century Irish Population: New Perspectives from Old Sources," *Journal of Economic History* 41 (1981), have dated the rapid growth somewhat earlier than the 1780s. Kevin O'Neill in *Family and Farm* asserts that the growth ought not to be identified with the lowest class of labourers, which had been another feature of the Connell interpretation, but rather with farmers and especially with middling farmers. Finally, the Malthusian overtones of aspects of the debate prompted Joe Mokyr to examine "Malthusian Models and Irish History" in the *Journal of Economic History* 40 (1980). He also offers qualified support for the traditional interpretation in his "Irish History with the Potato," *Irish Economic and Social History* 8 (1981). The classic account of the potato culture remains Redcliffe N. Salaman's *The History and Social Influence of the Potato* (1949) which has been revised and corrected by J.G. Hawkes (1985).

Joseph Lee attempted "to salvage something from the wreck" in "Marriage and Population in Pre-Famine Ireland," *Economic History Review* 2nd ser. 21 (1968). He admitted that Connell had lumped farmers and labourers together under the "obfuscatory term 'peasant'," conceded that the link between the potato and population was more complicated than Connell had recognized, but argued that the vegetable had been an important factor. By 1740 it was the winter diet of the southern labourer and cottier. Lastly, he sought to reestablish the credibility of the evidence given before the Poor Law Inquiry of 1836, on which Connell had based many of his findings. In *Irish Population, Economy and Society: Essays in Honour of the late K.H. Connell* (1981), edited by J.M. Goldstrom and L.A. Clarkson, Clarkson offers indirect support to the Connell thesis with his finding that the slowing of population growth after the French wars was the result of delayed marriages in the face of land hunger and landlord resistance to subdivision. Also, N.L. Tranter, *Population and Society 1750–1940: Contrasts in Population Growth* (1985) lends additional support to the Connell theory of earlier marriages as an explanation of the peculiarly rapid growth in the number of Irishmen. The modern debate on the causes of a mushrooming Irish population often echoes, as Mokyr pointed out, that among contemporaries on whether Ireland was overpopulated. In this dispute the Malthusians triumphed. There was general agreement that excess population created poverty and misery, and that they in turn led to crime. But in Ireland there was a widely recognized additional complication – sectarianism.

In *Orangeism in Ireland and Britain 1795–1836* (1966), Hereward Senior explored the lower-class origins of the Orange Order, as Protestants sought to protect their privileges. Aggressive conduct conjured up in turn the Defenders, who quickly became an exclusively Catholic secret order. Gradually the gentry asserted their leadership of the Orangemen while the suspicious authorities eventually compromised with them as allies in the struggle to maintain order. To the provocations Orangemen offered to Catholics must be added those of the proselytizers. Desmond Bowen has illustrated their disruptive contribution to Irish life in *The Protestant Crusade in Ireland 1800–70* (1978). Protestant triumphalism was another Catholic grievance. See Jacqueline R. Hill, "National Festivals, the State and 'Protestant Ascendancy' in Ireland, 1790–1829," *Irish Historical Studies* 24 (1984). The

Methodists also contributed to the sectarian animosity and fell victim to it, as D.N. Hempton shows in "The Methodist Crusade in Ireland, 1795–1845," *Irish Historical Studies* 22 (1980–81). But David Hempton has also argued that the conversions the Methodists made were more notable for the fuss made about them than for their number. Indeed, in "Methodism in Irish Society 1770–1830," *Transactions of the Royal Historical Society* 5th ser. 36 (1986), he suggests that it took root in those places where an Anglican population was only loosely committed to the Establishment, and appealed to urban rather than the less literate country dwellers. The internal reform of the State Church is the emphasis of Donald Harmon Akenson, *The Church of Ireland Ecclesiastical Reform and Revolution, 1800–1885* (1971). The parallel reform of the Catholic Church has been described by S.J. Connolly in *Priests and People in Pre-Famine Ireland 1780–1845* (1982). For the contentious issue of the priests' dues see J.A. Murphy, "The Support of the Catholic Clergy in Ireland 1750–1850," *Historical Studies* 5 (1965).

The most famous Irish Catholic was Daniel O'Connell. The indispensable source is Maurice O'Connell's *The Correspondence of Daniel O'Connell*, 8 vols. (1972–81), but his article "Daniel O'Connell and the Eighteenth Century," *Studies in Eighteenth Century Culture* 5 (1976), is a useful introduction to the Liberator. Denis Gwynn's *Daniel O'Connell The Irish Liberator* (1929) is now dated but Charles Chenevix Trench has written an eminently readable "nonacademic" account of *The Great Dan: A Biography of Daniel O'Connell* (1984). Gerard O'Brien has recently examined an important episode in the emergence of O'Connell as a significant figure in the politics of the Catholic question in his fresh analysis of "The Beginning of the Veto Controversy in Ireland," *Journal of Ecclesiastical History* 38 (1987). Interest has recently revived in O'Connell's vehicle of social and political change, the Catholic Association. Thomas Wyse's *Historical Sketch of the Late Catholic Association of Ireland*, 2 vols. (1829), is still of value. Of the modern studies, James A. Reynolds emphasized the role of the priesthood in *The Catholic Emancipation Crisis in Ireland 1823–1829* (1954 reprinted 1970). In *Catholic Emancipation: Daniel O'Connell and the Birth of Irish Democracy 1820–30* (1985) Fergus O'Ferrall has placed somewhat more weight on the contribution of the laity. See also W. Torrens McCullagh *Memoirs of the Right Honourable Richard Lalor Sheil*, 2 vols. (1855); the two articles by J.A. Whyte, "The Influence of the Catholic Clergy on Elections in Nineteenth-Century Ireland," *English Historical Review* 75 (1960), and "Landlord Influence at Elections in Ireland, 1760–1885," *English Historical Review* 80 (1965); and O. MacDonagh "The Politicization of the Irish Catholic Bishops 1800–1850," *Historical Journal* 18 (1975). The Catholic challenge and the rise of a popular press had encouraged Peel during his term as chief secretary to establish a more systematic policy for the management of "public opinion." Press enemies were disciplined more vigorously and allies rewarded more generously. A. Aspinall's *Politics and the Press c1780–1850* (1949) embraces Britain as well as Ireland but has much to say on policy in the latter country. His two short pieces in the *English Historical Review* 56 (1941), "The Irish Proclamation Fund" and "The Use of Irish Secret Money in subsidizing the Irish Press" briefly survey the use of these two instruments of influence. The standard work on Ireland is *Freedom of the Press in Ireland 1784–1841* (1954) by Brian Inglis. In an article, "O'Connell and the Irish Press 1800–42," *Irish Historical Studies* 8 (1952), Inglis demonstrates the Catholic leader's failings in his dealings with popular newspapers.

It was at the door of O'Connell and other agitators that the authorities laid much of the blame for the unrest which bedevilled the Irish countryside. The extent to which Ireland was endemically or abnormally violent, and the causes of the unrest, are two more areas of debate among historians. For a succinct and thoughtful introduction to these and other questions see David Fitzpatrick's review essay on "Unrest in Rural Ireland," *Irish Economic and Social History* 12 (1985). The study of "peasant" violence in Ireland is one area where Denis Smith's plea for greater interchange between historians and sociologists, in his article "Social History and Sociology – More than Just Good Friends," *Sociological Review* 30 (1982), had been anticipated. D. Frances Ferguson had suggested in "Rural/Urban Relations and peasant Radicalism: A Preliminary Statement," *Comparative Studies in Society and History* 28 (1976), that the peasantry require urban leadership if they are to be motivated politically. Marianne Elliot's "The Origins and Transformation of Early Irish Republicanism," *International Review of Social History* 23 (1978), described the process by which peasant dissent was transformed into something more subversive during the 1790s, and the temporary emergence of a Republican leadership. Carlo Geneletti, in "The Political Orientation of Agrarian Classes: A Theory," *Archives: European Journal of Sociology* 17 (1976), argued that smallholders were less dependent on their "betters" and therefore likely to be more assertive in political matters. But this was no more than George Cornewall Lewis had observed a century and a half earlier. In his classic account of Irish rural unrest, *On Local Disturbances in Ireland* (1836), Lewis also noted the existence of a "legitimizing notion" not unlike the "moral economy." Thus he depicted agrarian secret societies as "the expression of the wants and feelings of the great mass of the community" and as "administrators of a law of opinion generally prevalent among the classes to which they belong." Although persuaded of the non-political and essentially nonsectarian nature of the unrest, Lewis understood how and why it was misinterpreted as both political and sectarian. Indeed, the confusion at Dublin Castle is more understandable in the light of the continuing disagreement among historians. The most impressive recent publication is *Irish Peasants Violence and Political Unrest 1780–1914* (1983), edited by Samuel Clark and James S. Donnelly, Jr, but M.R. Beames's *Peasants and Power The Whiteboy Movement* (1983) is a useful if more limited work. See also Desmond T. Williams, ed., *Secret Societies in Ireland* (1973); T. Brown, "Nationalism and the Irish Peasant 1800–1848," *The Review of Politics* 15 (1953); Gale E. Christianson, "Secret Societies and Agrarian Violence in Ireland," *Agricultural History* 46 (1972); Tom Garvin, "Defenders, Ribbonmen and Others: Underground Political Networks in Pre-Famine Ireland," *Past and Present* 34 (1982); James W. O'Neill, "A Look at Captain Rock: Agrarian Rebellion in Ireland, 1818–45," *Eire-Ireland* 17 (1982).

Unlike the poor law system in Britain, that in Ireland failed to provide an effective safety net for the impoverished lower orders. The only substantial work remains Sir George Nicholls's, *A History of the Irish Poor Law in connexion with the Condition of the People* (1856), which chronicles the measures with were enacted and summarizes the reports of the select committees appointed to inquire into the condition of the Irish labouring poor. The growing agitation for an effective poor law is discussed by Thomas G. Conway "The Approach to an Irish Poor Law 1828–33," *Eire-Ireland* 6 (1971). In exceptional circumstances extensive emergency state aid was forthcoming. Stephen Royle, in his article "Irish Famine Relief in the Early Nineteenth Century: The 1822 Famine on the Aran Islands," *Irish Economic and Social History* 11 (1984), concludes that the famine was contained because the scale of relief compensated for its defective administration.

The Irish government attempted to reestablish the rule of law through an effective police force. J.J. Tobias's *Crime and Police in England 1700–1900* (1979) provides an introduction to the changing attitudes towards policing, while Galen Broeker has examined the conditions which in Ireland led the British to overcome their distaste for a species of gendarmerie. See *Rural Disorder and Police Reform in Ireland 1812–36* (1970). Also useful is T. O'Ceallaigh's article, "Peel and Police Reform in Ireland, 1814–18," *Studia Hibernica* 6 (1966). Another hope was that the Irish might be educated in docility. Brian Simon, *Studies in the History of Education 1780–1870* (1960), has analysed the revival of interest in education in the late eighteenth and early nineteenth centuries. Donald Akenson has written the standard work on *The Irish Education Experiment: The National System of Education in the Nineteenth Century* (1970). Peadar McCann, in "Charity-Schooling in Cork City in the Late 18th & Early 19th Centuries. Part 4: The Lancasterian Committee," *Cork Historical and Archeological Society* 87 (1982), reveals how Kildare Place schools immediately fell victim to sectarian hostility. A third solution to the poverty and unrest in Ireland was emigration. W.A. Carrothers, in *Emigration from the British Isles with Special Reference to the Development of Overseas Dominions* (1929, reprinted 1966), comments on "Malthusianism and Emigration." William Forbes Adams, *Ireland*

*and Irish Emigration to the New World from 1815 to the Famine* (1932, reprinted 1980), paints a suitably bleak portrait of Ireland in 1815 and points to the overwhelming influence of economic factors. David S. MacMillan does much the same in "Commercial and Industrial Society in Great Britain and Ireland 1814–1824: A Study of Australian Immigrant Applications," *Social History/Histoire Sociale* 6 (1973). In terms of the analysis of the Irish background to emigration Kirby A. Miller's *Emigrants and Exiles: Ireland and the Irish Exodus to North America* (1985) is a work of extraordinary detail. Donald Winch, *Classical Political Economy and Colonies* (1965), probes the difficulties state-assisted schemes of emigration posed for the political economists. The contemporary debate has been traced by Klaus E. Knorr, *British Colonial Theories 1570–1850* (1944). See also Peter Dunkley, "Emigration and the State, 1803–1842: The Nineteenth-Century Revolution in Government Reconsidered," *Historical Journal* 23 (1980). Oliver MacDonagh has studied the passenger acts and their enforcement in *Pattern of Government Growth 1800–60* (1961). Robert Wilmot Horton's activities are discussed by D.M. Young in *The Colonial Office in the Early Nineteenth Century* (1964), and analysed at some length by H.J.M. Johnston in *British Emigration Policy 1815–1830: Shovelling out Paupers'* (1972). In "Selecting Peter Robinson's Irish Emigrants," *Histoire Sociale/Social History* 9 (1976), Wendy Cameron concludes that the selection became another form of local patronage.

Michael Hechter's explanation of the rise of celtic nationalism and thus of the failure of the union, *Internal Colonialism: The Celtic Fringe in British National Development 1536–1966* (1975), owed much to the dependency theory which Theotonio Dos Santos defined in "The Structure of Dependence," *American Economic Review* 60: 2 (1970), as "a situation in which the economy of certain countries is conditioned by the development and expansion of another country to which the former is subject." But the notion of underdevelopment has been subjected to harsh criticism. See Tony Smith's article, "The Underdevelopment of Development literature: The Case of Dependency Theory," *World Politics* 31 (1978–9). The significance of unevent economic development as a cause of nationalism has also been challenged by A.W. Orridge, although his principal target was Tom Nairn's *The Break-Up of Britain* (1977). His two articles were published in *Political Studies* 29 (1981). Peter Alexis Gourevitch in "The Reemergence of 'Peripheral Nationalisms': Some Comparative Speculations on the Spatial Distribution of Political Leadership and Economic Growth," *Comparative Studies in Society and History* 21 (1979), followed Hechter in stressing the importance of the ethnic factor. The stronger the ethnic grievance the weaker the economic tension between core and periphery needed to be to produce nationalism. But William N. Sloan chastised Hechter in "Ethnicity or Imperialism: A Review Article," *Comparative Studies in Society and History*

21 (1979), for his "theoretical subordination of the fact of imperialism in Britain to the presence there of oppressed ethnic minorities." Other criticisms, both express and implied, have exposed Hechter's simplistic adaptation of the core-periphery model. Brian W. Ilbery in "Core-Periphery Contrasts in European Well-Being," *Geography* 69 (1984), has contrasted a central core of European nations with a peripheral zone of less advanced countries. Similarly, there has been a growing preoccupation with regional core-periphery divisions within a periphery of a larger national core. David Thurnock applied the model to Scotland in his *Historical Geography of Scotland since 1707: Geographical Aspects of Modernisation* (1982). So also did Munroe Eagles in "The Neglected Regional Dimension in Scottish Ethnic Nationalism," *Canadian Review of Studies in Nationalism* 12 (1985). Raymond R. Corrado had already found regional cleavages in Wales, between north and south, rural and urban communities. See "Nationalism and Communalism in Wales," *Ethnicity* 2 (1975). Indeed, the distinctiveness of Welsh nationalism, the "gulf between the Goidelic and the Brythonic variants of the Celt," has been discussed by Kenneth O. Morgan in *Wales: Birth of a Nation 1880–1980* (1981). In particular, Colin H. Williams has argued that Welsh nationalism remained latent so long as the external threat of Anglicization could be absorbed by Welsh culture. It was the danger posed by integration which revived it. See his article "Cultural Nationalism in Wales," *Canadian Review of Studies in Nationalism* 4 (1976) and the collection of essays he edited, *National Separatism* (1982). With respect to Ireland, internal colonialism has enjoyed a measure of acceptance from Hechter's fellow social scientists. D.G. Pringle's *One Island, Two Nations? A Political Geographical Analysis of the National Conflict in Ireland* (1985) conforms broadly to the model, and it provides the theoretical basis for Colin Anthony Regan's "Colonialism and Dependent Development in Ireland," a PHD thesis in historical geography (McGill University, 1980). Historians have continued to shun modular explanations. As a study in comparative history, *Celtic Nationalism* (1968), edited by Owen Dudley Edwards, is a disappointment but D. George Boyce has written an excellent account of *Nationalism in Ireland* (1982). In *New Nationalism of the Developed West* (1985), edited by Edward A. Tiryakian and Ronald Rogowski, Hechter responded to his critics. He concedes that the theory of internal colonialism has been dismissed by historians of Ireland, Scotland, and Wales but is proud of its acceptance by nationalists in those countries. He qualifies his description of Scotland as an internal colony and stresses his subsequent refinement of the theory. See, for example, "Group Formation and the Cultural Division of Labour," *American Journal of Sociology* 84: 1 (1978). In a recent assessment of "The Internal Colonial Concept" in *Comparative Studies in Society and History* 26 (1984), Robert J. Hind exposes its weaknesses and suggests ways in which it might still be of use to historians.

Since this study was sent to the printer a number of works have appeared which bear upon it. C.H.E. Philpin has edited a collection of essays on *Nationalism and Popular Protest in Ireland* (1987). Most of them were first published in *Past and Present* but there are four original contributions and an introduction by R.F. Foster. John Hutchinson's *The Dynamic of Cultural Nationalism: The Gaelic Revival and the Creation of the Irish Nation State* (1987) is principally concerned with a later period but offers a number of acute observations on the growth of nationalism during the late eighteenth and early nineteenth centuries. Unfortunately, the first of Oliver Mac-Donagh's projected two volumes on O'Connell, *The Hereditary Bondsman: Daniel O'Connell 1775–1829* (1988) appeared too late to be fully utilized.

# Index